AME ENGAGE™

Welcome to the fully integrated and interactive online learning hub for *Key Accounting Principles,* Volume Two, V5.0.

Online & Interactive

AME Learning's integrated and interactive online learning hub, AME Engage™, contextualizes the study of accounting in a hands-on, practical online learning environment. Designed to personalize the learning experience and engage students *before* class, our multi-sensory online tutorials guide students through the key accounting concepts for each chapter. These tutorials help students to *learn by doing,* using a variety of effective learning tools ranging from gaming to interactive problem solving.

In order to encourage students to truly understand the concepts rather than simply rely on memorization, AME Engage™ features randomized algorithmic homework questions, allowing students to practice the same concept repeatedly at their own leisure. The "Take me to the text" online homework feature links each question to the relevant examples in the digital textbook, immediately providing students the help they need at any time and from anywhere. Instructors have full control over all resources in AME Engage™ and can therefore effectively tailor their online environment according to their own teaching style.

Unique PIN Code

If you purchased this book brand-new, the PIN Card (image to the right) is attached to the front cover. Open this to get your unique **PIN Code**, then follow the instructions to log in to AME Engage™.

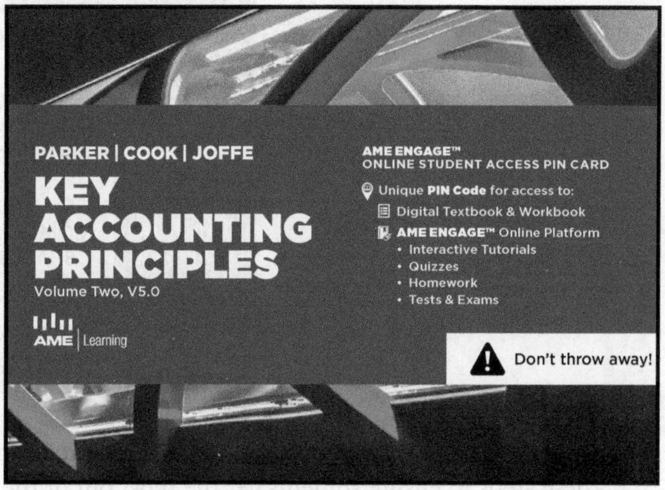

Don't have a PIN Card?

If you **did not** purchase this book brand-new, you will need to purchase your unique PIN Code at www.amelearning.com/store or contact your campus bookstore.

Instructor looking for access?

Please contact your AME Learning representative.

The AME Approach to Learning Accounting

AME utilizes a unique method to simplify accounting concepts, using step-by-step logic to ensure that the subject is extremely easy to understand. Accounting concepts are communicated using straightforward language and AME Accounting Maps™ that make potentially complex transactions simpler and easier to follow.

The AME Accounting Map™ is used throughout the textbook to show the impact of transactions on the financial statements. It is a visual representation of the balance sheet and income statement. The Accounting Map™ is also used in our interactive tutorials. Increases and decreases in values of specific items are clearly shown on the Map without needing to resort to technical accounting terminology.

The Accounting Map™

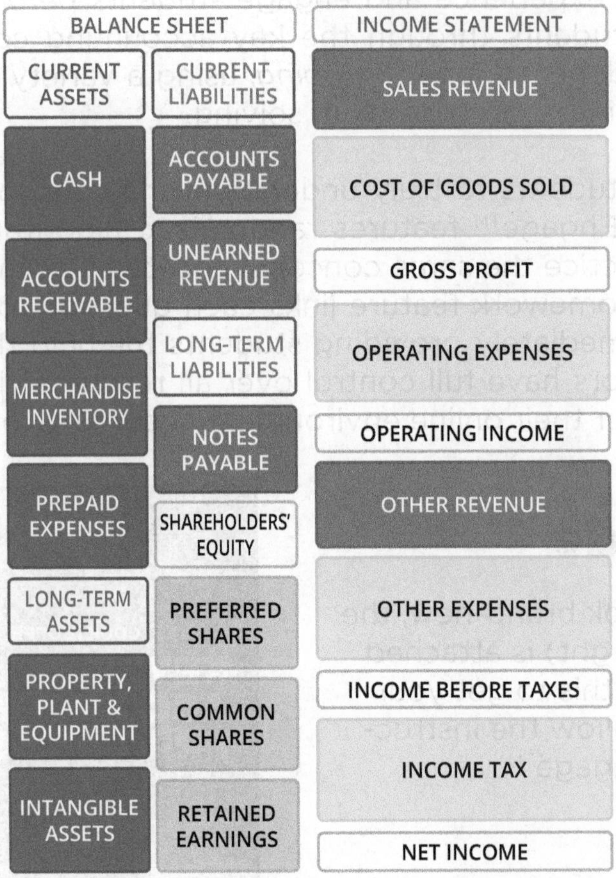

This textbook is part of a larger and blended program that is being used to teach the course. Instructors can follow these steps to ensure students get the most out of the program.

1. Encourage students to use the interactive online tutorials before attending each class.
2. Use the PowerPoint™ presentations to provide visuals to assist with teaching the material.
3. Assign online quizzes to test students' comprehension of the material. Quizzes can be used either before or after class.
4. Assign online homework questions to test students' ability to complete accounting problems. These should be used after class.

KEY ACCOUNTING PRINCIPLES

Volume Two, V5.0

Lead Authors

Penny L. Parker, MBA, CPA, CGA
Fanshawe College

Denise Cook, CPA, CA
Durham College

Contributing Writer

Shauna Roche, CPA, CMA, MBA
Fanshawe College

Reviewers

Rachel Bexon, CPA, CMA, MBA, PCP
Fanshawe College

Sheryl Boisvert, CPA, CGA, BEd
NorQuest College

Kolleen Brunton
Durham College

Crystal Buhler, CPA, CGA, CIRP

Kim Kennedy, CMrg, MBA, CPA, CGA, DBA
Olds College

Dan Kerr, BEd, PCP
triOS College

Athena Mailloux, PhD, MSL, CMA, CPA, CFF, CFE, CFCI, CCP
Sheridan College

Tanya McQueen, PID, LCI
Okanagan College

Dan Pasic, BComm, BEd
Fanshawe College

Cheryl Wilson, BBA, CPA, CA
Durham College

Lead Author of Key Accounting Principles, Volume Two, Fourth Edition © 2016

Neville Joffe

AME | Learning

Textbook ISBN: 978-1-989003-52-7
Workbook ISBN: 978-1-989003-53-4

Key Accounting Principles, Volume Two, V5.0
Authors: Penny L. Parker/Denise Cook/Neville Joffe
Publisher: AME Learning Inc.
Project Manager: Suzanne Schaan
Developmental Editors: Melody Yousefian/Graeme Gomes
Production Editors: Suzanne Schaan/Mark John Termoso
Photo and Permissions Research: A. Lloyd Permissions and Research Editing
Indexer: Elizabeth Walker
Typesetter: Paragon Prepress Inc.
VP Product Development and Technology: Linda Zhang
Cover Design: Soumik Dasgupta
Cover Photos: Valentyna Zhukova © 123RF.com
Online Course Design & Production: AME eLearning Team

3 4 5 Marquis 23 22 21

For more information contact:

AME Learning Inc.
1655 Dupont Street, Suite 101
Toronto, ON, Canada M6P 3T1
Phone: 416.479.0200
Toll-free: 1.888.401.3881
E-mail: info@amelearning.com
Visit our website at: www.amelearning.com

The AME Learning System™

It started 20 years ago when company founder Neville Joffe developed an innovative game-based methodology to help his employees understand basic financial concepts. Today, the AME Learning System™ is an award-winning teaching strategy. It's unique, it's patented and, most importantly, it works. Designed initially to teach the principles of accounting and financial literacy to people with no previous financial education, the AME Learning System™ has now accelerated learning for hundreds of thousands of students and professionals across North America.

The system incorporates the best of cognitive science, technology and learning principles into an active learning approach that emphasizes constant decision-making, real-world examples and impact over memorization.

The patented Accounting Map™ Tutorials are the foundation of the system. Using a logical, visually based approach that translates accounting concepts into common experiences and terminology, the interactive, online tutorials employ the "flipped classroom" strategy that is revolutionizing contemporary learning. Students complete tutorials *before* class, and in-class instruction consolidates their understanding of the material. Then, plain-language, real-world exercises help students practice and explore key lessons. When this system meets AME Engage—our distinctive online learning experience—it creates an unmatched connection between learners and content.

Our blended-learning packages offer print and digital resources that can support each other or stand alone to provide the learning experience that best fits everyone's needs. Our system is completely modular, allowing students, learners and clients to customize their learning goals and experiences, even as we continually update our content and technology.

Full-Cycle Support

The heart of the AME Learning System™ is our connection to you. We customize your experience, your content and your support because we know our customers personally. We ensure our technology is portable and interoperable with your platforms and we organize our materials to match your needs and processes. Behind it all, the AME Assistant Team—our in-house accounting and learning specialists—work as your virtual teaching assistants, helping you build the learning experience, develop tests and exams and refine your curriculum.

Who's It For?

The AME Learning System™ can support everyone looking to enhance their understanding of the financial world, including school-age and higher-education students, people starting their own businesses, employees preparing for their first management roles and people looking for new jobs or retraining in mid-career.

Virtual schools, online universities and traditional colleges are customizing the AME Learning System™ to train accounting majors, entrepreneurs, paralegals, human resources professionals and people working in agriculture, hospitality and sports management. Our system is for anyone who wants to learn more, retain more and understand more about accounting and finance.

About the Lead Authors

Penny L. Parker

Penny L. Parker is the Coordinator of the Business Fundamentals Program and Professor in the Lawrence Kinlin School of Business at Fanshawe College in London, Ontario. Shortly after joining the accounting faculty in 1990, she assumed the role of Coordinator of the Business Accounting Program, which she held for several years. She also serves the Canadian Academic Accounting Association (CAAA) as a member and past Chair of the Education Committee and Vice-President of Colleges. She earned her Master's in Business Administration from Laurentian University and is an active Certified Professional Accountant (CPA).

Penny's practical financial accounting experience began prior to her academic career, with Ernst & Young Chartered Accountants in London, Ontario, where she was employed as a Senior Client Accountant serving small and mid-sized businesses. Her duties included providing monthly accounting and bookkeeping services as well as preparing year-end financial statements and tax returns for her clients. Prior to working in public accounting, Penny held a junior accounting position at an electronic supply company, where she gained hands-on experience in processing accounts payable/receivable, inventory and other accounting-related transactions. It was here Penny realized she enjoyed working with numbers and began to pursue a professional accounting designation (1990) with the Certified General Accountant (CGA) Association of Ontario.

After working in accounting for several years, Penny was provided with an opportunity to teach introductory accounting at Fanshawe. It was then she realized her passion for teaching—a passion that dated back to when she was a child, playing school in the basement of her parents' home, where she handed out papers to a group of younger children and, using chalk to write on cement walls, taught them how to solve simple mathematical equations. Her years of education and experience working in both public and private accounting have helped her earn a reputation as a very knowledgeable and well-respected accounting professor. She also currently publishes a series of accounting practice sets, both manual and computerized, that are used by students at colleges and universities across the country.

In recent years, Penny has worked closely with AME Learning as a contributor on previous editions of *Key Accounting Principles*, Volumes 1 and 2, and is very excited to be involved as an author on the current edition.

Denise Cook

Denise Cook is an Accounting Professor in the School of Business, IT & Management (BITM), at Durham College. She has held previous accounting faculty positions in the Faculty of Business and Information Technology at the University of Ontario Institute of Technology (UOIT) and in the School of Continuing Education at Durham College; for seven years, she also held the role of Accounting Program Coordinator at Durham College. Denise has a Bachelor of Mathematics/Accounting (Honours Co-operative) from the University of Waterloo, and she has been an active Chartered Accountant (CA) since 1989 and a Chartered Professional Accountant (CPA) since the unification of the Canadian accounting bodies in 2013.

As a professor, Denise strives to educate students with basic accounting skills that apply to all aspects of their personal and professional lives. In her early years in the classroom, she taught accounting to health, sport and general business students, which required creativity to communicate transactions in a meaningful way in those respective disciplines. Shortly thereafter, the merger of professional accounting designations left a gap in the college curriculum for accounting majors. In her role as Accounting Program Coordinator, she has had the opportunity to develop and support new programs. Some of the programs Denise helped create are Accounting & Payroll (with an additional focus on Bookkeeping), Finance, and a university transfer program in conjunction with UOIT—most of which continue to be successful, in-demand programs at both the college and university level. All these experiences have attracted Denise to AME's philosophy of teaching and learning.

Prior to her academic career, Denise spent over 20 years gaining practical accounting experience in the corporate world. She held various senior managerial positions at major multinational corporations including McGraw-Hill Ryerson, EDS Canada (HP), Citibank Canada and Thorne Ernst & Whinney (KPMG). In these roles, Denise specialized in financial management, internal and external audit, financial analysis and compliance with internal controls. With her decades of experience and extensive knowledge in finance, audit and accounting, Denise has become more passionate about sharing past experiences and making education more applicable to the students.

In recent years, Denise has been a contributing editor on numerous accounting textbooks in both Canada and the United States. She's very excited to be a co-author on this edition of *Key Accounting Principles* and is proud to support AME Learning in delivering quality accounting education to the next generation.

Textbook and Workbook Features

AMEENGAGE™ Access **ameengage.com** for integrated resources including tutorials, practice exercises, the digital textbook and more.

Every chapter has reminders for students to check their online course for additional resources to help explain the accounting topics.

The learning objectives in each chapter are prepared using Bloom's taxonomy. In the textbook, each heading in the chapters is linked to one learning objective. The learning objectives are also linked to all the questions in the workbook.

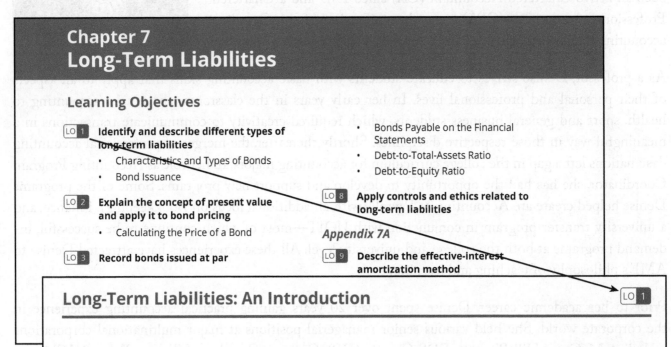

Chapter 7
Long-Term Liabilities

Learning Objectives

LO 1 **Identify and describe different types of long-term liabilities**

- Characteristics and Types of Bonds
- Bond Issuance

LO 2 **Explain the concept of present value and apply it to bond pricing**

- Calculating the Price of a Bond

LO 3 **Record bonds issued at par**

- Bonds Payable on the Financial Statements
- Debt-to-Total-Assets Ratio
- Debt-to-Equity Ratio

LO 8 **Apply controls and ethics related to long-term liabilities**

Appendix 7A

LO 9 **Describe the effective-interest amortization method**

Long-Term Liabilities: An Introduction LO 1

In previous chapters, we discussed some of the ways corporations finance their operations, through *short-term debt*, such as using credit to purchase goods and services on account, and offering *equity* in the business, such as issuing preferred or common shares to investors. In this chapter, we will look at another way that corporations finance their operations by using *long-term debt*, such as issuing bonds and notes payable.

At the end of the chapter is a summary, highlighting key points for each learning objective.

In Summary

LO 1 Identify and describe different types of long-term liabilities

- Corporations can finance their operations using long-term debt, such as bonds (borrowing from private investors) and notes payable (borrowing from the bank).
- The company that issues the bond is called the bond issuer. The investor who purchases the bond is the bondholder.
- The investor provides a principal loan to the issuing company. In return, the company makes interest payments to the investor, in addition to eventually repaying the principal.
- There are several types of bonds, such as term bonds, debenture bonds, redeemable bonds, mortgage bonds, convertible bonds, registered bonds and coupon bonds.

Within each chapter are several Pause & Reflect exercises for students to complete. These break down large chapters into smaller manageable parts to help enforce the concepts learned. Solutions to the Pause & Reflect exercises are in Appendix I of the textbook.

Pause & Reflect

Exercise 7-1

On January 1, 2020, Decorum Inc. issues 1,500 five-year bonds at par at a price of $200 each, with 9% interest paid annually. Show how the bond issuance transaction is recorded.

JOURNAL			
Date	**Account Title and Explanation**	**Debit**	**Credit**

See Appendix I for solutions.

Each chapter has a Review Exercise covering the major topics of the chapter. The Review Exercises are prepared so students can complete them and then compare their answers to the solutions. Solutions to the Review Exercises are in Appendix I of the textbook.

Review Exercise 7-1

Hohl Company is planning to expand its facilities by constructing a new building and installing new machines. To complete this project, the company has decided to issue $2,000,000 worth of 20-year, 4% callable bonds, with interest paid every six months.

On April 1, 2020, the company has completed all the necessary paperwork and is now ready to issue the bonds. Fortunately, just as Hohl Company is issuing its bonds, the current market rate drops to 3.5%. Its financial advisor recommends issuing the bonds at a premium of $142,968.

On March 31 of 2025, interest rates drop to 2%. At this point, the company issues $2,200,000 worth of 10-year, 2% bonds at par to redeem all outstanding 4% bonds. The company pays $2,110,000 to redeem the 4% bonds.

Required

a) Prepare the bond premium amortization table from period 1 to period 10 (covers 2020 to 2025), using the straight-line amortization method.

Straight-Line Amortization Table of Bond Premium

	A	B	C	D	E
Semi-Annual Interest Period	Interest Payment	Premium Amortization	Interest Expense	Premium Balance	Bond Book Value

The workbook is comprised of assessment and application questions.

- Assessment questions (AS) are designed to test theory and comprehension of topics.
- Application questions (AP) are split into Group A and Group B problems. These questions test students' ability to perform the accounting functions, such as creating journal entries and financial statements.
- A comprehensive case study tests students' ability to synthesize learning, including concepts from across the learning objectives.
- A critical thinking question tests students' ability to analyze situations and think beyond the numbers.

Assessment Questions

AS-1 LO 1

Name the typical forms of long-term debt.

AS-2 LO 1

What is a bond?

Application Questions Group A

Note: Round all calculations and final answers to the nearest whole dollar. When needed, use either the present value factors provided in the textbook or a financial calculator, as directed by your instructor. As noted in Appendix 7B in the textbook, rounding differences may exist depending on the method used to calculate the present values.

AP-1A LO 3

On September 1, 2020, Delia Company issued $264,000 worth of bonds at par, with an interest rate of 10% per annum. The bonds will mature on August 31, 2022. Interest will be paid annually on August 31. The company has a December 31 year end.

Calculate the accrued interest payable on December 31, 2020.

Case Study

CS-1 LO 1 2 4 10

You & Us Company issued $1,000,000 worth of redeemable six-year bonds on December 1, 2018. The interest rate was 4% per year and interest payment would be made semi-annually. In 2018, similar bonds were paying 6% interest on average.

On December 1, 2021, the average market interest rate for similar bonds had decreased to 2%. You & Us Company deci
have

In 20
book
whic

Critical Thinking

CT-1 LO 2 4

When it comes to bonds, IFRS requires using the effective-interest method while ASPE allows the straight-line method if the results do not differ significantly. Which method do you recommend for a private company following ASPE? Support your answer.

Some Additional Segments

This textbook was designed to make the learning experience productive and engaging. To that end, we have added some segments to each chapter that highlight learning objectives.

A Closer Look

A Closer Look segments examine a part of the chapter in detail to broaden students' understanding of an underlying concept. These boxes may also include an example that applies the concepts being learned in a way that is easy to understand and follow.

In the Real World

In the Real World segments provide applied examples. They put some of the concepts being learned in context and drive home the point that accounting eventually has to be done outside the classroom. We hope that these segments offer a sense of what "the real world" can be like for the accountant or business professional.

Worth Repeating

Worth Repeating segments remind students of accounting concepts already learned and highlight current concepts that are "worth repeating."

ASPE vs. IFRS

ASPE vs. *IFRS* segments discuss differences in the treatment of the topic being covered in the chapter based on the two different sets of accounting standards. Not all topics will have a difference between the two.

AME ENGAGE™

Welcome to the fully integrated and interactive online learning hub for *Key Accounting Principles,* Volume Two, V5.0.

The AME Learning™ Cycle for Students

The AME Learning Cycle is a unique learning method that integrates the textbook seamlessly with the online platform to achieve a fun and interactive learning experience. The online learning hub, AME Engage, guides students every step along the way to achieve successful knowledge retention. The pre-class interactive tutorials allow students to not only better prepare for in-class work but also engage with difficult concepts whenever and wherever. The post-class algorithmic homework provides a platform for students to practice workbook questions online and receive instant feedback.

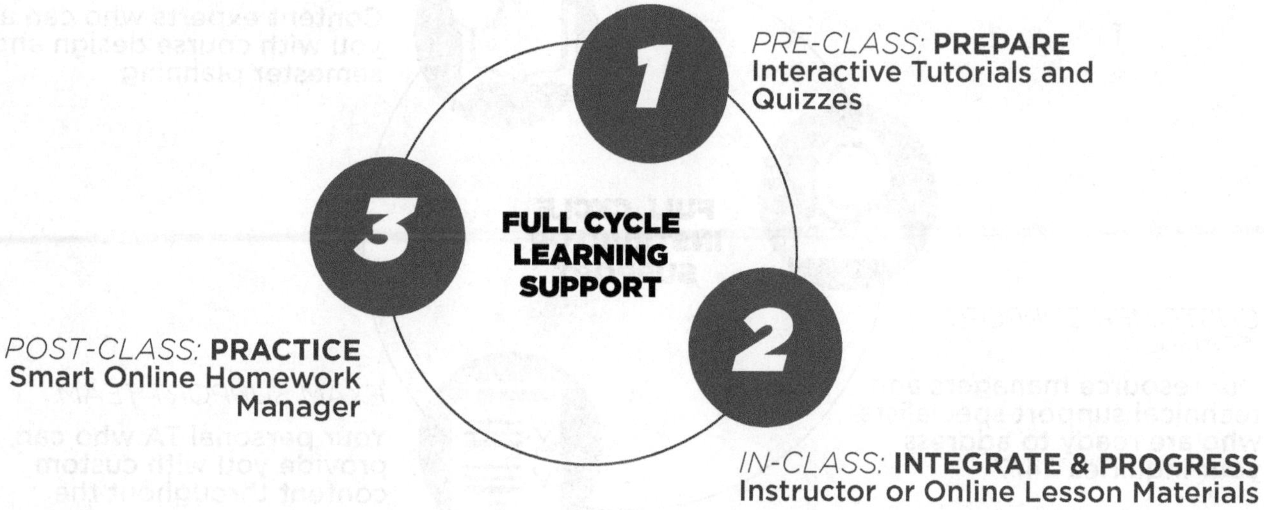

AME Engage: Features

Interactive Online Tutorials
Interactive multi-sensory video clips featuring hands-on practice with our innovative Accounting Map™.

Online Homework Manager
Algorithmic homework questions, assignments, projects, cases, tests and quizzes.

Resource Library
Focus on key lesson objectives with Microsoft Excel™ worksheet templates and our vast PowerPoint™ library.

Digital Textbook
Practical explanations and examples seamlessly integrated with workbook and online homework.

Digital Workbook
Hundreds of questions and cases perfectly integrated with textbook lessons and online homework.

Student Tech Support
Call 1(888) 401-3881 x 2 from 9 am to 5 pm EST Monday to Friday or email support@amelearning.com 24 hours a day and 7 days a week.

AME ENGAGE™

Welcome to the fully integrated and interactive online learning hub for *Key Accounting Principles,* Volume Two, V5.0.

Full Cycle Instructor Support

At AME Learning, we proudly provide full cycle instructor support for teaching a stimulating and rewarding class. Our AME Assistant™ Team consists of highly qualified content experts, technical support specialists and resource managers, who can provide you with personalized assistance from custom content development to on-demand training and technical support. Our AME Engage online learning hub offers you a resource centre that combines the best content with powerful teaching tools to achieve the desired flexibility and control.

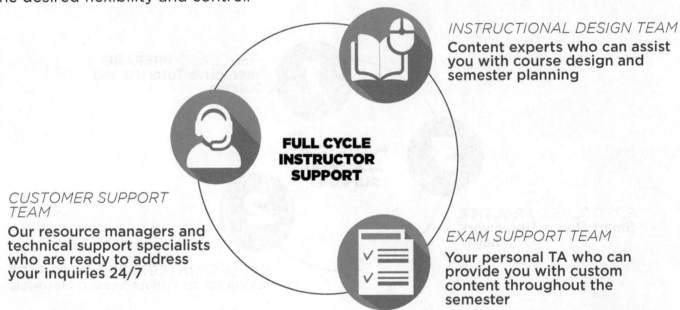

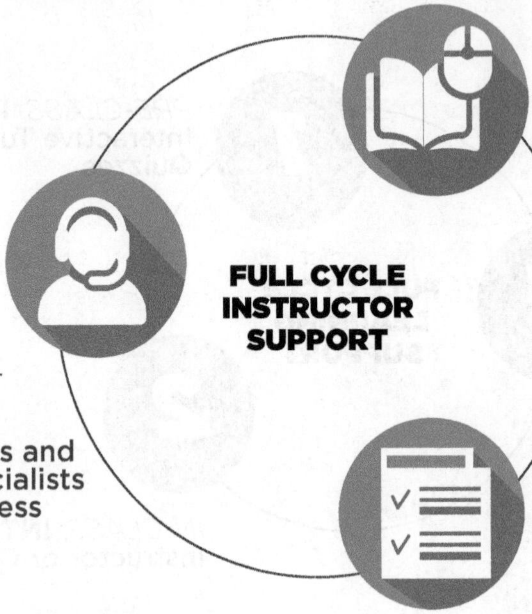

INSTRUCTIONAL DESIGN TEAM

Content experts who can assist you with course design and semester planning

CUSTOMER SUPPORT TEAM

Our resource managers and technical support specialists who are ready to address your inquiries 24/7

EXAM SUPPORT TEAM

Your personal TA who can provide you with custom content throughout the semester

Instructor Support: Features

Personalized Instructional Design
A unique and personalized service tailored to the needs of each curriculum and each instructor.

Personalized Exam Support
Custom content creation throughout the semester for both paper-based and online exams.

Online Question Bank
Over 1,500 questions organized by chapter and including multiple choice, matching and computational problems.

Workbook Solution Manual
Step-by-step solutions to all workbook questions available in print or in digital format.

Online Resource Library
Powerful online resource centre with additional teaching tools such as online cases, Microsoft PowerPoint© and Microsoft Excel© templates.

Instructor Training & Technical Support
On-demand support to integrate our products, technology and services into your course for optimum teaching and results.

Overview of Changes to This Version

New and Revised Features

Learning objectives better correspond to the depth of the material presented in each chapter, strictly following Bloom's taxonomy. The "In Summary" section has been revised to better link to the learning objectives.

A new section at the beginning of each chapter, "Making It Real to You," connects students with the content by showing them how accounting affects their everyday life.

In addition to the Review Exercises at the end of each chapter, Pause & Reflect Exercises are found throughout each chapter. These focus on an understanding of the content within one learning objective rather than the whole chapter, allowing students to test their knowledge before moving on to the next section. The solutions to the exercises are in an appendix at the end of the textbook.

The workbook features more application questions, in terms of both quantity and depth. There is an A set and a B set of questions for each chapter. Instructors can use the A set questions for illustration and allow students to practice with a corresponding B set question.

Each workbook chapter has a comprehensive case covering multiple learning objectives from that chapter. These cases help students consolidate the skills practiced in the application questions. A new critical thinking question at the end of each workbook chapter encourages analysis.

Both Accounting Standards for Private Enterprises (ASPE) and International Financial Reporting Standard (IFRS) are introduced. A comparison between ASPE and IFRS is included wherever applicable throughout the text; that information is summarized in Appendix IV.

Chapter Changes

Chapter 1: Accounting for Receivables

Revenue recognition criteria and methods in the sale of both goods and services are presented in context within this receivables chapter.

The chapter now covers two methods of accounting for bad debt: the allowance method and the direct write-off method.

Disposal of receivables through factoring and pledging has been added as a new learning objective.

The role of data analytics in accounting is highlighted in a new *In the Real World* box on credit checks. A sample accounts receivable dashboard is illustrated in *A Closer Look* box.

Overall, the content is more comprehensive. Terms such as *receivable*, *maker* and *payee* are explicitly defined and clearly explained. Information on credit card sales has been added, as has more detailed illustration of the computation of note interest and maturity date.

Chapter 2: Long-Term Assets

Throughout the chapter, information has been better explained for students, starting with a more comprehensive definition of long-term assets and discussion of their characteristics. The components included in the costs of building, machinery, equipment, land and land improvements are laid out in more detail. The discussion of residual and salvage values is simplified. The journal entry for natural resources is updated to include ore inventory.

The changes in property, plant and equipment are classified into betterment and ordinary repairs. Journal entries for both classifications are illustrated.

A clear explanation and illustration show how the depreciation calculation for federal income tax purposes using the capital cost allowance is usually different from the book depreciation.

A new *In the Real World* box discusses the use of predicative analytics in goodwill impairment.

A comprehensive figure summarizes the accounts used to record the purchase, depreciation and sale or disposal of long-term assets.

Discussion of trading an old asset for a new asset has been moved to an appendix at the end of the chapter.

Chapter 3: Current Liabilities

A new figure provides a visual summary of taxes paid by employer and employee. Journal entries illustrate employee benefits as part of estimated liabilities.

Basic and extended warranties are clearly explained in their own sections. A new *In the Real World* box highlights the use of analytic software in managing and improving the warranty process.

Contingent liabilities are clearly categorized, and a new figure summarizes accounting practices for those categories.

Chapter 4: Partnerships

A comprehensive figure summarizes and compares the characteristics of partnerships to both sole proprietorships and corporations.

Coverage of income division where salary and interest allowances exceed net income is added, as is discussion of how income is allocated in case of the death of a partner.

The section on partner bonuses has been improved visually by dividing the topic into clearly labelled subsections.

Chapter 5: Corporations: Contributed Capital and Dividends

The introductory discussion of the characteristics, advantages and disadvantages of corporations is improved. New subheadings and new and modified figures make the content easier to read and understand.

An explanation has been added on how to journalize organization costs.

More detailed explanations are provided for preferred shares, including discussion of participating and nonparticipating preferred shares. Restrictions on the use of retained earnings are covered as well.

More real-life examples are provided.

Chapter 6: Corporations: The Financial Statements

This chapter has been thoroughly updated to better distinguish between ASPE and IFRS in regard to preparing financial statements. It begins with a focus on ASPE and the format of its financial statements. A separate learning objective is then fully dedicated to IFRS and its financial statements.

The discussion of accounting changes and prior period adjustments has been expanded to include more detail as well as journals, financial statements and updated figures.

The section on ratios has been expanded to include the dividend yield ratio in addition to the dividend payout ratio.

A new *In the Real World* box highlights the use of eXtensible Business Reporting Language (XBRL) in sharing financial information digitally.

Chapter 7: Long-Term Liabilities

The introductory section on bonds includes more detail and a new figure showing a bond certificate. The concept of financial leverage is more clearly and explicitly illustrated at the start of this chapter.

The concept of present value is better illustrated by focusing on calculating the price of a bond.

New *In the Real World* boxes highlight bond ratings and the use of data analytics in pricing bonds.

Two bonds-related ratios (debt-to-total-assets and debt-to-equity) are introduced.

A new section on calculating time value of money (TVM) using a financial calculator appears as an appendix at the end of the chapter.

Chapter 8: Investments

Overall, the content has been updated to provide an easy-to-understand look at the complexities of accounting for various long-term investments. The chapter is focused on ASPE, with a separate learning objective listing the highlights under IFRS.

Both debt and equity investments are more clearly classified and explained.

Updated figures and summary tables on different classes of investments have been added for easy reference.

Presentation of investments on the financial statements is better illustrated with proper subheadings and more detail.

Chapter 9: The Statement of Cash Flows

The presentation has been improved through the addition of new figures, such as one that shows how various cash-related transactions impact the three sections of the statement of cash flow.

The accounting equation, along with a step-by-step process, is used in explaining the logic behind the indirect method.

The usefulness of the statement of cash flows is now specified for both internal and external financial statement users.

A new *In the Real World* box highlights the use of data analytics software to examine and predict cash flow.

The appendix to this chapter has been updated to illustrate a step-by-step process for the direct method. For example, a summary table has been added to outline the many adjustments made to net income in order to arrive at net cash under the operating activities of the direct method.

Chapter 10: Financial Statement Analysis

Throughout the whole chapter, the financial statements of Leon's Furniture Limited are used to provide a real-life analysis.

Ratios have been recategorized based on what they are intended to measure, such as liquidity, profitability and capital market performance. Return on common shareholders' equity ratio has been added, and dividend payout ratio has been replaced by dividend yield.

Management's Discussion and Analysis (MD&A) is introduced as an information source to be consulted in addition to the financial statements.

Deeper ratio interpretation is provided by offering alternative points of view. For example, a decrease in profit margin from the previous period is not necessarily interpreted negatively if it resulted from intentional actions and led to an increase in market share.

An updated summary table lists the formula for and purpose of each ratio, for quick reference.

A new section on computerized financial accounting briefly introduces tools to increase efficiency and ensure decision-makers have access to current and accurate information.

Brief Table of Contents

Detailed Table of Contents

Chapter 1
Accounting for Receivables

Learning Objectives

LO 1 Explain the importance of accounts receivable
- Accounts Receivable
- Revenue Recognition

LO 2 Account for bad debts using the allowance method
- The Allowance Method
- Approaches to Estimating Bad Debts

LO 3 Account for bad debts using the direct write-off method

LO 4 Record promissory notes and notes receivable

LO 5 Utilize reports, including the accounts receivable subledger, to manage accounts receivable information
- The Accounts Receivable Subledger
- Alternative Presentation Formats

LO 6 Calculate financial ratios pertaining to accounts receivable
- Accounts Receivable Turnover Ratio
- Days' Sales Outstanding

LO 7 Account for the disposal of receivables using factoring and pledging
- Factoring Receivables
- Pledging Receivables

LO 8 Apply internal controls relating to accounts receivable
- Credit Approval
- Credit Information
- Credit Terms
- Credit Collection

LO 9 Apply ethics relating to accounts receivable and notes receivable

AMEENGAGE™ Access **ameengage.com** for integrated resources including tutorials, practice exercises, the digital textbook and more.

MAKING IT REAL TO YOU

For most companies, extending credit to customers means revenues will increase. Why is this true? To answer this question, consider the following scenario.

You want to buy a television from a local electronics store and will not have the cash to make the purchase for at least 30 days. But it would be so nice to purchase the unit today so you could watch the hockey playoffs! The store offers credit terms of 2/10, n/30, which means you would get a 2% discount if you paid the invoice within 10 days, or you could simply pay the full amount in 30 days.

By offering credit terms, the store is likely to attract more customers, which should mean more revenues, since most people would rather enjoy their purchase earlier than later. However, on the downside for the retailer, the reality is that some customers will not pay on time or even not pay at all.

This chapter deals with recording accounts and notes receivable transactions, including accounting for customers who do not pay. Businesses have options for accounting for bad debts. As a credit customer, you should be aware of the credit terms being offered so you can take advantage of discounts being offered and understand the consequences of not paying your account on time.

Accounts Receivable: An Introduction

LO 1

You have been introduced to many common assets and liabilities on the balance sheet. You know their definitions and how to record them as debits and credits. However, there are more complex accounts and processes that companies use to account for assets and liabilities. These topics will be covered in depth as we explore the balance sheet in more detail.

Accounts Receivable

On a company's balance sheet, presented below cash and short-term investments (which may also be referred to as cash equivalents), is a category of current assets known as receivables, which represent amounts due from other businesses, customers or financial institutions. As with other assets on the balance sheet, receivables are listed in order of liquidity, from most to least liquid. Common types of receivables are accounts receivable, notes receivable, interest and taxes. This chapter focuses on one of the largest of these amounts: accounts receivable.

Accounts receivable are amounts owing from customers for credit sales, that is, sales billed on account for goods and services. You may recall that when a sale is made on account, it is recorded as a debit to accounts receivable and a credit to sales. The debit to accounts receivable increases the assets of the business while the credit to sales increases equity. When the customer pays the amount owed, the business records the transaction as a debit to cash and a credit to accounts receivable. The remaining amount that has not been received from customers at the end of an accounting period is reported as accounts receivable on the balance sheet. Accounts receivable amounts are normally due to be paid within 30 or 60 days; therefore, they are current assets.

When customers purchase a product or service from a company, they are issued an invoice that shows the **payment terms**, which are the conditions for customer payment. Also known as *credit terms*, they specify the payment due date and any other conditions on that payment, such as the discount rate for early payment. For example, the term 2/10, n/30 means that the customer will get a 2% discount if payment is received within 10 days; otherwise, the full amount (net) is due within 30 days. Payment terms ensure that the customer pays the invoice in a reasonable amount of time. They are an example of an internal control that a company uses to manage its assets.

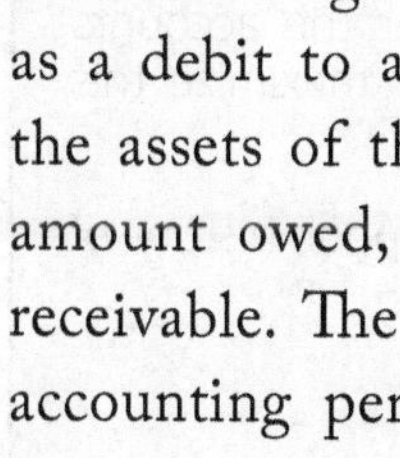

FIGURE 1.1

Figure 1.1 highlights a portion of the current assets section of the classified balance sheet. (It is assumed here that there is no short-term investment.) Starting with cash and cash equivalents, as we move down the accounts, there is a decrease in liquidity. Accounts receivable is less liquid than cash because it takes some time for accounts receivable to be converted into cash through collection from customers. In addition, there is some risk that customers will not pay the amount they owe.

Accounts receivable is an integral part of doing business in a modern economy. Sales may be increased by allowing customers to pay at a later date, since some customers may be unable to pay for their purchases immediately. Many businesses have accounts receivable on their books, so it is important to know how to record and manage them. Throughout this chapter, we will look at how this is achieved.

Compared to cash and cash equivalents, accounts receivable requires more hands-on administration, because it involves debt collection and management of debtor information. The information can include a debtor's company name, full address, contact information, what the company bought, the cost of the item(s) bought, delivery details and payment or credit terms.

In the Real World

One of the most prominent business trends of the past decade has been outsourcing, whereby one company hires another company to take over a certain business function, whether it is call centre duties or specialized manufacturing capabilities.

The accounts receivable department has not escaped this outsourcing trend. Accounts receivable is an important asset for most companies, and ensuring collection is necessary for success. Even in cases where accounts receivable represents only a small percentage of a company's total assets, the administrative aspect can be overwhelming, and a company's resources are often inadequate for the task.

To handle this challenge, companies have the option of hiring firms that specialize in taking over the accounts receivable function. Such specialists possess the technical hardware, expertise and experience to maximize this important asset.

Outsourcing accounts receivable offers certain advantages, especially for companies that have a poor history of managing this asset. Outsourcing can:

- improve a company's profitability by having the asset managed and controlled more efficiently
- make a company's accounts receivable function more consistent, thereby increasing customer satisfaction
- ensure accurate financial reporting
- allow a company to focus on its core business, while leaving some of the administrative duties to specialists

One disadvantage is that, when accounts receivable collection is outsourced, the company itself does not communicate directly with customers about any issues. As a result, it runs the risk of compromising relationships or even alienating some customers.

Even a business with a relatively small number of customers has many transactions to record and manage daily. To reduce time spent administering accounts receivable, many companies opt for the services of third-party credit card companies, as will be discussed next.

Credit Card Sales

Many businesses offer customers the choice to pay for goods and services using credit cards. Major credit cards such as Visa, Mastercard and American Express are known as third-party credit cards, because they accept customer payments on behalf of other businesses in return for a service fee. When a customer pays for a purchase using a third-party credit card, the sale is recorded as a cash sale by the vendor. The actual funds from the credit card sale are automatically and electronically deposited into the vendor company's bank account by the third party, so the sale is not a receivable for the vendor. The credit card company bills the customer directly, shifting the risk of uncollectible debt to that credit card issuer. For the vendor, this a good method of internal control, because it reduces the overall risk to its cash flow.

Most retailer-specific credit cards are managed by a finance company and offer customers the flexibility of using the card just like a standard Visa or Mastercard credit card at different retailers. For example, Canadian Tire offers the Triangle Mastercard, which customers can use not only for purchases at Canadian Tire but also for gasoline and other merchandise at several different retailers. Hudson's Bay is another retailer with a store-branded Mastercard, which can be used anywhere Mastercard is accepted.

Revenue Recognition

Revenue recognition refers to the principle that revenue can only be recorded (recognized) when goods are sold or when services are performed. It has become one of the most difficult concepts to understand because sales transactions are more complex now than they were in the past. Companies have also been accused of deliberately abusing the recognition of revenues in order to overstate or understate profits. International Financial Reporting Standards (IFRS) has identified several revenue recognition criteria for the sales of goods and services; Accounting Standards for Private Enterprises (ASPE) sets out similar guidelines.

Sale of Goods

The following five revenue recognition criteria have been defined for the sale of goods. All criteria must be met before revenue may be recognized.

1. The significant risks and rewards of ownership have been transferred to the buyer.
2. The seller no longer controls or manages the goods sold.
3. The amount of revenue can be measured reliably (agreed upon by both the buyer and seller).
4. It is probable that the seller will collect the economic benefits associated with the transaction.
5. The costs related to the sale of goods can be measured reliably.

In a typical retail environment, these criteria are generally all met at the point of sale. For example, a customer who purchases groceries for cash immediately assumes the risks and rewards of ownership. The customer may consume the goods as desired; the seller no longer controls them. At the point of sale, the customer has agreed to pay the specified price of the goods set by the seller and the economic benefit (cash) has already been transferred.

However, consider a customer who purchases furniture from a big box retailer. The retailer offers to deliver the goods within 10 business days from the sale. When can the seller recognize revenue for this sale? Even though the customer has already paid for the goods at the agreed-upon price, they have not yet received the risks and rewards of ownership. The customer cannot actually use and enjoy the furniture until it is delivered. Therefore, the seller must wait until the owner accepts and signs for the delivery before revenue can be recognized.

Now suppose the big box retailer purchases additional inventory from its supplier, but the inventory will not be shipped until next month. When can the supplier recognize the revenue? This depends on the shipping terms outlined in the sale. If the goods are shipped FOB (free on board) shipping point, the buyer assumes the risks of ownership at the time the goods are loaded onto the truck and shipped out. In this case, the seller may recognize revenue on the shipping date. If instead the goods are shipped FOB destination, the seller must remain responsible for the goods until they arrive at their destination. In this case, the seller may recognize revenue on the delivery date.

For example, assume that on February 1, 2020, Fred's Furniture sold inventory on account for $9,000, terms n/30, FOB shipping point. The inventory's cost was $5,000. The journal entries in Figure 1.2 would be recorded to recognize the revenue and cost of goods sold (assuming a perpetual inventory system is used).

JOURNAL

Date	Account Title and Explanation	Debit	Credit
Feb 1	Accounts Receivable	9,000	
	Sales Revenue		9,000
	To record sale on account		
Feb 1	Cost of Goods Sold	5,000	
	Inventory		5,000
	To record cost of goods sold		

FIGURE 1.2

Sometimes retailers will offer products such as furniture and appliances to customers for no money down and no payments for a specified period of time. This means that the products are transferred to the customer and the customer may use them for a period of time before they are required to pay for them. When can a retailer recognize revenue for these types of sales? Usually, these retailers perform credit checks on customers so that they can be reasonably sure that the customer will pay. All other recognition criteria are met when the goods are delivered to the customer, so these retailers do not have to wait until payments start to recognize the revenue.

Sale of Services

The following four revenue recognition criteria have been defined under IFRS for the sale of services, and ASPE has similar guidelines. Notice the similarity to the criteria for the sale of goods. Again, all criteria must be met before revenue may be recognized.

1. The amount of revenue can be measured reliably (agreed upon by both the buyer and seller).
2. It is probable that the seller will collect the economic benefits associated with the transaction.
3. The stage of completion can be measured reliably.
4. The costs related to the sale can be measured reliably.

Most commonly, services are rendered over a short period of time and the customer pays an agreed-upon price to the seller. The seller generally recognizes revenue after the service has been completed and payment has been made or has been agreed to. For example, a barber will cut a client's hair and recognize revenue after the customer is satisfied with the service.

However, the criterion does not state that the service must be completed in order for revenue to be recognized, only that the stage of completion needs to be known. This means that a service company can recognize a percentage of revenue for a service that is partially completed, which is called the **percentage-of-completion** method. This method is commonly used in the construction industry for projects that take years to complete.

ASPE vs IFRS

Under ASPE, companies are allowed to use the percentage-of-completion method as well as the completed-contract method. Under the completed-contract method, a company waits until the entire service has been completed and the contract fulfilled before any revenue or expenses are recognized.

The completed-contract method is not allowed under IFRS.

For example, Ketch Construction signs a contract to build a condominium. Work is scheduled to begin on June 1, 2020, and is estimated to take two years to complete. Ketch Construction charges $500 million for the project and expects to incur $400 million in costs. How much revenue should be recognized in 2020? We must first determine the stage of completion at the end of 2020. Due to factors such as weather or the complexity of the build, long-term construction projects are often not completed uniformly over time. Instead, the actual costs incurred in the year are divided by the total estimated costs for the project to calculate the percentage of completion, as shown in Figure 1.3.

$$\text{Percentage of Completion} = \frac{\text{Actual Costs Incurred in Current Year}}{\text{Total Estimated Project Costs}}$$

FIGURE 1.3

Suppose that the actual costs incurred by Ketch Construction for this project are $100 million in 2020, $280 million in 2021, and $20 million in 2022. After the percentage of completion is calculated for a given year, it is multiplied by the total revenue for the contract to calculate the amount of revenue to be recognized for that year. The calculations are performed in Figure 1.4.

Year	Actual Costs Incurred	Total Estimated Project Costs	Percentage of Completion	Total Revenue for Contract	Revenue Recognized
2020	$100 million	$400 million	25%	$500 million	$125 million
2021	280 million	400 million	70%	500 million	350 million
2022	20 million	400 million	5%	500 million	25 million
Total	$400 million		100%		$500 million

FIGURE 1.4

Therefore, Ketch Construction recognizes $125 million of revenue in 2020 for this project. It also incurred costs of $100 million, resulting in gross profit of $25 million in 2020.

The percentage-of-completion method relies on estimates. Estimates can be justified using historical data or industry analysis. If these figures cannot be estimated reliably, revenue may be recognized only to the extent that the costs are recoverable until the contract is completed.

Accounting for Bad Debts

LO 2

There is an upside and a downside to selling goods and services to customers on credit. The upside is that selling on credit encourages people to buy. For the most part, people pay their bills when they are due. The downside is that there are inevitably customers who delay paying their bills. There are also customers who never pay their bills, resulting in uncollectible accounts known as **bad debts.**

Bad debts are considered an operating expense and must be recorded in a way that is consistent with accounting principles. Because the **expense recognition** principle (also known as the matching concept) requires recording expenses during the same period in which the related revenue is generated, bad debt expense must be recorded during the same period in which credit sales are generated. Accurately determining the amount of bad debt in the same period as credit sales can be challenging, because it is sometimes difficult to know if a customer is just late with a payment or is unable to pay. Assumptions must be made in order for the records to reflect the company's current financial position as accurately as possible. There are two accepted accounting methods for doubtful accounts and bad debt: (1) the allowance method and (2) the direct write-off method. The allowance method is most common and will be discussed first. The direct method can only be allowed in very specific circumstances, which will be discussed in the following section.

The Allowance Method

To record bad debts in a way that satisfies expense recognition, accountants have created an account called **allowance for doubtful accounts (AFDA)**. It is located directly beneath accounts receivable on the Accounting Map, and it is a contra account. Recall that a **contra account** is linked directly to another account and is used to decrease the account balance. In this case, the AFDA contra account is linked directly to accounts receivable. The AFDA account has a normal credit balance, unlike accounts receivable, which has a normal debit balance. The use of the AFDA account in recording bad debts is referred to as the allowance method of accounting for bad debts.

The **allowance method** estimates an amount considered as uncollectible and records it in the books. The recording of bad debts decreases the equity of a business by recognizing an expense on the income statement, and decreases assets by using the AFDA account. Recall that expense recognition requires expenses to be recorded in the same period in which they were used to generate revenue. Expense recognition is closely tied to revenue recognition because there is often a direct association between incurring expenses and generating revenue. Since bad debt expense is directly associated with recording accounts receivable and sales, it should be recorded in the same period as the related revenue.

For example, assume that at the end of 2020, Columbo Company has an outstanding accounts receivable balance of $100,000. After analyzing the existing data and the current economy, it determines that $5,000 of the accounts receivable may not be collectible. However, since there is still a chance that Columbo will collect, the accounts are not removed from the accounts receivable list. Note that the amount estimated to be uncollectible is not based on one specific customer but is an overall estimate for the entire accounts receivable.

The accounts receivable account of $100,000 does not change. It remains as a debit on the balance sheet. Instead, the AFDA contra account is credited with $5,000, resulting in a net realizable value of $95,000. The **net realizable value** of accounts receivable is the amount of cash that the accounts receivable are likely to turn into; in other words, the accounts receivable balance net of the AFDA. For the debit side of this transaction, bad debt expense is increased by $5,000 and this amount is reported as an expense for the period on the income statement. The journal entry at the end of 2020 for this transaction is shown in Figure 1.5.

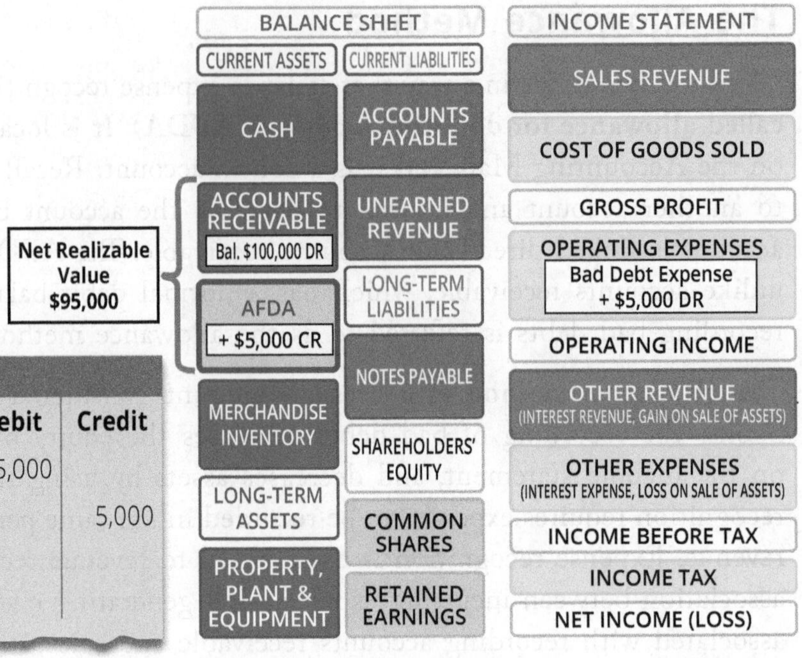

JOURNAL

Date	Account Title and Explanation	Debit	Credit
Dec 31	Bad Debt Expense	5,000	
	Allowance for Doubtful Accounts		5,000
	To record an allowance for doubtful accounts		

FIGURE 1.5

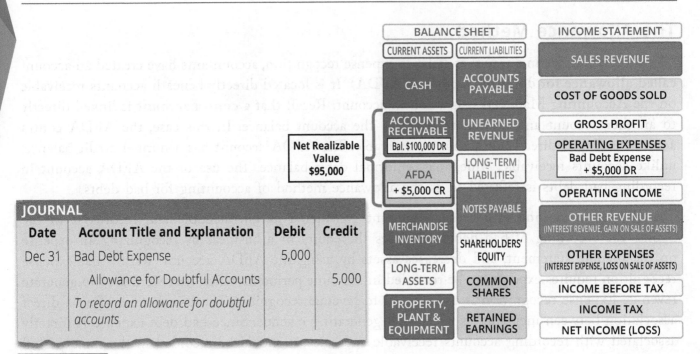

The net realizable value of accounts receivable is $95,000 and is presented on the balance sheet. The partial balance sheet for Columbo Company is shown in Figure 1.6.

Columbo Company Balance Sheet (partial) As at December 31, 2020		
Current Assets		
Cash		$12,500
Accounts Receivable	$100,000	
Allowance for Doubtful Accounts	(5,000)	
Net Accounts Receivable		95,000
Merchandise Inventory		210,000
Prepaid Insurance		12,000
Total Current Assets		$329,500

FIGURE 1.6

The AFDA contra account allows for the possibility that some of the accounts receivable generated in the current period will not be collected. The debit to bad debt expense supports expense recognition since this amount is deducted as an expense in the period when the sale was recorded. Note that the company's equity decreases as a result of recognizing the bad debt expense. Most companies show only the net balance of the accounts receivable account on the balance sheet. The details for the gross accounts receivable and the allowance for doubtful accounts are mainly reported in the notes to the financial statements.

A company must have a good reason to believe that some amounts will not be paid in order to justify the adjustments made to the assets and expenses. There should be some documentation to justify the amount of bad debt estimated. Such measures are warranted because estimates like AFDA are easy targets for manipulation by management.

After the above entries are recorded for an accounting period, the following scenarios may exist.

1. A customer is unable or unwilling to pay the debt and the amount is considered uncollectible.
2. After an account is written off as uncollectible, the customer informs the company that they are now able to pay the amount.
3. After an account is written off as uncollectible, the customer informs the company that they can pay part of the amount.

We will examine each scenario as a continuation of the estimation of bad debt from Figure 1.6.

Scenario 1: On February 16, 2021, Jacob Soloman, who owes $5,000, informs the company that he is unable to pay his account.

The amount is now considered uncollectible and needs to be written off.

Since the allowance method was used, the bad debt expense was previously entered to match prior period revenue, and the AFDA account was established. Now, the AFDA account is debited and the accounts receivable account is credited to remove the amount from the company's records. The entry shown in Figure 1.7 has no impact on the company's equity, since the amount was already accounted for by the original debit to bad debt expense in 2020.

Usually, a company attempts to collect outstanding payments from a customer for many months. If it is unsuccessful, the company writes off that account. The journal entry is shown in Figure 1.7.

JOURNAL

Date	Account Title and Explanation	Debit	Credit
Feb 16	Allowance for Doubtful Accounts	5,000	
	Accounts Receivable—Jacob Soloman		5,000
	To write off account as uncollectible		

FIGURE 1.7

Scenario 2: Jacob Soloman is now able to pay his account (which was previously written off as uncollectible). He pays the amount on June 25, 2021.

Two journal entries must be made in this scenario. The first journal entry is to reinstate the customer's account balance (by reversing the entry in Figure 1.7). This journal entry is required to reinstate the customer's balance in accounts receivable. Without it, there would be no balance to credit when the amount is paid. The second journal entry records the amount being paid. These journal entries are shown in Figures 1.8 and 1.9, respectively.

1. Reinstate the customer's account balance.

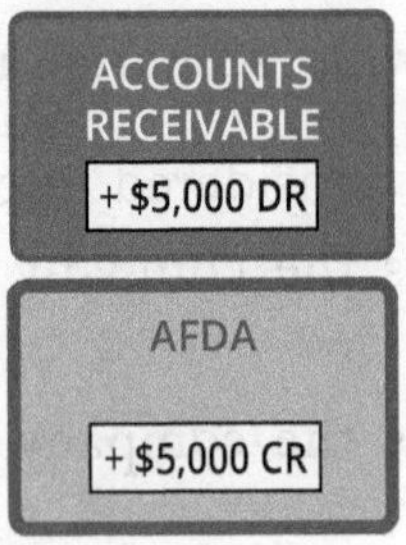

JOURNAL

Date	Account Title and Explanation	Debit	Credit
Jun 25	Accounts Receivable—Jacob Soloman	5,000	
	Allowance for Doubtful Accounts		5,000
	To reinstate amount previously written off		

FIGURE 1.8

2. Record receipt of payment on account.

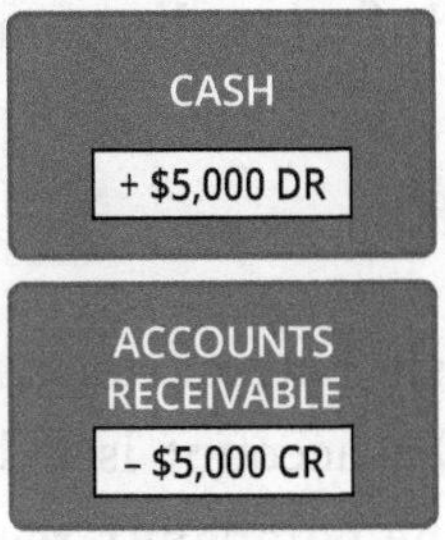

JOURNAL

Date	Account Title and Explanation	Debit	Credit
Jun 25	Cash	5,000	
	Accounts Receivable—Jacob Soloman		5,000
	To record receipt of payment from customer		

FIGURE 1.9

Scenario 3: Jacob Soloman notifies the company that he is able to pay half of the amount he owes, or $2,500.

Again, two journal entries are required, as shown in Figures 1.10 and 1.11. Note that, since the customer is able to repay only $2,500 and not the full amount owing, only $2,500 is reinstated as accounts receivable in Figure 1.10.

1. Reinstate the customer's account balance.

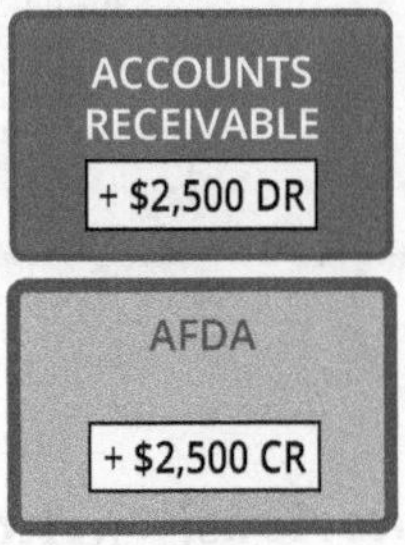

JOURNAL

Date	Account Title and Explanation	Debit	Credit
Jun 25	Accounts Receivable—Jacob Soloman	2,500	
	Allowance for Doubtful Accounts		2,500
	To reinstate amount previously written off		

FIGURE 1.10

2. Record receipt of payment on account.

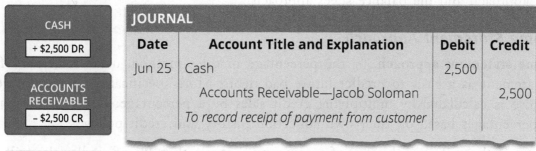

CASH
+ $2,500 DR

ACCOUNTS RECEIVABLE
- $2,500 CR

JOURNAL

Date	Account Title and Explanation	Debit	Credit
Jun 25	Cash	2,500	
	Accounts Receivable—Jacob Soloman		2,500
	To record receipt of payment from customer		

FIGURE 1.11

Even customers with a good credit record sometimes take time to settle their bills. After many months of attempting to collect from a customer, a company faces the decision of whether to write off the account as uncollectible. However, if it is relatively certain that the customer will pay eventually, the company can decide to take no action, except to periodically issue a reminder to the customer. The original amount in accounts receivable remains on the books and is credited when the account is finally paid. Another alternative is to convert the account receivable into a note receivable, which is covered later in this chapter.

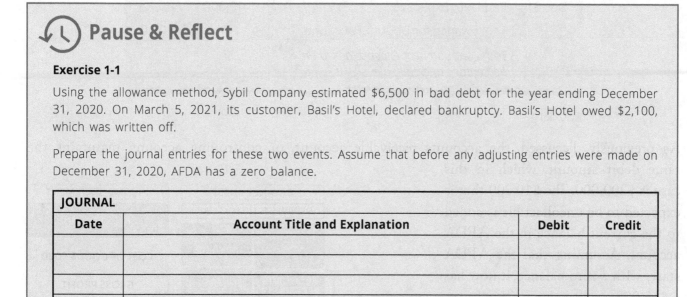

Pause & Reflect

Exercise 1-1

Using the allowance method, Sybil Company estimated $6,500 in bad debt for the year ending December 31, 2020. On March 5, 2021, its customer, Basil's Hotel, declared bankruptcy. Basil's Hotel owed $2,100, which was written off.

Prepare the journal entries for these two events. Assume that before any adjusting entries were made on December 31, 2020, AFDA has a zero balance.

JOURNAL

Date	Account Title and Explanation	Debit	Credit

See Appendix I for solutions.

Approaches to Estimating Bad Debts

Managing accounts receivable includes assessing what amount, if any, may end up as uncollectible. This has an impact on the financial statements of a business for the reporting period, and also has implications for meeting requirements for expense recognition.

We will examine two approaches for estimating bad debts under the allowance method: the income statement approach and the balance sheet approach.

The Income Statement Approach

The **income statement approach**, or the percentage of sales method, uses credit sales from the income statement as a basis to predict future bad debts. More specifically, the current year's bad debt expense is calculated by multiplying credit sales by a percentage. Different companies use different percentages based on their own collection history and credit policy.

For example, if the collection history of a company suggests that 1% of credit sales will result in bad debts, that rate is used to estimate the portion of each period's sales that will not be collectible.

Total credit sales for Columbo Company in 2020 amounted to $1,000,000, of which $200,000 is currently owed by customers. On the basis of historical sales, 1% of credit sales is expected to be uncollectible, which is $10,000 ($1,000,000 × 1%). The bad debt expense for the period is shown in Figure 1.12.

JOURNAL

Date	Account Title and Explanation	Debit	Credit
Dec 31	Bad Debt Expense	10,000	
	Allowance for Doubtful Accounts		10,000
	To record bad debt expense based on percentage of credit sales		

FIGURE 1.12

As previously discussed, the accounts receivable account, or controlling account, maintains the same debit amount, which in this case is $200,000. The $10,000 that is expected to be uncollectible is added to the current balance in the AFDA account. Assuming that the AFDA starts with a zero balance, it now has a $10,000 credit balance. This leaves a net realizable value of $190,000 in accounts receivable. The AFDA credit balance of $10,000 represents a decrease in the company's assets. The income statement includes a debit balance of $10,000 for bad debt expense. This is shown in Figure 1.13.

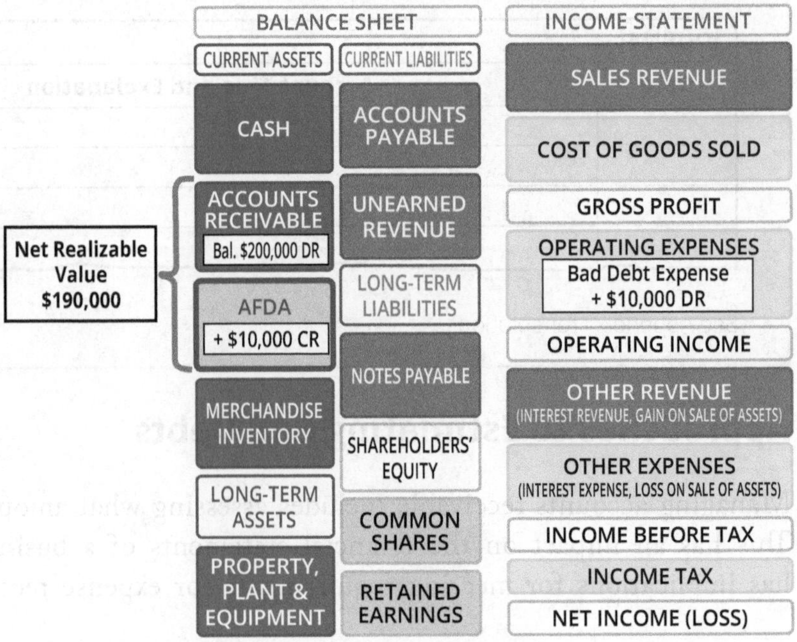

FIGURE 1.13

This approach is called the income statement approach because bad debt expense is calculated based on the credit sales figure from the income statement. Nevertheless, adjustments must be made to both the income statement and the balance sheet accounts when accounting for bad debt expense.

The Balance Sheet Approach

Under the **balance sheet approach**, a company can calculate the bad debt expense using either the percentage of total accounts receivable method or the aging method. The **percentage of total accounts receivable method**, as the name implies, uses a percentage of receivables to estimate bad debt. The percentage is applied to the ending accounts receivable balance. For example, if the accounts receivable balance at the end of the period is $200,000, and the company estimates, based on its experience, that 4% of total accounts receivable will become uncollectible, the allowance for bad debt in this period is $8,000 ($200,000 × 0.04). Therefore, the AFDA account must be adjusted to have a credit balance of $8,000. We will show entries to adjust the AFDA balance later in this section.

In the **aging method**, the second option under the balance sheet approach, percentages are applied to groupings based on the age of outstanding accounts receivable amounts. We will use an example to illustrate this procedure.

The chart in Figure 1.14 contains three groups of customers and their outstanding balances on December 31, 2020.

1. Those who have not paid within 30 days
2. Those who have not paid for 31 to 60 days
3. Those who have not paid for more than 60 days

Aging Category	Bad Debt %* (probability of being uncollectible)	Balance of Accounts Receivable
30 days	2%	$80,000
31–60 days	3%	90,000
More than 60 days	5%	30,000
Total		$200,000

*Percentages are based on historical collectability.

FIGURE 1.14

A percentage is applied to each aging category. A 2% rate is applied to the first group, 3% to the second group and 5% to the third group. These percentages are the probability, or likelihood, that these amounts will be uncollectible. The longer a customer takes to pay, the more likely the account will never be paid; that is why the highest rate is used for the third group.

The balance of accounts receivable column of the chart in Figure 1.15 shows the amount that each group still owes the company. The percentages are applied to these amounts to calculate the expected total bad debt per customer group. These amounts are then added to give the total amount of estimated bad debt.

Aging Category	Bad Debt % (probability of being uncollectible)	Balance of Accounts Receivable	Estimated Bad Debt*
30 days	2%	$80,000	$1,600
31–60 days	3%	90,000	2,700
More than 60 days	5%	30,000	1,500
Total		$200,000	$5,800

*Balance of Accounts Receivable × Bad Debt %

FIGURE 1.15

In this example, $5,800 of the gross accounts receivable balance of $200,000 is estimated to be uncollectible. The $5,800 of estimated bad debt becomes the ending balance of AFDA for the period regardless of AFDA's existing balance or which method was used, the percentage of total accounts receivable method or the aging method. Under the balance sheet approach, the adjustments required could be grouped into three different scenarios based on AFDA having a credit, zero or debit balance. These scenarios are presented through the following examples.

Scenario 1: AFDA has a credit balance of $3,000.

If there is already a credit balance in the AFDA account, it needs to be subtracted from the $5,800 total to give the bad debt expense for the period. A credit balance indicates the company has overestimated bad debt expense in the past. In this example, the AFDA account already has a credit balance of $3,000. Subtracting that from the calculated amount of $5,800 leaves an adjustment in the AFDA account of $2,800. In effect, this "tops up" the AFDA account, because it is being adjusted to reflect the total amount of bad debts expected. Figure 1.16 shows the journal entry for this transaction and Figure 1.17 shows its impact on the balance sheet and income statement.

Scenario 1

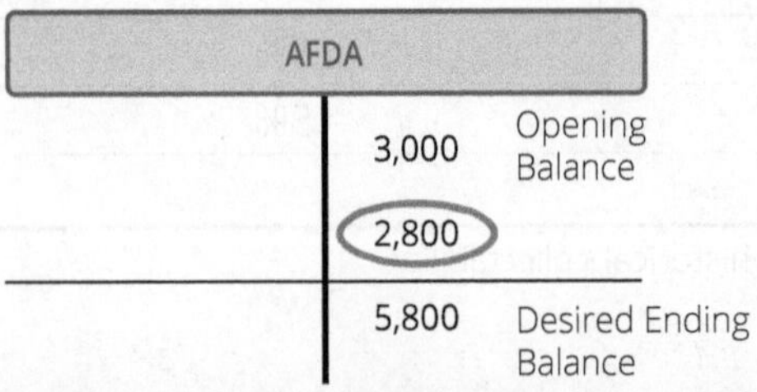

JOURNAL

Date	Account Title and Explanation	Debit	Credit
Dec 31	Bad Debt Expense	2,800	
	Allowance for Doubtful Accounts		2,800
	To adjust the AFDA account to the correct balance		

FIGURE 1.16

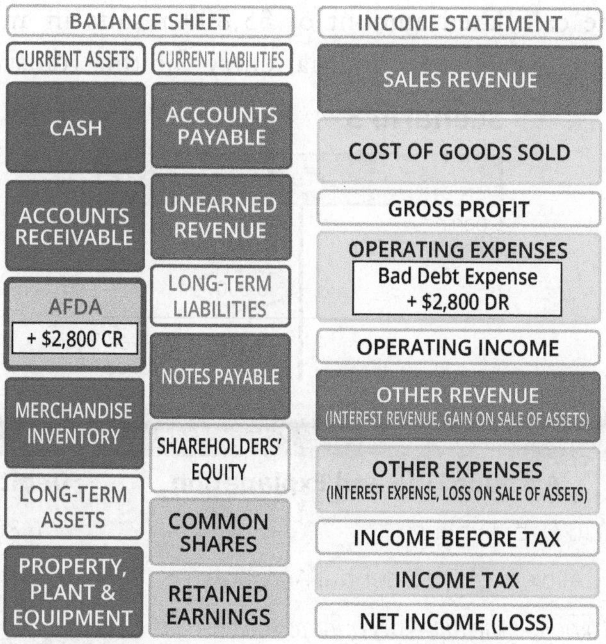

FIGURE 1.17

Scenario 2: AFDA has a balance of zero.

If AFDA has a zero balance, then the amount calculated as uncollectible becomes the amount of the adjustment. In our example, the amount of the credit to the AFDA account is $5,800. Figure 1.18 shows the journal entry for this transaction.

Scenario 2

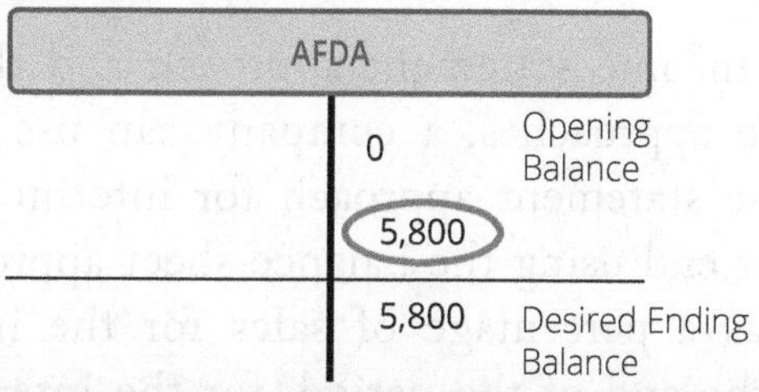

JOURNAL

Date	Account Title and Explanation	Debit	Credit
Dec 31	Bad Debt Expense	5,800	
	Allowance for Doubtful Accounts		5,800
	To adjust the AFDA account to the correct balance		

FIGURE 1.18

Scenario 3: AFDA has a debit balance of $1,000.

If there is already a debit balance in the AFDA account, it is added to the $5,800 total to give the bad debt expense for the period. A debit balance indicates the company has underestimated bad debt expense in the past. In this example, the AFDA account already has a debit balance of

$1,000. Adding that to the calculated amount of $5,800 results in an adjustment in the AFDA account of $6,800. Figure 1.19 shows the journal entry for this transaction.

Scenario 3

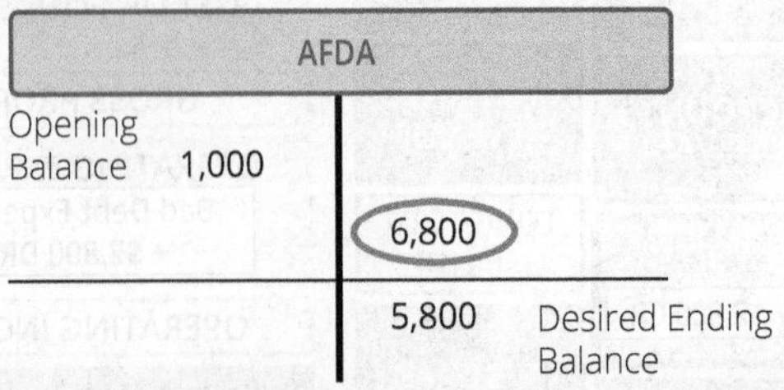

JOURNAL

Date	Account Title and Explanation	Debit	Credit
Dec 31	Bad Debt Expense	6,800	
	Allowance for Doubtful Accounts		6,800
	To adjust the AFDA account to the correct balance		

FIGURE 1.19

Note that the adjustment to accounts receivable and the allowance for doubtful accounts adheres to prudence, one of the related considerations within the conceptual framework of accounting. This concept requires assets to be valued at the lower amount of possible alternatives and, as a result, reflects a reduced net income for the period. This approach allows the business to make decisions based on figures that do not overstate assets, net income or the financial position of the company.

Figure 1.20 summarizes the income statement approach and the balance sheet approach. Rather than using only one of these approaches, a company can use a mix of procedures. Such a mix may involve using the income statement approach for interim periods (month, quarter or other) while adjusting AFDA at year end using the balance sheet approach. Those adopting this approach calculate bad debt expense as a percentage of sales for the interim period, while ignoring the existing AFDA balance. At the end of the period, for the interim period, the accounts receivable are reviewed to check the appropriateness of the AFDA balance, and adjustments to the AFDA balance are made as required.

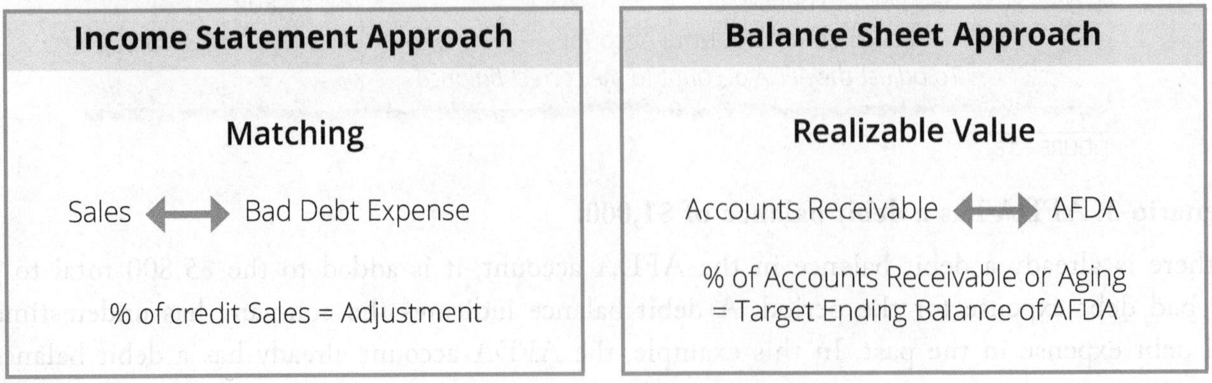

FIGURE 1.20

A Closer Look

For the income statement approach, the calculated amount is recorded as the bad debt expense regardless of what the existing balance of AFDA is. The calculated amount for the balance sheet approach is the ending balance of AFDA and not necessarily the amount of adjustment required.

Under the income statement approach, after the amount based on a percentage of credit sales is calculated, it is debited to bad debt expense and credited to AFDA. The expense is based on sales to appropriately match the bad debt expense with the credit sales of the period. The total amount of the allowance is essentially ignored. If the percentage of credit sales used realistically reflects the actual amount of bad debt experienced, the allowance account reflects a reasonable balance.

If the actual bad debt experienced is materially lower than the estimate (based on a percentage of sales), the allowance for doubtful accounts may build to an unrealistically large amount. This would occur because the increase in AFDA based on the estimate of bad debt is not consistent with a reduction from actual bad debt write-offs.

If the allowance account is becoming unusually large, a company could forgo recording additional bad debt expenses (and the corresponding credit to the allowance account), until debits (i.e. actual bad debt write-offs) reduce the allowance account to a reasonable balance. What is a reasonable balance? As with many items in accounting, the answer is based on professional judgment.

Pause & Reflect

Exercise 1-2

Manuel Enterprise is preparing its year-end adjustments for bad debt. Accounts receivable has a debit balance of $400,000 and allowance for doubtful accounts has a credit balance of $3,400. The aging breakdown of accounts receivable is shown below.

a) Calculate the estimated bad debt expense using the aging of accounts receivable method and complete the final column of the table.

Aging Category	Bad Debt %	Balance of Accounts Receivable	Estimated Bad Debt
30 days	1%	$200,000	
31-60 days	5%	120,000	
More than 60 days	10%	80,000	
Total		$400,000	

b) Prepare the journal entry to record the bad debt expense on December 31, 2020.

JOURNAL			
Date	**Account Title and Explanation**	**Debit**	**Credit**

See Appendix I for solutions.

The Direct Write-Off Method

LO 3

When a sale is made on account, it is recorded as a debit to accounts receivable and a credit to sales revenue. The debit to accounts receivable increases the assets of the business, while the credit to sales increases equity and is recorded as sales revenue. As we saw, under the allowance method, the AFDA account is used to estimate the accounts receivable amount that might not be collectible. However, under the **direct write-off method**, an account receivable is not written off until it has been determined to be uncollectible, and then it is written off directly to bad debt expense.

Consider this example. A customer informs you on March 3 that their company, Sweet Treats, is unable to pay its outstanding account balance of $5,000. When it is determined that the bill will not be paid, the direct write-off method requires a journal entry to increase (debit) bad debt expense and decrease (credit) accounts receivable. Note that the AFDA account is never used when the direct method is used, so it never shows up in the journal entries. Figure 1.21 shows the required journal entry for this transaction.

JOURNAL

Date	Account Title and Explanation	Debit	Credit
Mar 3	Bad Debt Expense	5,000	
	Accounts Receivable—Sweet Treats		5,000
	To record direct write-off of bad debt from accounts receivable		

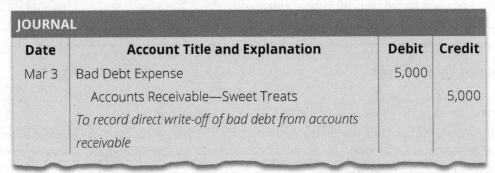

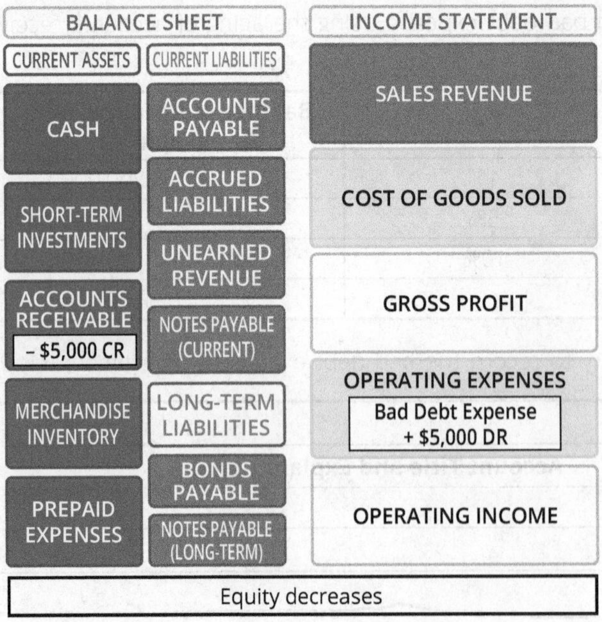

FIGURE 1.21

One drawback of using the direct method to write off bad debt is that it does not always satisfy expense recognition. Recall that expense recognition states that expenses must be recorded during the same period in which the related revenue is generated. However, the write-off under the direct method is usually made in later periods because it takes time to determine whether or not a customer will pay.

Since the direct method does not follow accounting standards, it is not used by most companies. This method should be used only if the uncollectible accounts are immaterial or if there is a small difference between using either the direct method or the allowance method. In the above example, assume that the year-end balance of accounts receivable was $50 million and credit sales for the year were $650 million. The company experiences very few write-offs and management considers $5,000 immaterial. In this case, using the direct method is acceptable.

The second drawback to using this method arises if the customer is able to repay the account *after* the account has been written off. For example, suppose the owner of Sweet Treats is able to pay her account of $5,000 on August 7, after the account has already been written off. Figure 1.22 shows the journal entries that are recorded if this occurs.

JOURNAL

Date	Account Title and Explanation	Debit	Credit
Aug 7	Accounts Receivable—Sweet Treats	5,000	
	Bad Debt Expense		5,000
	To reinstate the customer's account		
Aug 7	Cash	5,000	
	Accounts Receivable—Sweet Treats		5,000
	To record receipt of payment on account		

FIGURE 1.22

The amount needs to be reinstated into the customer's account. This requires a journal entry to increase (debit) accounts receivable and decrease (credit) bad debt expense, which causes a reduction in expenses and an overstatement of net income for the current period. Unless the write-off and the subsequent reinstatement occur in the same period, the expense recognition is violated.

After the amount is reinstated, a second journal entry is required to record the receipt of the payment from the customer.

Promissory Notes and Notes Receivable

LO 4

A **promissory note**, or **note receivable**, makes an account receivable resemble a formal loan by adding precise terms of repayment to which the customer adds their signature. The customer (the borrower) is known as the **maker** of the note, because they are the one making a promise to pay. The company (the lender) is known as the **payee**, because it is the one to whom the note is payable. Figure 1.23 shows an example of a promissory note. The face of a promissory note usually contains the information about the maker, the payee, the issuance date, the due date, the principal amount and the interest rate. The term of the note can be calculated as the duration between the issuance date and the maturity date. The term is sometimes specified on the face of the note in addition to the issuance date and the maturity date.

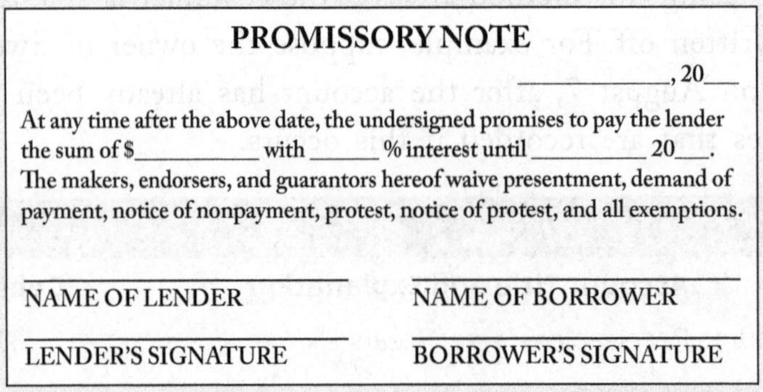
PROMISSORY NOTE

__________, 20__

At any time after the above date, the undersigned promises to pay the lender the sum of $________ with _____ % interest until ________ 20__.
The makers, endorsers, and guarantors hereof waive presentment, demand of payment, notice of nonpayment, protest, notice of protest, and all exemptions.

NAME OF LENDER NAME OF BORROWER

LENDER'S SIGNATURE BORROWER'S SIGNATURE

FIGURE 1.23

If a customer is overdue on their account, the company may request that the customer sign a promissory note to formalize the arrangements of the debt repayment, similar to how a formal loan specifies its terms of repayment. Both a loan and a promissory note can set terms that include naming the parties to the document, the amount to be paid (the *face value*), the rate of interest to be paid on the note and the *maturity date* or *due date* when the face amount of the note (plus interest) is to be paid.

A promissory note is used to formalize an accounts receivable item and also to extend unusual credit terms to a specific customer. For example, an agreement may involve lengthening the terms of repayment to more than one year. In addition, the note can be used to extend credit to a customer with no formal credit history. The stronger legal claim associated with a note provides greater protection for the selling company when dealing with uncertain or riskier customer accounts. Provided that the seller is confident the customer will eventually pay the note, there should be no objection to issuing the note.

Notes are often issued on a date other than the first or last day of the month. They can also have maturity dates that are less than a full year, such as 30, 60 or 90 days. In such cases, special calculations determine both the note's maturity date and the interest amount to be paid.

For example, assume a promissory note between two parties is issued on January 15, 2021. The face value of the note is $1,000 and the annual interest rate is 8%. The term of the note is 60 days. First, we will determine the maturity date.

The note has a maturity date of March 16, 2021, which is calculated as follows.

Days in January	31
Deduct: Note issuance date	15
Days remaining in January	16
Add: Days in February	28
Add: Days in March until due date	16
Term of note (in days)	60

Next, we can calculate the interest amount on the note.

The formula to calculate interest is shown in Figure 1.24.

$$\text{Interest} = \text{Face Amount of Note} \times \text{Annual Interest Rate} \times \left(\frac{\text{Term of Note}}{\text{365 days}}\right)$$

FIGURE 1.24

The note's interest rate is given as 8%, stated on an *annual* basis, but the term of the note is stated in *days* (60). Therefore, the interest needs to be adjusted for the partial year. Interest is calculated as shown here.

$$\text{Interest} = \$1{,}000 \times 8\% \times \left(\frac{60}{365}\right)$$
$$= \$13.15$$

Therefore, $13.15 in interest, along with the principal or face amount of the note ($1,000), is due on March 16, 2021.

To keep things simple, we will use a maturity date exactly one year away, and use the number of months instead of the number of days to calculate accrued interest in the following example.

On April 1, 2020, Kay Alonso has $1,000 of outstanding accounts receivable with Columbo Company. Columbo's year end is October 31. Kay cannot pay the amount immediately but is willing to sign a promissory note. The interest is 6% per annum, to be collected when the note is due. Kay promises to pay on April 1, 2021. The entry to record the conversion of the accounts receivable to a note receivable on April 1, 2020, is shown in Figure 1.25.

JOURNAL			
Date	**Account Title and Explanation**	**Debit**	**Credit**
Apr 1	Notes Receivable	1,000	
	Accounts Receivable		1,000
	To convert accounts receivable to a note receivable		

FIGURE 1.25

On October 31, when Columbo Company prepares its financial statements, it needs to accrue the interest earned from Kay. The interest earned from April 1 to October 31, 2020, which is seven months, is $35 ($1,000 × 6% × 7/12). Notice from Figure 1.26 that the interest earned is classified as other revenue rather than sales revenue.

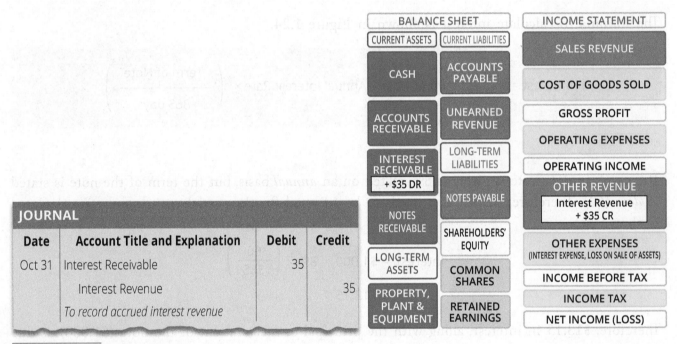

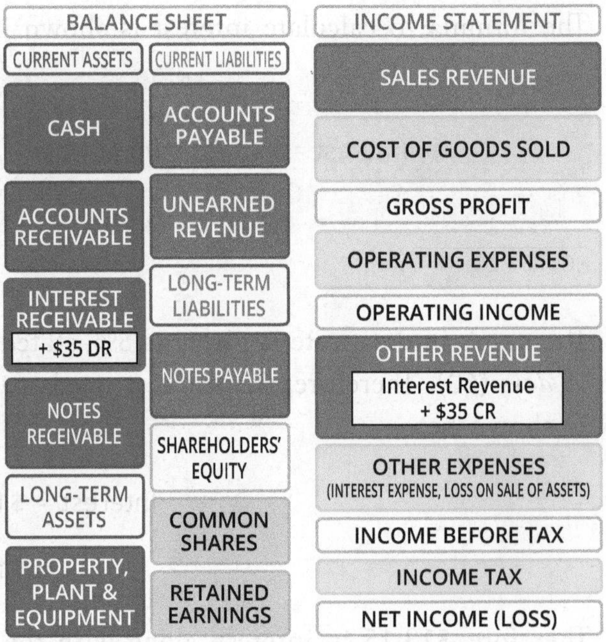

JOURNAL			
Date	**Account Title and Explanation**	**Debit**	**Credit**
Oct 31	Interest Receivable	35	
	Interest Revenue		35
	To record accrued interest revenue		

FIGURE 1.26

When Kay pays the amount due on April 1, 2021, the entry in Figure 1.27 is recorded on the statements of Columbo Company.

JOURNAL

Date	Account Title and Explanation	Debit	Credit
Apr 1	Cash	1,060	
	Interest Receivable		35
	Interest Revenue		25
	Notes Receivable		1,000
	To record the receipt of note principal and interest		

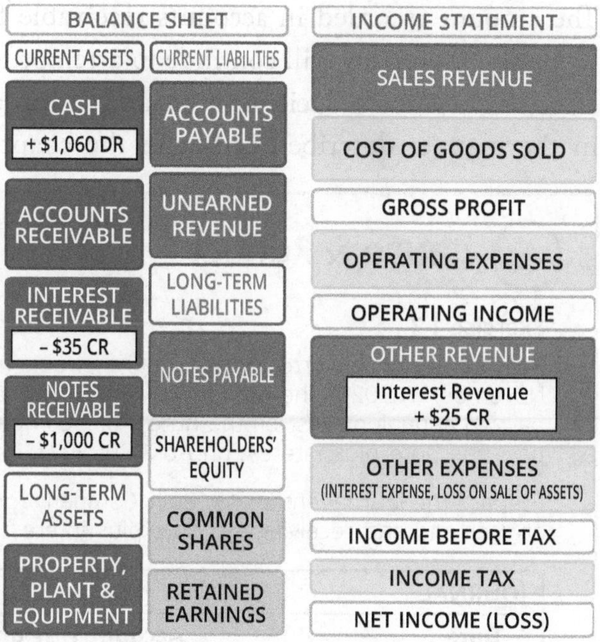

FIGURE 1.27

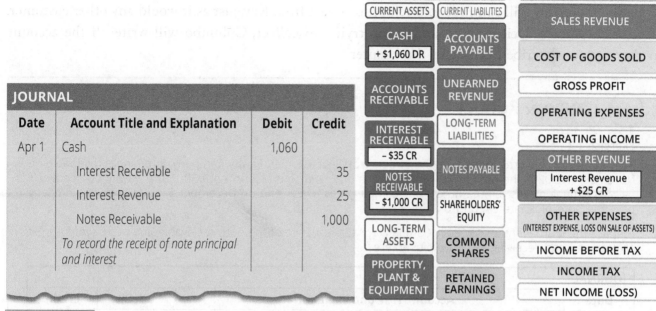

The explanation for this transaction is as follows.

- Kay paid $1,060 (debit to cash).
- The interest receivable of $35, which was recorded on October 31, 2020, was eliminated by crediting the account.
- An amount of $25 was recorded as interest revenue earned from November 1, 2020, to April 1, 2021 ($1,000 × 6% × 5/12), by crediting interest revenue.
- The note receivable of $1,000 was eliminated by crediting the notes receivable account.

It is possible that on April 1, 2021, Kay may not pay the amount owing to Columbo Company. If a note is not paid at maturity, it is considered a **dishonoured note**. Since the note receivable is no longer valid due to expiry, Columbo Company cannot keep it as a note receivable in its books. Thus, it will convert the note back to accounts receivable with the transaction shown in Figure 1.28.

JOURNAL

Date	Account Title and Explanation	Debit	Credit
Apr 1	Accounts Receivable—Kay Alonso	1,060	
	Interest Receivable		35
	Interest Revenue		25
	Notes Receivable		1,000
	To record a dishonoured note		

FIGURE 1.28

The amount recorded in accounts receivable for Kay is the total amount owing, including interest. Columbo Company will continue to attempt to collect from Kay, just as it would any other customer. If at some point a decision is made to stop trying to collect, Columbo will write off the account in the manner described earlier in the chapter.

Pause & Reflect

Exercise 1-3

Polly Company converted an account receivable from its customer, Fawlty Company, into a note receivable on November 1, 2020. The note is for $6,000 and is due in six months on April 30, 2021. Fawlty Company will pay 5% annual interest on the note. Polly Company has a year end on December 31, 2020. Fawlty Company pays the note plus interest on April 30, 2021.

Prepare the journal entries for Polly Company for the issuance of the note receivable, the accrual of interest at year end and receiving the note plus interest.

JOURNAL

Date	Account Title and Explanation	Debit	Credit

See Appendix I for solutions.

Managing Accounts Receivable Information Using Reports LO 5

Another important aspect of accounting for accounts receivable is managing or controlling them. It is important for a business to not only report the correct amount but also apply the policies and procedures that support collecting the maximum possible amount. This practice has a direct impact on the cash flow and working capital of the business, specifically on its ability to meet short-term debt obligations such as accounts payable, interest on loans and other current liabilities.

Today, most businesses use a computer software program to collect, organize and process accounting information involving accounts receivable transactions. These programs can generate reports that give management insight into financial affairs that goes beyond the raw data.

A Closer Look

A number of strategies ensure that a company effectively manages and controls its accounts receivable. These strategies include the following.

- **Commitment to efficiency**—Management commits to ensuring that accounts receivable are handled efficiently.
- **Measuring results**—After using ratios and reports to manage information, it is essential to determine whether these measures are working.
- **Cutting-edge technology**—Up-to-date technology provides accurate and useful information about accounts receivable and can support informed decision-making. For instance, data visualization software displays information graphically, making it simple to see patterns and trends among the data. The data displayed can also be easily customized using filters. This allows users to make decisions quickly without having to interpret spreadsheets or reports. Accounts receivable analytics software can alert a business to customers who are past due and provide information about what is outstanding in total. These key metrics for a business can be displayed in a dashboard like the one seen below from Sage Intelligence.

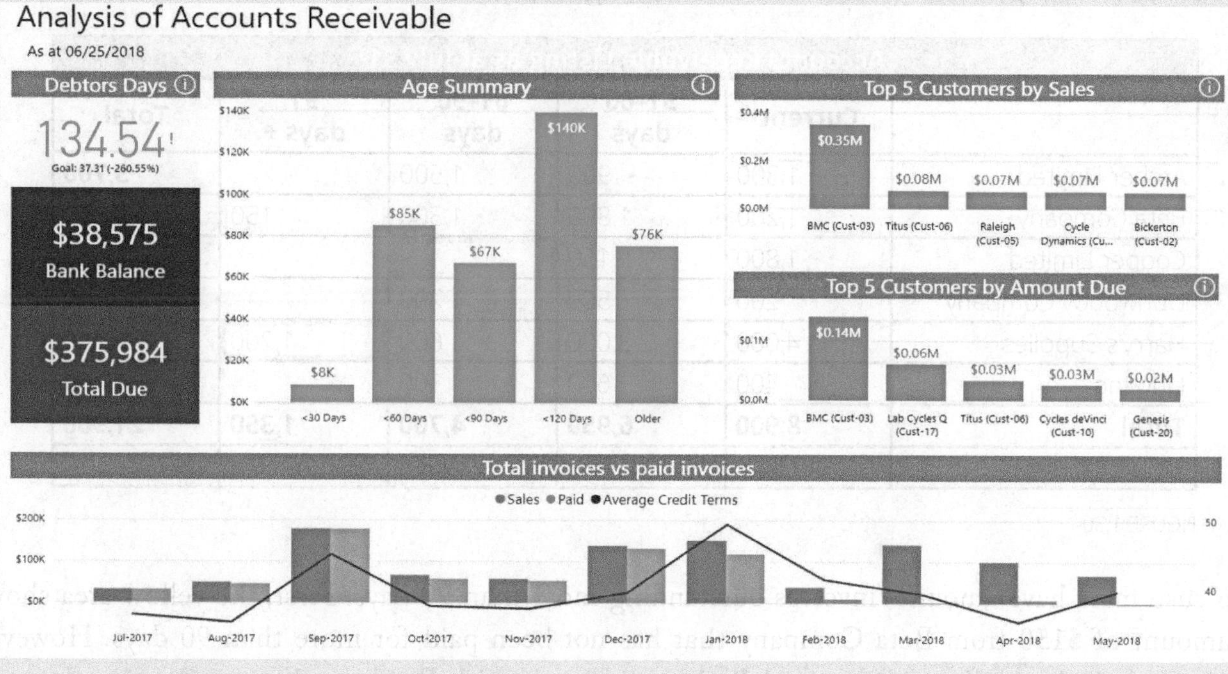

The Accounts Receivable Subledger

For most businesses, accounts receivable is considered a controlling account, as it reports the total of all amounts owed by customers listed in the **accounts receivable subledger**. The subledger contains individual customer accounts and is used to record the details of transactions affecting each account. Figure 1.29 is a customer-by-customer list of outstanding amounts owing to a business; the total is reported in the accounts receivable control account in the general ledger.

Accounts Receivable Listing as at July 31					
	Current	**31-60 days**	**61-90 days**	**91 days +**	**Total**
Archer Limited	1,300	900	1,500		**3,700**
Beta Company	1,200	1,800	1,300	150	**4,450**
Cooper Limited	1,800	150			**1,950**
Dunwoody Company	200	500	200		**900**
Harry's Supplies	4,000	3,000	1,600	1,200	**9,800**
Lino Inc.	400	600	100		**1,100**
Total	**8,900**	**6,950**	**4,700**	**1,350**	**21,900**
	40.64%	31.74%	21.46%	6.16%	

FIGURE 1.29

Presenting the data in this form facilitates the analysis of accounts receivable by customer. It also highlights the figures that stand out from the others. In this case, the areas to note are marked in yellow, red and green in the revised chart in Figure 1.30.

Accounts Receivable Listing as at July 31					
	Current	**31-60 days**	**61-90 days**	**91 days +**	**Total**
Archer Limited	1,300	900	1,500		**3,700**
Beta Company	1,200	1,800	1,300	150	**4,450**
Cooper Limited	1,800	150			**1,950**
Dunwoody Company	200	500	200		**900**
Harry's Supplies	4,000	3,000	1,600	1,200	**9,800**
Lino Inc.	400	600	100		**1,100**
Total	**8,900**	**6,950**	**4,700**	**1,350**	**21,900**
	40.64%	31.74%	21.46%	6.16%	

FIGURE 1.30

Two customers have amounts/invoices outstanding more than 90 days. First, the yellow area shows an amount of $150 from Beta Company that has not been paid for more than 90 days. However, this is a relatively small amount, especially in comparison with Beta's total amount owing. It could be the result of an invoice discrepancy or some other minor issue. Although Beta is one of only two customers with balances owing for more than 90 days, management may not be too concerned about this balance. There should be controls in place to follow up with the customer to either correct or adjust the amount.

The other customer with a balance exceeding 90 days, Harry's Supplies, is certainly cause for concern. The amount marked in red, $1,200, represents a significant portion of the outstanding balance. Furthermore, the amount might be even more problematic, given that the same customer was given $4,000 in credit in the current month. This account is not being well managed, and management should follow up and reconsider the credit policies that allowed this situation to develop.

The green area of this chart is notable because it shows that, unlike all the other customers on the list, Cooper Limited does not have an outstanding balance for the 61–90 day period. Furthermore, it has only $150 outstanding for the 31–60 day period. Therefore the $1,800 credit given to Cooper in the current period appears to be justified. This customer has paid bills promptly, and providing more credit for this customer makes good business sense.

Alternative Presentation Formats

The preceding examples represent just a few ways in which accounts receivable information can be organized and presented. Computer software allows for multiple methods of analysis. Management should use computer programs that meet the specific needs and objectives of the business with regard to information about accounts receivable, bad debts, internal controls and all other related issues.

The accounts receivable reports that can be generated include the following.

- Current active customers
- Past customers not active for the last 12 months
- Customer activities listing value of sales per month
- Customer activities listing value of sales per product
- Categorization of customers according to sales representative or geographic location
- Overdue accounts

Measuring the Effectiveness of Collections Using Ratios LO 6

Another approach to measuring the effectiveness of the company's collection efforts is financial ratios. This section examines two types of ratios: accounts receivable turnover and days' sales outstanding.

Accounts Receivable Turnover Ratio

The **accounts receivable turnover ratio (ART)** measures how often during the year a company collects its entire accounts receivable balance. This is done by using two basic figures from the financial records: average net accounts receivable and net credit sales for the past 12 months. Recall that the net accounts receivable is equal to the gross accounts receivable less allowance for doubtful accounts. The net credit sales is equal to the total of credit sales less sales discounts, returns and allowances. The formula to calculate ART is shown in Figure 1.31.

$$\text{Accounts Receivable Turnover (ART)} = \frac{\text{Net Credit Sales}}{\text{Average Net Accounts Receivable}}$$

FIGURE 1.31

The following two examples illustrate the use and function of this particular ratio.

Example 1: Juniper Company

Assume that Juniper Company has an average net accounts receivable of $200,000 and net credit sales of $1,200,000. The accounts receivable turnover is calculated as shown.

$$\text{ART} = \frac{\$1,200,000}{\$200,000}$$

$$= 6 \text{ times}$$

The turnover of six times per year means Juniper Company collects the entire amount of accounts receivable six times a year, or approximately every two months.

Example 2: Willow Company

Assume that Willow Company has an average net accounts receivable of $135,000 and net credit sales of $1,650,000. The accounts receivable turnover is calculated as shown.

$$\text{ART} = \frac{\$1,650,000}{\$135,000}$$

$$= 12.2 \text{ times}$$

The turnover of 12 times per year means Willow Company collects the entire amount of accounts receivable 12 times a year, or every month.

Days' Sales Outstanding

Another way of organizing accounts receivable information is to use days' sales outstanding. **Days' sales outstanding (DSO)** tracks how long customers take to pay their bills. The formula is shown in Figure 1.32.

$$\text{Days' Sales Outstanding (DSO)} = \frac{\text{Average Net Accounts Receivable}}{\text{Net Credit Sales}} \times 365$$

OR

$$\text{Days' Sales Outstanding (DSO)} = \frac{365}{\text{Accounts Receivable Turnover (ART)}}$$

FIGURE 1.32

As shown in the formula, the average net accounts receivable figure is divided by the net credit sales of the past 12 months. The result is then multiplied by 365 (days in the year). If ART has already been calculated, DSO can be found by simply dividing 365 by ART. The result provides the company with the average number of days that customers take to pay their bills.

Example 1: Juniper Company

From the previous example, the total average net accounts receivable amount for Juniper Company is $200,000, and the total net credit sales amount for the past year is $1,200,000. The DSO ratio is calculated as shown.

$$\text{DSO} = \frac{\$200{,}000}{\$1{,}200{,}000} \times 365$$
$$= 61 \text{ days}$$

Juniper Company collects amounts outstanding in an average of 61 days, or approximately two months.

Example 2: Willow Company

From the previous example, the total average net accounts receivable amount for Willow Company is $135,000, and the total net credit sales for the past year was $1,650,000. The DSO ratio is calculated as shown.

$$\text{DSO} = \frac{\$135{,}000}{\$1{,}650{,}000} \times 365$$
$$= 30 \text{ days}$$

Willow Company collects amounts oustanding in an average of 30 days, or approximately one month. On the basis of these calculations, Willow Company is collecting its accounts receivable from customers twice as fast as Juniper Company. Because of the importance of cash in operating a business, it is in the company's best interest to collect outstanding accounts receivable as quickly as possible. By quickly turning sales into cash, a company can effectively use the cash for reinvestment and to produce more revenue.

One of the most important factors that affects both ART and DSO is a company's credit terms. If both companies allow customers 30 days to pay for their purchases on account, Willow Company is doing well in terms of collection whereas Juniper Company is doing poorly.

Pause & Reflect

Exercise 1-4

The Practical Company obtained the following information from its financial records for 2020.

Net Credit Sales	$278,000
Average Net Accounts Receivable	$23,000

a) Calculate the accounts receivable turnover ratio. Explain what this result means.

b) Calculate the days' sales outstanding. Explain what this result means.

See Appendix I for solutions.

Disposal of Receivables

LO 7

Sometimes a business may want to speed up the collection of its accounts receivable by converting them into cash before they are due. The cash may be needed to purchase assets, cover operating expenses or pay debts. Alternatively, a business may dispose of its accounts receivable by converting them into cash using one of the following methods: (1) *factoring* (selling them), or (2) *pledging* them as collateral (security) for a loan.

Factoring Receivables

Factoring means that a company sells all or a portion of its accounts receivable to a factor, such as a bank or financial institution, in exchange for cash. The factor becomes the owner of the receivables and assumes the responsibility for collecting the amounts owing directly from the company's customers. It also assumes the risk of any bad debt. Factoring can help a company's cash flow and working capital in the short term.

The seller may also choose to have the factor take over the cost of the billing function. The factor charges a factoring fee, usually a percentage of the total receivables sold. For example, Zeta Inc. wants to dispose of $50,000 of its receivables by selling them to the bank in exchange for cash. The bank charges a 5% factoring fee. Figure 1.33 shows the journal entry for this transaction.

JOURNAL

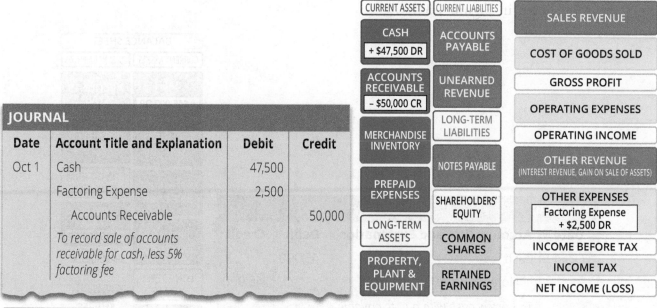

Date	Account Title and Explanation	Debit	Credit
Oct 1	Cash	47,500	
	Factoring Expense	2,500	
	Accounts Receivable		50,000
	To record sale of accounts receivable for cash, less 5% factoring fee		

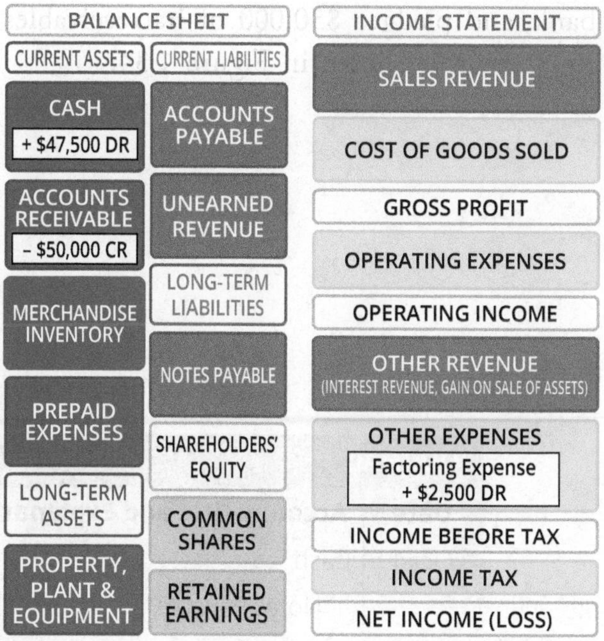

FIGURE 1.33

In a factoring arrangement, the company's customers are instructed to remit their payments directly to the factor. Because factoring expense is incurred in order to receive cash sooner, it is normally considered a part of the company's financing cost. Therefore, factoring expense, similar to interest expense, is classified as "other expenses" on the income statement.

In the Real World

As you just learned, factoring involves selling accounts receivable assets at a discount price to a third party, the factor. The factor is then responsible for collecting payment from the debtor.

At one time, a factor was brought in as a last resort—only after all previous attempts at collecting failed, including the use of a collection agency. However, factoring has become quite commonplace, with tens of billions of dollars being factored each year.

Today, as it becomes increasingly difficult for businesses to secure loans, factoring is turning into a viable option for raising funds. The cost to the seller involves receiving a discounted price for the total value of accounts receivable. In essence, this amounts to decreasing the value of the company assets. However, it receives cash for its accounts receivable, and the discount price may be worth more than the amount the company could hope to collect from its customers on its own.

Pledging Receivables

A company can also exchange its receivables for cash by **pledging** them as collateral for a loan. Pledging differs from factoring in that the borrower retains ownership of the pledged receivables. If the borrower is unable to pay back the loan, the lender is entitled to the cash receipts when the receivables are collected. For example, Jackman Company wants to borrow $45,000 from the bank, and pledges $50,000 of its receivables as collateral for the loan. The journal entry for this transaction is shown in Figure 1.34.

JOURNAL

Date	Account Title and Explanation	Debit	Credit
Oct 1	Cash	45,000	
	Notes Payable		45,000
	To borrow cash with a note payable secured by pledging receivables		

FIGURE 1.34

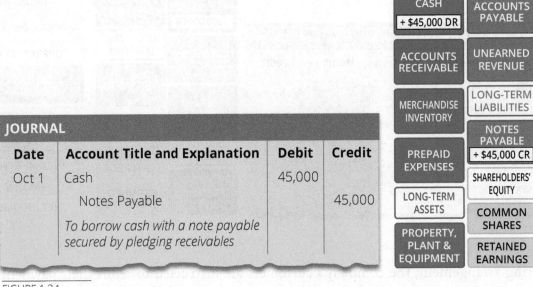

In addition to creating journal entries, Jackman Company is required to disclose the pledging of its accounts receivable in the notes to its financial statements. The note would be something similar to this: "Accounts receivable of $50,000 has been pledged as security for a $45,000 note payable."

Internal Controls for Accounts Receivable

LO 8

Now that we have examined various ways of recording, presenting and managing accounts receivable of a business in accordance with accounting standards, the information can be used to implement sound control policies.

Internal controls for accounts receivable help a company get the most out of one of its largest and most crucial assets. We will look specifically at how a credit policy can serve as a control mechanism to ensure that the accounts receivable asset is managed, protected and maximized in value.

Credit Approval

Providing payment terms to customers involves making unsecured loans to the customers so that they can buy the company's product or service. Instead of automatically offering these terms, a company can implement various measures to better understand its customers and follow up when necessary. This is the essence of credit approval. The company can have the customer complete a credit application and update the information regularly. It can also request a customer's financial statements to ensure the customer is in a position to pay the bills.

Credit Information

In a perfect world, all customers would pay their bills on time and businesses would not have to worry about collecting outstanding accounts receivable. However, since this is not the case, most businesses obtain credit information about their customers from independent credit reporting agencies such as Equifax and Dun & Bradstreet, financial institutions and other vendors.

Credit agency reports can be very useful in getting up-to-date information on current and potential customers. They can provide payment history, claims against the customer, banking information, existing credit granted and a record of recent inquiries, as well as any credit ratings.

In the Real World

Granting credit to customers can stimulate sales, but this approach comes with risk. The trade-off is that a business may never collect, and there is a cost associated with holding the receivable. To help mitigate the risk of default, a business can perform a credit check with a credit reporting agency. Credit agencies in Canada have tools that incorporate predictive analytics software to provide a more accurate estimate of creditworthiness.

Predictive analytics applies models, algorithms and machine learning to make predictions about the future. Algorithms are a set of instructions to perform a task, and deep learning means that the algorithms recognize patterns and learn over time. In the case of credit analysis, credit history, personal information and behavioural data, as well as alternative data sources, are analyzed by software to assess a customer's likelihood of paying. In the past, credit scores were based on credit history; however, now software can incorporate data from as many as 1,600 sources.

Expanding the amount of data that is analyzed and incorporating deep learning helps businesses make credit approval decisions more quickly and efficiently.

Credit Terms

One of the first decisions a business should make when establishing a credit policy is whether to adopt a lenient or restrictive approach to providing credit. This is an important decision because a business's credit policy can have a significant impact on sales volume. The more lenient a credit policy, the more likely it is to generate additional sales. A lenient credit policy provides potential customers with the incentive to buy goods without having to pay for them immediately; however, it also increases the risk of bad debts. In order to make credit policy decisions effectively, a business should take the following factors into consideration.

- The stronger the business's own financial situation, the better it can afford to make sales on credit. If a company is financially constrained, it probably cannot risk extending credit to customers.
- For a business dealing in custom-made products, low sales volume may leave less room to extend generous credit terms.

- The more competition in the market, the greater the pressure will be to extend credit in order to increase sales. A company with little or no competition does not need to increase market share and has little incentive to adopt lenient credit policies.

In general, a competitive market environment, homogeneous products and high sales volumes can encourage a company to offer more lenient credit terms to customers.

After analyzing the factors above, the company should set its credit terms, such as a period of 30 days. Industry standards differ, so assessing what the competition is doing, then setting a benchmark to meet or surpass those expectations, may be a wise business strategy. The terms should be communicated to and enforced with all approved customers.

As an ongoing control, the company should assess its collection period. Accounts receivable should not remain uncollected for more than 10 or 15 days beyond the credit terms. Setting a high standard and routinely enforcing it might improve the collection of accounts.

Credit Collection

Finally, deciding on the methods of collecting from customers is another control in credit policy. The invoice is always the first tool of collection. If a customer is overdue with payment, the company can send a copy of the invoice as a reminder. If that is unsuccessful, other measures such as letters, phone calls and even personal visits can be used to put pressure on the customer. If all else fails, a collection agency can be hired to enforce payment, especially when the account is long overdue.

Other controls for accounts receivable may include the following.

- Keeping individual records for each customer
- Following up on large accounts that are overdue
- Writing off a bad debt when all reasonable measures have been exhausted to collect the debt
- Ensuring that the original write-off is reversed when payments are received for a previously written-off account

A Closer Look

An important objective for any successful business is to maximize its control and management of accounts receivable. To that end, a company can establish a checklist of items to monitor how well it is doing in meeting this objective. Such a checklist may include the following items.

- Is the staff fully trained to handle accounts receivable issues?
- Is all sensitive accounts receivable information adequately secured?
- Are invoices being processed accurately?
- Are customers informed quickly enough of credit decisions made by the company?
- Are third-party collection agencies being properly monitored?

An Ethical Approach to Managing Accounts Receivable LO 9

The company and its accounting department are responsible for managing accounts receivable accurately and ethically. This includes properly recording credit sales and receipt of cash, as well as properly estimating bad debt. Accounts receivable is an important asset on the balance sheet and managing and accounting for this asset is open to manipulation.

Various ethical principles and standards have been established to prevent or detect manipulation of accounts receivable. The following case study illustrates unethical behaviour, which violates the full disclosure principle.

Charles owns a manufacturing business, which has been growing steadily. His bank wants to examine his financial statements before approving a loan to finance his increasing need for capital. His records show a total of $250,000 in accounts receivable, and he has earned a net income of $80,000 for the current year. Charles is aware that there is an amount of $50,000 that is likely to be uncollectible; however, he knows that if he allows for the bad debt in his statements, he may not be successful in securing the loan. Charles justifies his nondisclosure by committing himself to allowing for the bad debt the following year because there is a slight chance that he may still get paid.

What Charles did was unethical. He deliberately overstated the value of his assets to try to secure the loan. He believed that the debt was not going to be paid, but he represented it otherwise to distort the current value of the accounts receivable. Charles consciously violated the full disclosure principle by withholding information relevant to the valuation of these assets.

Consider another example of unethical behaviour. This time we will examine the importance of maintaining the integrity of the accounts receivable information that a company collects and manages. Failure to do so can put into doubt the accuracy of the company's books and the ethics of the people in charge.

Sophie is hired by the controller, Rick, to manage the company's accounts receivable. On first starting the job, Sophie notices that the company's accounts receivable has been poorly managed. The computer system is old and the invoices are not detailed enough, leading to customers questioning their invoices. Furthermore, the company had sometimes increased prices on the date of shipment instead of using the prices on the date the order was placed. Customers complained and did not want to pay invoices showing prices they had not agreed to.

Sophie brings her concerns to Rick, who asks her to keep quiet and do the best she can. Rick is afraid that he will be held accountable if upper management finds out, so he has tried to hide the problems. Sophie does not know what to do about the unethical accounting practices. If she remains silent, the integrity of the company's accounts receivable is in serious jeopardy.

An accountant is responsible for maintaining the integrity of the information in the books. Rick should have dealt with these problems as soon as he became aware of them. Instead, when these problems were identified, he tried to hide them and absolve himself of any responsibility. The company's customers are being treated unfairly, the integrity of the financial information of the company is compromised and the tactics used in response to the problems are ethical violations. Furthermore, Rick has imposed an unacceptable dilemma on his employee, Sophie, asking her to cover up the improper management of the company's assets. Unless Rick accepts responsibility for the problems and corrects them, he puts both himself and his company in a vulnerable position both financially and ethically.

Ethical lapses may be due to either deliberate decisions to falsify information or to poor day-to-day processes. Accountants must always prioritize the accuracy and integrity of the information they work with.

In Summary

LO 1 Explain the importance of accounts receivable

- Accounts receivable often represents a significant percentage of a business's assets.
- Allowing the existence of accounts receivable is instrumental in increasing sales in a modern economy. This includes allowing customers to buy on credit or make purchases using credit cards.
- IFRS and ASPE have identified revenue recognition criteria for sales of goods and sales of services.
- A service company can recognize a percentage of revenue for services partially completed; this is known as the percentage-of-completion method.

LO 2 Account for bad debts using the allowance method

- When accounts receivable are deemed uncollectible, they can be accounted for as bad debts using two different methods: the allowance method and the direct write-off method.
- The expense recognition principle requires bad debt expense to be estimated and accounted for in the same period that sales are recorded.
- The allowance method satisfies expense recognition through the use of an allowance for doubtful accounts (AFDA), which is a contra account attached to the accounts receivable account.
- The income statement approach estimates bad debts based on credit sales for the year.
- The balance sheet approach estimates bad debts based on the balance of accounts receivable or on the aging of accounts receivable at year end.

LO 3 Account for bad debts using the direct write-off method

- Under the direct write-off method, as soon as a receivable is determined to be uncollectible, it is written off by a debit (increase) to bad debt expense and a credit (decrease) to accounts receivable.

LO 4 Record promissory notes and notes receivable

- Accounts receivable can be converted into promissory notes, or notes receivable, which are legally binding documents. The conversion from accounts receivable to notes receivable is recorded in the journal with a debit to notes receivable and a credit to accounts receivable.
- The company that issued the notes receivable must record accrued interest revenue at the end of an accounting period.

LO 5 Utilize reports, including the accounts receivable subledger, to manage accounts receivable information

- The accounts receivable subledger shows accounts receivable balances by customer and by the length of time the debt has been outstanding. Detailed examination of the accounts receivable subledger can help the company highlight important areas that require management focus or changes in credit policies.
- Using computer software, a company can generate various accounts receivable reports that are tailored to management's needs.

LO 6 Calculate financial ratios pertaining to accounts receivable

- The effectiveness of accounts receivable collections can be gauged with the use of two ratios: accounts receivable turnover (ART) and days' sales outstanding (DSO).

LO 7 Account for the disposal of receivables using factoring and pledging

- A company can sell all or a portion of its accounts receivable to a factor, such as a bank or financial institution, in exchange for cash. The factor becomes the owner of the receivables and assumes responsibility for collecting them.
- While companies may find day-to-day administration of accounts receivable burdensome, effective and efficient management of accounts receivable by factoring (selling) them can help improve cash flows and customer satisfaction.
- A company can also exchange its receivables for cash by pledging them as collateral for a loan. The borrower retains ownership of the pledged receivables but must forfeit the proceeds to the lender if it defaults on the loan.

LO 8 Apply internal controls relating to accounts receivable

- Credit controls and policies are necessary to manage and protect the accounts receivable asset.
- Examples of controls relating to accounts receivable include setting competitive yet firm credit terms and getting independent credit information about customers before approving their credit.

LO 9 Apply ethics relating to accounts receivable and notes receivable

- Management must ensure that accounts receivable is properly managed and any estimates for bad debt are recorded as accurately as possible.

Review Exercise 1-1

ABC Company uses the allowance method to account for bad debts. During 2020, the company had $350,000 in sales, of which 80% were on account and 20% were cash sales. During the year, the company received $250,000 from customers as payment on their accounts. In June, it wrote off $1,500 for a customer who was not able to pay. However, some time after the account was written off, the customer notified ABC Company that she would to pay the account early in the new year. The company expects that $5,000 of the accounts receivable balance at the end of the year may be uncollectible.

Note: Do not consider cost of goods sold in any of the transactions.

Required

a) Using the general journal and December 31 as the date for all transactions, record the sales, collections for customers on account, write off of accounts and bad debt expense for 2020. You may omit explanations for each entry. Assume accounts receivable had a debit balance of $35,000 and that the AFDA had a credit balance of $2,500 at the beginning of the year (January 1, 2020).

JOURNAL

Date	Account Title and Explanation	Debit	Credit

b) Show how the transactions from part a) are posted in the related T-accounts.

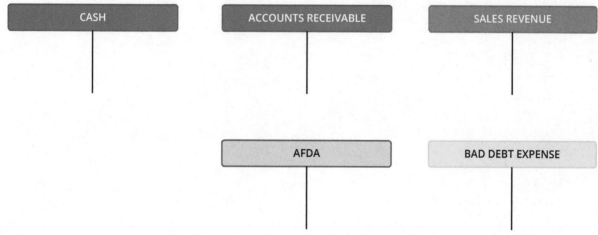

CASH		ACCOUNTS RECEIVABLE		SALES REVENUE	

AFDA		BAD DEBT EXPENSE	

c) Show how accounts receivable is reported on the December 31, 2020 balance sheet after the entries from part a) are posted.

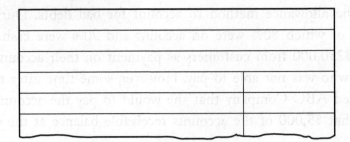

d) Assume that instead of using the balance sheet approach, the company uses the income statement approach and expects that 1% of credit sales may be uncollectible. Record the journal entry to estimate bad debt on December 31. Assume that AFDA has a credit balance of $2,500 at the beginning of the year.

JOURNAL

Date	Account Title and Explanation	Debit	Credit

See Appendix I for solutions.

Review Exercise 1-2

You are the accountant for Braham Company. Record the following transactions assuming the company has an August 31 year end.

1. Sale to Guy Tygart on account—1,000 gadgets for $5,000 on June 30, 2020.
2. Guy Tygart cannot pay on July 31, but signs a note with an annual 6% interest rate, to be collected on December 31, 2020.
3. Guy Tygart pays the amount due on December 31.
4. Assume instead that Guy dishonored the note on December 31.

Prepare the journal entries for the transactions. Do not record cost of goods sold.

JOURNAL

Date	Account Title and Explanation	Debit	Credit

See Appendix I for solutions.

Notes

Chapter 2
Long-Term Assets

Learning Objectives

LO 1 **Identify the characteristics of long-term assets**
- Classification of Long-Term Assets

LO 2 **Record the acquisition and changes in the value of property, plant and equipment**
- Recording the Acquisition of Property, Plant and Equipment
- Lump Sum Purchases of Property, Plant and Equipment
- Changes in Property, Plant and Equipment

LO 3 **Apply and compare three methods of depreciation of property, plant and equipment**
- Residual Value
- The Straight-Line Method
- The Declining-Balance and Double-Declining-Balance Methods
- The Units-of-Production Method
- Choosing a Depreciation Method
- Depreciation for Partial Years
- Revising Depreciation
- Depreciation for Federal Income Tax Purposes

LO 4 **Account for disposal of assets**

LO 5 **Account for natural resources**

LO 6 **Define and account for intangible assets and describe the different types of intangible assets**
- Intangible Assets with Finite Useful Lives
- Intangible Assets with Infinite Useful Lives

LO 7 **Calculate and interpret asset turnover and return on assets ratios**
- Asset Turnover
- Return on Assets
- Using the Ratios

LO 8 **Describe controls related to long-term assets**

LO 9 **Describe ethical approaches related to long-term assets**

Appendix 2A

LO 10 **Account for trading of long-term assets**
- Commercial Substance: Gain on Exchange
- Commercial Substance: Loss on Exchange
- Asset Exchange with No Commercial Substance

MAKING IT REAL TO YOU

When you buy a car, you are investing in a long-term personal asset, as you expect to drive it for a number of years. Its value will naturally deteriorate over time, but you can make upgrades or repairs that will increase the value at that point in time. When it is nearing the end of its useful life, you will consider what trade-in value it has toward the purchase of a new vehicle.

In the business world, accounting for long-term assets is complex. Recorded costs must be supported by verifiable information, such as an invoice, and later payments that change the efficiency or useful life of the asset must be added to its cost. Businesses must determine the useful life of each asset, its residual (trade-in) value and the method of depreciation (amortization) that best matches how the asset is used to generate revenues.

Different categories of long-term assets must be considered: tangible (physical), intangible (rights) and other assets that represent an investment or ownership. Proper classification and measurement are necessary, as these items usually represent the largest portion of the company's assets.

Decisions related to long-term assets can have an impact on reported profits for many years; therefore, it is very important that the accounting has been done properly.

Long-Term Assets

LO 1

Current assets are defined as those owned for the short term. **Long-term assets** are those that are owned and used by a company as part of normal operations for the long term. Specifically, long-term assets must possess the following three characteristics.

1. They provide the infrastructure necessary for operating the business.
2. They are expected to be used on an ongoing basis. Typically, this means longer than the business's operating cycle or one year.
3. They are not intended to be sold to customers.

Long-term assets are also commonly referred to as *long-lived assets, fixed assets* or *capital assets.*

Long-term assets can be either tangible or intangible by nature. **Tangible assets** have a physical existence, such as a machine or building. **Intangible assets** have no physical existence and can be perceived only by the mind or imagination, such as patents and trademarks. The long-term assets section of the Accounting Map is divided into separate parts containing tangible and intangible assets. As shown in Figure 2.1, property, plant and equipment, also called *plant assets,* are a company's long-term tangible assets, such as buildings, machinery, vehicles and computer equipment. Intangible assets include items such as patents and trademarks. Goodwill is also intangible by nature, but it has distinctive characteristics deserving of its own section. These three groups of assets are covered in this chapter. Long-term investments, also considered part of long-term assets, will be covered in a later chapter.

A company must have long-term tangible assets to accomplish physical tasks. Examples include machines that package bottles, trucks that deliver products, and computers that scan and calculate inventory data. Long-term tangible assets often form the physical backbone of a company. Without them, a business will not have the property, buildings and machinery it needs to deliver goods and services to its customers. This is particularly true for manufacturers or companies involved in the transportation industry, whose long-term assets are often the largest group of assets on the balance sheet.

For example, Figure 2.2 shows an excerpt from a balance sheet for Canadian Tire Corporation. The balance sheet shows values for the years ended December 29, 2018, and December 30, 2017.

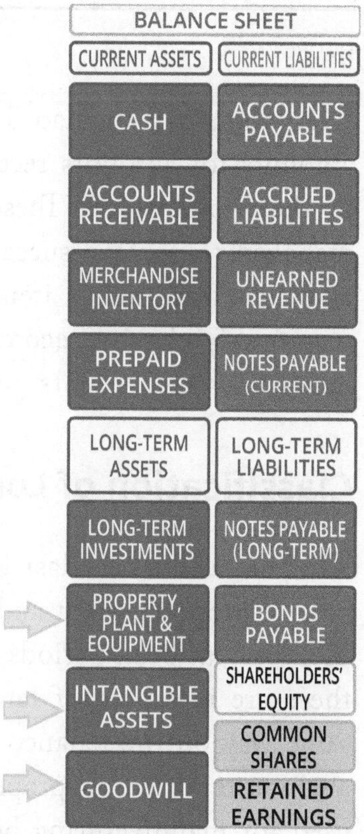

FIGURE 2.1

Canadian Tire Corporation Consolidated Balance Sheets (excerpt) As at December 29, 2018, and December 30, 2017 (C$ in millions)		
	December 29, 2018	**December 30, 2017**
ASSETS		
Cash and cash equivalents	$470.4	$437.0
Short-term investments	183.7	132.5
Trade and other receivables	933.3	681.1
Loans receivable	5,511.3	5,613.2
Merchandise inventories	1,997.5	1,769.8
Income taxes recoverable	15.3	48.3
Prepaid expenses and deposits	138.8	113.1
Assets classified as held for sale	5.5	1.1
Total current assets	9,255.8	8,796.1
Long-term receivables and other assets	742.6	717.8
Long-term investments	152.7	165.0
Goodwill and intangible assets	2,272.0	1,292.9
Investment property	364.7	344.7
Property and equipment	4,283.2	4,193.3
Deferred income taxes	215.8	117.2
Total assets	$17,286.8	$15,627.0

FIGURE 2.2

Even though Canadian Tire's main revenues are from selling merchandise, reporting significant amounts for accounts receivable and inventory, long-term assets also make up a large percentage of their total assets. These are important investments for the business and need to be properly managed to achieve success. Because long-term assets tend to be worth large amounts of money and constitute major items on a company's balance sheet, it is very important for management to properly classify, record and monitor the value of long-term assets. This chapter will discuss in detail how accountants perform these tasks.

Classification of Long-Term Assets

Tangible assets that last longer than one year and are used in normal operations are classified as part of property, plant and equipment. Items that are in use only some of the time (e.g. equipment used only at peak periods of activity) are also reported as property, plant and equipment. However, there are instances of tangible assets that last longer than one year but are not reported in the same way on the balance sheet. Specifically, tangible assets that are not used at all for operations are not reported as property, plant and equipment—for example, old equipment that was once used for manufacturing but is now sitting unused waiting to be sold as scrap metal.

Long-lived assets that are held for sale to customers and are not used in normal operations are classified as merchandise inventory. For example, vehicles held in merchandise inventory by an automotive dealership are intended for sale and therefore not considered as long-term assets of the dealership. Conversely, a delivery truck that is used in the daily operations of the dealership is classified as a long-term asset.

Land that is not used for daily operations but is held for resale or future expansion is classified on the balance sheet as a long-term investment. However, if the land holds a building that is used in normal operations, then that land is classified as a plant asset and is reported as part of property, plant and equipment on the balance sheet.

The Acquisition and Changes in Value of Long-Term Assets

LO 2

The initial purchase of property, plant and equipment requires a journal entry to record the value of the asset purchased. In accordance with the financial statement foundation of **measurement,** an asset must be recorded at its actual cost. However, when a company acquires physical items, such as land, buildings and equipment, there may be additional costs associated with the purchase. For example, when a company buys land for the purpose of building a factory, additional costs may be incurred for grading the property before construction can begin. Similarly, when a company buys a vehicle, it must pay for the vehicle's insurance and licence before the vehicle can be legally driven. Some of these expenditures have to be included in the cost of the asset and reported on the balance sheet, while others must be expensed and reported on the income statement. Accountants must pay attention to the nature of the expenditures related to asset acquisition to properly classify which costs should be included in the asset cost and which costs should be expensed.

> **Worth Repeating**
>
> Buying assets or selling assets at book value has no impact on the value of equity.

The costs necessary for getting the asset ready for use are those directly related to having the asset set up at its intended location and in a ready-to-use condition. These expenditures benefit the company not only in the current period, but also in future periods, as long as the long-term asset is still being used. Figure 2.3 lists the items that are usually included in the costs of acquiring the following classifications of long-term assets: (1) buildings, (2) machinery and equipment and (3) land and land improvements.

Expenditures Included in the Cost of a Long-Term Asset		
Buildings	**Machinery and Equipment**	**Land and Land Improvements**
• Purchase price • Sales taxes • Brokerage fees • Legal fees • Title fees • Design fees • Building permits • Betterments and major repairs of existing buildings • Insurance while under construction • Finance costs related to construction • Electrical system • Lighting fixtures • Plumbing • Flooring • Painting and wall coverings • Materials, labour and overhead costs of new building construction	• Purchase price • Sales taxes (PST) • Freight and delivery charges • Government permits • Insurance while in transit • Betterments and major repairs of existing machinery and equipment • Installation • Assembly • Testing prior to use	• Purchase price • Sales taxes • Brokerage fees • Delinquent property taxes • Legal fees • Title insurance • Government permits • Reclamation or remediation of land (if contaminated) to make it suitable for use • Removal of any existing structures • Land surveying fees • Preparation of land, such as clearing, grading, levelling, drainage, government assessments, installing sewers • Land improvements, such as driveways, walkways, paving, fences, landscaping, sprinkler systems, outdoor lighting

FIGURE 2.3

Since these expenditures are directly related to the asset itself, they are not treated as expenses but as part of the cost of the asset. This cost is then recorded on the company's balance sheet.

Other costs that are not directly attributable to getting the asset ready for use are expensed rather than capitalized. Examples include the costs of advertising products that a recently acquired machine will be producing, or unnecessary costs such as those arising from errors or damage in the installation of machinery. Recurring costs that benefit the company only in the current period without providing long-term benefits, such as the costs of a vehicle's licence and insurance, are also expensed.

The value of a long-term asset also dictates whether its purchase should be capitalized or expensed. The principle of **materiality** allows the company to expense low-cost, long-term assets that are below the company's materiality threshold. An item can be considered an expense on the income statement instead of a long-term asset on the balance sheet if it has no material value relative to the size of the business.

Recording the Acquisition of Property, Plant and Equipment

The asset's purchase price and the costs necessary for getting the asset ready for use are combined into a single account representing the cost of the asset.

For example, the Sunshine Juice Company purchased a new bottling machine for its orange juice line on February 1, 2021. It was purchased for $120,000, was shipped at a cost of $5,000 and had installation costs of $2,000. Assuming one invoice for all these costs, Figure 2.4 shows the journal entry for the acquisition of this long-term asset.

JOURNAL

Date	Account Title and Explanation	Debit	Credit
Feb 1	Machine	127,000	
	Accounts Payable		127,000
	To record the purchase of a machine for $120,000 plus $2,000 for installation and $5,000 for shipping		

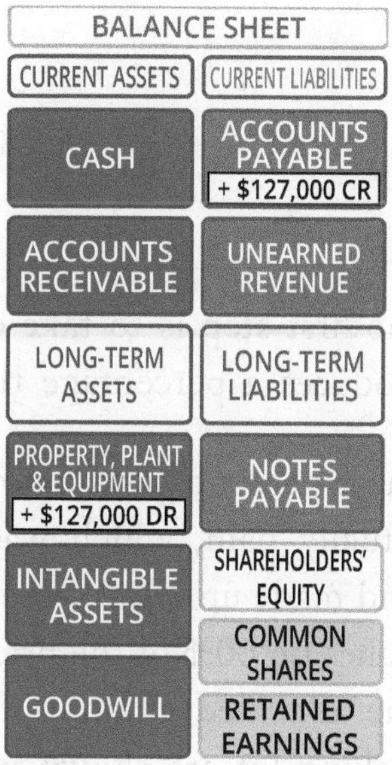

FIGURE 2.4

When totalled, the costs amount to $127,000. This is debited to an account that is part of property, plant and equipment and credited to accounts payable, since the company was invoiced and owes this amount to the bottling machine manufacturer. Of course, once the bill is paid, accounts payable is debited and cash is credited.

Although some prepared financial statements may show a single property, plant and equipment line item, there are actually separate accounts for each long-term asset within that category.

Lump Sum Purchases of Property, Plant and Equipment

Companies sometimes purchase property, plant and equipment in bundles, or what is known as a "basket of assets." Instead of buying property, plant and equipment individually from different vendors, a company may get a good price for a basket of assets by buying them from the same vendor in one transaction, called a **lump sum purchase** or a *basket purchase.*

The accounting challenge with this type of transaction is that, by paying a lower price for the assets, the buyer acquires them for less than their appraised value. In this case, the lump sum paid for all the assets is divided and allocated to each item according to percentages based on the appraised values or fair values. For example, on August 1, 2021, the Huge Bargain Store purchased land, a building and a parking lot to open a new store. It bought the assets in a bundle for the lump sum payment of $800,000. However, each asset has its own appraised value, as listed in

Figure 2.5. The total of all the appraised values is $1,000,000, which is $200,000 more than the purchase price.

Item	Appraised Value
Land	$600,000
Building	300,000
Parking Lot	100,000
Total	**$1,000,000**

FIGURE 2.5

The first step is to take each item's appraised value and divide it by the total appraised value. This produces a percentage that should be allocated to each asset, as shown in Figure 2.6.

These percentages are now allocated to the amount actually paid, which was $800,000. For example, land made up 60% of the total appraised value, so it makes up 60% of the price paid, which is $480,000. The allocated amounts for the land, building and parking lot are shown in Figure 2.7.

Land	(600,000 ÷ 1,000 ,000) × 100%	60%
Building	(300,000 ÷ 1,000,000) × 100%	30%
Parking Lot	(100,000 ÷ 1,000,000) × 100%	10%

FIGURE 2.6

Land	800,000 × 60%	$480,000
Building	800,000 × 30%	240,000
Parking Lot	800,000 × 10%	80,000
Total		**$800,000**

FIGURE 2.7

Figure 2.8 shows the journal entry after calculating the actual value applied to the assets. Each asset is debited by the value calculated (the book value), and cash is credited by the purchase price of $800,000.

JOURNAL

Date	Account Title and Explanation	Debit	Credit
Aug 1	Land	480,000	
	Building	240,000	
	Parking Lot	80,000	
	Cash		800,000
	To record the purchase of land, building and parking lot		

FIGURE 2.8

Pause & Reflect

Exercise 2-1

On May 1, 2021, Bristol Holding Company purchased land valued at $600,000, a building valued at $1,000,000 and a parking lot valued at $400,000. Bristol Holding paid $1,800,000 cash for these three assets.

a) Calculate the book value that should be recorded for these assets.

Asset	Appraised Value	Percentage	Book Value
Building	$1,000,000		
Land	600,000		
Parking Lot	400,000		
Total	$2,000,000		

b) Prepare the journal entry for this purchase.

JOURNAL			
Date	**Account Title and Explanation**	**Debit**	**Credit**

See Appendix I for solutions.

Changes in Property, Plant and Equipment

Property, plant and equipment can change in value as a result of two factors: depreciation, which will be examined shortly, and changes made to the asset itself. One challenge with property, plant and equipment is determining whether amounts paid subsequent to the initial purchase of the asset should be recorded as a betterment and added to the cost of the asset or simply recorded as an expense of the current year. If the amount paid either extends the useful life or improves the efficiency of the asset beyond the current period, it should be considered as a betterment, added to the cost of the asset and classified as a **capital expenditure**. Capital expenditures increase the net book value of the related asset accounts reported on the balance sheet. On the other hand, an expense that benefits the current period is known as a **revenue expenditure**. Revenue expenditures include ordinary repairs and maintenance and are reported on the income statement.

We will look at the different types of both capital expenditures and revenue expenditures in this section, starting with betterments.

Betterments

A **betterment** is an improvement that increases an asset's efficiency or effectiveness without necessarily increasing the asset's useful life. Some examples of betterments are plant expansions or major upgrades to equipment or vehicles used in the business. Betterments are capital expenditures and benefit future periods, so they are debited to the asset account (capitalized) and depreciated over the asset's remaining useful life. To illustrate, suppose a company replaces the engine in its existing equipment with a more powerful engine that will improve its efficiency. The new engine, including installation, costs $6,000. The journal entry is shown in Figure 2.9.

JOURNAL

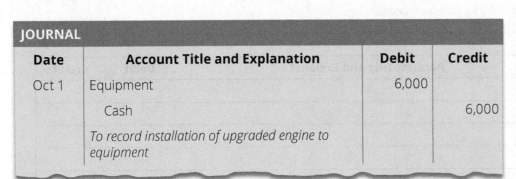

Date	Account Title and Explanation	Debit	Credit
Oct 1	Equipment	6,000	
	Cash		6,000
	To record installation of upgraded engine to equipment		

FIGURE 2.9

Similar to asset betterments, some other major repairs are costs incurred to extend an asset's useful life past the original estimate. Examples are replacing the existing roof of a building or repaving a parking lot. These major repairs are capital expenditures and benefit future periods, so they are recorded as a debit to the account for that asset. Because this journal entry changes the value of the asset, the depreciation charge needs to be recalculated and adjusted for the asset's remaining useful life.

> **ASPE vs. IFRS**
>
> Under IFRS, each significant part of an asset needs to be separately capitalized and depreciated. However, this is not required by ASPE.

Ordinary Repairs and Maintenance

Ordinary repairs and maintenance are expenditures made for the upkeep of existing assets, but they do not materially improve an asset's efficiency or effectiveness, nor do they extend the asset's useful life. Some examples are painting, minor wall and floor repairs, cleaning, and minor adjustments to equipment and machinery. Ordinary repairs and maintenance are revenue expenditures and benefit the current period, so they are debited to the related expense account. To illustrate, suppose a company pays to repair a hole in the drywall in one of its offices. The repair, including materials and labour, costs $325. The journal entry is shown in Figure 2.10.

JOURNAL

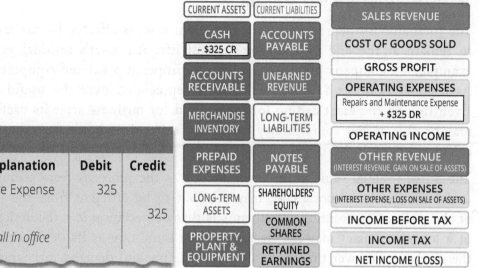

Date	Account Title and Explanation	Debit	Credit
Oct 1	Repairs and Maintenance Expense	325	
	Cash		325
	To record repairs to drywall in office		

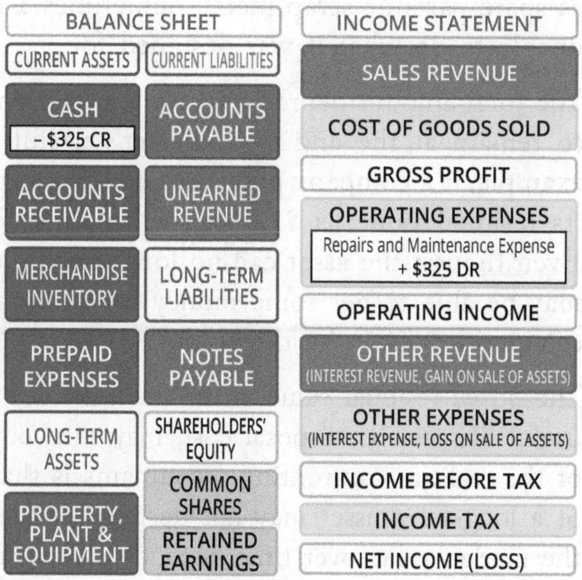

FIGURE 2.10

The Concept of Depreciation

LO 3

Recall that expense recognition (matching concept) requires expenses to be recorded in the same period in which they were used to generate revenue. Expense recognition is closely tied to revenue recognition because there is often a direct association between incurring expenses and generating revenue. For these types of expenses, recognition should occur in the same period as the related revenue, referred to as matching revenues and expenses.

Long-term assets such as property, plant and equipment are converted to expenses through **depreciation**, which means allocating the cost of a long-term asset over its useful life. This is done because the future economic benefits associated with these assets decrease over time. We will examine various aspects of depreciation and how long-term assets on the balance sheet are affected.

> **ASPE vs. IFRS**
>
> Under ASPE, the periodic allocation of property, plant and equipment cost is called *amortization,* although the term *depreciation* is also allowed.
>
> IFRS uses only the term *depreciation* for the same concept.

Residual Value

Before discussing specific methods of depreciation, we should first examine what an asset's residual value is and how it affects depreciation calculations. **Residual value** is the estimated value of an asset at the end of its useful life. An asset may still have some value, even if it is no longer useful to the company, or it may have a residual value of zero. Residual value is also referred to as *salvage value* or *scrap value.*

For example, a company has a delivery truck that has been on the road for many years and can no longer be fixed to continue running. A buyer might see some residual value in the truck, such as spare parts or scrap metal. Sometimes a long-term asset carries a residual value even after it is unable to do what it was designed for.

The total amount depreciated for a long-term asset is affected by the residual value that is expected to remain at the end of the asset's useful life. An asset's residual value is not depreciated. For example, if a company purchases an item of property, plant and equipment for $5,000 and estimates its residual value as $1,000, the amount depreciated over the useful life of the asset is $4,000. Even though the asset can no longer be used for business after its useful life expires, the company may be able to get some money for it and this price should be subtracted from the depreciation calculations made by the company.

The *actual* residual value of an asset, defined as the proceeds from selling the asset at the end of its useful life less its disposal cost, may turn out to be different from the *estimated* residual value. One of the realities confronting accountants is that depreciation is a theoretical concept. The market value of a long-term asset may not decrease at the same rate as its depreciation schedule. The decrease in the market value over time depends on the supply and demand mechanism of the market, which has nothing to do with how much the item has been depreciated in the books. Depreciation involves an accountant's best estimate, which requires justified calculations of a long-term asset's value over its useful life with the company. Depreciation does not dictate an asset's market value.

For example, Skyscape Company purchases a long-term asset at an initial cost of $100,000. The accountant will examine the asset, study its potential worth over time and make an educated guess at what someone might be willing to pay to salvage it. This is not an easy task. At the end of the asset's life, if the actual residual value is different from the accountant's original estimate, a gain (or loss) on asset disposal is recorded.

Assume that the accountant estimates the item's residual value to be $10,000. Ten years later, the item is sold for $6,000. Since the selling price is lower than the estimated residual value, the accountant records a loss of $4,000. The overestimation is not an issue, as long as the accountant was justified in making the initial estimate and adjusts for a loss once the asset is sold. Similarly, if the asset is sold for more than its estimated residual value, the difference is recorded as a gain.

In addition to estimating the residual value, an accountant must also decide which depreciation method to use, choosing the one that best reflects the pattern in which the asset will be used by the company in practice. The same depreciation method should generally be used throughout the life of the asset. However, there are times when the method may be changed, which is acceptable as long as there is justification for doing so.

We will now examine three methods of depreciation related to long-term assets. The three methods and their assumptions are listed in Figure 2.11.

Depreciation Method	Assumption
Straight-Line Method	Asset depreciates equally every year
Declining-Balance and Double-Declining-Balance Method	Asset depreciates faster at the beginning
Units-of-Production Method	Asset depreciates based on activity level

FIGURE 2.11

The Straight-Line Method

You were introduced to the straight-line method when learning about accounting adjustments. The **straight-line method of depreciation** produces an average depreciation expense, which is applied each year until the asset is sold or reaches the end of its useful life. Figure 2.12 shows the formula to calculate the amount of depreciation under the straight-line method.

$$\text{Straight-Line Depreciation} = \frac{\text{Cost of Asset} - \text{Residual Value}}{\text{Useful Life}}$$

FIGURE 2.12

The calculation has three components.

1. The total cost of the asset is the original purchase price of the asset and any additional costs required to get it in a ready-to-use condition.
2. The residual value is the estimated value of the asset at the end of its useful life. Since the residual value is not depreciated, it is subtracted from the total cost of the asset.
3. The useful life is an estimate of how long the asset is expected to be used by the business. Useful life is usually expressed in years.

For example, Smith Tools buys a machine for $5,000. The machine is expected to have a useful life of five years and its residual value is estimated to be $1,000. The calculation to determine the amount of depreciation applied annually for the machine is shown below.

$$\text{Straight-Line Depreciation} = \frac{\$5{,}000 - \$1{,}000}{5 \text{ years}}$$

$$= \$800/\text{year}$$

If the machine was purchased on January 1, 2019, the annual depreciation is applied to the machine as shown in Figure 2.13.

Year	Cost of Machine	Depreciation Expense	Accumulated Depreciation	Net Book Value
2019	$5,000	$800	$800	$4,200
2020	5,000	800	1,600	3,400
2021	5,000	800	2,400	2,600
2022	5,000	800	3,200	1,800
2023	5,000	800	4,000	**1,000** ← **Residual Value**

FIGURE 2.13

A depreciation of $800 is accumulated each year until the end of the asset's useful life. At that time, all that is left of the asset's book value is its residual value. In this case, the amount is $1,000, the final net book value.

Now assume that the asset has no residual value at the end of its useful life. This means that the total amount to be depreciated is $5,000, which was the original cost of the asset. The annual depreciation amount is calculated as $1,000 ($5,000 ÷ 5 years).

As is common in accounting, the calculations are only part of the process. The next step is to record the results of those calculations in the financial statements. Accountants want to see the original value of the asset and the change in the net book value over time. Contra accounts allow both values to be reflected on the balance sheet. Remember, a contra asset account is linked to another asset account to reduce the value of the asset. The contra account for a long-term asset is called **accumulated depreciation**. It reflects the decrease in value of the long-term asset over time. The original cost of the long-term asset account remains constant.

Figure 2.14 shows the corresponding journal entry for recording $1,000 of depreciation expense for the machine on December 31, 2019.

JOURNAL

Date	Account Title and Explanation	Debit	Credit
Dec 31	Depreciation Expense	1,000	
	Accumulated Depreciation—Machine		1,000
	To record the depreciation of machine for the first year		

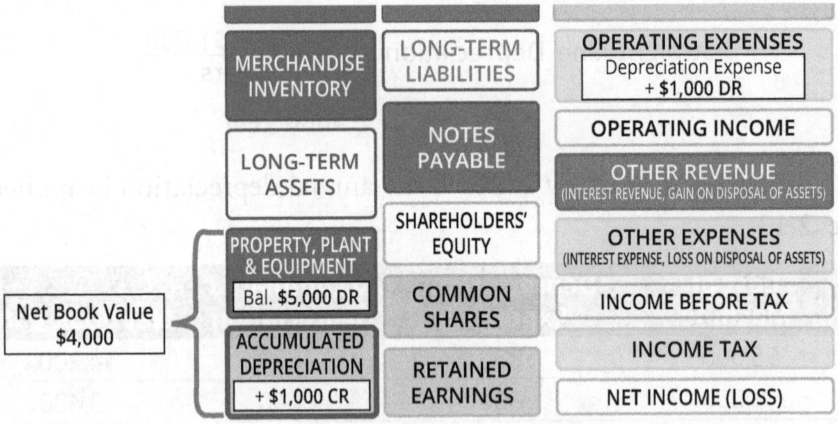

FIGURE 2.14

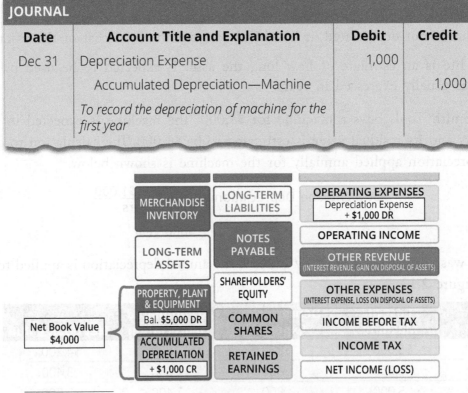

The initial purchase of the asset on January 1 is shown as a $5,000 debit balance in property, plant and equipment. The entry for depreciation on December 31 is recorded as a $1,000 credit to accumulated depreciation. This reduces the net book value of the machine to $4,000. Equity decreases with the depreciation expense that is recorded on the income statement under operating expenses.

Each year depreciation is recorded, the amount of accumulated depreciation increases and the net book value of the long-term asset decreases. This is illustrated in Figure 2.15. Notice that as accumulated depreciation increases by $1,000 each year, the net book value decreases by $1,000.

Year	Cost of Long-Term Asset	Depreciation Expense	Accumulated Depreciation	Net Book Value
2019	$5,000	$1,000	$1,000	$4,000
2020	5,000	1,000	2,000	3,000
2021	5,000	1,000	3,000	2,000
2022	5,000	1,000	4,000	1,000
2023	5,000	1,000	5,000	**0** ← **Residual Value**

FIGURE 2.15

The Declining-Balance and Double-Declining-Balance Methods

One drawback to the straight-line method is that it may not realistically reflect how the cost of the asset should be allocated. This is because the market value of long-term assets does not always decrease by the same amount each year. Alternative depreciation methods have been developed by the accounting profession, one of which is the declining-balance method.

The most common example of asset depreciation in everday life is a car. Usually, the largest decrease in the market value of a car occurs the moment it is driven off the dealership's lot. Since the greatest depreciation in value occurs during the early years of the car's useful life, the declining-balance method is used. This concept applies to many long-term assets.

While the straight-line method simply applies an average depreciation rate, the **declining-balance method** applies an annual percentage for the calculation of depreciation against the net book value of the asset. Since the net book value decreases each year, a higher level of depreciation is recorded in the early years of the asset's useful life. The formula to calculate the annual depreciation rate under the declining-balance method is shown in Figure 2.16.

$$\text{Declining-Balance Depreciation Rate} = \frac{100\%}{\text{Years of Useful Life}}$$

FIGURE 2.16

Consider the purchase of equipment worth $10,000 that has a useful life of five years with no residual value. The percentage for the declining-balance method is calculated as shown below.

$$\text{Declining-Balance Depreciation Rate} = \frac{100\%}{5\text{ years}} = 20\%$$

An annual depreciation rate of 20% is applied to the net book value of the asset to calculate depreciation for each year. In the first year, depreciation can be calculated by multiplying the depreciation rate of 20% by the asset's original cost of $10,000. Therefore, the first year's depreciation is equal to $2,000. The net book value of the asset after deducting the first year's depreciation is $8000 ($10,000 – $2,000). In the second year, depreciation is equal to $1,600 (20% × net book value of $8,000). As the asset's net book value decreases, the depreciation amount also gradually decreases from year to year.

Unlike the straight-line method, which applies the same dollar amount of depreciation every year, the declining-balance method applies the same depreciation *percentage rate* to the net book value every year. If the useful life of the asset is 10 years, the depreciation rate applied each year is 10% (100% ÷ 10 years); if the useful life is 20 years, the depreciation rate applied each year is 5% (100% ÷ 20 years); and so on.

The depreciation rate can be multiplied based on the accountant's estimation of how fast the asset's value will depreciate. One of the most commonly used depreciation rates is the **double-declining-balance method**, which doubles the declining-balance rate of depreciation. For example, a double-declining depreciation rate of 40% (20% × 2) is used when the useful life of an asset is five years. When the useful life is 10 years, a double-declining depreciation rate of 20% is used (10% × 2). For a useful life of 20 years, an annual rate of 10% is used (5% × 2).

The formula for calculating the double-declining depreciation rate is shown in Figure 2.17.

Double-Declining Depreciation Rate = Declining-Balance Depreciation Rate × 2

FIGURE 2.17

Using a double-declining rate exaggerates the declining effect, ensuring that much of the depreciation occurs during the early years of the asset's life span.

In the example of the $10,000 piece of equipment with a useful life of five years, assume the company uses the double-declining-balance method. The depreciation for the first year is calculated as follows.

$10,000 × 40% = $4,000

The net book value for the beginning of the second year is calculated as follows.

$10,000 − $4,000 = $6,000

The double-declining depreciation rate of 40% is applied to this new balance to determine the depreciation amount for the second year.

$6,000 × 40% = $2,400

The same double-declining rate is applied to a decreasing net book value on an annual basis. This means that over the years, the depreciation amounts are reduced substantially, which generally reflects the way long-term assets decline in value.

The rest of the depreciation amounts in the example are shown in Figure 2.18.

Year	Beginning of Year Book Value	@40% Double-Declining Depreciation Rate	Remaining Book Value
1	$10,000	$4,000	$6,000
2	6,000	2,400	3,600
3	3,600	1,440	2,160
4	2,160	864	1,296
5	1,296	518.40	**777.60**

FIGURE 2.18

Applying a percentage rate to a balance every year means there will always be a remaining balance when the declining-balance or double-declining-balance methods are used. In this example, the remaining book value at the end of five years under the double-declining-balance method is $777.60, despite the asset having a zero estimated residual value. Because a long-term asset is not fully depreciated by the end of its useful life under the double-declining-balance method, companies usually switch from the double-declining-balance method to the straight-line method when the asset reaches half of its useful life so the asset will be fully depreciated. If the asset has a residual value when the declining-balance (or double-declining-balance) method is used, the asset should not be depreciated below the residual value. For example, if the residual value is $1,000 for the example shown above, Figure 2.19 shows the depreciation amounts. Notice that in the last year, depreciation can only be $296 to drop the net book value to the residual amount of $1,000.

Worth Repeating

The straight-line method applies the same depreciation amount to the net book value of a long-term asset for each year of its useful life.

The declining-balance and double-declining-balance methods apply a depreciation percentage to the net book value of a long-term asset. Therefore, a larger amount of depreciation is applied in the early years of the asset's useful life. For many assets, this is a more realistic estimation of how the asset will depreciate each year.

Year	Beginning of Year Book Value	@40% Double-Declining Depreciation Rate	Remaining Book Value
1	$10,000	$4,000	$6,000
2	6,000	2,400	3,600
3	3,600	1,440	2,160
4	2,160	864	1,296
5	1,296	296*	1,000

*Only $296, instead of $518.40, is subtracted from the beginning of the year book value to avoid having the remaining book value drop below a residual value of $1,000.

FIGURE 2.19

Pause & Reflect

Exercise 2-2

On January 1, 2020, London Bridge Company purchased a hydraulic stamping machine for $5,000,000. It is expected to last five years and estimated to have a residual value of $400,000 at the end of the five years. London Bridge Company will depreciate the machine using the double-declining-balance method. Prepare the following chart to calculate the depreciation for each year.

Year	Beginning of Year Book Value	Depreciation	Remaining Book Value
2020			
2021			
2022			
2023			
2024			

See Appendix I for solutions.

The Units-of-Production Method

The **units-of-production method** involves a different procedure for depreciating property, plant and equipment. The level of asset usage is the basis for calculating depreciation. The methods studied so far use a predetermined formula that is not based on usage.

The following steps are involved when using the units-of-production method.

1. Choose a unit for measuring the usage of the long-term asset. For example, if the asset is a vehicle, the unit can be the number of kilometres driven. If the asset is a machine, the unit can be the number of hours operated. These measures are known as units of production, hence the name of this method.
2. Estimate the number of units used for the entire life of the asset. For example, an estimate for a vehicle may be 300,000 kilometres, or for a machine may be 600,000 hours.
3. Divide the total cost of the asset by the estimated number of units from step 2. This gives the cost per unit.
4. Multiply the cost per unit determined in step 3 by the number of units produced in a year to determine that year's depreciation amount.

Step 4 is repeated each year until the end of the asset's estimated useful life. Figure 2.20 shows how to calculate the cost per unit amount.

$$\text{Cost per Unit Amount} = \frac{\text{Cost} - \text{Residual Value}}{\text{Total Units of Production}}$$

FIGURE 2.20

Here is an example to illustrate how the units-of-production method is applied in the depreciation of property, plant and equipment.

Fenway Delivery bought a delivery truck for $110,000. The truck has an estimated residual value of $10,000. Fenway chooses a kilometre (km) as the unit for measuring usage (step 1). The company wants its trucks to be in top condition, so it retires them after 200,000 kilometres of usage (step 2). The calculation for the per unit amount (step 3) is shown here.

$$\text{Cost per Unit Amount} = \frac{\$110{,}000 - \$10{,}000}{200{,}000 \text{ km}}$$

$$= \$0.50/\text{km}$$

Using the cost per unit amount, the amount of depreciation applied for that period is shown in Figure 2.21

Units-of-Production Depreciation = Units of Production Used for Year × Cost per Unit Amount

FIGURE 2.21

If the truck is driven 30,000 kilometres in the first year, the depreciation for that year (step 4) is calculated as shown here.

$$\text{Units-of-Production Depreciation} = 30{,}000 \text{ km} \times \$0.50/\text{km}$$

$$= \$15{,}000$$

The amount of depreciation for a year is entirely dependent on the asset's usage. For example, if the truck was driven for 25,000 kilometres in the second year, the depreciation for that year is calculated as follows.

$$25{,}000 \text{ km} \times \$0.50/\text{km} = \$12{,}500$$

If the truck was driven for 35,000 kilometres in the third year, the depreciation for that year is calculated as follows.

$$35{,}000 \text{ km} \times \$0.50/\text{km} = \$17{,}500$$

This depreciation procedure is applied annually until the truck has been driven for 200,000 kilometres, the initial estimation for the life of the truck. Once the usage exceeds the estimated units of production, no additional depreciation expense should be allocated to the units produced.

Choosing a Depreciation Method

As is common in accounting, no single method of calculating a balance sheet item is necessarily better than or preferable to another. The challenge for the accountant is to choose a method that best reflects the usage and nature of the asset involved. For example, a company might use the straight-line method to depreciate an advertising sign but use the declining-balance method to depreciate a company-owned vehicle, since the value of cars and trucks decreases most during their early years.

A Comparison of Depreciation Methods

Figure 2.22 compares depreciation expense under the three different depreciation methods discussed in this chapter. Using numbers from our previous examples, although the depreciation expense for each period is different, the total over the asset's useful life remains the same under all methods.

Refer to the example of Fenway Delivery, who bought a delivery truck for $110,000. The truck's estimated residual value is $10,000. The company retires all of its trucks after 200,000 kilometres of use. The cost per unit of production (in which "production" was stated in kilometres of usage) was calculated as $0.50/km. For our example, the number of kilometres the truck was driven per year is shown in brackets under the units-of-production method. Assume that the 200,000 kilometres occur during a five-year period. This allows a comparison of all the depreciation methods based on an estimated useful life of five years.

	Depreciation Expense		
Year	Straight-Line Method $20,000/year[1]	Double-Declining-Balance Method 40%/year[2]	Units-of-Production Method
2019	$20,000	$44,000 ($110,000 × 40%)	$15,000 ($0.50 × 30,000 km)
2020	20,000	26,400 ($66,000 × 40%)	12,500 ($0.50 × 25,000 km)
2021	20,000	15,840 ($39,600 × 40%)	17,500 ($0.50 × 35,000 km)
2022	20,000	9,504 ($23,760 × 40%)	30,000 ($0.50 × 60,000 km)
2023	20,000	4,256[3]	25,000 ($0.50 × 50,000 km)
Total	$100,000	$100,000	$100,000

[1] ($110,000 − $10,000)/5 years
[2] 100%/5 years × 2
[3] The net book value of $14,256 × 40% gives a depreciation of $5,702; however, only $4,256 is applied because the truck cannot be depreciated beyond a residual value of $10,000.

FIGURE 2.22

Depreciation for Partial Years

Our examination of depreciation has been based on the assumption that property, plant and equipment are purchased on the first day of a year and sold on the last day of another year. Of course, depreciation methods do not dictate when assets are bought and sold. Various tactics can be employed to accommodate the realities of the calendar year when depreciating a company's long-term assets. Once a long-term asset has been purchased, the accountant must choose a depreciation method that best matches both the usefulness (ability to help generate revenues) and the expected life of the asset.

A number of possible methods are available to depreciate during the year (or month) of purchase or sale. One common approach, known as the "nearest month" rule, is to calculate the depreciation of the asset purchased between the 1st and 15th day of a month for the full month of purchase, as if the asset was purchased on the 1st day of the month, and not to apply any depreciation in the month of purchase if the asset is purchased between the 16th day and the last day of the month, as if the asset was purchased on the 1st day of the next month. The same logic is applied in the year the asset is sold or disposed of. That is, if the asset is sold by the 15th day of the month, it is not depreciated in the month of sale. If the asset is sold after the 15th day of the month, it is depreciated for a whole month of sale.

Examine the situation that arises from the purchase of a $120,000 packaging machine by the Jones Cookie Factory on March 27, 2012. The company determines that the packager has a useful life of 10 years, after which it will not be salvageable; thus no residual value needs to be estimated. The machine will be depreciated by $12,000 annually, which is equivalent to $1,000 monthly. The company has a December 31 year end. Jones decides to use the "nearest month" rule for calculating depreciation.

Figure 2.23 displays the annual depreciation for the machine. Note that for 2013 to 2021, each year includes 12 full months and has $12,000 of annual depreciation at $1,000 per month. However, since the asset was purchased almost at the end of March in 2012, it is assumed that the machine was purchased on April 1. Therefore, for that year, only $9,000 of depreciation will be taken, representing 9 months (April 1 to December 31). For the final year, 2022, there are 3 months (January 1 to March 31), or $3,000. If the company still owns and is still using the asset in 2023, no additional depreciation is recorded, as it has been fully depreciated as of March 31, 2022.

	Months	Depreciation
2012	9	$9,000
2013	12	12,000
2014	12	12,000
2015	12	12,000
2016	12	12,000
2017	12	12,000
2018	12	12,000
2019	12	12,000
2020	12	12,000
2021	12	12,000
2022	3	3,000
	Total	$120,000

FIGURE 2.23

Figure 2.24 illustrates the depreciation in the year of purchase. The chosen method dictates that there is no depreciation in the month of purchase if the asset is purchased after the 15th day of the month. That leaves 9 months of depreciation in the year, or $9,000.

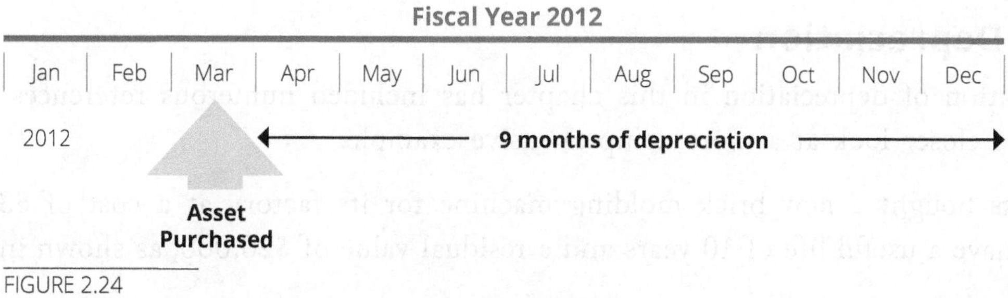

FIGURE 2.24

Figure 2.25 illustrates the depreciation in 2022, the last year of the packager's estimated useful life. Since 9 months were depreciated in 2012, then in 2022, the last year of the asset's estimated useful life, there are only 3 months left to depreciate, or $3,000.

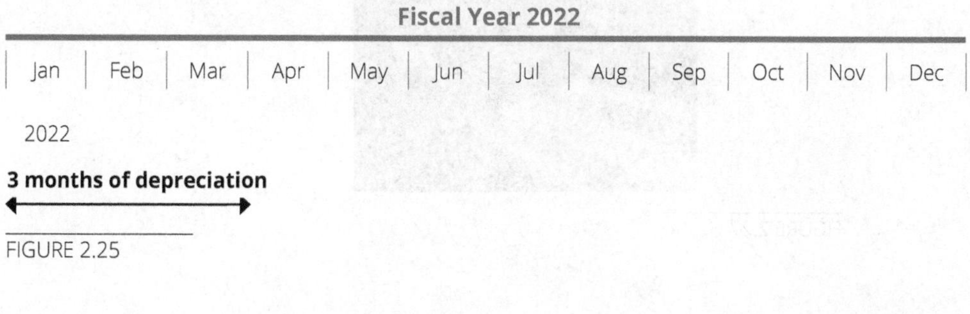

FIGURE 2.25

As Figure 2.23 shows, the total amount depreciated for the packaging machine after 10 years of use is $120,000. Subtracting this amount from the original purchase price of $120,000 produces a net book value of zero. The depreciation schedule can be used to determine the net book value (cost minus accumulated depreciation) at any point during the life of an asset. For example, Figure 2.26 shows the net book value of the packaging machine at the end of 2016.

FIGURE 2.26

Another common method for partial depreciation is a half-year of depreciation in the year of acquisition and a half-year of depreciation in the year of sale. It is worth noting that companies using the unit-of-production method do not need to worry about adopting a policy for partial year depreciation, as depreciation is based on output and not time.

Revising Depreciation

Our examination of depreciation in this chapter has included numerous references to estimates. Let us take a closer look at a more comprehensive example.

Brian's Bricks bought a new brick molding machine for its factory at a cost of $300,000. It is expected to have a useful life of 10 years and a residual value of $20,000, as shown in Figure 2.27.

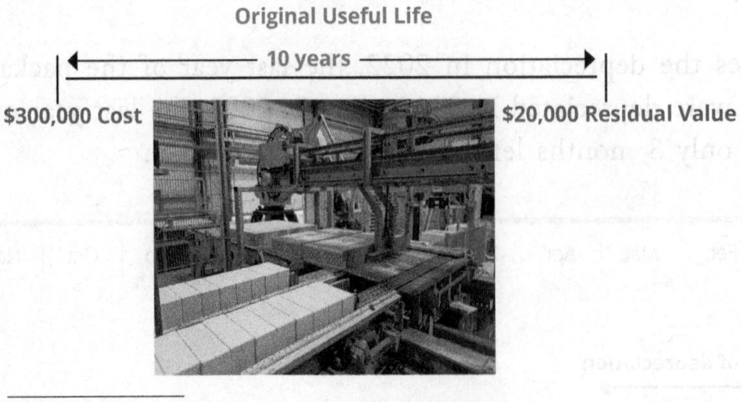

FIGURE 2.27

After five years of use, the molding machine is not deteriorating as quickly as expected. After consulting with the machine's manufacturer, management determines that the useful life of this asset could be extended to 15 years, and the residual value increased to $40,000, as illustrated in Figure 2.28.

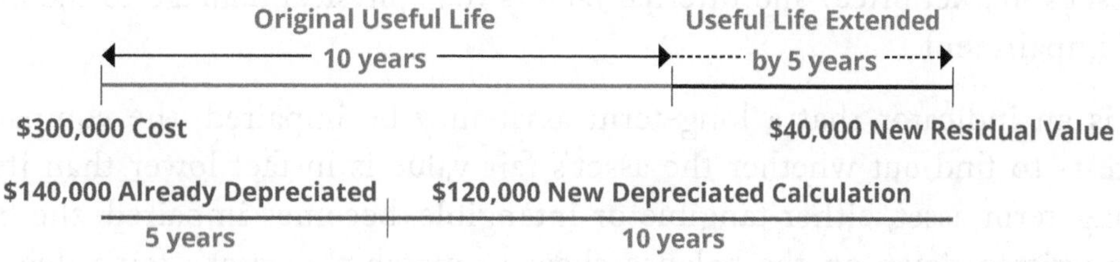

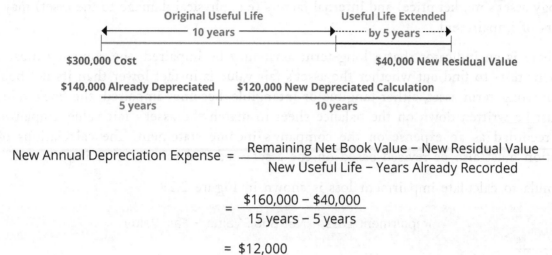

$$\text{New Annual Depreciation Expense} = \frac{\text{Remaining Net Book Value} - \text{New Residual Value}}{\text{New Useful Life} - \text{Years Already Recorded}}$$

$$= \frac{\$160{,}000 - \$40{,}000}{15 \text{ years} - 5 \text{ years}}$$

$$= \$12{,}000$$

FIGURE 2.28

Using the straight-line method, the company's accountants had already recorded a total depreciation of $140,000 over five years [(($300,000 - $20,000) ÷ 10 years) × 5 years], which produced a net book value of $160,000 ($300,000 - $140,000).

Brian's Bricks then started a new depreciation schedule, assuming the straight-line method again, in which the amount to be depreciated for the rest of the asset's new useful life would be $120,000 ($160,000 - $40,000), where $40,000 is the new residual value. This amount is divided by the number of years left in the new useful life of 10 years (15 years - 5 years already recorded), to produce an annual depreciation amount of $12,000.

Note that the company should not change the depreciation already accumulated during the first five years of using the molding machine. An accountant should only make or change depreciation estimates for the future. Any changes need to be justified with the appropriate documentation. In this case, that documentation would include a consultation with the asset's manufacturer.

ASPE vs. IFRS

There are two ways for a company to re-measure the value of long-term assets: the cost model and the revaluation model. Under ASPE, only the cost model is allowed, so long-term assets must always be recorded at cost (less accumulated depreciation and impairment). This means that if the market value of an asset increases, ASPE prohibits companies from recording the corresponding increase in the asset's book value.

However, under IFRS, companies may choose to account for long-term assets using either the cost model or the revaluation model. Under the revaluation model, assets are revalued periodically to reflect their fair market value. If the market value of a long-term asset is higher than the asset's net book value, the company increases the book value of the asset to match its market value. Unlike ASPE, IFRS requires an annual review of useful life and residual value estimates.

Depreciation also needs to be revised when the value of the asset decreases due to impairment. **Impairment** occurs when the asset's fair value appears to permanently drop to a point that is below its net book value. Both external factors (e.g. changes in technology that reduce the older-technology asset's market price) and internal factors (e.g. physical damage to the asset) may provide indicators of impairment.

When there is an indicator that a long-term asset may be impaired, the company must conduct impairment tests to find out whether the asset's fair value is in fact lower than its net book value. When any long-term asset, either tangible or intangible, becomes impaired, the book value of the asset must be written down on the balance sheet to match the asset's fair value. Impairment loss is then recorded as an expense on the company's income statement. The calculations of future depreciation must also be revised based on the asset's reduced value due to impairment.

The formula to calculate impairment loss is shown in Figure 2.29.

Impairment Loss = Net Book Value − Fair Value

FIGURE 2.29

Assume that on December 31, a company realizes that the value of its factory machinery has been impaired due to physical damage. The machinery's fair value is determined to be $60,000 while its original cost was $130,000. Up to this date, the accumulated depreciation was recorded as $40,000. The company must first determine the net book value of the machinery, as shown here.

Net Book Value = $130,000 − $40,000
= $90,000

Using this value and the formula from Figure 2.29, impairment loss is calculated as follows.

Impairment Loss = $90,000 − $60,000
= $30,000

The fair value of $60,000 is $30,000 less than the net book value of $90,000. Figure 2.30 shows that the $30,000 impairment is recorded by debiting the impairment loss account and crediting the accumulated depreciation account. As indicated by the Accounting Map, on the income statement, the loss increases the operating expenses; on the balance sheet, it decreases the net book value of the machinery by increasing the accumulated depreciation account.

JOURNAL			
Date	**Account Title and Explanation**	**Debit**	**Credit**
Dec 31	Impairment Loss	30,000	
	Accumulated Depreciation—Machinery		30,000
	To record impairment loss		

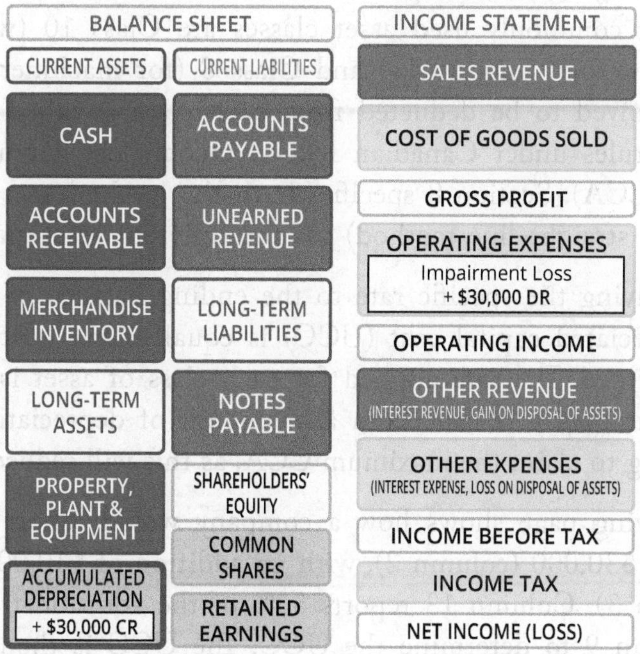

FIGURE 2.30

ASPE vs. IFRS

Under ASPE, the book value of an impaired plant asset is written down to its fair value. An impairment loss that has been previously recorded can never be reversed.

Under IFRS, the book value of an impaired plant asset is written down to its recoverable amount. An asset's recoverable amount is equal to the asset's market price less costs of disposal, or its future value, whichever is higher. Future value represents future revenue that the asset will generate for the company. IFRS allows reversal of previously recorded impairments for all tangible and intangible assets, except goodwill. Impairment reversal is recorded in income, while any increase in market value over the asset's original cost is recorded in comprehensive income.

Depreciation for Federal Income Tax Purposes

In Canada, businesses usually keep separate depreciation records for accounting versus tax purposes. Simply put, "book depreciation" is different from "tax depreciation." The purpose of financial accounting is to report a company's financial position and performance in accordance with ASPE and IFRS, while tax accounting is intended to adhere to the Income Tax Act and the section dealing with depreciable long-term assets.

The Canada Revenue Agency (CRA) assigns different classes to different types of assets. For instance, two of the most commonly used asset classes are Class 10 (which covers computers and lighter vehicles, such as cars and trucks) and Class 8 (for machinery and equipment). The maximum depreciation allowed to be deducted from each class is called **capital cost allowance** (CCA). The depreciation rules under Canadian federal income tax law are found in Section 8, Capital Cost Allowance (CCA). Section 8 specifies both the method and the rate of CCA to be used (declining-balance or straight-line method) for the different asset classes.

CCA is calculated by applying the specific rate to the ending balance of that class of asset. The ending balance or undepreciated capital cost (UCC) is equal to the cost of the asset minus all the accumulated CCA claimed. The rate applied for each class of asset is the maximum amount of deduction, meaning that taxpayers can claim any amount of depreciation from zero to CCA. Mostly taxpayers are willing to claim the maximum CCA, as this will reduce the tax amount owing.

Figure 2.31 on the following page shows how a company would report its Class 8 assets that have a beginning UCC of $30,000 (column 2), with an addition of $10,000 of assets to this class during the period (column 3). Column 13 reports 50% of the addition from column 3, which is then deducted from column 9 to determine the UCC. The UCC is then multiplied by the rate (column 14) to determine the maximum amount of CCA that can be claimed for the current year. In this case, that is $7,000 [($40,000 - $5,000) × 20%]. Note that the five-year class is depreciated over six years, and the seven-year class is depreciated over eight years. This is because, under CCA rules, all long-term depreciable assets are considered to be entered and removed from service in the middle of the year. The "half-year" rule is therefore used, where half of the regular rate is applied in the year of acquisition and in the year of disposal.

Because CCA is based on tax law and not ASPE or IFRS, it is not considered suitable for financial accounting purposes. It also does not take into account an asset's residual value when computing the annual amount. Also worth repeating is that the amount of CCA calculated for the year is the maximum deduction that can be taken. However, if the company has no taxable income, it may choose not to take any amount for the current year. As a result, the UCC moving forward to the next year would be $40,000 rather than $33,000 as shown in Figure 2.31.

Additional details of capital cost allowance classes and rates as set out in the Income Tax Act are beyond the scope of this course.

Canada Revenue Agency / Agence du revenu du Canada

Capital Cost Allowance (CCA) (2018 and later tax years)

Schedule 8
Code 1801
Protected B
when completed

Corporation's name	Business number	Tax year-end Year Month Day
SAMPLE CORPORATION	123456789 RT 1234	2019 12 31

For more information, see the section called "Capital Cost Allowance" in the T2 Corporation Income Tax Guide.

Is the corporation electing under Regulation 1101(5q)? **101** ☐ Yes ☑ No

1 Class number See note 1 **200**	2 Undepreciated capital cost (UCC) at the beginning of the year **201**	3 Cost of acquisitions during the year (new property must be available for use) See note 2 **203**	4 Cost of acquisitions from column 3 that are accelerated investment incentive property (AIIP) See note 3 **225**	5 Adjustments and transfers (show amounts that will reduce the undepreciated capital cost in brackets) See note 4 **205**	6 Amount from column 5 that is assistance received or receivable during the year for a property, subsequent to its disposition See note 5 **221**	7 Amount from column 5 that is repaid during the year for a property, subsequent to its disposition See note 6 **222**	8 Proceeds of dispositions See note 7 **207**	9 UCC (column 2 **plus** column 3 **plus or minus** column 5 **minus** column 8) See note 8
8	30,000	10,000				0		40,000

10 Proceeds of disposition available to reduce the UCC of AIIP (column 8 **plus** column 6 **minus** column 3 **plus** column 4 **minus** column 7) (if negative, enter "0")	11 Net capital cost additions of AIIP acquired during the year (column 4 **minus** column 10) (if negative, enter "0")	12 UCC adjustment for AIIP acquired during the year (column 11 **multiplied** by the relevant factor) See note 9	13 UCC adjustment for non-AIIP acquired during the year (0.5 **multiplied** by the result of column 3 **minus** column 4 **minus** column 6 **plus** column 7 **minus** column 8) (if negative, enter "0") See note 10 **224**	14 CCA rate % See note 11 **212**	15 Recapture of CCA See note 12 **213**	16 Terminal loss See note 13 **215**	17 CCA (for declining balance method, the result of column 9 **plus** column 12 **minus** column 13, **multiplied** by column 14 or a lower amount) See note 14 **217**	18 UCC at the end of the year (column 9 **minus** column 17) **220**
			5,000	20.00%			7,000	33,000
				Totals			7,000	

Enter the total of column 15 on line 107 of Schedule 1.
Enter the total of column 16 on line 404 of Schedule 1.
Enter the total of column 17 on line 403 of Schedule 1.

FIGURE 2.31

Disposal of Assets

LO 4

When a long-term asset is disposed of, a gain or loss is usually generated. The accountant must remove all the accumulated depreciation for the asset from the books, since the company no longer owns the item. The first step of disposal is to record the depreciation expense for the current year.

For example, a company has equipment that cost $5,000, with a useful life of five years and a residual value of $1,000, purchased on January 1, 2017. Assume that the company has not yet recorded depreciation expense for the year ended December 31, 2021. The first step is to update the depreciation as at the disposal date. For this scenario, we will assume an annual straight-line depreciation of $800 ([$5,000 – $1,000] ÷ 5 years). If we also assume the business takes depreciation to the nearest month in the year of acquisition (purchase) and disposal, the journal entry to update the depreciation before disposal is shown in Figure 2.32.

JOURNAL

Date	Account Title and Explanation	Debit	Credit
Dec 31	Depreciation Expense	800	
	Accumulated Depreciation—Equipment		800
	To record current period depreciation on equipment for disposal		

FIGURE 2.32

This entry brings the balance in the accumulated depreciation account to $4,000. The asset is eventually sold after five years on December 31, 2021, for $1,000. The journal entry to record the transaction is shown in Figure 2.33.

JOURNAL

Date	Account Title and Explanation	Debit	Credit
Dec 31	Cash	1,000	
	Accumulated Depreciation—Equipment	4,000	
	Equipment		5,000
	To record the sale of used asset for $1,000		

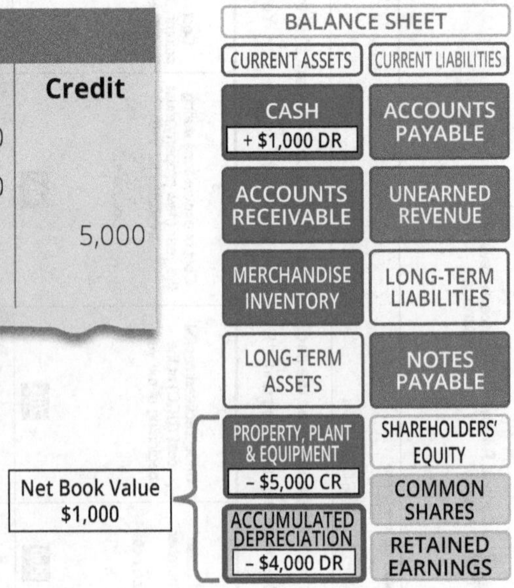

FIGURE 2.33

The amount of $1,000 is received for the asset and debited to cash. An amount of $4,000 is debited to the accumulated depreciation account, which initially had a credit balance of $4,000 due to adjusting entries made over the years. This amount is now cleared. Lastly, $5,000 is credited to the property, plant and equipment account to clear the value of the asset, since the company no longer owns it.

Now assume that the equipment was sold for $500, half the estimated residual value. As shown before, depreciation is first updated as at the disposal date. The $4,000 in accumulated depreciation is debited to that account, and the initial cost of $5,000 is credited to the property, plant and equipment asset account. Since only $500 was received for the asset, this amount is debited to cash and the $500 loss is recorded under other expenses on the income statement. The transaction is shown in Figure 2.34.

JOURNAL

Date	Account Title and Explanation	Debit	Credit
Dec 31	Cash	500	
	Accumulated Depreciation—Equipment	4,000	
	Loss on Disposal of Asset	500	
	Equipment		5,000
	To record the sale of used asset for $500		

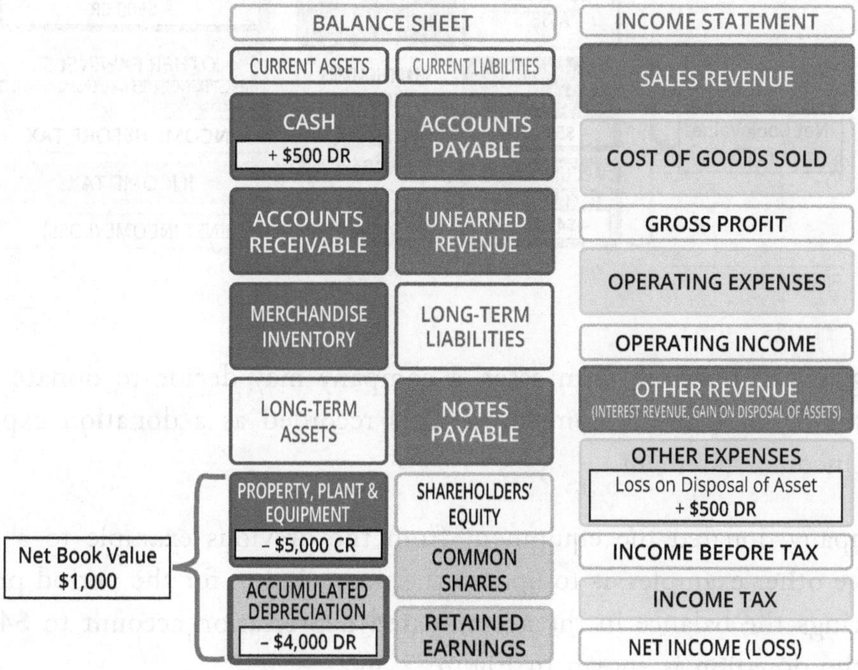

FIGURE 2.34

If the equipment was sold for $1,500, then a $500 gain is recorded under other revenue, since it was sold for more than the net book value. This is shown in Figure 2.35.

JOURNAL

Date	Account Title and Explanation	Debit	Credit
Dec 31	Cash	1,500	
	Accumulated Depreciation—Equipment	4,000	
	Gain on Disposal of Asset		500
	Equipment		5,000
	To record the sale of used asset for $1,500		

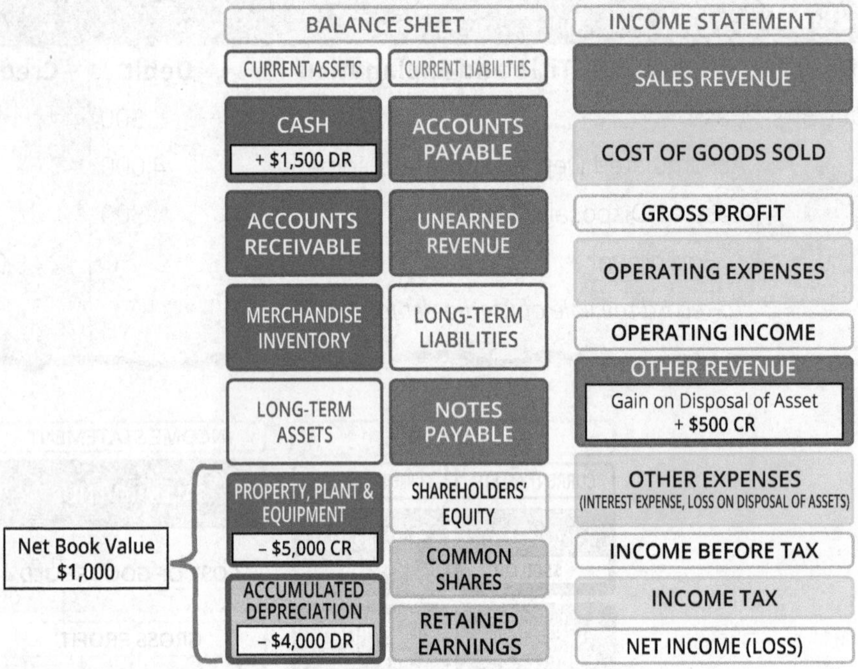

FIGURE 2.35

Instead of trying to sell the long-term asset, a company may decide to donate it to charity. The transaction involves a loss for the company and is recorded as a donation expense under other expenses on the income statement.

Assume the company donated the equipment from the previous example to a local charity. The first step, as in the other examples, is to update the depreciation for the period prior to disposal of the asset. This brings the balance in the accumulated depreciation account to $4,000. The journal entry to record the donation is shown in Figure 2.36.

JOURNAL			
Date	**Account Title and Explanation**	**Debit**	**Credit**
Dec 31	Accumulated Depreciation—Equipment	4,000	
	Donation Expense	1,000	
	Equipment		5,000
	To record the donation of used asset		

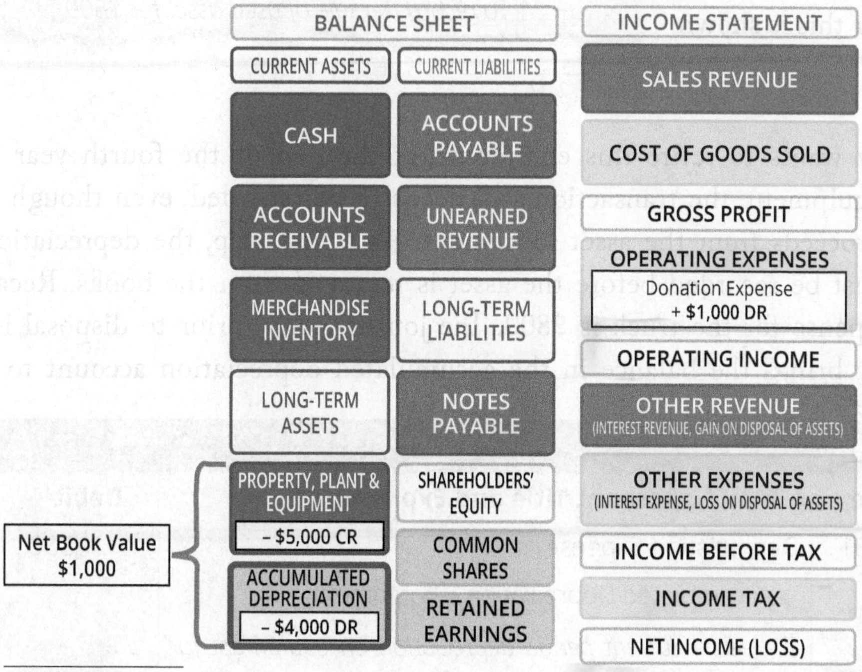

FIGURE 2.36

A long-term asset can be disposed of in many ways that do not involve selling the item; for example, the asset could be traded in or exchanged. In this chapter, we have discussed only the routine methods of disposal and provided a solid foundation for understanding the accounting concept in general. The details on trading long-terms assets are covered in the appendix to this chapter.

Here is one final change to the initial example in this section. Instead of five years, the life of the equipment ends up being four years, and the asset is sold for $500. When the useful life was five years, $4,000 of total depreciation had to be spread out over those five years, using the straight-line method. This amounted to $800 of depreciation per year. If the actual life of the asset ends up being four years, then only four years' worth of depreciation has accumulated, for a total of $3,200 ($800 × 4 years). The remaining book value, which is the residual value ($1,000) plus the amount yet to be depreciated ($800) is $1,800. Since the asset was sold for $500, this results in a loss of $1,300.

To record this as a journal entry, $500 is debited to cash, $3,200 in accumulated depreciation is taken off the books by debiting that amount, $1,300 is debited as a loss on the income statement, and the original cost of the asset ($5,000) is removed from the books by crediting that amount to the account. The journal entry for this is shown in Figure 2.37.

JOURNAL

Date	Account Title and Explanation	Debit	Credit
Dec 31	Cash	500	
	Accumulated Depreciation—Equipment	3,200	
	Loss on Disposal of Asset	1,300	
	Equipment		5,000
	To record the sale of used asset for $500		

FIGURE 2.37

If the company wants to retire this equipment at the end of the fourth year but cannot find a buyer for the equipment, the transaction still needs to be recorded, even though the company does not gain any proceeds from the asset retirement. As a first step, the depreciation expense for the current year must be recorded before the asset is removed from the books. Recall that the annual depreciation expense for the truck is $800. The journal entry prior to disposal is shown in Figure 2.38. This entry brings the balance in the accumulated depreciation account to $3,200.

JOURNAL

Date	Account Title and Explanation	Debit	Credit
Dec 31	Depreciation Expense	800	
	Accumulated Depreciation—Equipment		800
	To record current period depreciation on equipment for disposal		

FIGURE 2.38

When the equipment is retired, the accumulated depreciation of $3,200 and the original cost of $5,000 are removed from the books, while the loss on disposal of asset increases to $1,800. The journal entry for disposal of the equipment is shown in Figure 2.39.

JOURNAL

Date	Account Title and Explanation	Debit	Credit
Dec 31	Accumulated Depreciation—Equipment	3,200	
	Loss on Disposal of Asset	1,800	
	Equipment		5,000
	To record disposal of equipment		

FIGURE 2.39

In a different scenario where there is no gain or loss on the disposal of the asset, the journal entry still needs to be made whenever a long-term asset is retired. The retirement of an asset that has been fully depreciated without any residual value simply involves debiting accumulated depreciation and crediting the asset account at the original cost of the asset, as shown in Figure 2.40.

JOURNAL

Date	Account Title and Explanation	Debit	Credit
Dec 31	Accumulated Depreciation—Equipment	5,000	
	Equipment		5,000
	To record disposal of fully depreciated equipment		

FIGURE 2.40

This completely removes the asset and its accumulated depreciation from the company's books.

One final variation using our original example: If the company uses the asset for longer than the estimated useful life of five years, the remaining book value is $1,000, which is the estimated residual value. In this case, no adjustments are made and the company continues to use the asset without further depreciation.

Pause & Reflect

Exercise 2-3

Whitechapel Manufacturing sold an old piece of equipment on December 31, 2021, for $360,000. The company purchased it on January 1, 2013, for $3,000,000. It was estimated to last 10 years and have a residual value of $400,000. The depreciation for 2021 has not yet been recorded. Prepare the journal entries to record the yearly depreciation and the disposal of the asset on December 31, 2021. Assume Whitechapel uses the straight-line method of depreciation.

JOURNAL

Date	Account Title and Explanation	Debit	Credit

See Appendix I for solutions.

Natural Resources

LO 5

Natural resources have a physical nature but are different from the nature of property, plant and equipment. In fact, some companies place natural resources in a separate asset category on the balance sheet. **Natural resources** include things such as metal ores, minerals, timber, petroleum and natural gas. We will examine these special types of long-term assets and discuss how to account for natural resources in the company's books.

As with other long-term depreciable assets, we must determine their cost. This includes any expenditures to acquire the asset, such as preparing resources for extraction. It also includes any expenditure for restoring the land upon completion of use. The total cost is recorded in the appropriate asset account on the balance sheet.

Also similar to other long-term depreciable assets, the value of natural resources decreases over time as more natural resources are extracted from the ground or harvested from the land. As the resources are collected and sold, they must be allocated, or expensed, to the period in which they are consumed. This is called **depletion** and needs to be accounted for in the books just as depreciation is for property, plant and equipment. The resources must also be reported on the balance sheet at cost less accumulated depletion.

A Closer Look

Some companies still use the terms *amortization* or *depreciation* instead of *depletion* for natural resources.

Not all companies use the accumulated depreciation or depletion account. Instead, they credit the natural resource account directly and debit the expense account.

Our examination of depreciation introduced us to the units-of-production method of depreciation, the method that involves actual usage of an asset. It is appropriate for calculating the depletion of natural resources where actual units, such as ounces, barrels or metric tons, can be used in the calculation.

We can use the example of a mining company to illustrate how the units-of-production method is applied to a natural resource asset. The company has bought land containing an estimated 8,000,000 metric tons (t) of ore (rock from which minerals can be extracted), at a total cost of $10,000,000. It estimates that once all the ore has been extracted, the land will have zero residual value. Using this information, we can calculate depletion as follows.

1. Determine the depletion rate per unit using the formula shown in Figure 2.41.

$$\text{Depletion Rate} = \frac{\text{Total Cost} - \text{Residual Value}}{\text{Estimated Total Units of Resource}}$$

FIGURE 2.41

Using the values from the mining company example, the depletion rate is calculated as follows.

$$\text{Depletion Rate} = \frac{\$10{,}000{,}000 - \$0}{8{,}000{,}000\text{ t}}$$
$$= \$1.25/\text{t}$$

2. If 2,000,000 metric tons were mined and sold in the first year, the depletion expense for the year is calculated using the formula shown in Figure 2.42.

$$\text{Depletion Expense} = \text{Depletion Rate} \times \text{Quantity Extracted and Sold}$$

FIGURE 2.42

Using the depletion rate of $1.25 per metric ton, depletion expense is calculated as shown here.

$$\text{Depletion Expense} = \$1.25/\text{t} \times 2{,}000{,}000\text{ t}$$
$$= \$2{,}500{,}000$$

Figure 2.43 shows the journal entry at the end of the year.

JOURNAL

Date	Account Title and Explanation	Debit	Credit
Dec 31	Depletion Expense—Mineral Deposit	2,500,000	
	Accumulated Depletion—Mineral Deposit		2,500,000
	To record depletion of mineral deposit for year		

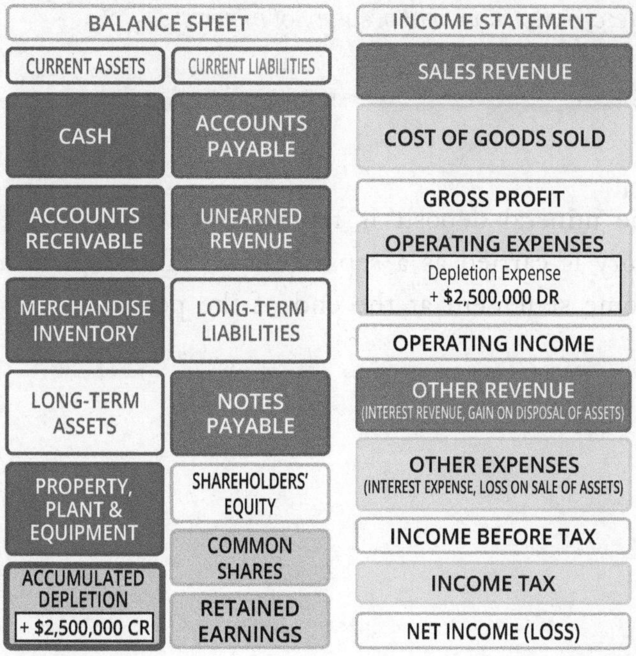

FIGURE 2.43

The $2,500,000 accumulated depletion for the year is reported on the year-end balance sheet as a contra asset to the mineral deposit account. The same amount is reported as an expense on the income statement at the end of the period.

This example assumes that all 2,000,000 metric tons of the ore mined in the year are sold within that same period. But suppose that in the second year, 1,000,000 metric tons of ore are mined but only 700,000 metric tons are sold, leaving 300,000 metric tons of ore unsold. The depletion on the unsold portion of ore must be carried forward as a current asset, called ore inventory, on the balance sheet. The depletion for the second year is calculated as follows.

$$\text{Depletion Expense} = \$1.25/\text{t} \times 700{,}000\ \text{t}$$
$$= \$875{,}000$$

The remaining 300,000 metric tons is carried as ore inventory, with a value of $375,000 ($1.25/t × 300,000 t).

The journal entry is shown in Figure 2.44.

JOURNAL

Date	Account Title and Explanation	Debit	Credit
Dec 31	Depletion Expense—Mineral Deposit	875,000	
	Ore Inventory	375,000	
	Accumulated Depletion—Mineral Deposit		1,250,000
	To record depletion and inventory of mineral deposit for year		

FIGURE 2.44

On the balance sheet, the mineral deposit is reported at its original cost less the accumulated depletion. The ore inventory is carried as a separate asset. The depletion of $875,000 is reported as an expense on the income statement at the end of the period.

Pause & Reflect

Exercise 2-4

GoodGold Inc. has just purchased a gold mine for $21,000,000. At the end of its life, the land for the gold mine is expected to be worth $1,000,000. GoodGold estimates that it will mine 500,000 ounces of gold. During its first year of operation, 14,000 ounces were mined and sold.

a) Calculate the depletion rate per unit.

b) Prepare the journal entry for the first year of depletion on December 31, 2021.

JOURNAL

Date	Account Title and Explanation	Debit	Credit

See Appendix I for solutions.

Natural Resources—A Real-World Example

Since we have learned the calculations and journal entries for natural resource transactions, we can look at how the information is presented by a Canadian company in the real world. Suncor Energy Inc. is one of the world's leaders in the oil and gas industry. Headquartered in Calgary, Alberta, and founded in 1919, Suncor Energy has operations in Canada and abroad. Mining requires a lot of investments in terms of property, plant and equipment. Figure 2.45 represents the components of Suncor property, plant and equipment.

Figure 2.45 shows the balances included in Note 15 in the Notes to the Consolidated Financial Statements section of Suncor Energy's 2018 annual report. It provides the details of Suncor's property, plant and equipment, which show net book values (in millions) of $74,245 and $73,493 on the 2018 and 2017 balance sheets, respectively.

Suncor Energy Inc.

Note 15: Property, Plant and Equipment

($ millions)	Oil and Gas Properties	Plant and Equipment	Total
Cost			
At December 31, 2016	$34,141	$73,537	$107,678
Additions	1,235	5,875	7,110
Acquisitions	25	310	335
Changes in decommissioning and restoration	821	22	843
Disposals and derecognition	—	(884)	(884)
Foreign exchange adjustments	(13)	(256)	(269)
Reclassified from assets held for sale	—	35	35
At December 31, 2017	$36,209	$78,639	$114,848
Additions	1,221	3,958	5,179
Transfers from exploration and evaluation	31	—	31
Acquisitions	289	948	1,237
Changes in decommissioning and restoration	85	(22)	63
Disposals and derecognition	(375)	(4,785)	(5,160)
Foreign exchange adjustments	385	291	676
At December 31, 2018	$37,845	$79,029	$116,874
Accumulated provision			
At December 31, 2016	($16,062)	($20,357)	($36,419)
Depreciation and depletion	(1,916)	(3,514)	(5,430)
Disposals and derecognition		368	368
Foreign exchange adjustments	3	126	129
Reclassified from assets held for sale	—	(3)	(3)
At December 31, 2017	(17,975)	(23,380)	(41,355)
Depreciation and depletion	(1,739)	(3,849)	(5,588)
Disposals and derecognition	255	4,545	4,800
Foreign exchange adjustments	(324)	(162)	(486)
At December 31, 2018	($19,783)	($22,846)	($42,629)
Net property, plant and equipment			
December 31, 2017	18,234	55,259	73,493
December 31, 2018	$18,062	$56,183	$74,245

	December 31, 2018			December 31, 2017		
($ millions)	Cost	Accumulated Provision	Net Book Value	Cost	Accumulated Provision	Net Book Value
Oil Sands	$80,295	($22,654)	$57,641	$79,625	($22,664)	$56,961
Exploration and Production	21,867	(14,075)	7,792	21,007	(12,990)	8,017
Refining and Marketing	13,627	(5,092)	8,535	13,137	(4,906)	8,231
Corporate, Energy Trading and Eliminations	1,085	(808)	277	1,079	(795)	284
	$116,874	($42,629)	$74,245	$114,848	($41,355)	$73,493

At December 31, 2018, the balance of assets under construction and not subject to depreciation or depletion was $4.7 billion (December 31, 2017 – $15.9 billion).
At December 31, 2018, Property, Plant and Equipment included finance leases with a net book value of $1.4 billion (December 31, 2017 – $1.4 billion).

FIGURE 2.45

Remember, all costs involved in preparing resources for extraction are capitalized. For a mining company, the costs of mine development include items such as expenses in constructing equipment used in mining natural resources. Construction may take more than a year to complete. At the end of the year, the costs associated with constructing assets that have not been finished are capitalized as construction-in-progress. Once construction is complete and the asset is ready for use, the balance is transferred from the construction-in-progress account to the appropriate account.

For example, if the company is constructing equipment, the balance is transferred from construction-in-progress to facilities and equipment once the equipment is ready for use. This is why the assets under construction are not depreciated, while all other four components of property, plant and equipment are. Depreciation does not start until the asset under construction is complete and ready for its intended use. Once this happens, the asset must be depreciated or depleted as discussed earlier.

> **ASPE vs. IFRS**
>
> Under IFRS, every company (regardless of whether it is in the natural resources industry or not) must show the reconciliation of the beginning and the ending balances for each class of property, plant and equipment.
>
> Under ASPE, such reconciliation is not required.

Intangible Assets and Goodwill

LO 6

The previous discussion of long-term assets covered tangible assets, which are physical in nature and can be touched or sensed. In contrast, intangible assets are conceptual in nature. They are *identifiable* assets that have no physical form and largely constitute intellectual property, such as patents and trademarks. An asset is considered to be identifiable if one of the following criteria applies.

1. It is separable, meaning it is capable of being separated from the company and sold.
2. It emerges from contractual or legal rights, regardless of whether it is separable or transferable from the company.

An asset that is not identifiable does not count as an intangible asset. Goodwill, for example, is not identifiable, since it does not fit either of the above two criteria. Therefore, it is accounted for differently and reported separately from other intangible assets. Goodwill is discussed at the end of this section.

Different intangible assets differ in their lengths of useful life. Some intangible assets benefit the company for a finite number of years, while others benefit the company indefinitely. Just as property, plant and equipment need to be depreciated, intangible assets with finite useful lives need to go through a similar process. However, the process of allocating the cost of intangible assets over their useful lives is usually called **amortization** instead of depreciation. The value of intangible assets (including both those with finite useful lives and those with infinite useful lives) may also decrease due to impairment, which is similar to the impairment of property, plant and equipment discussed earlier.

> **ASPE vs. IFRS**
>
> Under ASPE, intangible assets are reported and amortized only when they are purchased.
>
> However, under IFRS, any internally generated intangible asset can also be capitalized and amortized as long as it provides future benefits to the company.

Intangible Assets with Finite Useful Lives

Patents and copyrights are the most obvious examples of intangible assets that have limited useful lives.

Patents

Individuals and companies invent and develop innovative products, usually at an enormous cost of both money and time. Inventors need to protect their intellectual property and this is achieved through patenting.

A **patent** grants the patentee the exclusive right, for a set period of time, to prevent others from making, using, selling or distributing the patented invention without permission. In most international jurisdictions, a patent term lasts for 20 years, but the duration can differ according to the type of patent. This gives the inventor or inventing company the right to enjoy the rewards of creating a new and successful product.

A patent can be purchased from another party or filed by the company. If the company purchases the patent from another party, the cost of the patent is equal to the purchase price plus any legal costs involved. If the company files its own patent, the application process typically requires the use of patent lawyers (as does the defence and management of a patent). All legal and associated costs in acquiring and defending a patent are capitalized in the long-term assets section of the balance sheet. The value of the patent is then amortized for the amount of time left in the patent's legal term or its estimated useful life, whichever is shorter.

This example illustrates how to record journal entries for patent acquisition and amortization. Assume Henry's Lights purchases a patent from Pixie Light Bulbs for $28,000 on January 1, 2021. The patent has seven years remaining in its term and is expected to bring in revenues to the company for the whole seven years. The entries to record the purchase on January 1, 2021, as well as one year's amortization for the year ending December 31, 2021, are recorded as shown in Figure 2.46.

JOURNAL

Date	Account Title and Explanation	Debit	Credit
Jan 1	Patents	28,000	
	Cash		28,000
	To record purchase of patent with seven years remaining		
Dec 31	Amortization Expense—Patents	4,000	
	Accumulated Amortization—Patents		4,000
	To record amortization expense for one year		

FIGURE 2.46

The $4,000 annual amortization amount is calculated using the straight-line method. The straight-line method divides the amortizable amount ($28,000 less a residual value of zero) by the number of years remaining (seven years). This method is often used for amortizing patents and other intangible assets.

Copyright

Copyright is similar to a patent in that it gives exclusive rights of ownership to a person or group that has created something. The difference with copyright is that it applies to artistic work, such as music and literature, and can exist even if the work has not been registered. For example, it is automatically assumed that an article or photo posted on the internet is protected by copyright. A person cannot simply assume unlimited rights to use or copy a work found online. Registration with the Canadian Intellectual Property Office, however, puts a copyright holder in a stronger position if litigation arises over the copyright. In Canada, the laws regarding copyright are governed by the Copyright Act, which states that, generally, the life of a copyright lasts throughout the life of the author plus 50 years from the end of the calendar year of their death. This means that estimates of a copyright's legal life depend on when the work was first created and how long the author lives. The copyright's useful life, however, is usually shorter than its legal life in practice.

Overall, copyright is treated in much the same way as a patent. The costs may include the purchase price to obtain the copyright from someone else, legal fees paid to register and defend the copyright, and any other fees involved in its acquisition and defence. The cost of the copyright is amortized over the number of years of its legal term or its estimated useful life, whichever is shorter.

Intangible Assets with Infinite Useful Lives

Some intangible assets do not have an expiry date and will keep generating economic benefits for the company as long as the company still owns them. Some examples of these assets include trademarks, trade names, franchises and licences.

Trademark and Trade Name

A **trademark** is similar to a patent and copyright except that it grants ownership rights for a recognizable symbol or logo. A **trade name** grants exclusive rights to a name under which a company or product trades for commercial purposes, even though its legal or technical name might differ. Some corporations have numerous trademarks and trade names that they protect on a continuing basis. For example, McDonald's is not only a trade name that the company protects, but it serves as an umbrella brand for numerous other trademarks, such as the Golden Arches, the Extra Value Meal and Hamburger University.

Any internal costs incurred for developing and maintaining a trademark or trade name, such as those involved with advertising, are considered indistinguishable from other costs of developing the company's business and are expensed during the year they are incurred. However, just as with patents and copyrights, legal fees for registering the name or logo are capitalized. Alternatively, trademarks and trade names can be purchased from someone else. Because these can be separately measured, they are capitalized as intangible assets on the balance sheet.

Franchises and Licences

A **franchise** is a contract that allows the franchisee to operate a branch using the franchisor's brand name and business model. For example, one can buy a franchise to run a KFC branch, Circle K convenience store or Petro-Canada gas station. The franchisee receives operating support from the franchisor, such as marketing and training, while the franchisor maintains some control over how the franchisee operates the branch.

The franchisee usually has to pay initial fees when acquiring the franchise. These initial fees are capitalized as long-term assets on the balance sheet. Normally, there is no expiry date on the franchise, meaning the franchisee can keep operating the branch under the contract, as long as annual payments called royalties are made. Because there is no expiry date, if the franchisee plans to operate the franchise indefinitely, the initial fees are not amortized. Royalties that are paid annually are expensed.

A **licence** is a contract that permits the licensee to use the licensor's product or brand name under specified terms and conditions. For example, one can buy a licence from Marvel to sell T-shirts with Iron Man printed on them. A licence usually does not come with ongoing formal support from the licensor, and the licensor usually does not have much control over how the licensee operates the business. The same principles described above for franchises also apply to a licensee obtaining and using a licence.

Goodwill

Goodwill is an intangible asset that can be attributed to factors such as a recognizable brand name, experienced management, a skilled workforce or a unique product. As an accounting concept, goodwill arises when a company purchases another company at a cost that is greater than the market value of that company's net assets. The excess of the cost of the company over the total market value of its assets, less its total liabilities, is recorded as goodwill. Unlike other assets, items representing goodwill do not come with an easily determinable market price to be amortized over time. Nevertheless, businesses are willing to pay for goodwill, and it increases intangible assets on the balance sheet. We will use an example to explain how goodwill works and how accountants should record such items in the company's books.

Vicky's Entrepreneurial Enterprises decides to buy Jack's Sweets, an established candy maker, on June 1, 2021. The purchase price is $1,000,000. At the time of purchase, Jack's Sweets has assets with a market value of $1,500,000 and liabilities totalling $700,000, giving the purchased company a net asset value of $800,000. The breakdown of assets and liabilities is as shown in Figure 2.47.

Jack's Sweets Assets and Liabilities As at June 1, 2021	
Assets	
Accounts Receivable	$200,000
Inventory	400,000
Property, Plant & Equipment	900,000
Total Assets	**$1,500,000**
Liabilities	
Accounts Payable	$150,000
Unearned Revenue	200,000
Notes Payable	350,000
Total Liabilities	**$700,000**

FIGURE 2.47

The extra $200,000 in the company's purchase price constitutes goodwill. Vicky is willing to pay for the brand name, because Jack's Sweets is known for great-tasting candies. In addition, Jack's Sweets' memorable commercials featured a fictional "Uncle Jack" handing out treats to beloved customers. Vicky considers $200,000 for this brand to be a bargain and is willing to pay this amount for goodwill. However, she also expects a good return on her investment for the premium paid for the business.

To record the purchase of Jack's Sweets, Vicky's accountant adds the value of the assets and liabilities to Vicky's balance sheet. This results in a debit to the various asset accounts totalling $1,500,000 and a credit to the various liability accounts totalling $700,000. The cash payment amount of $1,000,000 is recorded as a credit to cash. The premium paid is recorded as goodwill and increases that asset account by $200,000. Figure 2.48 shows this transaction.

JOURNAL

Date	Account Title and Explanation	Debit	Credit
Jun 1	Accounts Receivable	200,000	
	Inventory	400,000	
	Property, Plant & Equipment	900,000	
	Goodwill	200,000	
	Accounts Payable		150,000
	Unearned Revenue		200,000
	Notes Payable		350,000
	Cash		1,000,000
	To purchase net assets of Jack's Sweets, including goodwill		

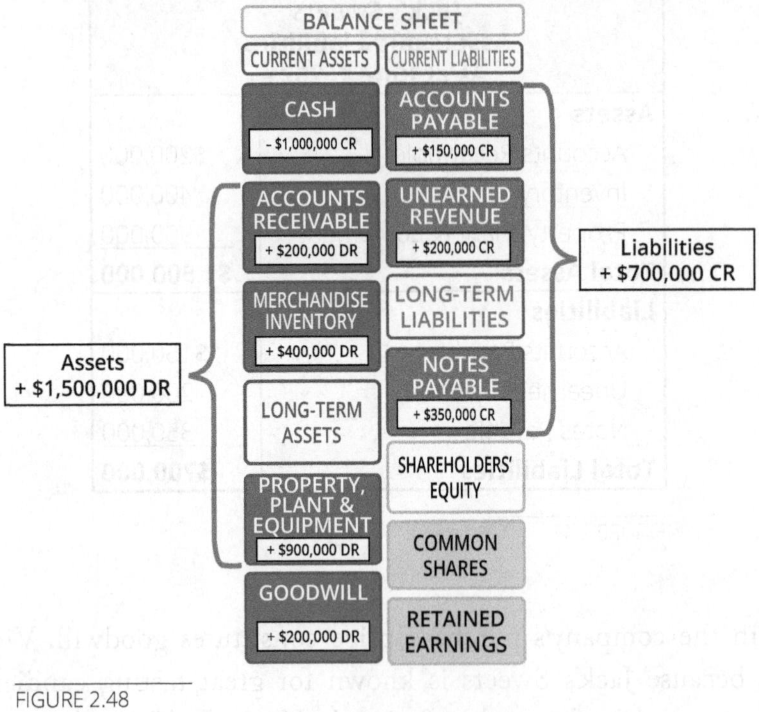

FIGURE 2.48

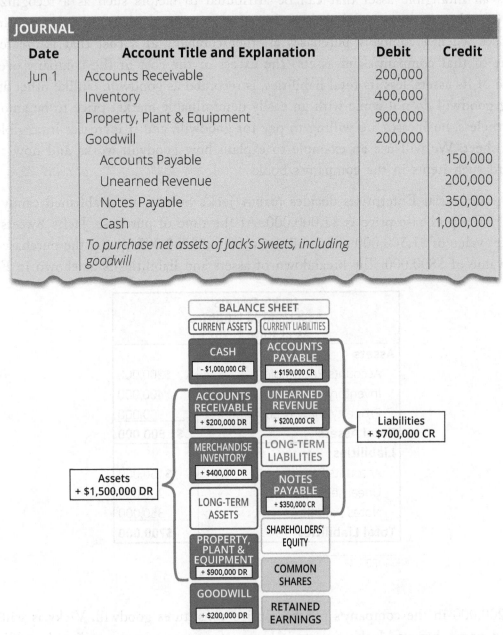

Unlike other intangible assets with infinite useful lives, items categorized as goodwill do not have their value amortized over time. However, this does not mean that the value of goodwill cannot decrease. Events may occur that impair the value of goodwill.

For example, assume that Company A bought Company B because the latter was producing a unique product that the rest of the market could not match. Company A paid a premium of $150,000 over the net asset value of Company B, so this premium is goodwill. However, since the purchase, advances in technology allowed a competitor to create a new product to compete with the one produced by Company B. The new product is still undergoing development and testing but will almost certainly enter the market within a year.

The value of goodwill associated with the innovative quality of Company B's product will be seriously reduced. But it will not be negated altogether, since it is estimated that the product will still be competitive, even after the introduction of another product.

A decrease in the value of goodwill for the current year is estimated at $50,000. The journal entry to record this is shown in Figure 2.49. The impairment of goodwill is recorded as an expense on the income statement, which reduces the equity of the company.

ASPE vs. IFRS

Under ASPE, a company must conduct impairment tests whenever the company becomes aware of an impairment indication.

Under IFRS, a company must conduct impairment tests on goodwill and intangible assets with indefinite lives every year, even if there is no indication of impairment. However, for intangible assets with finite lives and property, plant and equipment, IFRS requires the company to actively look for impairment indicators every year, and conduct impairment tests only if indicators exist.

JOURNAL

Date	Account Title and Explanation	Debit	Credit
Dec 31	Impairment Loss	50,000	
	Goodwill		50,000
	To record loss on impairment of goodwill		

FIGURE 2.49

The value of goodwill should never be adjusted upward above cost. This violates the accounting principle of prudence (conservatism). Internally generated goodwill also cannot be recognized or recorded on the balance sheet because the value of goodwill cannot be objectively separated from the value of the company's other assets.

Figure 2.50 summarizes the accounts used to record the purchase, depreciation and sale or disposal of long-term assets.

SUMMARY OF ACCOUNTS USED TO RECORD PURCHASE, DEPRECIATION AND SALE OR DISPOSAL OF LONG-TERM ASSETS

	Property, Plant & Equipment			Natural Resources			Intangibles		
	Account/Explanation	**Debit**	**Credit**	**Account/Explanation**	**Debit**	**Credit**	**Account/Explanation**	**Debit**	**Credit**
Purchase	Equipment	X		Mineral Deposit	X		Patent	X	
	Cash		X	Cash		X	Cash		X
	To record purchase of equipment			*To record purchase of mineral deposit rights*			*To record purchase of patent rights*		
Depreciation	Depreciation Expense	X		Depletion Expense	X		Amortization Expense	X	
	Accumulated Depreciation		X	Accumulated Depletion		X	Accumulated Amortization, or Patent		X
	To record depreciation of equipment			*To record depletion of natural resource*			*To record amortization of patent*		
Disposal	Cash	X		Cash	X		Cash	X	
	Accumulated Depreciation	X		Accumulated Depletion	X		Accumulated Amortization (if this account used above)	X	
	Loss on Disposal of Asset	X		Loss on Disposal of Asset	X		Loss on Sale of Asset	X	
	Equipment		X	Mineral Deposit		X	Patent		X
	To dispose of asset for less than net book value			*To dispose of asset for less than net book value*			*To record sale of patent rights for less than net book value*		
	Cash	X		Cash	X		Cash	X	
	Accumulated Depreciation	X		Accumulated Depletion	X		Accumulated Amortization	X	
	Equipment		X	Mineral Deposit		X	Patent		X
	Gain on Sale of Asset		X	Gain on Sale of Asset		X	Gain on Sale of Asset		X
	To dispose of asset for more than net book value			*To dispose of asset for more than net book value*			*To record sale of asset for more than net book value*		

FIGURE 2.50

In the Real World

Financial scandals in the early 2000s shook the confidence of investors. Some companies were found guilty of misrepresenting their financial statements to make their financial position appear better than it was. One of the ways this was achieved was through the inflation of goodwill by delaying goodwill impairments.

In response, changes in accounting rules were made to help regulate the practice of goodwill accounting for public companies, providing more transparency and greater accountability. In addition, predictive analytics, which can detect patterns in data, can be used to find anomalies in goodwill impairment and make predictions about future outcomes.

Predictive analytics allows companies to identify impairments and their impact on earnings before they occur. Models are used to forecast outcomes based on statistical relationships between factors. Factors found to be statistically related to goodwill impairment include management bonuses, firm size, market value to book value ratios and expected market delisting. The key with this technology is the use of effective models. Software is constantly evolving to improve the accuracy and effectiveness of the models.

Presentation and Financial Analysis of Long-Term Assets LO 7

The details of Suncor Energy's property, plant and equipment were examined in Figure 2.45. We will return to Suncor to see how the company's long-term assets and their depreciation and amortization are presented on its financial statements. Figure 2.51 shows the assets portion of Suncor's balance sheet.

As illustrated in Suncor's balance sheet, long-term assets are below current assets in the assets section. Tangible assets (property, plant and equipment) are separate from intangible assets. Notice that Suncor presents its long-term assets on the balance sheet at their net book value. The $74,245 balance of Suncor's property, plant and equipment on the company's 2018 balance sheet is the net book value, less accumulated depreciation. A company must always present the costs and accumulated depreciation or amortization of its long-term assets either in the notes or on the balance sheet itself. Suncor included this detail in the notes. Because Suncor's intangible assets constitute a relatively small portion of its total assets, Suncor includes intangible assets as part of "other intangible assets."

Figure 2.51 also shows a portion of Suncor's income statement. The statement presents depreciation, depletion, amortization and impairment of long-lived assets under expenses. Details of the depreciation methods and the impairments would be explained in the notes and are part of the complete set of financial statements.

Suncor Energy Inc.
Consolidated Balance Sheets (partial)

($ millions)	**December 31, 2018**	**December 31, 2017**
Assets		
Current assets		
Cash and cash equivalents	$2,221	$2,672
Accounts receivable	3,206	3,281
Inventories	3,159	3,468
Income taxes receivable	114	156
Total current assets	8,700	9,577
Property, plant and equipment, net	74,245	73,493
Exploration and evaluation	2,319	2,052
Other assets	1,126	1,211
Goodwill and other intangible assets	3,061	3,061
Deferred income taxes	128	100
Total assets	$89,579	$89,494

Consolidated Statements of Comprehensive Income (partial)

For the years ended December 31 ($ millions)	**2018**	**2017**
Revenues and Other Income		
Operating revenues, net of royalties	$38,542	$31,954
Other income	444	125
	38,986	32,079
Expenses		
Purchases of crude oil and products	14,133	11,121
Operating, selling and general	10,573	9,188
Transportation	1,319	997
Depreciation, depletion, amortization and impairment	5,738	5,601
Exploration	122	104
Gain on disposal of assets	(24)	(602)
Financing expenses (income)	2,142	(246)
	34,003	26,163
Earnings before Income Taxes	4,983	5,916
Income Tax Expense		
Current	1,250	1,209
Deferred	440	249
	1,690	1,458
Net Earnings	$3,293	$4,458

FIGURE 2.51

Asset Turnover

A turnover ratio measures how rapidly an asset's status changes and becomes productive. Recall that inventory turnover measures how quickly an asset converts from inventory to becoming a sale. **Asset turnover** measures how quickly a company converts its total assets, including long-term assets, into revenue.

To calculate asset turnover, we need net sales from the income statement and the average total assets, which is produced by taking the average of beginning and ending total assets. The formulas to do this are shown in Figure 2.52.

$$\text{Asset Turnover} = \frac{\text{Net Sales}}{\text{Average Total Assets*}}$$

*Average Total Assets = (Beginning of Year Total Assets + End of Year Total Assets) ÷ 2

FIGURE 2.52

Return on Assets

A company's return on assets is similar to asset turnover except that its focus is on net income instead of revenue. **Return on assets** measures the relationship between net income and assets. In other words, is the company making enough profit from investment in its total assets? Figure 2.53 shows the formula to calculate return on assets.

$$\text{Return on Assets} = \frac{\text{Net Income}}{\text{Average Total Assets}}$$

FIGURE 2.53

Note that the ratios to calculate asset turnover and return on assets both have the same denominator: average total assets. It is the numerators that differ. Asset turnover uses net sales, while return on assets uses net income. Another difference is that asset turnover is expressed as a decimal number, while return on assets is expressed as a percentage (that is, the ratio is multiplied by 100).

Using the Ratios

We can calculate and compare these two ratios by using the financial information from the financial statements of Suncor Energy for the years ended December 31, 2018 and 2017. Using the formulas already outlined, the ratios are calculated in Figure 2.54.

Selected Financial Information (in millions)			
		2018	**2017**
A	Net Sales	$38,542	$31,954
B	Total Assets—End of Year	$89,579	$89,494
C	Average Total Assets	$89,537	89,098*
D = A ÷ C	Asset Turnover	0.43	0.36
E	Net Income (Loss)	$3,293	$4,458
F = E ÷ C	Return on Assets	3.68%	5.00%

*Note that the total assets for 2016 were $88,702.

FIGURE 2.54

For 2018 and 2017, both net sales and net income were divided by average total assets to produce the two financial ratios. With regard to asset turnover, Suncor generated more revenue dollars per investment in assets in 2018 than 2017. With regard to return on assets, Suncor generated more net income per investment in assets in 2017 than 2018.

All financial ratios represent a simple snapshot of company performance; each ratio tends to focus on one aspect of a business. Calculation and interpretation of multiple ratios can provide a bigger picture of the overall well-being of a company, which will be discussed in a later chapter.

Controls Related to Long-Term Assets

LO 8

Tangible assets are purchased by a company, used to earn an income and eventually disposed of. The value of a long-term asset depreciates over the period of its estimated useful life. Accounting procedures are used to control and safeguard all tangible assets while the company possesses them. Different companies and industries depend on long-term assets to varying degrees. For instance, auto manufacturers General Motors and Ford rely heavily on long-term assets such as machines, robots and factories. It is sometimes possible for people to steal large assets from a company. Security measures, such as physical barriers and security personnel, can protect large items from theft.

Insurance is a more useful measure to protect large long-term assets. Insurance can protect not only in the case of theft but also in the event of catastrophic situations such as extreme weather or unforeseen breakdowns. It is important for management to make sure that the best possible insurance policies are in place and are updated or adjusted when needed. Some companies may even want to consider some self-insurance options to help protect their long-term assets from catastrophic risk.

In the Real World

Although businesses should make certain that all their assets are insured and that potential liabilities are also covered, this does not always mean that an insurance company needs to be involved. Businesses can self-insure to cover various risks. Companies that self-insure are sometimes regarded as being uninsured. In other words, "self-insurance" can be seen as an attempt to avoid paying for insurance. Indeed, this can be true, since some companies fail to adequately self-insure.

Proper self-insurance involves a company setting aside enough capital reserves to cover itself in case of a catastrophic event. If something happens to a company's long-term assets, these capital reserves can be used to cover the loss. The advantage of self-insurance is that a company avoids paying premiums that are often very high.

The disadvantage of self-insurance is that a company needs to tie up a certain amount of its capital to cover a disaster, and even that is sometimes insufficient. To minimize this disadvantage, there are alternative self-insurance strategies. For example, a business can still buy some insurance but add self-insurance. Alternatively, businesses can form collaborative self-insurance groups, whereby a group of companies contributes to a pool of funds that can be used if one or more of them suffer a catastrophic event.

As with most aspects of today's business environment, various innovative solutions can be found to resolve inadequacies in the market. Self-insurance is an example of one of these innovations.

Big or small, expensive or inexpensive, all types of tangible assets should be tracked properly and relevant transactions recorded accurately in the company's books. Experienced accountants should perform these control procedures.

Each long-term asset should be tagged in some way, perhaps by a bar code and scanner. The tags should be read and compared with accounting records, and vice versa. Physical audits should be performed on a regular basis to ensure that all assets on the books are on the premises, still in use and accounted for.

For all company assets, paperwork and records should be completed correctly and handled securely. The first priority is to record the correct cost for the long-term asset. As always, any costs related to the acquisition of the asset must be included in the total cost. These can include freight, installation and testing costs.

As emphasized throughout our discussion of asset controls, every company should have policies, plans and procedures in place and should follow regulations and laws. For example, a large company may have a policy of classifying items as long-term assets only if they cost more than $1,000. A smaller company may have a lower threshold for its policy. These policies need to be clearly communicated to the staff responsible for their implementation. Adherence to all related policies, plans, procedures, regulations and laws should be monitored, with audits when necessary.

Economical and efficient use of tangible assets involves purchasing assets at the best possible price. Internal controls should include a bidding process for suppliers, which helps to ensure the best possible price. Financial ratios, discussed in this chapter, can be used on a regular basis to monitor the efficient use of a company's long-term assets. If the ratios indicate an inefficient use of these assets, measures can be taken to either dispose of them or make better use of them. If sales are slow, this may mean that long-term assets are not being used to their full capacity. A business may also find that too much money has been invested in its long-term assets. Leasing them could free up some capital. As always, company goals and objectives related to long-term assets should be stated, implemented, reviewed and changed when necessary.

Controls related to intangible assets are not very different from those relating to tangible assets. Qualified staff should be available to ensure that transactions are recorded and classified properly in the company's books and that all payments are properly documented. Costs should be objectively verified and any supporting documentation should be properly maintained.

However, with intangible assets, the only physical evidence of their existence often comes in the form of contracts, accompanying invoices and supporting cost documentation. That is why it is so important to physically protect such documents. They can be placed in a vault on the premises or a safe deposit box in a bank. These documents can be referenced when changes are made or when the company's books need updating.

Beyond initial registration or purchase, ongoing valuation of intangible assets needs to take place. For example, market conditions may affect the value of goodwill, or competing trademarks may diminish the value of a brand name. Furthermore, companies that own patents, copyrights and trademarks should be on the lookout for entities that are using such intellectual property without permission. Any such use diminishes the value of the protected asset. All proper legal avenues should be pursued, including legal action or the threat of legal action, when improper use of protected intellectual assets has taken place.

An Ethical Approach to Long-Term Assets

LO 9

Accounting for a firm's long-term assets can be manipulated to produce fraudulent figures. Decisions about classifying long-term assets, depreciating them and estimating residual values can have a significant impact on a company's financial statements. Figures for long-term assets can be manipulated to present a financial picture that does not accurately reflect the financial state of the company.

One of the first decisions that an accountant must make is whether a long-term asset in question is in fact a long-term asset. An attempt to falsely classify a long-term asset as an expense understates the company's net income in the current period. Conversely, an attempt to classify an expense as a long-term asset overstates the company's equity in the current period. Any result that does not reflect the true nature of the asset is an ethical breach and should always be avoided.

In the Real World

The year 2001 saw the beginning of numerous corporate and accounting scandals that breached ethical standards. Authorities began investigating some of America's largest corporations regarding, among other things, accounting fraud. The corporations investigated included three telecommunications companies—Global Crossing, Qwest and WorldCom.

Some of these investigations found a distortion of gains and expenses as a result of misclassifying long-term assets. For example, both Global Crossing and Qwest engaged in billions of dollars of what are known as swaps. These companies purchased telecom capacity from customers who then bought it back from the companies. These were falsely treated as long-term assets rather than as current operating expenses. The result was that both companies recorded the revenue upfront, then expensed the amount over a period of time. This violates, among other things, the expense recognition principle.

In addition, WorldCom classified billions of dollars of current operating expenses as long-term assets. This was done over a period of 15 months. The auditing firm Arthur Andersen failed to raise any red flags over the practice.

Estimating the useful life of a long-term asset is also open to manipulation. Intentionally shortening an asset's life span can unduly increase the annual depreciation charges recorded in the company's books. Intentionally increasing a long-term asset's residual value decreases the amount to be depreciated and the depreciation charges. An accountant has an ethical obligation to avoid, or detect and correct, these abuses at all times.

Ethical considerations for intangible assets relate mostly to their correct reporting in financial statements. This includes determining the appropriate cost, calculating the correct amortization and impairment and accurately reporting all amounts on the income statement and balance sheet.

Companies should always set up internal controls to ensure that ongoing transactions involving intangible assets are expensed or capitalized properly. Following review procedures ensures that annual amortization is verified and properly reported. Any review procedure should be the joint responsibility of both management and company auditors. Executives and accountants must take responsibility for the company's books; not doing so can lead to serious consequences.

In Summary

LO 1 Identify the characteristics of long-term assets

- Long-term assets provide the infrastructure necessary for operating a business.
- They are expected to be used on an ongoing basis, typically longer than one year, and are not intended to be sold to customers.

LO 2 Record the acquisition and changes in the value of property, plant and equipment

- Cost of property, plant and equipment includes purchase price and expenditures necessary to get the asset ready for operation. The whole cost is debited to the appropriate long-term asset account.
- In a lump sum purchase, the amount paid for all the assets is divided and allocated to each item according to percentages based on the appraised values or fair values.
- After acquisition, changes made to property, plant and equipment are classified as a betterment, a major repair, or ordinary repairs and maintenance.
- Property, plant and equipment (except land) decrease in value (depreciate) over time. Depreciation is the process of allocating the cost of the asset over its useful life.

LO 3 Apply and compare three methods of depreciation of property, plant and equipment

- The straight-line method of depreciation uses a simple average, resulting in the same amount of depreciation every year.
- The declining-balance and double-declining-balance methods apply a depreciation rate to the remaining balance of the book value of the asset.
- The units-of-production method uses the level of asset usage as the basis for calculating depreciation.
- Accountants choose the depreciation method that best reflects the nature of the asset.
- Revisions can be made to a depreciation schedule. However, proper justification should always be used and prior depreciation deductions should never be changed.
- "Book depreciation" is different from depreciation for federal income tax purposes. The depreciation rules under Canadian federal income tax law are found in Section 8 of the Income Tax Act, Capital Cost Allowance (CCA).

LO 4 Account for disposal of assets

- The disposal of an asset usually involves a gain or loss relative to the item's book value. Gains and losses appear on the income statements.

LO 5 Account for natural resources

- The natural resources that a company owns—such as minerals, oil or timber—are physical in nature, and are capitalized under the long-term assets section on the balance sheet. Some companies categorize them separately from other long-term assets.
- A natural resource's value is depleted over time using the units-of-production method.

LO 6 Define and account for intangible assets and describe the different types of intangible assets

- Intangible assets are defined as identifiable assets that have no physical form. An asset is considered to be identifiable if it either is separable from the company or emerges from contractual or legal rights.
- The decrease in an intangible asset's value due to amortization and impairment is recorded as an expense or a loss on the income statement. While impairment loss may be recorded directly against the asset account, amortization must be recorded in an accumulated amortization account.
- A patent gives the inventor the exclusive right to use a product. The cost of the patent is for legal fees or the purchase of rights from someone else. This cost is amortized over the remaining term of the patent, or its expected useful life, whichever is shorter.
- Copyright gives exclusive rights of a creation to its creator. Copyright is granted automatically to works produced and published.
- A trademark gives exclusive rights to logos and other company symbols. A trade name provides exclusive rights to names of companies and products.
- A franchise is a contract that allows the franchisee to operate a branch using the franchisor's brand name and business model. A licence is a contract that permits the licensee to use the licensor's product or brand name under the specified terms and conditions. The initial franchise fees or licence fees are capitalized.
- Goodwill arises when a company purchases another company at a cost that is greater than the market value of that company's net assets. Unlike other intangible assets, goodwill is considered to be unidentifiable. Therefore, it is reported separately from other intangible assets.

LO 7 Calculate and interpret asset turnover and return on assets ratios

- Asset turnover measures the revenue a company generates relative to its investment in total assets.
- Return on assets measures the net income a company generates relative to total assets.

LO 8 Describe controls related to long-term assets

- Controls to protect a company's long-term assets can include accurate recording and tracking procedures, or proper insurance in case of catastrophic events. Qualified accounting personnel should always supervise the policies and measures that a company implements.

LO 9 Describe ethical approaches related to long-term assets

- Net income figures and net asset values can be distorted by manipulating decisions regarding the classification of long-term assets, the estimation of residual value and useful life, and other aspects of depreciation. Unethical manipulations must always be avoided.

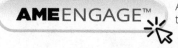

Review Exercise 2-1

Nelson Rugasa is an entrepreneur who has just started a consulting business. On December 31, 2021, Nelson used cash to purchase a laptop computer for $3,000 and office equipment for $10,000.

Required

a) Record the purchase of long-term assets.

JOURNAL

Date	Account Title and Explanation	Debit	Credit

Research Component (to be done outside of class time)

b) Research the useful life of long-term assets, and suggest the useful life for the computer and office equipment.

c) Research the way in which the value of long-term assets decline, and suggest the depreciation method(s) that should be used for the computer and office equipment.

d) Based on your research on useful life and the ways in which the value of long-term assets decline, prepare a table showing the cost, depreciation, accumulated depreciation and net book value of the computer and office equipment for the first three years.

Year	Cost	Depreciation	Accumulated Depreciation	Net Book Value

e) Explain how you calculate the profit or loss on the disposal of a long-term asset.

See Appendix I for solutions.

Review Exercise 2-2

Rulison Company had the following transactions during 2021.

Jan 1 Paid $250,000 to purchase Regnier Ltd., which had $500,000 in assets and $300,000 in liabilities.

Jan 1 Purchased patents from Sandra Raymond for $50,000. The remaining life of the patents is four years.

Jan 1 Purchased a trademark, which will be applied to the patented product, for $20,000. Management believes that the trademark's remaining useful life will be double that of the patent, and the trademark will have a residual value of $100.

Jan 30 Purchased a mineral deposit for $100,000. The company needs to extract a mineral that goes into the patented product. Rulison Company expects to extract 500,000 kilograms of the mineral before the rights expire.

Jun 30 The senior executives that came from Regnier Ltd. resigned en masse. The directors felt that the loss of the senior executives decreased the value of goodwill by $25,000.

Rulison Company prepares its financial statements with a year end of December 31. Amortization policy states that one half-year's amortization is taken in both the year of purchase and year of sale. Depletion is based on units extracted. The company extracted and sold 10,000 kilograms of mineral from the beginning of February to the end of December. Assume all purchases are made with cash and that the straight-line method of depreciation is used for the patent and trademark.

Prepare the journal entries to record the above transactions. Also prepare the year-end adjusting entries associated with the long-term assets.

JOURNAL

Date	Account Title and Explanation	Debit	Credit

See Appendix I for solutions.

Appendix 2A: Trading Long-Term Assets

LO 10

Rather than selling or donating an old asset that a company no longer wants, it may trade the old asset with its supplier for a newer one with a similar use. The supplier usually offers the buyer what is known as a trade-in allowance on the old asset that is being exchanged. The trade-in allowance may be either greater than or less than the old asset's book value. Often, the company has to pay cash in addition to giving up the old asset. Accounting for the exchange transaction depends on whether or not the exchange has commercial substance. Commercial substance exists when the exchange results in a change to the company's future cash flows.

As with all disposal scenarios, the first step is to update the depreciation as of the date of disposal. To record the exchange transaction, the old asset and its accumulated depreciation are removed from the company's books by crediting the original cost of the old asset and debiting the associated accumulated depreciation balance. Cash is credited for the amount paid. If the exchange has commercial substance, the new asset is debited at the fair value of the old asset plus the cash paid. The difference between the fair value of the old asset and its net book value is then recorded as a gain or loss on exchange of assets.

An asset exchange with commercial substance can result in a gain or a loss. We will look at both of these cases, starting with a gain on exchange. We will then discuss how to handle an asset exchange with no commercial substance.

Commercial Substance: Gain on Exchange

To illustrate a gain on exchange of assets, consider a company that exchanged its old truck for a new one valued at $120,000 at a truck dealership on June 1, 2020. The company's old truck and an additional $85,000 cash were given in exchange. The old truck originally cost $100,000. It had a fair market value of $35,000 and an accumulated depreciation of $70,000 on the day of the trade. (To keep things simple, we will assume that the $70,000 accumulated depreciation already includes the updated depreciation for the current period.) The gain on the exchange can be calculated in two different ways, both of which yield the same result.

The gain on exchange can be determined as the difference between the fair market value of the new asset received and the book value of the old asset given up plus cash paid on exchange, as shown in Figure 2A.1.

Price (Fair Market Value) of New Truck		$120,000
Less: Assets Given Up in Exchange		
Book Value of Old Truck ($100,000 - $70,000)	$30,000	
Cash Paid on Exchange	85,000	$115,000
Gain on Exchange of Assets		$5,000

FIGURE 2A.1

Alternatively, the gain on exchange can be determined as the difference between the fair market value (the trade-in allowance) of the asset given up and the book value of that asset, as shown in Figure 2A.2.

Fair Market Value (Trade-In Allowance) of Old Truck	$35,000
Less: Book Value of Old Truck ($100,000 – $70,000)	$30,000
Gain on Exchange of Assets	$5,000

FIGURE 2A.2

If the exchange is determined to have commercial substance, the journal entry in Figure 2A.3 is made to record the truck exchange.

JOURNAL

Date	Account Title and Explanation	Debit	Credit
Jun 1	Truck (new)	120,000	
	Accumulated Depreciation—Truck	70,000	
	Gain on Exchange of Assets		5,000
	Truck (old)		100,000
	Cash		85,000
	To record exchange of old truck and cash for new truck		

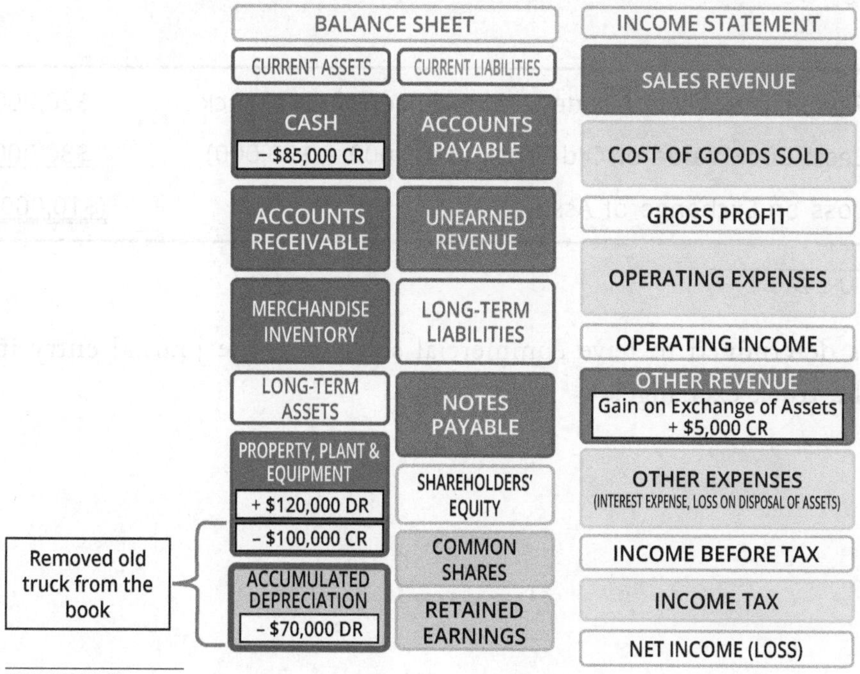

FIGURE 2A.3

Commercial Substance: Loss on Exchange

Now assume that the company exchanged its old truck for the new one valued at $115,000 on June 1, 2020. The company's old truck and an additional $95,000 cash were given in exchange. The old truck originally cost $100,000. It had a fair market value of $20,000 and an accumulated depreciation of $70,000 on the day of the trade. (Assume that the $70,000 accumulated depreciation already includes the updated depreciation for the current period.) The loss on the exchange can be calculated in two different ways, both of which yield the same result.

The loss on exchange can be determined as the difference between the fair market value of the new asset received and the book value of the old asset given up plus cash paid on exchange, as shown in Figure 2A.4.

Price (Fair Market Value) of New Truck		$115,000
Less: Assets Given Up in Exchange		
Book Value of Old Truck ($100,000 - $70,000)	$30,000	
Cash Paid on Exchange	95,000	$125,000
Loss on Exchange of Assets		($10,000)

FIGURE 2A.4

Alternatively, the loss on exchange can be determined as the difference between the fair market value (the trade-in allowance) of the asset given up and the book value of that asset, as shown in Figure 2A.5.

Fair Market Value (Trade-In Allowance) of Old Truck	$20,000
Less: Book Value of Old Truck ($100,000 - $70,000)	$30,000
Loss on Exchange of Assets	($10,000)

FIGURE 2A.5

If the exchange is determined to have commercial substance, the journal entry in Figure 2A.6 is made to record the truck exchange.

JOURNAL

Date	Account Title and Explanation	Debit	Credit
Jun 1	Truck (new)	115,000	
	Accumulated Depreciation—Truck (old)	70,000	
	Loss on Exchange of Assets	10,000	
	Truck (old)		100,000
	Cash		95,000
	To record exchange of old truck and cash for new truck		

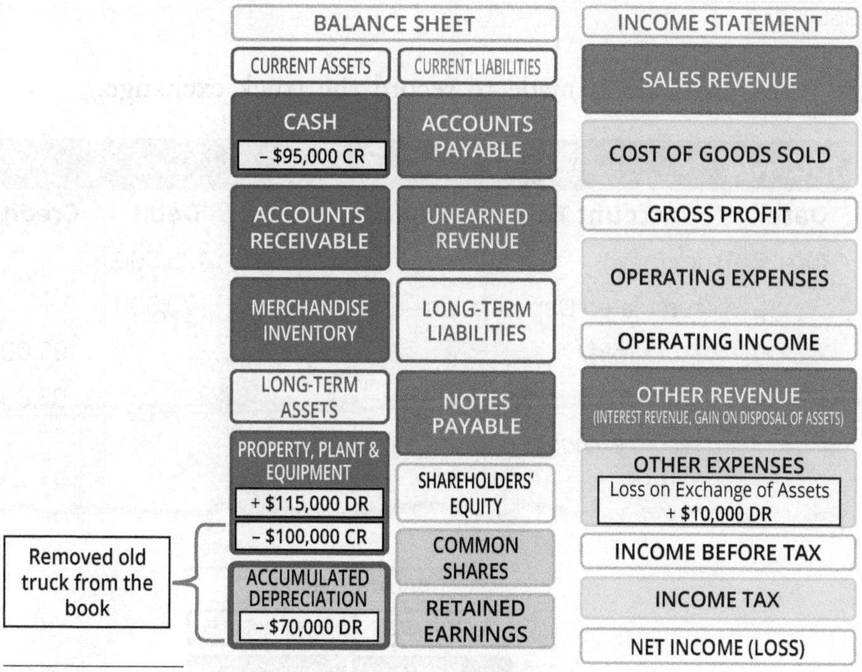

FIGURE 2A.6

Asset Exchange with No Commercial Substance

If an asset exchange has no commercial substance (i.e. the exchange will have no effect on the company's future cash flows), no gain or loss is recorded. Instead, the book value of the new asset received is based on the book value of the old asset given up. We can use the previous example to illustrate what happens when the exchange lacks commercial substance.

As before, the company exchanged its old truck for the new one valued at $115,000 on June 1, 2020. The company's old truck and an additional $95,000 cash were given in exchange. The old truck originally cost $100,000. It had a fair market value of $20,000 and an accumulated depreciation of $70,000 on the day of the trade. (Assume that the $70,000 accumulated depreciation already includes the updated depreciation for the current period.)

The cost of the new equipment when there is no commercial substance can be determined as shown in Figure 2A.7.

Cost of Old Truck	$100,000
Less: Accumulated Depreciation	70,000
Book Value of Old Truck	30,000
Cash Paid on Exchange	95,000
Cost of New Truck	$125,000

FIGURE 2A.7

The journal entry in Figure 2A.8 is made to record the truck exchange.

JOURNAL

Date	Account Title and Explanation	Debit	Credit
Jun 1	Truck (new)	125,000	
	Accumulated Depreciation—Truck	70,000	
	Truck (old)		100,000
	Cash		95,000
	To record exchange of old truck and cash for new truck		

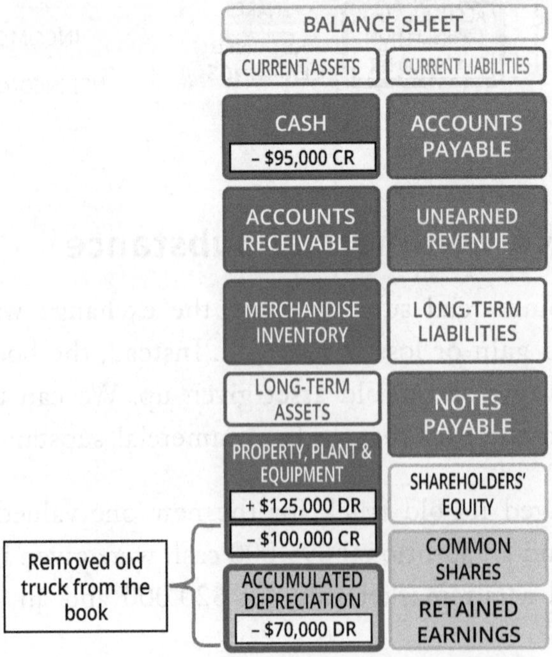

FIGURE 2A.8

In Summary

LO 10 Account for trading of long-term assets

- Accounting for the exchange transaction depends on whether or not the exchange has commercial substance. Commercial substance exists when the exchange results in a change to the company's future cash flows.
- An asset exchange with commercial substance can result in a gain or loss.
- An asset exchange with no commercial substance does not produce a gain or a loss.

Review Exercise 2A-1

On November 30, 2020, Absolute Manufacturing exchanged a unit of old machinery for some new machinery valued at $150,000. The company gave its old machinery plus $120,000 cash in exchange for the new machine. The old machinery originally cost $125,000. It had a fair market value of $30,000 and accumulated depreciation of $103,750 on the day of the trade. (Assume that the accumulated depreciation includes the updated depreciation for the month of November.) Assume that the transaction has commercial substance.

Required

a) Calculate the gain (loss) on the exchange.

b) Record the journal entry for the above transaction.

JOURNAL			
Date	**Account Title and Explanation**	**Debit**	**Credit**

c) Journalize the exchange transaction, assuming instead that the transaction has no commercial substance.

JOURNAL			
Date	**Account Title and Explanation**	**Debit**	**Credit**

See Appendix I for solutions.

Review Exercise 2A-2

On April 30, 2020, Victory Fabrications exchanged an old delivery vehicle for a new one valued at $60,000. The company gave its old vehicle plus $55,000 cash in exchange for the new vehicle. The old delivery vehicle originally cost $45,000. It had a fair market value of $5,000 and accumulated depreciation of $39,000 on the day of the trade. (Assume that the accumulated depreciation includes the updated depreciation for the month of April.) Assume that the transaction has commercial substance.

Required

a) Calculate the gain (loss) on the exchange.

b) Record the journal entry for the above transaction.

JOURNAL			
Date	Account Title and Explanation	Debit	Credit

c) Journalize the exchange transaction, assuming instead that the transaction has no commercial substance.

JOURNAL			
Date	Account Title and Explanation	Debit	Credit

See Appendix I for solutions.

Notes

Chapter 3
Current Liabilities

Learning Objectives

LO 1 **Define and differentiate between determinable and non-determinable liabilities**
- Bank Overdraft and Operating Line of Credit

LO 2 **Record accounts payable and accrued liabilities**
- Accrued Payroll Liabilities
- Utilities and Other Accrued Liabilities

LO 3 **Record transactions with sales tax**
- Provincial Sales Tax
- Goods and Services Tax
- Harmonized Sales Tax
- Sales Tax Remittances
- Returns and Sales Tax

LO 4 **Record unearned revenue**

LO 5 **Record short-term notes payable**
- Extending Credit Terms
- Borrowing from a Bank
- Accrued Interest and Notes Payable

LO 6 **Record transactions related to the current portion of long-term liabilities**

LO 7 **Record estimated liabilities**
- Employee Benefits
- Product Warranties
- Customer Loyalty Programs
- Contingent Liabilities

LO 8 **Apply internal controls relating to current liabilities**

MAKING IT REAL TO YOU

No matter their size, all businesses account for current liabilities. You may have owned your own business or worked somewhere that had several different current liability accounts, such as accounts payable, payroll liabilities, sales taxes and other liabilities for various accrued expenses. How important do you think it was that you paid these accounts on time? Did you have sufficient cash flow to make those payments? If not, did you have to secure some short-term financing from your bank?

These are questions that most businesses have to deal with on a daily basis. Your ability to manage these payments is a reflection of your understanding of and adherence to management policies related to current liabilities. It is also important that you are able to distinguish between determinable and non-determinable assets, and that you know when using an estimate is appropriate. Proper management of current liabilities has a direct impact on a company's current ratio calculation and therefore requires constant attention if the business is to maintain a good reputation with creditors.

Current Liabilities

LO 1

This chapter deals with current liabilities, which are obligations expected to be paid within one year of the balance sheet date or within the company's normal operating cycle if it is more than one year. Obligations due beyond this period are classified as long-term liabilities, which are covered in a later chapter.

The balance sheet presentation of current liabilities is comparable to the balance sheet presentation of current assets. The main difference is that the order of liabilities is dictated by the due date, while assets are placed in order of liquidity. Figure 3.1 illustrates this difference. Bank overdraft and operating line of credit are listed first among the current liabilities, followed by accounts payable (a common type of trade payable), then accrued liabilities (including payroll liability accounts, utilities payable, sales taxes payable to the government and interest payable on notes and loans). Unearned revenue and the current portion of long-term notes payable are also listed as current liabilities.

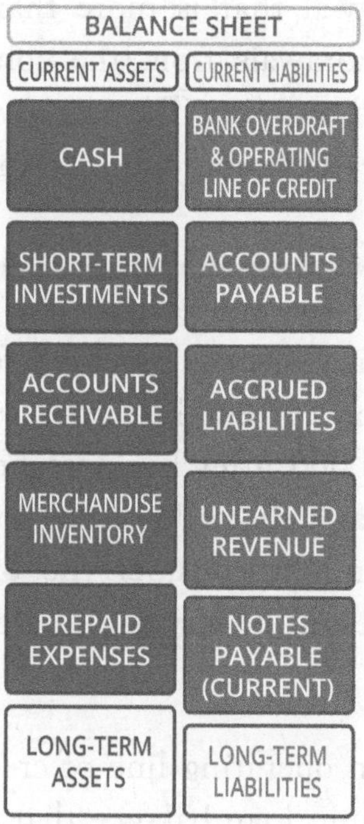

FIGURE 3.1

A company's liabilities can be divided into two categories: known liabilities and unknown liabilities. These categories are sometimes referred to as determinable liabilities and non-determinable liabilities, respectively.

Determinable liabilities have a precise value; businesses that have determinable liabilities know exactly who and how much they owe and when amounts are due. Amounts owed to suppliers (trade payables), employees (payroll liabilities), utilities providers and the government (sales taxes) are determinable liabilities. All determinable liabilities should leave an easily recognizable and traceable paper trail, which may include documents such as invoices and contracts. The exact amounts due, and when they are due, should be clearly identified.

A company's unknown or **non-determinable liabilities** include estimated and contingent liabilities. They are non-determinable because the exact amount and/or due date is unknown as of the financial statement date. We also used estimates when calculating bad debt and depreciation expenses and their related contra asset accounts (allowance for doubtful accounts and accumulated depreciation) in earlier chapters.

We will first discuss each important type of determinable liability, starting with bank overdraft and operating line of credit. Non-determinable liabilities, as well as controls and ethics related to current liabilities, are examined at the end of the chapter.

Bank Overdraft and Operating Line of Credit

A company faced with short-term financial needs can borrow from a financial institution through a bank overdraft or a line of credit. **Bank overdraft** is a financial institution's extension of credit to cover the portion of cash withdrawal that is more than the company's account balance. The financial institution will honour withdrawals from the company's cash account if it goes into a negative balance up to a pre-specified amount. The negative balance could be due to issues with cash flow or simply timing differences between deposits and withdrawals.

For example, suppose a company's cash account has a balance of $1,500 on the same day that a cheque for $2,000 clears the bank. At the end of that day, the company's bank account will have a negative balance of $500. If a balance sheet is prepared for that day, the company would report the overdraft balance as –$500 in the current liabilities section. Further, assume the company's bookkeeper deposits a cheque for $5,000 after business hours on same day. The company has a bank overdraft agreement with the bank that allows the company to be up to $3,000 overdrawn. Without that agreement, the bank might consider the $2,000 withdrawal to be *non-sufficient funds* (NSF), as the cheque was processed by the bank before the night deposit was added to the account balance.

Alternatively, many businesses have an operating line of credit with their financial institution. An **operating line of credit** is the maximum loan balance that a business may draw upon at any time without having to visit or request approval from the bank. The business negotiates a predetermined maximum balance that it is allowed to owe, as well as the interest rate charged on the outstanding balance of the account.

If the company's cash account has a negative balance as of the balance sheet date, the bank overdraft is reported as a current liability. Likewise, if the company owes a financial institution on its line of credit as of the balance sheet date, the line of credit is reported as a current liability. Both bank overdraft and line of credit are reported ahead of accounts payable and any other determinable liabilities on the balance sheet.

Accounts Payable and Accrued Liabilities

LO 2

Accounts payable is a determinable liability. A company purchases goods or services from a vendor and that vendor issues the company an invoice, which must be paid by a certain date. The terms of the liability are easily recognized and recorded by the company. Both ASPE and IFRS rely on **accrual-based accounting**. This means that transactions must be recorded *when they occur*, not when cash is paid or received, following the recognition principle that requires including an item on the financial statements. For example, a company must record a maintenance expense at the time the maintenance is performed, even if the bill is not paid until the next month.

In previous chapters, we pointed out that selling an item on account means debiting accounts receivable and crediting sales. With accounts payable, there is a mirror transaction; an asset or expense account is debited and the accounts payable account is credited.

The amount of money owed by customers is controlled by using an accounts receivable subledger (or subsidiary ledger). The same principle applies to the amount of money owed to suppliers, which is controlled by using the accounts payable subledger.

For accounts payable, the controlling account in the general ledger includes the total amount of credit balances in an individual subledger accounts.

Figure 3.2 shows the required journal entry when a company incurs a repair service on credit from Plumbers Inc. for $1,000 on September 30, 2020.

JOURNAL

Date	Account Title and Explanation	Debit	Credit
Sep 30	Repairs Expense	1,000	
	Accounts Payable		1,000
	To record repairs expense owing to Plumbers Inc.		

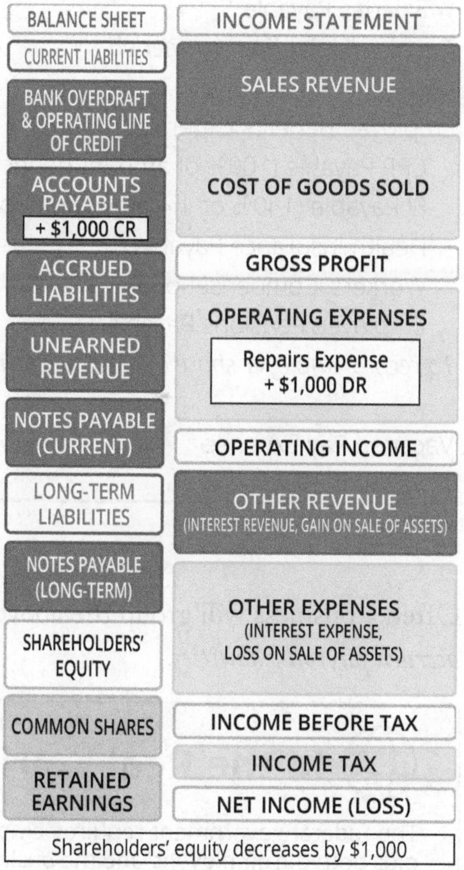

FIGURE 3.2

Since the purchase was for repairs, the repairs expense account is debited for $1,000 and is listed under operating expenses on the income statement. Accounts payable is credited for the same amount, showing that an invoice was received and must be paid in the future.

Accrued Payroll Liabilities

You will have learned about payroll earlier in your studies. However, note that this topic involves reporting many current liability accounts, as they represent accrued liabilities. Figure 3.3 provides a brief summary of the accounts used in the journal entries for recording payroll.

Expense Accounts	Debit	Credit
Salaries or Wages Expense	X	
CPP Payable		X
EI Payable		X
Income Tax Payable		X
Union Dues Payable		X
Charitable Donations Payable		X
Health Insurance Payable		X
Employee Pensions Payable		X
Salaries Payable		X
To record payroll for pay period		
Employee Benefits Expense	X	
CPP Payable (100% of amount deducted from employee)		X
EI Payable (140% or 1.4 times amount deducted from employee)		X
Health Insurance Payable		X
Workers' Compensation Payable		X
Employee Pensions Payable		X
To record employer share of employee benefits		
Vacation Pay Expense	X	
Vacation Pay Payable		X

FIGURE 3.3

Often a business will group the above liability accounts together and report them on the balance sheet as *accrued payroll liabilities.*

In the Real World

The federal government requires employers to remit the amounts deducted from employees for income tax, plus both the employees' and the business's share of CPP and EI, on a monthly basis. Failure to do so will result in interest and penalties being charged to the business. The government considers failure to remit these amounts a serious offence punishable by law.

Utilities and Other Accrued Liabilities

A business will usually not receive a bill for utilities such as heating, electricity or telephone until the next accounting period. These bills normally require payment within a short period of time (less than one month), and a journal entry is required to record the accrual of the expense and liability in the current accounting period. Consider the example where Critter Company receives a $300 electricity bill for the month of September 2020, on October 5, 2020. The journal entry shown in Figure 3.4 is required for the period ended September 30, 2020.

JOURNAL

Date	Account Title and Explanation	Debit	Credit
Sep 30	Utilities Expense	300	
	Utilities Payable		300
	To record accrual of expense		

FIGURE 3.4

Other common types of accruals for most businesses are property taxes and accrual for professional services used and billed but not yet paid, such as accounting or legal fees.

Pause & Reflect

Exercise 3-1

Cranberry Pickers is determining the payroll amounts for the month ending April 30, 2020. Its employees earned a total of $10,000 in gross pay. Assume the following rates.

Federal Income Tax	25%
Canada Pension Plan (CPP)	$490
Employment Insurance (EI)	$190
Health Insurance	$200

Assuming the employer is required to pay 100% of the amount deducted from employees for CPP and health insurance, and 140% of EI, calculate the net pay to be paid to the employees, as well as the total employee benefits expense for the pay period.

See Appendix I for solutions.

Sales Tax

LO 3

Sales tax is a tax applied by the government to goods or services that are sold. Sales taxes can be applied by both the federal and provincial government. They are calculated as a percentage of a sale, and the percentages can vary from province to province. Some provinces have a provincial sales tax (PST) that is applied by the provincial government. The federal government applies a federal sales tax called the goods and services tax (GST). Some provinces have partnered with the federal government and combined both the provincial and federal sales tax into a harmonized sales tax (HST). Figure 3.5 shows examples of provinces and the sales taxes they charge.

FIGURE 3.5

Although sales tax must be paid to the government, it would be impractical, if not impossible, for individual customers to send the sales tax owed to the government every time they bought something. Imagine buying a coffee and having to send the government a few cents in sales tax.

Instead, businesses act as tax collectors for the government by collecting the sales tax from their customers and sending (remitting) it to the government. Businesses must be careful to accurately account for sales taxes collected from customers. The amount collected does not belong to the business; it belongs to the government.

For example, imagine a business receives $1,650 from a customer for the purchase of a TV. Of that amount, $1,500 is for the actual TV and $150 is the amount of sales tax. The business has to eventually send (remit) the $150 sales tax to the government, as illustrated in Figure 3.6.

FIGURE 3.6

The due date for a business to remit the collected sales tax to the government can vary and depends on the amount of sales and the applicable rules for a given tax. Companies that have a very small amount of sales may be required to send in the sales tax once a year. As the amount of sales increases and the amount of sales tax collected also increases, the business may be required to remit the amount collected on a quarterly or monthly basis. Failure to remit, or late remittance, results in interest and penalties being charged to the business by the government.

Provincial Sales Tax

Provincial sales tax (PST) is paid by the final consumer of a product. A retailer buying inventory for resale from a supplier does not pay the PST because the retailer is not the final consumer of the inventory. But when the retailer sells the inventory to customers, the customers pay the PST. The retailer is responsible for collecting the PST from the customers and eventually remitting the amount collected to the provincial government. The amount collected is recorded in a current liability account until it is remitted.

As an example, assume Hardware Store sells inventory to a customer for $1,000 cash on June 15, 2020. The provincial sales tax rate is 6%. The transaction is shown in Figure 3.7. For this example, ignore the cost of goods sold.

JOURNAL

Date	Account Title and Explanation	Debit	Credit
Jun 15	Cash	1,060	
	PST Payable		60
	Sales Revenue		1,000
	To record sale of inventory		

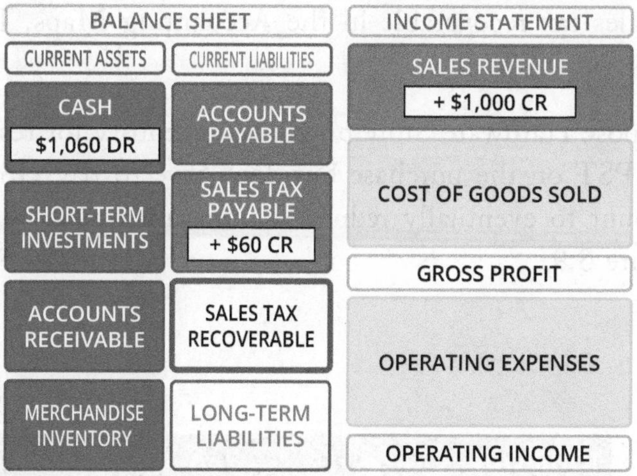

FIGURE 3.7

Each sale gradually increases the amount in the PST payable account until it is time for the company to send it to the provincial government. Assume the payment is made on August 31, 2020, and the account has only a $60 credit balance. Figure 3.8 shows the transaction.

The PST payable account essentially acts as a clearing account. It accumulates the PST collected over a period of time and then is cleared to $0 when a payment is sent to the provincial government. Note that, in the Accounting Map illustrations, PST payable is included in a general sales tax payable category. However, in a company's books, PST payable is a separate account, as are GST payable and HST payable.

JOURNAL

Date	Account Title and Explanation	Debit	Credit
Aug 31	PST Payable	60	
	Cash		60
	To remit PST to government		

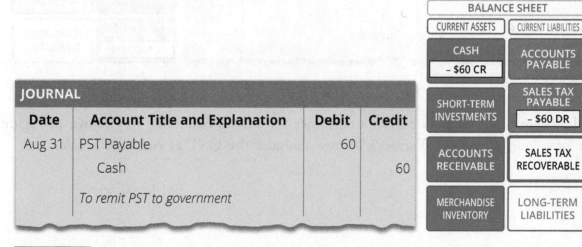

FIGURE 3.8

The retailer must pay PST on purchases that will not be resold to customers. In this case, the retailer is considered the final consumer of the product and must pay the PST. The PST is calculated and added to the cost of the asset or expense that is being purchased.

Goods and Services Tax

The **goods and services tax (GST)** is a sales tax imposed by the federal government on most transactions between businesses and between businesses and consumers. The GST rate is currently 5% of the sales amount. As with the provincial sales tax, the business that is selling a product or service must collect the GST on the sale and record it in a liability account.

Where the GST differs from the provincial sales tax is that it is considered a recoverable sales tax. This means that a business is able to reduce the amount of GST that must be paid to the government by the amount of GST the business spends. The amount of GST that the business spends is usually recorded in a contra liability account called **GST recoverable**. Again, note that GST recoverable and HST recoverable are separate accounts, although they are shown together as sales tax recoverable in the Accounting Maps. The following transactions illustrate how these accounts are used.

Suppose Hardware Store purchases inventory for resale on June 1. As discussed, it does not have to pay PST on the purchase but does have to pay GST. The GST is recorded in the contra liability account to eventually reduce the amount owing to the government. The transaction is shown in Figure 3.9.

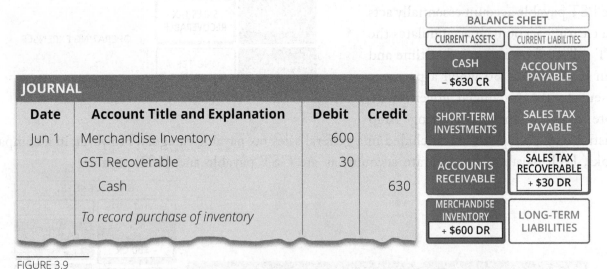

JOURNAL

Date	Account Title and Explanation	Debit	Credit
Jun 1	Merchandise Inventory	600	
	GST Recoverable	30	
	Cash		630
	To record purchase of inventory		

FIGURE 3.9

Now, Hardware Store makes a sale to a customer for $1,000 cash. This was shown in Figure 3.7, but the new journal entry in Figure 3.10 now includes the GST as part of the sale.

JOURNAL

Date	Account Title and Explanation	Debit	Credit
Jun 15	Cash	1,110	
	PST Payable		60
	GST Payable		50
	Sales Revenue		1,000
	To record sale of inventory		

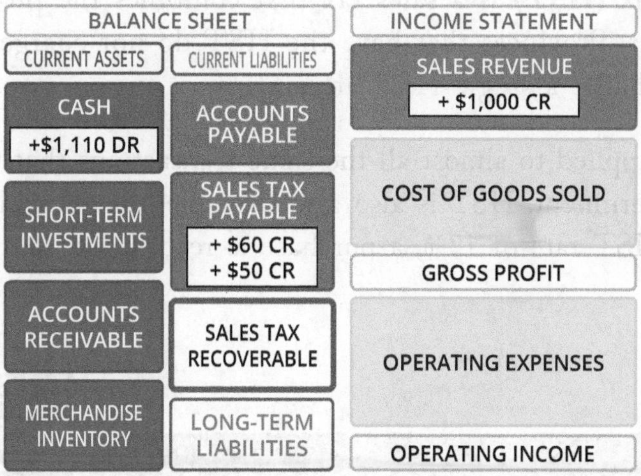

FIGURE 3.10

As we focus on the GST in Figure 3.10, Hardware Store owes the government $50 from the sale. However, it can reduce the amount owing by the $30 it spent earlier in the month. To make the payment to the federal government on June 30, the transaction shown in Figure 3.11 must be made.

JOURNAL

Date	Account Title and Explanation	Debit	Credit
Jun 30	GST Payable	50	
	GST Recoverable		30
	Cash		20
	To remit GST to government		

FIGURE 3.11

The cash payment is for the difference between the two accounts ($20). Both GST accounts act as clearing accounts. They accumulate the GST collected and GST paid over a period of time, and then the accounts are cleared to $0 when a payment is made to the federal government.

In the end, the customer pays the entire amount of GST, but the amount sent to the government is sent by different companies. In the example, the customer paid $50 GST to Hardware Store. Hardware Store sent $20 to the government and its supplier of inventory sent the other $30.

Harmonized Sales Tax

The **harmonized sales tax (HST)** is a sales tax that combines the provincial and federal taxes into one sales tax amount. Provinces that have the HST do not charge separate PST and GST amounts. Instead, they charge a single HST amount.

Harmonized sales tax is applied to almost all the same transactions that GST is applied to, and it is sent to the federal government. HST is also a recoverable sales tax, like GST. Using Hardware Store and assuming an HST rate of 13%, a purchase is recorded as shown in Figure 3.12.

JOURNAL

Date	Account Title and Explanation	Debit	Credit
Jun 1	Merchandise Inventory	600	
	HST Recoverable	78	
	Cash		678
	To record purchase of inventory		

FIGURE 3.12

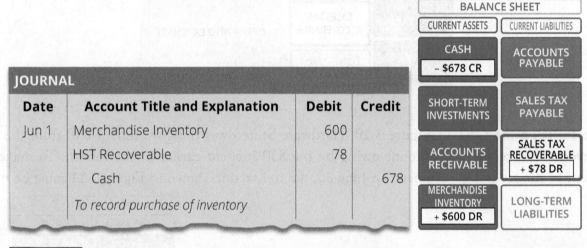

The cash sale for $1,000 is shown in Figure 3.13.

JOURNAL

Date	Account Title and Explanation	Debit	Credit
Jun 15	Cash	1,130	
	HST Payable		130
	Sales Revenue		1,000
	To record sale of inventory		

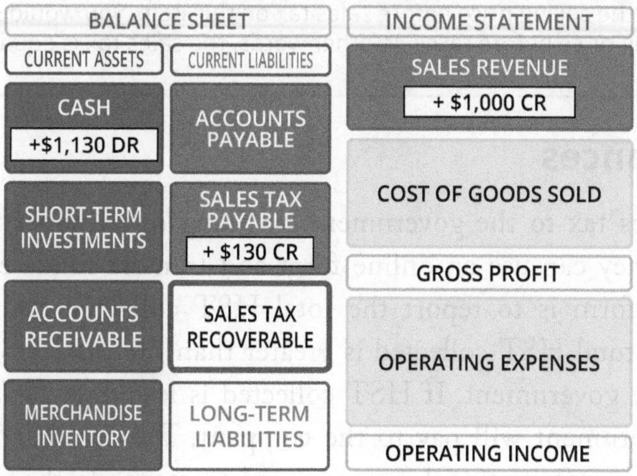

FIGURE 3.13

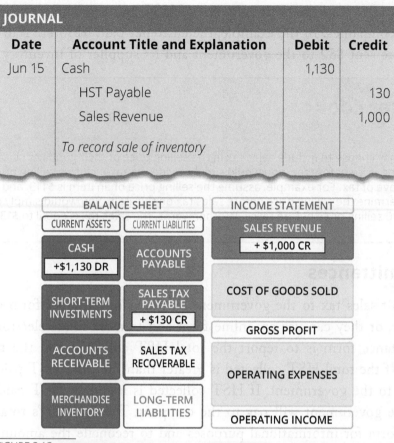

The payment to the federal government is similar to a GST payment. Both the HST recoverable account and the HST payable account are cleared when the payment is made. The journal entry for the HST payment transaction is shown in Figure 3.14.

JOURNAL

Date	Account Title and Explanation	Debit	Credit
Jun 30	HST Payable	130	
	HST Recoverable		78
	Cash		52
	To remit HST to government		

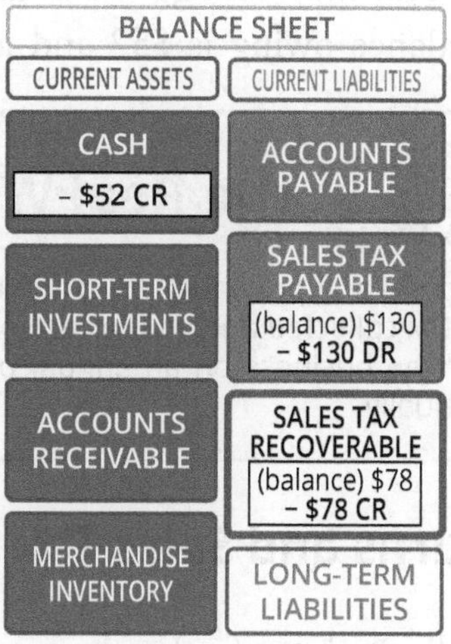

FIGURE 3.14

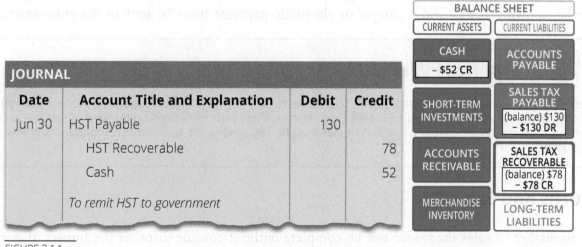

The cash payment is for the difference between the two accounts ($52). Both HST accounts act as clearing accounts. They accumulate the HST collected and HST paid over a period of time, and then they are cleared to $0 when a payment is made to the federal government.

In the end, the customer pays the entire amount of HST, but the amount sent to the government is sent by different companies. In the example, the customer paid $130 HST to Hardware Store. In turn, Hardware Store sent $52 to the government and its supplier of inventory sent the other $78.

A Closer Look

Some companies may choose to include sales tax in the selling price of their goods or services. To determine the amount of selling price before tax, you would simply divide the tax-inclusive selling price by 1 plus the applicable percentage of tax. For example, assume the selling price of an item is $113, and it already includes HST of 13%. To determine the selling price before sales tax on this item, you would simply divide $113 by 1.13, resulting in the $100 selling price before taxes. In other words, the sales tax is equal to $13 ($113 − $100).

Sales Tax Remittances

Businesses can remit sales tax to the government by filling out a paper form and sending it with payment by cheque, or they can use an online form and transfer funds electronically. The purpose of the HST remittance form is to report the total HST collected and the total HST paid out during the period. If the total HST collected is greater than the total HST paid out, the difference is a balance owing to the government. If HST collected is less than HST paid out, the difference is a refund that the government will pay to the company. The company's total sales before tax is also listed on the form for informational purposes and to reconcile the amount of HST collected.

Returning to Hardware Store, we will determine the company's HST balance owing or refund. From Figure 3.13, the HST collected is $130. From Figure 3.12, the HST paid is $78. The difference, also known as net tax, is $52 ($130 − $78). There are various adjustments that might be made after this point that may change the balance owing or refund. In this case, assuming there are no adjustments, the balance owing is $52 and a cheque or electronic payment must be sent to the government.

In the Real World

Federal and provincial governments require businesses to file information returns that summarize the amount of tax collected and, in the case of HST, paid. Due dates for these returns depend on the level of sales reported for the business on an annual basis. Businesses may be required to file their returns monthly, quarterly or annually.

Returns and Sales Tax

Our discussion of sales tax would not be complete without consideration of the impact of purchase and sales returns. Assume that on June 20, 2020, a customer of Hardware Store returned $200 worth of goods (cost $120) purchased on account. The journal entries shown in Figure 3.15 would be recorded. Note that the HST payable account is debited for the amount of HST charged on the sale amount of the transaction, which will reduce the amount of tax the business owes to the government.

JOURNAL

Date	Account Title and Explanation	Debit	Credit
Jun 20	Sales Returns & Allowances	200	
	HST Payable	26	
	Accounts Receivable		226
	To record return of goods by customer		
Jun 20	Merchandise Inventory	120	
	Cost of Goods Sold		120
	To record cost of goods returned by customer		

FIGURE 3.15

Pause & Reflect

Exercise 3-2

On March 13, 2020, Jerrod Furniture Shop sold products for $50,000 cash. The products cost Jerrod $22,000. Jerrod Furniture Shop operates in a province that charges 13% HST. Assume Jerrod Furniture Shop uses a perpetual inventory system. Prepare the journal entries for the sale of the products.

JOURNAL

Date	Account Title and Explanation	Debit	Credit

See Appendix I for solutions.

Unearned Revenue

LO 4

The accrual basis of accounting applies to both expenses and revenues. As you have learned, expenses are recognized during the period in which they are incurred and not when they are actually paid. The same applies to unearned revenue: it is recognized in the period in which it was earned and not when payment was actually received. As shown in Figure 3.16, current liabilities are recorded in the first period for both accrued expense and unearned revenue.

Accrued Expense		Unearned Revenue	
Expense Incurred	Expense Paid	Cash Received	Revenue Earned
Period 1	Period 2	Period 1	Period 2
DR Expense CR Accounts Payable	DR Accounts Payable CR Cash	DR Cash CR Unearned Revenue	DR Unearned Revenue CR Revenue

FIGURE 3.16

For accrued expense, accounts payable is recorded in the first period because the expense is incurred in the first period, but the company has not yet paid for it. Accounts payable has been covered in a previous section in this chapter. This section focuses on unearned revenue, which is recorded when the company receives cash before rendering goods or services to customers.

For example, a publishing company might receive payment in advance for a one-year subscription to its magazine. The money is received, but the magazine has not yet been supplied to the customer. Until the product changes hands, the amount received in advance cannot be recognized as revenue. The cash receipt is therefore considered unearned revenue, which is a liability.

Business owners sometimes misunderstand how accruals work. This can lead to mistakes and bad decisions. For example, management may be tempted to treat unearned revenue as though it is already earned. Using the example of a magazine subscription again, what would happen if the customer decided to cancel the subscription and the magazine publisher had considered the money as earned? Until the product has been delivered, no transaction has been finalized with the customer. The money should be paid back to the customer when the subscription is cancelled.

With a non-refundable subscription, the same principle would apply. It is still the obligation of the company to deliver goods or services that have been paid for and to treat the money as unearned until completion of the transaction.

What happens if a customer voluntarily cancels the rights to the goods or services and notifies the company to that effect? An example of this might be a subscriber moving overseas and informing the publisher that delivery of the magazine is no longer necessary. If the subscription is non-refundable, the customer has no right to request repayment and the company can continue to recognize revenue as it is earned. Of course, if the subscription is refundable, the publisher has to reverse all or part of the initial transaction and refund the subscriber for any remaining unused months of the subscription.

Here is an example to illustrate the concept of accruals and revenue. Tracking Time is the publisher of a magazine with a fiscal year end of December 31. In December 2019, Tracking Time receives $120,000 from subscribers to cover the monthly delivery of magazines for one year, starting on January 1, 2020. The transaction is recorded in the company's books as shown in Figure 3.17.

JOURNAL

Date	Account Title and Explanation	Debit	Credit
Dec 31	Cash	120,000	
	Unearned Revenue		120,000
	To record the deposit of subscription sales		

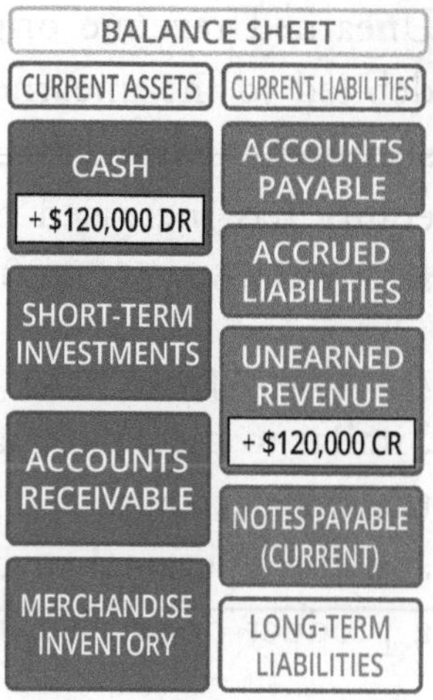

FIGURE 3.17

The money is received and debited to the cash account on December 31, 2019. However, the revenue is yet to be earned (i.e. it is earned when the magazines are delivered), so the amount is credited to the unearned revenue account. Since revenue is not yet earned, there is no change to the company's equity.

On January 1, the magazine is delivered to customers for that month. This means that Tracking Time's obligation to the customers has been met for the month and the corresponding revenue is now earned. One month of subscriptions equals one-twelfth of the annual subscriptions; therefore, $10,000 is recognized as revenue for the month of January, as shown in Figure 3.18.

JOURNAL

Date	Account Title and Explanation	Debit	Credit
Jan 1	Unearned Revenue	10,000	
	Sales Revenue		10,000
	To record delivery of magazines for January		

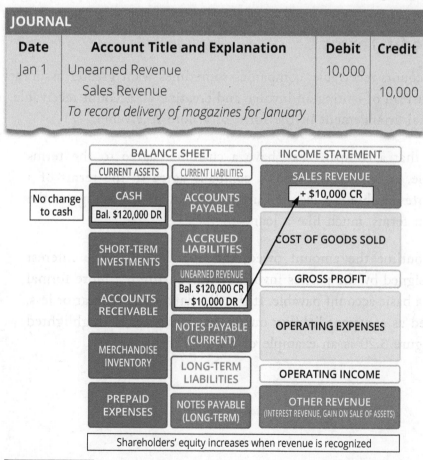

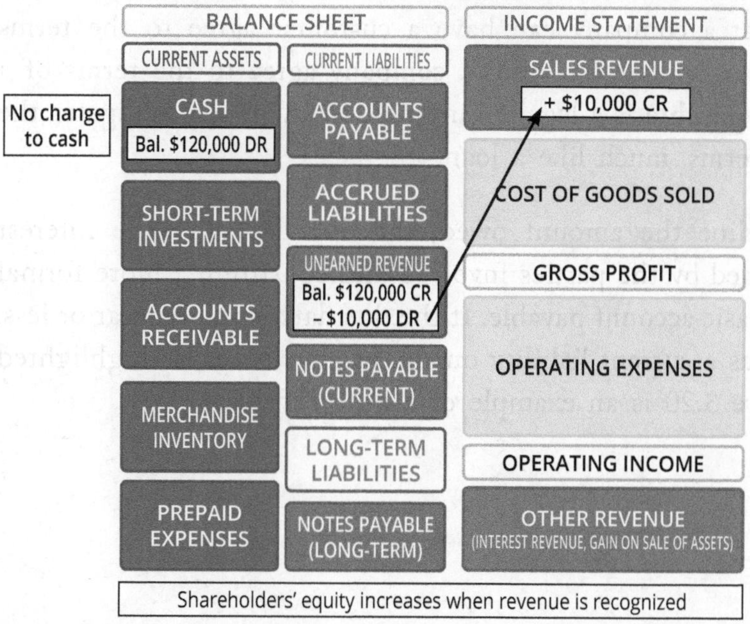

FIGURE 3.18

Unearned revenue originally had a credit balance of $120,000. Of that amount, $10,000 is now debited to the unearned revenue account and credited to the sales revenue account on the income statement. Although cash remains the same, the recognition of the unearned revenue means that equity has increased by $10,000. The obligation that Tracking Time now has to its customers is reduced from $120,000 to $110,000.

Another type of unearned liability gaining popularity in recent years is gift cards or gift certificates. Similar to the Tracking Time example above, when a business sells a gift card or certificate, it debits the cash account and credits an unearned revenue account. The sales revenue account is credited, and the unearned revenue account debited, only when the gift card or certificate is redeemed for a product or service.

Short-Term Notes Payable

LO 5

Short-term notes payable (notes payable that are considered current, due within 12 months) can be issued for different reasons.

- To extend credit terms—A company that purchases goods on credit can extend its credit term by replacing an account payable with a note payable.
- To borrow from a bank—A company may borrow from a bank by signing a note payable.

Extending Credit Terms

With regard to accounts receivable, companies sometimes want greater assurance that a customer will pay the bill. Instead of issuing an invoice and creating an account receivable, a company might make a more formal arrangement in the form of a note receivable.

In the same way that a company can have a customer agree to the terms of a note receivable, a supplier can have a company agree to the terms of a note payable. A **note payable** is a legally binding document that obligates the borrower to certain terms, much like a loan.

Such documents outline the amount owed, the due date and the interest payable. They are signed by the parties involved and constitute a more formal arrangement than a basic account payable. If the due date is in one year or less, the note is reported as a current liability on the balance sheet, as highlighted in Figure 3.19. Figure 3.20 is an example of a note payable.

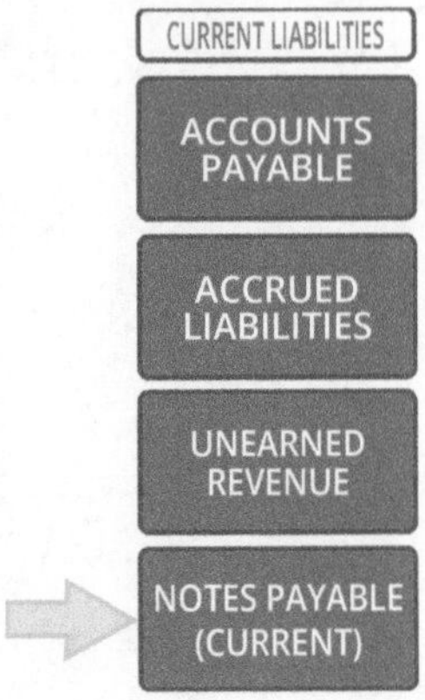

FIGURE 3.19

In addition to the note payable for $5,000, the company would report interest payable of $104 on its June 30 year-end balance sheet within the accrued liabilities sections.

On July 31, both principal and interest will be paid to Carson Bank. The remaining interest expense is calculated as $21 ($5,000 × 5% × 1/12) since interest was already accrued up until June 30. The entry to record repayment of the note, plus interest, is presented in Figure 3.26.

JOURNAL

Date	Account Title and Explanation	Debit	Credit
Jul 31	Interest Payable	104	
	Interest Expense	21	
	Notes Payable	5,000	
	Cash		5,125
	To record interest and payment for a six-month, 5% note payable		

FIGURE 3.26

Note that the interest payable account is debited to remove the accrual recorded in the previous period, and interest expense is debited with $21, which represents the interest expense for the month of July. In total, six months' worth of interest has been recorded: five months in the previous period and one month in the current period.

Pause & Reflect

Exercise 3-3

Bach Supplies has a short-term cash flow problem. On September 1, 2020, it approaches its bank and receives a $20,000 short-term note payable. The note is due in six months on February 28, 2021. The annual interest rate on the note payable is 6%. Bach Supplies has a December 31 year end. Record the journal entries for the issuance of the note payable, the accrued interest and the payment of the note when it is due.

JOURNAL

Date	Account Title and Explanation	Debit	Credit

See Appendix I for solutions.

Current Portion of Long-Term Liabilities

LO 6

When the term of a note payable is longer than one year, there will be two components to the note payable. The portion of the loan principal that will be paid within the next 12 months is considered current. This amount must be reported separately when the balance sheet is prepared, in a section under current liabilities called notes payable, current portion. The remaining amount of the note payable that is due beyond one year is reported on the balance sheet under long-term liabilities as notes payable, long-term portion. (Note that this account can also be called notes payable, noncurrent portion.)

For example, a company manufactures a wide range of products for consumers. It wants to purchase a new processing machine to keep up with growing demand for its product. The company has insufficient cash to finance the purchase. Management decides to obtain a loan from a bank to finance this important capital investment.

On January 2, 2020, the company negotiates a loan from the bank of $50,000 with a term of five years, bearing an annual interest rate of 5%. Of that debt, $10,000 plus interest is payable every December 31. The full amount of the loan is recorded as a note payable in the journal entry. When the balance sheet is prepared, the current portion of $10,000 is presented separately from the long-term portion of $40,000. Figure 3.27 shows how the note payable is recorded in the company's books.

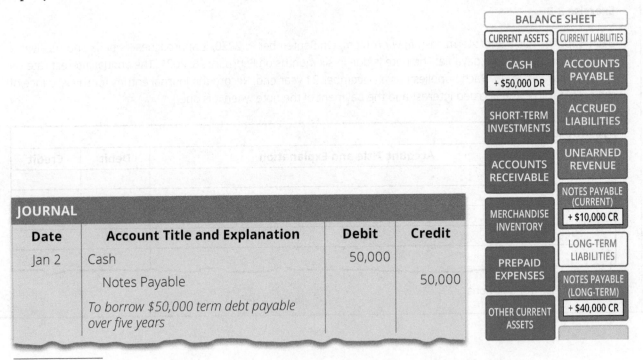

JOURNAL

Date	Account Title and Explanation	Debit	Credit
Jan 2	Cash	50,000	
	Notes Payable		50,000
	To borrow $50,000 term debt payable over five years		

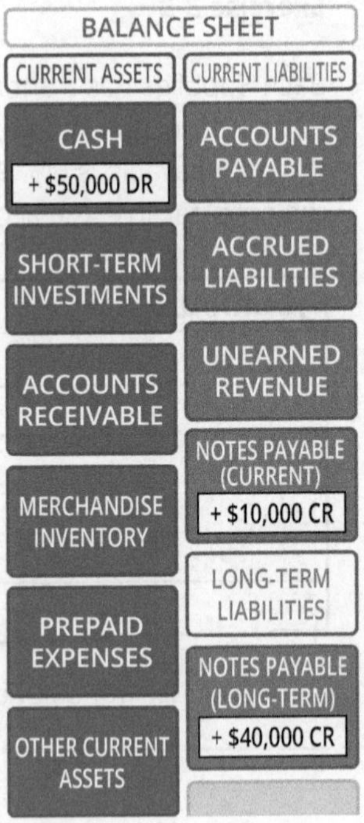

FIGURE 3.27

On December 31, the first installment plus interest is paid. The transaction is recorded as shown in Figure 3.28.

JOURNAL

Date	Account Title and Explanation	Debit	Credit
Dec 31	Notes Payable	10,000	
	Interest Expense	2,500	
	Cash		12,500
	To record payment for first notes payable installment plus interest		

FIGURE 3.28

After the first payment, the balance of the note payable decreases to $40,000, $10,000 of which is still considered current. When the balance sheet is prepared at the year end, $10,000 is included as part of current liabilities and $30,000 is included as part of long-term liabilities.

Estimated Liabilities

LO 7

We have already discussed various forms of known liabilities, also referred to as determinable liabilities, which are debts taken on by a company for which the terms are readily known. However, for other liabilities, the exact terms are not precisely known and cannot be determined until future events occur. These unknown liabilities are referred to as non-determinable liabilities, and can be divided further into estimated liabilities and contingent liabilities (using ASPE terminology).

Estimated liabilities are financial obligations that a company cannot exactly measure. Examples include employee benefits, product warranties and customer loyalty programs. A company needs to adhere to the expense recognition principle when it makes an estimate of the amount of the upcoming liability.

Employee Benefits

Employee benefits are an expense to the employer. According to the expense recognition principle, the cost of these benefits must be estimated and recorded in the period in which they are incurred—that is, in the period in which the employee earns the benefits. We will now look at some common employee benefits in more detail: paid vacations, pension benefits, health benefits and employee bonuses.

Vacation Pay

In Canada, every employee is entitled to receive vacation pay based on a percentage of their earnings. Depending on the arrangement, vacation pay may be paid to an employee each pay period (normally for part-time employees) or accrued and paid out when the employee takes their vacation. The employer estimates and records the amount to pay for employee vacations as an accrued liability for the period, either by pay period or at the end of the year. For example, assume that a salaried employee has earned an estimated $560 in vacation pay for the month of January. The company accrues its estimated vacation pay liabilities at the end of each month. On January 31, the employer makes the journal entry shown in Figure 3.29.

JOURNAL

Date	Account Title and Explanation	Debit	Credit
Jan 31	Vacation Pay Expense	560	
	Vacation Pay Payable		560
	To accrue estimated vacation pay payable for the month		

FIGURE 3.29

In many cases, whether by personal choice or by employer policy, the employee uses the vacation entitlement within the year. In this case, any accrued vacation pay at the end of the year is reported on the company's balance sheet as a current liability. Sometimes, employees are allowed to accumulate vacation entitlement and carry it over into another period. If the employee does not plan to take the vacation entitlement within the next year, the estimated vacation pay payable is reported on the company's balance sheet as a long-term liability.

When the employee in our example takes vacation, the employer records a journal entry to debit vacation pay payable and credit cash. The employer must also record the normal entries related to taxes and withholdings in the payroll records.

Pension Benefits

Some employers contribute to *pension plans* for their employees, which allow employees to receive cash payments from the company after they retire. Employee pension rights are accrued during the period of time that the employee works for the company. There are different types of pension plans, known as defined contribution and defined benefit plans. Details of these plans are beyond the scope of this textbook. However, in simple terms, the employer accrues employee pensions each period (assume one year) as shown in Figure 3.30.

When the employee retires and the former employer starts paying out the pension benefits, the company records the payments by decreasing (debiting) employee pensions payable and crediting the cash account.

JOURNAL

Date	Account Title and Explanation	Debit	Credit
Dec 31	Employee Benefits Expense	5,000	
	Employee Pensions Payable		5,000
	To record accrued pension benefits		

FIGURE 3.30

Health Benefits

Some employers provide continuing health benefits to their employees after they retire by paying for their medical and dental insurance coverage. The journal entry to record the accrued benefits for the period is shown in Figure 3.31.

JOURNAL			
Date	**Account Title and Explanation**	**Debit**	**Credit**
Dec 31	Employee Benefits Expense	2,000	
	Employee Medical Insurance Payable		2,000
	To record accrued medical insurance benefits		

FIGURE 3.31

When the medical insurance premiums are paid, the company records the payments by decreasing (debiting) employee medical insurance payable and crediting the cash account.

Employee Bonuses

Some employers offer employee bonuses based on a percentage of the company's net income for a period. Assume an employer plans to pay its staff a bonus equal to 5% of the company's net income. It estimates the total amount of the bonus as $5,000. The company records an accrual with the journal entry shown in Figure 3.32.

JOURNAL			
Date	**Account Title and Explanation**	**Debit**	**Credit**
Dec 31	Employee Bonus Expense	5,000	
	Employee Bonus Payable		5,000
	To record accrued employee bonus payable		

FIGURE 3.32

When the bonuses are paid, the company records the payments by decreasing (debiting) employee bonus payable and crediting the cash account.

Product Warranties

Just as a company needs to estimate how much bad debt it will have in the upcoming period, when a company sells products with warranties it needs to estimate how much warranty liability it will have. Warranties are one way a company reassures customers that its products are free of defects for a certain period of time, and any defects during that period are the responsibility of the company. By estimating the warranty liability, the company can expense this liability in the period in which related revenues are generated. Any errors in estimation can be adjusted once the actual figures are known.

There are two types of product warranties: basic and extended. A basic warranty is included in the price of the product. For example, when you buy a brand new cell phone, the price already includes a one-year warranty. There may be an option to purchase an extended warranty separately. This extended warranty will cover a specific period after the basic warranty expires. Basic warranties and extended warranties are accounted for differently.

Basic Warranties

A basic warranty must be accounted for using the expense warranty approach, which we will now discuss using the example of a company called Star Machines. Star Machines manufactures industrial labelling machines. A basic warranty of three years is included with the purchase of each machine. If a machine breaks down during this warranty period, Star Machines is obligated to repair it, provide parts and, if necessary, replace the machine.

Based on an analysis of historical company trends, the company's accountant determines that an average of $100 per machine is paid out in warranty obligations. The company has sold 50 labelling machines during the 2020 fiscal year; therefore, the journal entry in Figure 3.33 is made to recognize the warranty expense for 2020.

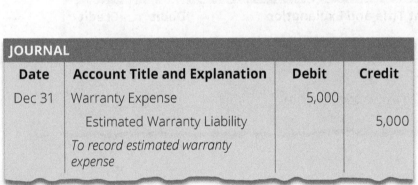

JOURNAL

Date	Account Title and Explanation	Debit	Credit
Dec 31	Warranty Expense	5,000	
	Estimated Warranty Liability		5,000
	To record estimated warranty expense		

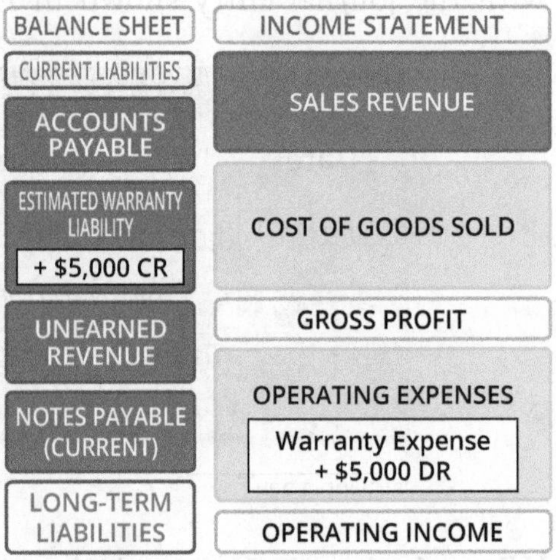

FIGURE 3.33

The $5,000 is expensed for this period on the income statement since this estimate covers expected warranties for the year. The estimated warranty liability of $5,000 is credited to the corresponding liability account.

During the next year, Star Machines receives some warranty claims and has actual expenditures in meeting those claims. Let us assume that Star Machines uses $500 in parts from its own inventory, and maintenance staff reports $1,500 worth of billable hours related to warranty claims. Figure 3.34 illustrates how Star Machines' accountant records these transactions.

JOURNAL			
Date	**Account Title and Explanation**	**Debit**	**Credit**
Jan 31	Estimated Warranty Liability	2,000	
	Parts Inventory		500
	Cash		1,500
	To record inventory and wages for warranty work		

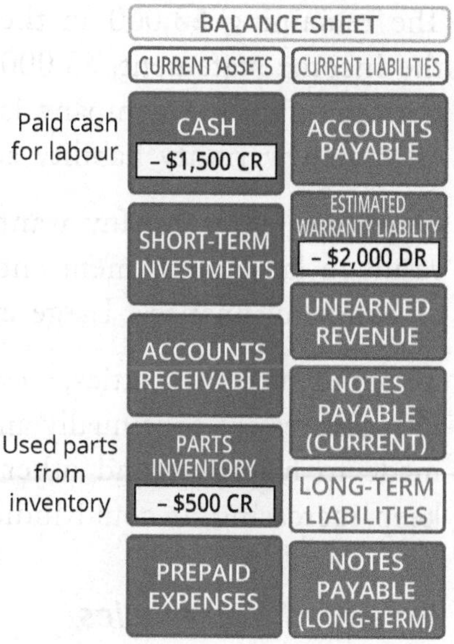

FIGURE 3.34

The estimated warranty liability account is debited with $2,000, leaving a balance of $3,000 to satisfy warranty claims over the remaining two-year period. On the credit side, $500 worth of inventory is taken off the books, and $1,500 is recorded as a decrease to cash.

There is no change to the income statement since the estimated warranty was expensed in the year the machines were sold. The company calculates and records a debit to warranty expense and a credit to estimated warranty liability accounts on the basis of the number of machines sold that year.

Assuming that this amount does not change for the remainder of the warranty period (i.e. no one else makes any warranty claims), Star Machines has to remove the remaining amount of the original estimate from the books. Figure 3.35 shows the journal entry to record this transaction.

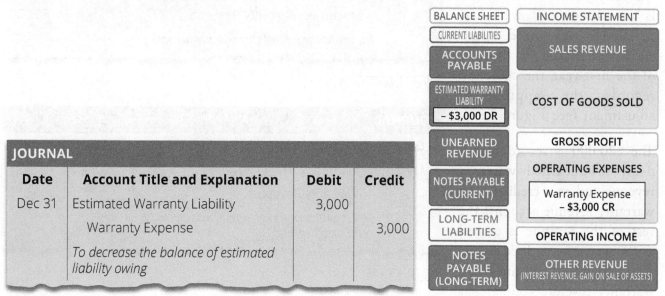

JOURNAL			
Date	**Account Title and Explanation**	**Debit**	**Credit**
Dec 31	Estimated Warranty Liability	3,000	
	Warranty Expense		3,000
	To decrease the balance of estimated liability owing		

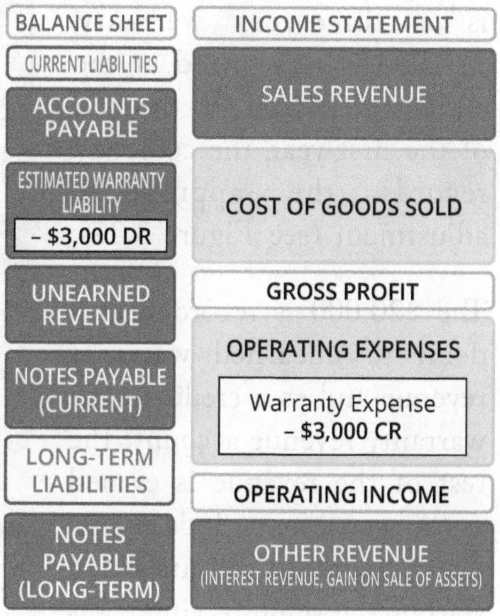

FIGURE 3.35

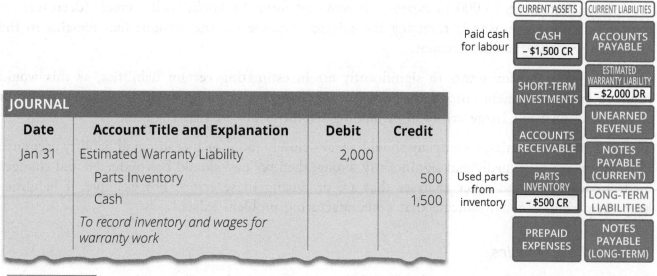

The remaining $3,000 in the estimated warranty liability account is removed with a debit. On the income statement, $3,000 in expenses is removed from the books with a credit (decrease) for that amount. The company is reversing the original expense for the amount that remains in the estimated warranty liability account.

Of course, no company wants to significantly err in estimating certain liabilities, as this would result in large adjustment entries after the fact. Accountants should provide an accurate snapshot of company finances. Large errors in estimating liabilities distort that snapshot.

To avoid such difficulties, a company should always closely monitor its estimated liability accounts. If estimates are continually and significantly wrong, then reviews should be conducted and changes made to historical and other analyses that are producing these errors. For example, if liabilities keep increasing, it could indicate that a manufacturing problem exists.

Extended Warranties

We will now look at accounting for extended warranties, which are warranties sold separately to customers. This type of warranty must be accounted for using the sales warranty approach. Under this approach, journal entries are made separately for the warranty revenues and the warranty expenses.

Let us assume that Star Machines sold $60,000 worth of three-year warranties as a separate product to its customers on June 1, 2020. Figure 3.36 illustrates how the transaction is recorded in the company's books.

The receipt of $60,000 is recorded as a debit to cash and a credit to unearned warranty revenue. Since this is a three-year warranty, $20,000 is recognized at the end of each year. At the end of the first year, the company records the appropriate adjustment (see Figure 3.37).

JOURNAL

Date	Account Title and Explanation	Debit	Credit
Jun 1	Cash	60,000	
	Unearned Warranty Revenue		60,000
	To record the sale of three-year warranties		

FIGURE 3.36

JOURNAL

Date	Account Title and Explanation	Debit	Credit
May 31	Unearned Warranty Revenue	20,000	
	Warranty Revenue		20,000
	To recognize one year unearned warranty revenue as earned		

FIGURE 3.37

The $20,000 is recorded as a debit to unearned warranty revenue and as a credit to the warranty revenue account. The rest of the revenue is earned as the warranty periods elapse. At present, the unearned warranty revenue account has a $40,000 balance because there are two years left in the warranty period. Note that only the unearned revenue in the next 12 months is reported on the balance sheet as a current liability.

The journal entries in Figures 3.36 and 3.37 are for the revenue side of the warranty. On the expense side, the journal entries that have to be made are quite similar to what was already shown in Figures 3.33 and 3.34. For example, if Star Machines' customers make warranty claims in 2020 that cost the company $8,000 in total (including $3,000 worth of inventory parts and $5,000 cash for labour), Star Machines would record a credit to parts inventory of $3,000, a credit to cash of $5,000, and a debit to warranty expense of $8,000.

In the Real World

Warranty claims can be expensive for businesses and hard to predict accurately, resulting in estimate adjustments. According to data compiled from the 2016 annual reports of US-based manufacturing companies, warranty expenses account for 1.4% of revenue, on average. Warranty expense rates vary by industry and are affected by many factors.

Analytic software solutions can help businesses leverage data to better understand the warranty process, highlighting areas for improvement to reduce expense. Products like IBM's Warranty Analytics review a company's warranty data—including customer complaints, call centre records, product data, sales reports, maintenance logs and service technician notes—to help uncover where product defects are occurring and to predict future issues.

With this information, businesses can take a proactive approach to ensure product quality and provide suggested maintenance schedules to customers to prevent future product failures. Overall, this can lower the cost of warranty claims and allows accountants to more accurately predict the value of warranty liabilities for the future.

Pause & Reflect

Exercise 3-4

Crystal Cleaners sells high-end vacuum cleaners. Every vacuum comes with a two-year warranty on parts and labour. The accountant estimates that an average of $50 worth of warranty work is done on each vacuum sold. During the year ending December 31, 2020, 8,000 vacuums were sold. Prepare the journal entry to record the estimated warranty expense.

JOURNAL

Date	Account Title and Explanation	Debit	Credit

See Appendix I for solutions.

Customer Loyalty Programs

Customer loyalty programs have gained popularity in recent years as companies look for creative ways to retain or attract customers. Such programs require a business to record an estimated liability for the amount the customers will receive in the future if they use up their accumulated rewards. The rewards are often in the form of points, store currencies or travel miles. Reward redemption by a customer represents a reduction in future sales. Therefore, when rewards are issued to a customer, a sales discounts account is normally debited instead of an expense account, and a redemption rewards liability account is credited. The dollar amount of redemption rewards liability recognized is estimated based on past redemption history.

For example, assume that Zen Gen is a teahouse chain that offers a customer loyalty program. Customers are rewarded one loyalty point for every dollar of tea and other refreshments purchased. One hundred loyalty points can be redeemed for a one-dollar discount on a future purchase. In June 2020, Zen Gen sold $150,000 worth of refreshments. Historically, an average of 70% of the points issued are redeemed. Following past experience, Zen Gen's accountant recognizes a redemption rewards liability of $1,050 ($150,000 × 70% × $0.01). Figure 3.38 shows the journal entry to record Zen Gen's customer loyalty points issued in June 2020.

JOURNAL

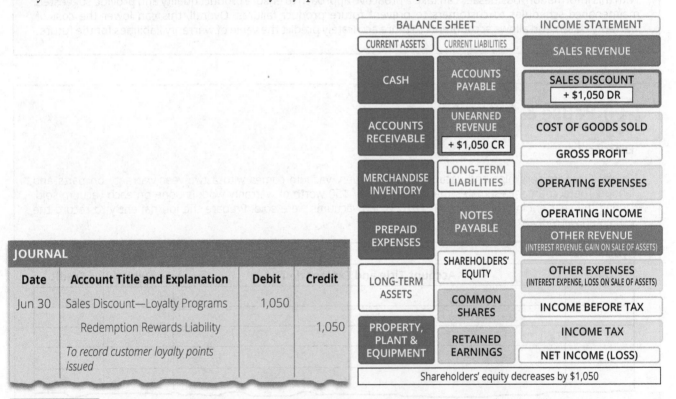

Date	Account Title and Explanation	Debit	Credit
Jun 30	Sales Discount—Loyalty Programs	1,050	
	Redemption Rewards Liability		1,050
	To record customer loyalty points issued		

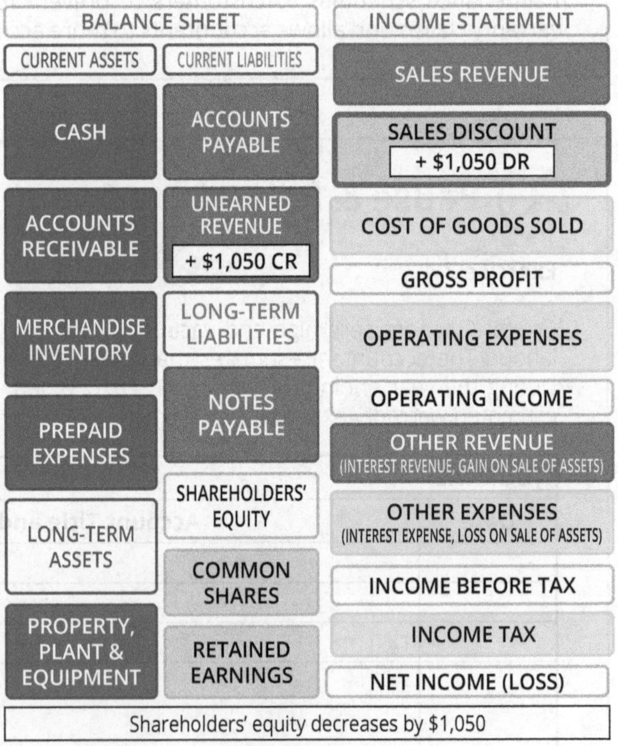

FIGURE 3.38

As a result of this transaction, net sales (and thus equity) decrease and liabilities increase. Similar to the sales returns and allowances account, the sales discount account is a contra account linked to the sales revenue account. Both sales discounts and sales returns and allowances are deducted from sales revenue to reveal the net sales amount on an income statement.

Redemption rewards liability is a current liability. The redemption rewards liability account is considered unearned revenue, because issuing loyalty points based on a current transaction's sales dollar amount is similar to Zen Gen accepting money from a customer in advance in exchange for a potential future discount. Once loyalty points are redeemed, Zen Gen's obligation or liability is nullified, and its unearned revenue becomes earned.

Zen Gen's sales transaction in July is used to illustrate an example of a loyalty point redemption journal entry. Assume that the total value of sales in July was $180,000 worth of refreshments, of which $179,250 was received in cash and $750 was redeemed in points. Figure 3.39 shows the journal entry to record the sales through cash and loyalty point redemption in July. For simplicity, the cost of goods sold is ignored, as is the fact that customers would earn additional loyalty points on the cash sales.

JOURNAL

Date	Account Title and Explanation	Debit	Credit
Jul 31	Redemption Rewards Liability	750	
	Cash	179,250	
	Sales Revenue		180,000
	To record July sales through cash and loyalty point redemption		

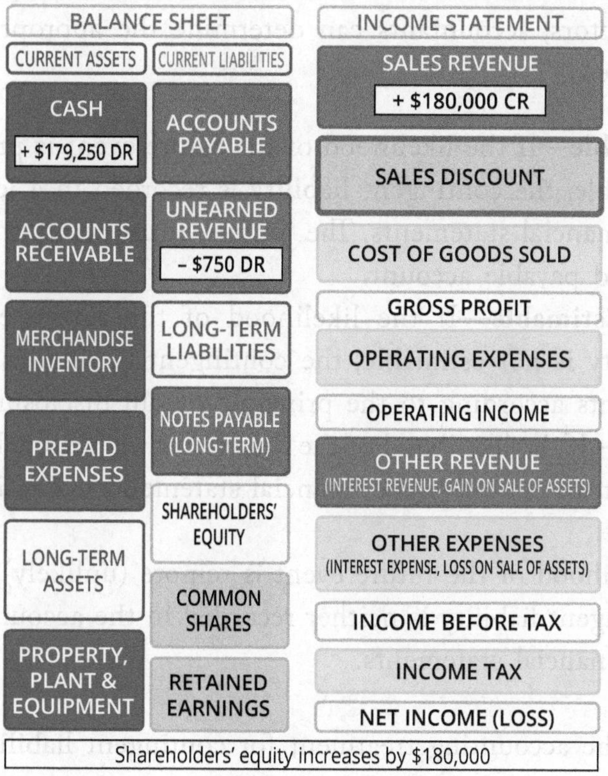

FIGURE 3.39

From Figure 3.39, you can see that even though Zen Gen sold $180,000 worth of refreshments in July, the company received only $179,250 in cash due to the sales discount through loyalty points. Because sales discount was recorded at the time of loyalty point issuance in June, the difference between sales amount and cash receipt of $750 in July is recorded as a reduction in redemption rewards liability. The redemption rewards liability account should be reviewed regularly and adjusted as needed to make sure that the balance always reflects the company's best estimate based on past redemption rates.

Contingent Liabilities

Unlike estimated liabilities, a company's **contingent liabilities** involve a financial obligation that occurs only if a certain event takes place in the future. As a result, not only are contingent liabilities estimated, but they are also dependent upon another event taking place. Since it is difficult to determine what is and is not possible, and how much of a contingency should be estimated, these items usually involve discretion and judgment by the accountants on behalf of the company.

According to accounting rules, the accounting treatment of contingent liabilities depends on the following two factors.

- The likelihood that the event will occur, which is classified as probable, reasonably possible or remote
- Whether the amount of the liability is estimable (measurable) or not estimable

By assessing these two factors, accountants can determine the appropriate accounting treatment for the contingent liabilities.

- **Probable and Estimable**—If the likelihood of the future event is probable and the amount of the liability is estimable, the contingent liability is recorded in a journal entry and disclosed in the notes to the financial statements. The journal entry debits the related expense account and credits the related payable account.
- **Probable and Not Estimable**—If the likelihood of the future event is probable but the amount of the liability is not estimable, the contingent liability is disclosed in the notes to the financial statements according to the principle of full disclosure.
- **Reasonably Possible**—If the likelihood of the future event is reasonably possible, the contingent liability is disclosed in the notes to the financial statements according to the principle of full disclosure.
- **Remote**—If the likelihood of the future event is remote (unlikely), and if the amount is not significant, the contingent liability is neither recorded in the accounting records nor disclosed in the notes to the financial statements.

Figure 3.40 summarizes the accounting treatment for contingent liabilities.

Contingent Liability: Likelihood of Future Event	Amount of Liability	Accounting Treatment
Probable	Estimable	Record the potential liability in accounting records Disclose in notes to financial statements
	Not Estimable	Disclose in notes to financial statements
Reasonably Possible		Disclose in notes to financial statements
Remote	Not significant	None required

FIGURE 3.40

ASPE vs. IFRS

The financial obligation that occurs if a certain event takes place is referred to as a "contingent liability." Both ASPE and IFRS require the contingent liability to be recognized as an actual liability when the company determines that the payment is probable. However, IFRS defines the word probable as "more likely than not," whereas ASPE defines it as "likely to occur." IFRS uses the term "provision" where ASPE would use the term "contingent loss." Under IFRS, a contingent liability is not recognized in the financial statements; however, provisions are recorded in the financial statements.

Perhaps the most common reason to establish a contingent liability is to anticipate a costly lawsuit. Being found guilty in a lawsuit could seriously affect a company's bottom line. If the likelihood of losing the case is probable and the amount of liability is estimable, in addition to disclosing the contingency in the notes, the company will also debit a related expense account (such as litigation expense) and credit a related liability account (such as litigation liability) for the estimated amount. If the likelihood of losing the case is either probable or reasonably possible, and the amount of liability is not estimable, then the company must include in the notes to its financial statements any contingencies that may lead to a liability.

In summary, Figure 3.41 shows an example of how both determinable and non-determinable liabilities appear in the current liabilities section of a business's balance sheet. The Note 4 beside Contingent Liabilities refers to an explanation in the notes to the financial statements.

Red Carpet Inc. Balance Sheet (partial) As at December 31, 2020	
Current Liabilities	
Accounts Payable & Accrued Liabilities	$15,760
Unearned Revenue	2,500
Notes Payable, Current Portion	10,000
Salaries & Wages Payable	10,000
Employee Payroll Deductions Payable	5,960
Estimated Warranty Liabilities	3,457
Contingent Liabilities (Note 4)	28,500
Total Current Liabilities	76,177

Note 4. Contingent Liabilities: Represents the amount the company is expecting to have to pay as a result of a pending lawsuit that the company does not anticipate being able to successfully defend.

FIGURE 3.41

Internal Controls Relating to Current Liabilities

LO 8

One of the first, basic controls over a company's liabilities involves a simple principle: keep track of company bills and budget well enough to pay them on time. Not paying suppliers on time may damage a company's reputation and its ability to do business with others in the future. Controls are implemented to ensure that the right bills are paid at the right time. To that end, all relevant documents are gathered, such as purchase orders, packing slips, receipts and original invoices, to verify the legitimacy of the invoices.

After an invoice is paid, it is marked as such and kept on file for verification purposes. A company never wants to pay the wrong bills or pay the same bills more than once. Controls related to invoices should prevent this from happening.

Accounting controls also ensure that a company's resources are used efficiently and economically. This includes paying bills on time and making use of any payment discounts that are available. Automated systems can alert the appropriate personnel when payments should be made. Manual systems can make use of date-labelled folders that help make time-sensitive documents quickly and easily accessible.

The amount of current liabilities a company has can play a part in applying for a bank loan. Too many current liabilities compared to current assets may prevent the company from securing a loan. The comparison of current assets to current liabilities is called the current ratio and is an indicator of how liquid the company is. A higher current ratio indicates better liquidity.

If the company is showing poor liquidity, this might lead management to either hide current liabilities by not recording them or reclassify them as long-term liabilities. Both actions are unethical and could lead to fines if discovered.

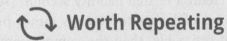

Worth Repeating

If a company has a current ratio of 1.5, this means they have $1.50 in current assets for every $1 in current liabilities.

In Summary

LO 1 Define and differentiate between determinable and non-determinable liabilities

- The listing order of liabilities on the balance sheet is dictated by the timing of the amount owed.
- A company's known liabilities, or determinable liabilities, are financial obligations with fixed terms that can be traced using documentation (e.g. accounts payable).
- Non-determinable liabilities include estimated liabilities for amounts that are not known as of the balance sheet date.

LO 2 Record accounts payable and accrued liabilities

- Accounts payable is the mirror image of accounts receivable. Instead of sending a customer a bill, accounts payable involves receiving an invoice for goods or services received.
- Payroll accounting includes several current liability accounts.
- Utility and other expenses involve recording accrued liabilities at the end of the accounting period.

LO 3 Record transactions with sales tax

- Sales taxes are charged on sales. The amount collected by the business must be sent to the government.
- Some provinces have a provincial sales tax (PST) that is applied by the provincial government. The federal government applies a federal sales tax called the goods and services tax (GST). Some provinces have partnered with the federal government and combined both the provincial and federal sales tax into a harmonized sales tax (HST).

LO 4 Record unearned revenue

- Unearned revenue relates to the way revenues are reconciled with the revenue recognition principle. Even though an amount may have been paid by customers, the revenue itself can be recognized only in a later period when goods or services are delivered.

LO 5 Record short-term notes payable

- Notes payable are the mirror image of a promissory note from a customer. They represent a more formal contract between a company and a supplier after a sale has been made, as opposed to a standard bill or invoice.
- Short-term notes payable can be used to extend credit terms or to borrow from a bank.

LO 6 Record transactions related to the current portion of long-term liabilities

- If a liability will be paid out over several years, the amount to be paid within 12 months is separated on the balance sheet and called the current portion of long-term liabilities.

LO 7 Record estimated liabilities

- Estimated liabilities, such as product warranties, represent financial obligations whose specific amount will not be known until some future time.
- Certain employee benefits, such as paid vacations, pension benefits, health benefits and employee bonuses, must be estimated and recorded in the period in which the employee earns the benefits.
- A company that sells products with warranties needs to estimate how much warranty liability it will have and expense that liability in the period in which related revenues are generated.
- Customer loyalty programs require a business to record an estimated liability for the amount that customers will receive in the future if they use their accumulated rewards.
- Contingent liabilities represent a financial obligation that needs to be met only if a certain event occurs. The possibility of a lawsuit might necessitate the establishment of a contingent liability.

LO 8 Apply internal controls relating to current liabilities

- Controls related to current liabilities should include proper tracking and monitoring of invoices and all related documentation. This ensures that the correct bills are paid on time, which is a crucial part of maintaining the company's finances.
- A company should not attempt to understate current liabilities by not recording them or by reclassifying them as long-term.

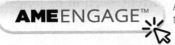

Review Exercise 3-1

Elnora Yearby Limited buys and resells machines. During 2020, the following transactions took place.

Jan 15	Bought a machine for resale for $105,000 plus 13% harmonized sales tax (HST), which is recoverable. The amount is payable in 30 days. The company uses a perpetual inventory system.
Jan 30	Sold the machine for $214,000 plus 13% HST cash including a five-year warranty. Based on past experience, the accountant determines that an amount of $20,000 will be paid out in warranty obligations.
Jan 30	Paid the HST amount owing.
Feb 15	Paid for the machine purchased on January 15.
Mar 27	Elnora Yearby must repair the machine under warranty. The company uses $200 in parts from its own inventory.

Record the journal entries for the above transactions.

JOURNAL

Date	Account Title and Explanation	Debit	Credit

See Appendix I for solutions.

Notes

Chapter 4
Partnerships

Learning Objectives

LO 1 Describe the characteristics, advantages and disadvantages of a partnership
- Characteristics of a Partnership
- Advantages of a Partnership
- Disadvantages of a Partnership

LO 2 Describe different types of partnerships
- General Partnership
- Limited Partnership
- Limited Liability Partnership
- Partnerships, Proprietorships and Corporations—A Summary of Characteristics

LO 3 Record the formation of a partnership

LO 4 Record the division of income or loss
- Dividing Profits Equally
- Dividing Profits According to an Agreed-Upon Ratio
- Dividing Profits According to the Capital Contribution of Each Partner
- Dividing Profits According to Agreed-Upon Salary and Interest Allocations, Plus a Share of the Remainder
- When Allowances Exceed Net Income

LO 5 Record partners' withdrawals

LO 6 Prepare financial statements for a partnership

LO 7 Account for the addition or withdrawal of a partner
- Addition of a Partner
- Withdrawal of a Partner
- Death of a Partner
- Partner Bonuses

LO 8 Record the liquidation of a partnership
- Liquidation with No Capital Deficiency
- Liquidation with a Capital Deficiency

AMEENGAGE™ Access **ameengage.com** for integrated resources including tutorials, practice exercises, the digital textbook and more.

MAKING IT REAL TO YOU

Your childhood best friend has asked you to form a partnership with them to sell 3D printers. Having both worked in the industry for several years, together you would bring a lot of knowledge and experience into the business. However, after learning that your friend was recently involved in another partnership that went bankrupt, you are wondering if entering a partnership with them would be a good idea.

Although forming a partnership can be as easy as shaking hands and verbally agreeing, you should do some research to determine whether or not this form of business is for you. While the combination of resources (both financial and human) would provide more investment in the business, you should also consider what would happen if you and your partner had a disagreement, or if your partner decided they no longer wanted to operate as a partnership. What would you do?

This chapter takes a closer look at the advantages and disadvantages of the partnership form of business and provides insight into the importance of having a partnership agreement. It covers methods for allocating profit (loss) as well as accounting for the addition or withdrawal of a partner and the liquidation of the business.

The Partnership Form of Business

LO 1

In previous chapters, you learned about the three primary options for structuring the ownership of a business.

1. A sole proprietorship is owned by only one person who keeps all the profits, which are taxed at the personal level. The owner is also personally responsible for all the liabilities of the business. This means that if the business is unable to pay its debts, creditors will pursue the owner's personal assets for payment should there not be sufficient funds in the business.

2. A **partnership** is an association of two or more people who jointly own a business, its assets and liabilities, and who share in gains or losses; profits are taxed personally. In Canada, partnerships are governed by the Partnerships Act, which deals with the formation, operation and dissolution of business partnerships. Some partners may be brought in for their technical expertise and others for their ability to raise capital. There are many similarities in accounting for partnerships and sole proprietorships.

3. In a corporation, there can be a large number of owners known as shareholders, many of whom may not participate in the running of the business. A corporation has many rights and duties because it is a legal entity distinct from its owners. All profits are taxed at the corporate level when they are earned and at the personal level when dividends are distributed to shareholders. Any capital gains from the sale of shares are also taxed. Corporations can raise funds from the general public by issuing shares. The shareholders (owners) of a corporation are not personally responsible for the company's debt.

While other chapters of this textbook focus on sole proprietorships and corporations, this chapter examines the characteristics of partnerships in detail. We will explore business partnerships, demonstrate the effect of transactions and financial reporting on the asset, liability and partners' equity accounts, and discuss how various accounting standards are applied.

Figure 4.1 shows a simple comparison of the equity component of a proprietor's balance sheet to that of a partnership. In a sole proprietorship, the owner's capital account records the total equity of the business (shown on the left). The total investment by the owner, plus any profit or loss, is reported in this one account. In a partnership, each partner has a separate capital account (shown on the right). Details on each partner's investment and share of profit or loss are recorded separately.

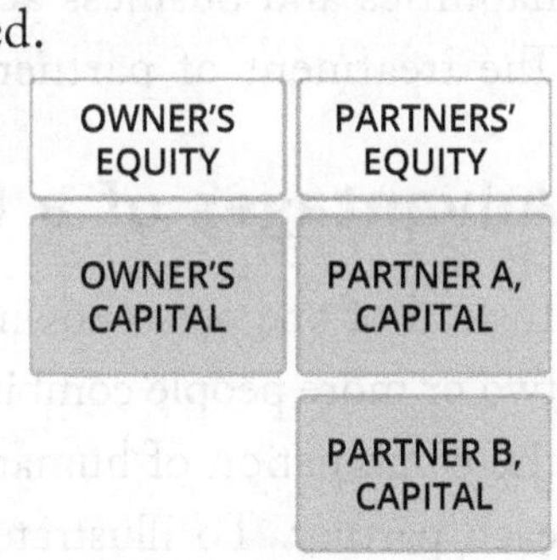

FIGURE 4.1

Many professional businesses are structured as partnerships, such as consulting firms, law firms and accounting firms. Regardless of which industries they operate in, all partnerships have characteristics in common that govern the duties, rights and responsibilities of the partners. Certain advantages and disadvantages are associated with conducting a business as a partnership. The characteristics, advantages and disadvantages of the partnership form of business will be discussed in detail.

Characteristics of a Partnership

Legal Entity

Although a partnership is considered a legal entity, for some purposes it is not considered legally separate from its owners. While the partnership itself does not pay taxes, it must still file a report on the profits of the partnership and each partner's share of those profits. Each partner is then required to report their share of profits (or losses) on an individual tax return, and (as with a sole proprietorship) they must pay taxes at a specific personal tax rate regardless of whether the profits were actually withdrawn from the partnership.

Division of Profit and Losses

Even though not formally required for a partnership, it is generally advisable for partners to draw up a *legal partnership agreement* that specifies the division of partnership profits and losses. If partners consent to change the terms of the agreement, a new one is drawn up, which cancels and replaces the previous agreement. The division of profits and losses are discussed later in this chapter.

Right to Own Property

A partnership can own assets in its name, such as property, plant and equipment. In fact, partners often bring existing individual assets into the partnership for use by the business. The partnership's assets are jointly owned by all partners. This means that if a partner brings an existing individual asset into the partnership, the asset becomes the partnership's, and it is not legally returnable to the partner who contributed it. If the partnership dissolves, the asset is sold along with other partnership assets and the proceeds (or losses) are divided according to the terms of the current partnership agreement. Also, just as in a sole proprietorship, the accounting records for all partnership assets, liabilities and business activities are kept separately from the partners' personal accounting records. The treatment of partnership assets will be discussed in more detail later in the chapter.

Advantages of a Partnership

Instead of one person owning and operating a business as in a sole proprietorship, a partnership involves two or more people combining resources, both human and financial. This provides two advantages. First, the combination of human resources means that the business benefits from the skills and experience of each partner. To illustrate, assume two lawyers, Helen White and Greg Harris, form the partnership White & Harris Law. Helen specializes in family law and Greg specializes in criminal law. Together, they are able to service twice as many clients in two different areas of law. Second, due to their combined financial resources, they are more likely than a sole proprietorship to provide sufficient cash flow to the business without having to rely on external financing.

Another advantage of the partnership form of business is the relative ease of formation. Some small partnerships of two or more individuals may be based on just a verbal agreement or a handshake.

On the other hand, many professional partnerships, such as those of legal and accounting firms, may have hundreds of partners located world-wide. Regardless of the number of partners, it is always wise to have a legal partnership agreement setting out the rights and obligations of all partners. A legal partnership agreement formalizes the arrangement for sharing profits and losses and for other eventualities, such as the addition or withdrawal of a partner, or the dissolution of the partnership. In the absence of a written agreement, individuals could be liable for the actions of other partners, regardless of their involvement in decisions made on behalf of the partnership. Partnership agreements are discussed in more depth later in the chapter.

Disadvantages of a Partnership

Perhaps the biggest disadvantage of the partnership form of business is that each partner is responsible for the liabilities of the business, referred to as **unlimited liability**. Consider the legal partnership, White & Harris Law. Assume that Helen White has no personal assets other than what she invested in the partnership. Greg Harris, on the other hand, owns his own home, rental property, cottage, sailboat and several valuable paintings. The business suffered losses for several years and was then sued for $1.5 million by a dissatisfied client. As the partnership had very little remaining cash and few assets, the partners were personally liable for the $1.5 million liability. Since Helen had no assets, Greg was required to pay the debt on behalf of the partnership, because of unlimited liability.

As with a sole proprietorship, a second disadvantage of a partnership is its limited life. In the event of the death of one of the partners, bankruptcy or the addition or withdrawal of a partner, the existing partnership ends (although not necessarily the business). A new partnership can be formed based on the new circumstance, and with the agreement of all partners, the business can continue.

A third disadvantage is **mutual agency**, which means that each partner can authorize contracts and transactions on behalf of the partnership, provided the activity is within the scope of the partnership's business. This ability places the other partners at risk if the authorizing partner does not act in the best interests of the partnership.

To overcome the most serious disadvantage of the partnership form of business, which is unlimited liability, different types of partnerships have been introduced to limit liability. These are known as limited partnerships and limited liability partnerships. In addition to the general form of partnership, these two special types of partnership are discussed in detail in the following section.

Types of Partnerships

LO 2

Partnerships can take different forms, each of which has a different way of dealing with liability issues. Owners must determine the type of partnership that best suits their business needs.

General Partnership

A **general partnership** means that all partners share the responsibility for the liabilities of the business; that is, they have unlimited liability.

Limited Partnership

Businesses are sometimes legally obligated to pay other parties a considerable amount of money. These obligations can include debt owed to creditors or financial sums awarded to other parties in a lawsuit. Sole proprietorships and partnerships generally extend unlimited liability to all the owners of the business. Unlimited liability in a partnership can be particularly damaging because, if one partner is unable to meet liability obligations related to the partnership, the other partners are legally required to pay. This could mean having to sell off personal assets such as houses, cars and investments. Limited partnerships resolve the potential problem of unlimited liability by creating two categories of partners within the business: the general partner and the limited partner. Unlimited liability is assigned to a **general partner**, who is legally authorized to manage the day-to-day operations of the business and to make decisions on behalf of the business. Each partnership must have at least one general partner.

Limited liability is a type of liability that extends only to the amount a person has invested in a partnership. Limited liability is assigned to a **limited partner**, also known as a "silent partner," who is responsible only for providing the capital to finance the business. This partner is not involved in day-to-day operations and is therefore not considered liable for decisions made by the business that can lead to a liability. Limited partners are liable only for the amount they have invested in the business.

Limited Liability Partnership

Another business legal entity—the **limited liability partnership** or **LLP**—has been developed to deal with liability. Unlike in a limited partnership, the limited partners in an LLP usually participate in managing the business. LLPs are primarily used in professional partnerships to protect one partner from another partner's negligence. For example, if a lawyer is sued for violating standards of professional conduct, other lawyers in the firm are not automatically considered liable. However, as with limited partnerships, partners usually cannot escape liability entirely. In the case of LLPs, all partners are still liable for any unpaid debts to creditors. Although the details of an LLP vary from province to province, generally an LLP can protect partners from some forms of liability but not all.

Since LLPs are governed by provincial or territorial legislation that differs in terms of the protection provided, partners should be aware of the rules for the province or territory in which they reside. For example, in Alberta and Manitoba, LLPs offer "partial shield protection," which limits the partner from acts of negligence, wrongful acts or omissions, malpractice or misconduct committed by other partners during the provision of services. It may also protect against similar wrongful acts committed by employees who are supervised by other partners. It does not, however, protect against general contractual claims against the firm. Other provinces, such as British Columbia and Ontario, provide "full shield protection," which protects the partner from all claims against the partnership, whether contractual or due to the malpractice or wrongdoing of other partners. Partners are still liable for their own wrongful acts.

Partnerships, Proprietorships and Corporations—A Summary of Characteristics

Figure 4.2 summarizes the characteristics of partnerships and compares them with the characteristics of sole proprietorships and corporations. You will notice both similarities and differences among the three forms of business ownership.

Characteristics	Sole Proprietorship	Partnership	Corporation
Number of Owners	One	Two or more	One or more (called "shareholders")
Control	Owner has complete control	Decisions are shared among partners, with possibility of disagreement and conflict	Depends on size of company, type and number of shares held (voting rights) In larger corporations, management is separate from ownership
Ability to Raise Capital	Small, since only one person is raising money	Moderate to large, since more than one person is responsible for raising money	Can be very large, depending on share issuance
Profits	Proprietor receives 100% of profits	Partners share profits according to terms of the partnership agreement	Owners (shareholders) receive profits when dividends are declared and paid
Formation	Relatively simple to set up	Simple to set up, but details require close attention	Moderately complex to set up; articles of incorporation, by-laws and other legal documents need to be filed with government
Liability	Proprietor is responsible for all debts and/or legal obligations	Partners are responsible jointly and individually for actions of other partners	Shareholders' liability is limited to their investment
Skills	Reliance on the skills of the proprietor alone	Skills in various areas of the business brought by each partner	More opportunity to hire highly skilled employees depending on needs of company
Dissolution	Relatively simple to dissolve	May be dissolved upon death or withdrawal of a partner; partnership has limited life	May continue despite addition, withdrawal or death of shareholders; business can have unlimited life
Taxation	Profits are taxed whether or not cash is withdrawn from the business	Partners share profits and are taxed whether or not cash is withdrawn; the partnership pays no income tax	Profits are taxed in the hands of the corporation; corporate tax return is filed

FIGURE 4.2

Formation of a Partnership

LO 3

In the formation stage of a partnership, all partners should collectively draw up a legal partnership agreement as a written contract. A partnership agreement lessens the chance of legal and ethical conflicts between partners, and it specifies the purpose of the business as well as the relationships between partners. In the absence of a partnership agreement, individuals could find themselves liable for the actions of their partners. Also, without an agreement, all partnership profits and losses must be shared equally, which may not be what the partners intended.

A partnership agreement should normally include the following elements.

- Date of creation of the partnership
- Legal name and address of the business
- Purpose of the business
- Names and addresses of all partners
- Contribution of each partner
- Duties, rights and responsibilities of the partners
- Terms for sharing profits and losses
- Procedures for addition or withdrawal of a partner
- Terms of withdrawal of assets from the business
- Provisions for the death of a partner
- Terms for liquidation of the partnership

Partnership agreements can be as varied as the businesses themselves, but any contract should include clear provisions for a full range of eventualities.

Once the partnership agreement has been drawn up, the next step is to record the initial journal entries to set up the asset, liability and equity accounts. The partners may have assets (other than cash) and liabilities that they would like to bring into the business. In order to have an objective valuation of each partner's contribution, an independent market evaluation (appraisal) of the items should be done.

Assume that on January 1, 2020, Lee Wang and Kim Chow decide to form the partnership Wang & Chow. Figure 4.3 is a summary of the amounts contributed by each partner.

Lee Wang	
Cash	$8,000
Accounts Receivable	10,000
Allowance for Doubtful Accounts	890
Equipment	18,000
Accumulated Depreciation—Equipment	2,000
Accounts Payable	1,800
Notes Payable	6,000

Kim Chow	
Cash	$10,000
Building	170,000
Notes Payable	100,000

FIGURE 4.3

An independent appraiser determined that the allowance for doubtful accounts should be $1,200 and the market value of the equipment is $11,000. All other assets and liabilities are recorded at the values presented. Notice that assets are recorded in the partnership's books at their market value and that their accumulated depreciation is not carried over when the partnership is formed. The journal entries to set up assets, liabilities and equity accounts based on Wang's and Chow's initial investments in the partnership are shown in Figure 4.4.

JOURNAL

Date	Account Title and Explanation	Debit	Credit
Jan 1	Cash	8,000	
	Accounts Receivable	10,000	
	Equipment	11,000	
	Allowance for Doubtful Accounts		1,200
	Accounts Payable		1,800
	Notes Payable		6,000
	Wang, Capital		20,000
	To record Wang's investment in the partnership		
Jan 1	Cash	10,000	
	Building	170,000	
	Notes Payable		100,000
	Chow, Capital		80,000
	To record Chow's investment in the partnership		

FIGURE 4.4

Pause & Reflect

Exercise 4-1

On September 1, 2020, Miko Akazi and Gayle Warren formed a general partnership for their bakery. They each brought to this new partnership the following assets and liabilities.

Miko Akazi		**Gayle Warren**	
Cash	$5,000	Cash	$15,000
Building	250,000	Equipment	60,000
Accumulated Depreciation—Building	120,000	Accumulated Depreciation—Equipment	25,000
Notes Payable	80,000	Accounts Payable	10,000

An independent appraiser determined that the market value of the building is $275,000 and the market value of the equipment is $20,000. Prepare the journal entries to set up the partnership.

JOURNAL

Date	Account Title and Explanation	Debit	Credit

See Appendix I for solutions.

Division of Income or Loss

LO 4

A key difference between a sole proprietorship, partnership and corporation is the way in which profits are distributed. In a sole proprietorship, the proprietor simply receives all the profits. In a corporation, profits are distributed in the form of dividend payments (profits paid out to shareholders). If all the assets are sold and all debts are paid, the remaining cash is distributed among the shareholders in proportion to the number of shares owned. For example, a shareholder with 10 times more shares than another shareholder receives 10 times more of the remaining cash. (Shares and dividends are discussed later on in the text.)

In a partnership, profits are distributed differently than they are in a sole proprietorship or corporation. Since partners are involved, profits must be shared, but not necessarily on an equal basis. A partnership agreement sets out the terms of ownership, including how profits are divided. In the absence of a partnership agreement, all profits and losses are shared equally among the partners. A partnership's equity account on the balance sheet is referred to as the capital account. Figure 4.5 shows an example of how partnership equity changes over a period of time.

	J. Witner	R. Pierce	Total
Capital Balance (beginning)	$25,000	$50,000	$75,000
Add: Additional Contribution	0	0	0
Share of Partnership Net Income for the Period	75,000	75,000	150,000
Subtotal	100,000	125,000	225,000
Less: Withdrawals	40,000	80,000	120,000
Capital Balance (ending)	$60,000	$45,000	$105,000

FIGURE 4.5

The partnership's capital account is broken down by partner. In this case, J. Witner had a beginning capital balance of $25,000 and R. Pierce had a beginning capital balance of $50,000. During the year, they did not contribute additional capital to the business. At the end of the year, J. Witner's share of net income is $75,000 and $40,000 was withdrawn. R. Pierce's share of net income is $75,000 and $80,000 was withdrawn. The closing capital account balance is the net worth of the partnership.

One of the primary purposes of a partnership agreement is to stipulate how earnings are divided. Each partner's share of profits and losses is determined by the partnership's profit and loss ratio. In Figure 4.5, it is assumed that the net income is split equally between the partners.

Profit and loss ratios can take many forms including, but not limited to, the following.

- Dividing profit or loss equally among all partners
- According to an agreed-upon ratio, such as 2:1, or 60% to 40%
- According to the capital contribution of each partner
- According to agreed-upon salary and interest allocations, plus a share of the remainder

Each of these methods will be examined separately.

Dividing Profits Equally

The simplest method of dividing profits is on an equal basis. For example, assume Wang & Chow earned $46,000 in net income for the year. The net income is credited to the income summary account after the revenue and expense accounts have been closed. For the partners to share the profits equally, a debit is then made to the income summary account for the entire amount, while a credit of $23,000 ($46,000 ÷ 2) is made to the capital account of each partner, as shown in the journal entry in Figure 4.6.

JOURNAL			
Date	**Account Title and Explanation**	**Debit**	**Credit**
Dec 31	Income Summary	46,000	
	Wang, Capital		23,000
	Chow, Capital		23,000
	To adjust partners' capital accounts for their share of net income		

FIGURE 4.6

Worth Repeating

Closing the books for a company, at year end, transfers the values in the revenue and expense accounts to the income summary account, leaving the revenue and expense accounts with a zero balance. The income summary account is then closed to the capital account. If the company had a net income for the year, the income summary account is debited and the capital account is credited, leaving the income summary account with a zero balance.

Dividing Profits According to an Agreed-Upon Ratio

The allocation of business profits can be done according to an agreed-upon ratio. For example, if Lee Wang receives 60% of the profits and Kim Chow receives 40%, the split is recorded in the books as shown in Figure 4.7.

JOURNAL			
Date	**Account Title and Explanation**	**Debit**	**Credit**
Dec 31	Income Summary	46,000	
	Wang, Capital		27,600
	Chow, Capital		18,400
	To adjust partners' capital accounts for their share of net income		

FIGURE 4.7

As a result of the $46,000 net income, Wang's capital balance increases by $27,600 ($46,000 × 60%), and Chow's capital balance increases by $18,400 ($46,000 × 40%).

Dividing Profits According to the Capital Contribution of Each Partner

Another method of allocating the profits among partners is to base it on the amount that each partner invested in the business. For example, Lee Wang and Kim Chow contributed a total of $100,000 to the partnership. Wang contributed $20,000 (one-fifth or 20%) of the capital and Chow contributed $80,000 (four-fifths or 80%). Therefore, Wang and Chow are entitled to 20% and 80% of the profits, respectively. The journal entry to record this is shown in Figure 4.8.

JOURNAL

Date	Account Title and Explanation	Debit	Credit
Dec 31	Income Summary	46,000	
	Wang, Capital		9,200
	Chow, Capital		36,800
	To adjust partners' capital accounts for their share of net income		

FIGURE 4.8

To allocate the $46,000 net income, Wang's capital balance increases by $9,200 ($46,000 × 20%), and Chow's capital balance increases by $36,800 ($46,000 × 80%).

Dividing Profits According to Agreed-Upon Salary and Interest Allocations, Plus a Share of the Remainder

Profits can also be divided by using a fixed salary allocation, interest allocation, or both for each partner, and then dividing the remaining profits equally. For example, if the partnership agreement stipulates that Lee Wang's salary is $18,000, Kim Chow's salary is $20,000, and interest allowance is 5% of each partner's capital balance at the beginning of the year, then those are the first amounts to be deducted from the net income of the business and distributed to the partners. These amounts are shown in the top half of Figure 4.9.

	Total	Wang	Chow
Net Income	$46,000		
Salary to Wang	−18,000	$18,000	
Salary to Chow	−20,000		$20,000
Interest allowance to Wang ($20,000 × 5%)	−1,000	1,000	
Interest allowance to Chow ($80,000 × 5%)	−4,000		4,000
Remainder	3,000		
Share of profit to Wang ($3,000 × 50%)	−1,500	1,500	
Share of profit to Chow ($3,000 × 50%)	−1,500		1,500
Transferred to partners' capital accounts	−$46,000	$20,500	$25,500

FIGURE 4.9

The $3,000 remaining after the salaries are distributed is divided equally between the partners. These amounts are shown in the lower portion of Figure 4.9.

If the distributed amounts are added up for each partner, the totals come to $20,500 ($18,000 + $1,000 + $1,500) for Wang and $25,500 ($20,000 + $4,000 + $1,500) for Chow, as shown in the bottom row of Figure 4.9. Figure 4.10 then shows how the allocations are recorded to each partner's capital account.

JOURNAL

Date	Account Title and Explanation	Debit	Credit
Dec 31	Income Summary	46,000	
	Wang, Capital		20,500
	Chow, Capital		25,500
	To adjust partners' capital accounts for their share of net income		

FIGURE 4.10

The number of ways that profits can be divided between partners is unlimited. As another example, interest can first be allocated (out of net income) at a fixed rate on each partner's capital account; the remaining amount of net income can then be divided according to a predetermined ratio or salary. The method chosen should meet the needs and interests of the partners involved and be clearly stated in the partnership agreement. The salary and interest allocations are not expenses and are not to be deducted from the partnership's revenues in determining net income for the period.

It is important to note that the method of distributing the earnings is just allocation, not actual payments and not actual expenses. Even the salary and interest amounts are allocations. The allocation assigns to each partner's capital account their share of the earnings. If they wish to take money from the business, it is considered a withdrawal, which is discussed in the next section.

When Allowances Exceed Net Income

The preceding example was based on a net income of $46,000 for the year. The total salary was $38,000 ($18,000 for Wang and $20,000 for Chow). The total interest allowance was $5,000 ($1,000 for Wang and $4,000 for Chow). This means that the net income exceeded the salary and interest allowances.

If the partners have agreed to allocate salary and interest, then salary and interest are allocated regardless of whether or not the net income can cover all the salary and interest amounts. Suppose the net income is only $40,000. In this case, the remainder is –$3,000, indicating an over-allocation of salary and interest. To compensate for the over-allocation, $1,500 is subtracted from each partner, reducing the total allocation of income to their capital accounts.

Figure 4.11 shows the final allocation of net income between Wang and Chow.

	Total	Wang	Chow
Net Income	$40,000		
Salary to Wang	−18,000	$18,000	
Salary to Chow	−20,000		$20,000
Interest allowance to Wang ($20,000 × 5%)	−1,000	1,000	
Interest allowance to Chow ($80,000 × 5%)	−4,000		4,000
Remainder	−3,000		
Less excess of allowance over net income, Wang (−$3,000 × 50%)	1,500	−1,500	
Less excess of allowance over net income, Chow (−$3,000 × 50%)	1,500		−1,500
Transferred to partners' capital accounts	−$40,000	$17,500	$22,500

FIGURE 4.11

In this case, the allocations are recorded to each partner's capital account as shown in Figure 4.12.

JOURNAL

Date	Account Title and Explanation	Debit	Credit
Dec 31	Income Summary	40,000	
	Wang, Capital		17,500
	Chow, Capital		22,500
	To adjust partners' capital accounts for their share of net income		

FIGURE 4.12

If Wang and Chow experience a net loss for the year, the partners share the net loss in the same way, only they begin their calculations with a negative amount. They still allocate the salary and interest allowances, except this adds to the negative balances. The total negative balance *after* these allocations is divided equally between Wang and Chow.

Pause & Reflect

Exercise 4-2

Eric Banner and David Martin operate a general partnership. At year end on December 31, 2020, the partnership reported a net income of $90,000. In the partnership agreement, Eric receives a salary allowance of $45,000 per year and David receives a salary allowance of $35,000 per year. Any excess is shared equally between the two.

a) Calculate how much each partner is allocated from the net income.

	Total	Eric Banner	David Martin
Net Income			

b) Prepare the journal entry to close the income summary to the capital accounts.

JOURNAL			
Date	**Account Title and Explanation**	**Debit**	**Credit**

See Appendix I for solutions.

Partner Withdrawals

LO 5

During the year, partners may withdraw cash or other assets from the business for personal use. This amount is reported as the amount that has been withdrawn from the partner's equity. Assume that on November 5, 2020, Lee Wang and Kim Chow withdrew from the partnership $8,000 and $15,000, respectively. The journal entries to record the withdrawals are shown on the left side of Figure 4.13. The journal entries to record the related year-end closing entries for the Wang & Chow partnership are shown on the right side.

JOURNAL			
Date	**Account Title and Explanation**	**Debit**	**Credit**
Nov 5	Wang, Withdrawals	8,000	
	Chow, Withdrawals	15,000	
	Cash		23,000
	To record partners' withdrawals during the year		

JOURNAL			
Date	**Account Title and Explanation**	**Debit**	**Credit**
Dec 31	Wang, Capital	8,000	
	Chow, Capital	15,000	
	Wang, Withdrawals		8,000
	Chow, Withdrawals		15,000
	To close each partner's withdrawals account		

FIGURE 4.13

Partnership Financial Statements

LO 6

Four basic financial statements are prepared by partnerships: the income statement, the statement of partners' equity, the balance sheet and the statement of cash flows. Partnership financial statements are quite similar to those of sole proprietorships. The main difference is that a partnership is an association of two or more people, and so there is a bit more involved in accounting for equity and the division of profits and losses of the partners.

For instance, Figure 4.14 shows an income statement for Wang & Chow. We have assumed all the balances in the statement simply for demonstration purposes.

Wang & Chow Income Statement For the Year Ended December 31, 2020		
Revenue		
Service Revenue		$60,000
Expenses		
Depreciation Expense	$1,000	
Bank Charges Expense	230	
Insurance Expense	425	
Professional Fees Expense	945	
Property Taxes Expense	1,300	
Repairs & Maintenance Expense	100	
Salaries Expense	10,000	
Total Expenses		(14,000)
Net Income		$46,000

FIGURE 4.14

Notice that the partnership income statement is almost identical to a sole proprietorship income statement. Partners' share of the income is divided according to the terms in the partnership agreement. Any detailed calculations for the distribution of profit (or losses) is usually included as a separate schedule in notes to the income statement.

Partnerships must also prepare a **statement of partners' equity**, which explains the changes to the balance of each partner's capital account from the beginning to the end of the year. Changes are normally in the form of withdrawals from the business, investments added to the business and each partner's share of profit or loss.

Now look at a statement of partners' equity for Wang & Chow. Using the partners' beginning capital balance information from the journal entry in Figure 4.4, a statement can be prepared for Wang & Chow for the year ended December 31, 2020 (Figure 4.15). For simplicity, assume the following events occurred.

- The partnership was formed on January 1, 2020.
- Lee Wang added an investment of $4,500 during the year.
- The two partners share profits and losses equally.
- Lee Wang withdrew $8,000 and Kim Chow withdrew $15,000 from the business in 2020.

Note that net income is taken from the partnership's income statement in Figure 4.14.

Wang & Chow Statement of Partners' Equity For the Year Ended December 31, 2020			
	Lee Wang	**Kim Chow**	**Total**
Partners' Capital, January 1	$0	$0	$0
Add: Investments	24,500	80,000	104,500
Net Income	23,000	23,000	46,000
Subtotal	47,500	103,000	150,500
Less: Withdrawals	8,000	15,000	23,000
Partners' Capital, December 31	$39,500	$88,000	$127,500

FIGURE 4.15

The information for the statement of partners' equity is taken from the partnership income statement, the partners' capital accounts and the partners' withdrawals accounts. The opening balance of the partners' capital is $0, since the partnership formed this year. For next year, the opening balance of the partners' capital will be equal to the December 31 balance shown in Figure 4.15.

A partnership balance sheet is very similar to that of a sole proprietorship. The main difference is that a partnership balance sheet shows the balance of each partner's capital account in a section called partners' capital. Using the partners' ending capital balance information from the statement of partners' equity in Figure 4.15, a balance sheet can be prepared for Wang & Chow for December 31, 2020, as shown in Figure 4.16.

Wang & Chow Balance Sheet As at December 31, 2020			
Assets		**Liabilities and Partners' Capital**	
Cash	$32,500	**Liabilities**	
Accounts Receivable	16,750	Accounts Payable	$40,500
Equipment	11,000	Notes Payable	52,000
Accumulated Depreciation—Equipment	(1,500)	**Total Liabilities**	92,500
Building	170,000	**Partners' Capital**	
Accumulated Depreciation—Building	(8,750)	Wang, Capital	39,500
		Chow, Capital	88,000
Total Assets	$220,000	**Total Liabilities and Partners' Capital**	$220,000

FIGURE 4.16

The partnership statement of cash flows is omitted in this section because it is similar to that of a sole proprietorship. Preparation of the statement of cash flows is covered in a later chapter.

Addition or Withdrawal of a Partner

LO 7

The legal basis for any partnership is the partnership agreement. Once a partner leaves, or another is added, a new partnership agreement should be prepared and signed by all parties. However, this does not mean that the business needs to open a new set of books. Instead, adjustments can be made to the current set of books to reflect any change in partner status.

Addition of a Partner

An existing partnership may want to add a new partner if it requires additional capital or another skilled person. The new partner will either invest assets in the partnership (similar to Figure 4.4) or purchase part of an existing partner's equity. To illustrate the transactions to add or remove a partner from a partnership, we will examine a sample partnership with three existing partners, A, B and C.

In Figure 4.17, the first row shows the existing capital balances of the three partners before the addition of Partner D.

	Partner A	Partner B	Partner C	Partner D	Total
Capital balance before admitting new partner (includes all earnings to date)	$120,000	$150,000	$50,000		$320,000
Admission of new partner				$100,000	100,000
Capital balance after admitting new partner	$120,000	$150,000	$50,000	$100,000	$420,000

FIGURE 4.17

Partner D is the new addition; therefore, their opening balance is zero. The total of the opening balances for Partners A, B and C is $320,000. On January 1, 2020, Partner D contributes $100,000 to the partnership, which creates a new balance of $420,000 (shown in the second and third rows).

Figure 4.18 shows how the admission of the new partner is recorded as a journal entry.

JOURNAL

Date	Account Title and Explanation	Debit	Credit
Jan 1	Cash	100,000	
	Partner D, Capital		100,000
	To record admission of new partner		

FIGURE 4.18

The receipt of $100,000 is debited to the company's cash account, and a corresponding credit of $100,000 is added to Partner D's capital account.

Another way a partner can be added is if they purchase part of the equity of one or more existing partners. In this scenario, part of the capital of one or more partners is transferred to the new partner. In Figure 4.19, $100,000 of Partner A's capital is transferred to Partner D.

	Partner A	Partner B	Partner C	Partner D	Total
Capital balance before admitting new partner (includes all earnings to date)	$120,000	$150,000	$50,000		$320,000
Admission of new partner	−100,000			$100,000	0
Capital balance after admitting new partner	$20,000	$150,000	$50,000	$100,000	$320,000

FIGURE 4.19

In the second row, $100,000 is deducted from Partner A's balance and added to Partner D's balance. The journal entry is shown in Figure 4.20.

JOURNAL

Date	Account Title and Explanation	Debit	Credit
Jan 1	Partner A, Capital	100,000	
	Partner D, Capital		100,000
	To record admission of new partner		

FIGURE 4.20

Note that the above transaction did not involve cash of the business. In cases like this, any cash that changes hands between Partner A and Partner D is done personally between the two partners;

that is, it is done outside of the partnership's books. In fact, the amount of cash paid by Partner D could be more or less than $100,000; however, for the partnership's books, that is irrelevant. Only the transfer of capital is what is recorded.

Since equity was simply transferred from Partner A to Partner D, no additional equity was brought into the partnership. Therefore, the partnership's total net assets after the transfer remain at $320,000.

Withdrawal of a Partner

At times, a partner may wish to leave the partnership, or the others may wish a partner to leave. When a partner leaves, their capital account is closed and the partner receives a cash payout. The cash payout can be a private transaction between partners, or the partnership itself can pay the leaving partner. Figure 4.21 illustrates a private cash transaction between partners. Partners A and B each use their personal cash to pay Partner C for a portion of C's capital.

	Partner A	Partner B	Partner C	Total
Capital balance before withdrawal of Partner C	$120,000	$150,000	$50,000	$320,000
Withdrawal of Partner C	25,000	25,000	-50,000	0
Capital balance after withdrawal of Partner C	$145,000	$175,000	$0	$320,000

FIGURE 4.21

After the withdrawal of Partner C, the total partnership capital of the business remains the same. It is important to understand that the cash payment to Partner C is not recorded using the cash account because Partner C's share was paid by Partners A and B personally, and not by the business. Assuming Partners A and B each receive an equal share of Partner C's capital, the capital of both Partners A and B increases by $25,000 and the capital of Partner C decreases by $50,000.

Figure 4.22 shows how the withdrawal of Partner C is recorded as a journal entry when Partners A and B have personally bought C's share in the business.

JOURNAL

Date	Account Title and Explanation	Debit	Credit
Jan 1	Partner C, Capital	50,000	
	Partner A, Capital		25,000
	Partner B, Capital		25,000
	To record withdrawal of Partner C		

FIGURE 4.22

Now consider the accounting if the withdrawal of Partner C is paid from partnership assets instead of by other partners as a private transaction. This reduces both net assets and total partnership capital, as shown in Figure 4.23.

	Partner A	Partner B	Partner C	Total
Capital balance before withdrawal of Partner C	$120,000	$150,000	$50,000	$320,000
Withdrawal of Partner C			−50,000	−50,000
Capital balance after withdrawal of Partner C	$120,000	$150,000	$0	$270,000

FIGURE 4.23

Figure 4.24 shows how the withdrawal of Partner C is recorded as a journal entry when the business pays for the withdrawal.

JOURNAL

Date	Account Title and Explanation	Debit	Credit
Jan 1	Partner C, Capital	50,000	
	Cash		50,000
	To record withdrawal of Partner C		

FIGURE 4.24

Death of a Partner

As you learned earlier in this chapter, when a partner dies the existing partnership ends, but not necessarily the business. The remaining partners have two choices: liquidate the business, or form a new partnership agreement and continue the business. Whatever the decision, several things must happen upon a partner's death. First, the partnership accounts must be closed as of the date of the partner's death in order to determine the net income or loss for the current period. The net income or loss must then be divided among all partners' capital accounts. The assets and liabilities should be adjusted to their current market values, and the amount of any adjustments must be divided among all partners' capital accounts. The deceased partner's estate is entitled to that partner's equity. Therefore, the remaining partners and the deceased partner's estate must come to an agreement about the settlement of that partner's equity. Once a settlement amount has been established, a journal entry is made to close (debit) the deceased partner's capital account and record (credit) a liability for the amount payable to the partner's estate. This entire process can go much more smoothly if the original partnership agreement and legal contract include detailed provisions for such circumstances.

Partner Bonuses

The discussion so far has assumed that the cash received from a new partner or paid to a leaving partner is the same as the value shown in the capital account. However, sometimes the cash amount is different from the capital amount. When new partnership agreements are negotiated, the partners usually come to an understanding of what the business is really worth, relative to its stated book value. This understanding then forms the foundation of how much of a *bonus* (or premium) new partners must pay the existing partners in order to receive a share of ownership in the business or, conversely, how much the existing partners are willing to pay a new partner to join the partnership.

Figure 4.25 shows the original opening balances for Partners A, B and C. The following examples will illustrate the *bonus method* of adding a partner.

	Partner A	Partner B	Partner C	Partner D	Total
Capital balance before admitting new partner (includes all earnings to date)	$120,000	$150,000	$50,000		$320,000

FIGURE 4.25

Bonus to Existing Partners from New Partner

In the first example, assume that Partner D (the new partner) is willing to pay a bonus to the existing partners for a share of the business. Partner D would be willing to do this if the business has a value that is not reflected in the capital account, such as an increase in the value of the good name of the business (goodwill) or a higher market value for assets, such as land or copyright.

After negotiating the new partnership agreement, Partner D agrees to pay $200,000 on January 1, 2020, to receive a $130,000 share of the business's book value, which amounts to a quarter of the business. Figure 4.26 shows how each partner's capital is affected by the admission of Partner D.

	Partner A	Partner B	Partner C	Partner D	Total
Capital balance before admitting new partner (includes all earnings to date)	$120,000	$150,000	$50,000		$320,000
Admission of new partner	23,334	23,333	23,333	$130,000	200,000
Capital balance after admitting new partner	$143,334	$173,333	$73,333	$130,000	$520,000

FIGURE 4.26

Partner D's $200,000 contribution increases the total net assets from $320,000 to $520,000. One quarter of the new total is $130,000, which is Partner D's new share. The remaining balance of Partner D's $200,000 investment, $70,000, is divided equally as a bonus among the other three partners, as shown in the journal entry in Figure 4.27. (The $1 difference for Partner A is due to rounding the values to whole dollars.) We assume the bonus is divided equally in this example, but it would be divided in whatever way the partnership agreement states.

JOURNAL			
Date	**Account Title and Explanation**	**Debit**	**Credit**
Jan 1	Cash	200,000	
	Partner A, Capital		23,334
	Partner B, Capital		23,333
	Partner C, Capital		23,333
	Partner D, Capital		130,000
	To record admission of new partner		

FIGURE 4.27

Bonus to New Partner

In the second example, assume that Partner D adds value to the business, perhaps by bringing a client list or an area of expertise that the partnership is looking for. Figure 4.28 shows what happens when Partner D pays $100,000 on January 1, 2020, to receive a quarter share of the business, for a value of $105,000.

	Partner A	Partner B	Partner C	Partner D	Total
Capital balance before admitting new partner (includes all earnings to date)	$120,000	$150,000	$50,000		$320,000
Admission of new partner	−1,666	−1,667	−1,667	$105,000	100,000
Capital balance after admitting new partner	$118,334	$148,333	$48,333	$105,000	$420,000

FIGURE 4.28

The $100,000 contribution made by Partner D increases total net assets to $420,000. One quarter of the new total is $105,000, which is Partner D's share. Since Partner D paid only $100,000 for this share, the $5,000 difference is a bonus to the new partner, paid for by the capital of the original partners. Therefore, approximately $1,667 is deducted from the account balances of Partners A, B and C, as shown in Figure 4.29. (Again, the slight difference for Partner A is due to rounding.)

JOURNAL			
Date	**Account Title and Explanation**	**Debit**	**Credit**
Jan 1	Cash	100,000	
	Partner A, Capital	1,666	
	Partner B, Capital	1,667	
	Partner C, Capital	1,667	
	Partner D, Capital		105,000
	To record admission of new partner		

FIGURE 4.29

Bonus on Withdrawal of Partner

The withdrawal of a partner can also create a situation where the cash given to a leaving partner is not equal to the capital in their account. Suppose Partner D has never joined the partnership, and instead Partner C wants to leave the business. This could be due to unresolved conflict with the other partners, unexpected life changes or any other reason. The desire to leave immediately may lead Partner C to accept a lesser amount of cash than what their capital account says should be received.

Suppose Partner C decides to leave and accepts $40,000 cash. In this scenario, both of the remaining partners receive a bonus based on the amount of Partner C's capital that was not paid out. This bonus to the remaining partners is split evenly. The impact on capital is shown in Figure 4.30.

	Partner A	Partner B	Partner C	Total
Capital balance before withdrawal of Partner C	$120,000	$150,000	$50,000	$320,000
Withdrawal of Partner C	5,000	5,000	-50,000	-40,000
Capital balance after withdrawal of Partner C	$125,000	$155,000	$0	$280,000

FIGURE 4.30

Equity and net assets decrease by $40,000, which is the amount of cash received by the departing partner. The remaining $10,000 is divided equally between Partners A and B. The journal entry to record this transaction is shown in Figure 4.31.

JOURNAL

Date	Account Title and Explanation	Debit	Credit
Jan 1	Partner C, Capital	50,000	
	Cash		40,000
	Partner A, Capital		5,000
	Partner B, Capital		5,000
	To record the withdrawal of a partner		

FIGURE 4.31

Alternatively, a partner may be leaving because the remaining partners want them out of the business. In this case, the incentive to Partner C to leave is cash payment in excess of the stated value of their capital.

Suppose Partner C is willing to leave if they receive $58,000 cash. In this scenario, both remaining partners give a bonus to the leaving partner. This bonus to the leaving partner is split evenly between the remaining partners. The impact on capital is shown in Figure 4.32.

	Partner A	Partner B	Partner C	Total
Capital balance before withdrawal of Partner C	$120,000	$150,000	50,000	$320,000
Withdrawal of Partner C	−4,000	−4,000	−50,000	−58,000
Capital balance after withdrawal of Partner C	$116,000	$146,000	$0	$262,000

FIGURE 4.32

Equity and net assets decrease by $58,000, which is the amount of cash received by the departing partner. Partners A and B must each give $4,000 of their capital to Partner C as a bonus, so their capital accounts are debited for that amount. The journal entry to record this transaction is shown in Figure 4.33.

JOURNAL

Date	Account Title and Explanation	Debit	Credit
Jan 1	Partner C, Capital	50,000	
	Partner A, Capital	4,000	
	Partner B, Capital	4,000	
	Cash		58,000
	To record the withdrawal of a partner		

FIGURE 4.33

Pause & Reflect

Exercise 4-3

Kelsey and Zac run a general partnership together. Kelsey has a capital balance of $110,000 and Zac has a capital balance of $150,000. They are looking to expand and want to bring in a new partner to help them grow the company. They find an interested person, Yelena, who has a good client list. They offer Yelena a one-third share in the partnership for an investment of $100,000. Any bonus will be shared evenly between Kelsey and Zac. Calculate the new balances of all three partners after the admission.

	Kelsey	Zac	Yelena	Total
Capital balance before admission				
Admission of new partner				
Capital balance after admission				

See Appendix I for solutions.

Liquidation of a Partnership

LO 8

A partnership has a limited life. If the partnership changes due to the addition or withdrawal of a partner, the existing partnership ends and a new partnership begins. Similarly, if the partners decide to end or sell the business, or if the partnership dissolves due to disagreement between partners or other factors, a process known as a **partnership liquidation** takes place. Liquidation means that the partnership as a business entity will legally cease to exist. The liquidation process involves selling off any partnership assets, paying off liabilities and distributing any remaining proceeds to the partners according to their individual profit and loss ratios.

As with the end of any business, the accounting cycle must first be completed to determine a starting point for the liquidation process. By now you have a firm understanding of the entire accounting cycle: journalizing and posting transactions, preparing a trial balance, preparing the financial statements, and preparing closing entries and the post-closing trial balance. Once these tasks are complete, the liquidation process can begin. This involves the following steps.

a. Sell off the partnership's non-cash assets for cash, and realize a gain or loss.
b. Allocate any gain or loss to the partners according to their individual profit and loss ratios.
c. Pay partnership liabilities (in cash) to creditors.
d. Distribute remaining proceeds to partners based on the balances in their capital accounts.

The last step is to distribute the remaining proceeds to partners according to their capital account balances. In many cases, all partners will have credit balances in their capital accounts. However, one or more partners may have a debit balance in their capital account, known as a capital deficiency. Both situations will be examined, starting with the most straightforward situation, where there is no capital deficiency.

Liquidation with No Capital Deficiency

First, consider a partnership liquidation based on the simplified balance sheet for ABC Partnership, in which there is no capital deficiency.

Suppose that before liquidation, ABC Partnership had assets valued at $700,000 and liabilities valued at $600,000, as shown on the balance sheet in Figure 4.34. Thus, net assets are equal to $100,000.

ABC Partnership Balance Sheet As at December 31, 2020			
Assets		**Liabilities and Partners' Capital**	
Cash	$100,000	**Liabilities**	
Land	600,000	Notes Payable	$200,000
		Accounts Payable	400,000
		Total Liabilities	600,000
		Partners' Capital	
		Partner A, Capital	35,000
		Partner B, Capital	40,000
		Partner C, Capital	25,000
		Total Partners' Capital	100,000
Total Assets	$700,000	**Total Liabilities and Partners' Capital**	$700,000

FIGURE 4.34

For this example, we will assume that profits and losses are divided equally among the three partners, that is, one-third each. The steps for liquidation are as follows.

ⓐ Sell off the partnership's non-cash assets for cash, and realize a gain or loss

Assume that on December 31, the business sells its non-cash asset, land, for $570,000. This represents a loss of $30,000 ($570,000 – $600,000). The journal entry for the sale is shown in Figure 4.35.

JOURNAL

Date	Account Title and Explanation	Debit	Credit
Dec 31	Cash	570,000	
	Loss on Sale of Assets	30,000	
	Land		600,000
	To record sale of land at a loss		

FIGURE 4.35

After the sale, the balance in the cash account is $670,000 ($100,000 + $570,000).

ⓑ Allocate any gain or loss to the partners according to their individual profit and loss ratios

The $30,000 loss is allocated as one-third ($10,000) to each partner. The journal entry for the allocation of the loss is shown in Figure 4.36.

JOURNAL

Date	Account Title and Explanation	Debit	Credit
Dec 31	Partner A, Capital	10,000	
	Partner B, Capital	10,000	
	Partner C, Capital	10,000	
	Loss on Sale of Assets		30,000
	To allocate loss on sale of assets		

FIGURE 4.36

c Pay partnership liabilities (in cash) to creditors

From the existing cash balance of $670,000, the partnership pays its liabilities as in the journal entry in Figure 4.37.

JOURNAL

Date	Account Title and Explanation	Debit	Credit
Dec 31	Notes Payable	200,000	
	Accounts Payable	400,000	
	Cash		600,000
	To pay liabilities		

FIGURE 4.37

After paying the partnership liabilities, the balance in the cash account is $70,000 ($670,000 – $600,000). With the non-cash assets sold and the liabilities paid, Figure 4.38 shows the effect on the partners' capital accounts and the balance of each before the cash is distributed to the partners.

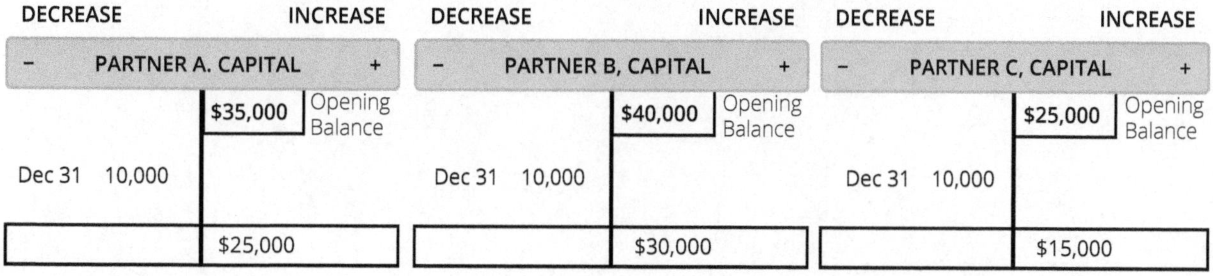

FIGURE 4.38

d Distribute remaining proceeds to partners based on the balances in their capital accounts

The entry to distribute the remaining cash to the partners is shown in Figure 4.39.

JOURNAL			
Date	**Account Title and Explanation**	**Debit**	**Credit**
Dec 31	Partner A, Capital	25,000	
	Partner B, Capital	30,000	
	Partner C, Capital	15,000	
	Cash		70,000
	To record cash distribution among partners		

FIGURE 4.39

Figure 4.40 summarizes the steps involved in the liquidation. The numbers in blue circles correspond to the steps already described.

	Assets		= Liabilities		+ Partners' Capital		
	Cash	**Land**	**Loan Payable**	**Accounts Payable**	**Partner A, Capital**	**Partner B, Capital**	**Partner C, Capital**
Before liquidation	$100,000	$600,000	$200,000	$400,000	$35,000	$40,000	$25,000
a b Sell assets and realize loss	570,000	-600,000			-10,000	-10,000	-10,000
c Pay partnership liabilities	670,000	0	200,000	400,000	25,000	30,000	15,000
	-600,000		-200,000	-400,000			
d Distribute remaining proceeds to partners	70,000	0	0	0	25,000	30,000	15,000
	-70,000				-25,000	-30,000	-15,000
Final balances	$ 0	$ 0	$ 0	$ 0	$ 0	$ 0	$ 0

FIGURE 4.40

This example involved allocating a loss on sale of assets. Any gain is allocated in the same manner—equally, unless otherwise provided for—and the cash is divided according to each partner's final balance of equity in the business.

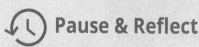

Pause & Reflect

Exercise 4-4

On November 30, 2020, Diana and Kate liquidated their general partnership. Before the liquidation, Diana had a capital balance of $70,000 and Kate had a capital balance of $90,000. The partnership has a cash balance of $30,000, non-cash assets worth $240,000 and liabilities worth $110,000. The non-cash assets are sold for $200,000. Any gain or loss on the sale of assets is split evenly between Diana and Kate.

Prepare the journal entries to liquidate the partnership and distribute any remaining cash to the partners.

JOURNAL			
Date	**Account Title and Explanation**	**Debit**	**Credit**

See Appendix I for solutions.

Liquidation with a Capital Deficiency

Sometimes, one or more partners have a debit balance in their capital account, known as a **capital deficiency**. Capital deficiencies occur for many reasons, including normal business losses, cash withdrawals that exceed a partner's capital account balance or a negative balance that arises during the process of liquidation. Let us look again at the previous example, but under different circumstances.

We will assume that the non-cash assets have been sold and the liabilities have been paid. Prior to distributing the remaining proceeds to the partners, the balances of the partners' capital accounts are as follows: Partner A, $25,000; Partner B, $30,000; and Partner C, –$2,500. Partner C's account has a capital deficiency of $2,500, and so Partner C owes the partnership that amount. Legally, Partner A and Partner B have a claim against Partner C's personal assets. One of two situations can exist: Partner C has enough personal cash to pay the $2,500, or Partner C is unable to pay what is owed.

Partner Can Pay Deficiency

If Partner C has sufficient personal cash to pay the $2,500 deficit to the partnership, the journal entry in Figure 4.41 is made to record the payment. This payment brings Partner C's capital account balance to zero, thereby fulfilling their obligation to the partnership and completing the liquidation process.

JOURNAL			
Date	**Account Title and Explanation**	**Debit**	**Credit**
Dec 31	Cash	2,500	
	Partner C, Capital		2,500
	To record the payment of capital deficiency by Partner C		

FIGURE 4.41

Partner Cannot Pay Deficiency

What if Partner C does not have enough cash to pay the $2,500 owed to the partnership? The partnership characteristic of unlimited liability means that if one partner is unable to meet obligations related to the partnership, the other partners are obligated to pay. Partner A and Partner B must absorb the loss according to their agreement—in this case, equally. Partner A and Partner B each need to decrease their own capital by $1,250 to cover the $2,500 capital deficiency, bringing Partner C's capital account balance to zero. The journal entry for this transaction is shown in Figure 4.42.

JOURNAL			
Date	**Account Title and Explanation**	**Debit**	**Credit**
Dec 31	Partner A, Capital	1,250	
	Partner B, Capital	1,250	
	Partner C, Capital		2,500
	To record the payment of Partner C's capital deficiency by Partner A and Partner B		

FIGURE 4.42

The partners are now able to close the partnership accounts and complete the liquidation process. Beyond this, Partners A and B may decide to pursue Partner C legally to get back the money they lost, although if Partner C cannot pay the partnership the amount owed, it is unlikely they would be able to pay Partners A and B.

In Summary

LO 1 Describe the characteristics, advantages and disadvantages of a partnership

- A partnership is an association of two or more people who jointly own a business, for which earnings are taxed at a personal level only.
- A partnership is a legal entity; however, partners generally have unlimited liability.
- Partnership advantages include raising more capital and having more expertise, since more people are involved in creating the business. Partnerships can also be easy to create.
- Disadvantages can include unlimited liability and mutual agency.

LO 2 Describe different types of partnerships

- A general partnership means that all partners have unlimited liability.
- A limited partnership divides a company's partners into two categories: general partners and limited partners. General partners have unlimited liability because they are involved in the day-to-day decision-making of the business. Limited partners, on the other hand, are liable for only the amount of capital they invest in the business. This is known as limited liability.
- A limited liability partnership, or LLP, is a legal ownership structure used in some jurisdictions that usually protects professionals from a partner's negligence. If one partner is sued, the others are not necessarily liable. However, all partners are liable for any debts owed to regular day-to-day creditors.

LO 3 Record the formation of a partnership

- Even though a partnership agreement in the form of a legal written contract is not required to form a partnership, having such an agreement lessens the chance of legal and ethical conflict between partners and specifies the purpose of the business and the relationships between the partners.
- Assets that partners bring into the business are recorded at their fair market values. Each partner's opening capital is calculated by deducting the total amount of liabilities from the total amount of assets that each partner brings into the business.

LO 4 Record the division of income or loss

- A partnership's earnings can be divided in a number of different ways; these are usually outlined in the partnership agreement. Four common methods of dividing earnings are the following: equally; based on a ratio; based on the capital contribution of each partner; and withdrawing salaries and interest before dividing the rest.
- To record the division of income, the income summary account is debited and the partners' capital accounts are credited. To record the division of loss, the partners' capital accounts are debited and the income summary account is credited.

LO 5 Record partners' withdrawals

- When a partner withdraws cash from the business for personal use, the partner's withdrawals account is debited and cash is credited.
- Each partner's withdrawals account is closed at the end of each accounting period by debiting the partner's capital account and crediting the partner's withdrawals account.

LO 6 Prepare financial statements for a partnership

- Four basic financial statements are prepared by partnerships: the income statement, the statement of partners' equity, the balance sheet and the statement of cash flows. Partnership financial statements are quite similar to those of sole proprietorships, except that they include capital accounts for each partner.

LO 7 Account for the addition or withdrawal of a partner

- A new partner can simply add a new portion of partner's equity, or they can purchase some or all of another partner's share.
- When a partner withdraws from a partnership, the capital of the withdrawn partner can be bought out using either the existing partners' personal assets or the partnership's assets. If the personal assets of the existing partners are used, a credit or an increase in the existing partners' capital is recorded in the partnership's journal. If the partnership's assets are used, a credit or a decrease in the partnership's assets is recorded.
- If the amount of capital allocated to a new partner is different from the cash invested, a bonus is allocated to either the existing partners or the new partner.
- If the amount of cash paid to a departing partner is different from their capital account, a bonus is allocated to either the existing partners or the leaving partner.

LO 8 Record the liquidation of a partnership

- The partnership agreement should stipulate how the liquidation is to be done. If assets are sold above or below book value, the corresponding gains or losses are shared among the partners. The remaining cash can be distributed according to the balance in each partner's capital account.

Review Exercise 4-1

On January 1, 2020, Zelma Rapoza, Serena Dennen and Sharon Thorne have decided to set up a spa and operate it as a general partnership. They will each contribute $10,000 to buy equipment and help pay for lease expenses. Zelma is also contributing $25,000 of her own equipment.

They agree to pay themselves an annual salary of $5,000 each. Since Zelma contributed the equipment, she expects $3,000 "rent" per year on the equipment for ten years. Each partner is to earn 5% on her investment (cash contribution). The net income for the year 2020 was $25,000. The profit remaining after salaries, rent and interest is to be distributed at the ratio of each partner's cash contribution.

Required

a) Prepare a schedule showing the changes in capital during 2020.

b) Prepare journal entries for the following transactions.

Jan 1	The initial cash contribution
Jan 1	The equipment contribution
Dec 31	The division of partnership income, assuming that revenues and expenses have already been closed to the income summary account
Jan 2, 2021	Sharon retires from the partnership. In order to exit the partnership, she decides to sell her share to Zelma and Serena, who contribute $10,000 and $7,333 of their personal assets, respectively.

JOURNAL

Date	Account Title and Explanation	Debit	Credit

See Appendix I for solutions.

Notes

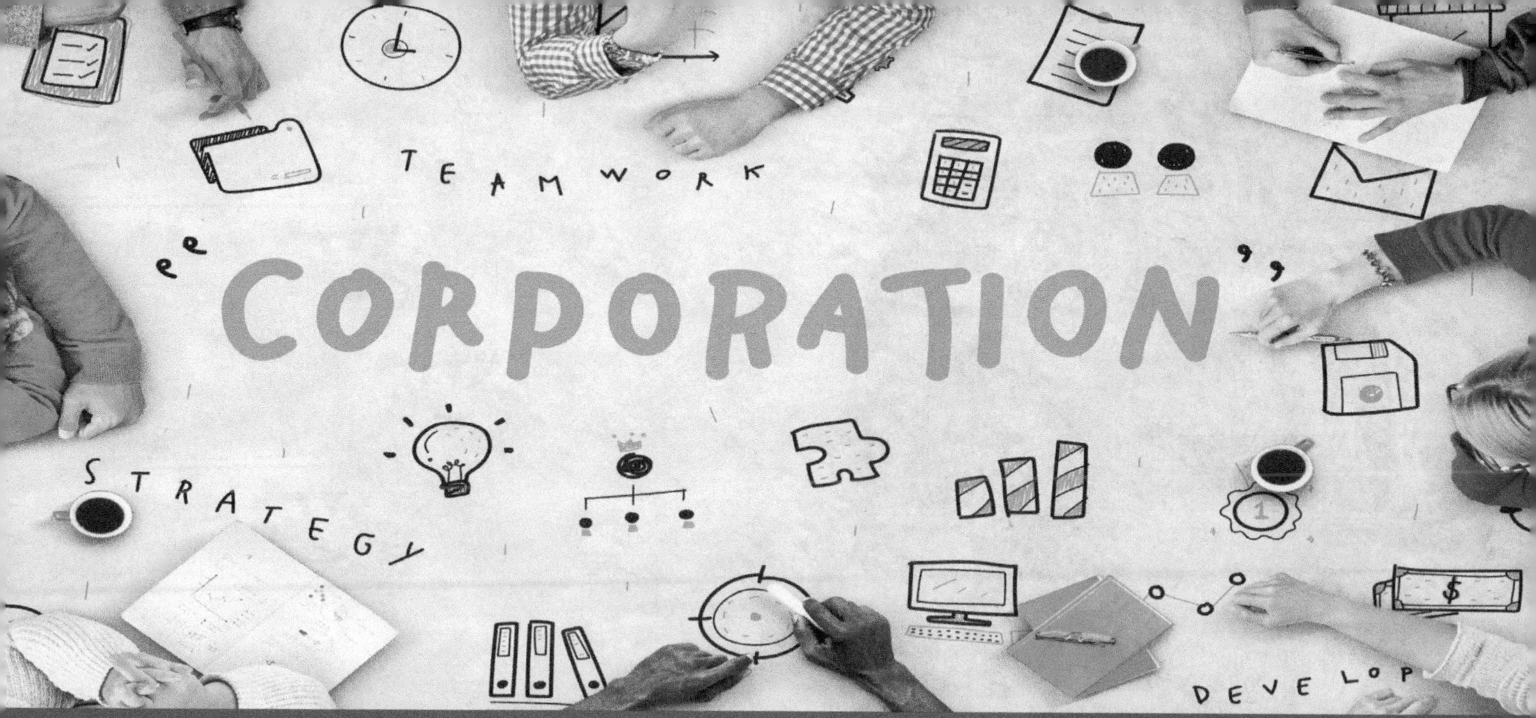

Chapter 5
Corporations: Contributed Capital and Dividends

Learning Objectives

LO 1 Describe the characteristics of corporations
- Characteristics of a Corporation
- Organization Costs

LO 2 Describe differences between public and private corporations
- IFRS vs. ASPE Reporting Requirements

LO 3 Explain shareholders' equity
- Par Value Shares and No-Par Value Shares
- The Classes of Shares: Common and Preferred

LO 4 Record the issuance of shares
- Issuing Shares for Cash
- Issuing Shares in Exchange for Non-Cash Assets or Services
- Accounting for Share Issue Costs

LO 5 Record the payment of cash dividends
- On the Date of Declaration
- On the Date of Record
- On the Date of Payment
- Dividends in Arrears

LO 6 Record stock splits and stock dividends
- Stock Split
- Stock Dividend
- Restrictions on the Use of Retained Earnings

LO 7 Record income tax expense

LO 8 Record closing entries for corporations

LO 9 Calculate retained earnings

LO 10 Explain the importance of ethics for corporate reporting

Appendix 5A

LO 11 Record the reacquisition of shares
- Average Cost of Shares
- Reacquiring Shares: Less Than the Average Cost
- Reacquiring Shares: More Than the Average Cost

AMEENGAGE™ Access **ameengage.com** for integrated resources including tutorials, practice exercises, the digital textbook and more.

MAKING IT REAL TO YOU

You may recall the concept of net worth. Your personal net worth is what is left if you cash out—that is, successfully sell your assets and get the value equivalent to the recorded amount—and pay everything you owe (your liabilities). Tracking the amount you are worth is a fundamental component of accounting in both your personal life and business life.

For a business, net worth is referred to as equity. Amounts that increase equity but are not earned are known as capital. A corporation raises capital, and therefore increases its equity, by issuing new shares. On the other hand, dividends paid out by a corporation decrease its equity. They are similar to withdrawals out of your bank account in relation to your own personal net worth.

In this chapter, you will learn about the corporate form of business and about corporate equity.

The Corporate Form of Organization

LO 1

So far we have demonstrated accounting practices related to sole proprietorships and partnerships. These two types of business are usually operated and managed by their owners. In sole proprietorships and partnerships, the owners provide their own funding for the business. They can fund the business with their personal assets or by taking out a loan and incurring debt. Whether the owners use their own assets or borrow money, they are personally liable for all debts of the business. A sole proprietorship or a partnership exists as long as the owners are alive and decide to continue its operation.

There is a different type of business known as a corporation. A **corporation** is a legal entity that is separate from its owners. In a corporation, the owners are known as **shareholders**, because they hold **shares** of equity in the corporation. A corporation is granted a charter, or articles of incorporation, under federal, provincial or territorial law, which formally creates the corporation. The corporation's management and board of directors then establish a set of bylaws, the rules and procedures that govern how the corporation's affairs are to be conducted. Figure 5.1 shows how sole proprietorships and partnerships differ from corporations in terms of equity.

SOLE PROPRIETORSHIP	PARTNERSHIP	CORPORATION
OWNER'S EQUITY	PARTNERS' EQUITY	SHAREHOLDERS' EQUITY
OWNER'S CAPITAL	PARTNER A, CAPITAL	COMMON SHARES
	PARTNER B, CAPITAL	RETAINED EARNINGS

FIGURE 5.1

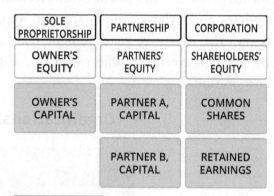

Characteristics of a Corporation

All corporations have certain characteristics in common that govern their duties, rights and responsibilities, and we will look at each one in more detail. Note that the accounting practices of for-profit corporations are different from those of nonprofit organizations; this textbook focuses on the accounting practices of for-profit corporations.

Separate Legal Existence

A corporation is a separate legal entity that has the rights and responsibilities of a person. This means that the corporation is legally separate from its owners, known as shareholders. As a distinct entity, the corporation itself owns the business's assets and liabilities and, like a person, can enter into its own contracts, such as those for the purchase or sale of property. It is responsible for its own actions and for its own debts. It has the right to sue and can be sued.

Limited Liability of Shareholders

Because a corporation is legally separate from its owners, the shareholders are not responsible for any actions or debts of the business. Shareholders are liable for only the amount that they have invested in the company, giving them what is called limited liability. In other words, the shareholders cannot be held personally liable for the debts of the corporation. The concept of limited liability was introduced in the partnership chapter, specifically in the discussion of limited partnerships and limited liability partnerships.

Formal Organizational Structure

At the heart of a corporation is the separation of ownership and management. In a large corporation, the company's shareholders may have very little to do with managing the business. As owners of the business, shareholders are responsible for electing a board of directors to oversee the business on their behalf. The board of directors is responsible for deciding on the corporation's operational policies and bylaws. The board also appoints the external auditors and an executive management team. The executive management team acts as the company's legal agents and is usually headed by a chief executive officer (CEO). Figure 5.2 shows the typical organizational structure of a corporation.

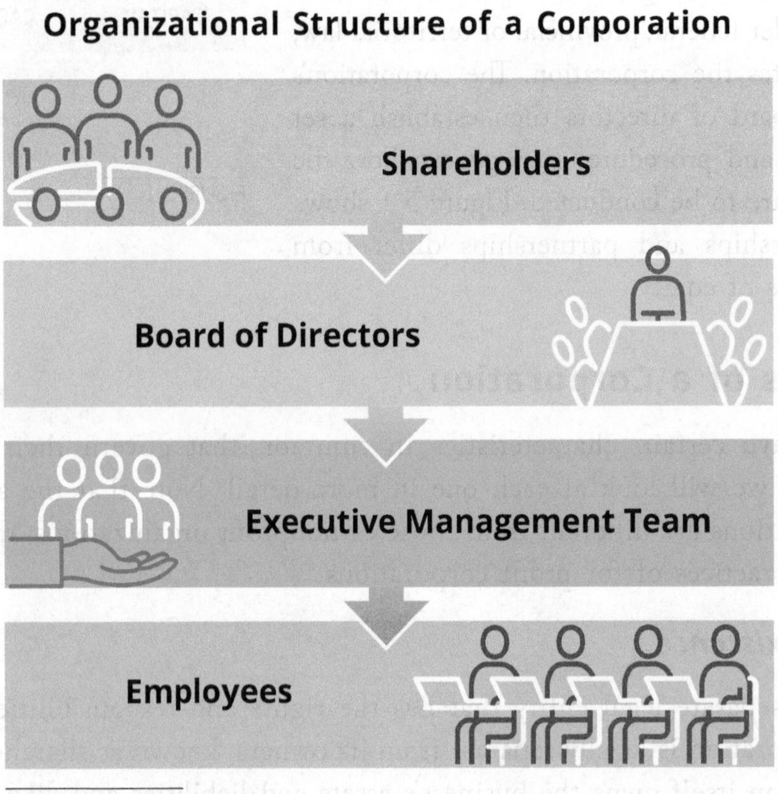

FIGURE 5.2

Lack of Mutual Agency

In contrast to owners of proprietorships and partnerships, owners of a corporation (i.e. shareholders) lack *mutual agency*, meaning they cannot act as agents of the business. Any contract signed by shareholders would not be binding for the whole business. Only managers and officers of a corporation have the power to commit the business to a contract.

Unlimited Life

The life of a corporation continues despite the death of any shareholders. Shares can be bequeathed or sold with no interruption to the continuation of the company's operations. As you have learned previously, this is not the case with either a partnership or a sole proprietorship.

Ability to Raise Capital

When a corporation needs to raise capital to finance day-to-day operations or to invest in property and equipment, it can issue shares. Shares are an attractive investment because they offer limited liability and have the potential to increase in value. They also offer liquidity, which is the investor's ability to quickly buy and sell them.

When an investor buys shares, the corporation sometimes issues a share certificate as proof of the shareholder's ownership in the corporation. The share certificate is a printed document that includes the company's name, the shareholder's name and the number of shares owned. Printed share certificates are not always issued unless requested by the investor, because many investors now maintain accounts with brokerages who keep these records electronically for their clients.

Income Tax Treatment

As a separate legal entity, a corporation must file a tax return and pay income tax on its earnings. Shareholders do not pay income tax on the earnings of the corporation. They are, however, required to pay personal income tax on any income that they receive in the form of dividends. A **dividend** is a distribution of the corporation's earnings (net income) to shareholders based on the shares that they own. You will learn more about dividends later in this chapter.

The term **double taxation** refers to the fact that a corporation pays income tax on its earnings and shareholders pay personal income tax on their dividends. This requirement does not necessarily mean the government receives $2 in income tax instead of $1. It simply means that tax is paid twice (at different rates) on earnings. The corporation earns income, pays corporate income tax and, from the remaining income after tax, pays dividends to shareholders. Shareholders then pay personal income tax on the dividends.

Government Requirements

A corporation is owned by its shareholders, and it is responsible to them for its financial results. Corporations are required to meet strict federal and provincial or territorial government regulations. When a corporation is formed, it must file government documents known as articles of incorporation. The **articles of incorporation** (or *corporate charter*) contain the operational details of the corporation, including its name, purpose and general objectives.

Corporations must also meet certain requirements for issuing shares and distributing income to shareholders. They must regularly report on their financial results and operations and conduct formal shareholder meetings. Although the corporate structure has many advantages, it also has legal obligations that require lawyers to be hired, forms to be completed and documents to be prepared and filed.

Figure 5.3 compares the characteristics of a sole proprietorship, a partnership and a corporation.

Characteristics of Business Organizations			
	Sole Proprietorship	**Partnership**	**Corporation**
Owners	One individual	Two or more individuals	One or more shareholders
Owner liability	Unlimited	Unlimited	Limited
Life of business	Limited	Limited	Unlimited
Taxation of earnings	• Taxed at the individual's personal tax rate • Paid by owner	• Taxed at each partner's personal tax rate • Paid by partners	• Taxed at corporate tax rate • Paid by corporation
Example	Indra's Bookkeeping Services	PricewaterhouseCoopers	General Electric Company

FIGURE 5.3

The corporate form of organization allows businesses to do things on a larger scale and in a formally structured way. It also brings certain duties, rights and responsibilities that can be viewed as advantages and disadvantages, as shown in Figure 5.4.

Advantages of a Corporation	Disadvantages of a Corporation
• Separate legal existence • Limited liability of shareholders • Formal organizational structure • Lack of mutual agency • Unlimited life • Ability to raise capital	• Strict government requirements • Double taxation of corporation and shareholders • Potentially high cost of government registration and ongoing compliance

FIGURE 5.4

Organization Costs

Organization costs are the initial expenditures incurred to organize or form a corporation, such as incorporation fees, legal fees, taxes and licence fees. These costs are generally recorded as a debit to an asset account called organization costs, as they are

> **ASPE vs. IFRS**
>
> ASPE allows organization costs to be capitalized as an intangible asset or to be treated as an expense, as long as the same accounting policy is applied to all such costs.
>
> IFRS treats organization costs as an expense, except in special circumstances.

associated with forming an organization. Many companies treat this cost as an intangible asset and amortize it over a short period of time. Under specific conditions, companies might be able to expense this cost instead of capitalizing it. Figure 5.5 illustrates the journal entry for a corporation's organization costs of $1,500 on September 1, 2020.

JOURNAL

Date	Account Title and Explanation	Debit	Credit
Sep 1	Organization Costs	1,500	
	Cash		1,500
	To record costs incurred in organizing the corporation		

FIGURE 5.5

Public vs. Private Corporations

LO 2

As a separate legal entity, a corporation has the right to be formed as either a public or a private corporation. A **public corporation** is one that trades its shares on a stock exchange, such as the Toronto Stock Exchange (TSX) or the Montreal Exchange (MX). Trading simply means buying or selling shares. That is, its shares are available to be traded publicly from one member of the general public (the seller) to another (the purchaser).

A **private corporation** is one that does not offer its shares to the public. The company's shares are instead owned and exchanged privately. For example, a private corporation may have a single owner who wishes never to sell the shares publicly. A private corporation may also have several owners who belong to the same family and who have no intention of selling shares on a stock exchange. A private corporation can also be referred to as a closed corporation or a privately held corporation.

In the Real World

A Canadian-controlled private corporation (CCPC) is a private corporation that is entitled to certain tax rates and deductions if it meets specific guidelines. Not all private corporations that operate in Canada are classified as CCPCs.

A private enterprise might choose to become a CCPC for the corporate tax advantages. A discussion of the specific tax benefits is outside the scope of this course, but they include additional time to pay some types of taxes, higher investment tax credits and potential capital gains exemptions.

Below are some of the requirements for a company to qualify as a registered CCPC in Canada.

- The company's shares are not traded on any stock exchange.
- The corporation is controlled by only Canadian residents.
- The corporation is not directly or indirectly controlled by a nonresident shareholder.

The financial reporting requirements for private companies are different from those of public companies. The reporting standards for public corporations are generally more strict and detailed than those for private companies, since more external users depend on the financial statements of public corporations.

IFRS vs. ASPE Reporting Requirements

In Canada, all publicly traded corporations must use International Financial Reporting Standards (IFRS). Private corporations have a choice of following IFRS or Accounting Standards for Private Enterprises (ASPE), as shown in Figure 5.6. A private corporation usually has only a few shareholders, most of whom may be closely related and involved in the day-to-day operation of the business. Given that a private corporation does not sell its shares to the general public, its shareholders may not see the need for the more stringent reporting standards required under IFRS. Some exceptions exist, including if a private corporation has issued publicly held bonds, in which case IFRS must be used.

Reporting Options for Private Corporations

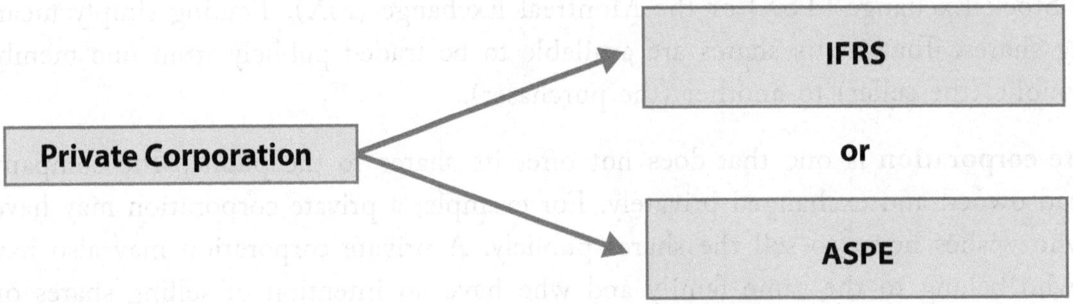

FIGURE 5.6

A private corporation may choose to use ASPE rather than incur the high costs of retraining staff and converting to IFRS. ASPE requires fewer disclosures in financial reporting than IFRS. IFRS can be much more technically complex.

On the other hand, a private corporation may choose to switch from ASPE to IFRS if its owners are considering making it a public corporation. In order to issue shares to the public, the corporation must comply with IFRS. A private corporation may also choose to switch to IFRS if it has international operations or wants the ability to compare its own financial statements to international competitors. Whichever standard the company decides to follow, it is required to include this information in its financial statements so that users are informed.

In the next chapter, financial statements will be shown in accordance with ASPE guidelines and differences under IFRS will then be discussed. But first, some of the specific accounting requirements of corporations will be discussed in more detail.

Accounting for Shareholders' Equity

LO 3

In a sole proprietorship, owner's equity is a simple figure that represents the net worth of the business. In a partnership, equity is divided into separate capital accounts for each partner's stake in the business. With a corporation, as the ownership structure gets more complicated, so does the recording and reporting of equity on the company's balance sheet. In the simplest terms, equity represents the owners' claims on the net assets of the business.

In a corporation, the shareholders actually own the company and so owners' equity is called **shareholders' equity**. Shareholders' equity is comprised of two components: contributed capital and retained earnings. These components are reported as separate items in the shareholders' equity section of the financial statements.

Contributed capital is generally comprised of two subcategories called share capital and contributed surplus, as shown in Figure 5.7. **Share capital** refers to capital raised from the sale of shares (common shares or preferred shares), and **contributed surplus** contains other types of additions to shareholders' contributions. The focus in this section will be on the issuance of shares, and the impact of accounting for contributed surplus will be discussed in more detail in the appendix to this chapter.

Retained earnings are the earnings that are kept and accumulated by the company after dividends have been paid to the shareholders. *Dividends* are distributions of the company's earnings to shareholders, and the earnings not paid out to shareholders are retained in the business. Net income is added to the retained earnings; net loss and dividends of the company are subtracted from the retained earnings. Since most companies generate net income and do not pay out all their earnings in dividends, the account of retained earnings generally has a credit balance. If the retained earnings account has a debit balance, it is called a *deficit*.

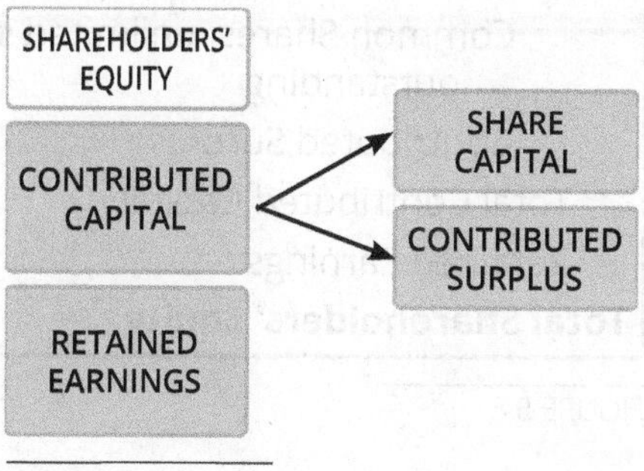

FIGURE 5.7

The articles of incorporation specify the number of shares a corporation is authorized to issue, the types of shares to be issued and the rights of the shareholders for each type of share. A corporation can offer for sale an unlimited number of shares, or it can specify a particular number of shares. Regardless of the stipulation in the articles of incorporation, a company will decide on the maximum number of shares that can legally be issued, known as the company's **authorized shares**. If the company later decides it needs to issue more shares, additional authorization is required.

When the company sells some shares out of its authorized shares, they become **issued shares**. Once shares have been issued, they can be sold by or transferred from one investor to other investors without involving the corporation. This is known as trading on the secondary market. **Outstanding shares** are shares that have been authorized and issued and are held by shareholders. Issued and outstanding shares would be either equal to or less than the total number of shares authorized at any given time. It is the shares issued that impact assets and equity of a corporation rather than the shares authorized.

In the secondary market, shares are sold at a price known as its **market value.** The market value is determined by the amount that investors are willing to pay for them. This means that the shares may be sold at a higher or lower price than what the original holder paid for them.

When we examine the balance sheet of a corporation, the share figure shows the total amount of money received by the corporation when it initially sold the shares to the shareholders. This value is the book value of the shares and has no bearing on the market value of the shares. If the company is doing well, the market value is likely higher than the book value. If the company is not doing well, the market value is likely lower than the book value.

Figure 5.8 shows the shareholders' equity section of a balance sheet, illustrating how the classes of shares are typically presented. Each component of this statement is explained in detail throughout this chapter, including the appendix.

Standard Corporation Balance Sheet (partial) As at December 31, 2020	
Shareholders' Equity	
Contributed Capital	
Preferred Shares, 7% noncumulative, 4,000 shares authorized and issued	$80,000
Common Shares, unlimited shares authorized, 50,000 shares issued, 49,000 shares outstanding	500,000
Contributed Surplus	70,000
Total Contributed Capital	650,000
Retained Earnings	300,000
Total Shareholders' Equity	$950,000

FIGURE 5.8

Par Value Shares and No-Par Value Shares

Shares may or may not have a par value. **Par value shares** are issued with an assigned value. **No-par value shares** are issued with no assigned value. When no-par value shares are issued, the equity account is credited for the entire proceeds of the sale. The Canada Business Corporations Act (CBCA) and most provincial and territorial business corporation acts prohibit the use of par value shares. For this chapter, we will assume all shares are no-par value shares.

The Classes of Shares: Common and Preferred

All public corporations must issue common shares. **Common shares** are a type of equity that gives shareholders ownership in the corporation, along with voting rights to elect a board of directors and the potential to receive a portion of the company's earnings in the form of dividends. Investors buy common shares with the expectation that the corporation will remain or become profitable, although the payment of dividends is not guaranteed. A corporation may offer several different classes of common shares with different voting rights in order for a specific group of investors to be able to maintain control of the company without having to buy more shares. For example, a corporation that has two classes of common shares may give 10 voting rights to a holder of Class A shares versus only one voting right to a holder of Class B shares.

A corporation may also issue preferred shares, a type of share with features that are not available with common shares. **Preferred shares** receive preference because dividends must first be paid on them before any dividends are paid on common shares. This preference, however, does not guarantee that dividends will be paid.

In the event of a company liquidation, preferred shareholders also have priority over common shareholders regarding the assets of the liquidating company. Preferred shareholders, however, have no voting rights to influence the direction of the company. Only common shareholders hold voting rights, an important aspect of company ownership.

Cumulative shares are a type of preferred shares that give shareholders the right to be paid the current year's dividends and to accumulate any unpaid dividends from previous years. With cumulative preferred shares, if no dividend is declared by the board of directors, or if a dividend payment is otherwise missed, the dividends owing will accumulate and must be paid before any dividends are paid to the common shareholders. With cumulative preferred shares, any unpaid dividends from prior periods are known as **dividends in arrears**. Preferred shares that do not have the right to receive any accumulated unpaid dividends are known as **noncumulative shares.**

Preferred shares usually indicate the amount of dividends that each share will receive on the share certificate, stated either as dollars per share or as a percent of par. To illustrate, a preferred share with a $20 value and a $2 per share dividend could be expressed as having dividends of either preferred $2 share at $20 or preferred 10% share at $20.

In terms of dividend entitlement, preferred shares can be designated as either participating or nonparticipating. **Nonparticipating preferred shares** limit the dividends that can be issued to preferred shareholders each year. The limit (or maximum) is the amount stated on the share certificates. This ensures that any dividend declared goes to the preferred shareholders first, protecting their entitlement. For example, suppose a company has 2,000 common shares outstanding, and 200 nonparticipating preferred shares with a stated dividend of $12 per share. The board of directors declares a dividend of $4,000. First, the preferred shareholders receive dividends of $2,400 (200 shares × $12 per share maximum). The common shareholders then receive the remaining dividends of $1,600 ($4,000 – $2,400).

Participating preferred shares entitle preferred shareholders to share with common shareholders any dividends paid in excess of the percentage stated on the preferred share certificates. This means that the dividend shown on the share certificate represents the minimum entitlement, and higher dividends could be paid out. It should be noted that participating preferred shares are not often issued by companies.

Figure 5.9 summarizes the most important features of common and preferred shares.

Features of Common Shares	Features of Preferred Shares
Common shareholders: • elect the board of directors • vote on corporate policy • rank after creditors and preferred shareholders in the event of a liquidation • have the right to receive dividends only if declared by the board of directors	Preferred shareholders: • have a higher claim on assets than do common shareholders in the case of a company liquidation • are paid first If dividends are declared, before any dividends are paid to common shareholders • have the right to accumulate unpaid dividends from previous years if their shares are cumulative • receive a limited (maximum) dividend per year if their shares are nonparticipating

FIGURE 5.9

ASPE vs. IFRS

ASPE is not as strict as IFRS when it comes to the disclosure of various classes of shares. Under ASPE, only the classes of shares that have been issued are required to be disclosed.

However, under IFRS, all classes of shares authorized must be disclosed, even if they are not issued.

Issuing Shares

LO 4

One of the advantages of the public corporate form of ownership is the company's ability to raise cash by selling shares to the public. We will look at the different ways a corporation can issue shares and how the transactions are recorded in the company's accounting records. The issuance of shares increases a company's assets and shareholders' equity. We will review accounting for issuances of shares for cash and also issuances for nonmonetary assets or services in the following sections.

Issuing Shares for Cash

When shares are issued, the common shares account (or the preferred shares account if preferred shares are issued) is credited for the entire proceeds of the sale. To illustrate, suppose that on April 10, 2020, a corporation issues 20,000 common shares for $20 per share. Figure 5.10 shows the journal entry for the transaction.

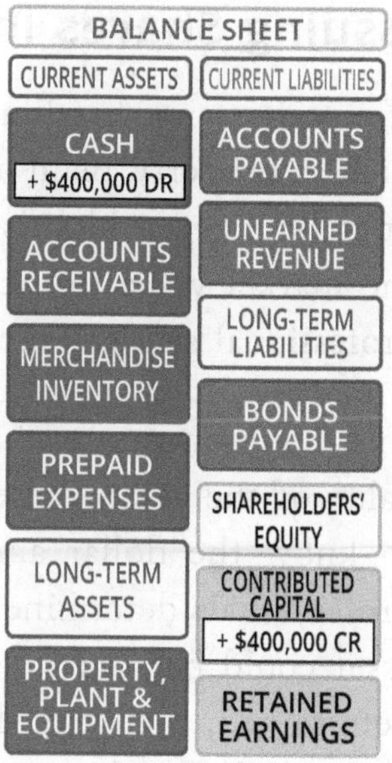

JOURNAL

Date	Account Title and Explanation	Debit	Credit
Apr 10	Cash	400,000	
	Common Shares		400,000
	To record issue of 20,000 common shares at $20 per share		

FIGURE 5.10

While the preceding example refers to the issuance of common shares, the accounting for issuing preferred shares would be similar. Recall that contributed capital within shareholders' equity includes capital raised from issuing both common and preferred shares.

To illustrate, suppose that on September 30, 2020, a corporation issues 30,000 preferred shares for $10 per share. Figure 5.11 shows the journal entry for this transaction.

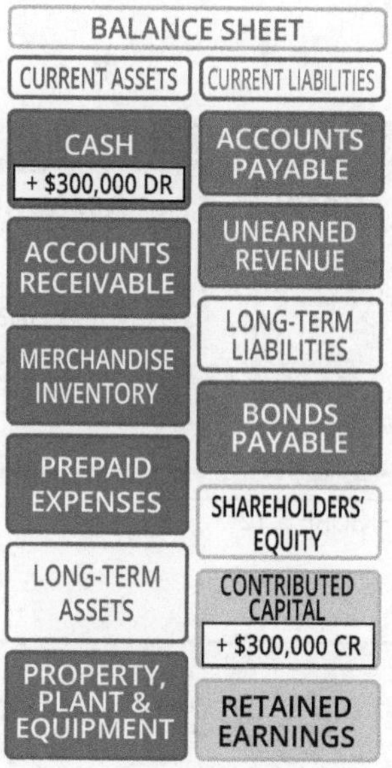

JOURNAL

Date	Account Title and Explanation	Debit	Credit
Sep 30	Cash	300,000	
	Preferred Shares		300,000
	To record issue of 30,000 preferred shares at $10 per share		

FIGURE 5.11

Issuing Shares in Exchange for Non-Cash Assets or Services

If a corporation has limited cash, it may offer shares to a supplier in exchange for non-cash assets, such as property, plant and equipment. Suppliers may be willing to make the exchange since shares offer liquidity, which is the ability to trade them at their market value, and there is potential for the market value to increase. Likewise, a corporation may offer shares instead of cash payment for professional services such as legal fees.

In a nonmonetary exchange, the parties involved with the transaction still need to determine the value of the assets or services that are being exchanged. Most importantly, the corporation needs to know the dollar amount at which the transaction will be recorded. Accountants and other professionals determine this amount using the concept of **fair value**, which is the amount that the asset could be sold for in the open market. Under IFRS, if the fair value of the asset cannot be determined, then the share issuance transaction is recorded at the fair value of the shares being exchanged. The fair market value of the shares of a public corporation can usually be taken from the stock market on the day of the transaction. ASPE requires recording based on the fair market value that is most reliable.

To illustrate, assume that on February 25, 2020, a corporation issues 20,000 common shares at the current market value of $40 in exchange for equipment. The fair value of the equipment cannot be determined. Therefore, the common shares account is credited at the the market value of the shares. Figure 5.12 shows how this transaction is recorded.

JOURNAL

Date	Account Title and Explanation	Debit	Credit
Feb 25	Equipment	800,000	
	Common Shares		800,000
	To record issue of 20,000 common shares for equipment		

FIGURE 5.12

ASPE vs. IFRS

To record the issuance of shares for non-cash items, ASPE allows using the fair market value of either the asset given up or the shares issued, whichever is more reliable.

IFRS, however, requires using the fair market value of the asset first. If that is not determined, then the fair value of shares can be used instead.

The share value of a private corporation may not be easy to determine, since a private corporation does not sell shares on a stock exchange. In this case, it is likely easier to determine the fair value of the asset or service and use that as the value for the transaction.

For example, on March 18, 2020, a private corporation issues 1,000 common shares in exchange for land that is appraised at $1,000,000. The transaction is recorded as shown in Figure 5.13.

The purchase increases land, a long-term asset account, with a debit. The corresponding $1,000,000 credit is recorded in the common shares account and reported in the shareholders' equity section of the balance sheet.

JOURNAL

Date	Account Title and Explanation	Debit	Credit
Mar 18	Land	1,000,000	
	Common Shares		1,000,000
	To record issue of 1,000 common shares for land valued at $1,000,000		

FIGURE 5.13

The concept and determination of fair value can also be used if a corporation wants to issue shares in exchange for professional services. Suppose that a new corporation requires the services of an accountant. The accounting services total $10,000. The corporation considers this expenditure costly and hard on its cash flow. On March 21, 2020, the company offers to issue to the accountant 1,000 common shares at their current market value of $10 per share, to equal the fair value of $10,000. The accountant accepts the offer of shares in exchange for accounting services. Figure 5.14 shows how the transaction is recorded on the company's books.

JOURNAL

Date	Account Title and Explanation	Debit	Credit
Mar 21	Accounting Fees Expense	10,000	
	Common Shares		10,000
	To record issue of 1,000 common shares in exchange for accounting services		

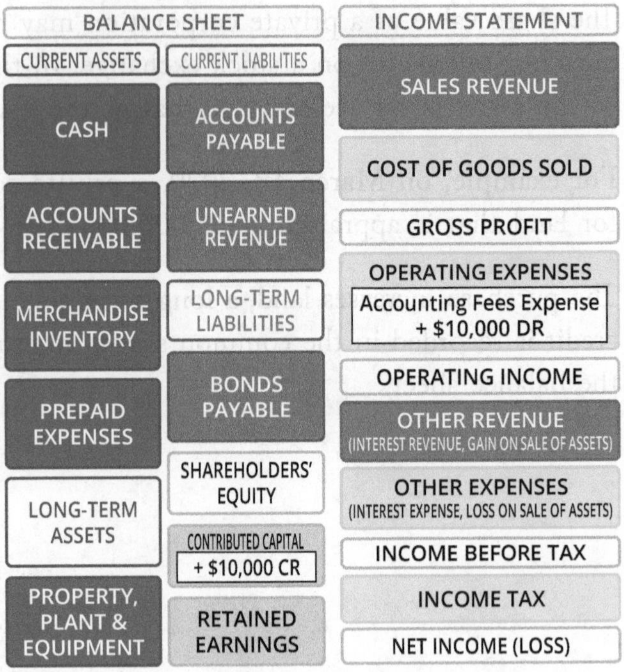

FIGURE 5.14

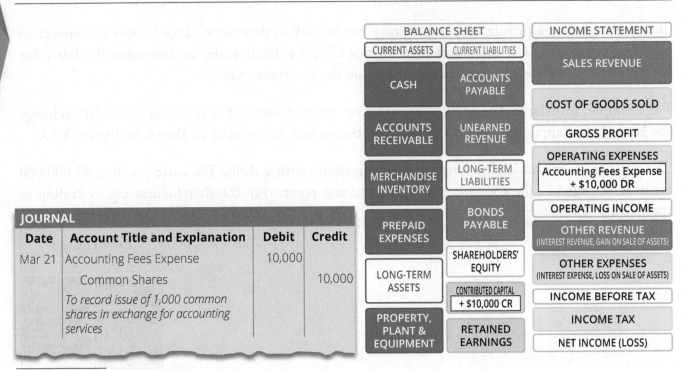

On the income statement, $10,000 is debited to an operating expense account, and the corresponding credit is made to the common shares account and reported in the shareholders' equity section of the balance sheet. Given the nature of such a transaction, the cash account remains untouched.

Accounting for Share Issue Costs

Earlier we established that all corporations have certain duties, rights and responsibilities. Along with the advantage of being able to raise large amounts of financial capital, public corporations are also responsible for the costs associated with raising that capital.

When a corporation issues shares to the public, there are certain costs associated with the share issue such as registration fees, legal and accounting fees, regulatory fees and printing of share certificates and other required documentation. These costs are not considered regular operating costs but are referred to as **share issue costs.** The share issue costs can be accounted for using either the offset method or the retained earnings method. If the offset method is used, then the share issue costs are recorded as a debit to the appropriate shares account (common or preferred). If the retained earnings method is used, then the share issue costs are debited directly to retained earnings.

For example, suppose that on February 10, 2020, a company issues 1,000 common shares in exchange for $10,000 cash and incurs a total of $600 in share issue costs. Figure 5.15 shows the entry that would be made for this transaction.

JOURNAL			
Date	**Account Title and Explanation**	**Debit**	**Credit**
Feb 10	Cash	9,400	
	Common Shares	600	
	Common Shares		10,000
	To record issue of 1,000 common shares for cash, with $600 in share issue costs		

JOURNAL			
Date	**Account Title and Explanation**	**Debit**	**Credit**
Feb 10	Cash	9,400	
	Retained Earnings	600	
	Common Shares		10,000
	To record issue of 1,000 common shares for cash, with $600 in share issue costs		

FIGURE 5.15

The journal entry on the left side shows the transaction using the offset method, which debits common shares by $600. The journal entry on the right side shows the transaction using the retained earnings method, which debits retained earnings by $600.

Pause & Reflect

Exercise 5-1

On January 7, 2020, Ketona Corporation issued 4,000 common shares at $8 per share and 1,000 preferred shares at $25 per share. The next day, on January 8, the corporation purchased land that was appraised at $400,000 by issuing 50,000 common shares. Prepare the journal entries for the share issuances.

JOURNAL			
Date	**Account Title and Explanation**	**Debit**	**Credit**

See Appendix I for solutions.

Accounting for Cash Dividends

LO 5

Corporations are able to raise capital by offering several attractive investment options to potential investors. Investors are attracted not only by the potential for increased market value of their shares, but also by an opportunity to receive a portion of the company's profits in the form of dividends. Dividends are commonly paid annually, biannually or quarterly. There are no set calendar dates to pay dividends; it depends on each individual company's fiscal calendar. Corporations commonly issue two types of dividends: cash dividends and stock dividends. We will discuss cash dividends first and stock dividends in a later section.

There are three important dates related to the accounting treatment of dividends.

- The **date of declaration** is the date on which the board of directors announces (declares) that dividends will be paid to shareholders.
- The **date of record** is the date on which the corporation lists all those who currently hold shares and are therefore eligible to receive dividend payments.
- The **date of payment** is the date on which the company actually makes the dividend payment to eligible shareholders.

Figure 5.16 demonstrates the timeline of these dates and the related journal entries (in green) if a cash dividend is announced and paid.

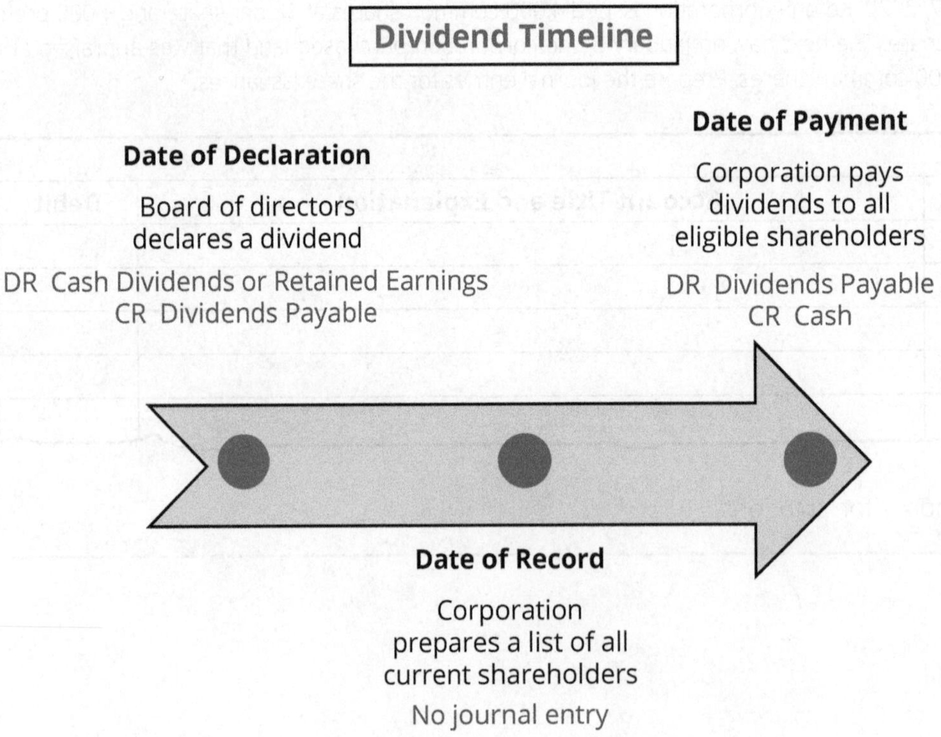

FIGURE 5.16

To illustrate the relationship between these three dates, suppose Zuti Corporation's board of directors declares a cash dividend on its common shares on March 31, 2020, and the dividend is to be paid on June 30, 2020. The board announces that all shareholders who hold common shares as of April 30, 2020, are eligible to receive the dividend. We would express this as follows: On March 31, 2020, Zuti Corporation declared a cash dividend to be distributed on June 30, 2020, to all shareholders of record as of April 30, 2020.

Next, we will examine Zuti Corporation's accounting responsibilities related to each of these dates.

A Closer Look

Before cash dividends can be paid, three important conditions must be met.

1. The board of directors must declare that a dividend will be paid.
2. The corporation must have enough cash to cover its ongoing operations and other obligations.
3. The corporation must have enough legal capital; that is, it must maintain enough assets to fulfill its obligations to creditors, and ensure that any dividend payments will not result in a deficit to retained earnings.

On the Date of Declaration

Suppose that Zuti Corporation's board of directors declares on March 31, 2020, that a dividend payment of $1 per share will be paid to shareholders of all 10,000 outstanding common shares.

Although the dividends are not paid right away, the company must record the obligation to pay them on the date that the dividends are declared. The accounting entry for a dividend declaration can be done in one of two ways: using a cash dividends account or using the retained earnings account.

Using the Cash Dividends Account

When the dividend is declared, a debit is made to a temporary account known as the cash dividends account, and a credit is made to the dividends payable account. The cash dividends account reduces the equity of the corporation and behaves like owner withdrawals in a sole proprietorship. It is used to accumulate all of the dividends declared for the period. Note that in the accounting records and financial statements, dividends must be divided between common shares and preferred shares. This example deals only with common shares.

Figure 5.17 shows the related accounting entry for Zuti Corporation. In this example, a debit of $10,000 is made to cash dividends. The debit to the cash dividends account eventually decreases the balance of retained earnings as part of the closing process on the balance sheet where retained earnings would be debited and the cash dividends would be credited at the end of the period. The credit appears on the balance sheet as an increase of $10,000 to the dividends payable account, which is considered a current liability; the dividend payment is accrued until the payment is finally made.

JOURNAL

Date	Account Title and Explanation	Debit	Credit
Mar 31	Cash Dividends—Common	10,000	
	Dividends Payable		10,000
	To record declaration of cash dividend on 10,000 common shares at $1 per share		

FIGURE 5.17

Using the Retained Earnings Account

Some companies choose an alternative method to record dividends on the date of declaration. Dividends eventually decrease the balance of retained earnings when the cash dividends account is closed to retained earnings at the end of the period. To save time and simplify their accounting entries, some companies choose to forgo using the cash dividends account and immediately debit the retained earnings account for the amount of the dividends. This method has the same effect on the balance sheet as the method that uses the cash dividends account. The related journal entry is shown in Figure 5.18.

JOURNAL

Date	Account Title and Explanation	Debit	Credit
Mar 31	Retained Earnings	10,000	
	Dividends Payable		10,000
	To record declaration of cash dividend on 10,000 common shares at $1 per share		

FIGURE 5.18

Whichever method is used, this transaction does not involve the income statement. Dividend payments are not an operating expense, but a distribution of the corporation's earnings to its shareholders.

On the Date of Record

The date of record is the date on which the corporation determines who the existing shareholders are and how many shares each shareholder owns. The company must do this so that it knows who is eligible for the declared dividend payment.

No accounting entry is made for the date of record, but the corporation does keep detailed records of all shareholders. The person responsible for this is the corporate secretary, who is in charge of all official company documentation. Among other duties, the corporate secretary maintains the company's share register, which is much like a subledger. Some large corporations use the services of a transfer agent to record changes in ownership of shares as a result of trading on the stock market.

On the Date of Payment

On the payment date, dividend payments are made to the shareholders by cheque or electronic transfer to their investment account at a financial institution. Using our previous example, assume that on June 30, 2020, Zuti Corporation pays the dividends that were declared on March 31, 2020. Figure 5.19 shows the related journal entry for this transaction.

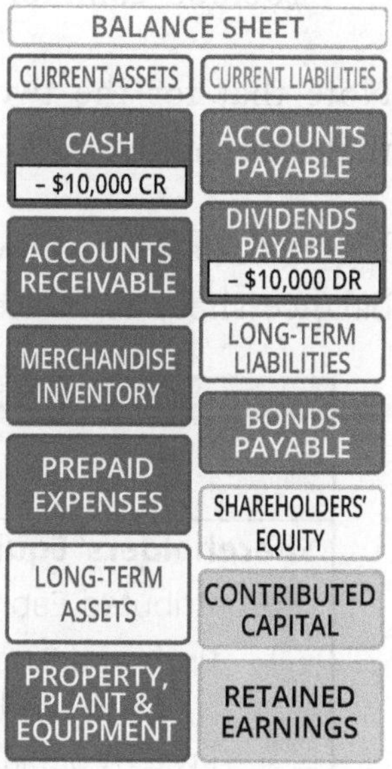

JOURNAL

Date	Account Title and Explanation	Debit	Credit
Jun 30	Dividends Payable	10,000	
	Cash		10,000
	To record payment of cash dividend declared on March 31, 2020		

FIGURE 5.19

The debit to dividends payable decreases the current liability on the balance sheet. The credit to cash decreases the current assets on the balance sheet. Note that this accounting entry will be the same no matter which method—the cash dividends method or the retained earnings method—was used to record the dividend declaration. This is because both methods originally set up the liability as a credit to dividends payable.

The preceding examples show the accounting entries for cash dividends on common shares. This was done to keep the examples easy to follow. The accounting entries are done in a similar manner if cash dividends are paid out only to preferred shareholders.

Dividends in Arrears

Cumulative preferred shares entitle shareholders to receive any unpaid dividends from prior periods—that is, dividends in arrears. Preferred shares without this cumulative feature are known as noncumulative shares. Noncumulative preferred shares do not accumulate unpaid dividends, and so they are treated in the accounting records in much the same way as common shares. The discussion that follows will demonstrate the accounting treatment for all three types of shares: noncumulative preferred shares, cumulative preferred shares and common shares.

Suppose that on December 31, 2020, Yarind Corporation had the following capital shares on its balance sheet.

- 10,000, $2 cumulative preferred shares with a total book value of $60,000
- 25,000, $2 noncumulative preferred shares with a total book value of $100,000
- 100,000 common shares with a total book value of $200,000

Note that for the two types of preferred shares, the $2 refers to the annual dividend per share that shareholders are entitled to receive when dividends are declared.

Figure 5.20 shows how the capital shares appear in the shareholders' equity section of the company's balance sheet on December 31, 2020.

Yarind Corporation Balance Sheet (partial) As at December 31, 2020	
Shareholders' Equity	
Contributed Capital	
Preferred Shares, $2 cumulative, 15,000 shares authorized, 10,000 shares issued and outstanding	$60,000
Preferred Shares, $2 noncumulative, 30,000 shares authorized, 25,000 shares issued and outstanding	100,000
Common Shares, unlimited shares authorized, 100,000 shares issued and outstanding	200,000
Total Contributed Capital	360,000
Retained Earnings	500,000
Total Shareholders' Equity	$860,000

FIGURE 5.20

Suppose that before the year 2020, Yarind Corporation paid dividends every year. However, during the year 2020, the company's board of directors neither declared nor paid any dividends. Then, on December 15, 2021, the board of directors declares $100,000 in dividends, payable on February 10, 2022, to the shareholders of record on December 31, 2021. No other dividends have been declared to date.

For the year ended December 31, 2020, dividends declared:	$0
For the year ended December 31, 2021, dividends declared:	$100,000

When dividends on cumulative preferred shares remain unpaid from prior periods, the corporation must keep track of the amount that is still owing to the cumulative preferred shareholders in the notes to the financial statements, regardless of whether dividends are declared or not. It is only when the board of directors declares the dividend that the dividends in arrears become a liability that needs to be paid out. This means the corporation owes the cumulative preferred shareholders a total of $40,000.

Dividends in arrears on cumulative preferred shares from 2020 ($2 × 10,000)	$20,000
Dividends on cumulative preferred shares for 2021 ($2 × 10,000)	20,000
Total cumulative preferred dividends	$40,000

For 2021, the corporation also owes the noncumulative preferred shareholders an amount equal to the dividends of 2021 only, for a total of $50,000 ($2 × 25,000).

Worth Repeating

Dividends accumulate for cumulative preferred shares, regardless of whether or not cash dividends were actually declared for that year. When dividends are declared and paid out, the corporation must first determine how much it owes cumulative preferred shareholders for dividends in arrears.

After the preferred shareholders are paid, the remainder of the dividends are paid to the common shareholders, as follows.

Dividends declared (December 15, 2021)		$100,000
Payable on cumulative preferred shares (2020 and 2021)	$40,000	
Payable on noncumulative preferred shares (2021)	50,000	
Total preferred dividends payable		90,000
Remainder of dividends—payable to common shareholders		$10,000

The journal entry to record the declaration of dividends on December 15, 2021, is shown in Figure 5.21. This accounting entry shows the cash dividends method of accounting for the dividend declaration, but Yarind Corporation could also use the retained earnings method.

JOURNAL

Date	Account Title and Explanation	Debit	Credit
Dec 15	Cash Dividends—Preferred, cumulative	40,000	
	Cash Dividends—Preferred, noncumulative	50,000	
	Cash Dividends—Common	10,000	
	Dividends Payable		100,000
	To record declaration of cash dividends on common and preferred shares		

FIGURE 5.21

The journal entry to record the subsequent payment of the dividends on February 10, 2022, and the effect on the balance sheet, is shown in Figure 5.22.

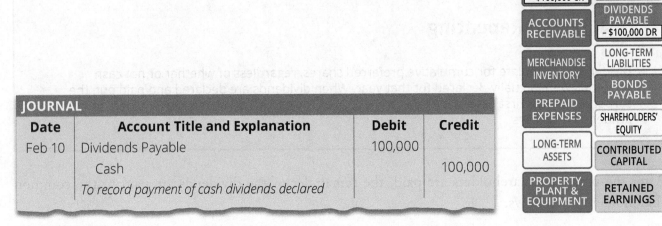

JOURNAL

Date	Account Title and Explanation	Debit	Credit
Feb 10	Dividends Payable	100,000	
	Cash		100,000
	To record payment of cash dividends declared		

FIGURE 5.22

As before, the payment reduces both the dividend liability and cash balances.

As mentioned at the beginning of the chapter, corporations can obtain financing by assuming debt. Payments on debt would be in the form of interest, compared to the preceding examples of dividends being paid on outstanding equity. The accounting for long-term liabilities will be covered in a later chapter.

Pause & Reflect

Exercise 5-2

SP Inc. has the following reported in the shareholders' equity section of its balance sheet.

- Preferred shares, 10%, $40 cumulative, 20,000 shares authorized, 5,000 issued and outstanding
- Preferred shares, 20%, $25 noncumulative, 15,000 shares authorized, 10,000 issued and outstanding
- Common shares, unlimited shares authorized, 50,000 issued and outstanding

SP Inc. last paid dividends in 2018. In May 25, 2020, the board of directors declared $120,000 in cash dividends, to be distributed on July 15, 2020 to all shareholders of record on June 20, 2020. The company uses the cash dividends method to record dividends. Prepare the required journal entries.

JOURNAL

Date	Account Title and Explanation	Debit	Credit

See Appendix I for solutions.

Stock Splits and Stock Dividends

LO 6

Among the advantages of the corporate form of organization is the right of a corporation to manage and reorganize its equity structure. For various reasons, a corporation's board of directors may decide to retain cash and, rather than declare a cash dividend, offer shareholders a different type of payment. This payment might be in the form of either a stock split or a stock dividend.

Stock Split

A **stock split** is an action that increases the number of a corporation's outstanding shares, which in turn decreases the individual price of each share traded on the stock market. For example, if a corporation declares a 2-for-1 stock split, it calls in all outstanding shares of existing shareholders and exchanges each share for two shares. The shareholder now owns two shares for every one share previously held in the company; however, the value of each share is reduced in half. Stock splits can be done with any ratio that the corporation decides on, such as 3-for-1 or 4-for-1. Consider this example of a stock split.

Suppose that as of December 31, 2020, Standard Corporation has 10,000 common shares outstanding, and the shares are currently traded at $40 per share on the stock market. The book value of the common shares on the balance sheet is $200,000. On January 15, 2021, the company's board of directors declares a 2-for-1 stock split. The stock split results in twice as many shares (10,000 shares × 2 = 20,000 shares), but the book value remains the same at $200,000. Each shareholder now owns two shares for every one that they originally held, but the market responds by dropping the market value from $40 per share to $20 per share.

Figure 5.23 shows the effect on Standard Corporation's shareholders' equity if it declares a stock split. As shown, a stock split increases the number of common shares issued with no impact on the total shareholders' equity. The overall result is that there is no change in each shareholder's percentage ownership and the total values of both capital and shareholders' equity remain the same after the stock split.

Standard Corporation Balance Sheet (partial) December 31, 2020 (before stock split)	
Shareholders' Equity	
Contributed Capital	
Common Shares, unlimited shares authorized, 10,000 shares issued and outstanding	$200,000
Retained Earnings	500,000
Total Shareholders' Equity	$700,000

Standard Corporation Balance Sheet (partial) January 15, 2021 (after stock split)	
Shareholders' Equity	
Contributed Capital	
Common Shares, unlimited shares authorized, 20,000 shares issued and outstanding	$200,000
Retained Earnings	500,000
Total Shareholders' Equity	$700,000

FIGURE 5.23

One of the main reasons for splitting shares is to increase their liquidity. If a share price is too high on the stock market, some investors may feel the shares are too expensive or unaffordable. A lower share price makes the shares attractive to more investors, which can potentially benefit all the investors. Because the total book value of the shares outstanding is not affected, no journal entry is needed to account for a stock split. A memorandum (note) is usually recorded to indicate the increased number of shares outstanding.

A Closer Look

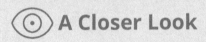

A corporation can do a stock split on preferred shares in addition to common shares. Increasing the number of preferred shares is handled the same as for common shares. The difference is how the dividends for preferred shares are handled. Suppose a corporation is going to issue a 2-for-1 preferred stock split, and there are 20,000 preferred shares that currently pay $4 dividends. After the stock split, there will be 40,000 preferred shares that will pay $2 dividends. The preferred stock split has to be mentioned in the notes to the financial statements.

Stock Dividend

A **stock dividend** may be issued in lieu of a cash dividend for several reasons. First, a company may wish to retain its cash in order to expand the business, which eventually increases the value for shareholders. Another reason is to keep the share price affordable for new investors; the company can increase the number of outstanding shares to reduce the market price per share. A stock dividend can also satisfy investors with a dividend, even though cash will not be paid. Stock dividends are normally issued to common shareholders only.

To demonstrate a stock dividend, we will return to Standard Corporation. Figure 5.24 shows the shareholders' equity section of the company's balance sheet before the stock dividend is declared. On December 31, 2020, Standard Corporation has 10,000 outstanding common shares. The current market price is $40 per share.

Standard Corporation Balance Sheet (partial) As at December 31, 2020 (before stock dividend)	
Shareholders' Equity	
Contributed Capital	
Common Shares, unlimited shares authorized, 10,000 shares issued and outstanding	$200,000
Retained Earnings	500,000
Total Shareholders' Equity	$700,000

FIGURE 5.24

On January 15, 2021, the company's board of directors decides to declare a 20% stock dividend on all 10,000 outstanding shares. The CBCA requires the value assigned to stock dividends to be at the market price on the declaration date. Therefore, this transaction is recorded at $40 per new share. The dividend is to be distributed on February 20, 2021, to all shareholders of record as of January 31, 2021. The value of the shares in this stock dividend is calculated as shown below.

Total number of outstanding common shares = 10,000

20% stock dividend on 10,000 shares = 10,000 × 0.20 = 2,000 shares

2,000 shares at a current market price of $40 per share = 2,000 × $40 = $80,000

Figure 5.25 shows the journal entry to record the declaration of the stock dividend, using the retained earnings method.

JOURNAL

Date	Account Title and Explanation	Debit	Credit
Jan 15	Retained Earnings	80,000	
	Common Stock Dividends Distributable		80,000
	To record declaration of 20% stock dividends on common shares		

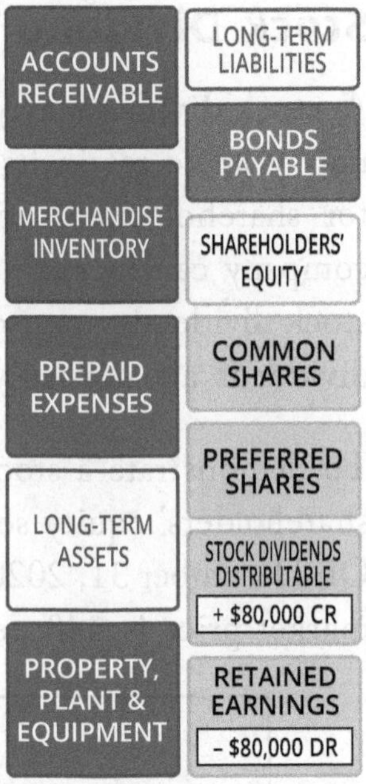

FIGURE 5.25

Stock dividends distributable is an equity account, not a liability, but it is used in a similar way to how the dividends payable account is used for cash dividends. It keeps track of the amount that will be distributed to the shareholders. The end result of a stock dividend is a rearrangement of the components of shareholders' equity; some of the value of retained earnings is shifted to the common shares account. Stock dividends are never considered a liability, because the company does not actually owe shareholders a stock dividend.

Figure 5.26 shows the journal entry to record the distribution of the stock dividend on February 20, 2021, and the effect on the shareholders' equity section of the balance sheet. The common stock dividends distributable account is debited and the common shares account is credited at the market value of the common stock dividends distributed.

JOURNAL

Date	Account Title and Explanation	Debit	Credit
Feb 20	Common Stock Dividends Distributable	80,000	
	Common Shares		80,000
	To record distribution of 20% stock dividends on common shares		

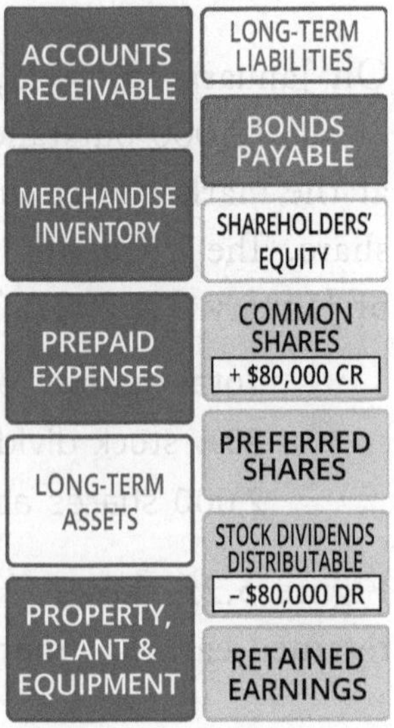

FIGURE 5.26

This distribution of the stock dividend completes the transfer of part of retained earnings to the value of common shares. Figure 5.27 shows the shareholders' equity section of the balance sheet for Standard Corporation before the stock dividend was declared and after the stock dividend was distributed. Notice that total shareholders' equity has not changed, just the values of retained earnings and common shares, and the number of common shares issued and outstanding.

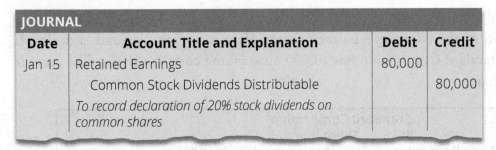

Standard Corporation Balance Sheet (partial) December 31, 2020 (before stock dividend)	
Shareholders' Equity	
Contributed Capital	
Common Shares, unlimited shares authorized, 10,000 shares issued and outstanding	$200,000
Retained Earnings	500,000
Total Shareholders' Equity	$700,000

Standard Corporation Balance Sheet (partial) February 20, 2021 (after stock dividend)	
Shareholders' Equity	
Contributed Capital	
Common Shares, unlimited shares authorized, 12,000 shares issued and outstanding	$280,000
Retained Earnings	420,000
Total Shareholders' Equity	$700,000

FIGURE 5.27

All of the above transactions illustrate how public corporations account for issuing shares and recording dividends. Private corporations record share issuance in the same manner. However, the recording and payment of dividends is usually less formal for private corporations because the shares are not publicly traded and the list of shareholders is usually quite short. Figure 5.28 shows the impact of cash dividends, stock dividends and stock splits.

	Common Shares		Retained Earnings	Shareholders' Equity	Assets
	Value	Quantity			
Cash Dividend	No Change	No Change	Decrease	Decrease	Decrease(1)
Stock Dividend	Increase	Increase	Decrease	No Change	No Change
Stock Split	No Change(2)	Increase	No Change	No Change	No Change

(1) Cash is reduced only when the declared cash dividend is paid out.
(2) For a stock split, the market value per share decreases, but the book value of the shares remains the same.

FIGURE 5.28

Restrictions on the Use of Retained Earnings

Sometimes a company's board of directors places restrictions on the use of retained earnings for the payment of dividends. Restricted retained earnings can be one of several types.

- *Statutory restrictions* are those required by provincial law. One example is limiting the amount of dividends to the amount of retained earnings minus the cost of treasury shares currently held by the company, so that legal capital is not used to pay dividends. Treasury shares are described in the appendix to this chapter.
- *Contractual restrictions* are those limited by legal contracts. A common example is a loan agreement that requires the company to restrict retained earnings so that money is available to repay the loan, rather than to pay out dividends.
- *Discretionary restrictions* are those voluntarily imposed by the company's board of directors. Such restrictions may be put in place so that retained earnings can be used to expand the company rather than pay out dividends.

Restrictions on retained earnings must be disclosed in the notes to the financial statements.

In the Real World

In a stock split, a corporation divides its existing outstanding shares into multiple shares. You may often see news of a company offering a 2-for-1 stock split, or perhaps a 3-for-1 stock split. The result is an increase in the number of shares outstanding.

Starbucks' Corporation (NASDAQ: SBUX), one of the world's leading specialty coffee retailers, has a long history of declaring stock splits. Since 1993, the company has offered six 2-for-1 stock splits on its common shares—the most recent of which was announced in March 2015. The 2-for-1 stock split reduced the company's stock from a then-current $94 per share (which was becoming too high for many investors) to a much more attractive price of about $47 per share. The multiple splits also mean that if you purchased 100 shares of Starbucks' stock in 1992 and held onto your shares until March 18, 2015, you would have 6,400 shares, a 160-fold increase in your holdings.

At the other end of the spectrum, Berskhire Hathaway, Inc. (NYSE: BRK.A)—a diverse company headed by investor Warren Buffett, with holdings in a wide variety of businesses including insurance, energy, transportation, manufacturing and retailing—has never offered a stock split. As of late 2019, Berskhire's stock was priced around $300,000 US per share.

Pause & Reflect

Exercise 5-3

StraightLine Industries has 400,000 common shares issued and outstanding, worth $1,200,000 in its books. Retained earnings has a value of $5,600,000. StraightLine is planning to issue a 2-for-1 stock split when the market price is $80 per share.

a) After the stock split, what will be the impact on the quantity and value of the common shares in the books?

b) What will be the impact on retained earnings?

c) What will be the impact on the share price?

See Appendix I for solutions.

Income Tax Expense for Corporations

LO 7

Unlike a sole proprietorship or partnership, a corporation is considered a separate legal entity from its owners. A corporation must therefore file and pay taxes on its net income; the amount that the corporation is obligated to pay is known as **income tax**. Federal income tax laws, including the income tax rates, are determined by the Government of Canada and published in the Income Tax Act.

Income tax expense is recorded in a corporation's accounting records on an accrual basis. For accounting purposes, the company applies the prescribed percentage from the Income Tax Act to its net income for its fiscal period. This amount is then recorded as its income tax expense and its income tax payable. Consider the following example.

Suppose that for the fiscal year ended December 31, 2020, Star Company reported a net income before tax of $266,000. Assume the company is subject to income tax at a rate of 30% on its net income for the period. Based on the net income according to its accounting records, Star Company would record an estimated income tax expense of $79,800 ($266,000 × 30%) for the year ended December 31, 2020. Figure 5.29 shows the recorded transaction, and the effects on the balance sheet and income statement.

JOURNAL

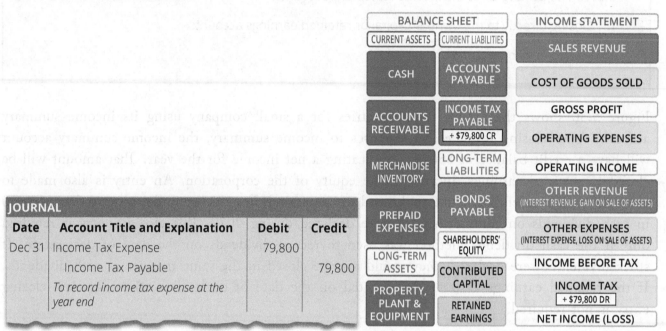

Date	Account Title and Explanation	Debit	Credit
Dec 31	Income Tax Expense	79,800	
	Income Tax Payable		79,800
	To record income tax expense at the year end		

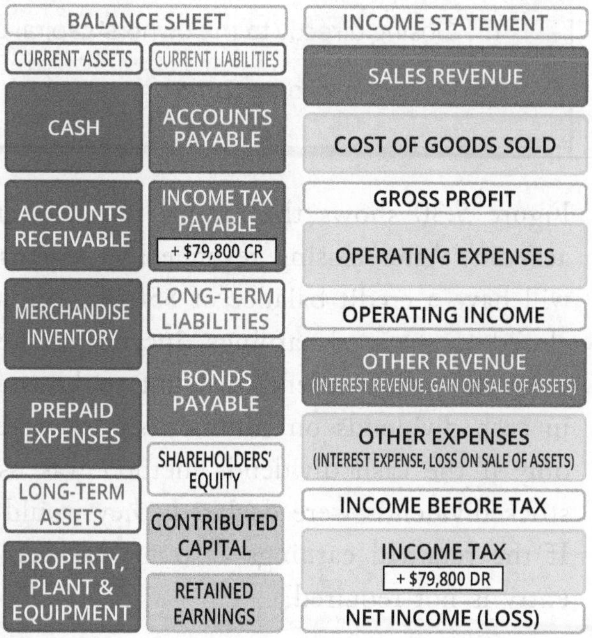

FIGURE 5.29

Note that the transaction is recorded with an increase to an expense and an increase to a liability. The liability will eventually be paid to the government.

We used the term "net income according to accounting records" because there is a difference between the Income Tax Act and accounting under both APSE and IFRS when it comes to calculating taxable income. As a result, different amounts of tax may be calculated depending on which income figures are used. A discussion of the difference is beyond the scope of this textbook, so we will simply use net income as calculated by the corporation for our tax calculations.

Closing Entries for Corporations

LO 8

At the end of a period, a business must close revenue and expense accounts to equity. A corporation is no different. At the end of the period, a corporation's revenue and expense accounts are closed to a temporary account called income summary. The income summary and any cash or stock dividends are then closed to retained earnings.

Worth Repeating

The term *closing the books* means updating the equity accounts by closing the income statement accounts to zero balances in preparation for the new accounting period. There are two methods that can be used to close the income statement accounts.

1. Closing directly to the owners' capital or retained earnings accounts
2. Using the income summary account

Figure 5.30 shows the sample closing entries for a small company using its income summary account. After closing revenue and expenses to income summary, the income summary account will have a credit balance of $50,000, indicating a net income for the year. That amount will be closed to retained earnings, increasing the equity of the corporation. An entry is also made to close the cash dividends account at the end of the period. For this example, assume that $10,000 in cash dividends on common shares were declared during 2020. This closing entry is required only if the cash dividends method was used to record dividends on the date of declaration. If stock dividends were declared, they would also be closed in the same manner as cash dividends. If the retained earnings account was debited on the date of declaration, then this last closing entry is not required.

JOURNAL

Date	Account Titles and Explanation	Debit	Credit
Dec 31	Sales Revenue	200,000	
	Income Summary		200,000
	To close revenue account		
Dec 31	Income Summary	150,000	
	Cost of Goods Sold		80,000
	Salaries Expense		35,000
	Rent Expense		25,000
	Income Tax Expense		10,000
	To close expense accounts		
Dec 31	Income Summary	50,000	
	Retained Earnings		50,000
	To close net income to retained earnings		
Dec 31	Retained Earnings	10,000	
	Cash Dividends—Common		10,000
	To close cash dividends account		

FIGURE 5.30

Calculating Retained Earnings

LO 9

Contributed capital and retained earnings are reported separately in the shareholders' equity section of the financial statements. As mentioned previously, one component of the contributed capital is share capital. Share capital is what has been invested by shareholders or the owners of a corporation when they purchase shares. This section illustrates how to calculate retained earnings and how retained earnings are presented in the shareholders' equity section of a company's balance sheet.

To calculate retained earnings, suppose Mamae Company started 2020 with a balance of $100,000 in its retained earnings account. During the year, the company earned a net income of $40,000. It also paid cash dividends to shareholders in the amount of $10,000, and stock dividends at a value of $5,000 (both dividends were paid on common shares). The balance of the retained earnings account on December 31, 2020, would be calculated as shown in Figure 5.31.

Calculation of Retained Earnings For the Year Ended December 31, 2020		
Retained Earnings, January 1, 2020		$100,000
Add: Net Income for Year		40,000
Less: Cash Dividends—Common	$10,000	
Stock Dividends	5,000	15,000
Retained Earnings, December 31, 2020		$125,000

FIGURE 5.31

Figure 5.32 shows how the December 31 balance of retained earnings fits into the shareholders' equity section of the balance sheet for Mamae Company as at December 31, 2020.

Mamae Company Balance Sheet (partial) As at December 31, 2020	
Shareholders' Equity	
Contributed Capital	
Preferred Shares, $2 cumulative, 10,000 shares authorized, 3,000 shares issued and outstanding	$12,000
Common Shares, unlimited shares authorized, 50,000 shares issued and outstanding	5,000,000
Total Contributed Capital	5,012,000
Retained Earnings	125,000
Total Shareholders' Equity	$5,137,000

FIGURE 5.32

The quantity of shares that have been sold (issued) through the stock market must be shown for all classes of shares (common and preferred). Also, the total value that the shares were sold for must be shown. This is considered the book value of the shares, and the value does not change as market prices for the shares increase or decrease.

For private corporations following ASPE, a calculation of retained earnings must be included in a formal statement of retained earnings. Under ASPE, a company is not required to disclose in the statement the number of authorized shares, only their rights and privileges. You will learn how to prepare a statement of retained earnings in the next chapter.

For all public corporations, and for private corporations that follow IFRS, a calculation of retained earnings must be included in a formal statement of changes in shareholders' equity, along with additional information that you will learn about when we discuss financial statements in the next chapter.

An Ethical Approach to Corporations and Insider Trading

LO 10

The stock market can be unpredictable at the best of times. Market trends can fluctuate, speculation can run rampant, and even the most informed investors can have a difficult time making the right decisions. One of the basic foundations of the stock market is fair and public access to all company-related information. If current or potential shareholders have a right to information about a company, then it should be disclosed to the public in a timely fashion.

An important ethical principle for all businesses, large or small, is the need to maintain the integrity of information released publicly, which is why insider trading is considered one of the worst violations at the corporate level. **Insider trading** occurs when anyone who has access to a company's private information uses such information to trade in the stock market for their own gain before the information is released publicly.

For example, imagine that a secretary in a company overhears information about an upcoming announcement of better-than-expected company earnings for the year. The secretary passes on this confidential information to a close friend. Knowing that the announcement will increase the price, the friend buys a large quantity of shares and even tells a few more friends, who also purchase the shares.

When the announcement is finally made, the price of the shares increases dramatically, and the friends who bought shares before the announcement make a substantial amount of money. This, of course, is highly illegal. Everyone involved, including the secretary and the friends, should be charged with insider trading. The crime is very serious and comes with some harsh penalties.

The purpose of insider trading laws is to give everyone the same amount of information at the same time, and a fair chance to make profits on the stock market. That is why securities regulators go to great lengths to detect the spread of information by way of insider activity. As tempting as it might be to act on private company information before anyone else knows, doing so violates the principle of fairness and openness that exists in world markets. Anything less threatens the way that capitalism and free markets should work.

In the Real World

Celebrity homemaking and insider trading are two concepts that do not often come to mind at the same time. However, Martha Stewart rose to fame and fortune by way of the stock market. In the late 1990s, she took Martha Stewart Living Omnimedia Inc. public and made a fortune on the subsequent rise of the company's stock.

Stewart's success with the stock market, however, started to unravel in late 2001 with events surrounding the stock of a company called ImClone Systems, a biopharmaceutical corporation. During that period, ImClone stock took a tumble as a result of regulatory procedures that were detrimental to the company. Records show that Stewart sold almost 4,000 shares in the company, making her a gain of $229,000, shortly before public disclosure about the regulations.

It appears that Stewart was good friends with Samuel Waksal, the CEO of ImClone. Investigations revealed that Stewart was advised by her stockbroker to sell her stock, based on information he was privy to regarding Waksal. The situation was a clear case of insider trading.

As is often the case with insider trading, however, it is very hard to prove who knew what and when. The investigators therefore focused on the cover-up, and discovered that Stewart had deceived investigators numerous times as they tried to gather information on insider activity in this case. In March of 2004, she was found guilty of obstructing justice and served a five-month prison sentence.

In Summary

LO 1 Describe the characteristics of corporations

- A corporation is a legal entity that is separate from its owners, known as shareholders.
- Some characteristics of corporations include limited liability of shareholders, formal organizational structure, lack of mutual agency, unlimited life and the ability to raise capital.

LO 2 Describe differences between public and private corporations

- Public corporations sell a portion of their shares to the public through stock markets. Private corporations do not sell their shares to the public.
- Publicly traded corporations must use IFRS. A private corporation may use either ASPE or IFRS.

LO 3 Explain shareholders' equity

- Shareholders' equity is made up of two components: contributed capital and retained earnings.
- Contributed capital generally consists of two subcategories, called share capital and contributed surplus.
- Par value shares are issued with an assigned value. No-par value shares are issued with no assigned value.
- Issuing no-par value shares involves the entire proceeds being credited to the equity account.
- There are two types of share capital: common shares and preferred shares.
- Common shares constitute ownership in the company, but do not come with guaranteed dividend payments.
- Preferred shares do not offer voting rights, but generally do come with regular dividend payments and a higher claim to company assets than common shares.

LO 4 Record the issuance of shares

- A company can issue shares in exchange for cash, assets owned or services rendered.
- When issuing shares for cash, the common shares (or preferred shares) account is credited for the entire proceeds of the sale.
- Issuing shares in exchange for non-cash assets or services must be recorded at the fair value of the assets or services received. If the fair value of assets or services cannot be determined, then the transaction is recorded at the fair value of the shares being exchanged.

LO 5 Record the payment of cash dividends

- There are three important dates related to the accounting treatment of dividends: the date of declaration, the date of record and the date of payment.

- The accounting entry for a dividend declaration can be made in one of two ways: using a cash dividends account or using the retained earnings account.
- The declared dividends must first go to preferred shareholders, including both the current year's dividends and dividends in arrears. Then, the remaining amount goes to common shareholders.

LO 6 Record stock splits and stock dividends

- A stock split is a corporate action that increases the number of a corporation's outstanding shares, which in turn decreases the individual market price of each share. No journal entry is required for a stock split.
- A stock dividend may be issued in lieu of a cash dividend if a company wants to retain its cash in order to expand the business, or to keep the share price affordable for new investors.

LO 7 Record income tax expense

- A corporation must file and pay taxes on its net income; the amount that the corporation is obligated to pay is known as income tax.
- Income tax expense is recorded in a corporation's accounting records periodically on an accrual basis.

LO 8 Record the closing entries for a corporation

- A corporation's revenue and expense accounts are closed at the end of the period either using the income summary account or directly to the retained earnings account.

LO 9 Calculate retained earnings

- Retained earnings represent the amount of equity that the company has earned and kept in the business and not distributed to shareholders.
- Contributed capital and retained earnings are reported separately in the shareholders' equity section of the financial statements.

LO 10 Explain the importance of ethics for corporate reporting

- Insider trading laws enforce the principle that everyone is given the same amount of information at the same time, and a fair chance to make profits on the stock market.

Review Exercise 5-1

Marcel Campos and Felicity Feisthamel have operated their company as a general partnership for several years. Over the years the company grew, and the partners decided to incorporate their company as Camphamel Inc., a publicly traded company, and raise more capital to expand.

Marcel and Felicity engaged a qualified bookkeeper to provide accounting services for their new corporation. The corporate charter authorized the company to issue an unlimited number of common shares and 200,000, 30% noncumulative preferred shares. On March 3, 2020, the partners transferred assets worth $2,000,000 and liabilities worth $1,250,000 to the company in exchange for 20,000 common shares.

Then, Marcel and Felicity sought investment capital from investors. On April 15, 2020, a group of investors agreed to buy an additional 20,000 common shares for $1,000,000 cash.

Instead of paying the accountant $100,000 of fees in cash, Marcel and Felicity gave her 10,000, 30% noncumulative preferred shares on April 30, 2020. The corporation cannot readily determine the fair value of the preferred shares.

To inject more capital into the business, on May 10, 2020, the company issued 5,000 additional common shares at their current market value of $50 each in exchange for equipment. The fair value of the equipment cannot be readily determined.

On September 15, 2020, the company declared a 5% stock dividend on all the common shares outstanding. The market value of each common share was $60 on this date. (For this transaction, use the retained earnings account to record the journal entry.) The stock dividend was later distributed to shareholders on October 2, 2020.

At the directors' meeting on October 15, 2020, Marcel, Felicity, and a director appointed by the shareholders decided to pay cash dividends of $180,000 to preferred and common shareholders of record on November 30, 2020. (For this transaction, use the cash dividends account to record the journal entry.) The cash dividend is paid on December 15, 2020. Assume net income was $900,000 for the year ended December 31, 2020.

Required

a) Record the required journal entries for 2020.

JOURNAL			
Date	Account Title and Explanation	Debit	Credit

b) Prepare the shareholders' equity section of the balance sheet as at December 31, 2020.

See Appendix I for solutions.

Appendix 5A: Reacquisition of Common Shares

LO 11

In addition to issuing shares, a corporation can also buy back its own shares from shareholders. The reacquisition of shares may take place for a number of different reasons. For example, a corporation may purchase its shares to reduce the number of shares outstanding, hence increasing earnings per share. A company may also purchase its own shares with the intention of increasing its shares' market price by attracting interest with a larger trading volume in the stock market. When they have enough cash on hand, some corporations may also reacquire shares to give back cash to shareholders or to remove a specific group of shareholders. Regardless of the reason for reacquisition, in most provinces and territories of Canada, the reacquired shares must be retired and cancelled. This means that those reacquired shares are brought back to the pool of authorized shares that remain unissued. However, in the United States and some Canadian provinces, those shares are allowed to be held as **treasury shares** to be reissued instead of being retired or cancelled. Treasury shares have no rights until they are reissued. Treasury shares are not common in Canada, and the accounting for them is covered in advanced accounting courses.

In this appendix, we will explore accounting treatments for the reacquisition of common shares that are cancelled by a corporation.

Average Cost of Shares

When a business retires or disposes of a long-term asset such as equipment, it removes the cost of that asset from the balance sheet. The same is true for retiring common shares. A corporation should remove from its books the cost of reacquired shares. However, since it would be nearly impossible to find out the exact cost of each share, an average cost per share is used instead. The **average cost per share** is calculated by dividing the book value of the common shares account by the number of common shares issued and outstanding at the transaction date. Usually shares would be reacquired at a price that is different from their average cost, as demonstrated in the following sections.

Reacquiring Shares: Less Than the Average Cost

If a corporation repurchases its shares for less than the average cost, a gain is made. However, since corporations are not allowed to record gains or losses from transactions with their shareholders, nothing can be recorded on the income statement. This gain is treated as an addition to shareholders' equity. More specifically, this gain is recorded as part of the contributed capital, as a contributed surplus.

Recall that contributed capital contains *share capital* and *contributed surplus* as shown in Figure 5A.1. Share capital is the capital raised from the sale of shares. Contributed capital can generally be referred to as share capital, since most of the corporation's transactions do not involve the contributed surplus account. However, contributed surplus contains other shareholder contributions, such as donations of assets to corporations. In this appendix, the focus will be on the accounting for reacquired shares using the contributed surplus account. We will illustrate how contributed surplus is affected when shares are reacquired for less than their average cost.

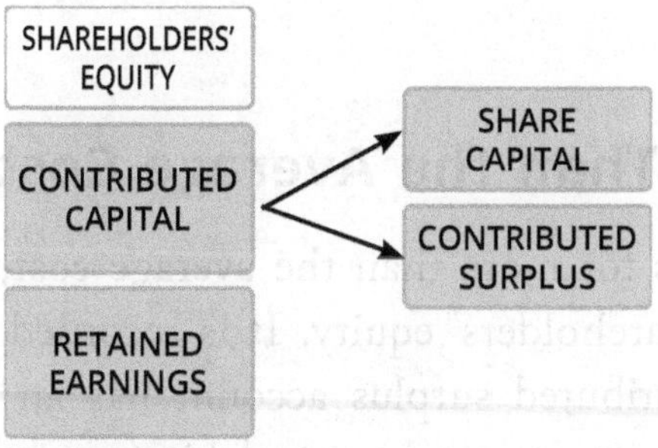

FIGURE 5A.1

Assume that Pokadot Corporation paid $15,000 to reacquire 5,000 of its own common shares on October 2, 2020. Prior to the share reacquisition, Pokadot had 100,000 outstanding common shares. Its balance sheet before recording the share reacquisition transaction shows a balance of $400,000 for the common shares. Thus, Pokadot's average cost per share is $4 ($400,000 ÷ 100,000 outstanding shares). Because the price of $3 ($15,000 ÷ 5,000 shares) that Pokadot paid for each share is lower than its average cost per share of $4, the difference is treated as an addition to shareholders' equity through the contributed surplus account. The journal entry to record the reacquisition of Pokadot's shares for less than its average cost per share and its impact on the balance sheet are shown in Figure 5A.2.

JOURNAL

Date	Account Title and Explanation	Debit	Credit
Oct 2	Common Shares	20,000	
	Contributed Surplus		5,000
	Cash		15,000
	To record reacquiring and retiring of shares		

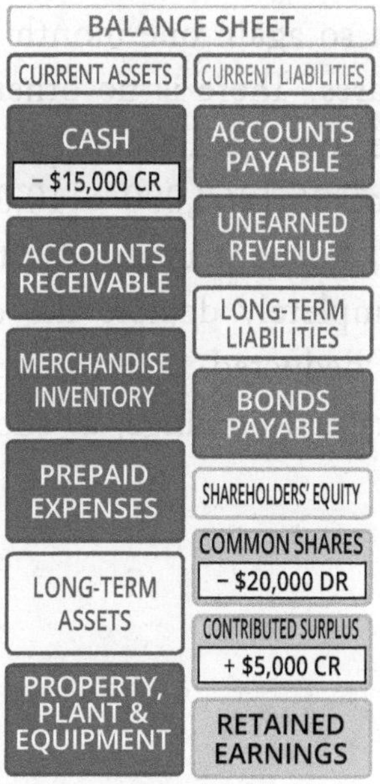

FIGURE 5A.2

The amount paid to buy back the shares is credited to cash. The 5,000 reacquired common shares are removed from the company's books by debiting the common shares account using the shares' average cost ($5,000 shares × $4 per share = $20,000). To balance the transaction, the difference of $5,000 ($20,000 – $15,000) is recorded as a credit to contributed surplus.

Pokadot now has 95,000 common shares outstanding (100,000 shares – 5,000 shares) with the remaining common shares balance of $380,000 ($400,000 – $20,000) after the share reacquisition.

The average cost per share remains the same ($380,000 ÷ 95,000 outstanding shares = $4 per share). Assuming that contributed surplus has a beginning balance of zero, the contributed surplus of $5,000 would be presented under contributed capital in the shareholders' equity section of the balance sheet.

Reacquiring Shares: More Than the Average Cost

If a corporation repurchases its shares for more than the average cost, a loss is incurred. This loss would be treated as a reduction in shareholders' equity. It is recorded by debiting the contributed surplus account, but only if the contributed surplus account has an existing credit (or positive) balance. The contributed surplus account cannot have a debit (or negative) balance. Therefore, if the size of the loss is larger than the existing balance of the contributed surplus account, or if the contributed surplus account has a zero balance, the part of the loss that cannot be absorbed by the contributed surplus is deducted against the retained earnings account, which can have a debit (or negative) balance. We will illustrate how to account for this loss when the contributed surplus account has a positive balance and when the contributed surplus account balance is zero.

Assume that after Pokadot Corporation reacquired a portion of its shares on October 2, 2020, it did so again one month later. On November 2, 2020, Pokadot paid $60,000 to repurchase 10,000 shares. There is no other change in the common shares between October 2 and November 2, so the average amount per share is still $4. Because the amount that Pokadot paid on November 2 of $6 ($60,000 ÷ 10,000 shares) per share is higher than Pokadot's average cost per share of $4, Pokadot incurred a total loss of $20,000 [($6 per share - $4 per share) × 10,000 shares]. To completely deplete the contributed surplus account, $5,000 of the total loss of $20,000 would be deducted against that account. The remaining $15,000 loss would then be deducted against retained earnings, as shown in the journal entry in Figure 5A.3.

JOURNAL

Date	Account Title and Explanation	Debit	Credit
Nov 2	Common Shares	40,000	
	Contributed Surplus	5,000	
	Retained Earnings	15,000	
	Cash		60,000
	To record reacquiring and retiring of shares		

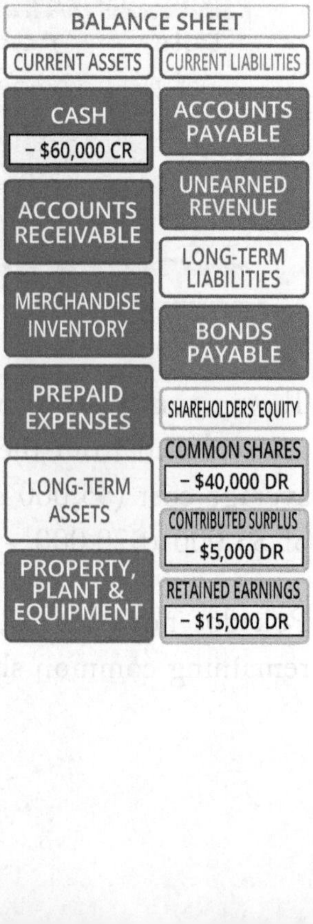

FIGURE 5A.3

Pokadot now has 85,000 common shares outstanding (95,000 shares - 10,000 shares) with the remaining common shares balance of $340,000 ($380,000 - $40,000) after the share reacquisition on November 2, 2020. The average cost per share remains the same ($340,000 ÷ 85,000 outstanding shares = $4 per share). Because the contributed surplus has been completely depleted, the account now has a zero balance.

If the company reacquires its shares for more than the average cost when the contributed surplus account has no balance, the loss is recorded directly to retained earnings. Assume that Pokadot reacquired an additional 1,000 shares on January 17, 2021, with $4,500 cash. There is no other change in the common shares between November 2, 2020, and January 17, 2021, so the average cost per share is still $4. Because the amount that Pokadot paid on January 17 of $4.50 ($4,500 ÷ 1,000 shares) per share is higher than Pokadot's average cost per share of $4, Pokadot incurred a total loss of $500 [($4.50 per share - $4 per share) × 1,000 shares]. The whole $500 loss is recorded as a debit to retained earnings because there is a zero balance in the contributed surplus account, as shown in the journal entry in Figure 5A.4.

JOURNAL

Date	Account Title and Explanation	Debit	Credit
Jan 17	Common Shares	4,000	
	Retained Earnings	500	
	Cash		4,500
	To record reacquiring and retiring of shares		

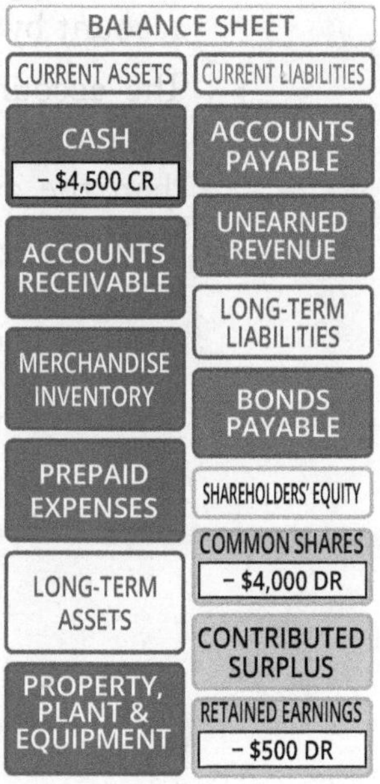

FIGURE 5A.4

The loss from share reacquisition that is recorded as a debit to retained earnings is never reversed, even if the company subsequently reacquires a portion of its shares at less than the average cost. In other words, whenever shares are reacquired at less than the average cost, the difference is always recorded as a credit to the contributed surplus account.

In Summary

LO 11 Record the reacquisition of shares

- The reacquisition of shares means that a corporation buys back its own shares from shareholders. In most provinces and territories of Canada, the reacquired shares must be retired and cancelled.
- A corporation reacquires its shares for a number of different reasons including reducing the number of shares outstanding, increasing share market price or giving back cash to shareholders.
- The average cost per share is calculated by dividing the book value of the common shares account by the number of common shares issued and outstanding at the transaction date.
- The accounts affected by share reacquisition depend on whether the repurchase price is more or less than the average cost per share. When shares are reacquired at less than the average cost, the difference is recorded as a credit to the contributed surplus account. When shares are reacquired for more than the average cost, the difference is first deducted against the contributed surplus account. Once the contributed surplus account is depleted, the remaining difference is debited to the retained earnings account.

Review Exercise 5A-1

Raktor Inc.'s balance sheet on December 31, 2020, reported that Raktor had 200,000 outstanding common shares with a book value of $1,000,000, and that Raktor had a contributed surplus account balance of zero. On March 10, 2021, Raktor paid $70,000 to repurchase 15,000 common shares. On June 15, 2021, Raktor repurchased an additional 15,000 common shares, but paid $90,000 this time. There had been no other changes in the number or value of the company's common shares.

Required

a) Record the share reacquisition journal entry on March 10, 2021.

Date	Account Title and Explanation	Debit	Credit

b) What is the average cost of shares after the share reacquisition on March 10, 2021?

c) Record the share reacquisition journal entry on June 15, 2021.

Date	Account Title and Explanation	Debit	Credit

See Appendix I for solutions.

Notes

Chapter 6
Corporations: The Financial Statements

Learning Objectives

LO 1 **Explain the different requirements for public and private companies when presenting financial statements**

LO 2 **Prepare an income statement**
- Continuing Operations
- Discontinued Operations

LO 3 **Prepare a statement of retained earnings**

LO 4 **Prepare a balance sheet**

LO 5 **Identify differences between ASPE and IFRS**
- Statement of Comprehensive Income
- Statement of Changes in Equity
- Statement of Financial Position

LO 6 **Describe and report accounting changes**
- Correction of Prior Period Errors
- Change in Accounting Policy
- Change in Accounting Estimate

LO 7 **Calculate and explain earnings per share**

LO 8 **Calculate ratios used to evaluate earnings and dividend performance**
- Book Value per Common Share
- Dividend Yield and Dividend Payout Ratio
- Price–Earnings Ratio

MAKING IT REAL TO YOU

Imagine you are part of the finance team at a small private corporation. You have been asked to help prepare a presentation on the financial position of the company for a group of potential investors. Where would you start?

Like sole proprietorships, corporations prepare financial statements, although the specific reporting requirements differ depending on whether the corporation is private or public. Public companies must use International Financial Reporting Standards (IFRS), and private companies may use either IFRS or Accounting Standards for Private Enterprises (ASPE). The documents prepared under each of these standards include various statements that provide clear reporting on all aspects of the company's financial status.

In order to communicate appropriate information to convince the potential investors, you will also need to calculate and interpret some of the key ratios used by the investor community. Key documents and ratios are covered in this chapter.

Preparation of Financial Statements

LO 1

In the news, you may come across articles about large companies, such as Google or Microsoft, releasing their quarterly or annual reports. These companies are presenting their financial performances for the last period. Most stock exchanges require public companies to prepare financial statements every three months in addition to their annual reports.

You have already learned how to prepare financial statements for a sole proprietorship and partnership. The logic behind preparing statements for a corporation is the same, although these statements are generally more complex than those of a sole proprietorship. Corporations have access to more sources of financing, so the debt and equity sections of the balance sheet are different. Additionally, a corporation may offer more diverse products and services, which can make the income statement more complex.

One reason for the complexity is that a corporation's financial statements serve a much wider audience. While a sole proprietorship may have a few financial statement users, a corporation can have hundreds or thousands. Corporation ownership is determined by shares, so all shareholders are considered users of the financial statements. Also, a public corporation has potential investors—that is, potential shareholders—who may use the financial information in deciding whether to purchase the corporation's shares. Users of a corporation's financial statements want different financial information to serve their respective purposes, so the corporation is subject to more complex disclosure requirements than a sole proprietorship or partnership.

This chapter illustrates how a corporation's financial statements can be prepared to satisfy disclosure requirements. Financial disclosure requirements for a corporation can be found in Accounting Standards for Private Enterprises (ASPE) and International Financial Reporting Standards (IFRS). As explained in previous chapters, in Canada, public companies are required to use IFRS and private corporations can prepare statements according to either IFRS or ASPE.

Figure 6.1 shows the adjusted trial balance of a fictitious company, Darma Corporation, at its year end, December 31, 2020. The section that follows will assume Darma Corporation is private and follows ASPE. Later in the chapter, the reporting requirements under IFRS will be covered for a public corporation. In that section, the adjusted trial balance will include a few additional financial statement elements applicable primarily to public company reporting requirements.

Darma Corporation Adjusted Trial Balance December 31, 2020		
Account Title	**Debit**	**Credit**
Cash and Cash Equivalents	$87,650	
Short-Term Investments	287,580	
Accounts Receivable (net)	685,725	
Merchandise Inventory	1,652,840	
Prepaid Expenses	16,840	
Property, Plant & Equipment	5,174,000	
Accumulated Depreciation		$1,967,260
Goodwill	877,185	
Accounts Payable		556,890
Salaries Payable		15,845
Notes Payable*		612,620
Long-Term Accrued Liabilities		24,800
Common Shares		4,000,000
Retained Earnings		1,340,000
Cash Dividends	400,000	
Sales Revenue		2,519,650
Sales Discounts	1,200	
Sales Returns & Allowances	3,800	
Gain on Sale of Assets		4,500
Income from Operating Discontinued Operations		125,000
Gain on Sale of Discontinued Operations		45,000
Cost of Goods Sold	1,100,000	
Interest Expense	21,000	
Sales Salaries Expense	150,000	
Office Salaries Expense	125,000	
Depreciation Expense—Store Equipment	23,000	
Depreciation Expense—Office Equipment	21,000	
Advertising Expense	230,000	
Miscellaneous Administrative Expenses	70,000	
Income Tax Expense	284,745	
Total	$11,211,565	$11,211,565

*Notes Payable balance consists of current and long-term portions of $43,870 and $568,750, respectively.

FIGURE 6.1

Income Statement

LO 2

Recall that the purpose of an **income statement** is to display the company's profitability during a specific period. The income statement shows the amount of revenue and the expenses that are deducted to provide the net income figure for the period. This section will show the requirements for reporting a company's profitabilty under ASPE; reporting under IFRS will be covered later in the chapter.

Worth Repeating

Chapter 5 discussed the different types of corporations, public and private. Canadian public corporations are chartered under federal, provincial or territorial law, and they trade shares on a stock exchange such as the Toronto Stock Exchange (TSX) or the Montreal Exchange (MX). Public corporations in Canada are required to report under IFRS, while privately held corporations can choose between IFRS and ASPE.

The sample income statement for Darma Corporation under ASPE is shown in Figure 6.2. ASPE requires companies to separate continuing operations from discontinued operations in their income statement presentation. Therefore, Darma Corporation's income statement is divided into two major components: continuing operations and discontinued operations.

Worth Repeating

Income statements can be set up in single-step or multi-step formats. The multi-step format, which divides revenues and expenses to show subtotals like gross profit, operating expenses by function, and other income and expenses, will be used in this chapter's illustrations and problems.

Darma Corporation Income Statement For the Year Ended December 31, 2020			
Sales Revenue			$2,519,650
Less: Sales Returns & Allowances		$3,800	
Sales Discounts		1,200	5,000
Net Sales			2,514,650
Cost of Goods Sold			1,100,000
Gross Profit			1,414,650
Operating Expenses			
Selling Expenses			
Sales Salaries Expense	$150,000		
Depreciation Expense—Store Equipment	23,000		
Advertising Expense	230,000		
Total Selling Expenses		403,000	
Administrative Expenses			
Office Salaries Expense	125,000		
Depreciation Expense—Office Equipment	21,000		
Miscellaneous Administrative Expenses	70,000		
Total Administrative Expenses		216,000	
Total Operating Expenses			619,000
Income from Operations			(a) 795,650
Other Income and Expenses			
Gain on Sale of Assets		4,500	
Interest Expense		(21,000)	(16,500)
Income (Loss) from Continuing Operations before Income Tax Expense			(b) 779,150
Income Tax Expense			(c) 233,745
Income (Loss) from Continuing Operations			(d) 545,405
Discontinued Operations			
Income from Operating Discontinued Operations (net of $37,500 tax)		87,500	
Gain on Sale of Discontinued Operations (net of $13,500 tax)		31,500	(e) 119,000
Net Income (Loss)			(f) $664,405

Continuing Operations (Sales Revenue through Income (Loss) from Continuing Operations)

Discontinued Operations (Discontinued Operations through Gain on Sale of Discontinued Operations)

FIGURE 6.2

As we discuss how to complete the income statement, we will refer to the lettered items in Figure 6.2.

Continuing Operations

Continuing operations refers to a company's normal day-to-day activities, such as the process required to make a product or service and deliver it to a customer. These operations are expected to continue in the near future. A large corporation may have several different lines of business that serve different types of customers or provide different goods and services. Each of these different operations is known as a **business segment**. Occasionally, a company may sell or discontinue a business segment. Companies are required to report the results of discontinued operations separately, as will be discussed later in this chapter.

Income (loss) from continuing operations shows the results of the company's operations that are ongoing. It represents the results of only business segments that have not been sold or discontinued. The income (loss) from continuing operations can be calculated in multiple steps. The first step is to calculate gross profit using the formula shown in Figure 6.3.

Gross Profit = Net Sales − Cost of Goods Sold

FIGURE 6.3

Using values for net sales and COGS from the income statement, gross profit is calculated as follows.

Gross Profit = \$2,514,650 − \$1,100,000
= \$1,414,650

Figure 6.4 shows the formula to calculate income from operations.

Income from Operations = Gross Profit − Total Operating Expenses

FIGURE 6.4

As seen in Figure 6.2, a multi-step income statement groups the operating expenses into subcategories such as selling and administrative expenses. Using the total of those subcategories and the value for gross profit already calculated, we can calculate income from operations.

Income from Operations = \$1,414,650 − \$619,000
= \$795,650 ⓐ

The next step is to calculate income (loss) from continuing operations before income tax expense, using the formula shown in Figure 6.5.

Income (Loss) from Continuing Operations before Income Tax Expense = Income from Operations + Other Income − Other Expenses

FIGURE 6.5

For this calculation, other income is added to, and other expenses are subtracted from, income from operations. **Other income (expenses)** includes items that are not part of the company's regular day-to-day operations. For example, any gain or loss on the sale of property, plant and equipment is listed as other income or expenses. In Darma's case, there is one gain and one loss (expense) from the other income (expenses) category. The calculation is shown here, with the value for income from operations taken from the calculation above.

$$\text{Income (Loss) from Continuing Operations before Income Tax Expense} = \$795{,}650 + \$4{,}500 - \$21{,}000 = \$779{,}150 \text{ (b)}$$

Next we will look at calculating continuing operations' taxes, which must be reported separately from discontinued operations' taxes. Continuing operations' income tax expense appears on the income statement following the income (loss) from continuing operations before income tax expense. Corporate income tax calculations in the real world can be quite complex and are beyond the scope of this textbook. For illustrative purposes, income tax presentation will be simply calculated by multiplying a tax percentage by an income figure. The formula to calculate income (loss) from continuing operations is shown in Figure 6.6.

Income (Loss) from Continuing Operations =
Income (Loss) from Continuing Operations before Income Tax Expense − Income Tax Expense

FIGURE 6.6

Assume Darma must pay income tax at 30%. Darma's income tax expense based on its income before taxes and discontinued operations is $233,745 (c) ($779,150 × 30%). This income tax expense is deducted from the income (loss) from continuing operations before income tax expense to determine the income (loss) from continuing operations, as shown here.

$$\text{Income (Loss) from Continuing Operations} = \$779{,}150 - \$233{,}745 = \$545{,}405 \text{ (d)}$$

Discontinued Operations

A **discontinued operation** is a business segment that is no longer part of the company's regular operating activities. The formula to calculate income from discontinued operations is shown in Figure 6.7.

Income (Loss) from Discontinued Operations = Income (Loss) from Operating Discontinued Operations, Net of Income Tax Expense (Benefit)
+ Gain (Loss) on Disposal of Discontinued Operations, Net of Income Tax Expense (Benefit)

FIGURE 6.7

During the year, Darma discontinued a segment of its business operations. This segment generated an income from operations of $125,000 before its disposal and a $45,000 gain on the sale of the assets. Darma must pay 30% tax on both the income and gain. These taxes are not reported as a separate line item; therefore, income from operating discontinued operations is reported as $87,000 ($125,000 – $37,500 in tax). The gain on disposal of discontinued operations is reported as $31,500 ($45,000 – $13,500 in tax). Using these values, income (loss) from discontinued operations is calculated as shown.

Income (Loss) from Discontinued Operations = ($125,000 − $37,500) + ($45,000 − $13,500)
= $119,000 ⓔ

We can now calculate net income (loss) using the formula shown in Figure 6.8.

Net Income (Loss) = Income (Loss) from Continuing Operations + Income (Loss) from Discontinued Operations

FIGURE 6.8

For Darma Corporation, we use the values that were just calculated to determine the total net income (loss), as shown here.

Net Income (Loss) = $545,405 + $119,000
= $664,405 ⓕ

The after-tax income from continuing operations and the after-tax income from discontinued operations leave Darma with a total net income of $664,405.

If the discontinued segment showed a loss from its operations or from the sale of assets, Darma would recognize a savings of income tax. For example, suppose Darma has an operating loss from the discontinued operations and the assets are sold at a loss for a total of $100,000. Darma saves 30% (or $30,000) of that in income tax, so the net loss is $70,000.

Another scenario is that Darma has income from operations from the discontinued segment but incurs a loss from the sale of assets. In this case, suppose Darma has income from operations of $100,000 from the discontinued segment but the assets are sold at a loss of $30,000. Darma needs to pay income tax of $30,000 ($100,000 × 30%) but also has an income tax benefit of $9,000 ($30,000 × 30%). The net effect is paying tax of $21,000 ($30,000 − $9,000) for this discontinued segment.

It is important to report the income from continuing operations and from discontinued operations separately because investors and creditors rely on this accounting information to make decisions. Reporting separately allows the users of financial information to identify what is not relevant to the company's ongoing performance. This especially helps users predict future results, such as how much profit the company will make in the following year and how competitive the company will be after eliminating a segment.

Shareholders' Equity

LO 3

Recall that the equity section of a sole proprietorship is referred to as owner's equity. In a corporation, this section of the financial statements is referred to as shareholders' equity, which is made up of contributed capital and retained earnings. The components of contributed capital were explained in Chapter 5. Contributed capital is also referenced in the IFRS reporting section later in this chapter.

Statement of Retained Earnings

All corporations are required to report on the changes to retained earnings during the accounting period. Retained earnings are the earnings that are kept and accumulated by the company after dividends have been paid to the shareholders. Note that the income statement must be prepared before the statement of retained earnings because the net income from the income statement must be added to (or the net loss subtracted from) the retained earnings at the beginning of the period. Retained earnings increase if the company reported a net income and decrease if the company reported a net loss or paid out dividends.

Under ASPE, the retained earnings account is the only equity account for which a private corporation must report changes in a separate statement, called the **statement of retained earnings**. ASPE also requires that changes in other shareholders' equity accounts be presented in the notes to the financial statements. You will learn more about the requirements under IFRS later in this chapter; for now, we will discuss the requirements under ASPE, using the example of Darma Corporation.

Assume Darma had an opening balance of retained earnings of $1,340,000 and paid $400,000 in cash dividends. As shown in Figure 6.9, the statement of retained earnings is prepared in a similar way to the statement of owner's equity in a sole proprietorship. The net income is taken from the income statement that was already prepared.

Darma Corporation Statement of Retained Earnings For the Year Ended December 31, 2020	
Retained Earnings, January 1, 2020	$1,340,000
Net Income	664,405
Less: Cash Dividends	400,000
Retained Earnings, December 31, 2020	$1,604,405

FIGURE 6.9

This statement is prepared based on the assumption that no adjustment needs to be made to the beginning retained earnings balance. Sometimes, this balance needs to be adjusted due to prior period adjustments, which are discussed later in the chapter. Figure 6.10 illustrates how the retained earnings balance is reported within the shareholders' equity section of the balance sheet for Darma Corporation for December 31, 2020.

Shareholders' Equity Section of Balance Sheet		
Shareholders' Equity		
Contributed Capital		
Common shares, unlimited shares authorized, 200,000 shares issued and outstanding	4,000,000	
Retained Earnings	1,604,405	
Total Shareholders' Equity		5,604,405

FIGURE 6.10

Balance Sheet

LO 4

The statement of retained earnings links the income statement and the balance sheet together. The net income figure from the income statement is used in the statement of retained earnings to calculate the ending balance of retained earnings. This ending balance is then presented under the shareholders' equity section on the balance sheet. The balance sheet under ASPE is illustrated next; reporting under IFRS will be covered in the next section.

A **classified balance sheet** prepared under ASPE looks very similar to a sole proprietorship's balance sheet. Assets and liabilities are listed on the basis of liquidity from most liquid to least liquid (i.e. the current items are listed first). ASPE allows a company the flexibility to call this statement either a balance sheet or a statement of financial position. The normal presentation of a balance sheet includes an asset section with the following classifications of assets.

- Current Assets
- Long-Term Investments (to be covered in later chapters)
- Property, Plant and Equipment
- Goodwill and Intangible Assets

The liabilities section has the following classification of liabilities.

- Current Liabilities
- Long-Term Liabilities

The shareholders' equity section includes the following sections.

- Contributed Capital
- Retained Earnings

As referenced in the previous section on shareholders' equity, contributed capital is generally made up of two subcategories called share capital and contributed surplus. Share capital refers to common or preferred shares and contributed surplus refers to other types of additions to shareholders' contributions. Accounting for share capital was covered in the previous chapter and contributed surplus is explained at a high level in the appendix of the previous chapter.

Figure 6.11 shows the classified balance sheet for Darma Corporation prepared according to ASPE.

Darma Corporation Balance Sheet As at December 31, 2020		
Assets		
Current Assets		
Cash and Cash Equivalents		$87,650
Short-Term Investments		287,580
Accounts Receivable (net)		685,725
Merchandise Inventory		1,652,840
Prepaid Expenses		16,840
Total Current Assets		2,730,635
Property, Plant & Equipment (net)		3,206,740
Goodwill		877,185
Total Assets		$6,814,560
Liabilities		
Current Liabilities		
Accounts Payable	$556,890	
Notes Payable, Current Portion	43,870	
Salaries Payable	15,845	
Total Current Liabilities		$616,605
Long-Term Liabilities		
Notes Payable, Long-Term Portion	568,750	
Long-Term Accrued Liabilities	24,800	
Total Long-Term Liabilities		593,550
Total Liabilities		1,210,155
Shareholders' Equity		
Contributed Capital		
Common Shares, unlimited shares authorized, 200,000 shares issued and outstanding	4,000,000	
Retained Earnings	1,604,405	
Total Shareholders' Equity		5,604,405
Total Liabilities and Shareholders' Equity		$6,814,560

FIGURE 6.11

The balance sheet in Figure 6.11 illustrates the common practice of presenting the individual items under each classification ordered by liquidity (most liquid to least liquid). Many companies choose to reverse the order of the individual items from least liquid to most liquid. There is currently no specific requirement for the order of these sections according to ASPE.

Financial Statements under IFRS

LO 5

The previous sections have illustrated preparation of financial statements under ASPE. Consider another fictitious company named SETUP Corporation, which is a public company. SETUP Corporation must prepare its financial statements under IFRS. This section will now illustrate IFRS reporting requirements.

Figure 6.12 shows the adjusted trial balance of SETUP Corporation assuming the company is public.

SETUP Corporation Adjusted Trial Balance December 31, 2020		
Account Titles	**Debit**	**Credit**
Cash	$87,650	
Short-Term Investments	287,580	
Accounts Receivable (net)	685,725	
Merchandise Inventory	1,652,840	
Prepaid Expenses	16,840	
Property, Plant & Equipment (net)	3,206,740	
Goodwill	777,185	
Accounts Payable		$556,890
Salaries Payable		15,845
Current Portion of Long-Term Debt		43,870
Long-Term Debt (Notes Payable)		568,750
Long-Term Accrued Liabilities		24,800
Common Shares		3,900,000
Retained Earnings		1,340,000
Cash Dividends	400,000	
Sales Revenue		2,505,750
Sales Discounts	1,200	
Sales Returns and Allowances	3,800	
Gain on Sale of Assets		4,500
Gain on Foreign Currency Translation		5,200
Unrealized Gain on Investments		8,700
Operating Income from Discontinued Operations		125,000
Gain on Sale of Assets from Discontinued Operations		45,000
Cost of Goods Sold	1,100,000	
Interest Expense	21,000	
Sales Salaries Expense	150,000	
Office Salaries Expense	125,000	
Depreciation Expense—Store Equipment	23,000	
Depreciation Expense—Office Equipment	21,000	
Advertising Expense	230,000	
Miscellaneous Administrative Expenses	70,000	
Income Tax Expense—Continuing Operations	233,745	
Income Tax Expense—Discontinued Operations	51,000	
Total	$9,144,305	$9,144,305

FIGURE 6.12

Statement of Comprehensive Income

Since SETUP Corporation is a public corporation, it will prepare a **statement of comprehensive income** under IFRS guidelines. Some of the IFRS requirements on how to present the statement of comprehensive income are similar to ASPE's requirements for presenting the income statement. For example, both must separate continuing operations income from discontinued operations. However, the comprehensive income statement under IFRS is more complex because of three additional requirements:

1. Comprehensive income
2. Presentation of expenses by function or by nature
3. Presentation of earnings per share

Each of these additional requirements is discussed below.

Comprehensive Income

Comprehensive income is the total of net income plus other comprehensive income (or loss). **Other comprehensive income** (**OCI**) is a category of income resulting from transactions that are beyond company owners' or management's control, such as a change in market value of investments. Other comprehensive income can arise from adjustments in fair value of investments, pension, or property, plant and equipment, and also from foreign currency translation transactions. IFRS does not allow these items to be reported as part of net income, but they do affect the equity accounts. Other comprehensive income is presented on the statement showing classification of expenses by function in Figure 6.13 below. (We will examine what "by function" means a little later.) As shown in Figure 6.13, a section called other comprehensive income appears below net income. Other comprehensive income (or loss) is added to net income to arrive at total comprehensive income. The details of the items in other comprehensive income are beyond the scope of this textbook.

IFRS requires that other comprehensive income (or loss) be reported either in its own section on the statement of comprehensive income or in a separate statement that accompanies the traditional income statement. This textbook will present other comprehensive income in its own section on the statement of comprehensive income. IFRS requires that each item listed under other comprehensive income be reported net of income tax. If the company chooses to report the total comprehensive income as one line item, the number shown must be net of income tax. This is why the sample statement in Figure 6.13 includes the heading "Other Comprehensive Income, Net of Tax."

Presentation of Expenses by Function

IFRS requires that expenses be analyzed and presented on the statement of comprehensive income either by function or by nature. A corporation is allowed to choose the more suitable of the two methods for its statement presentation, based on which format is considered most reliable and relevant to its users. IFRS also allows the expenses to be listed in any order within each classification.

Classifying expenses **by function** means that expenses are presented on the statement according to the various functions of the company, such as selling expenses and administrative expenses.

When a company uses the "by function" presentation for its income statement, it must still disclose the individual expenses by nature in notes to the statement. Figure 6.13 demonstrates how SETUP Corporation presents its statement of comprehensive income with expenses analyzed by function.

SETUP Corporation Statement of Comprehensive Income (by function) For the Year Ended December 31, 2020	
Sales (Net)	$2,500,750
Cost of Goods Sold	(1,100,000)
Gross Profit	1,400,750
Selling Expenses	(403,000)
Administrative Expenses	(216,000)
Other Income (Expenses)(1)	13,200
Operating Profit	794,950
Finance Costs	(21,000)
Profit before Income Tax	773,950
Income Tax Expense	(232,185)
Profit for the Year from Continuing Operations	541,765
Profit for the Year from Discontinued Operations(2)	119,000
Profit for the Year	660,765
Other Comprehensive Income, Net of Tax	
Foreign Currency Translation Adjustments (net of $1,560 tax)(3)	3,640
Total Comprehensive Income	$664,405
Basic and Diluted Earnings per Share*	
Continuing Operations	2.71
Discontinued Operations	0.60
Net Income (Loss)	3.30

(1) $4,500 Gain on Sale of Assets + $8,700 Unrealized Gain on Trading Investments = $13,200
(2) ($125,000 + $45,000) − 30% tax = $119,000
(3) $5,200 − 30% tax = $3,640
*Detailed calculations of the Earnings per Share figures are provided later in the chapter.

FIGURE 6.13

Presentation of Expenses by Nature

Classifying expenses **by nature** means that expenses are presented on the statement according to their natural classification, such as salary expense, employee benefits, advertising expense, depreciation, and so on. Expenses analyzed by nature are *not* allocated to the different functions of the business. Figure 6.14 demonstrates how SETUP Corporation presents its statement of comprehensive income with expenses analyzed by nature.

SETUP Corporation Statement of Comprehensive Income (by nature) For the Year Ended December 31, 2020	
Sales (Net)	$2,500,750
Cost of Goods Sold	(1,100,000)
Gross Profit	1,400,750
Salaries Expense	(275,000)
Depreciation Expense	(44,000)
Advertising Expense	(230,000)
Miscellaneous Administrative Expenses	(70,000)
Other Income (Expenses)	13,200
Operating Profit	794,950
Finance Costs	(21,000)
Profit before Income Tax	773,950
Income Tax Expense	(232,185)
Profit for the Year from Continuing Operations	541,765
Profit for the Year from Discontinued Operations	119,000
Profit for the Year	660,765
Other Comprehensive Income, Net of Tax	
Foreign Currency Translation Adjustments (net of $1,560 tax)	3,640
Total Comprehensive Income	$664,405
Basic and Diluted Earnings Per Share	
Continuing Operations	2.71
Discontinued Operations	0.60
Net Income (Loss)	3.30

FIGURE 6.14

Summary of Differences between ASPE's Income Statement and IFRS's Statement of Comprehensive Income

As illustrated earlier in the chapter assuming reporting under ASPE, the recognition and measurement of items on an income statement are intended to be much less complex under ASPE than IFRS. This is why ASPE does not require the recognition of other comprehensive income items and has no requirement to prepare income statements with expenses detailed by function or nature. ASPE does mandate minimum disclosures on the face of the financial statements to ensure that the information provided is useful. The main differences between ASPE's income statement and IFRS's statement of comprehensive income are summarized in Figure 6.15.

Topic of Interest	ASPE	IFRS
Statement name	Income Statement, or Statement of Income	Statement of Comprehensive Income, or Statement of Income and Comprehensive Income
Presentation of expenses	There is no specific rule on how to present the expenses as long as all items that are required are included.	Expenses should be classified by either their nature or their function.
Other comprehensive income/comprehensive income	All profit and loss items are included in net income without being separated into other comprehensive income.	Items must be classified as either comprehensive income or net income. Other comprehensive income must be presented either in a stand-alone statement or as a separate section within the statement of comprehensive income.
Earnings per share (EPS)	EPS is not mentioned.	Basic and diluted EPS must be presented in the statement.

FIGURE 6.15

Recall that the net income figure from the income statement is added to the beginning retained earnings balance in the statement of retained earnings under ASPE. Similarly, the net income figure from the statement of comprehensive income is added to the beginning retained earnings balance in the the statement of changes in equity (under IFRS), as explained in the next section.

Statement of Changes in Equity

IFRS requires that all changes to the equity accounts be shown on a **statement of changes in equity**. This statement must include changes in retained earnings, the changes in capital and any other items that affected equity during the period.

The statement of changes in equity has a column for each item that makes up shareholders' equity. Net income from the statement of comprehensive income is added to retained earnings, and dividends are subtracted from retained earnings. Any issuance of common or preferred shares is added to the respective capital account within shareholders' equity.

There are some differences in terminology between ASPE and IFRS. Companies that report under IFRS usually refer to some parts of shareholders' equity that are not common shares and retained earnings under the title "reserves." Treasury shares, for example, can be reported as part of the reserves. As you learned in the previous chapter's appendix, in addition to issuing shares, a corporation can also buy back its own shares from shareholders. Although not common in Canada, some shares are allowed to be held as treasury shares, meaning that they can be reissued instead of being retired or cancelled. Under IFRS, an alternative is to report treasury shares as a separate item, although doing so is not required, unlike under ASPE. In SETUP's example, the company reports treasury shares as reserve for own shares and reports foreign currency translation adjustments, which are a part of other comprehensive income, as foreign currency translation reserve. A total column combines all values and shows how equity changed from the beginning of the period to the end.

Figure 6.16 shows the statement of changes in equity under IFRS for SETUP Corporation for the year ended December 31, 2020. Note that SETUP does not have any preferred shares outstanding.

SETUP Corporation Statement of Changes in Equity For the Year Ended December 31, 2020						
				Reserves		
	Common Shares	Preferred Shares	Retained Earnings	Foreign Currency Translation Reserve	Reserve for Own Shares	Total Equity
Balance, January 1, 2020	$4,000,000		$1,340,000	$0	($100,000)	$5,240,000
Profit for the Year			660,765			660,765
Other Comprehensive Income						
Currency Translation Adjustments				3,640		3,640
Total Comprehensive Income			660,765	3,640		664,405
Transactions with Owners						
Dividends on Common Shares			(400,000)			(400,000)
Total Transactions with Owners	0	0	(400,000)	0	0	(400,000)
Balance, December 31, 2020	$4,000,000		$1,600,765	$3,640	($100,000)	$5,504,405

FIGURE 6.16

The statement of retained earnings in Figure 6.9 and the statement of changes in equity in Figure 6.16 are prepared based on the assumption that no adjustment needs to be made to the beginning retained earnings balance. Sometimes, this balance needs to be adjusted due to prior period adjustments, which is discussed later in the chapter.

Summary of Differences between ASPE's Statement of Retained Earnings and IFRS's Statement of Changes in Equity

The main differences between ASPE's statement of retained earnings and IFRS's statement of changes in equity are summarized in Figure 6.17.

Topic of Interest	ASPE	IFRS
Statement name	Statement of Retained Earnings	Statement of Changes in Equity
Content	Only changes in retained earnings are presented on the face of the statement. Changes in other shareholders' equity accounts are presented in the notes to the financial statements.	Changes in all equity accounts are presented on the face of the statement.

FIGURE 6.17

Statement of Financial Position

Preparing a **statement of financial position** under IFRS involves some similarities to, as well as some notable differences from, preparing a balance sheet under ASPE. Figure 6.18 shows the statement of financial position for SETUP Corporation under IFRS guidelines. Note that it shows reserves under equity attributable to owners, and this is where SETUP's treasury shares and foreign currency translation reserve are reported.

SETUP Corporation Statement of Financial Position As at December 31, 2020		
Assets		
Long-Term Assets		
Property, Plant & Equipment (net)		$3,206,740
Goodwill		777,185
Total Long-Term Assets		3,983,925
Current Assets		
Prepaid Expenses	$16,840	
Merchandise Inventory	1,652,840	
Accounts Receivable (net)	685,725	
Short-Term Investments	287,580	
Cash and Cash Equivalents	87,650	
Total Current Assets		2,730,635
Total Assets		$6,714,560
Equity Attributable to Owners		
Common Shares, unlimited shares authorized,		
200,000 shares issued and outstanding	$4,000,000	
Reserves	(96,360)	
Retained Earnings	1,600,765	
Total Equity Attributable to Owners		$5,504,405
Liabilities		
Long-Term Liabilities		
Notes Payable, Long-Term Portion	568,750	
Long-Term Accrued Liabilities	24,800	
Total Long-Term Liabilities		593,550
Current Liabilities		
Accounts Payable	556,890	
Notes Payable, Current Portion	43,870	
Salaries Payable	15,845	
Total Current Liabilities		616,605
Total Liabilities		1,210,155
Total Equity and Liabilities		$6,714,560

FIGURE 6.18

Summary of Differences between ASPE's Balance Sheet and IFRS's Statement of Financial Position

The main differences between ASPE's and IFRS's balance sheets or statements of financial position are summarized in Figure 6.19.

Topic of Interest	ASPE	IFRS
Statement name	Both Balance Sheet and Statement of Financial Position are acceptable, although Balance Sheet is more often used.	Both Balance Sheet and Statement of Financial Position are acceptable, although Statement of Financial Position is more often used.
Listing order	Listing order is not specified, but companies adopting ASPE tend to list items from most liquid to least liquid. Liabilities are usually presented before shareholders' equity.	Listing order is not specified, but companies adopting IFRS tend to list items from least liquid to most liquid. Shareholders' equity is usually presented before liabilities.
Shareholders' equity section	Because companies that use ASPE do not report other comprehensive income, the accumulated other comprehensive income (reserves) account does not exist on the balance sheet.	Retained earnings and accumulated other comprehensive income (reserves) are reported separately.

FIGURE 6.19

In the Real World

In Canada, all public companies must file their financial statements, annual reports and other required documents through the System for Electronic Document Analysis and Retrieval (SEDAR). SEDAR is an electronic filing system that provides public access to company financial information; it is managed by the Canadian Securities Administrators (CSA). Reports on SEDAR are uploaded and made available in PDF format. However, this format makes it difficult for analysts to compare or look for trends in financial information, especially between competitors. This is because the information would have to be manually input into a spreadsheet or other software system for analysis.

One solution to this issue is XBRL, which stands for eXtensible Business Reporting Language. XBRL is a standard language that allows financial information to be shared digitally. It uses tags to help identify data and can be transmitted easily between software systems. This standard is currently being adopted all over the world. In the United States, the Security and Exchange Commission (SEC) requires companies to provide filings in XBRL, and regulators in Canada are allowing companies to begin sharing their documents in this way. In addition, Canadian companies who are listed on a US stock exchange will need to comply with XBRL filing format rules.

Accounting Changes and Prior Period Adjustments

LO 6

Sometimes errors are discovered in the accounting records. A correcting entry can be made, but it must be journalized and posted before the closing entries at the end of that period. That way, the information will be included in the period to which it belongs. For example, if a company's accounting clerk discovers an error in a journal entry that was made on June 15, 2020, and corrects it on June 22, 2020, the financial statements for June will be accurate.

But what happens when an error is found after the period has been closed? The error must be corrected so that the information is included in the period to which it belongs and remains comparable from one period to the next. A correcting entry that is made to a previous period is known as a **prior period adjustment**. Prior period adjustments are particularly important because they can affect net income (or loss) of the prior period and therefore affect the beginning retained earnings balance for the current period.

Accounting errors are just one of three types of accounting changes that can affect a prior period's financial information. The three types of accounting changes are as follows.

- Correction of prior period errors
- Change in accounting policy
- Change in accounting estimate

The mechanics of how the prior period adjustments are made and how they are presented are similar for ASPE and IFRS. The illustration that follows shows a correction of a prior period error on the statement of retained earnings under ASPE for Darma Corporation.

Correction of Prior Period Errors

Errors are sometimes made in financial statements, which then require correction in a future period. Suppose a $25,000 purchase of equipment was mistakenly recorded as maintenance expense. The original entry was made in 2019 but is not discovered until 2020. Because the error overstated the repairs and maintenance expenses, income for 2019 was understated by $25,000. Simply transferring $25,000 from maintenance expense to equipment is not appropriate, because maintenance expense would then be understated for 2020. The transfer would also not address the fact that retained earnings should be increased when this error is corrected.

The solution is to increase the balance of the equipment account by $25,000 so that the asset is properly recorded. The balance in retained earnings should also increase; however, the income taxes that are now owed on the extra income must also be taken into account. If Darma pays 30% income tax, it will owe $7,500 in taxes based on the increase of $25,000 in income. The final journal entry is shown in Figure 6.20. Notice that this entry affects only balance sheet accounts and not the income statement.

JOURNAL			
Date	**Account Title and Explanation**	**Debit**	**Credit**
Jan 31	Equipment	25,000	
	Retained Earnings		17,500
	Income Tax Payable (25,000 × 30%)		7,500
	To record correction for error in June 15, 2019 journal entry, expensed to Repairs and Maintenance		

FIGURE 6.20

The error caused net income for 2019 to be understated by $17,500 ($25,000 less the income tax at a rate of 30%). By crediting retained earnings for the net effect of the error, this account was corrected to reflect the income that would have been recorded. Income taxes payable are also corrected to reflect the actual amount owing on the income earned.

When a company has a prior period error, adjustments to retained earnings must be included in the statement of retained earnings if the company uses ASPE or the statement of changes in equity if the company uses IFRS. Specifically, the adjustment to retained earnings is listed before any other items are added or subtracted. The statement of retained earnings with the prior period adjustment is shown in Figure 6.21.

Darma Corporation Statement of Retained Earnings For the Year Ended December 31, 2020	
Retained Earnings, January 1, 2020	$1,340,000
Add: Prior Year Adjustment	17,500
Add: Net Income for the Period	664,405
	2,021,905
Less: Cash Dividends	(400,000)
Retained Earnings, December 31, 2020	$1,621,905

FIGURE 6.21

Change in Accounting Policy

Suppose that in fiscal year 2020, Darma Corporation changes its method of depreciation from the straight-line to the double-declining balance method. The decision to change its depreciation method represents a **change in accounting policy**. Under IFRS, this can be undertaken by a company only if the change is required by IFRS or if the change will result in more reliable and relevant information for users of its financial statements. Under ASPE a company does not need to meet the reliability/relevance test to change an accounting policy.

If Darma always reports comparative numbers (statements for two or more years) on its financial statements, then this change in depreciation policy means the 2019 and 2020 values for depreciation expense and net income are not comparable. When there is a change in accounting policy, accounting standards require a restatement of previously reported information. The new accounting policy must be retroactively applied to the prior period's accounting information that is presented in comparison with the current period's information, as if the new accounting policy had always been used. This change to accounting information on prior period financial statements is also known as the **retroactive approach**.

Because of the change in accounting policy, Darma has to restate the 2019 comparative amounts in the 2020 financial statements. In addition, the beginning balances of 2019 and 2020 retained earnings have to be adjusted for the cumulative effect of using the double-declining balance method over the straight-line method. The adjustment would reflect a larger depreciation expense (lower net income) for prior periods up until 2019, assuming the asset is relatively new; therefore, depreciation expense under the double-declining balance method is higher than the depreciation expense under the straight-line method up until 2019. Similar to the correction of prior period errors, the cumulative effect of the change in accounting policy would be added to (or subtracted from) the beginning retained earnings balance in the statement of retained earnings.

Change in Accounting Estimate

Often, items that are recorded in a company's accounting records and reported on its financial statements are based on estimates. For example, the useful life of an asset is usually estimated to calculate its depreciation over time. But what if the useful life of an asset turns out to be significantly longer (or shorter) than originally estimated? This is not an error, but it represents a **change in accounting estimate**. In such a case, no prior period adjustment is necessary. This type of change would simply be handled by using the new estimate to calculate depreciation for the current and future periods, also known as the **prospective approach**.

Figure 6.22 summarizes the accounting treatment of three types of accounting changes previously discussed. As mentioned previously, these accounting changes are presented similarly in ASPE and IFRS.

Accounting Changes	Accounting Treatment
Correction of Prior Period Errors	Retrospective approach with restatement, including the presentation of prior period error corrections as an addition to (or deduction from) the beginning retained earnings balance in the statement of retained earnings
Accounting Policy Changes	Retrospective approach with restatement as if the new policy had always been used
Accounting Estimate Changes	Prospective approach affecting only current and future periods

FIGURE 6.22

A Closer Look

Since a company's financial statements are intended to communicate useful, relevant information to the investment community, it is imperative that accounting changes be disclosed and accounted for properly. Overlooking an accounting change or reporting it incorrectly (or not at all) has the potential to mislead the users.

In the example of Darma Corporation, if the error in reporting the purchase of equipment discussed above had been accounted for in the current year, the income would be understated. Shareholders could then be left with a false impression of the company's financial status.

Earnings per Share

LO 7

The previous chapter discussed how corporations raise capital by offering their shares to the public. For investors, there are two monetary reasons to buy shares in a company. One is the potential to make a profit from an increase in the share price (what is known as a *capital gain*). The other is the anticipation of regular payments of cash dividends.

Worth Repeating

Shares are an attractive investment because they offer limited liability and have the potential to increase in value. They also offer liquidity, which is the ability to sell or transfer shares at their market value. The market value of shares is determined by the amount that investors are willing to pay for them at that particular point in time. This means that the shares may be sold at a higher or lower price than the current holder paid for them.

Every corporation issues common shares. Common shares are a type of equity that gives shareholders ownership in the corporation, along with voting rights to elect a board of directors and the potential to receive a portion of the company's equity in the form of dividends. Investors buy common shares with the expectation that the corporation will remain or become profitable, although the payment of dividends is not guaranteed. Some corporations also offer another class of shares known as preferred shares.

When potential investors are deciding which company's shares to buy, they first want to know something about the company's profitability. One key indicator of a company's profitability is a value known as earnings per share. **Earnings per share** (**EPS**) is a ratio that indicates the profit earned by each common share. EPS enables shareholders to evaluate the potential return on their investment. We will look at the formula for calculating earnings per share.

First, recall the discussion about dividends from the previous chapter. When a company issues both preferred and common shares, dividends must be paid to preferred shareholders first. The remainder of profits available for dividends is then declared to the common shareholders. Because EPS is calculated only on common shares, the current year's preferred dividends are subtracted from net income, and the result is divided by the weighted average number of common shares outstanding. The **weighted average number of common shares outstanding** is determined by multiplying the number of shares outstanding by the fraction of the year during which those shares were outstanding. This ensures that the number of shares outstanding is matched to the amount of income that was earned on them.

The formula for calculating earnings per share is presented in Figure 6.23.

$$\text{Earnings per Share} = \frac{\text{Net Income} - \text{Preferred Dividends}}{\text{Weighted Average Number of Common Shares Outstanding}}$$

FIGURE 6.23

A Closer Look

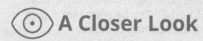

In the formula for calculating earnings per share, only the preferred dividends amount declared is deducted from net income. However, if the preferred shares are cumulative, the annual dividends should be deducted regardless of whether they have been declared or not.

Also note that the formula uses only net income, excluding any other comprehensive income (OCI). As mentioned earlier, OCI is any gain or loss that impacts equity and is not part of net income.

All calculations in this section are based on the example of SETUP Corporation, as a public company. From Figure 6.13 or 6.14, SETUP's 2020 net income of $660,765 is used. Assume that SETUP has 200,000 common shares outstanding on December 31, 2020, and no preferred shares outstanding. For now, also assume that there were no changes to the number of shares outstanding for 2020; that is, all 200,000 common shares were outstanding for the entire year. SETUP's earnings per share (EPS) is calculated as follows.

$$\text{Earnings per Share} = \frac{(\$660{,}765 - \$0)}{200{,}000}$$

$$= \frac{\$660{,}765}{200{,}000}$$

$$= \$3.30$$

For the year ended December 31, 2020, SETUP Corporation had a basic earnings per share (EPS) of $3.30, which means the company is earning a profit of $3.30 for every common share outstanding. The general interpretation is that the higher the EPS, the more profitable the company.

A Closer Look

When examining corporate financial statements, it is common to see two earnings per share figures: basic earnings per share and fully diluted earnings per share. **Basic earnings per share** is based on actual shares that have been issued to shareholders, and it is shown in this textbook. **Fully diluted earnings per share** is based on actual and potential shares that have or could be issued. Potential shares can arise from a few places.

- Management compensation—Some corporations give senior management options to purchase company shares at a reduced price.
- Convertible bonds—Corporations can sell bonds that are convertible into shares in the company.
- Convertible preferred shares—Corporations may issue preferred shares with the "convertible" feature, which allows preferred shareholders to convert their preferred shares into common shares.

The fully diluted EPS is calculated as if all existing management options, convertible bonds and convertible preferred shares were converted into common shares. This causes the fully diluted EPS to be a smaller figure than the basic EPS. The concept of fully diluted EPS is covered in more advanced accounting courses.

When earnings per share was calculated for the statement of comprehensive income, it was assumed that there was no change in the number of outstanding common shares for the entire year. That is, SETUP had 200,000 common shares outstanding on January 1, 2020, and 200,000 common shares outstanding on December 31, 2020. What if SETUP had 200,000 common shares outstanding on January 1, 2020, and issued an additional 10,000 common shares on July 1, 2020, which would mean 10,000 additional shares were outstanding for six months, from July 1 to December 31? This is where the calculation of weighted average number of shares is required. Figure 6.24 summarizes the numbers needed to calculate EPS for this situation.

Date 2020	Actual Number of Shares	Fraction of Year	Weighted Average Number of Shares
Jan 1	200,000	× 12 months/12 months	200,000
Jul 1	10,000	× 6 months/12 months	5,000
Total	210,000		205,000

FIGURE 6.24

In addition, assume that SETUP Corporation has preferred shares and declared preferred dividends of $50,000 for 2020. The calculation of earnings per share for 2020 using the formula from Figure 6.23 is shown here.

$$\text{Earnings per Share} = \frac{(\$660{,}765 - \$50{,}000)}{205{,}000}$$

$$= \frac{\$610{,}765}{205{,}000}$$

$$= \$2.98$$

For the year ended December 31, 2020, SETUP Corporation had earnings per share (EPS) of $2.98. Under these changed conditions, the company is earning a profit of $2.98 for every common share outstanding.

Under IFRS, corporations must disclose earnings per share (EPS) on their statement of comprehensive income, or on the income statement if it is presented separately. EPS must also be explained in notes to the financial statements. ASPE does not require EPS ratios to be shown on the income statement; however, most private companies present EPS ratios, as stakeholders find those calculations useful information.

Pause & Reflect

Exercise 6-1

The December 31, 2020 statement of comprehensive income for Digit Corporation shows profit from continuing operations was $850,000 and profit for the year was $925,000.

The company had 100,000 common shares outstanding on December 31, 2020, and no preferred shares outstanding. There were no changes to the number of shares during the year. Calculate the company's earnings per share from continuing operations and basic earnings per share.

Earnings per share from continuing operations	
Basic earnings per share	

See Appendix I for solutions.

Calculation of Financial Ratios

LO 8

In addition to earnings per share (EPS), there are several other ratios of interest to potential investors, shareholders and other users of financial information: book value per share, dividend yield, dividend payout ratio and price–earnings (P/E) ratio. This section discusses these ratios and how they are used to evaluate a company's earnings and dividend performance. To illustrate these ratios, the SETUP Corporation data reported under IFRS is used.

Book Value per Common Share

Like earnings per share (EPS), book value per share is considered a profitability ratio. It enables shareholders to evaluate the potential return on their investment. **Book value per share** is a value that indicates what a share would be worth to shareholders if the company were to be liquidated (dissolved).

A company's shares can be valued at either their market value or book value. Market value represents the price at which shares are publicly traded on the stock market. Book value represents the theoretical value of a share based on a shareholder's claim to the company's assets.

Theoretically, a share's market value should mirror its book value. What the company is worth according to its financial statements should be reflected in the price at which its shares are trading.

However, shares are often bought and sold for a very different price from what is reflected on the company's financial statements; the book value does not usually match the market value.

Book value per common share is calculated using the formula in Figure 6.25.

$$\text{Book Value per Common Share} = \frac{\text{Shareholders' Equity} - \text{Preferred Equity}}{\text{Number of Common Shares Outstanding}}$$

FIGURE 6.25

From Figure 6.18, the shareholders' equity section of SETUP's December 31, 2020 statement of financial position is used. The value of shareholders' equity (listed as total equity attributable to owners) is $5,504,405 and SETUP does not have any preferred shares. The number of common shares outstanding is 200,000. SETUP's book value per common share is calculated as follows.

$$\text{Book Value per Common Share} = \frac{\$5{,}504{,}405}{200{,}000}$$

$$= \$27.52$$

Therefore, as of December 31, 2020, SETUP Corporation's book value per common share is $27.52. This figure is of interest to investors and others who want to evaluate a share's value against its market price—that is, as a comparison to what a share in the company is currently selling for. Note that book value per share can be calculated per common share and per preferred share. This textbook shows the calculation for book value per common share.

Dividend Yield and Dividend Payout Ratio

The **dividend yield** shows potential investors what percentage of market value of a common share is paid out to shareholders in cash dividends. In other words, this ratio calculates a rate of return on investment in common shares. This helps investors evaluate which company they want to invest in. A stable dividend yield indicates that a company's board of directors has a consistent record of paying out dividends. For this reason, the dividend yield is considered a good market analysis tool. Having a low dividend yield is not necessarily a bad sign of a company's profitability; a company could be profitable but decide to mainly invest its profits in the growth of the company rather than paying them out to investors. In addition, some shareholders are more interested in increased share prices than in cash dividends, and they consider that a better indication of a company's future success.

The dividend yield is calculated using the formula shown in Figure 6.26.

$$\text{Dividend Yield} = \frac{\text{Cash Dividends per Common Share}}{\text{Market Price per Common Share}}$$

FIGURE 6.26

SETUP's statement of changes in equity shows that the company paid $400,000 in dividends to shareholders during 2020 and there were 200,000 common shares outstanding. This provides the numerator, which is a cash dividend per common share of $2.00 ($400,000 ÷ 200,000 shares). Assume that on December 31, 2020, SETUP's common shares were selling at $24 per share, which is the denominator. SETUP's dividend yield is calculated as follows.

$$\text{Dividend Yield} = \frac{\$2.00}{\$24}$$

$$= 0.083 \text{ or } 8.3\%$$

The company is paying out 8.3% of a share market price in the form of cash dividends to common shareholders.

A related calculation, the **dividend payout ratio**, shows potential investors what percentage of company earnings is paid out to shareholders in dividends. This enables investors to evaluate which company or companies they want to invest in. A stable dividend payout ratio indicates that a company's board of directors has a consistent record of paying out dividends. For this reason, the dividend payout ratio is considered a good market analysis tool.

The dividend payout ratio is calculated using the formula in Figure 6.27.

$$\text{Dividend Payout Ratio} = \frac{\text{Dividends Paid for the Year}}{\text{Net Income}}$$

FIGURE 6.27

SETUP's statement of changes in equity in Figure 6.16 shows that the company paid $400,000 in dividends to shareholders during 2020. This is the numerator. The denominator is the 2020 net income figure, $660,765, from SETUP's statement of comprehensive income in Figure 6.13 or 6.14. SETUP's dividend payout ratio would be calculated as follows.

$$\text{Dividend Payout Ratio} = \frac{\$400,000}{\$660,765}$$

$$= 0.61 \text{ or } \$61\%$$

The company is paying out 61% of its earnings in the form of dividends, and the rest of net income, which is 39%, is being kept in the business in the form of retained earnings.

Price-Earnings Ratio

Another good indicator of company performance is the **price-earnings (P/E) ratio**, which divides the market price per common share by earnings per share. The P/E ratio is considered a good market analysis tool that provides investors with an indicator of future growth, as well as risk, of the company's earnings. It is often used by investors and investment advisors as an indicator to buy, sell or hold on to shares.

The P/E ratio is calculated using the formula shown in Figure 6.28.

$$\text{Price–Earnings (P/E) Ratio} = \frac{\text{Market Price per Share}}{\text{Earnings per Share}}$$

FIGURE 6.28

SETUP had 2020 earnings per common share of $3.30. As mentioned previously, on December 31, 2020, SETUP's common shares were selling at $24 per share. SETUP's P/E ratio is calculated as follows.

$$\text{Price–Earnings (P/E) Ratio} = \frac{\$24.00}{\$3.30}$$

$$= 7.27$$

This price–earnings ratio indicates that, as of December 31, 2020, SETUP's common shares were selling at 7.27 times their earnings. If it is assumed that SETUP always reports comparative numbers (statements for two or more years) on its financial statements, then its P/E ratio can be compared from one period to the next. Investors generally look at a high P/E ratio as an indicator of earnings growth in the future. It can be useful to compare a company's ratio from one period to another, to the ratios of other companies within the same industry or to ratios in the market in general.

No single financial ratio tells the whole story about a company's performance. Investors and other users of financial information must evaluate a combination of factors when deciding whether and when to invest in a company.

Pause & Reflect

Exercise 6-2

a) The December 31, 2020 statement of retained earnings for Benning Corporation showed a net income of $1,462,000 and dividends paid on common shares in the amount of $300,000 for 100,000 common shares outstanding during the year. Each share has a market price of $50. Calculate the dividend yield and the dividend payout.

b) If Alpha Company has earnings per share of $3.15 and the current market price per share is $17.42, calculate the price–earnings ratio.

See Appendix I for solutions.

In Summary

LO 1 Explain the different requirements for public and private companies when presenting financial statements

- Public corporations must prepare financial statements according to IFRS, while private corporations can prepare statements according to IFRS or ASPE.
- ASPE and IFRS have different financial statement presentation requirements.

LO 2 Prepare an income statement

- The statement displaying a company's profitability is called an income statement under ASPE.
- ASPE requires companies to present income (or loss) and taxes from continuing operations separately from those from discontinued operations.

LO 3 Prepare a statement of retained earnings

- In the statement of retained earnings under ASPE, net income from the income statement is added to, and dividends are subtracted from, the beginning balance of retained earnings to determine the ending balance of retained earnings.
- Sometimes, the beginning retained earnings balance needs to be adjusted due to prior period adjustments.

LO 4 Prepare a balance sheet

- A statement that lists a company's assets, liabilities and shareholders' equity is called a balance sheet.
- Companies that use ASPE tend to list assets and liabilities on the basis of liquidity, from most liquid to least liquid.

LO 5 Identify differences between ASPE and IFRS

- Under IFRS, the statement of comprehensive income is comparable to ASPE's income statement, although it has additional requirements.
- Under IFRS, the statement of changes in equity is comparable to ASPE's statement of retained earnings, although it reports on all equity accounts, not just retained earnings.
- Under IFRS, the statement of financial position is comparable to ASPE's balance sheet, although it also includes other comprehensive income.
- Reporting requirements under IFRS are more rigorous than under ASPE.

LO 6 Describe and report accounting changes

- Three types of accounting changes are a correction of prior period errors, a change in accounting policy and a change in accounting estimate.
- A correction of prior period errors and a change in accounting policy both require the retrospective approach to adjustments.
- No prior period adjustment is required for a change in accounting estimate, which affects only current and future periods (the prospective approach).
- If prior period adjustments are needed, adjustments to retained earnings must be listed before any other items are added or subtracted on the statement of retained earnings under ASPE or on the statement of changes in equity under IFRS.

LO 7 Calculate and explain earnings per share

- Earnings per share (EPS) can be calculated by dividing the net income available for common shareholders by the weighted average number of common shares outstanding.
- EPS measures dollars of profit for every common share outstanding. The larger the EPS, the more profitable the company.

LO 8 Calculate ratios used to evaluate earnings and dividend performance

- Book value per common share is calculated by dividing equity net of preferred shares by the number of common shares outstanding. It indicates what a common share would be worth to common shareholders if the company were to be liquidated (dissolved).
- Dividend yield is calculated by dividing dividends paid per share for the year by the stock market price. It shows what percentage of market value of a common share was paid out to shareholders in dividends.
- Dividend payout ratio is calculated by dividing dividends paid for the year by net income after tax. It shows what percentage of company earnings is paid out to shareholders in dividends.
- The price–earnings (P/E) ratio is calculated by dividing market price per share by earnings per share. It compares a company's current share price to its EPS.

Review Exercise 6-1

The following information was taken from the accounting records of a Canadian private corporation called Shah Company at December 31, 2020. Assume the tax rate is 35% and the company follows ASPE.

FINANCIAL STATEMENT ITEMS	Amount
Prior-year error—debit to retained earnings	$7,500
Income tax expense on operating income from discontinued operations	12,250
Total dividends	25,000
Common shares, unlimited shares authorized, 15,500 shares issued and outstanding	155,000
Sales revenue	710,000
Interest expense	30,000
Operating income, discontinued operations	35,000
Loss due to lawsuit	11,000
Sales discounts	15,000
Income tax savings on sale of discontinued operations (sold at a loss)	14,000
Selling expenses	42,000
Administrative expenses	20,000
Income tax expense on continuing operations	74,200
Preferred shares, noncumulative, 10%, 10,000 shares authorized, 1,000 shares issued	50,000
Retained earnings, January 1, 2020 (prior to adjustment)	110,000
Loss on sale of discontinued operations	40,000
Cost of goods sold	380,000

Required

a) Prepare an income statement for the year ended December 31, 2020.

b) Prepare a statement of retained earnings for Shah Company for the year ended December 31, 2020.

c) Prepare a partial balance sheet that shows only the shareholders' equity portion as at December 31, 2020.

d) Calculate the EPS ratio.

See Appendix I for solutions.

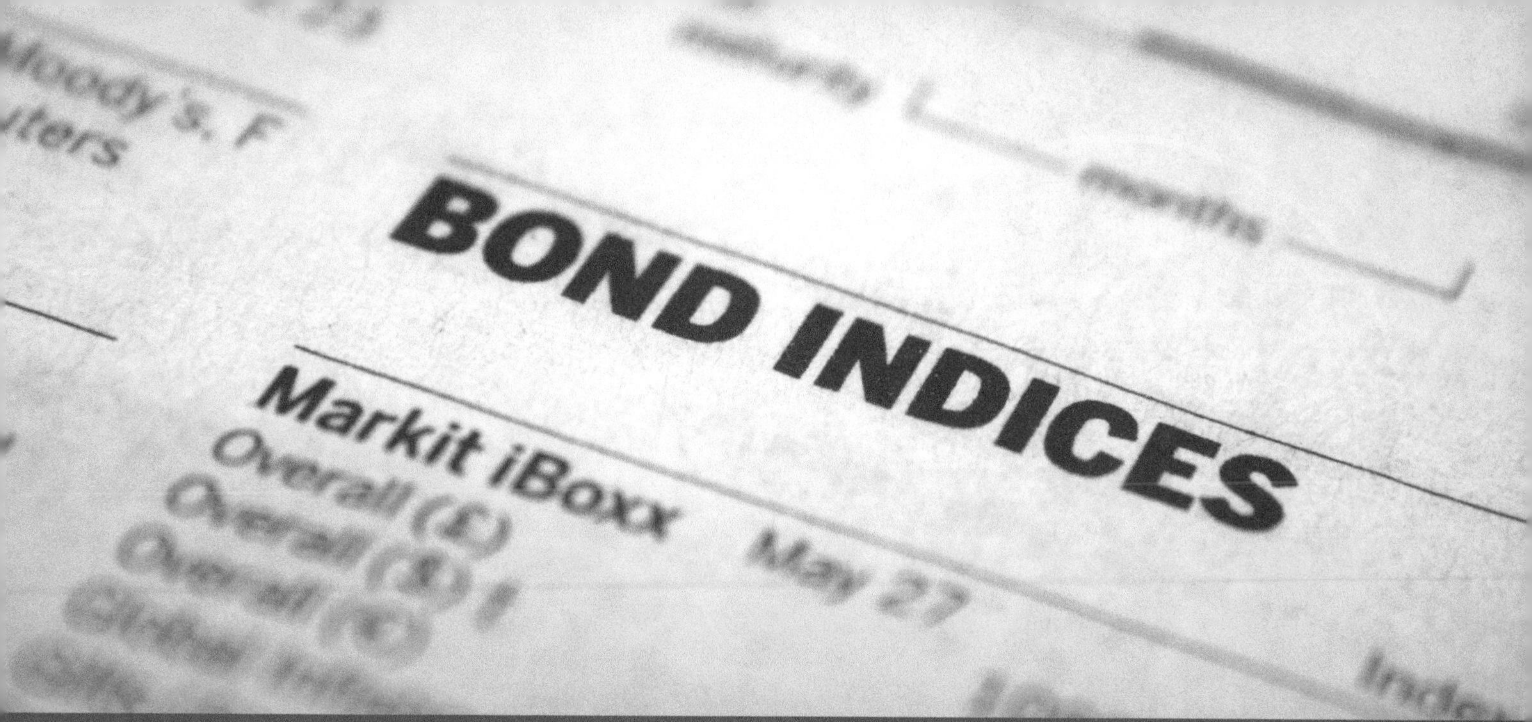

Chapter 7
Long-Term Liabilities

Learning Objectives

LO 1 Identify and describe different types of long-term liabilities
- Characteristics and Types of Bonds
- Bond Issuance

LO 2 Explain the concept of present value and apply it to bond pricing
- Calculating the Price of a Bond

LO 3 Record bonds issued at par

LO 4 Record bonds issued at a discount or a premium
- Issuing Bonds at a Discount
- Issuing Bonds at a Premium

LO 5 Record the retirement of bonds

LO 6 Record installment notes payable

LO 7 Describe how long-term liabilities are analyzed and presented on the balance sheet
- Notes Payable on the Financial Statements
- Bonds Payable on the Financial Statements
- Debt-to-Total-Assets Ratio
- Debt-to-Equity Ratio

LO 8 Apply controls and ethics related to long-term liabilities

Appendix 7A

LO 9 Describe the effective-interest amortization method
- Amortization of Bond Discount by the Effective-Interest Method
- Amortization of Bond Premium by the Effective-Interest Method

Appendix 7B

LO 10 Calculate TVM using a financial calculator
- Issuing Bonds at Par
- Issuing Bonds at a Discount
- Issuing Bonds at a Premium
- Calculating Notes Payable Monthly Installments

AMEENGAGE™ Access **ameengage.com** for integrated resources including tutorials, practice exercises, the digital textbook and more.

MAKING IT REAL TO YOU

Have you ever heard the phrase "stocks and bonds" when it comes to personal investing? These terms commonly go together, but do you know the difference? In previous chapters, we discussed equity financing such as shares traded on the stock market. This chapter focuses on long-term debt financing, with emphasis on corporations borrowing money by issuing long-term notes and bonds.

These investments tend to pay lower interest rates but provide more security than equity investments. For many years, Canada Savings Bonds issued by the government were a popular choice for risk-averse Canadians with a bit of money to invest.

The terms for these long-term notes and bonds are written in contracts, identifying the interest rates, dates for paying interest and principal, and the maturity date of the borrowed amounts. In the case of bonds, bondholders are investors in the corporation and receive regular interest payments as stated in the contract.

Long-Term Liabilities: An Introduction

LO 1

In previous chapters, we discussed some of the ways corporations finance their operations, through *short-term debt*, such as using credit to purchase goods and services on account, and offering *equity* in the business, such as issuing preferred or common shares to investors. In this chapter, we will look at another way that corporations finance their operations by using *long-term debt*, such as issuing bonds and notes payable.

Long-term debt is classified on the balance sheet under **long-term liabilities**, which are obligations due beyond one year (12 months) or beyond a company's operating cycle if the cycle is more than a year. Long-term liabilities are also sometimes referred to as *noncurrent liabilities*. The liabilities side of the balance sheet contains two main sections: current liabilities (discussed in an earlier chapter) and long-term liabilities (see Figure 7.1). Some common types of long-term liabilities of business organizations are bonds payable and notes payable with a due date beyond one year.

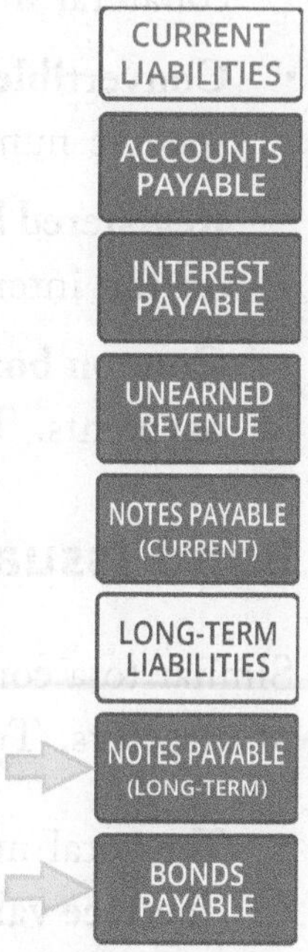

FIGURE 7.1

The most common form of long-term financing used by a company is signing a note payable to borrow a bank loan. Notes payable were partly covered in the current liabilities chapter because the portion of the note due within one fiscal period is presented as a current liability on the balance sheet. An alternative to borrowing money from a bank is to borrow money from private investors. This is done by issuing bonds, which can be sold to raise cash for the business.

Financing through debt and financing through equity each has its own advantages and disadvantages, which are covered in more advanced textbooks. This chapter focuses primarily on debt financing, with an emphasis on bonds.

Characteristics and Types of Bonds

A **bond** is an interest-bearing note that represents a promise to pay a specified amount to an investor on a specific date, known as the bond's maturity date.

The company that issues the bond is called the **bond issuer**. The investor who purchases the bond is known as the **bondholder**. The contract between the bond issuer and the bondholder is called a **bond indenture**. Like a company's shares, bonds are sold to investors on the stock (or securities) exchange. Bonds are typically sold in small denominations, in multiples of $1,000. Bond investors are often large organizations, such as pension funds, but can also include smaller institutions or individuals. The primary difference between a bond and a note is that there is a market in which bonds are actively traded. A note is usually a private agreement between two parties that is nontradeable.

There are several types of bonds.

- **Term bonds** mature on a specific date, whereas **serial bonds** are a set of bonds that mature at different intervals.
- **Debenture bonds**, often just referred to as "debentures," are unsecured bonds that are backed only by the bondholder's faith in the company's good reputation.
- **Redeemable bonds**, or *callable bonds*, have a feature whereby the bond issuer has the right to buy back the bonds before maturity at a set or "call" price.
- **Mortgage bonds**, or *secured bonds*, can be issued when a company puts up specific assets as collateral in the event that it defaults on interest or principal repayments.
- **Convertible bonds** give bondholders the option of converting or exchanging the bonds for a specific number of the company's shares.
- **Registered bonds** list the bondholders as registered owners who receive regular interest payments on the interest payment dates.
- **Coupon bonds** contain detachable coupons that state the amount and due date of the interest payments. These coupons can be removed and cashed by the holder separately.

Bond Issuance

Similar to a company's share issue, a bond issue must first be authorized by the corporation's board of directors. To authorize a bond issue, the board of directors must determine the following.

- The total number of bonds to authorize and issue.
- The **face value** of the bonds, which is the amount to be paid to the investor upon maturity date, and which is printed on the front (face) of the bond itself. The face value is also sometimes referred to as the bond's *par value*; the bond price is quoted as a percentage of the bond's face value.
- The **contractual interest rate**, which is the annual percentage rate of interest the investor receives on the face value of each bond. The contractual rate is also sometimes referred to as the bond's *coupon rate*.
- The **maturity date**, which is the date on which the final payment is due to the investor

All of these details are stated in a **bond certificate**, a document that is issued as an official record to investors when they purchase their bonds. An example of a bond certificate is presented in Figure 7.2.

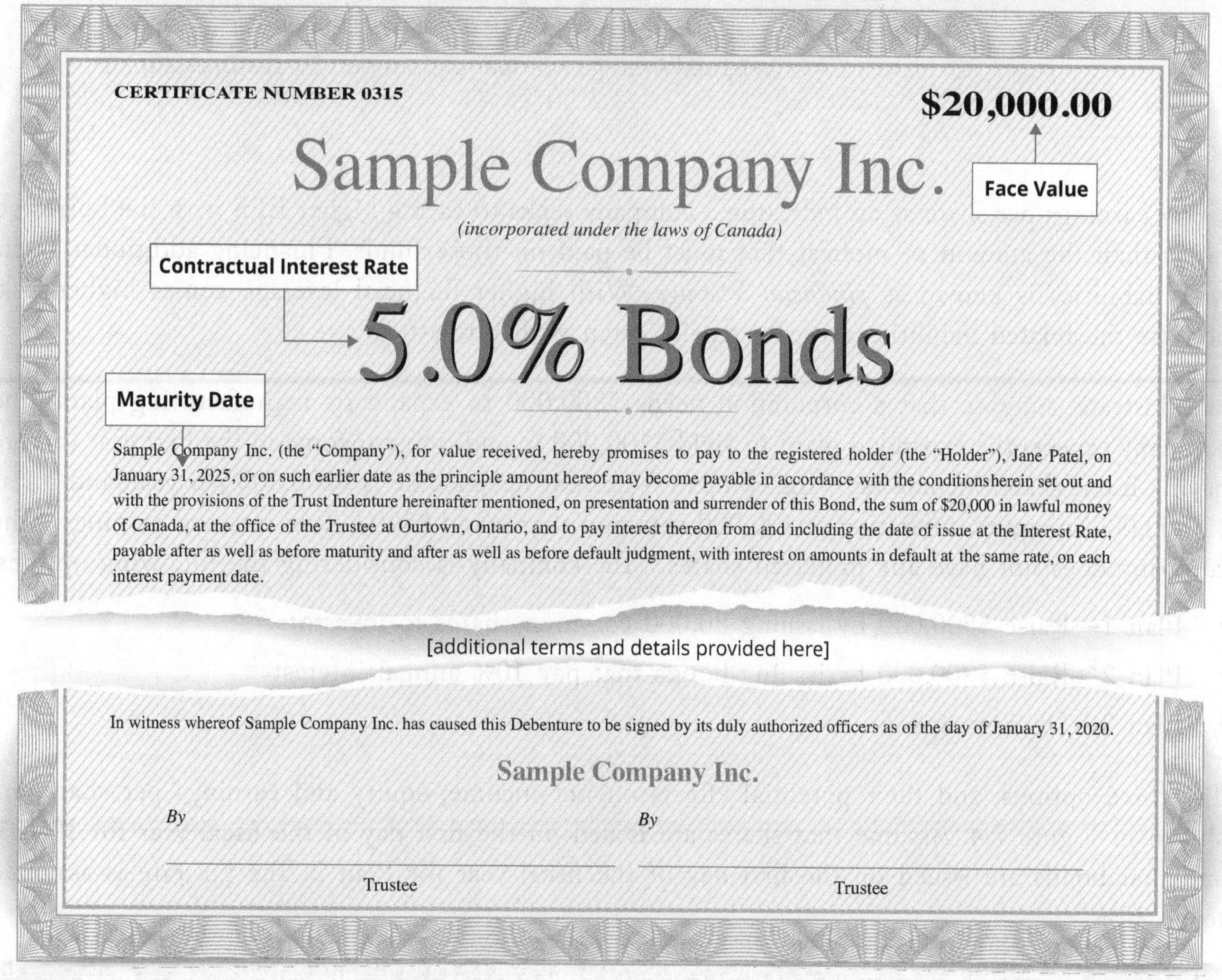

FIGURE 7.2

A bond is an interest-bearing investment vehicle whereby money is received from investors in exchange for interest payments. Interest payments are determined by the bond's contractual interest rate, which is written on the bond. The contractual interest rate is an annual rate. For example, if an investor buys a $100,000 bond with a 10% interest rate, the investor earns $10,000 every year ($100,000 × 10%). However, most bonds pay out interest semi-annually (twice a year). To calculate this, the annual interest is simply divided by two. So the semi-annual interest for the above bond is $5,000 ($10,000 ÷ 2).

When deciding whether to finance its operations using debt or equity, a company must assess the potential effects of the various alternatives. In other words, is it more advantageous for the company to seek financing through long-term liabilities or by issuing equity (i.e. shares) to investors? One way of assessing the various options is to calculate earnings per share (EPS). As you learned in the last chapter, EPS is calculated as shown in Figure 7.3.

$$\text{Earnings per Share (EPS)} = \frac{\text{Net Income} - \text{Preferred Dividends}}{\text{Weighted Average Number of Common Shares Outstanding}}$$

FIGURE 7.3

Using earnings per share as an indicator, a company seeks to earn a higher EPS with the borrowed funds than the amount of interest that must be paid on those funds. Financing additional assets with liabilities is known as *financial leverage.* With higher financial leverage comes higher risk, because the related liabilities must be repaid, often with interest.

To illustrate, suppose that a corporation needs $800,000 to expand its manufacturing plant. The company expects the expanded plant to yield $100,000 in additional income in the first year (before paying interest and income tax). The company's current net income is $200,000 per year, and it has $1,500,000 in equity, consisting of 100,000 common shares and $500,000 in retained earnings. (The company does not have any preferred shares.) The company is considering the following options.

- Plan 1—Raise $800,000 by issuing 80,000 common shares to investors
- Plan 2—Raise $800,000 by issuing bonds that pay 10% annual interest
- Plan 3—Do not expand

The three options, and their potential effects on net income, equity and earnings per share, are shown in Figure 7.4. Assume that shares are issued on the first day of the fiscal year for Plan 1, and that bonds are issued on the first day of the fiscal year for Plan 2. The tax rate is assumed to be 30%.

	Plan 1 Equity Financing	Plan 2 Debt Financing	Plan 3 Do Not Expand
Income before Interest Expense and Income Tax	$300,000	$300,000	$200,000
Less: Interest Expense	0	80,000	0
Income before Income Tax	300,000	220,000	200,000
Income Tax	90,000	66,000	60,000
Net Income	$210,000	$154,000	$140,000
Weighted Average Number of Common Shares Outstanding	180,000	100,000	100,000
Earnings per Share (EPS)	$1.17	$1.54	$1.40

FIGURE 7.4

As Figure 7.4 indicates, the company can earn the highest earnings per share if it expands through debt financing by issuing the 10% bonds. This is why many companies choose debt financing over equity financing, especially when they are confident that they can meet interest payment obligations.

Companies that issue bonds want to pay the lowest interest possible, but they must remain competitive with other investment opportunities or potential buyers will invest elsewhere. Therefore, companies generally issue bonds at the **market interest rate**, which is the interest rate that investors can demand in return for lending their money. For example, if the market rate is 10%, the company is likely to issue the bond with a 10% interest rate; this is known as issuing a bond at par (face value).

However, it can take several months to arrange the printing and distribution of bonds, and market rates tend to change. If the bonds' coupon rate differs from the market rate when the bonds are issued, the market responds by adjusting the prices of the bonds up or down from the bonds' face value, depending on whether the coupon rate is higher or lower than the market rate. Calculating the market price of bonds involves a concept known as the time value of money, which is discussed next.

In the Real World

The bond market is the largest securities market in the world. The volume of securities, along with constantly changing conditions, can make bond pricing difficult. Bond prices are largely market driven, as investors evaluate opportunities to find the best rate of return, given their risk preference.

To ensure competitive pricing, companies may work with a capital market underwriter to issue bonds and other debt securities. Underwriters are organizations that evaluate and/or assume a company's risk in bringing a security to market. Underwriters price bonds by examining both risk factors and market demand.

Pricing can be further complicated if a company has no other actively traded debt securities. Underwriters use analytics software to evaluate pricing and trading data from other corporate issues, while taking into consideration features of the debt, to get an overall picture of the market. Market complexity makes data analytics a necessity to help determine a competitive price.

The Concept of Present Value and Calculating the Price of a Bond LO 2

The value of money changes over time due to interest. If money is loaned, it is repaid with interest. When you deposit money in your bank account, you are essentially loaning your money to the bank. The bank pays you interest to "borrow" your money. Conversely, if you borrow money from the bank, you must pay back the principal you borrowed, plus interest as payment for the loan. Therefore, if you are given a choice whether to receive \$100 today or \$100 one year from now, receiving \$100 today is always a better choice because you can deposit \$100 today, and if the annual interest rate is 10%, the money will grow to \$110 by the end of the year. In other words, \$100 today is worth more than \$100 in the future.

The world of finance often refers to this phenomenon as the **time value of money**. It is important for accountants to be familiar with this because it is a basic principle of economics and finance. Furthermore, it affects the amounts in transactions that an accountant records over time. If a company keeps money in a bank, its value will change even if nothing is done with it.

The following simple example shows how the value of money changes over a longer period of time. Suppose Samuel has \$1.00 and invests it for one year at an interest rate of 10%. At the end of the year, Samuel has made 10 cents in interest and has a total of \$1.10.

At the start of the second year, Samuel starts with $1.10. The interest for the year amounts to 11 cents ($1.10 × 10%), for a year-end balance of $1.21.

There is a pattern developing. The more money that is left in an interest-bearing account, the more the interest grows each year. In the first year, interest was 10 cents. In the second year, it was 11 cents. Figure 7.5 shows the interest that would accumulate in the account over a period of 10 years.

Year	Opening Balance	Interest at 10%	Closing Balance
1	1.0000	0.1000	1.1000
2	1.1000	0.1100	1.2100
3	1.2100	0.1210	1.3310
4	1.3310	0.1331	1.4641
5	1.4641	0.1464	1.6105
6	1.6105	0.1611	1.7716
7	1.7716	0.1772	1.9487
8	1.9487	0.1949	2.1436
9	2.1436	0.2144	2.3579
10	2.3579	0.2358	2.5937

FIGURE 7.5

This phenomenon is referred to as **compound interest**, which is the growth effect that applying the same interest rate has on an account over a period of time. With each passing period, the interest rate is applied to interest on top of the principal. The amount of interest earned in Year 10 is over 23 cents, more than double the amount of interest earned in Year 1.

The closing balance in the second row of the chart ($1.21) is the value of the money in the account after Year 2, also referred to as the **future value**. Following this basic logic, the future value of the money after Year 5 is $1.61; after Year 10, it is $2.59.

Calculating the value of money can work in reverse, too. An accountant can try to calculate what amount needs to be invested today to produce a certain amount in the future. This is known as the **present value** and is also referred to as *discounting*.

Figure 7.6 shows the present values of $1.00 over 10 years, given an interest rate of 10%. The chart provides answers for the following question: What amount needs to be invested now to create $1 in x number of years, with x representing Years 1 to 10 and assuming an interest rate of 10%?

Year	Factor
1	0.9091
2	0.8264
3	0.7513
4	0.6830
5	0.6209
6	0.5645
7	0.5132
8	0.4665
9	0.4241
10	0.3855

FIGURE 7.6

An investor requiring $1.00 after one year would have to invest about 91 cents (as indicated on the first line of the chart). If the investor wanted $1.00 after 10 years, 39 cents would have to be invested now (as shown on the last line of the chart). The difference between the amounts is a testament to the power of compound interest. Waiting nine years to get the same payoff means initially investing less than half the money. The greater the interest rate, and the longer this interest rate is applied, the more compound interest is earned.

It should be noted that Figure 7.6 applies only to an interest rate calculation of 10%. Separate charts need to be used when other interest rates are involved in calculating present and future values. These charts, referred to as present value tables, can be found at the end of this chapter and also in Appendix II at the end of the book. The factors are calculated using a formula that is beyond the scope of this book. However, these factors can be found in many mathematics textbooks and are commonly included as tables in professional accounting exams. Most business calculators include functions that use the factors, as do common spreadsheet programs.

Calculating the Price of a Bond

In the context of the current discussion of bonds payable, the time value of money matters because it helps determine the price the bonds will sell for. The price of the bonds can be determined by calculating the present value of the principal and future interest payments. In other words, the price of a bond is essentially the present value of all the future cash flows. In the previous calculations, interest was stated at an annual rate and paid once per year. Interest on bonds is normally paid semi-annually. Therefore, when applying present value concepts, the number of periods is doubled and the interest rate is divided by two.

Some corporations also issue what are known as *zero-coupon bonds*, which pay zero interest but pay the full face value of the bond at maturity. These bonds sell at a discount (i.e. the buyer pays less than face value), at an amount equal to the present value of their face value.

A $100,000 bond issued with 10% interest payable semi-annually over the next five years is used for the following calculations.

Future Value *(FV)* = $100,000
Semi-Annual Interest Rate *(i)* = 10% × ½ = 5%
Semi-Annual Interest Payments *(PMT)* = $100,000 × 5% = $5,000
Number of Periods *(n)* = 5 × 2 = 10

Using the period 10 factor from Figure 7.7, which is 0.6139, the present value of the $100,000 principal repayment is calculated as follows.

$100,000 × 0.6139 = $61,390

The interest payments are different from the principal repayment in that they represent an **annuity**, meaning they are periodic and recurring fixed payments. One of two methods can be used to calculate the present value of the interest payment annuity.

Periods	Factor
1	0.9524
2	0.9070
3	0.8638
4	0.8227
5	0.7835
6	0.7462
7	0.7107
8	0.6768
9	0.6446
10	0.6139

FIGURE 7.7

1. The present value of each interest payment can be calculated individually. For example, the first interest payment of $5,000 in six months is multiplied by the period 1 factor from Figure 7.7 to determine the present value of that particular payment. To this amount, add the second $5,000 payment in 12 months and multiply it by the period 2 factor. After this, add the third $5,000 payment in 18 months and multiply it by the period 3 factor. This goes on for all 10 interest payments, which can get tedious and is prone to error. For a five-year bond, this calculation would be repeated 10 times (once for each semi-annual interest payment) to determine the present value of all the interest payments.

2. Since annuities are a common occurrence in the financial industry, tables containing factors for annuities have been developed (see Figure 7.8). Using this table, the present value of *all* interest payments can be made in just one calculation, as shown below.

Periods	Factor
1	0.9524
2	1.8594
3	2.7232
4	3.5460
5	4.3295
6	5.0757
7	5.7864
8	6.4632
9	7.1078
10	7.7217

FIGURE 7.8

Present Value of $5,000 payments (annuity) made over 10 periods
= $5,000 × 7.7217
= $38,608.50 (round to $38,610)*

Summary

Present value of principal	$61,390
Present value of interest payments	$38,610
Total proceeds	$100,000

*Note: The present value of the interest payments is rounded to $38,610 for illustrative purposes.

This text uses the tables at the end of the chapter for illustration and exercise purposes. Figures may be slightly different if a financial calculator or Excel spreadsheet is used. Illustrations of how to compute the price of bonds using a financial calculator are provided in Appendix 7B at the end of this chapter.

It is important to note that the present value of the principal and interest payments equal the face value of the bond ($100,000). This occurred because we have discounted the 5% bond using the 5% interest rate. This shows that the face value of the bond is equal to the present value of the payments when the market rate is equal to the interest rate of the bond. An easy rule of thumb is that, if the interest rate attached to the bond is the same as the market rate, the bonds will be issued at par. An investor would not pay any more or less than the face value of the bond, that is, what they can earn in the market. Examples showing what happens when these interest rates are different will follow later in this chapter.

A Closer Look

Present value (*PV*) and future value (*FV*) can also be calculated using either a business or financial calculator, or a spreadsheet program. These tools use the same factors found in charts or tables, but they allow you to eliminate steps in calculations. Rather than separately calculating the *PV* or *FV* of the bond's face value and then its interest, these tools enable you to find the total value using one calculation. All you need to know are the input values: the bond's face value, the market rate of interest per period (*i*), the number of periods (*n*), and the interest payment (*PMT*).

You may find that you get slightly different answers using the tables than you do using a digital tool; this is simply due to rounding factors used in the *PV* and *FV* tables. Different calculators may vary in their method of operation, but they are based on the same concepts and use the same inputs.

Refer to Appendix 7B at the end of this chapter for illustration of the calculator inputs for pricing bonds. Spreadsheet tips for present value functions can be found in the HELP function within Excel.

Issuing Bonds at Par

LO 3

Business Time Inc., a publisher of investment-related books, magazines and newspapers, wants to raise money for long-term financing by issuing bonds. On December 31, 2020, the company issues 1,000 10-year bonds at par, at a price of $100 each with 5% annual interest. Figure 7.9 shows the journal entry for the transaction.

The total amount of $100,000 is debited to the cash account. A corresponding liability shows a credit increase of $100,000 in the bonds payable account. Since the principal for the bonds is due in 10 years, the liability is classified as long-term and placed in that section of the balance sheet.

Issuing the bond for a 10-year term means that the company has to make interest payments to its bondholders every year for 10 years. Most bonds call for semi-annual (twice per year) interest payments. For simplicity, interest is paid annually in this illustration.

JOURNAL

Date	Account Title and Explanation	Debit	Credit
Dec 31	Cash	100,000	
	Bonds Payable		100,000
	To issue $100,000 worth of bonds at par (due in 2030)		

FIGURE 7.9

When an interest payment is made, a $5,000 credit represents a decrease in cash, while a $5,000 debit represents an increase in interest expense. This is illustrated in Figure 7.10.

JOURNAL

Date	Account Title and Explanation	Debit	Credit
Dec 31	Interest Expense	5,000	
	Cash		5,000
	To pay interest on bonds		

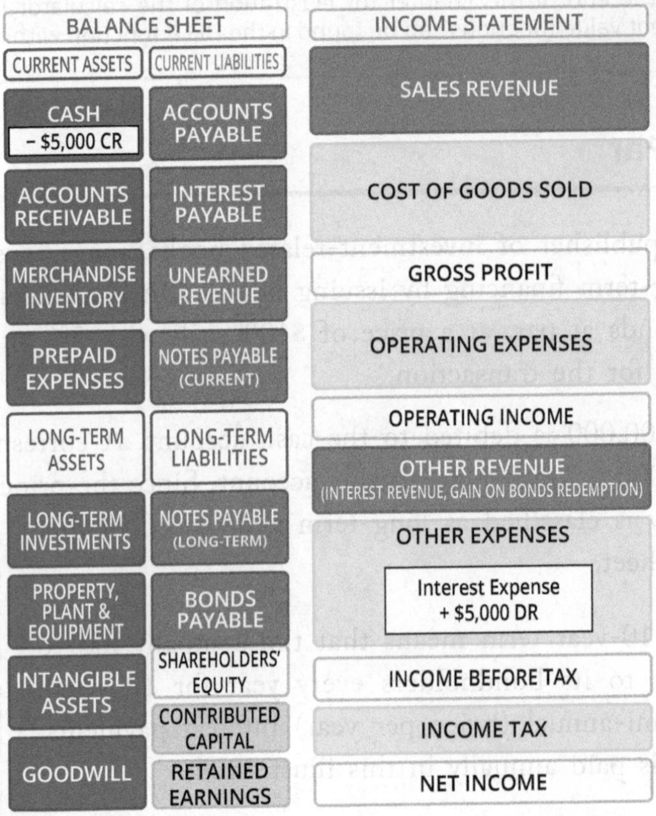

FIGURE 7.10

Depending on Business Time's fiscal year, its year end may occur before the payment is made. In that case, a portion of the interest must be accrued, even though the interest is actually paid in the following period. The company is therefore required to expense the interest during the period in which it was incurred; this is regarded as an accrual and represents a decrease in the company's equity for the period. Recognizing the interest expense in the same period as when the bond proceeds are used to generate revenue follows the expense recognition principle (matching concept) under the accrual basis of accounting. If the interest expense is not properly accrued, the current period's liability will be understated and equity will be overstated.

Assume for a moment that the company's year end is October 31, but the bond anniversary date is December 31. On October 31, when the company prepares its financial statements, it will accrue only 10/12 of the annual interest, as shown in Figure 7.11.

JOURNAL

Date	Account Title and Explanation	Debit	Credit
Oct 31	Interest Expense	4,167	
	Interest Payable		4,167
	To accrue interest on bonds ($5,000 × 10/12 months)		

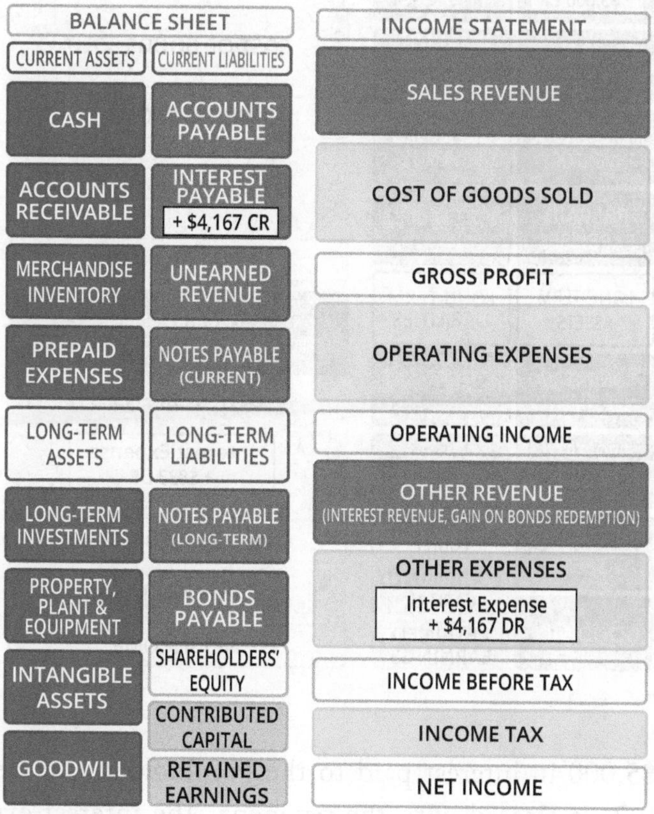

FIGURE 7.11

As with the other interest payments on the bond, $4,167 is expensed as a debit (increase) to bond interest on October 31. However, unlike the previous transaction, interest payable (accrued liabilities) is credited instead of cash.

Continuing the above example, when interest is paid on December 31, the payment is recorded as shown in Figure 7.12.

JOURNAL

Date	Account Title and Explanation	Debit	Credit
Dec 31	Interest Expense ($5,000 × $^{2}/_{12}$)	833	
	Interest Payable	4,167	
	Cash		5,000
	To pay interest		

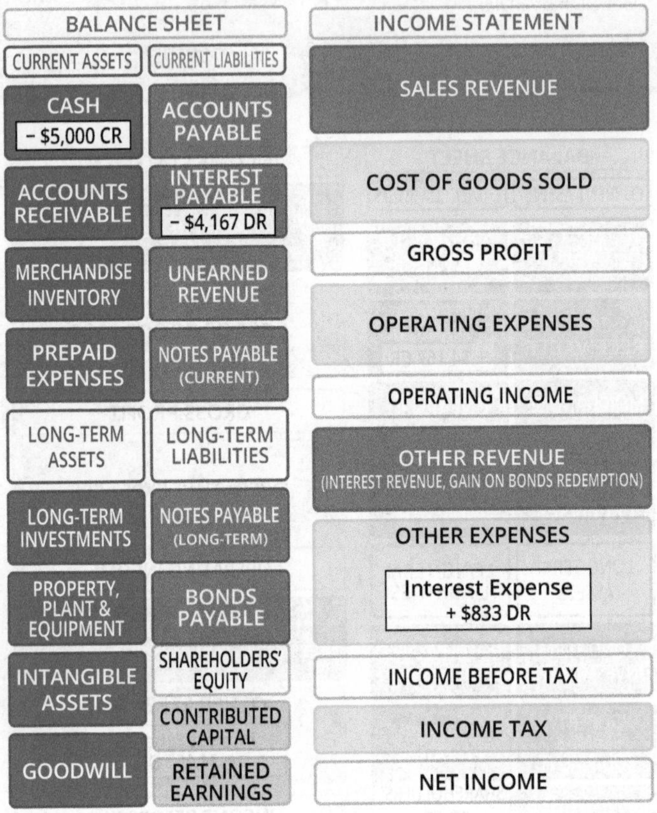

FIGURE 7.12

This transaction records $5,000 in interest paid to the bondholder as a credit to cash. The interest accrued at year end ($4,167) is cleared with the payment. The interest expense ($833) is recorded for the two months between the year end and the interest payment date.

It is important to distinguish how the accrued interest on the bonds is classified on the balance sheet compared to the original principal of the bond. On the first day of the fiscal year, the company knows that the accrued interest is due before the end of the year. Therefore, that year's interest payable is classified as a current liability. On the other hand, the original principal (which will be paid back at the end of the 10-year term of the bond) is classified as a long-term liability by the company. This is like a 10-year term loan where the borrower pays only the interest; that is, the principal is not repaid in annual installments, unlike for a note payable, which we will discuss later in this chapter.

The principal is the same as the face value of the bond, and that amount is paid back to the bondholder, regardless of any changes in market price. In other words, *regardless of the price paid for the bond*, the business needs to pay the full face value of the bond to the bondholder when the bond matures. For example, Figure 7.13 shows the journal entry when Business Time repays the bond principal on December 31, 2030.

JOURNAL			
Date	**Account Title and Explanation**	**Debit**	**Credit**
Dec 31	Bonds Payable	100,000	
	Cash		100,000
	To pay bond principal on maturity date		

FIGURE 7.13

In the next section, we will look at what happens when the market value and the face value of a bond are not the same.

Pause & Reflect

Exercise 7-1

On January 1, 2020, Decorum Inc. issues 1,500 five-year bonds at par at a price of $200 each, with 9% interest paid annually. Show how the bond issuance transaction is recorded.

JOURNAL			
Date	**Account Title and Explanation**	**Debit**	**Credit**

See Appendix I for solutions.

Issuing Bonds at a Discount or a Premium

LO 4

We have demonstrated how a bond issue is treated at par. However, the period from the time that a business decides to issue the bonds to the time they are printed for distribution can be several months. During that time, the market rate is likely to have changed. This means that the interest rate on the bond may end up being higher—or lower—than that of the market, which will affect the demand for the company's bonds. The price of the bond must therefore be adjusted accordingly.

There are two scenarios to consider.

Scenario 1: Market interest rate is more than coupon rate. The bond will be sold at a discount.

Scenario 2: Market interest rate is less than coupon rate. The bond will be sold at a premium.

Issuing Bonds at a Discount

When bonds are sold at par (or face value), the resulting transaction is relatively simple. From the previous example, Business Time Inc. received a lump sum of $100,000 and established bonds payable for that same amount.

The accounting changes when market interest rates rise above the interest rate attached to the bond. When that happens, investors can receive higher interest payments from other bonds and market investments. To deter investors from those other investments and attract them to the issuer's bonds, the company should offer the bonds at a better price—at a discount. The **discount** is the difference between the price paid and the par value.

How do firms establish an appropriate price in these situations? The company sets a discount price that compensates the investor for the money lost with the bond's lower interest rate. The following is a demonstration of how this is done.

Assume on January 1, 2020, when the market rate of interest is 12%, Energy Bite Inc. issues bonds with a maturity value of $100,000. The bonds have an annual contractual interest rate of 10% and mature in five years. Interest on the bonds is payable semi-annually on July 1 and January 1 of each year. The company's year end is September 30. Since the principal is $100,000, the semi-annual interest payment is $5,000 ($100,000 × 10% × ½).

With the market rate at 12%, an interest payment of 10% is not high enough to attract investors. Therefore, the company must lower the price of the bond below face value so that the buyer gets an *effective interest rate* of 12%. It is important to understand that the buyer still expects to get $100,000 for the bond when it matures plus the $5,000 interest every period, regardless of what was initially paid. Using the same present value concepts previously discussed, the following illustrates how the price of the bond is calculated.

> Note: Use Table 7.1 and Table 7.2 at the end of the chapter for present value factors in the following calculations.

Future Value *(FV)* = $100,000

Semi-Annual Payment *(PMT)* = (10% × ½) × $100,000 = $5,000

Semi-Annual Market Interest Rate *(i)* = 12% × ½ = 6%

Number of Periods *(n)* = 5 × 2 = 10

Present Value of the Principal *(PV)* = $100,000 × 0.5584 = $55,840
[6% Semi-Annual Market Interest Rate *(i)*, 10 periods *(n)*]

Present Value of Future Interest Payments *(PV)* = $5,000 × 7.3601 = $36,800
[6% Semi-Annual Market Interest Rate *(i)*, 10 periods *(n)*]

Total price bondholders are willing to pay for their investment = $55,840 + $36,800 = $92,640

Remember to always use the market interest rate to determine the present value factor, because that is what investors use to determine what they should pay for the bonds. However, the bond contractual rate (coupon or stated rate) should be used to determine the interest payment, as that is the rate attached to the bond. The price investors are willing to pay is lower than the par value because the market rate is 12%, meaning investors can easily get a return higher than 10% elsewhere in the market.

The difference between the price for the bond paid and its par value is known as the *discount.* Accounting for the bond discount requires the use of a contra account. As you learned in your previous accounting studies, a contra account is linked to another account and records decreases in the value of that other account. This is done so that the original value of the related account remains unchanged. An example of a contra account covered in a previous chapter is the accumulated depreciation account used in accounting for the depreciation of an asset such as property, plant and equipment.

Figure 7.14 shows how the receipt of $92,640 for the issue of Energy Bite Inc. bonds (at discount) is recorded by the company using the contra account called discount on bonds payable.

JOURNAL

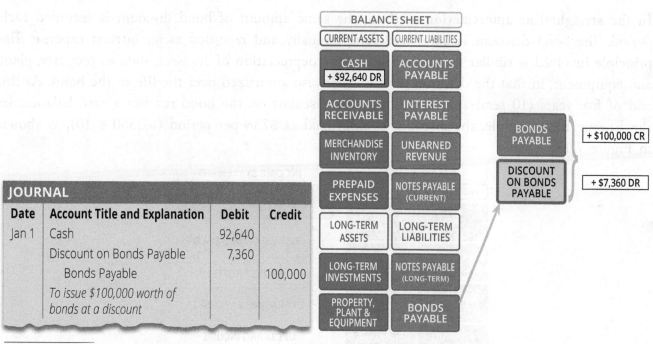

Date	Account Title and Explanation	Debit	Credit
Jan 1	Cash	92,640	
	Discount on Bonds Payable	7,360	
	Bonds Payable		100,000
	To issue $100,000 worth of bonds at a discount		

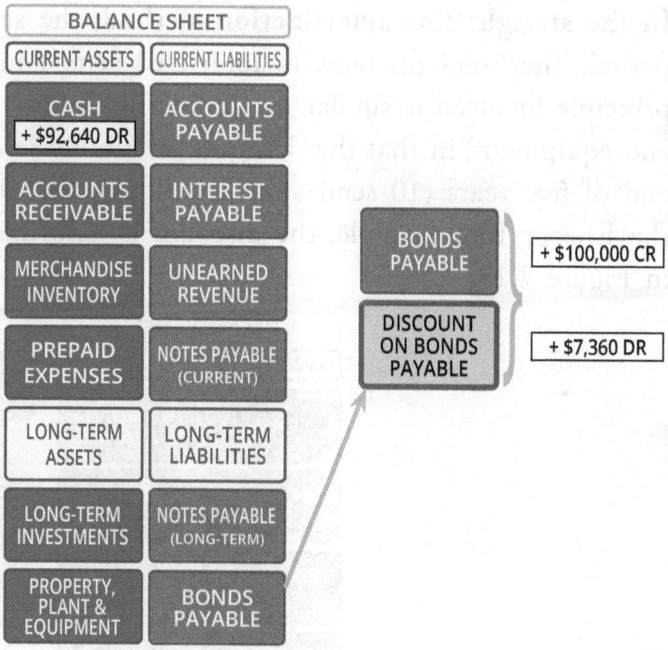

FIGURE 7.14

Although Energy Bite has issued a $100,000 bond and this amount must be paid when the bond matures, it received only $92,640 from the bondholder.

Issuing bonds below the market rate, meaning they are issued (or sold) at a discount, makes borrowing money more costly for a firm. At the maturity date, the company must repay the face value of $100,000 rather than the issue price of $92,640; the discount itself ($7,360) is an additional cost of borrowing. Over the life of the bonds, the total cost of borrowing (interest and discount) must be allocated to the interest expense account. This process is called **amortizing the discount** and increases the amount of interest expense reported in each period. We will amortize the discount using two different methods. One method of amortization (*straight-line amortization method*) is illustrated in this section. The other method (the *effective-interest amortization method*) is illustrated in Appendix 7A.

> **ASPE vs. IFRS**
>
> ASPE supports the use of the effective-interest method (also called the "interest method") but allows the straight-line method if the results are not significantly different from the effective-interest method. The straight-line method may be used by private companies because it is simpler.
>
> Under IFRS, companies are strictly required to use the effective-interest amortization method.

Amortization of Bond Discount by the Straight-Line Method

In the **straight-line amortization method**, the same amount of bond discount is recorded each period. The bond discount is amortized semi-annually and recorded as an interest expense. The principle involved is similar to accounting for the depreciation of an asset, such as property, plant and equipment, in that the discount on a bond is also amortized over the life of the bond. At the end of five years (10 semi-annual periods), the discount on the bond reaches a zero balance. In the Energy Bite example, the discount is amortized as $736 per period ($7,360 ÷ 10), as shown in Figure 7.15.

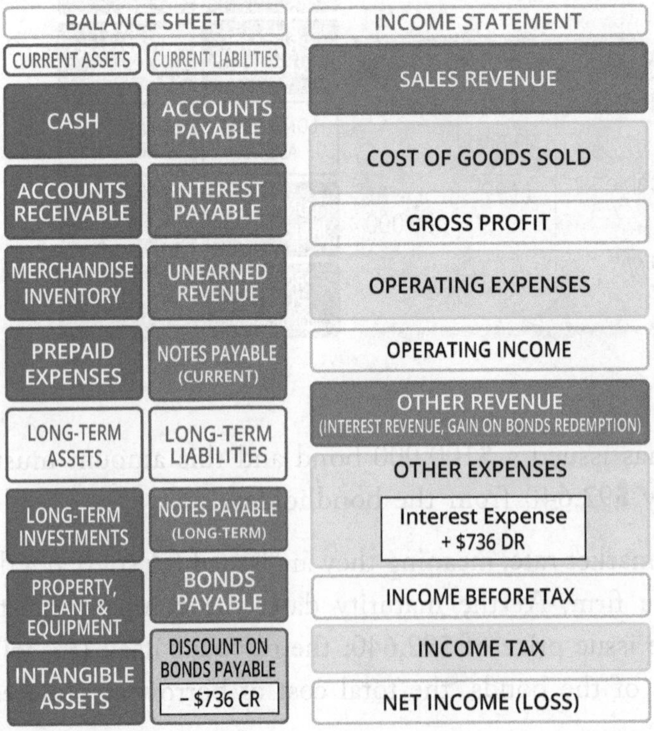

FIGURE 7.15

Figure 7.16 shows an amortization table of the bond for the 10 periods. Notice how the discount balance decreases while the bond book value increases.

Straight-Line Amortization Table of Bond Discount					
Semi-Annual Interest Period	A Interest Payment ($100,000 × 5%)	B Discount Amortization (Total Discount ÷ 10 periods)	C Interest Expense (A + B)	D Discount Balance (D [Previous Period] - B)	E Bond Book Value ($100,000 - D)
0				$7,360	$92,640
1	$5,000	$736	$5,736	6,624	93,376
2	5,000	736	5,736	5,888	94,112
3	5,000	736	5,736	5,152	94,848
4	5,000	736	5,736	4,416	95,584
5	5,000	736	5,736	3,680	96,320
6	5,000	736	5,736	2,944	97,056
7	5,000	736	5,736	2,208	97,792
8	5,000	736	5,736	1,472	98,528
9	5,000	736	5,736	736	99,264
10	5,000	736	5,736	0	100,000
Total	$50,000	$7,360	$57,360	-	-

FIGURE 7.16

At the end of the first period when the interest payment is made, the company records the total interest expense for the bond ($5,736), the amortization on the discount ($736) and the cash paid to the bondholder ($5,000). The journal entry and the effects on the company's account balances are shown in Figure 7.17.

JOURNAL

Date	Account Title and Explanation	Debit	Credit
July 1	Interest Expense	5,736	
	Discount on Bonds Payable		736
	Cash		5,000
	To record interest and the amortization of the bond discount for the current period		

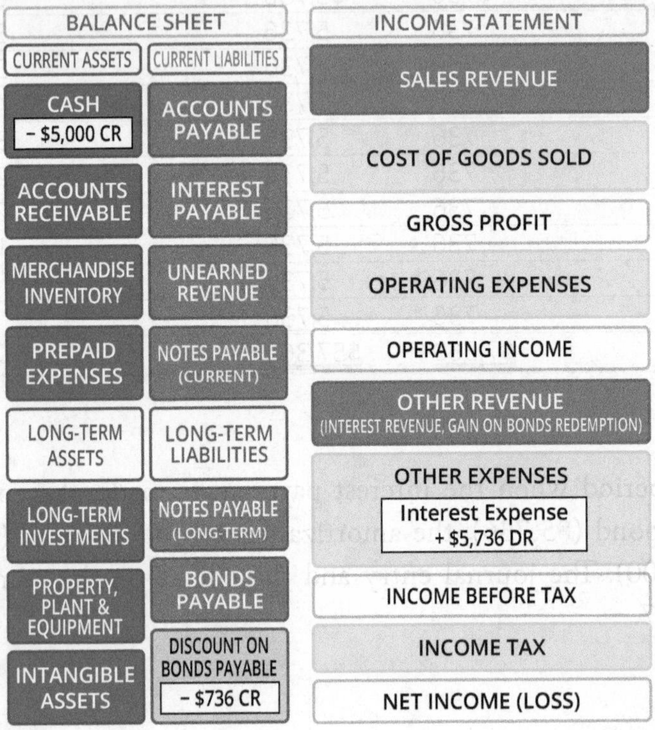

FIGURE 7.17

When financial statements are prepared, the discount on bonds is deducted from the face value of the bonds. The partial balance sheet at the end of the first period is shown in Figure 7.18, after 1/10 of the discount is applied.

Bonds Payable	$100,000
Less: Unamortized Discount	6,624
Book Value	$93,376

FIGURE 7.18

Over five years (10 semi-annual periods), interest is paid to the bondholder and the discount is amortized. As this happens, the value of the discount on the bonds decreases and the book value (or carrying value) of the bonds increases. By the end of the five years, the discount is reduced to zero and the book value of the bond is equal to its face value, $100,000.

Since the year end is September 30, 2020, Energy Bite needs to accrue interest expense before the second payment date on January 1, 2021. Figure 7.19 shows that at each year end for the next five years, the interest expense is accrued and the discount is amortized for three months, from July 1 to September 30. The interest expense and the amortized discounts for period 2 (six months) can be found in Figure 7.16. These numbers must be adjusted to reflect only three months instead of six months. As shown in Figure 7.19, the interest payable is credited for $2,500 ($5,000 × 3/6), discount on bond payable is amortized (credited) for $368 ($736 × 3/6) and interest expense is debited for 2,868 ($2,500 + $368).

JOURNAL

Date	Account Title and Explanation	Debit	Credit
Sep 30	Interest Expense	2,868	
	Discount on Bonds Payable		368
	Interest Payable		2,500
	To record accrued interest expense and amortized discount at year end		

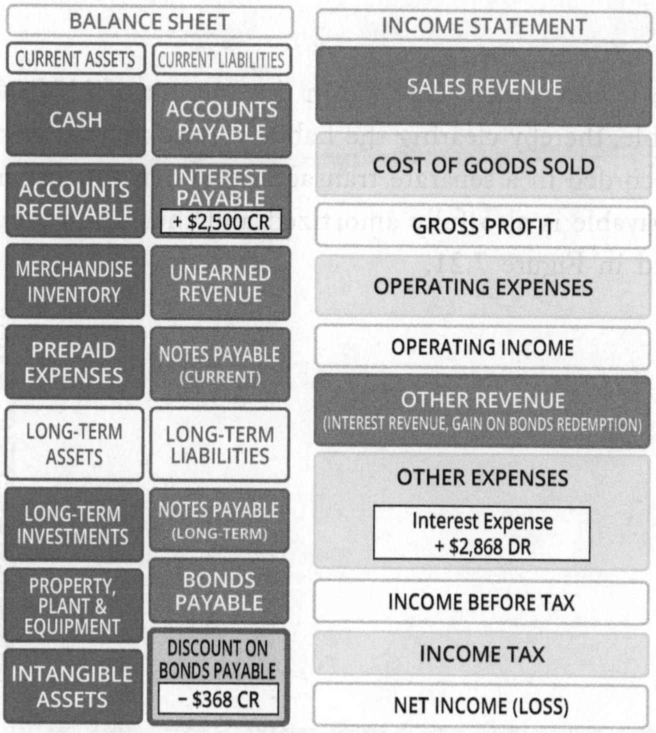

FIGURE 7.19

As shown in Figure 7.20, the cash payment of $5,000 is made on January 1, 2021. Interest payable is debited for $2,500 and interest expense is also debited for the remaining balance of period 2, which is $2,868 ($5,736 − $2,868). The rest of the discount on bonds payable of period 2 is also amortized and credited for $368 ($736 − $368).

JOURNAL

Date	Account Title and Explanation	Debit	Credit
Jan 1	Interest Payable	2,500	
	Interest Expense	2,868	
	Discount on Bonds Payable		368
	Cash		5,000
	To record payment of interest and amortized discount		

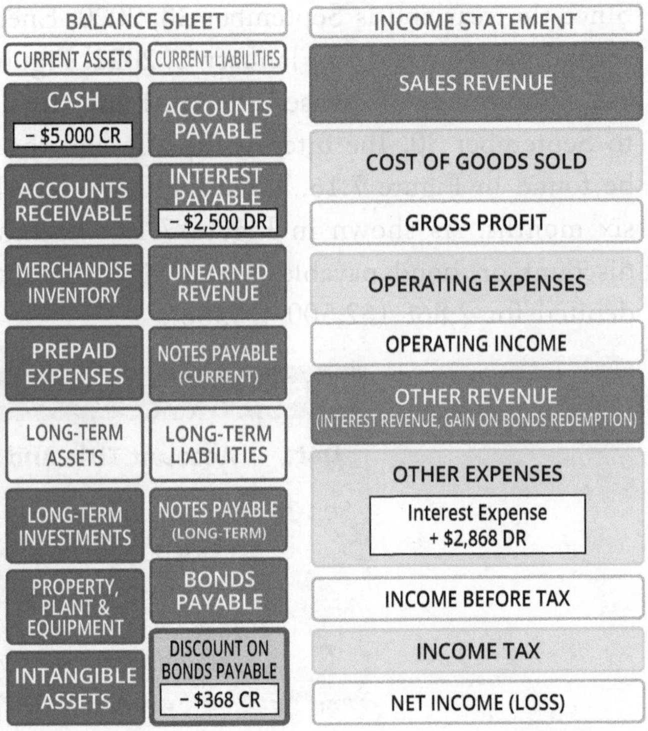

FIGURE 7.20

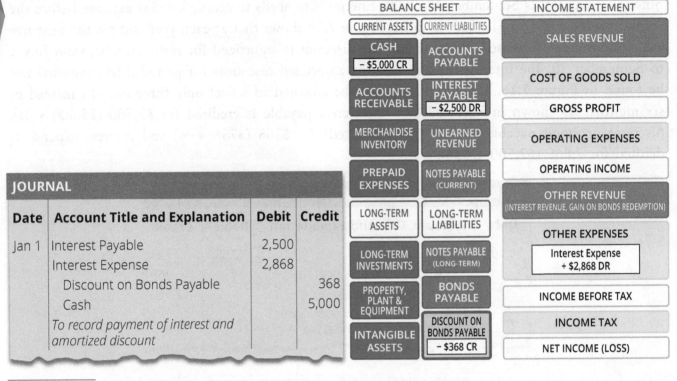

At the end of the five-year term, cash is credited in the amount of $100,000, and the same amount is debited to bonds payable, thereby clearing the liability. Assume that any outstanding interest has already been paid and recorded in a separate transaction. When the last interest payment is made, the discount on bonds payable is also fully amortized and thus has a zero balance remaining. The journal entry is presented in Figure 7.21.

JOURNAL

Date	Account Title and Explanation	Debit	Credit
Jan 1	Bonds Payable	100,000	
	Cash		100,000
	To repay $100,000 to bondholder		

FIGURE 7.21

Pause & Reflect

Exercise 7-2

On January 1, 2020, Draper Corporation issues $100,000 worth of 8%, two-year bonds with interest payable semi-annually. Just prior to the bond issue, the market interest rate increases to 10%.

a) Fill in the amortization table below.

Straight-Line Amortization Table of Bond Discount					
Semi-Annual Interest Period	**Interest Payment**	**Discount Amortization**	**Interest Expense**	**Discount Balance**	**Bond Book Value**
0					
1					
2					
3					
4					
Total					

b) Show how Draper Corporation records the bond issuance transaction.

JOURNAL			
Date	**Account Title and Explanation**	**Debit**	**Credit**

See Appendix I for solutions.

Issuing Bonds at a Premium

We have already discussed why companies issue bonds at a discount. The higher market interest rate makes the bond's interest rate less competitive, so the selling price is reduced to make up the difference with potential investors.

However, there is a flip side to that scenario. By the time a company's bond issue reaches the market, the market interest rate may have declined. The bond's interest rate is now higher than that of the market and will therefore produce a higher rate of return for an investor than what the market is currently offering. This creates a greater demand for the company's bond, which means the company can now sell the bond at a **premium** (at a price that is higher than its face value).

A company that issues bonds at a premium takes the same steps in recording the transaction as it would with a discount, except the journal entry is different. Let us review those steps with an example using Energy Bite Inc. again.

On January 1, 2020, Energy Bite Inc. issues bonds with a maturity value of $100,000. The bonds have an annual contractual interest rate of 10% and mature in five years. Interest on the bonds is payable semi-annually on July 1 and January 1 of each year. The company's year end is September 30. A market rate of 10% means that the bonds could be issued at par. A market rate of 12% means that the bonds would be issued at a discount as in our previous example. What happens when the market rate is 8%?

> Note: Use Table 7.1 and Table 7.2 at the end of the chapter for present value factors in the following calculations.

Future Value *(FV)* = $100,000
Semi-Annual Payment *(PMT)* = (10% × ½) × $100,000 = $5,000
Semi-Annual Market Interest Rate *(i)* = 8% × ½ = 4%
Number of Periods *(n)* = 5 × 2 = 10

Present Value of the Principal *(PV)* = $100,000 × 0.6756 = $67,560
[4% Semi-Annual Market Interest Rate *(i)*, 10 periods *(n)*]

Present Value of Future Interest Payments *(PV)* = $5,000 × 8.1109 = $40,555
[4% Semi-Annual Market Interest Rate *(i)*, 10 periods *(n)*]

Total price bondholders are willing to pay for their investment = $67,560 + $40,555 = $108,115

The price investors are willing to pay is higher than the par value because the market rate is 8%, meaning it is difficult for investors to get a return as high as 10% elsewhere in the market.

Figure 7.22 shows how this bond issue is recorded on the company's books. As always, proceeds from the sale are deposited and recorded as a debit to cash. On the other side of the balance sheet, the principal amount of the bond ($100,000) is credited to bonds payable (a long-term liability). Finally, the premium on the bond of $8,115 is recorded as a credit in an account called premium on bonds payable. Premium on bonds payable appears directly below the bonds payable account on the balance sheet. So far, there is no change to equity.

JOURNAL

Date	Account Title and Explanation	Debit	Credit
Jan 1	Cash	108,115	
	Premium on Bonds Payable		8,115
	Bonds Payable		100,000
	To issue $100,000 worth of bonds at a premium		

FIGURE 7.22

Unlike the discount on a bond, which is recorded in a contra liability account, the premium is recorded in an adjunct liability account. The nature of an **adjunct account** is opposite to that of a contra account; it is linked to another account to record increases in the value of that account. The balance of the discount on bonds payable account, which is a contra liability account, is deducted from the bonds payable balance on the balance sheet. The balance of the premium on bonds payable account, which is an adjunct liability account, is added to the bonds payable balance on the balance sheet. When the discount on a bond is amortized, it increases the interest expense. On the contrary, when the premium on a bond is amortized, it decreases the interest expense.

Because of the premium, issuing bonds above the market rate makes it less costly for the company to borrow money. At the maturity date, the company needs to repay the face value of $100,000, rather than the issue price of $108,115. In other words, the premium itself ($8,115) reduces the cost of borrowing. Over the life of the bonds, the total cost of borrowing (interest payment less premium) must be allocated to the interest expense account. This process of allocating the premium is called **amortizing the premium**, which decreases the amount of interest expense reported in each period.

Similar to the discount on a bond issue, a bond premium is amortized each period when the interest payments are made. In other words, the premium liability of $8,115 is amortized over the term of the bond.

Amortization of Bond Premium by the Straight-Line Method

This section illustrates the straight-line amortization method for the Energy Bite example. The effective-interest method is explained in Appendix 7A.

Using the straight-line method, the amount to be amortized comes to $812 ($8,115 ÷ 10, rounded to the nearest dollar) for each of the 10 semi-annual periods. Therefore, $812 is debited to the premium on bonds payable account every period until the amount is zero upon maturity of the bond.

Figure 7.23 shows an amortization table of the bond for 10 periods. Notice how the premium balance and the bond book value decrease.

Straight-Line Amortization Table of Bond Premium					
Semi-Annual Interest Period	A Interest Payment ($100,000 × 5%)	B Premium Amortization (Total Premium ÷ 10 periods)	C Interest Expense (A − B)	D Premium Balance (D [Previous Period] − B)	E Bond Book Value ($100,000 + D)
0				$8,115	$108,115
1	$5,000	$812	$4,188	7,303	107,303
2	5,000	812	4,188	6,491	106,491
3	5,000	812	4,188	5,679	105,679
4	5,000	812	4,188	4,867	104,867
5	5,000	812	4,188	4,055	104,055
6	5,000	812	4,188	3,243	103,243
7	5,000	812	4,188	2,431	102,431
8	5,000	812	4,188	1,619	101,619
9	5,000	812	4,188	807	100,807
10	5,000	807*	4,193	0	100,000
Total	$50,000	$8,115	$41,885	-	-

*$807 is due to rounding

FIGURE 7.23

Figure 7.24 shows how the transaction is recorded at the end of the first period. The $5,000 interest payment is recorded each period with a credit to cash. The expense to the company is $4,188, and the rest of the debit is taken care of by the $812 amortization of the premium calculated using the straight-line method.

JOURNAL			
Date	Account Title and Explanation	Debit	Credit
July 1	Interest Expense	4,188	
	Premium on Bonds Payable	812	
	Cash		5,000
	To record payment of interest and amortization of the bond premium		

FIGURE 7.24

When financial statements are prepared, the premium on bonds is added to the face value of the bonds. The partial balance sheet at the end of the first period is shown in Figure 7.25, after 1/10 of the premium is applied.

Bonds Payable	$100,000
Added: Unamortized Discount	7,303
Book Value	$107,303

FIGURE 7.25

Since the year end is September 30, 2020, Energy Bite needs to accrue interest expense before the second payment date on January 1, 2021. At each year end for the next five years, the interest expense is accrued and the premium is amortized for three months, from July 1 to September 30. The interest expense and the amortized premium for period 2 (six months) can be found in Figure 7.23. These numbers must be adjusted to reflect only three months instead of six months. As shown in Figure 7.26, the interest payable is credited for $2,500 ($5,000 × 3/6), premium on bonds payable is amortized (debited) for $406 ($812 × 3/6) and interest expense is debited for $2,094 ($2,500 – $406).

JOURNAL

Date	Account Title and Explanation	Debit	Credit
Sep 30	Interest Expense	2,094	
	Premium on Bonds Payable	406	
	Interest Payable		2,500
	To record accrued interest expense and amortized premium at year end		

FIGURE 7.26

As shown in Figure 7.27, the cash payment of $5,000 is made on January 1, 2020. Interest payable is debited for $2,500 and interest expense is also debited for the remaining balance of period 2, which is $2,094 ($4,188 – $2,094). The rest of the premium on bonds payable of period 2 should also be amortized and debited for $406 ($812 – $406).

JOURNAL

Date	Account Title and Explanation	Debit	Credit
Jan 1	Interest Payable	2,500	
	Interest Expense	2,094	
	Premium on Bonds Payable	406	
	Cash		5,000
	To record payment of interest and amortized discount		

FIGURE 7.27

At the end of five years, the company pays the bondholder $100,000 instead of the $108,115 that was originally received. Over the 10 periods, the journal entry shown in Figure 7.24 is repeated. As this happens, the value of the premium on the bonds decreases and the book value (or carrying value) of the bond decreases. By the end of the 10 periods, the premium is reduced to zero and the book value of the bond is the face value, $100,000.

Similar to Figure 7.14 from the discount discussion, on the maturity date, cash is credited in the amount of $100,000, and the same amount is debited to bonds payable to remove the debt from the books.

A Closer Look

Recording the bond premium or discount using a separate premium on bonds payable or discount on bonds payable account is called the gross method. Alternatively, a bond issuer can account for bond premiums or discounts using the net method by recording them directly in the bonds payable account. This method eliminates the use of separate accounts to track premiums or discounts. To illustrate the differences between the two methods, the transactions below compare how issuing bonds at a discount is recorded under the net method and the gross method.

Net Method

Jan 1	Cash	92,640	
	Bonds Payable		92,640

Gross Method

Jan 1	Cash	92,640	
	Discount on Bonds Payable	7,360	
	Bonds Payable		100,000

The transactions below compare how the interest payment and discount amortization are recorded under the net and gross methods.

Net Method

July 1	Interest Expense	5,558	
	Bonds Payable		558
	Cash		5,000

Gross Method

July 1	Interest Expense	5,558	
	Discount on Bonds Payable		558
	Cash		5,000

If the bonds are issued at a premium, the two methods of accounting work in a similar way. The premium amount is included in the bonds payable account on the date of bond issuance, making the balance of bonds payable higher than the par value. When the premium is amortized, instead of debiting the premium on bonds payable account, the bond issuer debits the bonds payable account, thus lowering its balance.

Pause & Reflect

Exercise 7-3

On January 1, 2020, The Kitchen Company issues $200,000 worth of 12%, two-year bonds with interest payable semi-annually. Just prior to issuing the bonds, the market interest rate decreases to 10%.

a) Fill in the premium amortization table below.

Straight-Line Amortization Table of Bond Premium					
Semi-Annual Interest Period	**Interest Payment**	**Premium Amortization**	**Interest Expense**	**Premium Balance**	**Bond Book Value**
0					
1					
2					
3					
4					
Total					

b) Show how The Kitchen Company records the bond issuance transaction.

JOURNAL			
Date	**Account Title and Explanation**	**Debit**	**Credit**

See Appendix I for solutions.

Retiring Bonds

LO 5

Regardless of the price at which a bond is issued, whether at par, discount or premium, the underlying terms of the bond remain the same. This means that an interest payment is made regularly according to the rate on the bond and that the principal amount is paid back in full at maturity. The original investor essentially loans the issuing company the principal amount, in exchange for regular interest payments.

When the bond matures, that principal amount is paid back to the investor (owner) of the bond. This transaction is also referred to as redeeming the bond or buying it back.

Using our example of Energy Bite Inc., let us look at how the final bond redemption is recorded. Cash is credited in the amount of $100,000. The original bonds payable, created five years earlier at the time of bond issue, is finally taken off the books with a $100,000 debit to that account. This transaction of bonds redemption, shown in Figure 7.28, is identical to what was shown earlier in Figures 7.13 (bonds issued at par) and 7.21 (bonds issued at a discount).

JOURNAL

Date	Account Title and Explanation	Debit	Credit
Jan 1	Bonds Payable	100,000	
	Cash		100,000
	To redeem $100,000 worth of bonds		

FIGURE 7.28

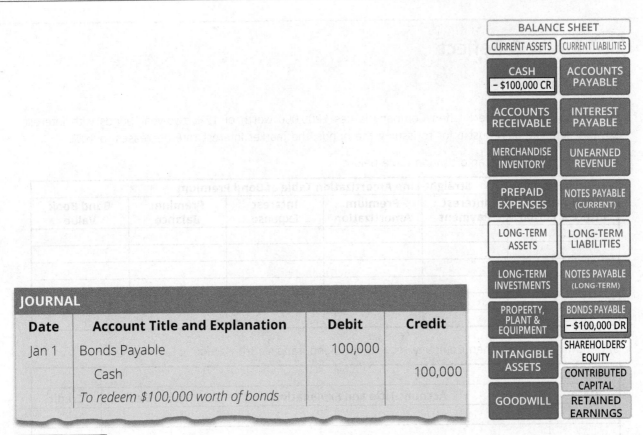

This transaction takes care of the redemption of the bond at maturity. However, a company may sometimes issue what are known as redeemable bonds, also called callable bonds. These give the issuing company the option to buy back the bonds before the stated maturity date. The issuer might want to do this to take advantage of lower market interest rates, which would then allow for the issuance of new bonds to match those lower rates. The company would then make lower annual interest payments on its new bonds.

When the bonds are redeemed, in addition to removing the bonds from the books, any remaining premium or discount must also be removed.

Consider our earlier example of Energy Bite Inc. bonds issued at a discount. If the company exercises a call option on the bonds at the end of Year 4 (which includes eight periods of paid interest), then according to the amortization table in Figure 7.16, the unamortized discount at the end of semi-annual interest period 8 amounts to $1,472.

The book value of the bond on this date is $98,528 ($100,000 - $1,472); however, it is likely that the amount of cash paid to redeem this bond early will be different from the book value. If the amount of cash paid is greater than the book value, a loss must be recognized. If the amount of cash paid is less than the book value, a gain must be recognized.

If Energy Bite pays $99,000 to redeem the bonds early, it records a loss of $472, as shown in Figure 7.29.

JOURNAL

Date	Account Title and Explanation	Debit	Credit
Jan 1	Bonds Payable	100,000	
	Loss on Bond Redemption	472	
	Discount on Bonds Payable		1,472
	Cash		99,000
	To redeem $100,000 worth of bonds		

FIGURE 7.29

The debit to bonds payable and the credit to discount on bonds payable are to remove both items from the balance sheet. The loss is reported on the income statement under other income and expenses. If the cash paid is less than the bond's book value, a gain is recorded and also reported on the income statement.

If we use the bonds that were issued at a premium, then the same type of transaction takes place, except that a debit is recorded to premium on bonds payable to close the account. Any gain or loss on the redemption is recorded in the same manner illustrated.

Pause & Reflect

Exercise 7-4

On June 30, 2020, the Goldstar Group has the following bond issue on its books.

Face value of bonds:	$2,000,000 of callable bonds
Premium on bonds payable:	$80,000

The company decides to redeem one-half of the bonds ($1,000,000) early. It pays $950,000 to redeem the bonds. Show how the company's accountant records the transaction.

JOURNAL

Date	Account Title and Explanation	Debit	Credit

See Appendix I for solutions.

Notes Payable

LO 6

A note payable is a legally binding document that represents money owed to the bank, an individual, a corporation or another lender. In a previous chapter you learned about short-term notes payable, which represent a current liability due within 12 months of the date of issue. Short-term notes payable are shown as current liabilities on the balance sheet at the end of the period.

Long-term notes payable, on the other hand, represent a long-term liability due beyond 12 months of the date of issue. A note that is used to purchase a particular asset, such as equipment or a building, is usually *secured* by the asset being purchased, meaning that the asset can be sold for cash by the lender if the borrower defaults on payment. A note secured by an asset is known as a **mortgage note**.

Notes payable are similar to bonds payable in some respects. Like bonds, notes represent the borrower's promise to repay the principal to the lender. Also, both bonds and notes require interest payments. However, while bonds have a stated contractual interest rate (or coupon rate), notes can have one of two types of interest rate. The first, a **fixed interest rate**, is a rate that remains constant for the entire term of the note. The second type, a **variable interest rate**, is also referred to as a *floating* rate because it fluctuates according to market interest rates.

Another difference between bonds and notes is that a bond's principal is repaid all at once on a single maturity date (except in the case of serial bonds), but a note's principal is repaid in periodic payments, such as monthly, quarterly or semi-annually. These periodic payments on the notes are usually referred to as **installments**. When the installments are paid on notes payable, the amount consists of both a payment toward the note's principal (its face value) and interest on the unpaid balance of the note.

Let us look at an example using a company called Trigraph Inc. Suppose that Trigraph issues a $300,000 five-year, 5% note payable on January 1, 2020. The journal entry to record the issue of the note payable is shown in Figure 7.30.

JOURNAL

Date	Account Title and Explanation	Debit	Credit
Jan 1	Cash	300,000	
	Notes Payable		300,000
	To issue a five-year, 5% note payable (due in 2025)		

FIGURE 7.30

According to the terms of the note, the note is repayable in 60 monthly installments. Therefore, the blended payments include the interest on the outstanding principal. This type of payment is often used for mortgages, car loans, student loan payments, and so on.

The installments are made in equal monthly payments that consist of both the reduction of the principal and the monthly interest expense of 0.417% (5% × 1⁄12) on the outstanding principal. Therefore, the interest expense decreases with each period. However, the portion of the payment that is applied to the principal increases with each period. Let us look at how this happens.

The equal installment payments can be calculated by applying the present value (*PV*) concepts you used earlier in the chapter. To illustrate, we can calculate the dollar value of the monthly installment payments using the concept of present value of an annuity. The formula to calculate the monthly installment payment is shown in Figure 7.31.

$$\text{Monthly Installment Payment} = \frac{\text{Note Payable Amount}}{\text{Present Value of an Annuity of \$1 for } n \text{ periods at } i\%}$$

FIGURE 7.31

The amount of Trigraph's monthly installment payment is calculated by dividing the total amount of the note principal ($300,000) by the present value of an annuity of $1 for 60 periods at 0.417% compound interest, which is 52.99071. (To determine the present value factor, you can use a calculator or a spreadsheet application. See Appendix 7B for an example.) The monthly installment payment is therefore as shown below.

$$\text{Monthly Installment Payment} = \frac{\$300{,}000}{52.99071}$$

$$= \$5{,}661$$

The key is determining how much of the installment payment of $5,661 is interest and how much is principal. Figure 7.32 shows an installment payment schedule for Trigraph Inc.'s note payable for the first four payment periods.

	A	B	C	D
Date	Cash Payment	Interest Expense (D × 5% × 1/12)	Reduction of Principal (A − B)	Principal Balance (D − C)
Jan 1				$300,000
Feb 1	$5,661	$1,250	$4,411	295,589
Mar 1	5,661	1,232	4,429	291,160
Apr 1	5,661	1,213	4,448	286,712

FIGURE 7.32

Column A represents the total cash payment, which is fixed for each interest period at $5,661. The interest expense (column B) is calculated by multiplying the interest rate by the outstanding principal (column D of the previous period). The principal reduction (column C) is equal to the difference between the fixed cash payment and the interest expense. As the payments are made, the principal balance (column D) decreases. Looking at the second row in Figure 7.32, the calculations for the February 1 payment are as follows.

Principal:	$300,000
Payment Terms:	60 equal installment payments of $5,661
Interest (5%):	($300,000 × 5% × $1/12$) = $1,250
Reduction of Principal:	$5,661 - $1,250 = $4,411
Principal Balance after Payment:	$300,000 - $4,411 = $295,589

The journal entry to record the first installment payment on the note payable is shown in Figure 7.33. Interest expense and notes payable are both debited, for $1,250 and $4,411 respectively. This is referred to as the blended payment method. Cash is also credited for $5,661. As shown in the Accounting Map, the interest expense for the period is shown on the income statement under other expenses. On the balance sheet, the principal amount of $4,411 reduces the current portion of the notes payable.

JOURNAL

Date	Account Title and Explanation	Debit	Credit
Feb 1	Interest Expense	1,250	
	Notes Payable	4,411	
	Cash		5,661
	To record monthly payment of principal and interest on note payable		

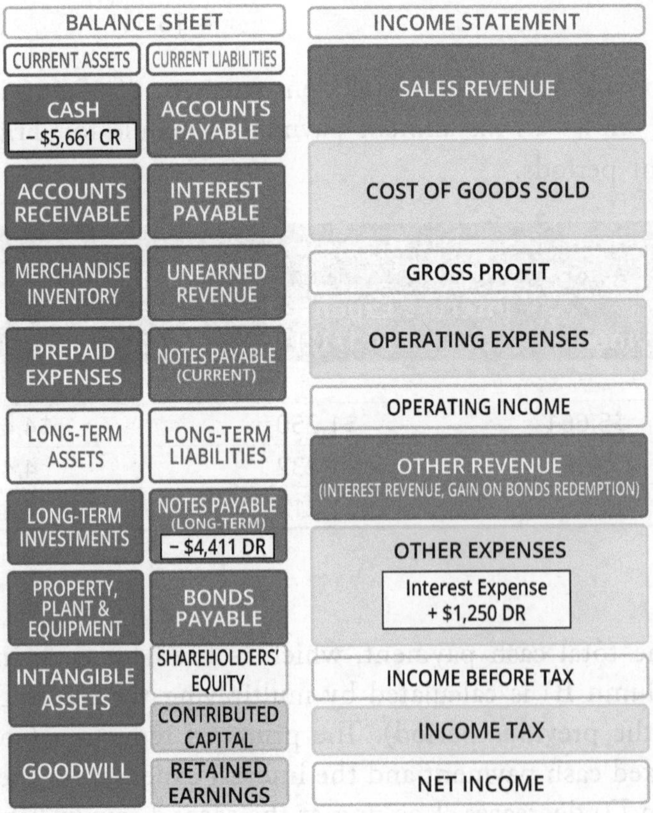

FIGURE 7.33

A similar journal entry is made monthly for the remainder of the term of the note. However, as more payments are made, the amount going toward reducing the principal increases while the amount of interest decreases.

Pause & Reflect

Exercise 7-5

The table below shows a portion of the installment payment schedule for Trigraph Inc.'s note payable that relates to 2021.

Date	A Cash Payment	B Interest Expense (D × 5% × 1/12)	C Reduction of Principal (A – B)	D Principal Balance (D – C)
Jan 1, 2021	$5,661	$1,044	$4,617	$245,840
Feb 1	5,661	1,024	4,637	241,203
Mar 1	5,661	1,005	4,656	236,547
Apr 1	5,661	986	4,675	231,872
May 1	5,661	966	4,695	227,177
Jun 1	5,661	947	4,714	222,463
Jul 1	5,661	927	4,734	217,729
Aug 1	5,661	907	4,754	212,975
Sep 1	5,661	887	4,774	208,201
Oct 1	5,661	867	4,794	203,408
Nov 1	5,661	848	4,813	198,594
Dec 1	5,661	827	4,834	193,761
Total	$67,932	$11,236	$56,696	-

Show how the July 1, 2021 interest payment is recorded.

JOURNAL

Date	Account Title and Explanation	Debit	Credit

See Appendix I for solutions.

Financial Statement Presentation and Analysis

LO 7

In the normal presentation of a balance sheet, assets and liabilities are classified as current and long-term. This level of detail is required by users of the financial statements so that they can fully understand and assess a company's financial position and its ability to pay its debts.

We have just discussed the concept of separately reporting current and long-term portions of notes payable on the balance sheet. This same practice applies to bonds payable, which was covered earlier in this chapter. Let us look at an example of financial statement presentation for both types of long-term liabilities, starting with notes payable.

Notes Payable on the Financial Statements

By now you are quite familiar with the difference between current and long-term (or noncurrent) liabilities: current liabilities are those payable within 12 months of the balance sheet date or within one operating cycle (whichever is longer), while long-term liabilities are those payable beyond 12 months or beyond the operating cycle. Using this concept and assuming the operating cycle is 12 months, a note payable must be reported on the balance sheet in its respective categories: the amount of principal to be reduced over the next 12 months from the balance sheet date is reported as notes payable, current portion, and the balance of the principal to be reduced beyond the 12-month period is reported as notes payable, long-term portion.

The example of the notes payable of Trigraph Inc. will be used to illustrate the balance sheet presentation. Fast-forward to the end of the first 12 months after the note was issued, to the balance sheet date of December 31, 2020. First, determine the current and long-term portions of the note as of December 31. Based on the installment payment schedule in Figure 7.32, the schedule for the year 2020 is shown in Figure 7.34.

Date	A Cash Payment	B Interest Expense (D × 5% × 1/12)	C Reduction of Principal (A − B)	D Principal Balance (D − C)
Jan 1, 2020				$300,000
Feb 1	$5,661	$1,250	$4,411	295,589
Mar 1	5,661	1,232	4,429	291,160
Apr 1	5,661	1,213	4,448	286,712
May 1	5,661	1,195	4,466	282,246
Jun 1	5,661	1,176	4,485	277,761
Jul 1	5,661	1,157	4,504	273,257
Aug 1	5,661	1,139	4,522	268,735
Sep 1	5,661	1,120	4,541	264,194
Oct 1	5,661	1,101	4,560	259,634
Nov 1	5,661	1,082	4,579	255,055
Dec 1	5,661	1,063	4,598	250,457
Total	$62,271	$12,728	$49,543	-

FIGURE 7.34

In Column C, the reduction of principal increases each month, with a total of $49,543 for 2020. Figure 7.35 shows the installment payment schedule over the five-year term of the note (for simplicity, this has already been calculated and condensed).

Year	A Beginning Balance	B Cash Payment	C Interest Expense	D Reduction of Principal	E Principal Balance
2020	$300,000	$62,271	$12,728	$49,543	$250,457
2021	250,457	$67,932	11,236	56,696	193,761
2022	193,761	$67,932	8,333	59,599	134,162
2023	134,162	$67,932	5,283	62,649	71,513
2024	71,513	$67,932	2,080	65,852	5,661
2025	5,661	5,661	0	5,661	0
Total	-	$339,660	$39,660	$300,000	-

FIGURE 7.35

So, as of December 31, 2020, the current portion of the note payable (that is, the amount to be paid over the next 12 months) is $56,696 (from Column D). As of December 31, 2020, the long-term portion of the note payable (that is, the amount to be paid beyond the next 12 months) is calculated as follows.

Long-Term Portion of Note Payable = Principal Balance (Dec 31, 2020) – Reduction of Principal over Next 12 Months
= $250,457 – $56,696
= $193,761

Figure 7.36 presents the partial balance sheet for Trigraph Inc., focusing on the liabilities section of the statement. Note that all other amounts in the partial balance sheet are assumed for illustration purposes.

Trigraph Inc. Balance Sheet (partial) As at December 31, 2020		
Current Liabilities		
Accounts Payable	$70,000	
Interest Payable	10,000	
Notes Payable, Current Portion	56,696	
Total Current Liabilities		$136,696
Long-Term Liabilities		
Notes Payable, Long-Term Portion	193,761	
Total Long-Term Liabilities		193,761
Total Liabilities		330,457

FIGURE 7.36

Bonds Payable on the Financial Statements

Bonds payable affect the balance sheet accounts in different ways, depending on whether the bonds are issued at par, at a discount or at a premium. Generally, the presentation of bonds payable on the balance sheet can be summarized as follows.

- Bonds issued at par—The balance sheet reports the long-term liability (as of the end of the period) equal to the bond's face value, until the bond's maturity.
- Bonds issued at a discount—The balance sheet reports the long-term liability (as of the end of the period) equal to the bond's carrying value (its book value), until the bond's maturity. For bonds issued at a discount, the carrying value is the bond's face value minus the total unamortized discount. Each year, the bond's carrying value increases until the amount reported on the balance sheet equals the bond's face value.
- Bonds issued at a premium—The balance sheet reports the long-term liability (as of the end of the period) equal to the bond's carrying value (its book value), until the bond's maturity. For bonds issued at a premium, the carrying value is the bond's face value plus the total unamortized premium. Each year, the bond's carrying value decreases until the amount reported on the balance sheet equals the bond's face value.

To illustrate the balance sheet presentation, we will use an example of bonds issued at a discount. Return to the earlier example in which Energy Bite issues $100,000 worth of five-year, 10% interest bonds on January 1, 2020. At the then-current market interest rate of 12% with semi-annual interest payments, the bonds were issued at a discount for $92,640, which is the carrying value of the bonds on their issue date. Referring to the amortization table in Figure 7.16, at the end of the first fiscal year of September 30 (half way between semi-annual interest periods 1 and 2), the unamortized discount on the bonds payable is $6,256 ($7,360 - $736 - $368). Since the year end is September 30, only three months of period 2 should be accounted for when calculating the year-end adjustments ($736 × 3/6 - $368). We know that the face value of the bonds is $100,000. Energy Bite's partial balance sheet for September 30, 2020, is shown in Figure 7.37.

Energy Bite Inc. Balance Sheet (partial) As at September 30, 2020	
Long-Term Liabilities	
Bonds Payable, 10%, due January 1, 2025	$100,000
Discount on Bonds Payable	6,256
Total Long-Term Liabilities	93,744

FIGURE 7.37

Note that as of September 30, 2020, the bonds' carrying value is now $93,744, which represents the amortized cost.

If instead Energy Bite issues the same bonds on January 1, 2020, at a then-current market interest rate of 8% with semi-annual interest payments, the bonds are issued at a premium for $108,115; this is the carrying value of the bonds on their issue date. Referring to the amortization table in Figure 7.23, at the end of the first fiscal year (half way between semi-annual interest periods 1 and 2), the unamortized premium on the bonds payable is $6,897 ($8,115 - $812 - $406). Since the year end is September 30, only three months of period 2 are accounted for when calculating the year-end adjustments ($812 × 3/6 = $406). We know that the face value of the bonds is $100,000. Energy Bite's partial balance sheet for September 30, 2020, is shown in Figure 7.38.

Energy Bite Inc. Balance Sheet (partial) As at September 30, 2020	
Long-Term Liabilities	
Bonds Payable, 10%, due January 1, 2025	$100,000
Premium on Bonds Payable	6,897
Total Long-Term Liabilities	$106,897

FIGURE 7.38

Interest expense and the amortization of bond discount and premium affect the income statement accounts in different ways, depending on whether the bonds are issued at par, at a discount or at a premium. Generally, the presentation of interest expense from the bonds payable on the income statement can be summarized as follows.

- Bonds issued at par—The income statement reports interest expense for the period equal to the bond's contractual interest rate.
- Bonds issued at a discount—The income statement reports interest expense for the period equal to the bond's contractual interest rate plus the amortized portion of the discount.
- Bonds issued at a premium—The income statement reports interest expense for the period equal to the bond's contractual interest rate minus the amortized portion of the premium.

As the Accounting Maps showed in the section on bonds payable, the income statement includes interest expense for the period under other expenses.

At the beginning of this section, you learned that users of the financial statements require this level of detail. Creditors and investors need complete and accurate financial information so that they can make informed business decisions. This is why accounting standards require full disclosure of all current and long-term debt.

In the next section, we will look at financial ratios related to liabilities and how to calculate the different ratios.

Debt-to-Total-Assets Ratio

The **debt-to-total-assets ratio** measures how much of a company's assets are financed through total liabilities. This ratio is an indicator of a company's financial leverage, a concept discussed at the beginning of this chapter. The higher the ratio, the greater the difficulty a company has in repaying its creditors. A high debt-to-total-assets ratio indicates that the company is at a greater risk of being unable to meet debt obligations. A low debt-to-total-assets ratio indicates that a company is in a favourable position to meet debt obligations, which is more desirable to creditors.

The debt-to-total-assets ratio is calculated by dividing a company's total liabilities by its total assets, as shown in Figure 7.39.

$$\text{Debt-to-Total-Assets Ratio} = \frac{\text{Total Liabilities}}{\text{Total Assets}}$$

FIGURE 7.39

To illustrate, assume that a corporation has $10,000,000 in total assets, $4,000,000 in total liabilities, and $6,000,000 in shareholders' equity. Its debt-to-total-assets ratio is calculated as follows.

$$\text{Debt-to-Total-Assets Ratio} = \frac{\$4{,}000{,}000}{\$10{,}000{,}000}$$

$$= 0.4 \text{ or } 0.4 \text{ to } 1$$

This means that 40% of the company's assets are financed by debt, and therefore 60% of the assets are financed by equity (its owners or shareholders). To determine if this is an acceptable level of financial leverage, decision-makers often compare a company's debt-to-total-assets ratio to the industry ratio (i.e. that of competitors in the same industry).

Debt-to-Equity Ratio

The **debt-to-equity ratio** is used to assess how much of a company is being financed by lenders and how much is being financed by the owners or shareholders. It measures the extent to which a business is indebted to lenders. Generally, owners or shareholders are expected to take a higher risk than lenders.

The debt-to-equity ratio is calculated by dividing a company's total liabilities by its total shareholders' equity, as shown in Figure 7.40.

$$\text{Debt-to-Equity Ratio} = \frac{\text{Total Liabilities}}{\text{Total Shareholders' Equity}}$$

FIGURE 7.40

To illustrate, we can use the information from the corporation in our previous example. The corporation's debt-to-equity ratio is calculated as follows.

$$\text{Debt-to-Equity Ratio} = \frac{\$4{,}000{,}000}{\$6{,}000{,}000}$$

$$= 0.67 \text{ or } 0.67 \text{ to } 1$$

This means that the company has 67 cents of debt for every $1 in equity. Ideally, a business should have a debt-to-equity ratio of 1:2, which would mean that the company has $1 of debt for every $2 of equity. Like other ratios, though, the debt-to-equity ratio must be compared to industry benchmarks to draw sound conclusions.

Controls and Ethics Related to Long-Term Liabilities

LO 8

Long-term liabilities play a key role in helping a company finance its business. At the same time, lenders and investors want assurance that they will receive their money back by the payment dates. That is why a company needs to monitor the level of debt and its accompanying interest expense. Taking on too much debt can jeopardize a company's ability to maintain a good credit rating and may consequently limit future borrowing from banks and other creditors.

In the Real World

When potential investors want to purchase bonds, they need to be able to assess the creditworthiness of the issuer and the securities that they are offering. They often rely on information from bond rating agencies such as Moody's, Standard & Poor's (S&P), and Fitch Ratings.

Bond rating agencies review and assign ratings to the issuers of bonds and other debt instruments. A company's credit grade indicates its financial health and how likely it will continue to pay interest and return the bond's principal at maturity. Each agency uses its own evaluation and grading system. For instance, S&P uses a rating grade system ranging from AAA (highest quality) to D (in default). Bonds rated from AAA to BBB are known as investment grade because they are of high to medium quality and considered safe investments. (These grades often include a plus (+) or a minus (−) to indicate their standing within their category.)

Ratings of BB+ and lower are considered noninvestment grade or junk bonds because of their higher risk level or potential to default on payments. Some investors, however, may be attracted to these lower-grade bonds because of the much higher rates of interest that they pay—that is, if the company behind them survives to pay its obligations.

In general, different financial measurements can be applied to monitor and control a company's ability to pay off its long-term debt. For example, analysts can look at the amount of a company's total assets financed by creditors or the amount of interest obligations, compared to its earnings. Beyond the ratios illustrated in the previous section, other financial ratios used for long-term liabilities and solvency analysis are discussed in detail in a later chapter.

A company must comply with all relevant policies, plans, procedures, laws and regulations. With regard to loans, this means that all documents pertaining to the loan should be reviewed by legal counsel. Strong controls surrounding the negotiation of long-term liabilities should result in obtaining the best possible interest rates. A lower interest rate increases cash flow, which can then be used for other activities of the business. In addition, robust cash controls ensure that interest and principal payments are made on time. Other controls include verifying that interest and principal payments have been received by lenders.

We will now consider ethical violations related to long-term liabilities. Companies assume long-term liabilities, such as term loans and bond issues, to finance large items and projects that often take years to complete. The sheer magnitude of these transactions makes them vulnerable to abuse.

Management is often closely involved when large sums of money are involved. Internal controls must be thoroughly documented and monitored, to help reduce the likelihood of fraudulent activities. Furthermore, both internal and external audits should be performed at least annually. Individuals may be tempted to siphon off or redirect money when dealing with large amounts. Staying alert and attentive to these risks is one of the primary responsibilities of those who own and run the company.

It is also necessary to be vigilant with transactions conducted with financial institutions, where unauthorized commissions may exist. Some part of the loan money might end up in the hands of individuals who work out a side deal for themselves. That is why it is always important for companies to keep track of all the money.

Another type of fraud is off-balance-sheet financing. Some companies engage in accounting practices that keep some large financing schemes off the books. This allows the company to keep its debt-to-equity and leverage ratios low, which might artificially inflate stock prices by overstating its equity position. Examples include joint ventures, research and development partnerships and operating leases.

A **lease** is a contract between the owner of an asset and another party who uses the asset for a given period of time. One form is an **operating lease**, such as a car rental, where the ownership is not transferred to another party over the term of the agreement.

Operating leases were once a common example of off-balance-sheet financing. Instead of owning the asset, a company could lease it and expense any rental fees. Depending on the terms, some leases are treated as a form of financing. This forces the company to record an asset and the accompanying liability on its balance sheet. This in turn increases its debt-to-equity ratio and gives users of its financial statements a more accurate picture of the company's financial position. Companies must always be careful to comply with the related requirements, whether reporting under ASPE or IFRS.

ASPE vs. IFRS

Given recent changes in lease accounting, IFRS requires almost all leases to be recognized as finance leases, meaning that they would be recorded on the balance sheet.

An operating lease is permitted under ASPE.

In the Real World

In the fall of 2008, the world was hit by the worst financial crisis since the Depression. Global financial institutions had too much money invested in bad credit, especially subprime mortgages. The economy started to slow down when these bad debts went unpaid and the credit market crashed as a result.

In the aftermath of the crash, leading financial minds looked for solutions to problems that had gone unsolved for years. Although many experts looked for ways to better regulate the markets, some analysts started pointing fingers at the accounting profession.

Specifically, a long-running criticism of accounting standards is that they do not require an appropriate level of disclosure. A perfect example of this is off-balance-sheet financing—the practice of keeping some forms of long-term financing off the company books.

Another example of poor disclosure is reporting pension fund assets and liabilities only in footnote form. Recent standards are now forcing companies to disclose a net amount on the balance sheet itself.

Critics of the accounting profession believe that it is only through fair and open reporting that companies can gain the trust of investment markets in general. How can companies expect people to trust them with money if they are not fully open about what is reported in the financial statements?

Open and fair accounting practices can help bring back some stability and trust in world markets at a time when it is most needed.

In Summary

LO 1 Identify and describe different types of long-term liabilities

- Corporations can finance their operations using long-term debt, such as bonds (borrowing from private investors) and notes payable (borrowing from the bank).
- The company that issues the bond is called the bond issuer. The investor who purchases the bond is the bondholder.
- The investor provides a principal loan to the issuing company. In return, the company makes interest payments to the investor, in addition to eventually repaying the principal.
- There are several types of bonds, such as term bonds, debenture bonds, redeemable bonds, mortgage bonds, convertible bonds, registered bonds and coupon bonds.

LO 2 Explain the concept of present value and apply it to bond pricing

- The time value of money involves the concept that interest is earned on top of interest year after year. This is called compound interest.
- Future value determines the value of an investment in the future if an amount is invested today. Present value determines the amount invested today required to produce a certain amount in the future. Another way to describe present value is *discounting*.
- A bond's price is determined by computing the present value of all the future cash flows, including interest and repayment of principal.

LO 3 Record bonds issued at par

- When the bond interest rate equals the market interest rate, the company can sell the bond at par.

LO 4 Record bonds issued at a discount or a premium

- When the bond interest rate is lower than the market interest rate, the company sells the bond at a discount.
- When the bond interest rate is higher than the market interest rate, the company can sell the bond at a premium.
- The discount or premium attached to a bond price should be amortized over the term of the bond until maturity.
- The straight-line amortization method records the same amount of interest expense each period.

LO 5 Record the retirement of bonds

- When the bond reaches maturity, it is time for the issuing company to repay the principal to whoever holds the bond at the time. This is also called bond redemption.
- The issuing company may have the option to redeem a bond early. Such securities are referred to as redeemable bonds, or callable bonds.

LO 6 Record installment notes payable

- A company usually has three basic options when it comes to long-term financing: bank loans, bond issues and notes payable.
- Long-term notes payable are repayable in periodic payments, such as monthly, quarterly or semi-annually.
- A long-term note payable represents a long-term liability that is due beyond 12 months of the date of issue.

LO 7 Describe how long-term liabilities are analyzed and presented on the balance sheet

- Long-term liabilities must be split into a current portion (typically, the amount owed in the next 12 months) and a long-term portion (amount owed beyond 12 months). These amounts are reported on the balance sheet in the current liabilities and long-term liabilities sections respectively.

LO 8 Apply controls and ethics related to long-term liabilities

- Controls related to long-term liabilities should ensure that all documentation is readily available, and that cash flow planning accommodates future payments for loans and bonds.
- Ethics related to long-term liabilities should ensure the integrity of large amounts of cash that upper management has the responsibility of handling.
- Off-balance-sheet financing is a practice that can skew the way in which company finances are reported to the public.

Table 7.1
Present Value of $1

Periods	1%	2%	3%	4%	5%	6%
1	0.9901	0.9804	0.9709	0.9615	0.9524	0.9434
2	0.9803	0.9612	0.9426	0.9246	0.9070	0.8900
3	0.9706	0.9423	0.9151	0.8890	0.8638	0.8396
4	0.9610	0.9238	0.8885	0.8548	0.8227	0.7921
5	0.9515	0.9057	0.8626	0.8219	0.7835	0.7473
6	0.9420	0.8880	0.8375	0.7903	0.7462	0.7050
7	0.9327	0.8706	0.8131	0.7599	0.7107	0.6651
8	0.9235	0.8535	0.7894	0.7307	0.6768	0.6274
9	0.9143	0.8368	0.7664	0.7026	0.6446	0.5919
10	0.9053	0.8203	0.7441	0.6756	0.6139	0.5584
11	0.8963	0.8043	0.7224	0.6496	0.5847	0.5268
12	0.8874	0.7885	0.7014	0.6246	0.5568	0.4970
13	0.8787	0.7730	0.6810	0.6006	0.5303	0.4688
14	0.8700	0.7579	0.6611	0.5775	0.5051	0.4423
15	0.8613	0.7430	0.6419	0.5553	0.4810	0.4173

Table 7.2
Present Value of Annuity of $1

Periods	1%	2%	3%	4%	5%	6%
1	0.9901	0.9804	0.9709	0.9615	0.9524	0.9434
2	1.9704	1.9416	1.9135	1.8861	1.8594	1.8334
3	2.9410	2.8839	2.8286	2.7751	2.7232	2.6730
4	3.9020	3.8077	3.7171	3.6299	3.5460	3.4651
5	4.8534	4.7135	4.5797	4.4518	4.3295	4.2124
6	5.7955	5.6014	5.4172	5.2421	5.0757	4.9173
7	6.7282	6.4720	6.2303	6.0021	5.7864	5.5824
8	7.6517	7.3255	7.0197	6.7327	6.4632	6.2098
9	8.5660	8.1622	7.7861	7.4353	7.1078	6.8017
10	9.4713	8.9826	8.5302	8.1109	7.7217	7.3601
11	10.3676	9.7868	9.2526	8.7605	8.3064	7.8869
12	11.2551	10.5753	9.9540	9.3851	8.8633	8.3838
13	12.1337	11.3484	10.6350	9.9856	9.3936	8.8527
14	13.0037	12.1062	11.2961	10.5631	9.8986	9.2950
15	13.8651	12.8493	11.9379	11.1184	10.3797	9.7122

Review Exercise 7-1

Hohl Company is planning to expand its facilities by constructing a new building and installing new machines. To complete this project, the company has decided to issue $2,000,000 worth of 20-year, 4% callable bonds, with interest paid every six months.

On April 1, 2020, the company has completed all the necessary paperwork and is now ready to issue the bonds. Fortunately, just as Hohl Company is issuing its bonds, the current market rate drops to 3.5%. Its financial advisor recommends issuing the bonds at a premium of $142,968.

On March 31 of 2025, interest rates drop to 2%. At this point, the company issues $2,200,000 worth of 10-year, 2% bonds at par to redeem all outstanding 4% bonds. The company pays $2,110,000 to redeem the 4% bonds.

Required

a) Prepare the bond premium amortization table from period 1 to period 10 (covers 2020 to 2025), using the straight-line amortization method.

Straight-Line Amortization Table of Bond Premium

Semi-Annual Interest Period	A Interest Payment	B Premium Amortization	C Interest Expense	D Premium Balance	E Bond Book Value

b) Record the journal entries for the following transactions.

- The issuance of bonds on April 1, 2020
- Any required entries for the company's year ended February 28, 2021 (note that the company pays interest semi-annually)
- The retirement of the 4% bonds and issue of the new 2% bonds
- The first interest payment on the 2% bonds

JOURNAL

Date	Account Title and Explanation	Debit	Credit

See Appendix I for solutions.

Review Exercise 7-2

On May 1, 2020, Hohl Company issues a two-year note payable for $200,000 in exchange for equipment from one of the company's suppliers. The interest rate is 4% and payments are made semi-annually. Assume all other conditions remain unchanged and the company's year end is March 31.

Required

a) Using the table below, calculate cash payment, interest expense, reduction of principal and principal balance on each payment date, with an equal installment payment of $52,525 using the blended payment method.

Date	A Cash Payment	B Interest Expense	C Reduction of Principal	D Principal Balance

b) Record journal entries of issuing day, first payment day, first year end and second payment day, using the blended payment method from part a).

JOURNAL

Date	Account Title and Explanation	Debit	Credit

See Appendix I for solutions.

Appendix 7A: Effective-Interest Amortization Method

LO 9

In this chapter, you learned about amortization of bond discount or premium using the straight-line method. In this appendix, we will look at amortization of bond discount or premium using the effective-interest method. This method more accurately reflects the change in value of an item over time.

Amortization of Bond Discount by the Effective-Interest Method

First, we will look at amortization of bond discount using the effective-interest method. We will illustrate this method using data from the chapter example of Energy Bite Inc. (in the section Issuing Bonds at a Discount). Keep in mind the following summary points.

- Face value of 10%, five-year bonds, interest paid semi-annually: $100,000
- Present value of bonds at market interest rate (effective rate) of 12%: $92,640
- Discount on bonds payable: $7,360

Figure 7A.1 shows how the receipt of $92,640 for the issue of Energy Bite Inc. bonds (at discount) is recorded by the company using the contra account called discount on bonds payable.

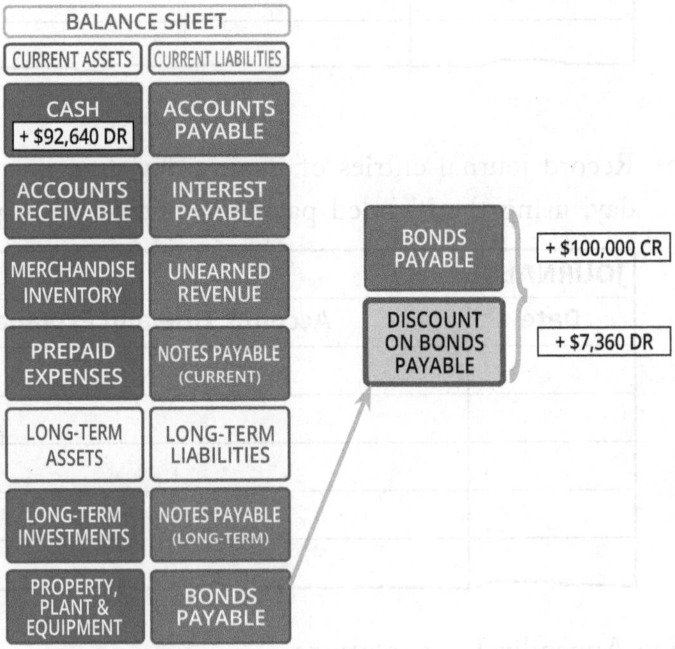

JOURNAL

Date	Account Title and Explanation	Debit	Credit
Jan 1	Cash	92,640	
	Discount on Bonds Payable	7,360	
	Bonds Payable		100,000
	To issue of $100,000 worth of bonds at a discount		

FIGURE 7A.1

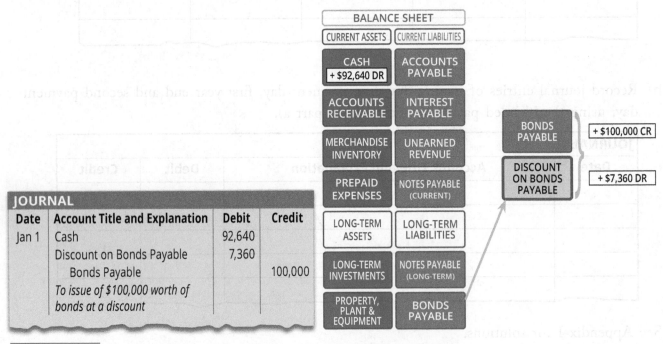

Although Energy Bite has issued a $100,000 bond and this amount must be paid when the bond matures, the company received only $92,640 from the bondholder.

The bond discount is amortized using the **effective-interest amortization method**, which uses the market interest rate at the date the bonds are issued as the basis to calculate the interest expense. The effective interest rate is applied to the amortized cost of the bonds payable and reflects the actual cost of borrowing.

Figure 7A.2 shows the amortization table of the bond over five years (10 periods). Column A shows the interest payment of $5,000, which is fixed in each period since the semi-annual contractual interest rate of 5% and the face value of $100,000 stay the same. Column B shows the interest expense, which is calculated by multiplying the semi-annual market rate of interest (6%) and the bond's amortized cost at the end of the previous period. The values in this column increase over time since, although the market rate is fixed, the bond's amortized cost increases over time. Column C shows the amount of discount amortized over the periods by calculating the difference between the interest expense and the interest payment. The values in this column increase as well, since the interest expense increases. Column D shows the bond's amortized cost. Note that this continues to increase by the amount of discounts amortized each period until it reaches the face value of $100,000.

Effective Interest Amortization Table of Bond Discount				
Semi-Annual Interest Period	A Interest Payment ($100,000 × 5%)	B Interest Expense (D × 6%)	C Discount Amortization (B − A)	D Bond Amortized Cost (D + C)
0				$92,640
1	$5,000	$5,558	$558	93,198
2	5,000	5,592	592	93,790
3	5,000	5,627	627	94,418
4	5,000	5,665	665	95,083
5	5,000	5,705	705	95,788
6	5,000	5,747	747	96,535
7	5,000	5,792	792	97,327
8	5,000	5,840	840	98,167
9	5,000	5,890	890	99,057
10	5,000	5,943	943	100,000
Total	$50,000	$57,360	$7,360	-

FIGURE 7A.2

On July 1, 2020, the first payment of interest is recorded as shown in Figure 7A.3. Going back to Figure 7A.2, in period 1, interest expense is debited for $5,558 (column B). Discount on bonds payable is also amortized and credited for $558 (column C). Cash is credited for the interest payment of $5,000 (column A).

JOURNAL

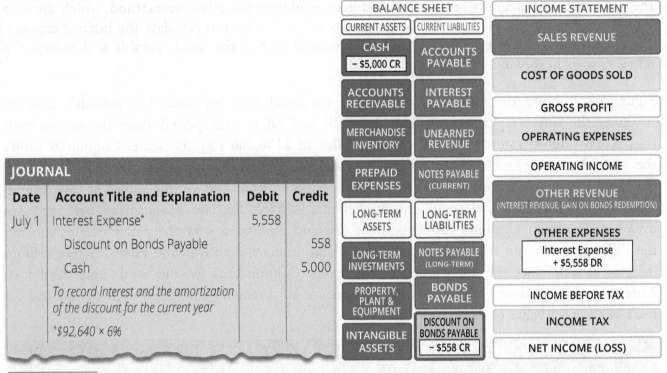

Date	Account Title and Explanation	Debit	Credit
July 1	Interest Expense*	5,558	
	Discount on Bonds Payable		558
	Cash		5,000
	To record interest and the amortization of the discount for the current year		
	**$92,640 × 6%*		

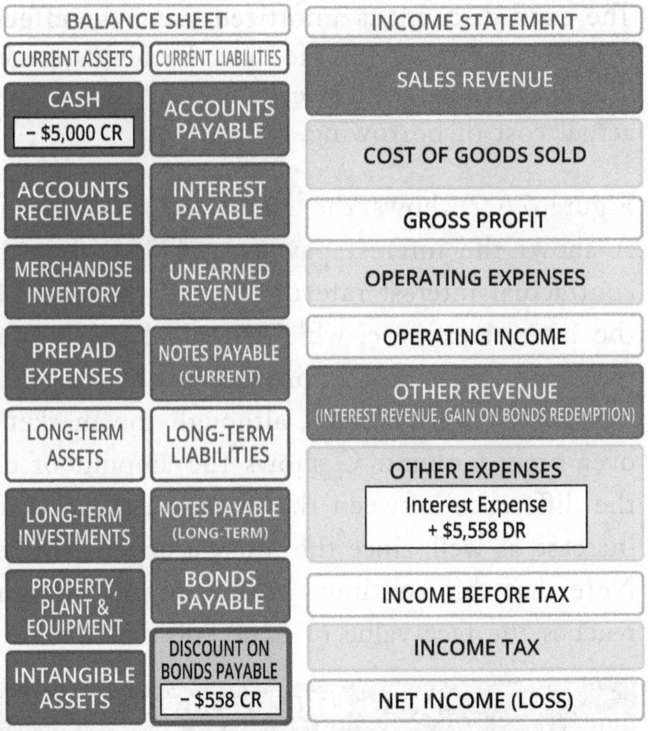

FIGURE 7A.3

On July 1 and January 1 in each of the next five years, the bond issuer will pay $5,000 interest on the bond in cash to the bondholder. The amortization of the discount is just an adjustment and is calculated as the difference between the interest payment and the interest expense. After each period, the value of the discount on the bonds decreases and the book value (or carrying value) of the bond increases. By the end of the five years, the discount is reduced to zero and the book value of the bond is the face value, $100,000.

Since the year end is September 30, 2020, Energy Bite needs to accrue interest expense before the second payment date on January 1, 2021. Figure 7A.4 shows that at each year end for the next five years, the interest expense is accrued and the discount is amortized for three months, from July 1 to September 30. The interest expense and the amortized discounts for period 2 (six months) can be found in Figure 7A.2. These numbers must be adjusted to reflect only three months instead of six months. As shown in Figure 7A.4, interest expense is debited for $2,796 ($5,592 × ³⁄₆), discount on bonds payable is amortized (credited) for $296 ($592 × ³⁄₆) and interest payable is credited for $2,500 ($2,796 - $296).

JOURNAL

Date	Account Title and Explanation	Debit	Credit
Sep 30	Interest Expense	2,796	
	Discount on Bonds Payable		296
	Interest Payable		2,500
	To record accrued interest expense and amortized discount at year end		

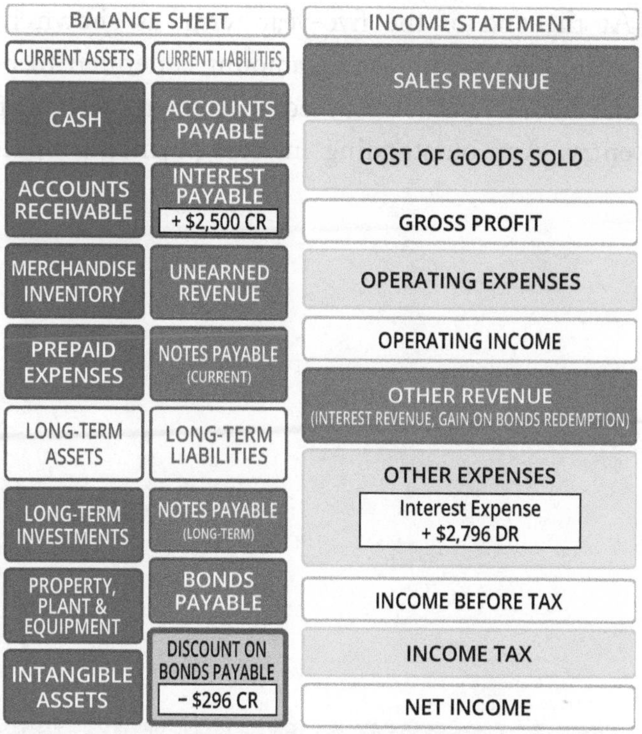

FIGURE 7A.4

As shown in Figure 7A.5, on January 1, 2021, the cash payment is made for $5,000. Interest payable is debited for $2,500 and interest expense is also debited for the remaining balance of period 2, which is $2,796 ($5,592 - $2,796). The rest of the discount of period 2 is also amortized and credited for $296 ($592 - $296).

JOURNAL

Date	Account Title and Explanation	Debit	Credit
Jan 1	Interest Payable	2,500	
	Interest Expense	2,796	
	Discount on Bonds Payable		296
	Cash		5,000
	To record payment of interest and amortized discount		

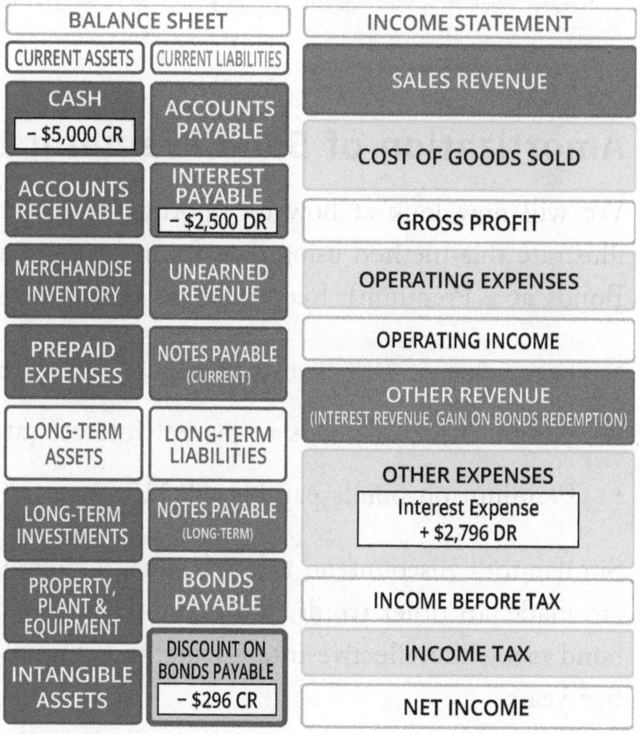

FIGURE 7A.5

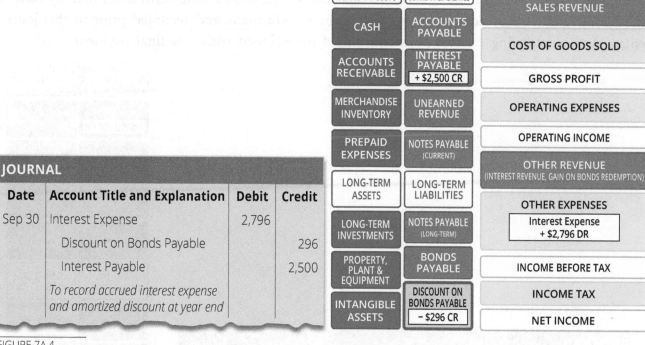

At the end of the five-year term, as shown in Figure 7A.6, cash is credited in the amount of $100,000, and the same amount is debited to bonds payable as a long-term debt, thereby clearing the liability. It is assumed that all interest payments are made and recorded prior to this journal entry. Any outstanding interest payments would be included with this final payment.

JOURNAL

Date	Account Title and Explanation	Debit	Credit
Jan 1, 2025	Bonds Payable	100,000	
	Cash		100,000
	To repay $100,000 to bondholder		

FIGURE 7A.6

Amortization of Bond Premium by the Effective-Interest Method

We will now look at how to amortize bond premiums using the effective-interest method. We will illustrate this method using data from the chapter example of Energy Bite Inc. (in the section Issuing Bonds at a Premium). Keep in mind the following summary points.

- Face value of 10%, five-year bonds, interest paid semi-annually: $100,000
- Present value of bonds at market interest rate (effective rate) of 8%: $108,115
- Premium on bonds payable: $8,115

Similar to a discount on a bond issue, a premium must be amortized as periodic interest payments are made. In other words, the premium liability of $8,115 should be amortized over the term of the bond using the effective-interest method. Figure 7A.7 shows the amortization table of the bond over five years.

Effective-Interest Amortization Table of Bond Premium				
	A	B	C	D
Semi-Annual Interest Period	Interest Payment ($100,000 × 5%)	Interest Expense (D × 4%)	Premium Amortization (A – B)	Bond Amortized Cost (D – C)
0				$108,115
1	$5,000	$4,325	$675	107,440
2	5,000	4,298	702	106,738
3	5,000	4,270	730	106,008
4	5,000	4,240	760	105,248
5	5,000	4,210	790	104,458
6	5,000	4,178	822	103,636
7	5,000	4,145	855	102,781
8	5,000	4,111	889	101,892
9	5,000	4,076	924	100,968
10	5,000	4,032*	968	100,000
Total	$50,000	$41,885	$8,115	-

* $7 difference due to rounding. The final interest expense is adjusted due to rounding to ensure the final bond amortized cost is equal to $100,000.

FIGURE 7A.7

Column A shows the interest payment of $5,000, which is fixed in each period since the semi-annual contractual interest rate of 5% and the face value of $100,000 stay the same. Column B shows the interest expense, which is calculated by multiplying the semi-annual interest market rate of 4% and the bond's amortized cost at the end of the previous period. The values in this column decrease over time since, although the market rate is fixed, the bond's amortized cost decreases over time. Column C shows the amount of premium amortized over the periods by calculating the difference between the interest expense and the interest payment. The values in this column increase, since the interest expense decreases while the interest payment remains constant. Column D shows the bond's amortized cost. Note that this continues to decrease by the amount of premium amortized each period until it reaches the face value of $100,000.

Figure 7A.8 shows how that transaction is recorded for the first year if the effective-interest rate method is used.

JOURNAL

Date	Account Title and Explanation	Debit	Credit
July 1	Interest Expense	4,325	
	Premium on Bonds Payable	675	
	Cash		5,000
	To record payment of interest and amortization of premium		

FIGURE 7A.8

On July 1, 2020, the first payment date, the $5,000 interest payment (column A) is recorded and is represented by a credit to cash. The expense to the company is only $4,325 (column B) and the remaining $675 debit is the first period's amortization of the premium calculated using the effective-interest rate method (column C).

On July 1 and January 1 in each of the next five years, the bond issuer pays $5,000 interest on the bond in cash to the bondholder. The amortization of the premium is just an adjustment and is calculated as the difference between the interest payment and the interest expense.

When financial statements are prepared, the premium on bonds payable is added to the face value of the bonds. The balance sheet at the end of the first period, after the amortization of the premium, is shown in Figure 7A.9.

Bonds Payable	$100,000
Add: Unamortized Premium	7,440
Book Value	$107,440

FIGURE 7A.9

Since the year end is September 30, 2020, Energy Bite needs to accrue interest expense before the second payment date on January 1, 2021. Figure 7A.10 shows that at each year end for the next five years, the interest expense is accrued and the premium is amortized for three months, from July 1 to September 30. The interest expense and the amortized premium for period 2 (six months) can be found in Figure 7A.7. These numbers must be adjusted to reflect only three months instead of six months. As shown in Figure 7A.10, interest expense is debited for $2,149 ($4,298 × $\frac{3}{6}$), premium on bonds payable is amortized (debited) for $351 ($702 × $\frac{3}{6}$) and interest payable is credited for $2,500 ($2,149 + $351).

JOURNAL

Date	Account Title and Explanation	Debit	Credit
Sep 30	Interest Expense	2,149	
	Premium on Bonds Payable	351	
	Interest Payable		2,500
	To record interest expense and amortized premium at year end		

FIGURE 7A.10

On January 1, 2021, the cash payment is made for $5,000, as shown in Figure 7A.11. Interest payable is debited for $2,500 and interest expense is debited for the remaining balance of period 2, which is $2,149 ($4,298 − $2,149). The rest of the premium of period 2 is also amortized and debited for $351 ($702 − $351).

JOURNAL

Date	Account Title and Explanation	Debit	Credit
Jan 1	Interest Payable	2,500	
	Interest Expense	2,149	
	Premium on Bonds Payable	351	
	Cash		5,000
	To record payment of interest and amortized discount		

FIGURE 7A.11

In Summary

LO 9 Describe the effective-interest amortization method

- In contrast to the straight-line amortization method (which records the same amount of interest expense each period), effective interest amortization records interest expense based on the amortized cost of the bond—that is, on the bond's book value at the end of the previous period.
- When amortizing a bond discount, the bond's amortized cost increases each period as the interest expense increases. Conversely, when amortizing a bond premium, the bond's amortized cost decreases each period as the interest expense decreases.

Review Exercise 7A-1

The following information was gathered from the records of Danbury Inc. after a bond issue on January 1, 2020. Interest is paid semi-annually on June 30 and December 31.

- Face value of 8%, five-year bonds, interest compounded semi-annually: $200,000
- Present value of bonds at market interest rate (effective rate) of 10%: $184,557
- Discount on bonds payable: $15,443

Required

a) Prepare the bond discount amortization table for periods 1 to 10 using the effective-interest amortization method.

Effective-Interest Amortization Table of Bond Premium				
Semi-Annual Interest Period (Date)	A Interest Payment	B Interest Expense	C Discount Amortization	D Bond Amortized Cost

b) Record the journal entry for the issuance of the bonds.

JOURNAL			
Date	Account Title and Explanation	Debit	Credit

c) Record the journal entry for the first interest payment date.

JOURNAL

Date	Account Title and Explanation	Debit	Credit

d) Record the journal entry for the end of the five-year term of the bonds. Assume the last interest expense payment has already been recorded.

JOURNAL

Date	Account Title and Explanation	Debit	Credit

See Appendix I for solutions.

Appendix 7B: Time Value of Money Using a Financial Calculator

LO 10

Throughout this chapter, we referred to tables to determine present value factors for our calculations. However, as mentioned, the price of a bond or the monthly installments for a note payable can also be calculated using a financial calculator or spreadsheet program such as Excel. This appendix focuses on using a financial calculator to discount the future cash flows pertaining to a bond. Compounding will not be addressed.

For these examples, a Texas Instruments BAII Plus is used; note that the key strokes on other financial calculators may differ slightly. The rounding on the calculator has been set to zero decimal places. Rounding differences may exist in the calculations of bond prices using the various methods (tables, financial calculators and Excel), so it is important to seek guidance from your instructor if you are uncertain about how to approach a question. As needed, refer to your user manual for more specific instructions.

The following examples mirror those in the chapter so that you can easily cross-reference those calculations.

Issuing Bonds at Par

As shown in Figure 7.9, Business Time Inc. issued 1,000, 10-year bonds at par, at a price of $100 each with 5% annual interest. The following calculator inputs are required.

TI BAII Plus Key Strokes

100,000	FV
10	N
5	I/Y
5,000	PMT
Compute	PV

ANSWER **100,000***

*Note that the PV answer will always show as a negative. The negative sign can be ignored for our calculations.

This answer represents the price of the bond (i.e. the amount of cash received by Business Time Inc.). Note that the answer, in this case, is the same as that obtained using the present value tables.

Issuing Bonds at a Discount

As shown in Figure 7.14, Energy Bite Inc. issued bonds with a maturity value of $100,000 when the market rate of interest was 12%. The bonds have an annual contractual interest rate of 10% payable semi-annually, and they mature in five years. The following calculator inputs are required.

TI BAII Plus Key Strokes

100,000	FV
10	N
6	I/Y
5,000	PMT
Compute	PV

ANSWER **92,640**

Notes:
1) N is calculated as 5 years × 2 (semi-annual).
2) I/Y is calculated as 12% × ½ (semi-annual).
3) PMT is calculated as $100,000 × (10% × ½).

As with the par value bond, the answer is the same as that obtained using the present value tables. Energy Bite Inc. would receive $92,640 from its investor when it issues this bond.

Issuing Bonds at a Premium

As shown in Figure 7.22, Energy Bite Inc. issued bonds with a maturity value of $100,000 when the market rate of interest was 8%. The bonds have an annual contractual interest rate of 10% payable semi-annually, and they mature in five years. The following calculator inputs are required.

TI BAII Plus Key Strokes

100,000	FV
10	N
4	I/Y
5,000	PMT
Compute	PV

ANSWER **108,111**

Notes:
1) N is calculated as 5 years × 2 (semi-annual).
2) I/Y is calculated as 8% × ½ (semi-annual).
3) PMT is calculated as $100,000 × (10% × ½).

A rounding issue exists in this situation. The price of the bond (i.e. the amount of cash received by Energy Bite Inc.) was $108,115. As discussed at the beginning of this appendix, answers may vary slightly depending on the method used to discount (tables, calculators or Excel). It is important to read instructions carefully and ask your instructor which method to use if there is any uncertainty.

Calculating Notes Payable Monthly Installments

As shown in Figure 7.30, Trigraph has issued a $300,000 five-year, 5% note payable. The following calculator inputs are required to determine the monthly installment payments.

TI BAII Plus Key Strokes

300,000	PV
60	N
.417	I/Y
0	FV
Compute	PMT

ANSWER **5,662**

Notes:
1) N is calculated as 5 years × 12 months.
2) I/Y is calculated as 5% ÷ 12 months.

Note that there is a slight different due to rounding; the value calculated using the tables was $5,661.

In Summary

LO 10 Calculate TVM using a financial calculator

- Time value of money can be calculated using a financial calculator.
- Rounding differences may exist in the calculations of bond prices using the various methods (tables, financial calculators and Excel).

Review Exercise 7B-1

Metal Machinery Inc. is in the process of seeking $3,500,000 worth of financing for an expansion and has decided to issue five-year bonds paying 3% annual interest. Using a financial calculator, calculate the bond issue price under each of the following market interest rates.

Market Interest Rate	Bond Price
2%	
3%	
4%	

See Appendix I for solutions.

Notes

Chapter 8
Investments

Learning Objectives

LO 1 Describe and classify different types of investments

- Debt Investments
- Equity Investments

LO 2 Prepare journal entries for debt investments

- Short-Term Investments in Bonds
- Long-Term Investments in Bonds

LO 3 Prepare journal entries for equity investments

- Investments with Insignificant Influence
- Investments with Significant Influence

LO 4 Describe how the different types of investments are presented in the financial statements

- Debt Investments
- Equity Investments

LO 5 Identify differences between ASPE and IFRS in accounting for investments

AMEENGAGE™ Access **ameengage.com** for integrated resources including tutorials, practice exercises, the digital textbook and more.

MAKING IT REAL TO YOU

Have you ever wondered how much you should be saving? Most people start to take charge of their personal finances early in their career in order to save for a big purchase like a car or house or big vacation. Ultimately, making good investment choices impacts the ability to meet goals. Investment choices include short-term and long-term goals and an understanding of your risk tolerance. Similar decisions must be made by financial managers, as they plan for the short-term and long-term cash flow needs of their business. Investing in either debt or shares of other companies is explored further in this chapter.

Investments: An Introduction and Classification

LO 1

Cash is the lifeblood of a business. Cash management is therefore of the utmost importance, to ensure not only that the business has enough cash to cover its operations and debt obligations, but also that it is able to maximize returns on its excess cash. When a company has more cash on hand than it immediately needs for general operations and debt repayment, the company can invest the surplus to generate investment income rather than leaving it in a bank account and receiving a much lower return. This chapter covers how to account for and report on these investments.

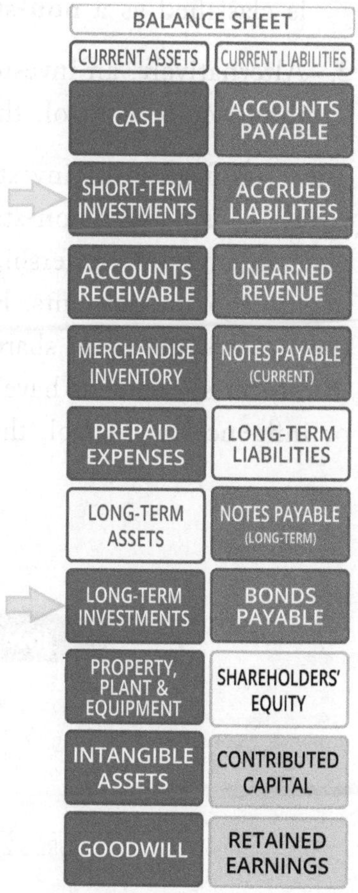

FIGURE 8.1

The Accounting Map in Figure 8.1 shows how investments appear on the balance sheet. The balance sheet presentation of an investment depends on whether the investment is considered short-term or long-term. A **short-term investment**, or *temporary investment*, is intended to be held for less than a year (or one operating cycle, whichever is longer) and is reported in the current assets section of the balance sheet. A **long-term investment** is intended to be held for longer than a year and is reported in the long-term (or noncurrent) assets section of the balance sheet.

There are two types of investments a company can make. One is lending money to someone else (debt). The other is buying a stake (equity) in the ownership of another company.

When a company loans excess cash to someone else, this is known as investing in a **debt investment** (also called a *debt security* or *debt instrument*). The company that purchases the debt is the **investor**. The company that issues (sells) the debt is the **investee**. The investee is obligated to pay back the principal amount of the loan, plus any interest, to the investor. Examples of debt investments include money market funds, term deposits, treasury bills and bonds. The focus of this chapter is investment in bonds from the investor's point of view. The issuance of debt on the investee's or borrower's books was covered in the long-term liabilities chapter, with a particular focus on bonds.

When a company invests excess cash by buying a stake in the ownership of another organization, this is known as investing in an **equity investment** (also called an *equity security* or *equity instrument*), such as the purchase of preferred or common shares of another company (discussed in the chapter on contributed capital and dividends). As with debt or bond investments, the company that purchases the equity is the investor, and the company that issues (sells) the equity is the investee. This chapter focuses on equity investments mostly from the investor's point of view.

On the investor's books, an investment is first classified based on the investor's *intent*. Investors may invest with either of the following intentions.

1. An investor may simply try to generate investment income without intending to establish a long-term business relationship with, or to influence or control, the investee. Such an investment is classified as a **non-strategic investment**.

2. Alternatively, an investor may intend to establish a long-term business relationship with, or to influence or control, the investee. Such an investment is classified as a **strategic investment**.

The classification of investments is summarized in Figure 8.2. Notice that debt investments are always considered a non-strategic investment. This is because purchasing debt investments does not give the investor ownership rights in the investee. Equity investments can be either non-strategic or strategic investments. For example, investors with ownership rights through investee's shares (particularly common shares) can vote on important matters, such as electing the investee's board of directors, and thus have an opportunity to establish and maintain a long-term relationship with, or influence or control, the investee.

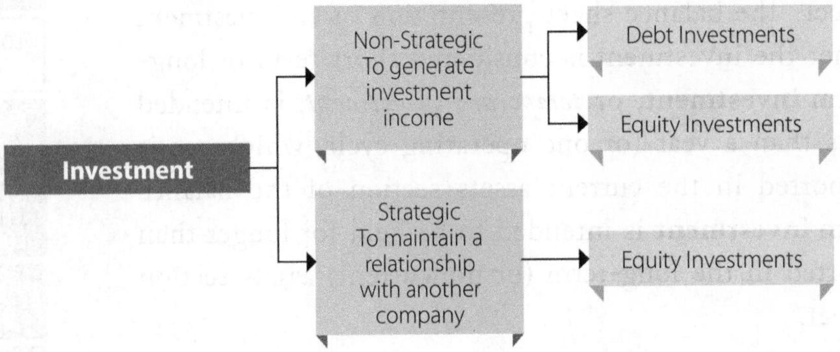

FIGURE 8.2

Let us look at the concept of intent in more detail. A company has a plan, or *strategy*, when it comes to investing. It may want to invest its money for a few months, or it may plan on getting long-term returns or having a long-term relationship with the investee. The plan of the company highlights its intent. It is important to note that the intent at the time the investment is purchased may not always be the actual outcome. For example, a company may plan to invest for the long term, but an unexpected event happens that causes it to sell its investment early to get the cash. In accounting, the intent at the purchase date determines how the investment is initially classified. Specifically, how an investment is accounted for is based on both the investor's intent (strategic or non-strategic, and short-term or long-term) and the type of investment (debt or equity).

> **Worth Repeating**
>
> Debt involves lending money to someone else in return for interest. Debt generally has a fixed maturity.
>
> Equity involves investing in another organization in the form of ownership, with the expectation that its value will increase over time while profits are shared in the form of dividends. Unlike debt, equity does not have a maturity.

This chapter illustrates how a corporation accounts for investments in both debt and equity. Guidance can be found in Accounting Standards for Private

Enterprises (ASPE) and International Financial Reporting Standards (IFRS). As explained in previous chapters, public companies are required to use IFRS, and private corporations can account for investments according to either IFRS or ASPE. The section that follows assumes reporting by a private company following ASPE. Later in the chapter, the reporting for investments under IFRS will be highlighted.

Debt Investments

Although all debt investments are non-strategic, they can be either short-term or long-term securities. Each has its own characteristics and associated method of accounting.

Short-Term Investments in Bonds

Short-term investments in bonds are intended to be held for the short term (typically up to one year) and then sold for a profit. These short-term debt investments are actively managed because the investor hopes to take advantage of changes in the market price. The investor may receive interest while holding the investment. This type of investment is rare in reality, as investors usually would like to earn investment income over a long period of time, and most bonds mature in more than one year. Short-term investments in bonds are reported as current assets on the balance sheet. The investment's value may fluctuate during the time it is held. Therefore, at the end of each period, the investment value must be adjusted to its fair value, or market price. This revaluation results in unrealized gains or losses for the period. The term *unrealized* is used because the investment has not yet been sold. The gain or loss is only shown on paper and is not realized until the investment is sold. Because of the short-term nature of this investment, any unrealized gain or loss is reported as part of net income on the income statement.

Long-Term Investments in Bonds

Long-term investments in bonds are intended to be held for the long term (until maturity) in order to earn interest revenue. Since these investments mostly mature beyond one year, they are reported as long-term assets. Unlike short-term investments in bonds, the book value of these long-term investments is not adjusted to their fair value at the end of each period. Therefore, unrealized gains or losses are never recorded for long-term investments in bonds. If the company later decides to sell the investment before the maturity date, any gain or loss is recorded as part of net income on the income statement.

Equity Investments

Equity investments are either non-strategic or strategic. Each type has its own characteristics and associated method of accounting.

Non-Strategic Equity Investments

When investors purchase common shares in a company, they become part-owner of that company. For many shareholders, the level of ownership is minimal because they own such a small percentage of the total outstanding shares. For instance, if you own 10 shares out of 1,000,000 common shares outstanding, your vote does little to elect a board of directors or influence the operation of the company you have invested in. Accordingly, you have an insignificant influence on the investee corporation. This typically applies to any shareholder who owns less than 20% of the common shares outstanding, which is usually considered a non-strategic investment.

Non-strategic equity investments can be either short-term or long-term depending upon management's intent when the shares are purchased, and they are recorded on the balance sheet based on the intent. Accounting for non-strategic equity investments is similar to accounting for short-term investments in bonds. The main difference for equity investments is that they pay out dividends, not interest, to the investor for as long as the investor holds the equity investment. Any gain or loss on the sale of the investment is recorded under the other income and expenses section of the income statement. As with short-term debt investments, unrealized gains or losses from non-strategic equity investments are reported as part of net income on the income statement. Non-strategic equity investments and short-term debt investments (bonds) share the same accounting method, called the fair value through net income method, which is discussed later in the chapter.

Strategic Equity Investments

A company may choose to invest in another corporation for strategic reasons. For example, the investor may want to build a long-term relationship with a key customer or vendor by investing in it. The company may want to venture into a new industry by investing in another company that is already established in that industry. Alternatively, the company may invest strategically in common shares of another company in the same industry because it wants to expand its market base, tap into new technologies used by that other company or eliminate competition.

Equity investments that are held for strategic purposes are always considered long-term investments. Strategic investments can be further classified as equity investments with significant influence and equity investments with controlling influence. The accounting method required for strategic investments depends on which type of influence the investor has over the investee.

Investments with Significant Influence

A company that owns between 20% and 50% of another company's common shares outstanding typically has a **significant influence** on the investee corporation. This gives the investor the right to participate in decisions about the investee's operating and financial policies. At this level of influence, the investor has a non-controlling interest in the investee company.

Investments with Controlling Influence

If one shareholder or investor owns more than 50% of a company's outstanding common shares, that investor typically has a **controlling influence**, which means that the investor company has control over how the investee company operates. At this level of share ownership, the investor has the right to direct the operating and financial activities of the investee.

When one company purchases more than 50% of the outstanding shares of another company, the transaction is known as a **business combination.** Such an arrangement is usually made in order to maximize the investor company's operating efficiency, expand its product offerings or minimize competition. The investor then becomes known as the **parent company**, and the investee becomes the **subsidiary company**.

Investments with controlling influence are accounted for using the *consolidation method*. This means that, although the parent and the subsidiary usually maintain separate accounting records and financial statements during the accounting period, at the end of the year the parent company combines all the financial statements into a set of **consolidated financial statements.** Consolidated financial statements are considered more meaningful to investors than separate reports. Note that an investor that has the ability to control a company, even without the intent to do so, will still be required to consolidate. The specifics of the consolidation method are beyond the scope of this textbook.

A Closer Look

It should be noted that, in special situations, an investor with less than 20% of a company's stake may have significant influence, if all other shareholders have a very small percentage of shares.

In a different scenario, an investor with more than 20% of shares would have no significant influence if another shareholder with more than 50% has a controlling interest.

Although these ownership benchmarks are helpful in grouping these securities in textbooks, in reality, other qualifying factors should be considered as well.

How a security is classified determines how it should be valued and presented on the financial statements. We will discuss how to account for investments in debt first, followed by investments in equity, specifically under ASPE.

Investments in Debt

LO 2

Debt investments are classified and reported according to their maturity and purpose. A debt investment that will mature within 12 months is considered a **short-term debt investment** (i.e. short-term investment in bonds). A short-term debt investment is usually a highly liquid, low-risk **money market instrument** such as a treasury bill, term deposit or money market fund.

A debt investment that will take more than 12 months to mature is considered a **long-term debt investment** (i.e. long-term investment in bonds). For example, most bonds mature in more than one year and they provide a steady source of interest income.

The accounting method for each classification of debt investment under ASPE is illustrated in Figure 8.3. In this section, we will look at how to account for each of these classifications in more detail.

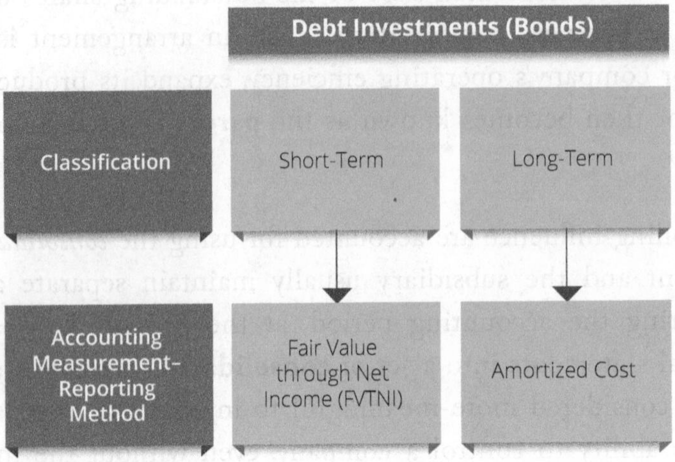

FIGURE 8.3

Short-Term Investments in Bonds

Similar to equity investments, some short-term debt investments (bonds) can be readily bought and sold on the open market, making them good trading investments. When debt investments are purchased for the primary purpose of trading, they are reported at their fair value. Fair value is the amount that an asset can be sold for in the public market. Recording investments at fair value enables investors to evaluate the issuer's financial solvency and predict its future cash flows. If no fair value is readily available, the historical cost method for reporting is permitted, although it is not commonly used for investments and is therefore not covered in detail in this chapter.

There are several important events during the lifetime of a debt investment that must be accounted for. These include the following:

- Acquisition, at the fair value of the investment
- Recording interest earned
- Fair value adjustments, to record changes from the original cost to the current market value
- Recording the realized gain or loss when the investment is sold

The accounting method used to report short-term investments in bonds is called the **fair value through net income (FVTNI) method,** also known as *fair value through profit or loss (FVTPL)*. We will demonstrate this method with an example.

Fair Value through Net Income Method

Suppose that on October 1, 2020, Vinyl Sound Company pays $10,500, including brokerage fees of $500, to purchase a *portfolio* (or group) of debt investments (bonds) paying 10% interest and intended to be sold within a year.

1. Acquisition. Vinyl Sound records the acquisition of the investments as in Figure 8.4. Note that all the individual investments are combined into one total portfolio cost of $10,000.

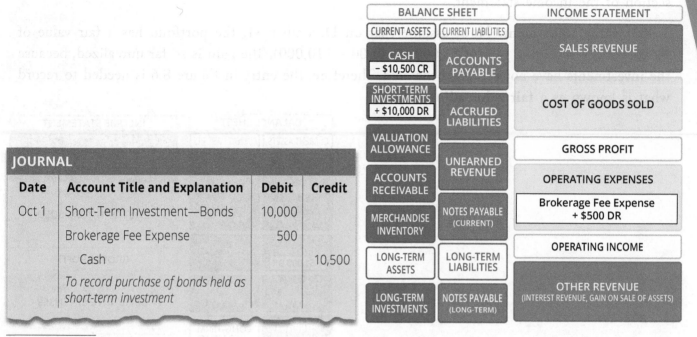

JOURNAL

Date	Account Title and Explanation	Debit	Credit
Oct 1	Short-Term Investment—Bonds	10,000	
	Brokerage Fee Expense	500	
	Cash		10,500
	To record purchase of bonds held as short-term investment		

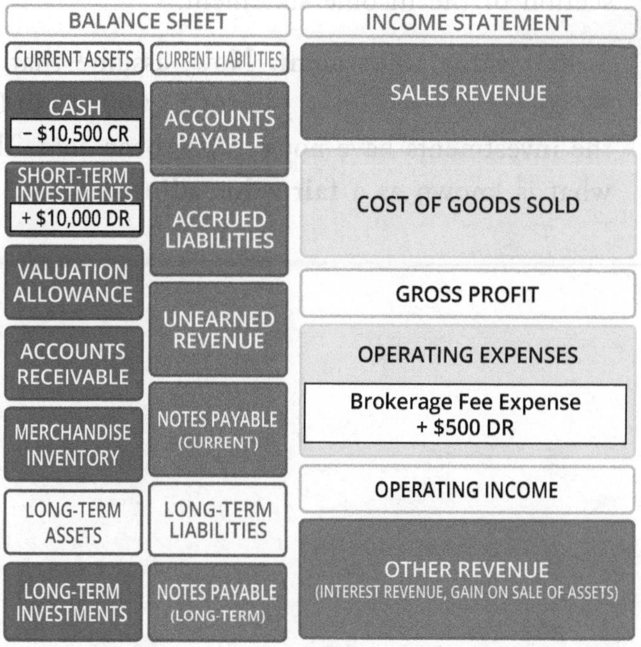

FIGURE 8.4

2. Recording interest earned. Assuming Vinyl Sound has a year end of December 31, the entry in Figure 8.5 is made to accrue the interest receivable on the bonds that make up the investment portfolio.

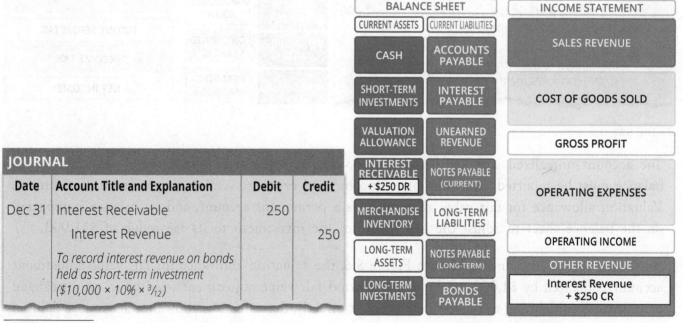

JOURNAL

Date	Account Title and Explanation	Debit	Credit
Dec 31	Interest Receivable	250	
	Interest Revenue		250
	To record interest revenue on bonds held as short-term investment ($10,000 × 10% × $^{3}/_{12}$)		

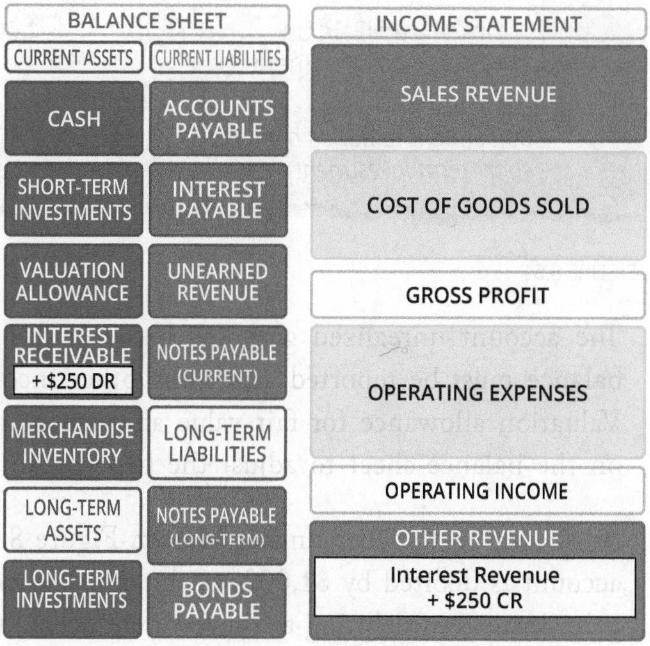

FIGURE 8.5

Note that for as long as the company owns these investments, regular journal entries must be made for any interest earned. Interest revenue is reported under the other income and expenses section of the income statement.

3. Fair value adjustment. Now, assume that on December 31, the portfolio has a fair value of \$11,000, representing a gain of \$1,000 (\$11,000 – \$10,000). The gain is so far unrealized, because the investments have not actually been sold. Therefore, the entry in Figure 8.6 is needed to record what is known as a **fair value adjustment.**

JOURNAL

Date	Account Title and Explanation	Debit	Credit
Dec 31	Valuation Allowance for Fair Value Adjustment	1,000	
	Unrealized Gain on Fair Value Adjustment		1,000
	To record fair value adjustment to bonds held as short-term investment		

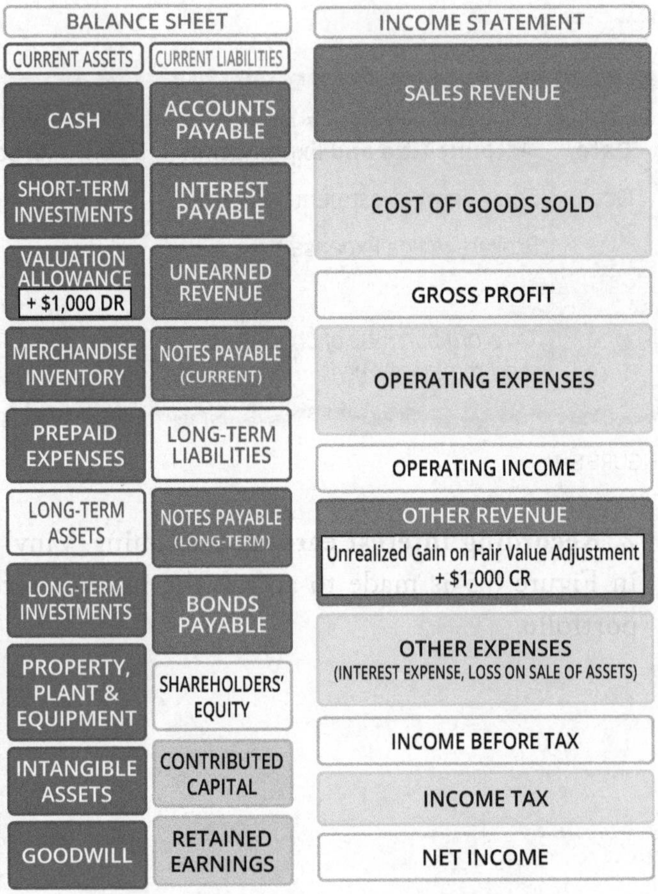

FIGURE 8.6

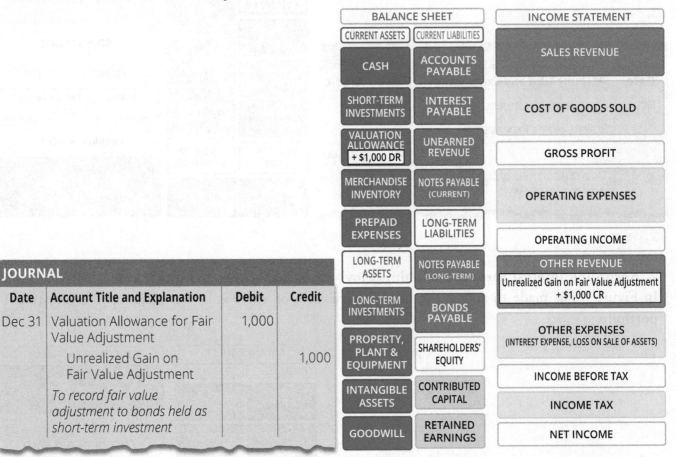

The account unrealized gain (or loss) on fair value adjustment is a temporary account, and its balance must be reported under the other income and expenses section on the income statement. Valuation allowance for fair value adjustment is a permanent account, and its balance is reported on the balance sheet to adjust the book value of the investment to its fair value of \$11,000.

As shown on the Accounting Map in Figure 8.6, the valuation allowance for fair value adjustment account is debited by \$1,000, as the end-of-period fair value adjustment resulted in an unrealized gain. Instead of debiting the investment account directly, the valuation allowance account is debited so that the original cost of the investment is always kept on record on the balance sheet. If an unrealized loss is incurred instead of an unrealized gain, unrealized loss on fair value adjustment would be debited and valuation allowance for fair value adjustment would be credited.

Therefore, the valuation allowance account could have either a debit or credit balance depending on the fair value adjustment required at the end of the period. If the fair value of the investment turns out to be more than its original cost, the valuation allowance account would have a debit balance, which adds to the cost of the investment. If the fair value is less than the original cost, the valuation allowance account would have a credit balance.

4. Realized gain or loss. Now, suppose that on January 15, 2021, Vinyl Sound sells some of the bonds in its portfolio. The bonds originally cost $1,800, and they are sold for $2,100. Vinyl Sound Company therefore realizes a gain of $300 ($2,100 – $1,800), which is recorded as shown in the journal entry in Figure 8.7.

JOURNAL

Date	Account Title and Explanation	Debit	Credit
Jan 15	Cash	2,100	
	Short-Term Investment—Bonds		1,800
	Gain on Sale of Investment		300
	To record sale of bonds held as short-term investment		

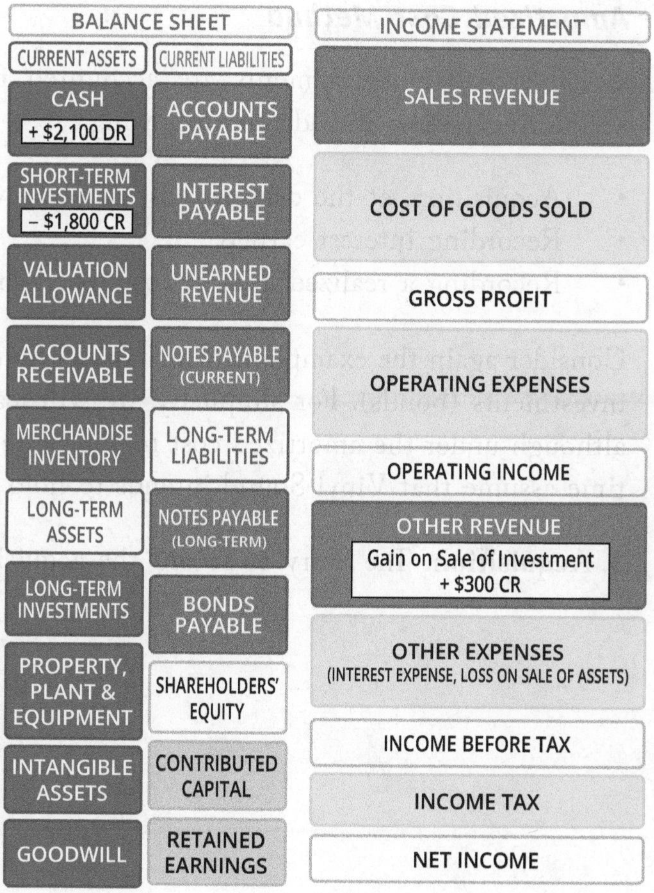

FIGURE 8.7

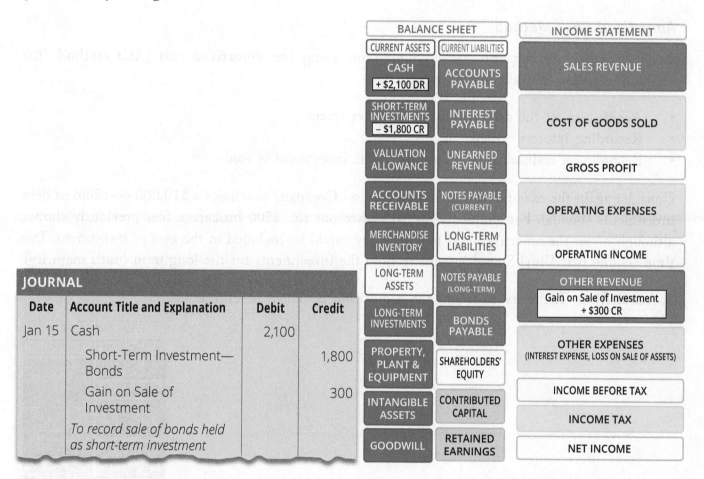

Note that the journal entry records the difference between the sale price and the original cost of the bonds, but does not include any amounts related to previous fair value adjustments. This is because the fair value adjustment in Figure 8.6 was applied to the value of the *entire* portfolio and not to the individual bond investments. At the end of the accounting period, the balance of the valuation allowance account would be adjusted so that the investment value would match its fair value. For example, if at Vinyl Sound's year end of December 31, 2021, the remaining investment, which had an original cost of $8,200 ($10,000 - $1,800), has a fair value of $8,500, Vinyl Sound will adjust its valuation allowance account to have a debit balance of $300 so that the value of the investment on the balance sheet (original cost of $8,200 plus valuation allowance of $300) is equal to the investment's fair value of $8,500.

Long-Term Investments in Bonds

In the first section of this chapter, you learned that long-term debt investments (e.g. notes or bonds) are intended to be held by the investor until they mature in order to earn interest revenue. Since most of these debt investments (bonds) are due to mature beyond one year, they are classified as long-term assets.

Amortized Cost Method

Long-term debt investments are accounted for using the **amortized cost (AC) method**. The accounting entries include the following:

- Acquisition, at the original cost of the investment
- Recording interest earned
- Recording a realized gain or loss when the investment is sold

Consider again the example in which Vinyl Sound Company purchases a $10,000 portfolio of debt investments (bonds). For simplicity, we will leave out the $500 brokerage fees previously shown, although under the amortized cost method, they would be included in the cost of investment. This time assume that Vinyl Sound intends to hold the investments for the long term (until maturity).

1. Acquisition. The entry to record the acquisition is shown in Figure 8.8.

JOURNAL

Date	Account Title and Explanation	Debit	Credit
Oct 1	Long-Term Investment—Bonds	10,000	
	Cash		10,000
	To record purchase of bonds held as long-term investment		

FIGURE 8.8

2. Recording interest earned. Assuming Vinyl Sound has a year end of December 31, the entry in Figure 8.9 is made to accrue the interest receivable on the bonds that make up the investment portfolio.

JOURNAL

Date	Account Title and Explanation	Debit	Credit
Dec 31	Interest Receivable	250	
	Interest Revenue		250
	To record interest revenue on bonds held as long-term investment ($10,000 × 10% × 3/12)		

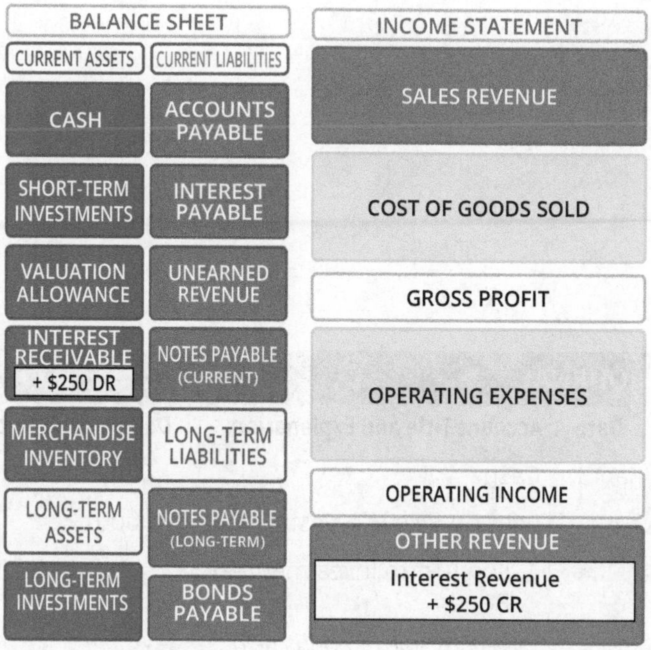

FIGURE 8.9

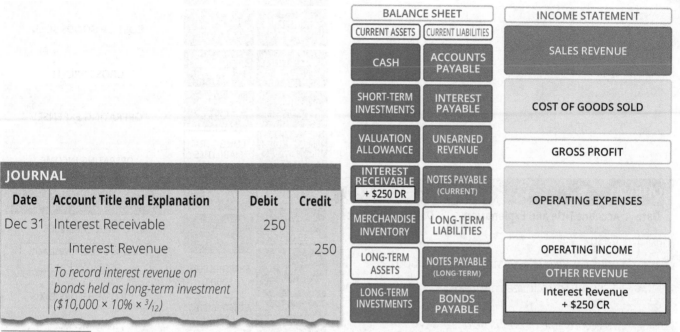

As mentioned previously in this chapter, the book value of long-term investments is not adjusted to the investments' fair value at the end of the accounting period. Therefore, unrealized gains or losses are never recorded for long-term investments. In other words, an entry similar to that shown in Figure 8.6 for the short-term investment would not be recorded.

As you know from the chapter on long-term liabilities, bonds are often issued at a discount or a premium. That means the issuer (borrower) has sold the bonds for less or more than their par value. For the investor (lender) purchasing a discount or premium bond, the discount or premium would be amortized using either the straight-line method or the effective-interest method over the life of the investment. Essentially, the amortization of the discount or premium on a bond investment affects interest revenue and the carrying value of the bond, similar to how it affects the interest expense and the carrying value of the bond on the books of the issuer. The journal entries related to a discount or premium bond under the amortized cost method are not specifically covered in this chapter.

3. Realized gain or loss. Now, suppose that on January 31, 2021, Vinyl Sound sells half of the bonds in its portfolio for $4,000. Therefore, bonds that originally cost $5,000 are sold at a loss of $1,000 ($4,000 – $5,000). The journal entry to record this loss is shown in Figure 8.10 below.

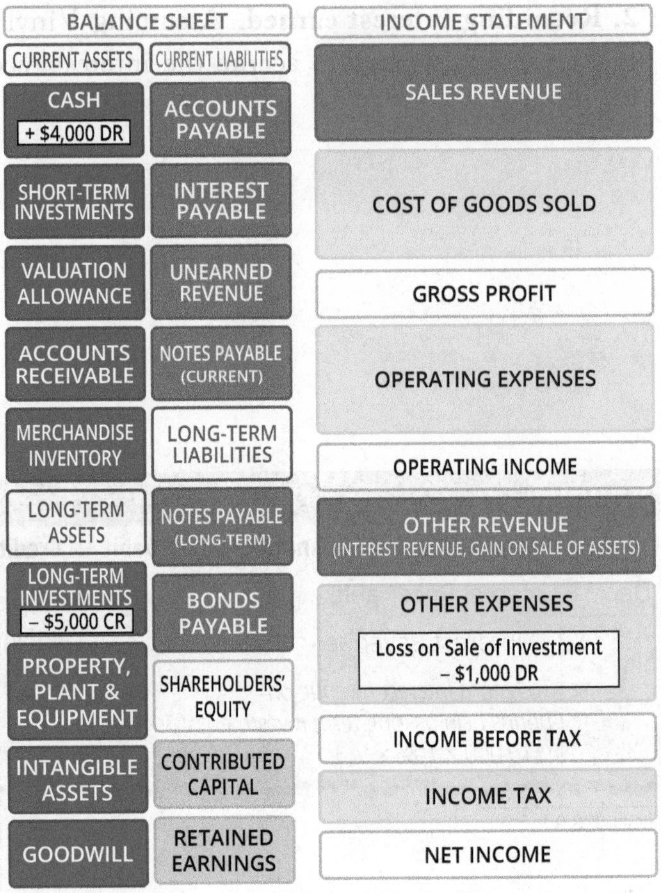

JOURNAL

Date	Account Title and Explanation	Debit	Credit
Jan 31	Cash	4,000	
	Loss on Sale of Investment	1,000	
	Long-Term Investment—Bonds		5,000
	To record sale of bonds held as long-term investment		

FIGURE 8.10

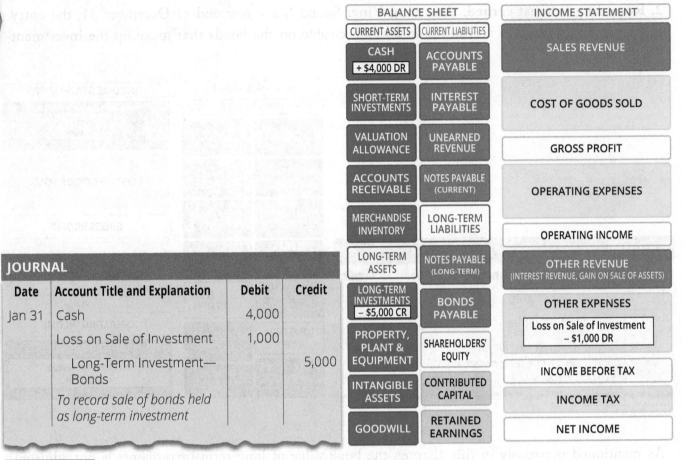

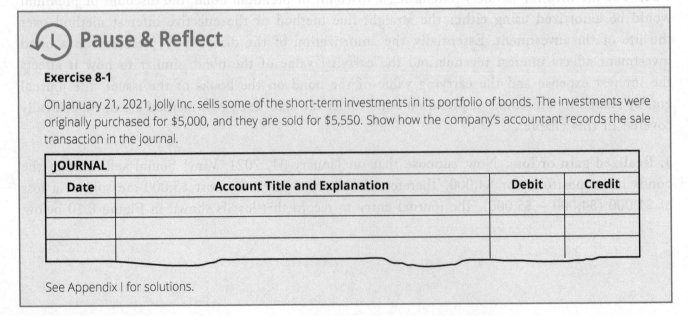

This is similar to the accounting for the gain on the sale of the short-term investment in bonds in Figure 8.7 above.

The key difference between short-term and long-term investment accounting is that there are no fair value adjustments made on long-term investments under the amortized cost method.

Pause & Reflect

Exercise 8-1

On January 21, 2021, Jolly Inc. sells some of the short-term investments in its portfolio of bonds. The investments were originally purchased for $5,000, and they are sold for $5,550. Show how the company's accountant records the sale transaction in the journal.

JOURNAL

Date	Account Title and Explanation	Debit	Credit

See Appendix I for solutions.

Investments in Equity

LO 3

As you learned in the first section of this chapter, non-strategic equity investments are typically investments in shares where less than 20% of the common shares are owned by the investor. A strategic investment means an investment of 20% or more of the common shares issued by an investee. Strategic investments are further classified into investments with significant influence and investments with controlling influence. Figure 8.11 shows the classification of equity investments and the accounting methods used for each.

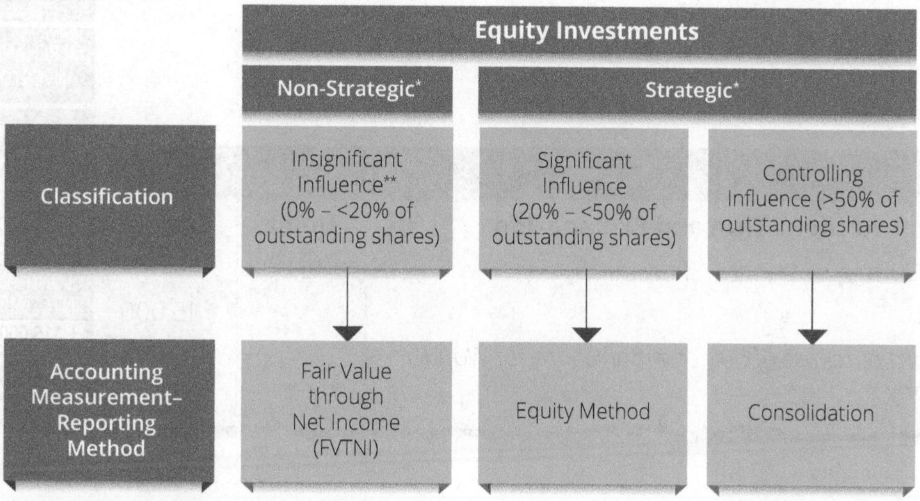

*Non-strategic equity investments could be either short-term or long-term; strategic equity investments are always long-term.
**In this textbook, it is assumed that the security is actively traded in the market; otherwise, the historical cost method is used.

FIGURE 8.11

Investments with Insignificant Influence

Notice that the non-strategic equity investment of insignificant influence uses the fair value through net income method. This is the same method used for short-term investments in bonds. Thus, the transactions to acquire, record fair value adjustments and sell the investment are similar to what we have learned already.

Assume Vinyl Sound Company purchases 500 common shares in Wonder Company on January 1, 2020, at $30 per share. The 500 common shares represent only 1% of Wonder's outstanding common stock, which means Vinyl Sound has insignificant influence over Wonder and this is a non-strategic investment. Vinyl Sound intends to hold these shares for more than one year; therefore, this investment is considered long-term. If Vinyl Sound's intention were to sell these shares within a year, then this investment would be considered short-term and reported under current assets on the balance sheet. The same accounting treatment applies to the short-term equity investment.

1. **Acquisition**. The shares are recorded in a long-term investment in shares account. The entry to record the acquisition is shown in Figure 8.12.

JOURNAL

Date	Account Title and Explanation	Debit	Credit
Jan 1	Long-Term Investment—Shares	15,000	
	Cash		15,000
	To record purchase of 500 common shares of Wonder Company		

FIGURE 8.12

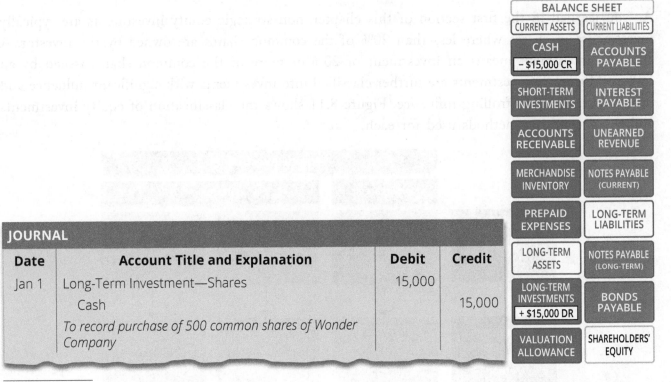

2. **Recording dividend revenue**. Suppose Vinyl Sound received $400 in cash dividends from Wonder Company on August 31, 2020. The journal entry to record the dividend revenue is shown in Figure 8.13.

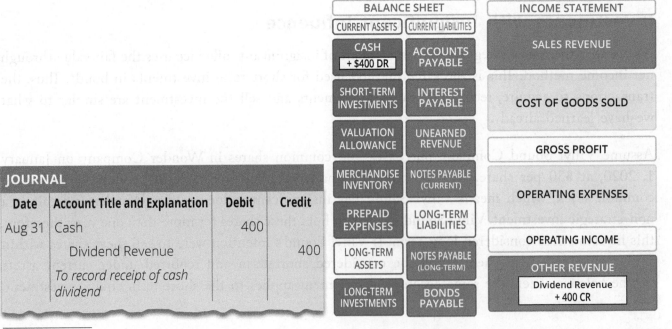

JOURNAL

Date	Account Title and Explanation	Debit	Credit
Aug 31	Cash	400	
	Dividend Revenue		400
	To record receipt of cash dividend		

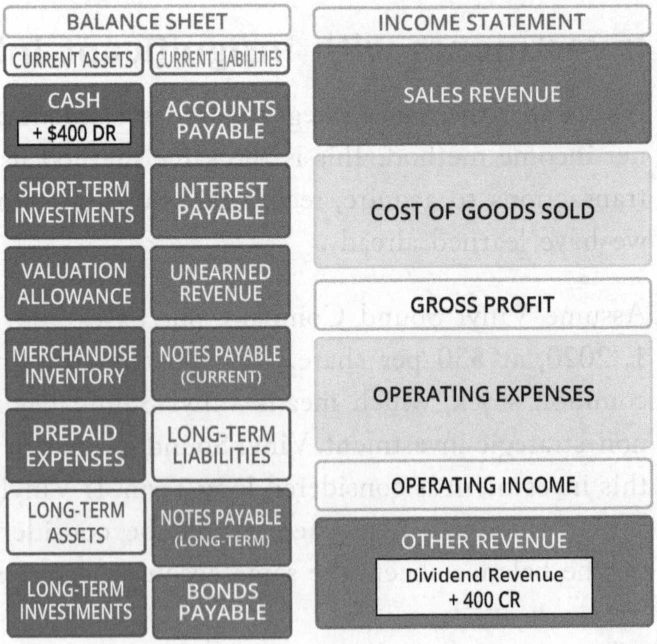

FIGURE 8.13

3. **Fair value adjustment**. By Vinyl Sound's year end, December 31, 2020, the market value of Wonder Company's shares has increased to $35 per share. This represents an increase of $2,500 in the value of the investment. As with short-term investments in bonds, this is an unrealized gain since the shares have not been sold. The journal entry in Figure 8.14 is made to record the fair value adjustment.

JOURNAL

Date	Account Title and Explanation	Debit	Credit
Dec 31	Valuation Allowance for Fair Value Adjustment	2,500	
	Unrealized Gain on Fair Value Adjustment		2,500
	To record fair value adjustment		

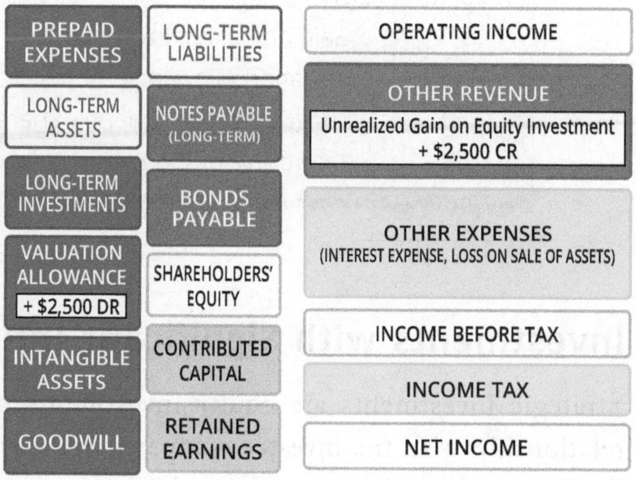

FIGURE 8.14

The reporting of the change in value of the investment is treated the same way as was done for short-term debt investments. The unrealized gain (or loss) is reported under the other income and expenses section of the income statement. The valuation allowance is reported in the asset section of the balance sheet and is added to or subtracted from the investment account to arrive at the fair value of $17,500.

Worth Repeating

For short-term or long-term non-strategic equity investments with insignificant influence, if the security is actively traded in the market, the fair value method of accounting is used. If the equity investment is not active in the market, the historical cost method of recording is used.

In cases where a company has a non-strategic equity investment consisting of a single company's shares, any sale of those shares should take into account the current carrying value. This carrying value will reflect the most recent fair value entry related to the shares. This means the valuation allowance account will be affected when calculating the gain or loss connected to the shares being sold.

For example, suppose Vinyl Sound sells all the shares of Wonder Company at a price of $38 on February 16, 2021. It will receive $19,000 cash and will clear out the long-term investment account and the accompanying valuation allowance account. Thus, the carrying value of $17,500 ($15,000 cost + $2,500 valuation allowance) is removed from the balance sheet, and the remaining $1,500 is recorded as a realized gain on the sale of the shares. Figure 8.15 shows the journal entry made to record this transaction.

JOURNAL

Date	Account Title and Explanation	Debit	Credit
Feb 16	Cash	19,000	
	Gain on Sale of Investment		1,500
	Valuation Allowance for Fair Value Adjustment		2,500
	Long-Term Investment—Shares		15,000
	To record sale of shares at a gain		

FIGURE 8.15

Investments with Significant Influence

Strategic investments are equity investments purchased with the intention to build a long-term relationship with the investee company. Specifically, the investor intends to participate in or control the investee's decisions on how the investee company operates its business. Recall that strategic equity investments can be classified as investments with significant influence or investments with controlling influence. Investments with controlling influence are accounted for using the consolidation method. The specifics of this type of accounting method are beyond the scope of this textbook. This section will focus on accounting for investments with significant influence.

The **equity method** is used to record and report strategic equity investments when the investor owns 20% to 50% of the investee's outstanding common shares. The equity method records the purchase of the investment at its original cost, and any brokerage fees should be expensed. Thereafter, the investor adjusts its investment account for its share of the investee's net income and dividends. While the historical cost method can also be used to account for such investments under ASPE, this chapter presents only the equity method.

When accounting for strategic investments under the equity method, the important events that require journal entries are as follows:

- Acquisition, at cost (the purchase price) of the instrument on the date of purchase
- Recording investment revenue (the share of the investee's profit or loss) as an adjustment to the investor's equity account
- Recording dividends received, recognized when the investor becomes entitled to the dividend

We will once again use the example of Vinyl Sound Company, but this time we will apply the equity method for recording and reporting the investment. For this purchase, there are some transaction costs (i.e. brokerage fees) for purchasing shares, but we will ignore those expenses for simplicity.

Assume that Vinyl Sound Company purchases 1,000 common shares in Dempton Corporation on January 1, 2020, at $400 per share. The 1,000 common shares represent 25% of Dempton's total outstanding common shares, which means that Vinyl Sound has a significant influence over Dempton.

1. **Acquisition.** When the shares are initially purchased, they are recorded at cost in a long-term asset account, in this case called investment in Dempton Corporation shares. It is listed on the balance sheet under the category of long-term investments. The entry to record the acquisition is shown in Figure 8.16.

JOURNAL

Date	Account Title and Explanation	Debit	Credit
Jan 1	Investment in Dempton Corporation Shares	400,000	
	Cash		400,000
	To record purchase of 1,000 shares of Dempton Corporation common shares		

FIGURE 8.16

2. **Recording investment revenue and dividends received.** Assume that for the year ended December 31, 2020, Dempton Corporation has a profit of $200,000. It also declares and pays a $20,000 cash dividend. Vinyl Sound Company owns a 25% stake in Dempton's total outstanding common shares. Vinyl Sound must first calculate its share of Dempton's profit, which is $50,000 ($200,000 × 25%). Then, Vinyl Sound calculates its cash dividend, which is $5,000 ($20,000 × 25%). The cash dividend of $5,000 is a reduction of Vinyl Sound's investment, since Dempton Corporation's net assets are reduced as a result of the dividends paid. Vinyl Sound records the investment revenue and dividend received as in Figure 8.17.

JOURNAL

Date	Account Title and Explanation	Debit	Credit
Dec 31	Investment in Dempton Corporation Shares	50,000	
	Revenue from Investment in Dempton Corporation		50,000
	To record 25% profit on equity investment in Dempton Corporation		

JOURNAL

Date	Account Title and Explanation	Debit	Credit
Dec 31	Cash	5,000	
	Investment in Dempton Corporation Shares		5,000
	To record dividends received on equity investment in Dempton Corporation		

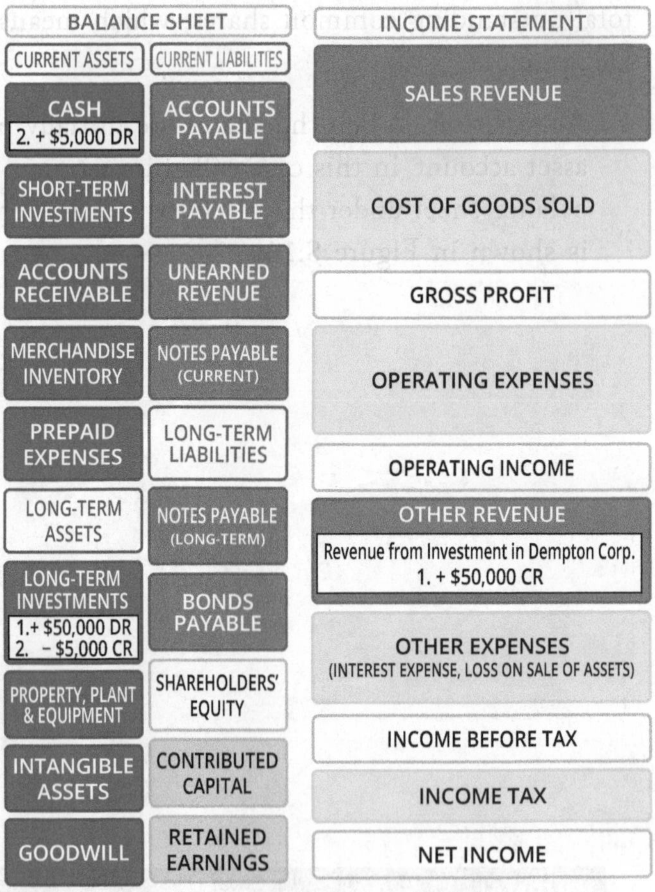

FIGURE 8.17

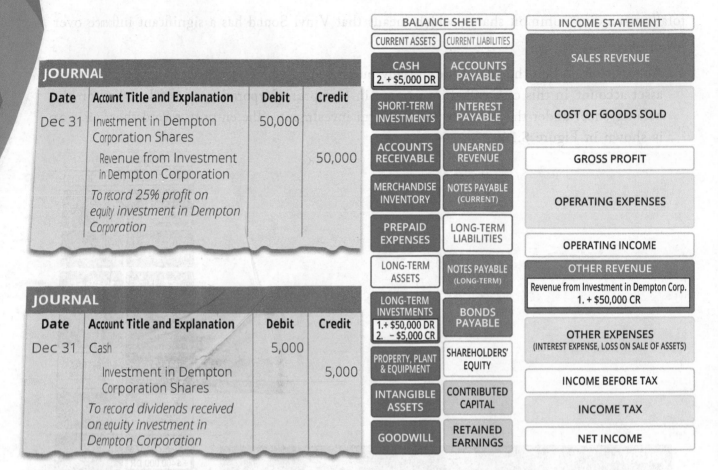

As a result of these transactions, the balance of the investment in Dempton Corporation shares account on Vinyl Sound Company's books as of December 31, 2020, is calculated as follows.

Investment in Dempton Shares = Initial Investment + Revenue from Investment – Cash Dividend Received
= $400,000 + $50,000 – $5,000
= $445,000

Under the equity method, when two companies are closely related, any transaction that increases or decreases the investee's shareholders' equity will increase or decrease the investor's investment as well. For example, if Dempton Corporation had a loss of $200,000 instead of a profit in 2020, Vinyl Sound would have recorded a reduction of $50,000 ($200,000 × 25%) on its investment instead of an addition.

Summary

Figure 8.18 summarizes the levels of influence that investors can have, the portions of investees' shares that investors generally own in order to obtain those levels of influence and the associated reporting requirements.

Portion of Outstanding Common Stock Owned by Investor	Investor's Level of Influence on Investee	Method of Accounting and Reporting Required
Less than 20%	Insignificant influence	Fair value through net income (FVTNI) method
20% to 50%	Significant influence	Equity method
More than 50%	Controlling influence	Consolidation method

FIGURE 8.18

Note that in the real world, an investor's level of influence can often be affected by other circumstances, such as hostile takeovers or legal issues. However, such situations are beyond the scope of this textbook.

Pause & Reflect

Exercise 8-2

During 2020, Andover Company purchased $250,000 worth of common shares in Blackstar Limited. This represents 30% of the outstanding common shares of Blackstar. For the year ended December 31, 2020, Blackstar made a profit of $200,000. Also during 2020, Blackstar declared and paid a cash dividend of $10,000.

Calculate Andover's net investment in Blackstar Limited as of December 31, 2020.

See Appendix I for solutions.

Presentation of Investments on the Financial Statements

LO 4

In the first section of this chapter, we discussed the importance of *intent* when determining how to classify and account for investments in debt and equity securities. In other words, an investor's intent at the purchase date determines an investment's accounting treatment—its classification, its valuation and its presentation on the financial statements. Referring once again to Figure 8.3 and Figure 8.11, we can get a visual summary of the investor's intent by looking across the classifications row. In this section, we will illustrate how the different classifications of investments are presented in the financial statements. We will look at the financial statement presentation for debt investments first.

Debt Investments

We have already discussed that debt investments can be classified as either short-term or long-term. To demonstrate how each class is reported on the balance sheet and income statement under ASPE, we will return to the Vinyl Sound Company examples from earlier in the chapter. (Note that some accounts displayed on the financial statements that follow, such as cash and cash equivalents, income from operations and contributed capital, have been added simply to show where they fit into the statement format.)

Short-Term Investments in Bonds (Short-Term Debt Securities)

The following is a reminder of the accounting events that occurred during the year ended December 31, 2020.

- On October 1, 2020, Vinyl Sound Company paid $10,500 to purchase a portfolio of debt (bonds) for the cost of $10,000 and brokerage fee of $500. Vinyl Sound intends to hold the bonds for a short time and then sell them to make a profit.
- On its December 31, 2020 year end, Vinyl Sound recorded $250 in interest revenue on the bonds in its trading portfolio.
- By its December 31, 2020 year end, Vinyl Sound's portfolio of debt securities had a fair value of $11,000, representing an unrealized gain of $1,000 and requiring a fair value adjustment in that amount.

Recall that short-term investments in bonds are accounted for using the fair value through net income (FVTNI) method.

Income Statement

Brokerage fee expense, interest revenue and unrealized gain on fair value adjustment are part of purchasing and recording the debt investment, and their balances must be reported in the other income and expenses section on the income statement (see Figure 8.19).

Vinyl Sound Company Income Statement (partial) For the Year Ended December 31, 2020		
Income from Operations		$765,000
Other Income and Expenses		
Interest Revenue	$250	
Unrealized Gain on Fair Value Adjustment	1,000	
Brokerage Fee Expense	(500)	750
Income before Income Taxes		765,750

FIGURE 8.19

Balance Sheet

Vinyl Sound's December 31, 2020 partial balance sheet is shown in Figure 8.20. Note that valuation allowance for bonds is reported on the balance sheet to show the calculation of the assets' fair value, which is $11,000.

Vinyl Sound Company Balance Sheet (partial) As at December 31, 2020		
Current Assets		
Cash and Cash Equivalents		$70,000
Short-Term Investment—Bonds (at Cost)	$10,000	
Valuation Allowance for Fair Value Adjustment	1,000	
Short-Term Investment—Bonds (at Fair Value)		11,000
Interest Receivable		250

FIGURE 8.20

Long-Term Investments in Bonds (Long-Term Debt Securities)

If Vinyl Sound Company had classified its $10,000 investment in debt securities as long-term, the company would report this investment on its financial statements using the amortized cost method, as shown below.

Income Statement

Under the amortized cost method, the investment is not adjusted to its market value. Therefore, unrealized gain or loss is not recorded in the journal and thus not reported on the income statement. Interest revenue is reported on the income statement as shown in Figure 8.21.

Vinyl Sound Company Income Statement (partial) For the Year Ended December 31, 2020	
Income from Operations	$765,000
Other Income and Expenses	
Interest Revenue	250

FIGURE 8.21

Balance Sheet

Unlike short-term investments in bonds, the long-term debt investments are reported on the balance sheet at their amortized cost instead of at their market value. Figure 8.22 shows how the investments are reported on the balance sheet. Since their maturity date is more than one year from the balance sheet date, they are classified as long-term investments. In our example above, Vinyl Sound purchased these bonds at par ($10,000) rather than at a premium or discount (i.e. more or less than $10,000). The journal entries related to a discount or a premium under the amortized cost method are not illustrated in this textbook. Balance sheet reporting under the amortized cost method should reflect the original investment at par (net of the premium or discount amortized) as at the reporting date.

Vinyl Sound Company Balance Sheet (partial) As at December 31, 2020	
Long-Term Investments	
Long-Term Investment—Bonds (at Amortized Cost)	$10,000

FIGURE 8.22

Equity Investments

Equity investments are treated differently on the financial statements depending on whether they have insignificant or significant influence.

Insignificant Influence

As mentioned earlier, non-strategic long-term equity investments of less than 20% or short-term equity investments are accounted for similarly to how debt (bond) or short-term investments are accounted for. Thus, the presentation on the income statement would be similar to Figure 8.19, except dividend revenue would be reported instead of interest revenue. The balance sheet would also be similar to Figure 8.20, showing the valuation allowance as an increase or decrease to the cost of the initial investment. However, because equity investments do not generate interest, interest receivable would not appear on the company's balance sheet. The equity investment would be classified as either a short-term investment or a long-term investment, depending on management's intent to hold the investment for less than or longer than one year. If management intends to liquidate the investment within one year, then the investment is classified as a short-term investment and reported under the current assets section of the balance sheet. If management intends to hold the investment for longer than one year, then the investment is reported under the long-term investments section of the balance sheet.

Significant Influence

When an investor owns 20% to 50% of the investee's outstanding shares, the equity method records the purchase of the investment at its original cost. We will return to the Vinyl Sound Company example for the equity method from earlier in the chapter.

The following is a reminder of the accounting events that occurred during the year ended December 31, 2020.

- On January 1, 2020, Vinyl Sound Company purchased 1,000 common shares from Dempton Corporation at $400 per share. The 1,000 shares represent 25% of Dempton's total outstanding common shares, giving Vinyl Sound a significant influence over Dempton's business.
- For the year ended December 31, 2020, Dempton Corporation had a profit of $200,000. Vinyl Sound's share of Dempton's profit was $50,000.
- During the year ended December 31, 2020, Dempton declared and paid a cash dividend of $20,000. Vinyl Sound's share of the cash dividend was $5,000.

Income Statement

Vinyl Sound's income statement will include its share of Dempton's profits, which is reported as part of other income, as shown in Figure 8.23.

Vinyl Sound Company Income Statement (partial) For the Year Ended December 31, 2020	
Income from Operations	$765,000
Other Income and Expenses	
Revenue from Investment in Dempton Corporation	50,000

FIGURE 8.23

Balance Sheet

Recall that, as a result of these transactions, Vinyl Sound's *net* equity investment in Dempton as of December 31, 2020, was $445,000 ($400,000 + $50,000 – $5,000). The investment is reported on Vinyl Sound's balance sheet at cost, along with any other long-term investments, as shown in Figure 8.24.

Vinyl Sound Company Balance Sheet (partial) As at December 31, 2020	
Long-Term Investments	
Investment in Dempton Corporation (Equity Method)	$445,000

FIGURE 8.24

As previously mentioned, investments with controlling influence are reported in a set of consolidated financial statements, which are beyond the scope of this textbook.

Accounting for Investments under IFRS

LO 5

The previous sections have illustrated accounting for investments under ASPE. We will now briefly look at IFRS reporting requirements.

As mentioned earlier in this chapter, on the investor's books under ASPE, an equity investment is classified based first on the investor's intent. However, according to IFRS, equity investments are classified based on *ability* to influence or control, not necessarily on intent. That is, a company might be able to exercise influence even if it does not intend to. In that case, the investment would be classified as strategic under IFRS, although it would be non-strategic under ASPE.

Figure 8.25 summarizes accounting for debt and equity under IFRS compared to ASPE.

	Investment	Method under ASPE	Method under IFRS
Non-Strategic	Short-term debt (bonds)	Fair value through net income (FVTNI) method Use the historical cost method if no market value is available.	Fair value through net income (FVTNI) method Use the historical cost method if no market value is available.
Non-Strategic	Long-term debt (bonds)	Amortized cost (AC) method Any premium or discount can be amortized using either the straight-line or the effective-interest rate method.	Amortized cost (AC) method Any premium or discount must be amortized using the effective-interest rate method.
Non-Strategic	Equity with insignificant influence (less than 20% ownership)	Fair value through net income (FVTNI) method Use the historical cost method if no market value is available. Gains and losses are reported in net income.	Fair value through net income (FVTNI) method or fair value through other comprehensive income (FVTOCI) method, depending on the circumstances. FVTOCI is beyond the scope of this textbook. Gains and losses are reported in either net income or other comprehensive income (OCI). Accounting for items reported in OCI is beyond the scope of this textbook.
Strategic	Equity with significant influence (20% to 50% ownership)	Equity or historical cost method	Equity method
Strategic	Equity with controlling influence (greater than 50% ownership)	Consolidation (if the parent company chooses)	Consolidation (required)

FIGURE 8.25

As you can see, the accounting is similar under both ASPE and IFRS. This accounting was illustrated previously in this chapter. For short-term investments, ASPE allows reporting using the historical cost method if fair value is not available or is too difficult and costly to obtain. IFRS requires that investments accounted for using the amortized cost method use the effective-interest rate method for amortization, whereas ASPE permits either the effective-interest method or straight-line amortization method.

These accounting methods have all been discussed in detail in previous sections, with the exception of fair value through other comprehensive income (FVTOCI), which is used under IFRS for non-strategic equity investments, and consolidation, which can be used under ASPE and must be used under IFRS for strategic equity investments with controlling influence.

In Summary

LO 1 Describe and classify different types of investments

- Investments can be made by purchasing debt, such as money market funds, term deposits, treasury bills and bonds. Investments can also be made by purchasing equity, such as preferred and common shares of another company.
- Investors can purchase debt and equity investments with an intention to generate investment income only (a non-strategic investment) or to establish a long-term relationship with another company (a strategic investment).
- Equity investments held for strategic purposes are always considered long-term investments.
- A shareholder owning less than 20% of an investee's common shares outstanding typically has an insignificant influence on the investee corporation.
- A significant influence exists if one shareholder owns between 20% and 50% of the common shares outstanding.
- An investor owning more than 50% of the common shares outstanding typically has a controlling influence.

LO 2 Prepare journal entries for debt investments

- Debt securities purchased with the intent of selling them in the short term at a gain are known as short-term debt investments (bonds).
- A debt investment that will mature within 12 months is considered a short-term debt investment.
- Short-term investments in debt (bonds) are accounted for using the fair value through net income method, or the historical cost method if no market price is available.
- Long-term investments in debt (bonds) are accounted for using the amortized cost method.

LO 3 Prepare journal entries for equity investments

- Investments with insignificant influence (short-term or long-term) are considered non-strategic investments and are accounted for using the fair value through net income method, or the historical cost method if fair value is too difficult or costly to obtain.
- Investments with significant influence are accounted for using the equity or historical cost method.
- The equity method records the purchase of the investment at its original cost.
- The investor's investment account must be adjusted to account for its share of the investee's net income and dividends.
- Investments with controlling influence are accounted for using the consolidation method.

LO 4 Describe how the different types of investments are presented in the financial statements

- Short-term investments in bonds are always classified as current assets on the investor's balance sheet.
- When bonds are purchased as long-term investments, they are classified on the balance sheet according to their time to maturity, with most investments maturing beyond 12 months classified as long-term assets.
- Equity investments with insignificant influence can be classified as either current or long-term assets based on management's intent.
- Gain or loss from fair value adjustments are reported as part of net income for short-term investments in bonds or non-strategic equity investments. Fair value adjustments are not reported for long-term investments in bonds (debt).

LO 5 Identify differences between ASPE and IFRS in accounting for investments

- Both ASPE and IFRS require short-term debt investments to be measured and reported using fair value. The historical cost method is used if there is no market price available.
- Long-term debt investments are accounted for using the amortized cost method under both ASPE and IFRS.
- Equity investments with insignificant influence must be measured at fair value under both IFRS and ASPE.
- Investments with 20% to 50% ownership must be accounted for using the equity method under IFRS, but either the cost or equity method is permitted under ASPE.

Review Exercise 8-1

Benita Sikorsky is the controller for Travel Time Inc., a medium-sized enterprise that has a December 31 year end. From time to time, her company has surplus cash on hand that it uses to make short-term and long-term investments. The types of investments vary from period to period, depending on which investments produce the highest return for the company.

During the past year, the company completed the following transactions.

Jan 1	Paid $450,000 to purchase 6,000 common shares in Tamalie Inc. for strategic reasons. The 6,000 shares represent 30% of Tamalie's total outstanding common shares.
Apr 1	Paid $101,500 to purchase a portfolio of bonds with an intention to hold until maturity, which is over one year from now
May 10	Paid $50,000 to purchase 4% of the outstanding common shares in Pergola Inc. Management hopes that their prices will rise quickly and that the shares can be sold for a gain within one year.
Jul 1	Received $3,000 in interest revenue from the debt securities purchased on April 1
Jul 10	Received a $100 cash dividend from the equity securities purchased on May 10
Jul 31	Tamalie Inc. announced that its net income for the year ended July 31, 2020 was $80,000
Aug 20	Tamalie Inc. declared and paid a $10,000 cash dividend to its common shareholders
Oct 1	Sold 10% of the portfolio that was purchased on April 1, 2020 for $10,000
Dec 15	Sold half of the shares that were purchased on May 10, 2020, for $26,800
Dec 31	At the company's year end, the market values of the portfolio purchased on April 1 is $92,000 and the value of the shares in Pergola Inc. is worth $24,000.

Record journal entries for each of the above transactions.

JOURNAL

Date	Account Title and Explanation	Debit	Credit

See Appendix I for solutions.

Notes

Chapter 9
The Statement of Cash Flows

Learning Objectives

LO 1 Classify operating, investing and financing activities

- Three Categories of Cash Flow Activities

LO 2 Prepare a statement of cash flows using the indirect method

- A Step-by-Step Approach to the Statement of Cash Flows
- Analysis of the Statement of Cash Flows

LO 3 Calculate book value and cash received for selling long-term assets

- Property, Plant and Equipment with Depreciation
- Long-Term Investments

LO 4 Explain the concept of free cash flow and its importance for potential investors

LO 5 Discuss ethical issues related to cash flow

Appendix 9A

LO 6 Prepare a statement of cash flows using the direct method

- Cash Receipts
- Cash Payments

Appendix 9B

LO 7 Prepare a statement of cash flows in a spreadsheet using the indirect method

- Preparing the Spreadsheet
- Analyzing Account Changes
- Preparing the Statement of Cash Flows

MAKING IT REAL TO YOU

We have examined the financial statements prepared by corporations and learned about how they are used in making decisions for internal and external purposes. In your own personal finances, understanding cash inflows and outflows is very important for decision-making. It not only helps you manage your day-to-day bill payments but also provides a way to plan for larger purchases in the future and to be prepared for the unexpected. Similarly, a statement of cash flows helps corporations understand their sources and uses of cash and provides important information to all users about operating, investing and financing activities.

The Importance of Cash Flow LO 1

Most of our discussion of accounting procedures and principles so far has focused on two types of financial statements: the balance sheet and the income statement. When people think about business finance, they usually think about these financial statements.

Unfortunately, analyzing the income statement and balance sheet does not provide all the information needed by users. This is because balance sheets and income statements are prepared on an accrual basis. Revenue and expense recognition dictate that revenues and expenses be recorded for the period in which they are earned or incurred. However, these types of transactions do not always involve an actual exchange of cash or cash equivalents. In contrast, other transactions, such as borrowing or repaying loans, affect cash but do not affect net income.

Why is cash so important? Without cash, a company cannot pay its bills. Without cash, a company cannot purchase and pay for new inventory or other assets required to run the business. Therefore, determining how cash is generated and spent is an important way to assess how well the company is performing.

To some extent, recording accruals masks the sources and uses of cash in a business. Thus, accounting standards require the preparation of a **statement of cash flows**, sometimes also referred to as a *cash flow statement*, to track a company's sources and uses of cash. You will have been briefly introduced to the statement of cash flows earlier in your studies. This chapter examines the statement in more depth and discusses how to prepare it.

The statement of cash flows ignores accruals and focuses just on cash. Internal users of financial statements (e.g. company managers and executives) rely on the statement of cash flows to help them evaluate operations and to make financing and investing decisions. These decisions include whether the company can pay for expenses in its day-to-day operations, or whether it must borrow cash to make large asset purchases. External users (e.g. shareholders, potential investors, creditors and lenders) use the statement of cash flows to assess the company's overall cash position and potential to make a profit. They make judgments such as whether the company can pay its debts as they mature (to lenders and creditors), or whether it will be able to pay dividends (to investors and shareholders).

Three Categories of Cash Flow Activities

A company generates and consumes cash in one of the following three ways:

- Operating activities
- Investing activities
- Financing activities

All statements of cash flow have three sections showing how cash flows in and out of a company.

Cash flow from operating activities is the movement of cash within a company as a result of day-to-day activities. All items in this section are directly related to revenues and expenses on the income statement, and current assets and current liabilities on the balance sheet. This includes transactions involving customers, suppliers, inventory, and so on. It is the most important section because the company's future largely depends on operating activities.

Cash flow from investing activities is the movement of cash on the basis of the purchases and sales of long-term (noncurrent) assets. This section shows how the company is investing cash back into itself. For example, if a truck was sold during the year, cash flow would have increased. Alternatively, if the company purchased land, cash flow would have decreased, since the company had to use cash to invest in the land.

Cash flow from financing activities is cash received from investors and lenders to help run, or finance, the company. It is also cash paid back to the investors (dividends) and lenders (principal repayments). This section shows financing that generally deals with long-term liabilities, such as notes payable, and equity financing, such as selling shares. Payments toward notes payable and dividend payments to shareholders are also reported here.

Figure 9.1 summarizes what is recorded in each section of the statement of cash flows.

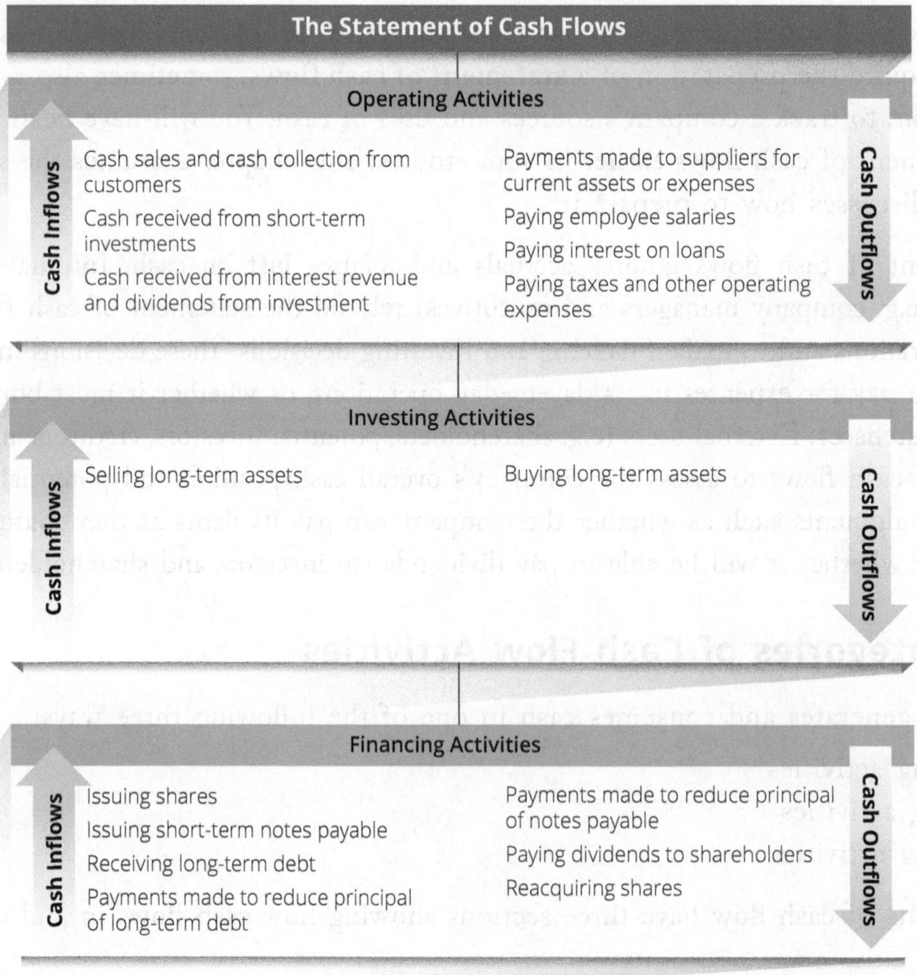

FIGURE 9.1

Figure 9.2 shows the format of the statement of cash flows. The individual cash inflow and outflow items, similar to those shown in Figure 9.1, are listed below their respective headings. There may also be non-cash investing and financing transactions, such as the company issuing shares to pay off a note payable or buying assets in exchange for shares. These non-cash transactions must be disclosed in a separate schedule either at the bottom of the statement of cash flows, as shown in Figure 9.2, or in the notes to the financial statements.

ABC Company Statement of Cash Flows For the Year Ended MM-DD-YYYY		
Cash Flow from Operating Activities		
(Individual cash inflows and outflows are listed here)	$xxx	
Net Cash Provided (Used) by Operating Activities		$xxx
Cash Flow from Investing Activities		
(Individual cash inflows and outflows are listed here)	xxx	
Net Cash Provided (Used) by Investing Activities		xxx
Cash Flow from Financing Activities		
(Individual cash inflows and outflows are listed here)	xxx	
Net Cash Provided (Used) by Financing Activities		xxx
Net Increase (Decrease) in Cash		xxx
Cash at the Beginning of the Year		xxx
Cash at the End of the Year		$xxx
Non-Cash Investing and Financing Activities		$xxx

FIGURE 9.2

ASPE vs. IFRS

Although both standards require the creation of the statement of cash flows, IFRS does allow for some options on how a few items are reported.

Under ASPE, interest or dividends received from a short-term or long-term investment are reported as operating activities. IFRS, however, allows the option to report these items as either operating or investing activities.

Under ASPE, interest paid on loans is an operating activity, and dividends paid to shareholders are a financing activity. IFRS, however, allows the option to report these items as either operating or financing activities. Of course, for IFRS statements to be consistent, once a decision is made about where to report interest and dividends, they must always be reported in that manner.

ASPE requires that cash outflows for income tax always be classified as operating activities but does not require a separate line disclosure. Under IFRS, cash flows to pay taxes are reported as a separate line in the operating activities, unless they are specifically identified with financing or investing activities.

Preparing a Statement of Cash Flows

LO 2

Two methods are used to prepare a statement of cash flows: the indirect method and the direct method. Both methods are allowed under both ASPE and IFRS, with some differences, as referred to in the *ASPE vs. IFRS* feature box on the previous page. Where applicable in the illustrations that follow, we will highlight ASPE reporting.

There are some similarities between the indirect method and the direct method. Both methods break down the three ways of generating and using cash into operating, investing and financing activities. The investing activities and financing activities sections are prepared in exactly the same way under both methods. Specifically, investing activities and financing activities are determined by analyzing the long-term assets, long-term liabilities and equity portion of the balance sheet.

The only difference between the indirect method and the direct method is how the cash flow from operating activities section is prepared. The **indirect method** *indirectly* analyzes cash flow from operating activities by starting with accrual-based net income, and then adding or subtracting certain items from the income statement as well as changes in current assets and current liabilities from the balance sheet.

Unlike the indirect method, the direct method calculates cash flow from operating activities by *directly* analyzing cash received from sales and collections and *directly* analyzing cash spent on expenses. As you will learn by the end of this chapter, the net cash flow from operating activities is the same no matter which method is used; it is simply the way of calculating and presenting the information that differs, not the actual amount. ASPE encourages private companies to use the direct method, mainly due to the fact that it does provide more detailed information on cash flow from operating activities. However, the indirect method is most commonly used since it is generally easier to prepare. Preparation of the statement of cash flows using the direct method is illustrated in Appendix 9A. In this section, we will demonstrate the step-by-step approach to creating the statement of cash flows using the indirect method.

In the Real World

Academic studies have shown that if two versions of the statement of cash flows are shown (i.e. direct and indirect method), investors can make better decisions. By disclosing both the direct and indirect methods, a company improves its accounting transparency. Statistical studies suggest that the indirect method is more useful than the direct method, although the studies do not reveal a reason for this discrepancy. On the other hand, the direct method is usually more easily understood by users than the indirect method.

A Step-by-Step Approach to the Statement of Cash Flows

The statement of cash flows is easiest to prepare using the following six steps.

Step 1. Calculate the net increase (or decrease) in cash during the period.

Step 2. Calculate the net cash provided (or used) by operating activities using the indirect method.

Step 3. Calculate the net cash provided (or used) by investing activities.

Step 4. Calculate the net cash provided (or used) by financing activities.

Step 5. Calculate the *total* net cash provided (or used) by operating, investing and financing activities combined.

Step 6. Verify that the total net cash flow equals the ending cash balance less the beginning cash balance.

Step 7. Identify all non-cash transactions for disclosure in the notes to the financial statements.

We will follow this process using the example of Soho Supplies, a manufacturer of office supplies with a year end of December 31, 2020. Before preparing the statement of cash flows, we must examine Soho's balance sheet and income statement.

Step 1. Calculate the net increase (or decrease) in cash during the period.

Figure 9.3 on the next page is a comparative balance sheet for two periods and shows both periods' cash balances. We will use this specific balance sheet for Soho Supplies for the remainder of the chapter.

The last column of the balance sheet shows the difference between 2019 and 2020 period-end account balances. This difference is used when preparing the statement of cash flows. The first line of the balance sheet shows that the cash account decreased from $396,142 in 2019 to $349,935 in 2020. Therefore, the net decrease in cash for the year was $46,207, as shown in blue on the first line of the change column. Alternatively, we could say that Soho's net cash flow was -$46,207.

Step 2. Calculate the net cash provided (or used) by operating activities using the indirect method.

The indirect method of analyzing cash flows from operating activities begins with the period's net income (from the income statement), which is then adjusted as necessary. These adjustments include adding back non-cash expenses to net income and deducting non-cash increases from net income.

At this point, some additional information will help in our cash flow analysis. The indirect method of preparing a statement of cash flows follows the logic of the basic accounting equation.

Assets = Liabilities + Shareholders' Equity

The accounting equation enables us to analyze changes in one balance sheet account by examining changes in the other balance sheet accounts. Even by analyzing non-cash balance sheet accounts, we can determine indirectly how they affect the cash account (hence, the term indirect method). To demonstrate, we can also express the basic accounting equation as follows.

Cash + Non-Cash Assets = Liabilities + Shareholders' Equity

and therefore,

Cash = Liabilities + Shareholders' Equity – Non-Cash Assets

It then follows that any changes in the cash balance can be determined from changes in liabilities, shareholders' equity and non-cash assets.

Changes in Cash = Changes in Liabilities + Changes in Shareholders' Equity – Changes in Non-Cash Assets

This relationship will become apparent as we work through the example in this section.

Soho Supplies Balance Sheet As at December 31, 2020	2020	2019	Change
Assets			
Current Assets			
Cash	$349,935	$396,142	**($46,207)**
Accounts Receivable	1,286,138	1,065,812	220,326
Merchandise Inventory	1,683,560	840,091	843,469
Prepaid Insurance	48,612	42,625	5,987
Total Current Assets	3,368,245	2,344,670	1,023,575
Long-Term Assets			
Land[1]	0	50,000	(50,000)
Equipment[2]	322,518	120,000	202,518
Accumulated Depreciation	(79,262)	(36,000)	(43,262)
Total Long-Term Assets	243,256	134,000	109,256
Total Assets	$3,611,501	$2,478,670	$1,132,831
Liabilities			
Current Liabilities			
Accounts Payable	$783,602	$475,645	$307,957
Salaries Payable	25,000	50,000	(25,000)
Interest Payable	15,650	23,500	(7,850)
Income Taxes Payable	280,117	250,000	30,117
Notes Payable, Current Portion	380,000	240,000	140,000
Total Current Liabilities	1,484,369	1,039,145	445,224
Long-Term Liabilities			
Notes Payable, Long-Term Portion	420,000	356,000	64,000
Bonds Payable[3]	170,000	200,000	(30,000)
Total Long-Term Liabilities	590,000	556,000	34,000
Total Liabilities	2,074,369	1,595,145	479,224
Shareholders' Equity			
Contributed Capital			
Preferred Shares	10,000	0	10,000
Common Shares	5,000	5,000	0
Total Contributed Capital	15,000	5,000	10,000
Retained Earnings[4]	1,522,132	878,525	643,607
Total Shareholders' Equity	1,537,132	883,525	653,607
Total Liabilities and Shareholders' Equity	$3,611,501	$2,478,670	$1,132,831

Additional Information

(1) During 2020, land that cost $50,000 was sold for $60,000, resulting in a $10,000 gain on sale. The gain is reported on the income statement in the other income and expenses section.

(2) During 2020, Soho made purchases of equipment for $202,518.

(3) The bonds were issued at par.

(4) Soho declared and paid $10,000 in dividends in 2020.

FIGURE 9.3

Soho's income statement is shown in Figure 9.4.

Soho Supplies Income Statement For the Year Ended December 31, 2020		
Sales Revenue		$8,685,025
Cost of Goods Sold		5,998,612
Gross Profit		2,686,413
Operating Expenses		
Salaries Expense		1,416,135
Depreciation Expense		43,262
Insurance Expense		16,000
Other Operating Expenses		235,417
Total Operating Expenses		1,710,814
Income from Operations		975,599
Other Income and Expenses		
Gain on Sale of Land		10,000
Interest Expense		(51,875)
Income before Income Taxes		933,724
Income Tax Expense		280,117
Net Income		**$653,607**

FIGURE 9.4

The company's net income is $653,607 for 2020. This income statement will be used for the remainder of the chapter, so refer to it as we assemble the statement of cash flows for 2020.

Remember that cash flow from operating activities under the indirect method starts with net income and then adds or subtracts certain items from the income statement and from changes on the balance sheet. In the current example, the company's net income for 2020 is $653,607, shown in blue at the bottom of the income statement in Figure 9.4. However, in reality, not all revenues and expenses involve cash, due to the accrual basis of accounting required under ASPE and IFRS. Since the focus is on cash flow instead of accruals, only the money that actually changes hands during a period needs to be accounted for. Therefore, in the cash flow from operating activities section, we begin with net income and add or subtract non-cash items that appear on the income statement.

Add or subtract non-cash and non-operating items from the income statement.

Non-cash and non-operating items from the income statement include things such as depreciation and amortization, gains (losses) from the sale of assets and gains (losses) on the retirement of debt (discussed in the chapter on long-term liabilities, in the section on retiring bonds). These and other non-cash or non-operating items either have no effect on actual cash inflows or outflows or are not classified as operating activities; therefore, their amounts must be cancelled by adjusting net income. In our example, there are two non-cash or non-operating items affecting Soho's cash flow from operating activities: depreciation and gain on the sale of land.

To help illustrate how the cash balance changes using the indirect method, we will start with the opening cash balance in 2020 (or the ending cash balance in 2019). Figure 9.5 shows a partial statement of cash flows that includes cash flow from operating activities. At the top of the statement is the opening cash balance, which is $396,142. If the whole amount of net income was received in cash, then cash would be increased by the net income amount. This is why net income (a) is added to the opening cash balance in Figure 9.5. At this point, cash is updated to $1,049,749, which is equal to the opening cash balance of $396,142 plus the net income amount of $653,607. However, not all components of the net income are cash, and not all components are classified as operating activities. To prepare the cash flow from operating activities section of the statement of cash flows, items that are non-cash or unrelated to operating activities must be taken out. Consequently, as shown in Figure 9.5, depreciation (b) is added to net income, and gain on sale of land (c) is subtracted from net income in order to adjust accrual-based net income to cash-based operating income.

Soho Supplies
Statement of Cash Flows (partial)
For the Year Ended December 31, 2020

	Amount	Updated Cash Balance
Opening Cash Balance		$396,142
Cash Flow from Operating Activities		
Net Income	$653,607 (a)	1,049,749
Adjustments to Reconcile Net Income to Net Cash Provided (Used) by Operating Activities		
Depreciation Expense	43,262 (b)	1,093,011
Gain on Sale of Land	(10,000) (c)	1,083,011

The Updated Cash Balance column is used to calculate the updated cash balance to help you understand the process. **You will not see this theoretical column illustrated in a proper statement of cash flows. It is a learning tool only.**

FIGURE 9.5

Depreciation Expense. Depreciation is a non-cash expense that simply decreases the book value of an asset without any change to cash. Therefore, depreciation must be excluded from any equations involving cash flow. To illustrate this point, a journal entry for depreciation debits depreciation expense and credits accumulated depreciation for the particular asset—neither the debit nor the credit involves cash. Therefore, Soho Supplies' depreciation expense of $43,262 from the income statement in Figure 9.4 is added to the net income, as shown in Figure 9.5, item (b).

Gain on Sale of Land. In 2020, Soho Supplies' land with a book value of $50,000 was sold for $60,000. This means that the company made a profit (or gain) of $10,000, which appears in the other income and expenses section of Soho Supplies' income statement.

Soho Supplies' net income of $653,607 includes the $10,000 gain on sale of land. However, because the gain is not part of day-to-day operating activities, it must be removed from the cash flow from operating activities section of the statement of cash flows. This is why the $10,000 gain on sale of land is deducted from net income in the cash flow from operating activities section, in item (c). Although the gain is removed from this section, the $60,000 proceeds from the sale of land are reported in the cash flow from investing activities section, which is explained later. Therefore, the $10,000 gain is deducted from net income in the cash flow from operating activities section to avoid double counting. If, instead, Soho incurred a *loss* from the sale of land, the amount would be added back to net income in the cash flow from operating activities section.

Add or subtract operating activities that do not flow through the income statement.

The next step is to add or subtract changes in items related to operating activities that do not flow through the income statement. These items include all the current assets and current liabilities (except the current portion of long-term debt) on the balance sheet.

Figure 9.6 shows the rest of the cash flow from operating activities with all the changes in current assets and current liabilities, items (d) to (k). A discussion of these items follows after the figure.

Soho Supplies
Statement of Cash Flows (partial)
For the Year Ended December 31, 2020

	Amount		**Updated Cash Balance**
Opening Cash Balance			$396,142
Cash Flow from Operating Activities			
Net Income	$653,607		1,049,749
Adjustments to Reconcile Net Income to Net Cash Provided (Used) by Operating Activities			
Depreciation Expense	43,262		1,093,011
Gain on Sale of Land	(10,000)		1,083,011
Changes in Operating Assets and Liabilities			
Increase in Accounts Receivable	(220,326)	(d)	862,685
Increase in Prepaid Insurance	(5,987)	(e)	856,698
Increase in Merchandise Inventory	(843,469)	(f)	13,229
Increase in Accounts Payable	307,957	(g)	321,186
Decrease in Salaries Payable	(25,000)	(h)	296,186
Decrease in Interest Payable	(7,850)	(i)	288,336
Increase in Income Taxes Payable	30,117	(j)	318,453
Net Cash Provided (Used) by Operating Activities	($77,689)	(k)	

FIGURE 9.6

(d) The first listed current asset in the comparative balance sheet (after cash) is accounts receivable. The balance sheet in Figure 9.3 showed that this account increased by $220,326 from 2019 to 2020. Remember that since accounts receivable increased, cash will decrease because the amount is yet to be collected. We therefore deduct this amount from the cash balance of $1,083,011. As indicated in Figure 9.6, the updated cash balance is $862,685.

(e) Prepaid insurance increased by $5,987, decreasing the cash balance to $856,698 because the prepaid insurance must have been paid with cash.

(f) Merchandise inventory increased by $843,469, decreasing the cash balance to $13,229 because cash must have been used to pay for the additional inventory.

(g) Accounts payable increased by $307,957. This resulted in more cash in the bank since Soho deferred paying their suppliers, increasing the cash balance to $321,186.

(h) Salaries payable decreased by $25,000. This means Soho paid out cash owing for salaries, decreasing the cash balance to $296,186.

(i) Interest payable decreased by $7,850, meaning Soho used cash to pay for the interest owed. The cash balance decreased to $288,336.

(j) Income taxes payable increased by $30,117. This means Soho has deferred payment of income taxes and therefore has more cash. This increases the cash balance to $318,453.

(k) The updated cash balance has gone from the beginning balance of $396,142 to $318,453. This indicates that cash decreased by $77,689 due to operating activities.

Figure 9.7 outlines the impact an increase or decrease to current assets or current liabilities has on the statement of cash flows under the indirect method of preparing a statement of cash flows.

		Change from Beginning of Period	
		Increase	**Decrease**
Category	**Current Assets**	***Deduct*** *from cash flow*	***Add*** *to cash flow*
	Current Liabilities	***Add*** *to cash flow*	***Deduct*** *from cash flow*

FIGURE 9.7

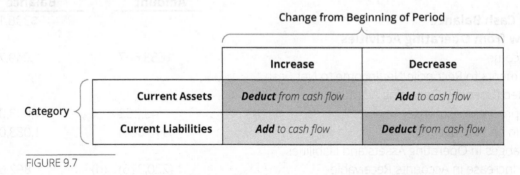

Step 3. Calculate the net cash provided (or used) by investing activities.

Changes in the value of long-term assets (i.e. property, plant and equipment) affect cash flow. However, measuring the effect is not as straightforward as observing the change in the property, plant and equipment balance from one year to the next.

In Figure 9.8, the cash flow from investing activities section is added to the statement of cash flows. This section of the statement of cash flows deals with the way cash flow changes through the investment in or sale of long-term assets. In the current example of Soho Supplies, the information required to complete the cash flow from investing activities section is provided in the additional information portion below Soho's balance sheet (Figure 9.3). We will analyze the items from this additional information, shown in Figure 9.8 as items (l) to (n).

Soho Supplies Statement of Cash Flows (partial) For the Year Ended December 31, 2020			
	Amount		Updated Cash Balance
Opening Cash Balance			$396,142
Cash Flow from Operating Activities			
Net Income	$653,607		1,049,749
Adjustments to Reconcile Net Income to Net Cash Provided (Used) by Operating Activities			
Depreciation Expense	43,262		1,093,011
Gain on Sale of Land	(10,000)		1,083,011
Changes in Operating Assets and Liabilities			
Increase in Accounts Receivable	(220,326)		862,685
Increase in Prepaid Insurance	(5,987)		856,698
Increase in Merchandise Inventory	(843,469)		13,229
Increase in Accounts Payable	307,957		321,186
Decrease in Salaries Payable	(25,000)		296,186
Decrease in Interest Payable	(7,850)		288,336
Increase in Income Taxes Payable	30,117		318,453
Net Cash Provided (Used) by Operating Activities	(77,689)		
Cash Flow from Investing Activities			
Sale of Land	60,000	(l)	378,453
Purchase of Equipment	(202,518)	(m)	$175,935
Net Cash Provided (Used) by Investing Activities	($142,518)	(n)	

FIGURE 9.8

(l) The proceeds from the sale of the land in the amount of $60,000 are added to the updated cash balance since the transaction represents a cash inflow. The proceeds include the $10,000 gain, which was previously deducted from the operating activities section of the statement of cash flows.

(m) The $202,518 purchase of equipment is deducted from the updated cash balance because it represents a cash outflow.

(n) The updated cash balance has dropped from $318,453 to $175,935. This indicates that net cash provided (used) by investing activities was –$142,518.

The updated partial statement of cash flows now shows the net cash used by operating activities, which is $77,689, and the net cash used by investing activities, which is $142,518.

Step 4. Calculate the net cash provided (or used) by financing activities.

The last section prepared for the statement of cash flows is cash flow from financing activities. This section includes borrowing money or receiving cash as a result of issuing shares. It also includes any payments involved with financing, such as dividend payments or loan repayments. Therefore, the cash flow in this section is affected by changes in liabilities based on which interest must be paid, such as notes payable (current and long-term portions), and changes related to preferred shares, common shares and contributed surplus (if any exists) as a result of shares being issued.

The liabilities and shareholders' equity portion of Soho Supplies' balance sheet from Figure 9.3 is shown in Figure 9.9.

Soho Supplies Balance Sheet (partial) As at December 31, 2020			
	2020	**2019**	**Change**
Liabilities			
Current Liabilities			
Accounts Payable	$783,602	$475,645	$307,957
Salaries Payable	25,000	50,000	(25,000)
Interest Payable	15,650	23,500	(7,850)
Income Taxes Payable	280,117	250,000	30,117
Notes Payable, Current Portion	380,000	240,000	**140,000**
Total Current Liabilities	1,484,369	1,039,145	445,224
Long-Term Liabilities			
Notes Payable, Long-Term Portion	420,000	356,000	**64,000**
Bonds Payable	170,000	200,000	(30,000)
Total Long-Term Liabilities	590,000	556,000	34,000
Total Liabilities	2,074,369	1,595,145	479,224
Shareholders' Equity			
Contributed Capital			
Preferred Shares	10,000	0	10,000
Common Shares	5,000	5,000	0
Total Contributed Capital	15,000	5,000	10,000
Retained Earnings	1,522,132	878,525	643,607
Total Shareholders' Equity	1,537,132	883,525	653,607
Total Liabilities and Shareholders' Equity	$3,611,501	$2,478,670	$1,132,831

Sum = $204,0000

FIGURE 9.9

The following account balances changed between 2019 and 2020: notes payable, bonds payable, dividends (included in retained earnings) and preferred shares (including any contributed surplus). We will look at each of these items, labelled (o) to (r) on the statement of cash flows in Figure 9.10, to which the cash flows from financing activities section has been added.

Soho Supplies Statement of Cash Flows (partial) For the Year Ended December 31, 2020			
	Amount		**Updated Cash Balance**
Opening Cash Balance			$396,142
Cash Flow from Operating Activities			
Net Income	$653,607		1,049,749
Adjustments to Reconcile Net Income to Net Cash Provided (Used) by Operating Activities			
Depreciation Expense	43,262		1,093,011
Gain on Sale of Land	(10,000)		1,083,011
Changes in Operating Assets and Liabilities			
Increase in Accounts Receivable	(220,326)		862,685
Increase in Prepaid Insurance	(5,987)		856,698
Increase in Merchandise Inventory	(843,469)		13,229
Increase in Accounts Payable	307,957		321,186
Decrease in Salaries Payable	(25,000)		296,186
Decrease in Interest Payable	(7,850)		288,336
Increase in Income Taxes Payable	30,117		318,453
Net Cash Provided (Used) by Operating Activities	(77,689)		
Cash Flow from Investing Activities			
Sale of Land	60,000		378,453
Purchase of Equipment	(202,518)		175,935
Net Cash Provided (Used) by Investing Activities	(142,518)		
Cash Flow from Financing Activities			
Proceeds from Notes Payable[1]	204,000 [2]	(o)	379,935
Payment toward Bonds Payable	(30,000)	(p)	349,935
Payment of Cash Dividends	(10,000)	(q)	339,935
Issuance of Preferred Shares	10,000 [3]	(r)	349,935
Net Cash Provided (Used) by Financing Activities	$174,000	(s)	

[1] Soho Supplies did not sign any additional notes payable during the year.
[2] The $204,000 proceeds from the notes payable is from the calculation in Figure 9.9.
[3] Increase in preferred shares of $10,000.

FIGURE 9.10

(o) First, we will look at notes payable. As shown in Figure 9.9, the notes payable is reported in two areas of the balance sheet: in the current portion under current liabilities, and in the long-term portion under long-term liabilities. From 2019 to 2020, the current portion of the notes payable increased by $140,000. The long-term portion of the notes payable increased by $64,000. Therefore, the total increase in the notes payable balance is $204,000 ($140,000 + $64,000). This amount is an increase to cash—or a cash inflow—since Soho received additional money.

(p) The decrease in bonds payable of $30,000 indicates that cash also decreased by $30,000 from 2019 to 2020 due to principal repayment. Since the notes indicate that the bonds were sold at par, there is no discount or premium to be included in the statement of cash flows.

(q) Dividends are considered next. In the additional information section under Soho's balance sheet (Figure 9.3), it is mentioned that Soho declared and paid $10,000 in dividends during 2020. This represents a decrease to cash because it is a cash outflow.

Although there is a note regarding the amount of dividends paid, the amount of dividends paid can also be calculated by examining the financial statements.

Previous chapters explained that the retained earnings account will increase if there is a net income for the year and decrease if there is a net loss for the year. Additionally, dividends are paid out of the retained earnings account, decreasing its value. The partial balance sheet in Figure 9.9 shows that the retained earnings account increased by $643,607 in 2020; however, the income statement shows that net income was $653,607. Therefore, the difference of $10,000 must be the dividends paid, as illustrated in the T-account in Figure 9.11. This represents a decrease in cash flow in the financing section of the statement of cash flows.

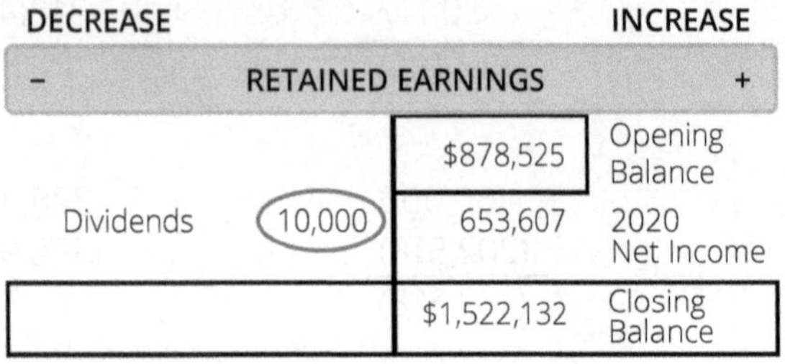

FIGURE 9.11

A Closer Look

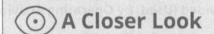

Note that under ASPE, dividend income and interest received or paid on investments belong to the operating activities of the cash flow. Dividends paid to shareholders impact the cash flow from financing activities.

(r) The balance of preferred shares increased by $10,000 from 2019 to 2020. The shares were issued for $10 per share and therefore the $10,000 is recorded as a credit to the preferred share account. The cash receipt of $10,000 from the sale of preferred shares is reported in the financing section of the cash flow statement as an increase to cash.

(s) Net cash provided (used) by financing activities accounts for an increase to the cash account of $174,000 ($204,000 - $30,000 - $10,000 + $10,000).

Step 5. Calculate the *total* net cash provided (or used) by operating, investing and financing activities combined.

Three sections of the statement of cash flows have been completed: net cash provided (or used) from operating activities, investing activities and financing activities. They can now be put all together to form one complete statement of cash flows in proper format for 2020, as shown in Figure 9.12.

Soho Supplies Statement of Cash Flows For the Year Ended December 31, 2020		
Cash Flow from Operating Activities		
Net Income	$653,607	
Adjustments to Reconcile Net Income to Net Cash Provided (Used) by Operating Activities		
Depreciation Expense	43,262	
Gain on Sale of Land	(10,000)	
Changes in Operating Assets and Liabilities		
Increase in Accounts Receivable	(220,326)	
Increase in Prepaid Expenses	(5,987)	
Increase in Merchandise Inventory	(843,469)	
Increase in Accounts Payable	307,957	
Decrease in Salaries Payable	(25,000)	
Decrease in Interest Payable	(7,850)	
Increase in Income Taxes Payable	30,117	
Net Cash Provided (Used) by Operating Activities		($77,689)
Cash Flow from Investing Activities		
Sale of Land	60,000	
Purchase of Equipment	(202,518)	
Net Cash Provided (Used) by Investing Activities		(142,518)
Cash Flow from Financing Activities		
Proceeds from Notes Payable	204,000	
Payment toward Bonds Payable	(30,000)	
Payment of Cash Dividends	(10,000)	
Issuance of Preferred Shares	10,000	
Net Cash Provided (Used) by Financing Activities		174,000
Net Increase (Decrease) in Cash		(46,207)
Cash at the Beginning of the Year		396,142
Cash at the End of the Year		$349,935

FIGURE 9.12

Step 6. Verify that the total net cash flow equals the ending cash balance less the beginning cash balance.

To finish the process, we must verify that the net cash provided (or used) by operating, investing and financing activities combined, or the net increase (or decrease) in cash, equals the difference between the cash balance at the beginning of the year and the cash balance at the end of the year.

The bottom three lines on the statement of cash flows in Figure 9.12 verify that the net decrease in cash of $46,207 accounts for the difference.

Step 7. Identify all non-cash transactions for disclosure in the notes to the financial statements.

Companies sometimes engage in financing or investing activities that do not involve cash. These transactions must be reported in the notes to the financial statements. The consolidation of these non-cash transactions would be summarized in one line item at the bottom of the statement of cash flows, as illustrated in Figure 9.2.

To demonstrate these transactions, suppose Mory Inc. purchased land by issuing 100,000 common shares with a market value of $9 per share on June 1, 2020. Mory Inc. would make the journal entry shown in Figure 9.13.

JOURNAL

Date	Account Title and Explanation	Debit	Credit
June 1	Land	900,000	
	Common Shares		900,000
	To record purchase of land with common shares		

FIGURE 9.13

This non-cash activity would be included in the notes to the financial statements and also consolidated with other such transactions on the statement of cash flows.

Analysis of the Statement of Cash Flows

Once the statement of cash flows is completed, it is analyzed to see if there are any concerns. The first item to note is that cash decreased during the year even though there was a net income. Part of that decrease was due to an outflow of cash from operating activities of $77,689. This can be a problem for the company, since it indicates that day-to-day operations are not generating a cash inflow. In other words, the company is not being self-sufficient with its operations.

The two major contributors to this cash outflow from operations were an increase in accounts receivable and an increase in inventory. Both can indicate trouble for the company. An increase in accounts receivable can result from an increase in sales on account instead of cash, or from customers taking longer to pay their bills. Either situation means the company is not receiving cash on a timely basis. The large increase in inventory can indicate that the company is buying too much inventory, which eventually has to be paid for with cash. Alternatively, it could mean that inventory is not turning into cost of goods sold, which would mean that the amount of sales has decreased.

The company purchased some new equipment during the year and also sold some land. Both can be considered normal, assuming the equipment is needed and the plan was to sell the land. However, considering the cash flow problems from operations, the question may be asked whether the sale of land was simply to raise some cash to pay for operating expenses. Financing operations by selling long-term assets is not a sustainable practice.

The financing activities section of the statement of cash flows is the only one showing a cash inflow. This is primarily due to a large bank loan. The bank loan may have been borrowed to pay for the equipment. Overall, there are concerns due to the negative cash flow from operations and the apparent financing of operating activities by selling assets and taking loans.

In the Real World

Understanding cash flow is essential to a company's overall financial performance and success. Fundamentally, the ability to generate cash flow determines the value that is created for shareholders. Having positive cash flow allows a business to take advantage of opportunities that arise and provides financial reserves when needed. Companies often rely on cash flow statements generated by accounting software, ledgers and bank statements to get an overall picture of their cash situation. However, this process is static and may not incorporate all relevant and current information, making it more difficult to assess the present position.

Data analytics software can be used to examine and predict cash flow and to provide forecasts tailored to the user's needs. It can include integrations with financial institutions to ensure all investment and banking data is updated in real time. Cash flow analytics software provides drill-down ability in reports so that transaction data can be viewed at a high level or in detail, providing more flexibility and access. The system also ensures accuracy through features such as highlighting any duplicate data.

Pause & Reflect

Exercise 9-1

For each item in the schedule below, indicate whether the amount should be added to or subtracted from net income to reconcile it to the net cash provided (used) by operating activities.

Reconciliation of Net Income to Net Cash Provided (Used) by Operating Activities	
	Add or Subtract?
Net Income	
Adjustments to Reconcile Net Income to Net Cash Provided (Used) by Operating Activities	
Depreciation Expense	
Amortization Expense	
Loss on Sale of Land	
Gain on Retirement of Debt	
Changes in Current Assets and Current Liabilities	
Increase in Accounts Receivable	
Increase in Prepaid Expenses	
Decrease in Merchandise Inventory	
Decrease in Accounts Payable	
Increase in Salaries Payable	
Decrease in Interest Payable	
Increase in Income Taxes Payable	
Net Cash Provided (Used) by Operating Activities	

See Appendix I for solutions.

Selling Long-Term Assets

LO 3

In the example of Soho Supplies, land was sold and reported in the investing activities section of the statement of cash flows. Since land does not depreciate, the decrease in the value of land was equal to the book value of the land. A gain is reported if the amount received is greater than the book value of the land, and a loss is reported if the amount is less than the book value of the land.

When selling equipment or any other long-term asset that depreciates in value, determining the book value of the item is an important step in calculating cash flow. Figure 9.14 presents the assets section of the balance sheet for Soho Supplies. For demonstration purposes, information in the long-term assets section has been changed; it is now different from Figure 9.3.

Soho Supplies Balance Sheet (partial) As at December 31, 2020			
	2020	**2019**	**Change**
Assets			
Current Assets			
Cash	$349,935	$396,142	($46,207)
Accounts Receivable	1,286,138	1,065,812	220,326
Merchandise Inventory	1,683,560	840,091	843,469
Prepaid Insurance	48,612	42,625	5,987
Total Current Assets	3,368,245	2,344,670	1,023,575
Long-Term Assets			
Long-Term Investments(1)	400,000	500,000	(100,000)
Equipment(2)	420,000	170,000	250,000
Accumulated Depreciation	(61,262)	(36,000)	(25,262)
Total Long-Term Assets	758,738	634,000	124,738
Total Assets	$4,126,983	$2,978,670	$1,148,313

Additional Information
(1) During 2020, Soho did not purchase any long-term investments.
(2) During 2020, Soho made purchases of equipment for $375,000.

FIGURE 9.14

The additional information indicates that there were no purchases of long-term investments, so the decrease in that account is due only to the sale of investments. However, the actual cash received does not necessarily match the decrease in value. Also, Soho purchased equipment worth $375,000; however, the value of that account increased by only $250,000. This indicates that some equipment was sold. The income statement in Figure 9.15 provides more information about these accounts. For demonstration purposes, the other income and expenses section has been changed; it is now different from Figure 9.4.

Soho Supplies Income Statement For the Year Ended December 31, 2020	
Sales Revenue	$8,685,025
Cost of Goods Sold	5,998,612
Gross Profit	2,686,413
Operating Expenses	
Salaries Expense	1,416,135
Depreciation Expense	43,262
Insurance Expense	16,000
Other Operating Expenses	235,417
Total Operating Expenses	1,710,814
Income from Operations	975,599
Other Income and Expenses	
Loss on Sale of Investments	(5,000)
Gain on Sale of Equipment	16,000
Income before Income Tax Expense	986,599
Income Tax Expense	(280,117)
Net Income	$706,482

FIGURE 9.15

Property, Plant and Equipment with Depreciation

The cash involved for both the sale of long-term investments and the sale and purchase of equipment is reported in the investing activities section. In this example, the income statement (from Figure 9.15) indicates that some equipment has been sold for a gain. To determine how much cash was actually received, the book value of the asset must be determined. This is done by examining the changes in the balance sheet accounts. Figure 9.16 helps illustrate this.

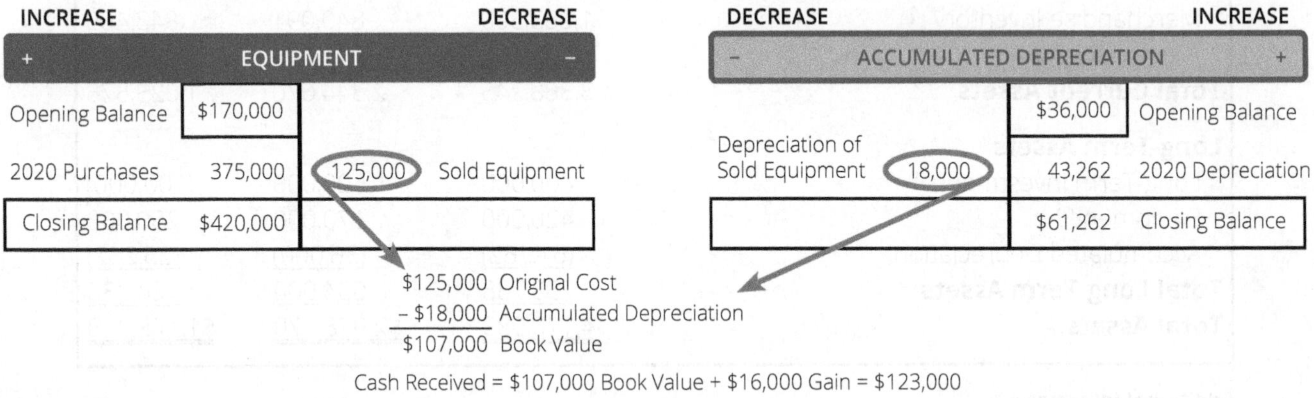

FIGURE 9.16

The balance sheet shows that equipment increased by $250,000; however, the additional information indicates that $375,000 was purchased during the year. The $125,000 difference represents the original cost of the equipment that was sold in 2020. Also from the balance sheet, accumulated depreciation increased by $25,262; however, depreciation expense on the income statement was $43,262. This means that $18,000 was removed from accumulated depreciation when the equipment was sold.

The difference between the cost of the equipment and the associated accumulated depreciation indicates the equipment had a book value of $107,000 when it was sold. The income statement tells us that the equipment was sold at a gain of $16,000, which means the total amount of cash received was $123,000 ($107,000 + $16,000). If there was a loss instead of a gain on the sale of the equipment, the cash received would be calculated by deducting the loss from the book value of the equipment. The proceeds from the sale of equipment represent an increase in cash flow in the investing activities section of the statement of cash flows.

Long-Term Investments

Long-term investments held at cost were also sold during the year, as shown by the account's decrease on the balance sheet in Figure 9.14.

However, the $100,000 decrease represents the cost of the investment, not necessarily the amount of cash received. The income statement indicates there was a loss of $5,000 when the investment was sold. Thus, the amount of cash received, as shown in Figure 9.17, was $95,000 ($100,000 – $5,000), representing an increase in cash flow in the investing activities section of the statement of cash flows. Note that a gain on the sale would be added to the cost of the investment for calculating the amount of cash received on the sale.

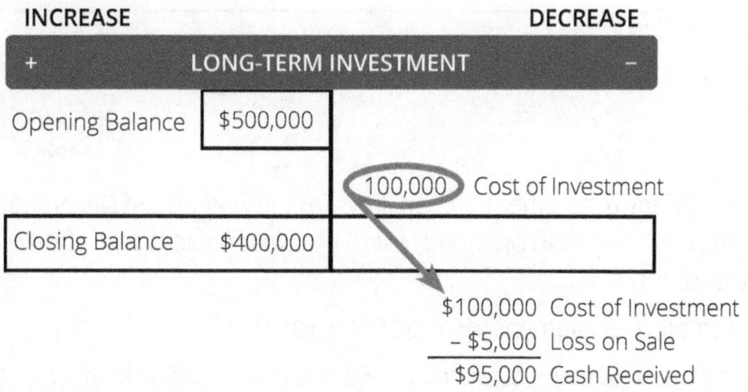

FIGURE 9.17

In this example for long-term investments, it was assumed that there were no additional purchases in the year. If there were in fact purchases of long-term investments during the year, the amount would be added to the debit side of the investment account and then the amount (cost) of investment sold would be calculated. The calculation is similar to the example shown in the equipment account from Figure 9.16.

Based on the information given in Figures 9.14 and 9.15, the investing activities section of the statement of cash flows would be reported as in Figure 9.18.

Soho Supplies Statement of Cash Flows (partial) For the Year Ended December 31, 2020		
Cash Flow from Investing Activities		
Sale of Equipment	$123,000	
Sale of Investments	95,000	
Purchase of Equipment	(375,000)	
Net Cash Provided (Used) by Investing Activities		($157,000)

FIGURE 9.18

Pause & Reflect

Exercise 9-2

Altitude Sportswear Inc. is preparing a statement of cash flows for the year ended December 31, 2020. The accountant needs to determine the company's net cash provided (used) by investing activities. The accounting records show the following events that occurred during 2020.

- The company purchased office equipment for $250,000 cash.
- Long-term investments had an opening balance of $155,000 and a closing balance of $70,000. Altitude's income statement reports a loss on sale of investments of $5,000. No investment was purchased during the year.
- Land that cost $850,000 was sold for cash. The gain on sale of land was $50,000.
- The company sold its old production equipment for cash and did not purchase any production equipment during the year. The production equipment had an original cost of $200,000. The accumulated depreciation related to this equipment had an opening balance of $130,000 and a closing balance of $0. Altitude's 2020 income statement shows the production equipment's depreciation expense of $30,000 and a loss on its sale of $25,000.

Use this information and the template below to prepare the cash flows from investing activities section for Altitude's statement of cash flows.

Altitude Sportswear Inc. Statement of Cash Flows (partial) For the Year Ended December 31, 2020	
Cash Flow from Investing Activities	
______________	$______
______________	______
______________	______
______________	______
Net Cash Provided (Used) by Investing Activities	$______

See Appendix I for solutions.

Free Cash Flow

LO 4

Throughout this course, it is continually emphasized that the fundamental objective of accounting is to provide financial information that readers can use to make appropriate decisions. One group of readers is made up of those outside the organization, primarily consisting of current and potential investors, creditors and lenders. These external users want to ensure that their investment or loan is protected, and so they require information on the company's financial resources and any claims on those resources. Some of the information most crucial to their decisions can be found on the statement of cash flows, in a concept known as *free cash flow.*

Free cash flow is the amount of cash remaining after a company has covered the operating activities and capital expenditures (investing in long-term assets) that are required to maintain its existing production capacity. This remaining cash is available for uses such as reducing debt, buying back shares or paying dividends. Free cash flow relies partly on the company's cash from operating activities, which in turn is based on the company's net income. However, the investing activities section of the statement of cash flows does not separate capital expenditures that are required to maintain the current capacity from those that are additional investments to expand the capacity. Since it can be difficult to determine exactly which items in the investing section are only related to the maintenance of the existing capacity, companies quite often just use net cash from investing activities in the calculation of free cash flow.

Free cash flow is typically calculated by deducting the net cash used by investing activities from the net cash provided by operating activities. If the net cash provided (used) by investing activities is negative, it means that cash has been spent on assets. This number must be subtracted from the cash flow from operating activities. If the net cash provided (used) by investing activities is positive, it means that cash was received from selling assets. This number must be added to the cash flow from operating activities. The equation to calculate free cash flow as defined in this textbook is shown in Figure 9.19. Note that different companies may have different definitions of free cash flow; therefore, they may use different equations from what is presented in here.

Free Cash Flow = Net Cash Provided by Operating Activities – Net Cash Used by Investing Activities

FIGURE 9.19

The information from Soho's statement of cash flows in Figure 9.12 can be used to calculate free cash flow. Soho Supplies' statement of cash flows for the year ended December 31, 2020, reported a decrease in cash due to operations of $77,689 and a decrease in cash due to investments of $142,518. Using the equation from Figure 9.19, Soho's free cash flow can be calculated as follows.

$$\text{Free Cash Flow} = -\$77{,}689 - \$142{,}518$$

$$= -\$220{,}207$$

The negative free cash flow is an unfavourable indicator of Soho's financial health. Investors and lenders often use free cash flow as a measure of a company's ability to grow its capacity and to pay them back in the form of loan repayment and dividends. Therefore, they are looking for a positive or increasing cash flow. Despite generating over half a million dollars in net income, Soho has a negative free cash flow, mainly due to inventory and equipment purchases. Because the income statement does not include such transactions as asset purchases, financial statement users should not assess a company's financial well-being only from the income statement. The statement of cash flows provides additional insight into Soho's activities during the year.

External users of the financial statements must be aware that many factors affect a company's reported cash flow and that different companies may interpret accounting guidelines differently.

As well, companies can influence their cash flow in various ways, and external users need to be particularly well informed before making any decisions.

> **Pause & Reflect**
>
> **Exercise 9-3**
>
> Pacific Property Management Inc. has just prepared its statement of cash flows for December 31, 2020. It shows an increase in cash from operations of $235,000 and a decrease in cash due to investments of $78,000.
>
> a) Calculate Pacific's free cash flow.
>
> b) Is Pacific's free cash flow a favourable or unfavourable indicator of the company's financial health? Explain.
>
> See Appendix I for solutions.

An Ethical Approach to Cash Flow

LO 5

The accounting scandals that began in 2001 with Enron served as a warning to much of the financial community that income statements and balance sheets can be manipulated to present a false financial picture of a company. As a result, an increasing number of people started using the statement of cash flows as a more revealing snapshot of a company's financial well-being.

Indeed, the motivation behind relying more on a statement of cash flows to analyze company performance is understandable. Statements of cash flows are supposed to show where the money is coming from and where it is going. However, no financial statement is immune from flaws, and this is certainly also the case with statements of cash flows.

The following three situations should be viewed with caution when analyzing a company's statement of cash flows.

- **Some companies may stretch out their payables.** One way of artificially enhancing a company's cash position from operations is to deliberately delay paying bills. In fact, some companies will even go so far as to institute such a policy and label it as a form of good cash flow decision-making. Of course, the company has not improved its underlying cash flow but has simply manipulated it.
- **Some companies may finance their payables.** Some companies try to manipulate their statement of cash flows by having a third party pay their payables for them, although regulators have tried to crack down on this practice. This means that the company itself shows no payments in its cash flow and instead pays a fee to the third party at a later date. Picking and choosing the periods in which this is done artificially manipulates the statement of cash flows.

- **Some companies may shorten their collection of receivables.** While not necessarily a bad decision to collect faster from customers, this can have implications if it is done just to improve perceived cash flow. If collections that would normally happen in the next fiscal year are collected immediately to improve the cash flow in the current fiscal year, then the next fiscal year may show poor cash flow. This type of action merely delays reporting a poor cash flow.

In Summary

LO 1 Classify operating, investing and financing activities

- Balance sheets and income statements are prepared on an accrual basis, which involves recording transactions that do not necessarily involve any exchange of money. Statements of cash flows differ in that they reveal both the sources and uses of cash within a company.
- The statement of cash flows contains three sections: cash flow from operating activities, cash flow from investing activities and cash flow from financing activities.
- The cash flow from operating activities tracks the movement of cash related to day-to-day activities of the company.
- The cash flow from investing activities tracks the movement of cash on the basis of the purchases and sales of long-term assets.
- The cash flow from financing activities tracks the movement of cash related to the way a company receives money for financing purposes and pays it back.

LO 2 Prepare a statement of cash flows using the indirect method

- The indirect method of preparing a statement of cash flows starts with accrual-based net income from the income statement and adjusts it by adding or subtracting non-cash items and changes in current assets and current liabilities to reveal net cash flow from operating activities.
- The indirect method tends to be more commonly used in preparing a statement of cash flows, since the direct method takes a more burdensome approach to tracking cash receipts and payments.

LO 3 Calculate book value and cash received for selling long-term assets

- When selling long-term assets, the accumulated depreciation must also be cleared out. Accumulated depreciation, along with an asset's book value and gain (or loss) on disposal, must be taken into account in calculating cash proceeds from the disposal.

LO 4 Explain the concept of free cash flow and its importance for potential investors

- Free cash flow is the amount of cash remaining after a company has covered its operating activities and capital expenditures.
- Investors often use free cash flow as a measure of a company's cash-generating ability and its overall financial health.

LO 5 Discuss ethical issues related to cash flow

- Three situations should be viewed with caution when analyzing a company's statement of cash flows: some companies may stretch out their payables; some companies may finance their payables; and some companies may shorten their collections.

Review Exercise 9-1

Shown below is the balance sheet, income statement and notes for Dellray Inc.

Dellray Inc. Balance Sheet As at December 31		
	2020	**2019**
Assets		
Current Assets		
Cash	$1,085,700	$27,000
Accounts Receivable	370,000	400,000
Merchandise Inventory	290,000	250,000
Prepaid Expenses	29,000	21,000
Total Current Assets	1,774,700	698,000
Long-Term Assets		
Long-Term Investments[1]	560,000	600,000
Equipment[2]	1,300,000	1,100,000
Accumulated Depreciation	(206,000)	(156,000)
Total Long-Term Assets	1,654,000	1,544,000
Total Assets	$3,428,700	$2,242,000
Liabilities		
Current Liabilities		
Accounts Payable	$461,000	$342,000
Notes Payable, Current Portion[3]	75,000	65,000
Total Current Liabilities	536,000	407,000
Long-Term Liabilities		
Notes Payable, Long-Term Portion[3]	275,000	215,000
Bonds Payable[4]	96,000	90,000
Total Long-Term Liabilities	371,000	305,000
Total Liabilities	907,000	712,000
Shareholders' Equity		
Common Shares	400,000	320,000
Retained Earnings	2,121,700	1,210,000
Total Shareholders' Equity	2,521,700	1,530,000
Total Liabilities and Shareholders' Equity	$3,428,700	$2,242,000

Additional Information

(1) During 2020, Dellray Inc. did not purchase any long-term investments.
(2) During 2020, Dellray Inc. made purchases of equipment for $400,000.
(3) Dellray Inc. did not repay any notes payable during the year.
(4) The bonds were issued at par.

Dellray Inc. Income Statement For the Year Ended December 31, 2020	
Sales Revenue	$5,600,000
Cost of Goods Sold	2,968,000
Gross Profit	2,632,000
Operating Expenses	
Selling Expenses	
Depreciation Expense	80,000
Insurance Expense	8,000
Other Operating Expenses	367,300
Total Selling Expenses	455,300
Administrative Expenses	
Salaries Expense	766,000
Total Administrative Expenses	766,000
Total Operating Expenses	1,221,300
Income from Operations	1,410,700
Other Income and Expenses	
Gain on Sale of Investments	8,000
Loss on Sale of Factory Equipment	(10,000)
Income before Income Tax Expense	1,408,700
Income Tax Expense	422,000
Net Income	$986,700

Required

a) Prepare the statement of cash flows for 2020 using the indirect method. Include any notes if necessary.

b) Calculate and analyze Dellray's free cash flow for 2020.

See Appendix I for solutions.

Appendix 9A: The Direct Method

LO 6

Earlier in this chapter, a statement of cash flows was assembled using the indirect method. As you learned, the net cash flow from operating activities is the same whether the indirect method or the direct method is used—it is simply the way of calculating and presenting the information that differs, not the actual amount. The term "indirect" refers to tracking the changes to cash without direct reference to cash receipts or payments. The indirect method analyzes cash flow by starting with accrual-based net income and making related adjustments for changes on the balance sheet and income statement.

The **direct method** is the other way to prepare the statement of cash flows. Like the indirect method, the direct method breaks down the three ways of generating and using cash into operating activities, investing activities and financing activities. The difference is that the direct method prepares the operating activities section so that each income statement item is reported on a cash basis; that is, each item is adjusted to remove any accruals and report just cash. Therefore, the only difference in the step-by-step approach to preparing the statement of cash flows is step 2, as follows.

Step 1. Calculate the net increase (or decrease) in cash during the period.

Step 2. Calculate the net cash provided (or used) by operating activities using the direct method.

Step 3. Calculate the net cash provided (or used) by investing activities.

Step 4. Calculate the net cash provided (or used) by financing activities.

Step 5. Calculate the *total* net cash provided (or used) by operating investing and financing activities combined.

Step 6. Verify that the total net cash flow equals the ending cash balance less the beginning cash balance.

Step 7. Identify all non-cash transactions for disclosure in the notes to the financial statements.

To illustrate the direct method, we will use the same Soho Supplies balance sheet and income statement that were used for the indirect method. The balance sheet is shown in Figure 9A.1 and the income statement is shown in Figure 9A.2.

Soho Supplies
Balance Sheet
As at December 31, 2020

	2020	2019	Change
Assets			
Current Assets			
Cash	$349,935	$396,142	($46,207)
Accounts Receivable	1,286,138	1,065,812	220,326
Merchandise Inventory	1,683,560	840,091	843,469
Prepaid Insurance	48,612	42,625	5,987
Total Current Assets	3,368,245	2,344,670	1,023,575
Long-Term Assets			
Land[1]	0	50,000	(50,000)
Equipment[2]	322,518	120,000	202,518
Accumulated Depreciation	(79,262)	(36,000)	(43,262)
Total Long-Term Assets	243,256	134,000	109,256
Total Assets	$3,611,501	$2,478,670	$1,132,831
Liabilities			
Current Liabilities			
Accounts Payable	$783,602	$475,645	$307,957
Salaries Payable	25,000	50,000	(25,000)
Interest Payable	15,650	23,500	(7,850)
Income Taxes Payable	280,117	250,000	30,117
Notes Payable, Current Portion	380,000	240,000	140,000
Total Current Liabilities	1,484,369	1,039,145	445,224
Long-Term Liabilities			
Notes Payable, Long-Term Portion	420,000	356,000	64,000
Bonds Payable[3]	170,000	200,000	(30,000)
Total Long-Term Liabilities	590,000	556,000	34,000
Total Liabilities	2,074,369	1,595,145	479,224
Shareholders' Equity			
Contributed Capital			
Preferred Shares	10,000	0	10,000
Common Shares	5,000	5,000	0
Total Contributed Capital	15,000	5,000	10,000
Retained Earnings[4]	1,522,132	878,525	643,607
Total Shareholders' Equity	1,537,132	883,525	653,607
Total Liabilities and Shareholders' Equity	$3,611,501	$2,478,670	$1,132,831

Additional Information

(1) During 2020, land that cost $50,000 was sold for $60,000, resulting in a $10,000 gain on sale. The gain is reported on the income statement in the other income and expenses section.
(2) During 2020, Soho made purchases of equipment for $202,518.
(3) The bonds were issued at par.
(4) Soho declared and paid $10,000 in dividends in 2020.

FIGURE 9A.1

Soho Supplies Income Statement For the Year Ended December 31, 2020	
Sales Revenue	$8,685,025
Cost of Goods Sold	5,998,612
Gross Profit	2,686,413
Operating Expenses	
Salaries Expense	1,416,135
Depreciation Expense	43,262
Insurance Expense	16,000
Other Operating Expenses	235,417
Total Operating Expenses	1,710,814
Income from Operations	975,599
Other Income and Expenses	
Gain on Sale of Land	10,000
Interest Expense	(51,875)
Income before Income Tax Expense	933,724
Income Tax Expense	280,117
Net Income	$653,607

FIGURE 9A.2

For the operating activities section, the focus is on operating items that affect cash. Thus, depreciation is ignored, since depreciation is a transaction that does not affect cash. Also, the gain on the sale of land is ignored, since the sale of land is an investing activity. All other items on the income statement are examined and recorded on the statement of cash flows. These items are labelled (a) to (g) to correspond with the operating activities section of the statement of cash flows as shown in Figure 9A.10.

Cash Receipts

(a) Cash Received from Customers

The first item on the statement of cash flows prepared using the direct method is cash receipts. For simplicity, let us assume that Soho Supplies' only source of cash receipts is from sales to its customers. Also assume that all sales are credit sales. In preparing the statement of cash flows, the credit sales balance has to be converted to the actual amount of cash collected from customers during 2020. The amount of sales revenue from Soho's income statement and the beginning and ending accounts receivable balances from Soho's balance sheet can be used to calculate the amount of cash collection from customers.

An analysis of the T-account in Figure 9A.3 will help visualize the calculation.

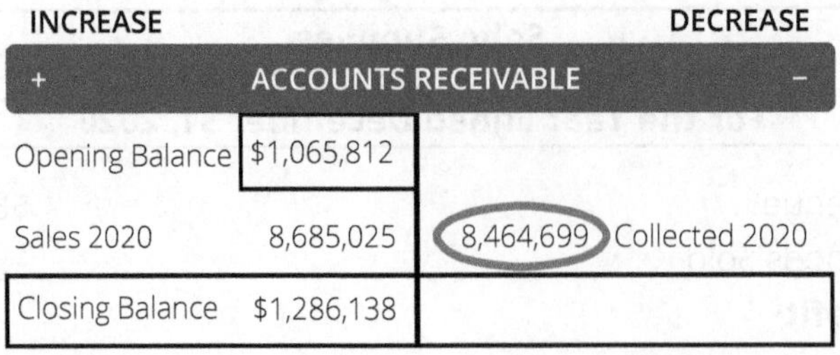

FIGURE 9A.3

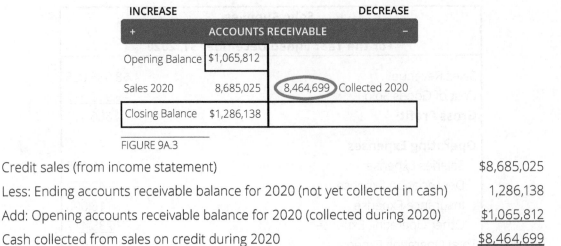

Credit sales (from income statement)	$8,685,025
Less: Ending accounts receivable balance for 2020 (not yet collected in cash)	1,286,138
Add: Opening accounts receivable balance for 2020 (collected during 2020)	$1,065,812
Cash collected from sales on credit during 2020	$8,464,699

We now know that $8,464,699 cash was collected from sales during 2020.

Cash Payments

Next, Soho's cash payments are calculated by analyzing the changes to each of the expenses listed on the income statement and their related balance sheet accounts.

(b) Cash Payments for Merchandise Inventory

There are two steps involved in calculating the cash payments for inventory purchased.

First, the amount of inventory purchased during the year must be calculated. From the balance sheet, we know the beginning and ending balances of inventory. The income statement tells us the cost of goods sold. Based on COGS and inventory balances, the amount of purchases can be calculated by solving the missing number in the merchandise inventory T-account, as shown in Figure 9A.4.

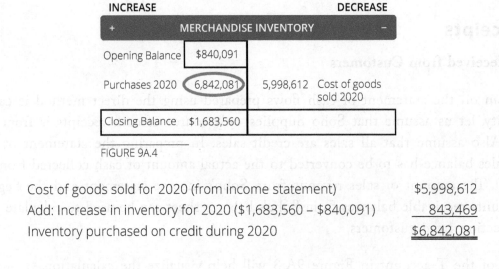

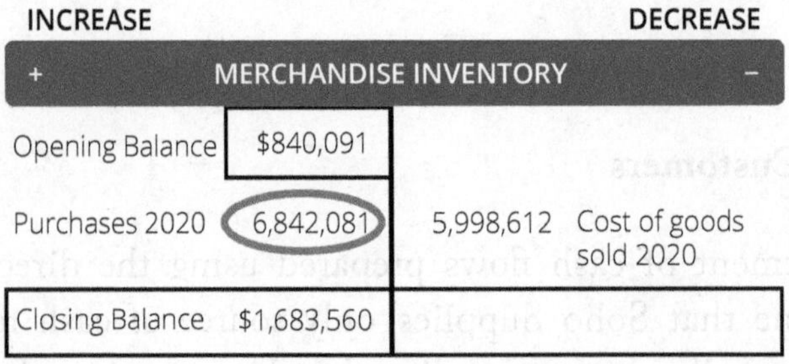

FIGURE 9A.4

Cost of goods sold for 2020 (from income statement)	$5,998,612
Add: Increase in inventory for 2020 ($1,683,560 – $840,091)	843,469
Inventory purchased on credit during 2020	$6,842,081

Now that the amount of inventory purchased during the year is known, this figure can be used to determine the cash payments for inventory.

A few assumptions have to be made about how inventory is purchased and paid for. One assumption is that inventory is purchased on credit and paid for at a later date. Another assumption is that accounts payable is used only for suppliers of inventory. With two assumptions in place, the inventory purchases for 2020 can be added to accounts payable to determine how much cash was paid for inventory.

This is shown in the T-account in Figure 9A.5.

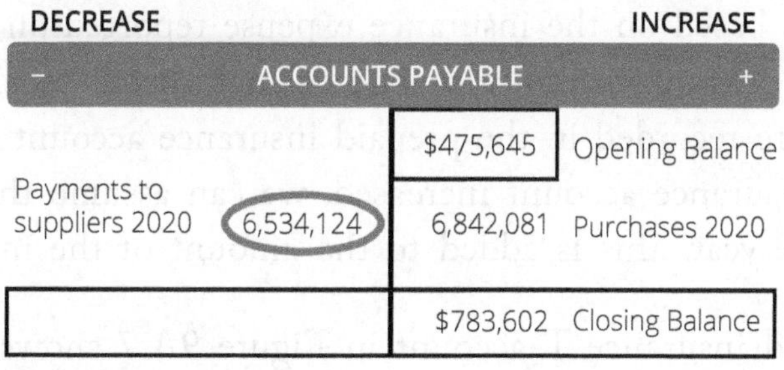

FIGURE 9A.5

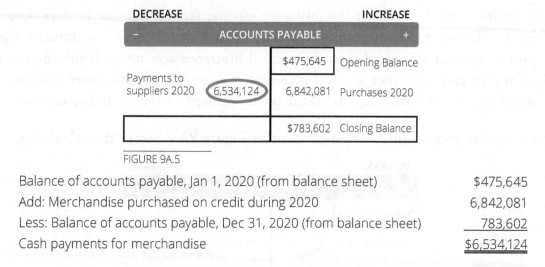

Balance of accounts payable, Jan 1, 2020 (from balance sheet)	$475,645
Add: Merchandise purchased on credit during 2020	6,842,081
Less: Balance of accounts payable, Dec 31, 2020 (from balance sheet)	783,602
Cash payments for merchandise	$6,534,124

(c) Cash Payments to Employees

To analyze Soho's cash payments to employees for salaries expense for the year, start with the expense on the income statement. Next, adjust this amount by the change in salaries payable during the year. Because salaries are normally paid within a short time period of when they are accrued (usually weeks or a month), we will assume that all salaries payable at January 1, 2020, were fully paid during the year.

The analysis of the salaries payable T-account in Figure 9A.6 shows the calculation.

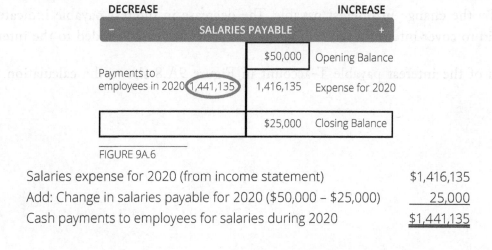

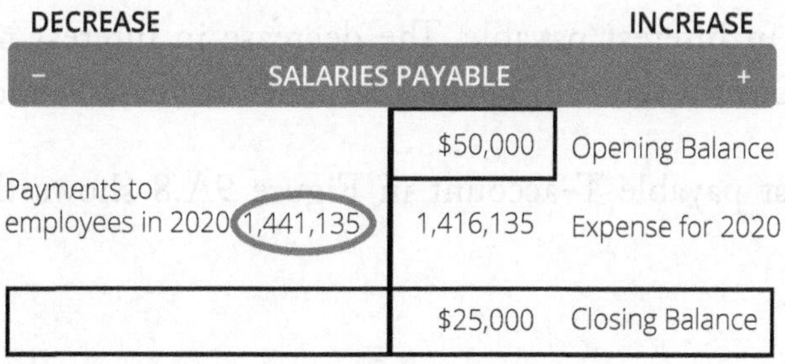

FIGURE 9A.6

Salaries expense for 2020 (from income statement)	$1,416,135
Add: Change in salaries payable for 2020 ($50,000 – $25,000)	25,000
Cash payments to employees for salaries during 2020	$1,441,135

(d) Cash Payments for Other Operating Expenses

The next expense on the income statement is other operating expenses. None of the remaining current assets or current liabilities are related to this item on the income statement. For example, prepaid insurance is related to insurance expense and interest payable is related to interest expense.

Thus, there are no adjustments to the amount of cash for other operating expenses, and the amount shown on the income statement ($235,417) is the amount reported as cash payments on the statement of cash flows.

(e) Cash Payments for Insurance

Cash paid for insurance is based on the insurance expense reported on the income statement and adjusted by the change in prepaid insurance on the balance sheet. Recall that insurance premiums that are paid in advance are recorded in the prepaid insurance account until the amount has been used. Since the prepaid insurance account increased, we can assume that more cash was paid for prepaid insurance over the year. This is added to the amount of the insurance expense.

The analysis of the prepaid insurance T-account in Figure 9A.7 shows the calculation.

INCREASE +	PREPAID INSURANCE		DECREASE −
Opening Balance	$42,625		
Paid during 2020	21,987	16,000	Insurance expense 2020
Closing Balance	$48,612		

FIGURE 9A.7

Insurance expense incurred during 2020 (from income statement)	$16,000
Add: Change in prepaid insurance for 2020 ($48,612 – $42,625)	5,987
Cash payments for insurance during 2020	$21,987

(f) Cash Payments for Interest

Interest expense is the next cash item on the income statement. The amount reported as an expense is adjusted by the change in interest payable. The decrease in interest payable indicates that more cash was paid to cover interest owed during the year. This decrease is added to the interest expense.

The analysis of the interest payable T-account in Figure 9A.8 shows the calculation.

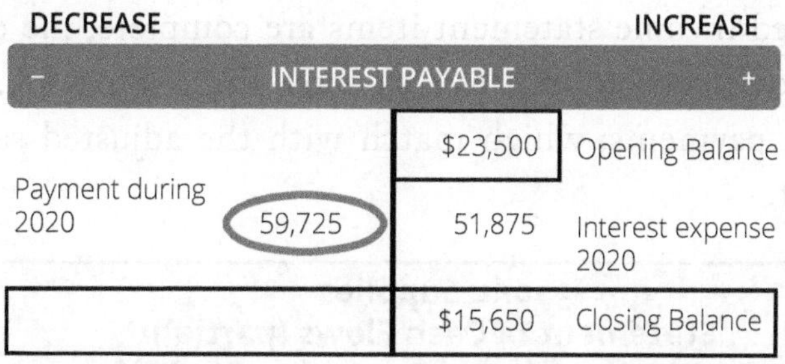

FIGURE 9A.8

Interest expense incurred during 2020 (from income statement)	$51,875
Add: Change in interest payable for 2020 ($23,500 – $15,650)	7,850
Cash payments for interest during 2020	$59,725

(g) Cash Payments for Income Taxes

The last cash expense is income taxes. The balance sheet account, income tax payable, is used to adjust the expense to determine the actual cash amount paid. Since income tax payable increased over the year, it indicates that the company was able to defer paying income taxes. This saves cash, thus reducing the amount of cash paid for income tax during 2020 to $250,000.

The analysis of the income tax payable T-account in Figure 9A.9 shows the calculation.

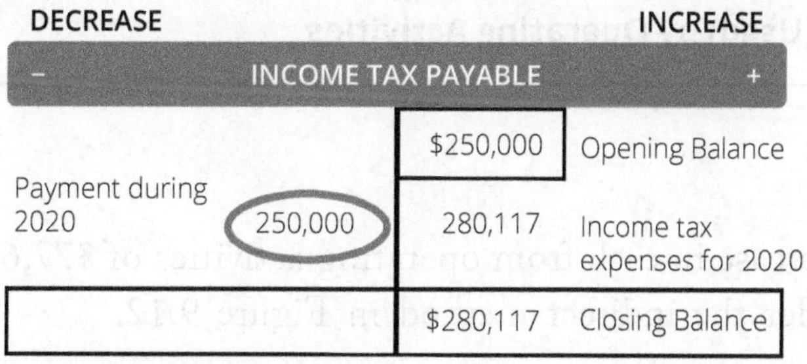

FIGURE 9A.9

Income tax expense for 2020 (from income statement)	$280,117
Less: Change in income tax payable for 2020 ($250,000 – $280,117)	(30,117)
Cash payments for income tax during 2020	$250,000

Now that all the cash-related income statement items are complete, the operating activities section of the statement of cash flows can be prepared, as shown in Figure 9A.10. The section is divided into cash receipts and cash payments, which match with the adjusted sales and adjusted expenses from the income statement.

Soho Supplies Statement of Cash Flows (partial) For the Year Ended December 31, 2020		
Cash Flow from Operating Activities		
Cash Receipts		
Cash Received from Customers		$8,464,699 (a)
Cash Payments		
Payments for Merchandise Inventory	$6,534,124 (b)	
Payments to Employees	1,441,135 (c)	
Payments for Other Operating Expenses	235,417 (d)	
Payments for Insurance	21,987 (e)	
Payments for Interest	59,725 (f)	
Payments for Income Taxes	250,000 (g)	
Total Cash Payments		8,542,388
Net Cash Provided (Used) by Operating Activities		($77,689)

FIGURE 9A.10

You will notice that the decrease in cash from operating activities of $77,689 matches the statement of cash flows prepared under the indirect method in Figure 9.12.

The investing and financing activities of the statement of cash flows under the direct method are analyzed and prepared in the same manner as for the indirect method. These two sections are explained in the main part of this chapter. The completed statement of cash flows prepared using the direct method is shown in Figure 9A.11. Notice that the bottom part of the statement provides a schedule reconciling net income to the net cash flows from operating activities. This schedule is similar to the cash flow from operating activities section in the statement of cash flows prepared by the indirect method (see Figure 9.12).

Soho Supplies Statement of Cash Flows For the Year Ended December 31, 2020		
Cash Flow from Operating Activities		
Cash Receipts		
Cash Received from Customers		$8,464,699
Cash Payments		
Payments for Merchandise Inventory	$6,534,124	
Payments to Employees	1,441,135	
Payments for Other Operating Expenses	235,417	
Payments for Insurance	21,987	
Payments for Interest	59,725	
Payments for Income Taxes	250,000	
Total Cash Payments		8,542,388
Net Cash Provided (Used) by Operating Activities		(77,689)
Cash Flow from Investing Activities		
Sale of Land	60,000	
Purchase of Equipment	(202,518)	
Net Cash Provided (Used) by Investing Activities		(142,518)
Cash Flow from Financing Activities		
Proceeds from Notes Payable[1]	204,000	
Payments toward Bonds Payable	(30,000)	
Payment of Cash Dividends	(10,000)	
Issuance of Preferred Shares	10,000	
Net Cash Provided (Used) by Financing Activities		174,000
Net Increase (Decrease) in Cash		(46,207)
Cash at the Beginning of the Year		396,142
Cash at the End of the Year		$349,935
Reconciliation of Net Income with Net Cash Provided (Used) by Operating Activities		
Cash Flow from Operating Activities		
Net Income	$653,607	
Adjustments to Reconcile Net Income to Net Cash Provided (Used) by Operating Activities		
Depreciation	43,262	
Gain on Sale of Land	(10,000)	
Changes in Operating Assets and Liabilities		
Increase in Accounts Receivable	(220,326)	
Increase in Prepaid Expenses	(5,987)	
Increase in Merchandise Inventory	(843,469)	
Increase in Accounts Payable	307,957	
Decrease in Salaries Payable	(25,000)	
Decrease in Interest Payable	(7,850)	
Increase in Income Taxes Payable	30,117	
Net Cash Provided (Used) by Operating Activities	($77,689)	

Additional Notes

[1] Soho Supplies did not borrow any additional notes payable during the year.

FIGURE 9A.11

Summary of the Statement of Cash Flows—Direct Method

This appendix demonstrates many of the adjustments made to net income in order to arrive at the net cash provided (used) by operating activities under the direct method. Figure 9A.12 summarizes these adjustments.

Income Statement Adjustments to Cash Flows from Operating Activities—Direct Method		
Income Statement Item	**Adjustments**	**Cash Flows from Operating Activities**
Sales	Increase (–) or decrease (+) in Accounts Receivable	Cash Received from Customers
Cost of Goods Sold	Increase (+) or decrease (–) in Merchandise Inventory and Increase (–) or decrease (+) in Accounts Payable	Cash Payments for Merchandise Inventory
Salaries Expense	Increase (+) or decrease (–) in Salaries Payable	Cash Payments to Employees
Other Operating Expenses	Increase (+) or decrease (–) in Prepaid Expenses and Increase (–) or decrease (+) in Accrued Liabilities	Cash Payments for Other Operating Expenses
Insurance Expense	Increase (+) or decrease (–) in Prepaid Insurance	Cash Payments for Insurance
Interest Expense	Increase (+) or decrease (–) in Interest Payable	Cash Payments for Interest
Income Tax Expense	Increase (–) or decrease (+) in Income Tax Payable	Cash Payments for Income Taxes

FIGURE 9A.12

Note that two of the items on the income statement do not appear as adjustments to cash flows from operating activities: depreciation and gain on sale of land. As you learned earlier in the chapter, depreciation does not involve a cash outflow so it is not reported in the statement of cash flows prepared using the direct method. The gain on the sale of land is not an operating activity; however, the proceeds from the sale of land are an investing activity and are therefore reported in the cash flow from investing activities section.

ASPE vs. IFRS

Under ASPE, net income must be reconciled to net cash provided (used) by operating activities under both direct and indirect methods.

Under IFRS, net income must be reconciled to net cash provided (used) by operating activities only under the indirect method.

In Summary

LO 6 Prepare a statement of cash flows using the direct method

- The direct method applies only to the operating activities section of the statement of cash flows.
- Under the direct method, all cash items on the income statement are reported separately on the statement of cash flows, after being adjusted by changes in related accounts from the balance sheet.
- Under the direct method, a schedule reconciling net income to the net cash flows from operating activities is included at the bottom of the statement of cash flows. This schedule is similar to the cash flow from operating activities section in the statement of cash flows prepared by the indirect method.

Review Exercise 9A-1

The balance sheet, income statement and notes for Harmony Inc. are as follows.

Harmony Inc. Balance Sheet As at December 31		
	2020	**2019**
Assets		
Current Assets		
Cash	$1,085,700	$27,000
Accounts Receivable	370,000	400,000
Merchandise Inventory	290,000	250,000
Prepaid Insurance	29,000	21,000
Total Current Assets	1,774,700	698,000
Long-Term Assets		
Long-Term Investments[1]	560,000	600,000
Equipment[2]	1,300,000	1,100,000
Accumulated Depreciation	(206,000)	(156,000)
Total Long-Term Assets	1,654,000	1,544,000
Total Assets	$3,428,700	$2,242,000
Liabilities		
Current Liabilities		
Accounts Payable[3]	$461,000	$342,000
Notes Payable, Current Portion	75,000	65,000
Total Current Liabilities	536,000	407,000
Long-Term Liabilities		
Notes Payable, Long-Term Portion	275,000	215,000
Bonds Payable[4]	96,000	90,000
Total Long-Term Liabilities	371,000	305,000
Total Liabilities	907,000	712,000
Shareholders' Equity		
Common Shares	400,000	320,000
Retained Earnings	2,121,700	1,210,000
Total Shareholders' Equity	2,521,700	1,530,000
Total Liabilities and Shareholders' Equity	$3,428,700	$2,242,000

Additional Information

[1] During 2020, Harmony Inc. did not purchase any long-term investments.

[2] During 2020, Harmony Inc. made purchases of equipment for $400,000.

[3] Assume accounts payable is only used for suppliers of inventory.

[4] The bonds were issued at par.

Harmony Inc. **Income Statement** **For the Year Ended December 31, 2020**	
Sales Revenue[1]	$5,600,000
Cost of Goods Sold	2,968,000
Gross Profit	2,632,000
Operating Expenses	
Salaries Expense	766,000
Depreciation Expense	80,000
Insurance Expense	8,000
Other Operating Expenses	367,300
Total Operating Expenses	1,221,300
Income from Operations	1,410,700
Other Income and Expenses	
Gain on Sale of Investments	8,000
Loss on Sale of Factory Equipment	(10,000)
Income before Income Tax Expense	1,408,700
Income Tax Expense	422,000
Net Income	$986,700

Additional Information

(1) Assume sales in 2020 were all received in cash.

Prepare the statement of cash flows for 2020 using the direct method. Show your calculations separately.

See Appendix I for solutions.

Appendix 9B: Preparing a Statement of Cash Flows Using a Spreadsheet—Indirect Method

LO 7

This appendix shows how to use a spreadsheet (work sheet) to prepare a statement of cash flows under the indirect method. A spreadsheet is a valuable tool to help organize and verify all the transactions that affect a company's cash balance.

To illustrate, we will once again use the example of Soho Supplies. We will use Soho's comparative balance sheet from Figure 9.3 (including the additional information), and its income statement from Figure 9.4. We will also identify all the transaction items in the spreadsheet using the same alphabetical codes that we used throughout the chapter examples.

- Cash flows from operating activities, items (d) to (k)
- Cash flows from investing activities, items (l) to (n)
- Cash flows from financing activities, items (o) to (s)

Soho's transactions for the year ended December 31, 2020, are shown below. (They include the additional information that accompanies Soho's balance sheet in Figure 9.3.)

(a) Net income for the year, $653,607

(b) Depreciation expense, $43,262

(c) Gain on sale of land, $10,000

(d) Increase in accounts receivable, $220,326

(e) Increase in prepaid insurance, $5,987

(f) Increase in merchandise inventory, $843,469

(g) Increase in accounts payable, $307,957

(h) Decrease in salaries payable, $25,000

(i) Decrease in interest payable, $7,850

(j) Increase in income taxes payable, $30,117

(k) Net cash provided (used) by operating activities, ($77,689)

Additional Information from Balance Sheet (Figure 9.3)

(l) During 2020, land that cost $50,000 was sold for $60,000, resulting in a $10,000 gain on sale

(m) During 2020, Soho made purchases of equipment for $202,518

(n) Net cash provided (used) by investing activities, ($142,518)

(o) Increase in (i.e. proceeds from) notes payable (total), $204,000: current portion, $64,000; long-term portion, $140,000

(p) Decrease in (i.e. payment toward) bonds payable, $30,000

Additional Information from Balance Sheet (Figure 9.3)

(q) Soho declared and paid $10,000 in cash dividends in 2020

(r) Increase in (i.e. issuance of) preferred shares, $10,000

(s) Net cash provided (used) by financing activities, $174,000

Preparing the Spreadsheet

To prepare the spreadsheet using a spreadsheet application, refer to Figure 9B.1 and follow these steps.

Step 1. Set up a spreadsheet with separate columns for the following items: the names of the balance sheet accounts; the December 31, 2019 balances of those accounts; a column for changes that are debits; a column for changes that are credits; and the December 31, 2020 balances of the balance sheet accounts. It is also a good idea to add some narrow columns in which to enter alphabetical codes (as in Figure 9B.1), so that you can track and cross-reference the entries that you make.

Step 2. In the first column, list the name of each balance sheet account.

Step 3. In the second column, enter the balance for each balance sheet account as at December 31, 2019. In the last column, enter the corresponding balances as at December 31, 2020. Use parentheses for all credit balances. Total each of these columns, ensuring that each one totals zero.

Step 4. Start a statement of cash flows section below the balance sheet accounts. Enter the amount of net income (debit) as your first entry, and make a corresponding (credit) entry to the retained earnings account in the balance sheet section.

Step 5. Analyze the change in each non-cash account to determine the net increase (decrease) in cash flows. Enter the amount of the change as an adjustment in the appropriate changes column in the balance sheet section (debit or credit). In the statement of cash flows section, enter a corresponding entry for each adjustment under the appropriate classification: operating, investing, financing, or non-cash investing and financing activity, if any. (Note that Soho does not have any non-cash investing and financing activities—this is simply mentioned for completeness.)

Step 6. When all changes have been analyzed and entered, calculate the net increase (decrease) in cash, and enter the amount of the change in the cash account.

Step 7. Total each changes column (debit and credit) for the balance sheet accounts. These two totals should be equal. Do the same for the debit and credit columns for the statement of cash flows section, and ensure that they too are equal.

Analyzing Account Changes

When you begin to analyze the accounts, you may notice that many of the changes are fairly straightforward while some are a bit more complex. Just as we used T-account analysis to help explain some of the account changes earlier in the chapter, it may help to practice with something similar to journal entries when working through some of the adjustments in the spreadsheet approach. The following items are some of the more complex adjustments.

Retained earnings increased by $643,607 during 2020, which breaks down as follows.

(a) Net Income (operating activities)	653,607	
Retained Earnings		653,607
(q) Retained Earnings	10,000	
Payment of Cash Dividend (financing activities)		10,000

During 2020, land that cost $50,000 was sold for $60,000, resulting in a $10,000 gain on sale.

(c)(1) Proceeds from sale of land (investing activities)	60,000	
Land		50,000
Gain on sale of land (operating activities)		10,000

Preparing the Statement of Cash Flows

Once you have completed all the steps to prepare the spreadsheet, the statement of cash flows can be prepared using the information from the bottom section of the spreadsheet. In fact, if you compare the spreadsheet in Figure 9B.1 with the statement of cash flows in Figure 9.12, you will notice that they are the same.

	A	B	C	D	E	F	G
1	**Soho Supplies**						
2	**Spreadsheet for Statement of Cash Flows**						
3	**For the Year Ended December 31, 2020**						
4		**Balance**		**Changes**			**Balance**
5		**Dec 31, 2019**		**Debit**		**Credit**	**Dec 31, 2020**
6	**Balance Sheet Accounts**						
7	Cash	396,142			(s)	46,207	349,935
8	Accounts Receivable	1,065,812	(d)	220,326			1,286,138
9	Merchandise Inventory	840,091	(f)	843,469			1,683,560
10	Prepaid Insurance	42,625	(e)	5,987			48,612
11	Land	50,000			(c)	50,000	0
12	Equipment	120,000	(m)	202,518			322,518
13	Accumulated Depreciation	(36,000)			(b)	43,262	(79,262)
14	Accounts Payable	(475,645)			(g)	307,957	(783,602)
15	Salaries Payable	(50,000)	(h)	25,000			(25,000)
16	Interest Payable	(23,500)	(i)	7,850			(15,650)
17	Income Taxes Payable	(250,000)			(j)	30,117	(280,117)
18	Notes Payable	(596,000)			(o)	204,000	(800,000)
19	Bonds Payable	(200,000)	(p)	30,000			(170,000)
20	Preferred Shares	0			(r)	10,000	(10,000)
21	Common Shares	(5,000)					(5,000)
22	Retained Earnings	(878,525)	(q)	10,000	(a)	653,607	(1,522,132)
23	Totals			1,345,150		1,345,150	
24							
25	**Statement of Cash Flows**						
26	Operating Activities						
27	Net Income		(a)	653,607			
28	Depreciation		(b)	43,262			
29	Gain on Sale of Land				(c)	10,000	
30	Increase in Accounts Receivable				(d)	220,326	
31	Increase in Prepaid Insurance				(e)	5,987	
32	Increase in Merchandise Inventory				(f)	843,469	
33	Increase in Accounts Payable		(g)	307,957			
34	Decrease in Salaries Payable				(h)	25,000	
35	Decrease in Interest Payable				(i)	7,850	
36	Increase in Income Taxes Payable		(j)	30,117			
37	Investing Activities						
38	Sale of Land		(c)	60,000			
39	Purchase of Equipment				(m)	202,518	
40	Financing Activities						
41	Proceeds of Bank Loan		(o)	204,000			
42	Payment on Notes Payable				(p)	30,000	
43	Payment of Cash Dividend				(q)	10,000	
44	Issuance of Preferred Shares		(r)	10,000			
45	Net Increase (Decrease) in Cash		(s)	46,207			
46	Totals			1,355,150		1,355,150	

FIGURE 9B.1

In Summary

LO 7 Prepare a statement of cash flows in a spreadsheet using the indirect method.

- A spreadsheet is a valuable tool to help organize and verify all the transactions that affect a company's cash balance. It is divided into two sections: the balance sheet accounts and the statement of cash flows.
- A spreadsheet allows you to analyze the change in each non-cash account to determine the net increase (decrease) in cash flows.
- The statement of cash flows is prepared using the information from the bottom section of the spreadsheet, which shows the net increase (decrease) in cash from operating, investing and financing activities.

Review Exercise 9B-1

The balance sheet and income statement for Mountain Slope Merchandise Inc. are presented below.

Mountain Slope Merchandise Inc. Balance Sheet As at December 31		
	2021	**2020**
Assets		
Cash	$6,300	$69,000
Accounts Receivable	63,000	36,000
Merchandise Inventory	63,000	75,000
Total Current Assets	132,300	180,000
Land	300,000	300,000
Equipment	510,000	450,000
Accumulated Depreciation	(85,800)	(75,000)
Total Assets	$856,500	$855,000
Liabilities		
Current Liabilities		
Accounts Payable	$69,000	$99,000
Notes Payable, Current Portion	36,000	36,000
Total Current Liabilities	105,000	135,000
Notes Payable, Long-Term Portion	144,000	180,000
Total Liabilities	249,000	315,000
Shareholders' Equity		
Contributed Capital		
Preferred Shares	15,000	0
Common Shares	45,000	45,000
Total Contributed Capital	60,000	45,000
Retained Earnings	547,500	495,000
Total Shareholders' Equity	607,500	540,000
Total Liabilities and Shareholders' Equity	$856,500	$855,000

Mountain Slope Merchandise Inc. Income Statement For the Year Ended December 31, 2021	
Sales	$483,000
Cost of Goods Sold	338,100
Gross Profit	144,900
Operating Expenses	
Depreciation Expense	10,800
Other Operating Expenses	59,100
Total Operating Expenses	69,900
Income before Income Tax Expense	75,000
Income Tax Expense	22,500
Net Income (Loss)	$52,500

Notes: The company did not sell any equipment during the year. They also did not sign any additional note payable in 2021. No dividends were declared or paid during the year.

Using the information above, prepare a statement of cash flows under the indirect method using a spreadsheet.

See Appendix I for solutions.

Chapter 10
Financial Statement Analysis

Learning Objectives

LO 1 Explain the importance of analyzing financial statements

LO 2 Calculate and apply liquidity ratios
- Working Capital
- Current Ratio
- Quick Ratio

LO 3 Calculate and apply profitability ratios
- Gross Profit Margin
- Net Profit Margin
- Return on Equity
- Return on Common Shareholders' Equity
- Return on Assets
- Asset Turnover

LO 4 Calculate and apply operations management ratios
- Inventory Turnover Ratio
- Days' Sales in Inventory
- Days' Sales Outstanding
- Accounts Receivable Turnover Ratio

LO 5 Calculate and apply solvency ratios
- Debt-to-Equity Ratio
- Times Interest Earned Ratio
- Debt-to-Total-Assets Ratio

LO 6 Calculate and apply capital market ratios
- Book Value per Common Share
- Dividend Yield
- Earnings per Share
- Price–Earnings Ratio

LO 7 Conduct a horizontal and vertical analysis of financial statements
- Horizontal Analysis—Balance Sheet
- Vertical Analysis—Balance Sheet
- Horizontal Analysis—Income Statement
- Vertical Analysis—Income Statement
- Computerized Financial Analysis

LO 8 Identify the limitations of financial statement analysis

MAKING IT REAL TO YOU

A friend has come to you seeking advice about investing in the stock market. They know you have just finished taking an accounting course that included a chapter on financial statement analysis. While you are no expert, you can advise them on where to locate a company's financial statements and what information would be most important to them as an investor.

Financial statement analysis may also be important when you are considering employment with a company. Trend analysis and ratios can reveal how well the company manages its business and provide insight into its overall profitability. This may help you determine whether or not the company would offer a stable work environment where you would not have to worry about it going out of business.

If you were a creditor or supplier looking to extend short-term credit, you would be interested in determining how able the company is to pay its current debts, and whether this ability has improved or deteriorated over the past few years.

This chapter provides information from the financial statements of a real Canadian company from which you may have purchased goods or services, making the results of the financial analysis even more real to you!

The Importance of Financial Statement Analysis

LO 1

In your studies so far, you have learned how to prepare the financial statements for sole proprietorships, partnerships and corporations. These statements provide a basic set of information about a company and are used in decision-making, both internally and externally. Internal users, such as managers and executives, analyze financial information to correct negative results and take advantage of positive results. External users, such as investors and suppliers, analyze financial information to determine whether to invest money or extend credit terms. Financial statement analysis focuses on four areas of information that are critical to decision-making:

- Liquidity—a company's ability to convert current assets into cash
- Profitability—a company's ability to generate profits
- Operations management—a company's ability to manage its assets, such as inventory and accounts receivable
- Solvency—a company's ability to cover its long-term debt obligations as they become due

Financial statement analysis also uses *capital market ratios* to assess a company's potential to generate positive returns for shareholders.

All of these areas of financial statement analysis are related. For instance, a company's ability to convert its current assets into cash (liquidity) can affect its ability to take advantage of profit-generating opportunities (profitability). Liquidity also affects the company's ability to purchase assets or inventory (operations management) and to cover its debts as they become due (solvency). If the company is unable to purchase inventory or expand its operations, this in turn can affect its profitability. Furthermore, if the company cannot meet its debt obligations, this affects its credit standing and hence its ability to obtain any necessary financing.

There are different ways to analyze a company's financial statements. One way is to calculate ratios based on the numbers from the financial statements. While each ratio has its own merits, one ratio alone does not provide users with a complete picture of the company's financial health. Another way is to perform a horizontal or vertical analysis of the financial statements, looking at trends or the relationship between items.

Other key information comes from additional official sources. The first source is **Management's Discussion and Analysis (MD&A)**, a special section that is included in a company's annual report filed with the security regulators for each province or territory. In the MD&A, management provides shareholders with an analysis of the company's past and current performance, and a discussion of its future plans and projected performance. The second source is the report on internal control by management, which is required for corporate governance. In this report, the CEO and CFO certify the fairness of the financial statements and the effectiveness of the company's internal controls. A report on internal control must be accompanied by formal verification made by a public accounting firm; both must be included in the company's annual report.

This chapter illustrates how to calculate important ratios and how to analyze them to better understand the complex nature of a corporation's financial status. Our calculations are based on the financial results of Leon's Furniture Limited, a well-known, successful Canadian retailer in the home furniture and appliance industry. We will begin our discussion with coverage of the liquidity ratios.

Liquidity Analysis

LO 2

The comparative balance sheet for Leon's Furniture Limited is shown in Figure 10.1. A **comparative balance sheet** is a balance sheet that shows the balances for multiple years. For readability, a single column is used for each year. Leon's Furniture is made up of several subsidiary companies, many of which also sell furniture, and so it reports using consolidated financial statements. (The company calls this the consolidated statements of financial position; recall that is the usual term under IFRS.) The comparative balance sheet allows users to easily calculate various financial ratios for a company to better understand its finances. Note that throughout the chapter, all of Leon's data is presented in thousands, with the exception of share data. You will also notice that Leon's uses some terminology that is more common under IFRS, such as "non-current" instead of "long-term."

Leon's Furniture Limited
Consolidated Statements of Financial Position
As at December 31, 2018 and 2017

($ in thousands)	2018	2017
ASSETS		
Current assets		
Cash and cash equivalents	$90,267	$36,207
Restricted marketable securities	5,994	13,778
Debt securities	54,759	41,128
Equity securities	33,862	26,199
Trade receivables	122,131	138,516
Income taxes receivable	8,413	2,042
Inventories	329,317	317,914
Deferred acquisition costs	7,899	5,841
Deferred financing costs	276	541
Prepaid expenses and other assets	8,335	6,382
Total current assets	$661,253	$588,548
Non-current assets		
Other assets	484	
Deferred acquisition costs	11,751	14,632
Loan receivable	13,191	-
Property, plant and equipment	321,597	336,748
Investment properties	17,072	17,529
Intangibles	300,896	306,286
Goodwill	390,120	390,120
Deferred income tax assets	7,208	7,592
Total non-current assets	$1,062,319	$1,072,907
Total assets	$1,723,572	$1,661,455

Leon's Furniture Limited Consolidated Statements of Financial Position (continued) As at December 31, 2018 and 2017		
($ in thousands)	**2018**	**2017**
LIABILITIES AND SHAREHOLDERS' EQUITY		
Current liabilities		
Trade and other payables	$247,136	$234,478
Provisions	11,687	8,791
Income taxes payable	7,338	7,517
Customers' deposits	146,362	128,078
Finance lease liability	1,415	1,421
Dividends payable	10,690	9,140
Deferred warranty plan revenue	38,180	24,979
Loans and borrowings	144,712	-
Other liabilities	-	5,434
Total current liabilities	$607,520	$419,838
Non-current liabilities		
Loans and borrowings	-	194,439
Convertible debentures	48,435	48,004
Finance lease liability	7,784	9,053
Deferred warranty plan revenue	110,126	122,773
Redeemable share liability	13	157
Deferred rent liabilities and lease inducements	11,021	10,791
Deferred income tax liabilities	81,311	83,352
Total non-current liabilities	$258,690	$468,569
Total liabilities	$866,210	$888,407
Shareholders' equity		
Common shares	$111,956	$93,392
Equity component of convertible debentures	3,546	3,555
Retained earnings	743,399	674,883
Accumulated other comprehensive income	(1,539)	1,218
Total shareholders' equity	$857,362	$773,048
Total liabilities and shareholders' equity	$1,723,572	$1,661,455

FIGURE 10.1

We will dissect sections of the balance sheet to perform our initial analysis: the calculation of ratios. Ratios measure four different aspects of a company's financial situation: liquidity, profitability, operations management and solvency. For a public company, we can also measure corporate performance. By comparing ratios for Leon's Furniture to industry averages, we can assess if the company is performing relatively well or relatively poorly.

Industry averages are available online through many financial research websites. Industry financial ratios are grouped by a six-digit code within the North American Industry Classification System (NAICS) Canada. NAICS is used by government agencies to classify business entities by industry. For instance, Leon's Furniture Limited is classified as NAICS Code 442110–Furniture Stores. However, as current information for the Canadian industry is not available as of this writing, we have used ratios for the furniture and fixtures industry in the United States, provided by CSIMarket, a digital financial media company. (Note that some industry ratios have been rounded to whole numbers for simplicity.)

In our discussion of Leon's Furniture, we will compare its ratios from one year to the next and to sample industry averages. Both Leon's ratios and the industry averages are presented here for illustrative purposes only.

Liquidity refers to the ability of a company to convert current assets into cash in order to repay its short-term debt obligations. The more liquid a company is, the more easily it can cover obligations, such as accounts payable and loan payments. There are several ways to measure liquidity: working capital, current ratio and quick ratio, which were introduced in a previous chapter.

Working Capital

Working capital is a measure of liquidity that assesses the adequacy of a company's current assets to cover its current liabilities. The formula for working capital is shown in Figure 10.2.

$$\text{Working Capital} = \text{Current Assets} - \text{Current Liabilities}$$

FIGURE 10.2

A positive working capital indicates that the company has enough liquid assets to pay off its upcoming debts. Specifically, the positive working capital is the amount of money left over from paying short-term debt that can be used to expand the business. On the other hand, a negative working capital indicates that current assets alone are not enough to pay off short-term debt, and that the company may have to sell some long-term assets in order to meet short-term debt obligations. If the company is forced to sell long-term assets that are necessary for generating sales, that may lead to a decrease in revenue and net income, which can put the company's long-term prospects in jeopardy.

Leon's working capital is calculated in Figure 10.3 for 2018 and 2017. Remember that the numbers are all in thousands, as shown in Leon's statement.

	2018	**2017**
Total Current Assets	$661,253	$588,548
Total Current Liabilities	$607,520	$419,838
Working Capital—Leon's Furniture	**$53,733**	**$168,710**
Industry Average(1)	**$75,000**	**$125,000**

(1) This industry average is estimated based on available information about current and quick ratios.

FIGURE 10.3

Leon's had enough current assets to cover its current liabilities, as evident by its positive working capital in both 2017 and 2018. Its working capital decreased from 2017 to 2018, indicating decreased liquidity. Leon's working capital was higher than the estimated industry average in 2017 and lower in 2018. However, because working capital is calculated in dollars rather than in the form of a ratio, it may not provide a very meaningful comparison. For this reason, it is better to also calculate current and quick ratios in order to more clearly understand a company's liquidity and to compare it to the industry as a whole or to a specific competitor.

Current Ratio

The **current ratio** is a useful ratio for determining a company's ability to repay its upcoming debts and obligations. The current ratio is calculated as shown in Figure 10.4.

$$\text{Current Ratio} = \frac{\text{Current Assets}}{\text{Current Liabilities}}$$

FIGURE 10.4

The current ratio assesses a company's liquidity by determining the extent to which current assets can cover current liabilities. This means establishing its ability to pay off its debt due within one year. No company wants to find itself in a position of having to sell long-term assets to pay current bills. A current ratio of 1.0 indicates that the company has just enough current assets to pay for its current liabilities. A ratio above 1.0 would be considered more favourable, as it indicates that the company has more than enough current assets to cover current liabilities.

Depending on the industry, the higher the current ratio, the more assurance that the company can afford to pay off its current liabilities without being forced to liquidate its long-term assets to do so. However, a very high current ratio could indicate poor management of current assets. For example, if the current ratio of a business is 5.0, it has $5.00 in current assets for every dollar that it owes in the next 12 months. This indicates that the company may have too much cash. Money in a bank account earning 0.1% interest is not an efficient use of assets, especially if a better rate of return is available elsewhere. Cash should be invested in either new long-term assets or perhaps a short-term investment until a better use for the cash can be established.

Figure 10.5 calculates the current ratio using the numbers provided in Leon's financial statements.

	2018	2017
Total Current Assets	$661,253	$588,548
Total Current Liabilities	$607,520	$419,838
Current Ratio—Leon's Furniture	**1.09**	**1.40**
Industry Average[(1)]	**1.71**	**1.56**

[(1)] CSIMarket refers to this ratio as the working capital ratio.

FIGURE 10.5

In this case, the ratio indicates a healthy situation for both Leon's and the industry. All ratios are more than 1.0, so there seems to be enough current assets to pay for the current liabilities. However, Leon's experienced a decrease in this ratio, which could indicate that Leon's ability to pay its short-term debts as they come due has declined. In contrast, the industry shows an increase in the ratio over the two years and also a more favourable situation in each year compared to Leon's.

Quick Ratio

Another ratio that is relevant to the analysis of a company's liquidity is the **quick ratio** (also known as the *acid test*). This ratio measures the adequacy of highly liquid assets (including cash, short-term investments and accounts receivable) to cover current liabilities. The formula for the quick ratio is shown in Figure 10.6.

$$\text{Quick Ratio} = \frac{\text{Cash + Short-Term Investments + Accounts Receivable}}{\text{Current Liabilities}}$$

FIGURE 10.6

The quick ratio is much like the current ratio; the only difference is that the quick ratio excludes some current assets that cannot be quickly converted to cash (e.g. inventory and prepaid expenses). Short-term investments occur when a company has excess cash and wishes to invest it. This cash can be invested in debt and equity instruments, such as bonds and shares of other companies.

The quick ratio assesses the ability of the company to meet its most immediate debt obligations without relying on the liquidation of inventory (which may take some time to sell). A quick ratio of 1.0 indicates that the company has just enough liquid assets to pay for its current liabilities, so a ratio higher than 1.0 is preferable. Anything below 1.0 might mean that it has too much of its money tied up in inventory or other less liquid assets and may be unable to pay its short-term bills.

Quick ratios have been calculated in Figure 10.7 using the numbers from Leon's balance sheet.

	2018	**2017**
Cash + Short-Term Investments[(1)] + Accounts Receivable	$307,013	$255,828
Total Current Liabilities	$607,520	$419,838
Quick Ratio—Leon's Furniture	**0.51**	**0.61**
Industry Average	**0.21**	**0.19**

(1) Short-Term Investments = Restricted marketable securities + Debt securities + Equity securities

FIGURE 10.7

The above chart reveals that Leon's ability to pay its current liabilities as they come due with quick assets has declined from 2017 to 2018, but that it is in a better position than the industry average.

Since the balance sheet provides only a snapshot of the financial position, further analysis would be required to identify and rectify any potential problems, and to ensure that bills can be paid on time.

In the Real World

Liquidation is a process through which a company ceases to operate. In general, a liquidator is appointed by either the shareholders (in the case of a voluntary liquidation) or a court of law (in the case of a compulsory liquidation). The liquidator is a third party who represents the interests of the creditors and supervises the liquidation. First, the company's assets are collected and turned into cash. The company's liabilities are then paid off, first to secured creditors (i.e. banks), then to unsecured creditors (including amounts owed to suppliers and bondholders, taxes owed to the government, and any unpaid wages or other obligations to current employees). Finally, any funds left over are distributed to shareholders according to the articles of incorporation, with preferred shareholders having priority over common shareholders. After these steps are complete, a company is formally dissolved.

Pause & Reflect

Exercise 10-1

Stellar Corporation includes the following items on its December 31 comparative balance sheet.

Stellar Corporation
Comparative Balance Sheet (partial)
As at December 31, 2020 and 2019

	2020	2019
Cash	$10,918	$6,501
Short-Term Investments	$81	$220
Accounts Receivable	$4,026	$4,368
Merchandise Inventory	$221	$123
Prepaid Expenses	$485	$190
Deferred Income Tax Asset	$699	-
Current Liabilities	$23,684	$11,061

a) Calculate the company's working capital for both years.

b) Calculate the company's current ratio for both years.

See Appendix I for solutions.

Profitability Analysis

LO 3

Profitability refers to the ability of a company to generate profits. The greater the profitability, the more valuable the company is to shareholders. A consistently unprofitable company is likely to go bankrupt. There are several ratios available to help analyze the profitability of a company. They are calculated using figures from the income statement as well as the balance sheet. Leon's income statement (consolidated statements of income) in Figure 10.8 allows users to easily compare the financial results of the company over the years.

Leon's Furniture Limited
Consolidated Statements of Income (partial)
As at December 31, 2018 and 2017

($ in thousands)	**2018**	**2017**
Revenue	$2,241,437	$2,215,379
Cost of sales	1,264,561	1,261,112
Gross profit	$976,876	$954,267
Operating expenses		
Selling, general and administrative expenses	825,276	809,025
Operating profit	151,600	145,242
Finance costs	(9,396)	(11,952)
Finance income	2,468	1,450
Change in fair value of derivative instruments	5,918	(3,311)
Net income before income tax	150,590	131,429
Income tax expense	39,560	34,836
Net income for the year	$111,030	$96,593

FIGURE 10.8

For example, we can instantly see that Leon's has generated increasing revenue for the past two years. We can see that expenses have also increased but not to the same degree as revenue, resulting in a higher net income in 2018. In addition to these observations, several more ratios can be calculated to assess profitability: gross profit margin, net profit margin, return on equity, return on common shareholders' equity, return on assets and asset turnover.

Gross Profit Margin

The gross profit margin is used to demonstrate the impact of cost of goods sold (cost of sales) on the income statement. In other words, the gross profit margin subtracts cost of goods sold from sales revenue, the result of which is divided by net sales. The formula is shown in Figure 10.9.

$$\text{Gross Profit Margin (\%)} = \frac{\text{Gross Profit*}}{\text{Net Sales}}$$

*Gross Profit = Sales Revenue − Cost of Goods Sold

FIGURE 10.9

Gross profit margin reveals the percentage of revenue left after the costs that are directly involved in producing the goods or services (for manufacturers) or in buying the goods for resale (for retailers) are deducted. The remaining profit is used to pay for operating and other expenses, so a higher value is more favourable. Figure 10.10 calculates the gross profit margin related to the sale and cost of furniture and other products using figures from Leon's income statement for 2017 and 2018.

	2018	2017
Gross Profit	$976,876	$954,267
Net Sales	$2,241,437	$2,215,379
Gross Profit Margin—Leon's Furniture	**0.44 or 44%**	**0.43 or 43%**
Industry Average	**0.32 or 32%**	**0.35 or 35%**

FIGURE 10.10

Leon's gross profit margin increased slightly from 2017 to 2018, as a result of a larger increase in revenue compared to the increase in cost of sales. This is a positive sign, as is the fact that, for both periods, it was above the industry average.

The industry averages in 2017 and 2018 indicate that the industry, which includes Leon's competitors, experienced a lower gross profit margin than Leon's. The lower gross profit margin for the industry could be due to the high competitive pressure, or it could be that competitors intentionally keep the gross profit margin low as part of a marketing strategy to gain a bigger market share.

Net Profit Margin

The **net profit margin** assesses a company's profitability after all expenses have been deducted. This is the amount of net profit or loss per dollar of revenue. The formula is shown in Figure 10.11.

$$\text{Net Profit Margin} = \frac{\text{Net Income}}{\text{Total Revenue}}$$

FIGURE 10.11

As with the gross profit margin, a higher net profit margin is generally considered a better sign than a lower one, although it should always be compared to the industry average and previous results. Figure 10.12 calculates the net profit margin for Leon's Furniture for both 2017 and 2018.

	2018	2017
Net Income (Loss)	$111,030	$96,593
Total Revenue	$2,241,437	$2,215,379
Net Profit Margin—Leon's Furniture	**0.05 or 5%**	**0.04 or 4%**
Industry Average	**0.06 or 6%**	**0.07 or 7%**

FIGURE 10.12

Leon's total revenue, net income and net profit margin have all increased for 2018 over 2017. This could be a positive sign for the shareholders, because earnings on their investments have increased from 2017 to 2018. To perform a complete analysis of net profit margin, comparisons should be made on a monthly and yearly basis to historical company performance, industry averages and direct competitors. Conclusions can be drawn only when net income figures are placed in context.

The industry also reported positive net profit margins for both years that were higher than those reported by Leon's. This is an interesting result given that Leon's gross profit margin was higher than the industry average. How can this be so? One explanation could be that Leon's was not as efficient in controlling the operating costs that are reflected in its net profit margin.

Return on Equity

Return on equity (ROE) is a measure of what the owners are getting out of their investment in the company. It is often the most important ratio for investors because it has a large impact on the value of an investment. This ratio requires calculations using information from both the balance sheet and income statement. The formula is shown in Figure 10.13.

$$\text{Return on Equity (ROE)} = \frac{\text{Net Income}}{\text{Average Shareholders' Equity}}$$

FIGURE 10.13

Notice that the calculation requires *average* shareholders' equity. Whenever a ratio is calculated that uses some information from the balance sheet and some from the income statement, the balance sheet information is always averaged. This is because the balance sheet represents a snapshot in time while the income statement represents an entire accounting period. By averaging the balance sheet accounts, we are simulating a figure that covers the same period of time as the income statement. This makes the ratio more comparable and reliable.

Although it is not shown in Figure 10.1, we need to know the balance of Leon's shareholders' equity at December 31, 2016, to calculate the average shareholders' equity for 2017. The balance on this date was $659,553. The calculations of ROE for Leon's Furniture in 2017 and 2018 are shown in Figure 10.14.

	2018	**2017**
Net Income (Loss)	$111,030	$96,593
Average Shareholders' Equity[1]	$815,205	$716,300
Return on Equity—Leon's Furniture	**0.14 or 14%**	**0.13 or 13%**
Industry Average	**0.17 or 17%**	**0.21 or 21%**

[1] Average Shareholders' Equity for 2017: ($659,553 + $773,048) ÷ 2 = $716,300
Average Shareholders' Equity for 2018: ($773,048 + $857,362) ÷ 2 = $815,205

FIGURE 10.14

A high ROE is desirable because it means that investors made a good decision to invest in the company. A negative ROE indicates that shareholders lost money on their investments over the year. It deters investors from investing more money because of the risk of loss. Leon's return on equity has remained positive and consistent from 2017 to 2018, but it was lower than the industry averages for both years, which may indicate that other companies in this industry might be a better investment. Shareholders like to see a return that is as good as or better than they could have received by investing elsewhere.

Return on Common Shareholders' Equity

Return on common shareholders' equity is a measure of the profits earned on the investment of common shareholders. This differs from the return on equity (ROE), which assumes that there is no preferred share equity included in shareholders' equity. As with ROE, this ratio requires information from both the balance sheet and income statement. If preferred equity exists, the correct formula is shown in Figure 10.15.

$$\text{Return on Common Shareholders' Equity} = \frac{(\text{Net Income} - \text{Preferred Dividends})}{\text{Average Common Shareholders' Equity}}$$

FIGURE 10.15

In the numerator of this equation, preferred dividends are subtracted from net income. This takes into account the fact that preferred shareholders have the first claim on earnings, before common shareholders. If the preferred shares are cumulative, dividends must be subtracted whether or not they have been declared or if they are in arrears. If the preferred shares are non-cumulative, dividends are subtracted only if they have been declared. The denominator of this calculation is average common shareholders' equity.

The shareholders' equity section of Leon's consolidated statements of financial position (balance sheets) in Figure 10.1 indicates that there are no preferred shares authorized or issued. Therefore, the numerator in the equation will simply be equal to the net income for the respective periods. Therefore, in this particular example of Leon's Furniture, we will arrive at the same returns as we did for ROE.

In the Real World

One of the most important assessments business owners can make is to know if they are getting a decent return on their investment. How is this done?

Any determination of return on investment revolves around shareholders' equity. That is, how much cash would the owners have left if they sold all the assets of the company and paid off all its debt? This is a hypothetical question, as there are other ways of assessing the value of the investment in the business.

For example, the owners could ask themselves another practical question: Should we keep our money in the company or put it elsewhere? Safe investments, such as fixed deposit accounts, come with relatively lower returns on investment. Investing in a friend's new business comes with a potentially much larger return on investment—but also with greater risk.

In fact, a general rule of thumb can be applied to assessing return on investment associated with certain levels of risk. Generally speaking, investments in publicly traded companies come with the expectation of a return of about 10%. The rate of return associated with private companies is expected to be much higher. In fact, it is not unusual to expect a rate of return of 100% or more for an investment in a small private company.

As with most things in life, everything comes at a price. With return on investment, the price can be a matter of risk. If owners want a better return, they must have a greater tolerance for risk.

Return on Assets

Return on assets (ROA) provides an assessment of what the company does with what it has; it measures every dollar earned against each dollar's worth of assets. (Return on assets was introduced in Chapter 2.) A business invests in assets for the purpose of generating sales and making a profit. ROA is a measure of how effective that investment is. Although assessing ROA depends on the type of business being analyzed, a higher ROA number is generally considered better than a lower one; it means the company is earning more money on its investment in assets. Figure 10.16 shows the equation to calculate ROA.

$$\text{Return on Assets (ROA)} = \frac{\text{Net Income}}{\text{Average Total Assets}}$$

FIGURE 10.16

Now we will calculate ROA for Leon's Furniture. The net income (loss) comes from the income statement. The total asset figures are found on the balance sheet. The balance of total assets at year end in 2016 was $1,611,662. The calculation is shown in Figure 10.17.

	2018	2017
Net Income (Loss)	$111,030	$96,593
Average Total Assets[(1)]	$1,692,514	$1,636,559
Return on Assets—Leon's Furniture	**0.07 or 7%**	**0.06 or 6%**
Industry Average	**0.07 or 7%**	**0.08 or 8%**

[(1)] Average Total Assets for 2017: ($1,611,662 + $1,661,455) ÷ 2 = $1,636,559
Average Total Assets for 2018: ($1,661,455 + $1,723,572) ÷ 2 = $1,692,514

FIGURE 10.17

There was a slight increase in the ROA in 2018. What the ROA means is that in 2017, Leon's gained $0.06 for every $1 invested in assets. In 2018, the company's returns increased to $0.07 for every $1 invested in assets. This improvement is likely the result of the company's growth in net income. In 2018, Leon's return on assets was the same as the industry's, although the industry average declined slightly from 2017, while Leon's experienced an increase.

As a general rule, a low industry ROA usually indicates that the industry is capital-intensive or asset-heavy. This means that companies are investing a considerable amount in assets relative to profits. Industries that tend to display low ROA figures include manufacturers and large transportation companies such as railroads. Alternatively, a business in an industry with a high ROA is less capital-intensive or asset-heavy. Examples include professional practices, software companies and retailers. Since Leon's ROA can be considered on the lower side, it makes sense to say that they are more capital intensive; that is, a higher percentage of their assets are non-current (long-term) than current.

Asset Turnover

Another way to assess how well business assets are being used is to calculate the **asset turnover,** which measures a company's ability to generate sales revenue from asset investments. (Asset turnover was discussed in Chapter 2.) This is calculated by dividing revenue by average total assets, as shown in Figure 10.18.

$$\text{Asset Turnover} = \frac{\text{Total Revenue}}{\text{Average Total Assets}}$$

FIGURE 10.18

Since this is a measurement of generating sales, the higher the number, the better. Figure 10.19 shows the asset turnover for Leon's Furniture.

	2018	2017
Total Revenue	$2,241,437	$2,215,379
Average Total Assets[1]	$1,692,514	$1,636,559
Asset Turnover—Leon's Furniture	**1.32 times**	**1.35 times**
Industry Average	**1.12 times**	**1.19 times**

[1] Average Total Assets for 2017: ($1,611,662 + $1,661,455) ÷ 2 = $1,636,559
Average Total Assets for 2018: ($1,661,455 + $1,723,572) ÷ 2 = $1,692,514

FIGURE 10.19

For 2018, an asset turnover of 1.32 means Leon's generated $1.32 of revenue for every dollar tied up in assets. This is a slight decrease from the previous year, which indicates the company was slightly less efficient at generating revenue with its assets. Despite this decline, Leon's performed better than the industry overall.

Pause & Reflect

Exercise 10-2

Vernacular Inc. reports the following key items on its comparative income statement for the year ended December 31, 2020.

Vernacular Inc. Comparative Income Statement For the Period Ended December 31, 2020 and 2019		
	2020	**2019**
Sales Revenue	$28,172	$27,188
Cost of Goods Sold	7,679	4,054
Gross Profit	20,493	23,134
Operating Expenses	47,525	30,503
Net Income (Loss)	($27,032)	($7,369)

a) Calculate the company's gross profit margin for both years.

b) Calculate the company's net profit margin for both years.

See Appendix I for solutions.

Operations Management Analysis

LO 4

Operations management refers to the ability of a company to manage its assets, such as inventory and accounts receivable. Inventory is converted into cash by selling it, but it must be managed properly to ensure that it can be sold in a timely manner. To determine whether inventory is being managed properly, two ratios can be calculated: inventory turnover ratio and days' sales in inventory.

The other aspect of operations management is the ability to collect on bills. Accounts receivable may be a large source of cash for a company, but it is not worth anything if it cannot be collected. When customers buy a product or service on credit, they have to pay within a reasonable amount of time to ensure proper cash flow and good financial health for the company. To determine whether accounts receivable is being managed properly, two ratios can be calculated: days' sales outstanding and accounts receivable turnover.

Inventory Turnover Ratio

Management is often concerned with the company's ability to sell, or *turn over*, inventory. In industries that deal with food and beverage sales, it is especially important because of the short shelf life of the inventory. Throwing away expired products is just like throwing away cash. The **inventory turnover ratio** represents the number of times that a company sold its entire inventory within the given period, and it is calculated as shown in Figure 10.20.

$$\text{Inventory Turnover Ratio} = \frac{\text{Cost of Goods Sold}}{\text{Average Inventory}}$$

FIGURE 10.20

The industry the company is in determines the desirable value for this ratio. For example, hardware stores may turn over inventory only once or twice per year because the goods do not expire or become obsolete very quickly. The fashion industry may turn over inventory four times per year because fashion trends tend to change quickly and with the seasons. Similarly, the furniture industry may follow the same trend as fashion, as home furnishings typically change with the seasons.

Leon's inventory turnover ratio is calculated in Figure 10.21. The inventory balance at December 31, 2016, was $308,801.

	2018	2017
Cost of Goods Sold (Cost of Sales)	$1,264,561	$1,261,112
Average Inventory[1]	$323,616	$313,358
Inventory Turnover—Leon's Furniture	**3.91 times**	**4.02 times**
Industry Average	**3.81 times**	**3.97 times**

[1] Average Inventory for 2017: ($308,801 + $317,914) ÷ 2 = $313,358
Average Inventory for 2018: ($317,914 + $329,317) ÷ 2 = $323,616

FIGURE 10.21

Leon's inventory turnover is consistent with that expected from a company operating in the retail furniture industry; that is, their inventory turns over approximately 4 times per year, possibly due to changing styles and seasons. Even though Leon's inventory turnover decreased slightly, from 4.02 in 2017 to 3.91 in 2018, it remained above the industry average for both years.

To get a better understanding of what this ratio means in a more general sense, we can also calculate the days' sales in inventory.

Days' Sales in Inventory

This ratio states the same thing as the inventory turnover ratio but in a different way. **Days' sales in inventory** is the average number of days that it took to turn over inventory during the year. Some users prefer this ratio because they are familiar with working in units such as days and months. Figure 10.22 shows two different ways to calculate days' sales in inventory.

$$\text{Days' Sales in Inventory} = \frac{\text{Average Inventory}}{\text{Cost of Goods Sold}} \times 365$$

or

$$\text{Days' Sales in Inventory} = \frac{365}{\text{Inventory Turnover Ratio}}$$

FIGURE 10.22

This ratio converts the number of times inventory is turned over into the average number of days it took to turn over inventory. For example, a company that sells its entire inventory twice a year has an inventory turnover ratio of 2 and a days' sales in inventory of 182.5 days. The ratio is calculated for Leon's Furniture in Figure 10.23.

	2018	2017
Average Inventory[(1)]	$323,616	$313,358
Cost of Goods Sold (Cost of Sales)	$1,264,561	$1,261,112
Days in a Year	365	365
Days' Sales in Inventory—Leon's Furniture	**93.4 days**	**90.7 days**
Industry Average	**95.8 days**	**91.9 days**

[(1)] Average Inventory for 2017: ($308,801 + $317,914) ÷ 2 = $313,358
Average Inventory for 2018: ($317,914 + $329,317) ÷ 2 = $323,616

FIGURE 10.23

The lower the number, the faster inventory is sold on average. As we saw with inventory turnover, Leon's days' sales in inventory for 2017 and 2018 reflect the nature of its inventory (furniture) and is also consistent with, though slightly better than, the overall conditions within the industry.

Days' Sales Outstanding

As noted, the ability to collect accounts receivable is critical to a company's financial health. **Days' sales outstanding (DSO)** measures the average number of days that a company takes to collect its receivables. The formula for DSO is shown in Figure 10.24.

$$\text{Days' Sales Outstanding (DSO)} = \frac{\text{Average Net Accounts Receivable}}{\text{Net Credit Sales}} \times 365$$

FIGURE 10.24

Leon's accounts receivable is primarily comprised of customer trade receivables. From an external point of view, we do not know what portion of its total revenue is cash versus credit. For our discussion, we will assume that all revenue is on credit. The DSO provides an indication of how many days it takes for customers to pay their accounts. This number is important because late payments can cost a company lost interest from cash deposits in a bank, or result in additional administration costs to collect payments from customers.

The calculation of DSO for Leon's Furniture is shown in Figure 10.25. The accounts receivable balance at year end in 2016 was $128,142.

	2018	**2017**
Average Accounts Receivable[1]	$130,324	$133,329
Net Credit Sales (Total Revenue)	$2,241,437	$2,215,379
Number of Days in the Year	365	365
Days' Sales Outstanding—Leon's Furniture	**21 days**	**22 days**
Industry Average	**43 days**	**41 days**

[1] Average Accounts Receivable for 2017: ($128,142 + $138,516) ÷ 2 = $133,329
Average Accounts Receivable for 2018: ($138,516 + $122,131) ÷ 2 = $130,324

FIGURE 10.25

As you can see, the business is improving its ability to collect from customers. The DSO decreased slightly from 22 days in 2017 to 21 days in 2018. This is significantly lower than the industry values, which indicates that Leon's is performing much better than the industry in collecting from customers. The industry average has in fact increased from 2017 to 2018. For an individual company, that might be an indication of disputes with customers, a slowdown in sales resulting in slower payments to the company, or problems in the billing and credit function of the company. None of these reasons would be considered favourably by owners, investors or analysts.

There are some cautionary notes to keep in mind related to using the DSO for analysis in the real world. First, the revenue figure used in the ratio should exclude all cash sales, since only sales on account (credit sales) are relevant to collecting customer payments. Second, outliers in sales data, such as sales to a major customer who was given a different credit policy from other customers, should be kept out of the total revenue figure used to calculate DSO, because they can skew the ratio. While data such as credit sales as a percentage of total sales and credit policies to franchisees are not available on the public financial statements, management should track and analyze credit sales and receivables data internally to manage the company's DSO.

Accounts Receivable Turnover Ratio

The **accounts receivable turnover ratio (ART)** is similar to days' sales outstanding. It involves dividing a company's net credit sales by the average amount of accounts receivable. Figure 10.26 shows the formula to calculate accounts receivable turnover.

$$\text{Accounts Receivable Turnover (ART)} = \frac{\text{Net Credit Sales}}{\text{Average Net Accounts Receivable}}$$

FIGURE 10.26

The calculation for Leon's Furniture is shown in Figure 10.27.

	2018	2017
Net Credit Sales (Total Revenue)	$2,241,437	$2,215,379
Average Accounts Receivable[(1)]	$130,324	$133,329
Accounts Receivable Turnover—Leon's Furniture	**17.2 times**	**16.6 times**
Industry Average	**8.45 times**	**9.01 times**

(1) Average Accounts Receivable for 2017: ($128,142 + $138,516) ÷ 2 = $133,329
Average Accounts Receivable for 2018: ($138,516 + $122,131) ÷ 2 =$130,324

FIGURE 10.27

Note that the *net credit sales* amount is not usually reported to external users of the financial statements; therefore, external users would simply use the *net sales* figure as the numerator in their ART calculations.

A higher ratio indicates a greater ability to convert accounts receivable into cash. If a company turns over its receivables 12 times per year, it is collecting the average balance of receivables every month. In Leon's case, an accounts receivable turnover of 16.6 in 2017 means that it collected receivables once every 22 days on average. By 2018, Leon's ART had improved to 17.2 times, or nearly once every 21 days. For both 2018 and 2017, Leon's performed better than the industry, which indicates better management of collections from credit customers than other companies in the industry.

Pause & Reflect

Exercise 10-3

Reaper Company reports the following key items on its comparative financial statements for the year ended December 31, 2020 (numbers in thousands).

Reaper Company	2020	2019
Average Inventory	$172	$130
Cost of Goods Sold	$7,679	$4,054

Calculate the company's days' sales in inventory for each of the two years.

See Appendix I for solutions.

Solvency Analysis

LO 5

There are two ways to finance a business: debt and equity. Debts are the company's liabilities, such as bank loans and accounts payable. Equity is generated by selling shares and generating profits. **Solvency** refers to the company's ability to cover its long-term debt obligations, and it relates to the amount of debt and risk the company has. Companies often take on debt to finance the purchase of large assets. They then use these assets to expand operations and generate sales. However, there is usually a high cost of debt in the form of interest expense, which is where the risk comes in. A company must be able to increase profits by more than the interest expense to benefit the shareholders. There are three measurements of solvency: debt-to-equity ratio (from Chapter 7), times interest earned, and debt-to-total assets ratio (from Chapter 7).

Debt-to-Equity Ratio

The **debt-to-equity (D/E) ratio** is used to assess a company's balance of debt and equity. The debt-to-equity ratio is calculated as shown in Figure 10.28.

$$\text{Debt-to-Equity (D/E) Ratio} = \frac{\text{Total Liabilities}}{\text{Total Shareholders' Equity}}$$

FIGURE 10.28

It is not healthy for a company to borrow too much relative to what it is worth, because there is a cost of debt in the form of interest. The industry a company is in usually influences how much should be borrowed. For example, capital-intensive industries, such as car manufacturers, have higher debt-to-equity ratios than software developers. Leon's Furniture's debt-to-equity ratios for the years 2017 and 2018 are calculated in Figure 10.29.

> **Worth Repeating**
>
> Acquiring loans or paying back loan principal has no effect on equity. However, paying interest on a loan has a negative effect on equity.

	2018	**2017**
Total Liabilities	$866,210	$888,407
Shareholders' Equity	$857,362	$773,048
Debt-to-Equity Ratio—Leon's Furniture	**1.01**	**1.15**
Industry Average	**1.13**	**1.15**

FIGURE 10.29

As you can see, the debt-to-equity ratio decreased from 2017 to 2018, which is a positive sign. In fact, it has been decreasing since 2016. In 2016, reported total liabilities and shareholders' equity were $952,109 and $659,553 respectively, which resulted in a debt-to-equity ratio of 1.44. Part of the reason for this decrease could be that Leon's is a well-established, successful business that has been able to pay off more long-term debt than it has taken on. Leon's is also in a slightly better position than the industry average, which has also decreased over the past two years.

There are a few ways a company can improve its debt-to-equity ratio. First, making more profit directly results in an increase to shareholders' equity, although this may not be easy. Second, the company might consider issuing more shares in exchange for cash.

Times Interest Earned Ratio

There is a cost to borrowing money. The **times interest earned ratio** is used to determine whether the company is able to cover the interest charged on its debt. This ratio divides earnings before interest expense and income tax by the interest expense. Figure 10.30 shows the formula to calculate times interest earned.

$$\text{Times Interest Earned} = \frac{\text{Earnings before Interest Expense and Income Tax}}{\text{Interest Expense}}$$

FIGURE 10.30

For example, times interest earned of only 1 time means that the business has just enough earnings (before interest and tax expenses are deducted) to cover the amount of interest paid during the year. A higher ratio is considered more favourable.

For Leon's Furniture, the calculation of the times interest earned ratio is shown in Figure 10.31. Earnings before interest and taxes is simply adding back income taxes and interest expense to net income.

	2018	2017
Earnings before Interest Expense and Income Tax(1)	$159,986	$143,381
Interest Expense(2)	$9,396	$11,952
Times Interest Earned—Leon's Furniture	**17.03 times**	**12.00 times**
Industry Average	**16.96 times**	**21.03 times**

(1) For this illustration based on Leon's consolidated statements of income:
Earnings before Interest Expense and Income Tax = Net income for the year + Income tax expense + Finance costs
Earnings before Interest Expense and Income Tax for 2017: $96,593 + $34,836 + $11,952 = $143,381
Earnings before Interest Expense and Income Tax for 2018: $111,030 + $39,560 + $9,396 = $159,986

(2) On Leon's statement, this item is called financing costs.

FIGURE 10.31

The amount of interest expense has decreased while income before interest and tax has increased from 2017 to 2018. Therefore, it makes sense that Leon's times interest earned ratio has improved over this period of time. This is a key ratio that a lender would be interested in when making a decision whether to lend money to a company. The industry average decreased from 2017 to 2018, and it was slightly lower than Leon's for 2018. A poor times interest earned, or a continual drop in that figure from year to year, may mean a company will have difficulty securing loans in the future.

Debt-to-Total-Assets Ratio

The **debt-to-total-assets ratio** shows how much debt a company has as a percentage of assets. The formula to calculate the debt-to-total-assets ratio is shown in Figure 10.32.

$$\text{Debt-to-Total-Assets Ratio} = \frac{\text{Total Liabilities}}{\text{Total Assets}}$$

FIGURE 10.32

The calculation for Leon's Furniture is shown in Figure 10.33.

	2018	2017
Total Liabilities(1)	$866,210	$888,407
Total Assets	$1,723,572	$1,661,455
Debt-to-Total-Assets Ratio—Leon's Furniture	**0.50 or 50%**	**0.53 or 53%**
Industry Average(1)	**1.12 or 112%**	**1.14 or 114%**

(1) CSIMarket refers to this ratio as the leverage ratio.

FIGURE 10.33

As the debt-to-total-assets ratio decreases, this indicates that less debt is being used to finance the business relative to its assets. This reduces the risk the company will not be able to meet its interest or principal repayments as they come due.

Different industries have different tolerances for the amount of debt a company should incur. In 2017, Leon's had a debt-to-total-assets ratio that was less than half of the industry average. In 2018, Leon's ratio improved to be only 0.50 in comparison to the industry average of 1.12, meaning that the industry as a whole was more than twice as dependent on debt financing as Leon's was. The significance of this ratio is that Leon's is in a much better position to handle its long-term debt repayments than the majority of companies in the retail furniture industry.

Capital Market Performance Analysis

LO 6

In addition to financial ratios for internal measurements, there are ratios that are used by investors to determine whether a public corporation's shares are a desirable purchase. Shares that are publicly traded on the stock markets can experience price changes daily, hourly or even by the minute. The changes in market value affect investors as they buy and sell shares, but the corporation does not record any of these changes in its books. The ratios that measure share performance of a public corporation—book value per common share, dividend yield, earnings per share and price-earnings ratio—were covered in Chapter 6 and are reviewed here using Leon's Furniture as an illustration. Leon's does not have any preferred shares; however, its consolidated balance sheet shows that it had 77,490,893 common shares outstanding at the year end of 2018. The company ended 2017 with 76,188,143 common shares outstanding.

Book Value per Common Share

Book value per common share represents the theoretical value of a common share based on a shareholder's claim to the company assets. This assumes that all assets would be sold for their book value and all liabilities would be paid off. However, book value will not necessarily match the market value of the shares. The calculation of book value per common share is shown in Figure 10.34.

$$\text{Book Value per Common Share} = \frac{\text{Shareholders' Equity} - \text{Preferred Equity}}{\text{Number of Common Shares Outstanding}}$$

FIGURE 10.34

Note that the value for preferred equity includes preferred dividends if there are any preferred dividends outstanding. The formula calculates the amount of money that the holder of each common share would receive if all the company's assets were immediately liquidated.

For Leon's Furniture, the book value per common share at the end of 2018 is calculated below. Note that, unlike the numbers from the statements used in calculating the ratios in the earlier part of this chapter, these are expressed in full rather than in thousands.

$$\text{Book Value per Common Share} = \frac{\$857{,}362{,}000}{77{,}490{,}893}$$

$$= \$11.06$$

Based on the above, Leon's 2018 book value per common share is approximately $11.06. This indicates that if Leon's were to liquidate immediately, shareholders could expect to receive this value per share, but only if creditors and other loan holders are paid what they are owed first.

Dividend Yield

Since dividends, or at least the potential for dividends, must form part of the analysis of a company, the investing community developed a ratio to assess just how much in dividends a corporation is paying out to shareholders. This is called the **dividend yield** and calculates dividends paid as a percentage of market price per share. Figure 10.35 shows how to calculate the dividend yield.

$$\text{Dividend Yield} = \frac{\text{Cash Dividends per Common Share}}{\text{Market Price per Common Share}}$$

FIGURE 10.35

Leon's Furniture paid $0.52 per common share in dividends in 2018, when the current share price was $14.62. The calculation of the dividend yield is shown below.

$$\text{Dividend Yield} = \frac{\$0.52}{\$14.62}$$

$$= 0.04 \text{ or } 4\%$$

The dividend yield for Leon's in 2018 was 4%. This means that if the investor paid $14.62 to purchase a common share and in turn received a cash dividend of $0.52, then the investor's rate of return for investing in Leon's Furniture's shares in the form of a dividend was 4% in 2018. While a higher dividend yield provides investors with a higher return on investment, paying too high a dividend may not leave enough cash for the company to grow its operations. Therefore, a high dividend yield may not always be interpreted positively by investors. While some investors may prefer to invest in a company that gives a higher dividend yield in order to get a higher return on investment, other investors may prefer to make a long-term investment in a company that currently pays a lower dividend yield but has higher growth potential.

Earnings per Share

Earnings per share (EPS) is a key corporate measure for investors. This measures how much profit is earned for each outstanding common share. The formula for earnings per share is shown in Figure 10.36.

$$\text{Earnings per Share (EPS)} = \frac{\text{Net Income} - \text{Preferred Dividends}}{\text{Weighted Average Number of Common Shares Outstanding}}$$

FIGURE 10.36

Leon's financial statements present the weighted average number of common shares for 2018 as 76,368,088. We will use this number in our calculation.

$$\text{Earnings per Share} = \frac{\$111{,}030{,}000}{76{,}368{,}088}$$

$$= \$1.45$$

Not only did Leon's have a positive EPS for 2018, that amount was also greater than the previous year's EPS of $1.32.

We learned in Chapter 6 how to calculate the weighted average number of common shares; however, companies may use slightly different variations in their calculation. Thus, since Leon's Furniture provided its weighted number of common shares, we used that in our calculation. If we had to calculate the weighted number based on the information given, we might end up with a slightly different weighted average and a different EPS. It is also important to mention that this amount represents *basic* earnings per share. Where the company also reports convertible accounts in the shareholders' equity section (meaning debt or other equity accounts are convertible into common shares), the company is required to report fully diluted earnings per share that represent the amount that would be reported for EPS if all conversions had taken place.

Price-Earnings Ratio

Another ratio commonly used by shareholders to evaluate their investment in a corporation is the **price-earnings ratio (P/E)**, which provides the investor with a measurement of share price compared to actual earnings of the corporation. It is used as an indicator of company growth and risk. It can be used as a sign to buy, sell or hold shares. P/E ratios and dividend yields are found in the daily stock market quotations listed in many publications, such as the *Globe and Mail*, and from numerous online sources, such as *Yahoo Finance*. The formula is shown in Figure 10.37.

$$\text{Price-Earnings (P/E) Ratio} = \frac{\text{Market Price per Share}}{\text{Earnings per Share}}$$

FIGURE 10.37

Leon's Furniture had a year end of December 31, 2018. On that date, the market value of its shares was $14.62 per share. Thus, the price–earnings ratio for Leon's is calculated below.

$$\text{Price–Earnings Ratio} = \frac{\$14.62}{\$1.45}$$
$$= 10.08$$

When a company has a positive P/E ratio, as Leon's does, the ratio indicates the shares are selling for a multiple of its earnings. The fact that Leon's has a higher P/E ratio of 10.08 means that investors are willing to pay a price 10.08 times the earnings per share as reported for same period. However, if Leon's future earnings do not match the market's expectations, then the investors may decide to sell their shares, which (all things being equal) will cause the market price to decrease, which in turn will effect the P/E calculation in the future.

Pause & Reflect

Exercise 10-4

Peach Tree Company does not have any preferred shares. However, the company's financial statement notes show that it had 9,903,045 common shares outstanding at its 2019 year end. Toward the end of 2020, the company issued an additional 2,927,900 common shares and ended 2020 with 12,830,945 common shares outstanding. The company reported total shareholders' equity of $24,994,000 in its balance sheet as at December 31, 2020. Calculate the company's book value per common share at the end of 2020.

See Appendix I for solutions.

We have just examined many different ratios. Examining only one ratio does not provide a complete picture of the financial status of a company. Many values are needed to form a proper picture. Figure 10.38 summarizes the formulas used to determine different valuations.

Ratio	Formula	Is a measure of
Liquidity		
Working Capital	Current Assets − Current Liabilities	Ability to cover current liabilities using current assets
Current Ratio	$\frac{\text{Current Assets}}{\text{Current Liabilities}}$	Ability to cover current liabilities using current assets
Quick Ratio	$\frac{\text{Cash + Short-Term Investments + Accounts Receivable}}{\text{Current Liabilities}}$	Ability of *highly liquid* assets to cover current liabilities
Profitability		
Gross Profit Margin	$\frac{\text{Gross Profit}}{\text{Net Sales}}$	Percentage of profit remaining after deducting cost of goods sold
Net Profit Margin	$\frac{\text{Net Income}}{\text{Total Revenue}}$	Percentage of profit remaining after deducting all expenses

Ratio	Formula	Is a measure of
Return on Equity	$\frac{\text{Net Income}}{\text{Average Shareholders' Equity}}$	Profitability of shareholders' investments
Return on Common Shareholders' Equity	$\frac{\text{(Net Income − Preferred Dividends)}}{\text{Average Common Shareholders' Equity}}$	Profits earned on investment of common shareholders
Return on Assets	$\frac{\text{Net Income}}{\text{Average Total Assets}}$	Effectiveness of the company's investment in assets
Asset Turnover	$\frac{\text{Total Revenue}}{\text{Average Total Assets}}$	Ability to generate sales revenue from asset investments
Operations Management		
Inventory Turnover Ratio	$\frac{\text{Cost of Goods Sold}}{\text{Average Inventory}}$	Efficiency of inventory management
Days' Sales in Inventory	$\frac{\text{Average Inventory}}{\text{Cost of Goods Sold}} \times 365$ or $\frac{365}{\text{Inventory Turnover Ratio}}$	Average number of days to turn over inventory during the year
Days' Sales Outstanding	$\frac{\text{Average Net Accounts Receivable}}{\text{Net Credit Sales}} \times 365$	Average number of days to collect accounts receivable
Accounts Receivable Turnover Ratio	$\frac{\text{Net Credit Sales}}{\text{Average Net Accounts Receivable}}$	Efficiency of accounts receivable collections
Solvency		
Debt-to-Equity Ratio	$\frac{\text{Total Liabilities}}{\text{Total Shareholder's Equity}}$	Relative amount of debt vs. shareholders' equity that is being used to finance a company's assets
Times Interest Earned	$\frac{\text{Earnings before Interest Expense and Income Tax}}{\text{Interest Expense}}$	Ability to cover interest on debt
Debt-to-Total-Assets Ratio	$\frac{\text{Total Liabilities}}{\text{Total Assets}}$	Amount of debt being financed by creditors
Capital Market Performance		
Book Value per Common Share	$\frac{\text{Shareholders' Equity − Preferred Equity}}{\text{Number of Common Shares Outstanding}}$	Theoretical value of a share based on shareholders' claims to a company's assets
Dividend Yield	$\frac{\text{Cash Dividends per Common Share}}{\text{Market Price per Common Share}}$	Rate of return to common shareholders
Earnings per Share	$\frac{\text{Net Income − Preferred Dividends}}{\text{Weighted Average Number of Common Shares Outstanding}}$	Profit earned by investors per common share
Price-Earnings Ratio	$\frac{\text{Market Price per Share}}{\text{Earnings per Share}}$	Market value of a common share related to its earnings

FIGURE 10.38

Throughout the chapter, we have discussed whether the ideal value for each ratio is higher or lower. However, keep in mind that an extremely high value on a ratio where higher is better, or an extremely low value on a ratio where a lower value is better, may not always be a good outcome. For example, if days' sales in inventory is too low, it could indicate a situation where the company is always running out of products. A quick ratio that is too high may indicate the company is not reinvesting cash into the business to improve operations. As with any analysis, the numbers must be considered in context.

Horizontal and Vertical Analyses

LO 7

We will now look at Leon's Furniture's profitability by applying horizontal and vertical analysis to its balance sheet and income statement. Such an analysis can be used by a company to make decisions about its future, such as possible expansion of operations.

Horizontal Analysis—Balance Sheet

Leon's Furniture's consolidated statements of financial position, or comparative balance sheet, for the years 2016–2018 is presented in Figure 10.39. (This figure adds the information for 2016 to what was presented for 2017 and 2018 in Figure 10.1.)

Leon's Furniture Limited
Consolidated Statements of Financial Position
As at December 31, 2018, 2017 and 2016

($ in thousands)	2018	2017	2016
ASSETS			
Current assets			
Cash and cash equivalents	$90,267	$36,207	$43,985
Restricted marketable securities	5,994	13,778	16,600
Available-for-sale financial assets[(1)]	88,621	67,327	39,079
Trade receivables	122,131	138,516	128,142
Income taxes receivable	8,413	2,042	2,042
Inventories	329,317	317,914	308,801
Deferred acquisition costs	7,899	5,841	7,643
Deferred financing costs	276	541	775
Prepaid expenses and other assets	8,335	6,382	8,225
Total current assets	$661,253	$588,548	$555,292
Non-current assets			
Other assets	484	-	-
Deferred acquisition costs	11,751	14,632	13,128
Loan receivable	13,191	-	-
Property, plant and equipment	321,597	336,748	315,500
Investment properties	17,072	17,529	17,984
Intangibles	300,896	306,286	311,464
Goodwill	390,120	390,120	390,120
Deferred income tax assets	7,208	7,592	8,174
Total non-current assets	$1,062,319	$1,072,907	$1,056,370
Total assets	$1,723,572	$1,661,455	$1,611,662

Leon's Furniture Limited
Consolidated Statements of Financial Position (continued)
As at December 31, 2018, 2017 and 2016

($ in thousands)	**2018**	**2017**	**2016**
LIABILITIES AND SHAREHOLDERS' EQUITY			
Current liabilities			
Trade and other payables	$247,136	$234,478	$214,838
Provisions	11,687	8,791	5,468
Income taxes payable	7,338	7,517	12,641
Customers' deposits	146,362	128,078	117,990
Finance lease liability	1,415	1,421	1,421
Dividends payable	10,690	9,140	7,183
Deferred warranty plan revenue	38,180	24,979	39,839
Loans and borrowings	144,712	-	25,000
Other liabilities	-	5,434	2,124
Total current liabilities	$607,520	$419,838	$426,504
Non-current liabilities			
Loans and borrowings	-	194,439	214,436
Convertible debentures	48,435	48,004	93,520
Finance lease liability	7,784	9,053	10,474
Deferred warranty plan revenue	110,126	122,773	105,289
Redeemable share liability	13	157	503
Deferred rent liabilities and lease inducements	11,021	10,791	11,380
Deferred income tax liabilities	81,311	83,352	90,003
Total non-current liabilities	$258,690	$468,569	$525,605
Total liabilities	$866,210	$888,407	$952,109
Shareholders' equity			
Common shares	$111,956	$93,392	$39,184
Equity component of convertible debentures	3,546	3,555	7,089
Retained earnings	743,399	674,883	613,426
Accumulated other comprehensive income	(1,539)	1,218	(146)
Total shareholders' equity	$857,362	$773,048	$659,553
Total liabilities and shareholders' equity	$1,723,572	$1,661,455	$1,611,662

(1) In Leon's Furniture Limited's reporting for 2018, the line for available-for-sale financial assets is replaced with two separate lines for debt securities and equity securities.

For demonstration purposes, information from Leon's Furniture Limited's Consolidated Statements of Financial Position for 2018 and 2017 has been put together in this figure. Values for 2018 and 2017 are taken from the 2018 report; those for 2016 are taken from the 2017 report.

FIGURE 10.39

The comparative balance sheet is a tool used to perform a **horizontal analysis,** which involves comparing information from one accounting period to another, usually from year to year. This means that you can compare similar line items to see how that item has changed from year to year, providing what is known as a **trend analysis.** Trend analysis compares line items in terms of two things:

- The *dollar change* (increase or decrease) compared to a base year
- The *percentage change* (increase or decrease) compared to a base year

A **base year** is usually the earliest year shown and is used as the basis for comparison.

Figure 10.40 summarizes some key financial information for Leon's previous three years.

Leon's Furniture Limited Key Figures ($ in thousands) As at December 31, 2016–2018			
	2018	**2017**	**2016**
Cash	$90,267	$36,207	$43,985
Total Current Assets	661,253	588,548	555,292
Total Non-Current Assets	1,062,319	1,072,907	1,056,370
Total Assets	1,723,572	1,661,455	1,611,662
Total Current Liabilities	607,520	419,838	426,504
Total Shareholders' Equity	857,362	773,048	659,553

FIGURE 10.40

In this example, 2016 (the earliest year shown) is the base year. If we start our comparison with the cash balance of the current year (2018), we can see that compared to 2016, the following things happened. (Recall that numbers are expressed in thousands.)

- Cash increased by $46,282 ($90,267 – $43,985).
- Total assets increased by $111,910 ($1,723,572 – $1,611,662).
- Total current liabilities increased by $181,016 ($607,520 – $426,504).
- Total shareholders' equity increased by $197,809 ($857,362 – $659,553).

Using the comparative balance sheet, we can easily see the increases and decreases in assets and liabilities. While total assets have increased, so have total liabilities and total shareholders' equity. We can see that the company's cash balance has increased; however, so have current liabilities, which indicates the extra cash will be needed to pay current liabilities as they come due. It should be obvious that examining the above dollar amounts does not reveal trends in the company. To really explore the financial health of the company, more in-depth information is needed. For that purpose, the values can be expressed as percentages, or more specifically, *trend percentages.*

To perform a trend analysis, we can calculate trend percentages using the formula in Figure 10.41.

$$\text{Trend Percentage} = \frac{\text{New Account Balance} - \text{Base Year Account Balance}}{\text{Base Year Account Balance}}$$

FIGURE 10.41

As before, 2016 is selected as the base year. For cash, we subtract $43,985 from the year we are examining and divide the result by $43,985. For example, the balance of cash in 2018 was $90,267.

$$\frac{\$90{,}267 - \$43{,}985}{\$43{,}985} = 1.05 \text{ or } 105\%$$

A way to describe this trend is that the cash balance increased by 105% from 2016 to 2018. However, since cash actually went down in 2017, additional years may have to be analyzed to determine whether an increasing or decreasing trend exists. Figure 10.42 shows the trend percentages for Leon's Furniture, based on the key figures from its comparative balance sheet.

Leon's Furniture Limited Trend Percentage As at December 31, 2016–2018			
	2018	**2017**	**2016**
Cash	105%	−18%	0%
Total Current Assets	19%	6%	0%
Total Non-Current Assets	1%	2%	0%
Total Assets	7%	3%	0%
Total Current Liabilities	43%	−2%	0%
Total Shareholders' Equity	30%	17%	0%

FIGURE 10.42

One item to note in Figure 10.42 is the 0% changes for 2016. There is no percent change from the base year figure, because there is no previous year to compare it to.

Using this method, the company can see trends emerging in the data. While there is no evident trend in cash, total current assets have been steadily increasing. Current liabilities had a small decrease in 2017 with a significant increase in 2018, while shareholders' equity has continued to grow over the years. There are no major concerns with these observations.

Vertical Analysis—Balance Sheet

The balance sheet can also be used to perform a **vertical analysis**, in which a line item is compared to a base figure within the same year. This type of analysis provides information on the *relationship* between the balance sheet components. Usually, the **base figure** is a total dollar amount, such as total assets.

To calculate the percentages, we use the formula shown in Figure 10.43.

$$\text{Percentage} = \frac{\text{Line Item Account Balance}}{\text{Base Figure Account Balance}}$$

FIGURE 10.43

To start, a base figure must be selected. In 2018, Leon's Furniture had a total asset balance of $1,723,572; this amount is the base figure. Next, divide all line items in the 2018 balance sheet by the base figure. For example, for cash, divide the balance of $90,267 by the total assets. The result is 0.05 or 5%.

$$\frac{\$90,267}{\$1,723,572} = 0.05 \text{ or } 5\%$$

Figure 10.44 shows a horizontal analysis in which the individual line items from the balance sheet are stated as a percentage of total assets.

Leon's Furniture Limited Key Percentages As at December 31, 2016–2018			
	2018	**2017**	**2016**
Cash	5%	2%	3%
Total Current Assets	38%	35%	34%
Total Non-Current Assets	62%	65%	66%
Total Assets	100%*	100%	100%
Total Current Liabilities	35%	25%	26%
Total Shareholders' Equity	50%	47%	41%

*$1,723,572 ÷ $1,723,572 = 100%

FIGURE 10.44

This type of analysis reveals that, for 2018, current assets represent 38% of total assets while current liabilities are 35%. As shown from calculation of the current ratio in the previous section, Leon's appears to be in a healthy position and able to pay its current liabilities as they come due. Being able to analyze percentages instead of dollar amounts allows the user to easily identify variances without having to do additional calculations as required with ratio analysis. This information helps confirm that Leon's Furniture is in an overall healthy financial position and can be used to support its decisions about future plans.

Horizontal Analysis—Income Statement

The next step is to use the same tools to analyze the company's income statement. Horizontal analysis is done in much the same way on the income statement as it is on the balance sheet.

Leon's Furniture's comparative income statement for the past three years is shown in Figure 10.45. (This figure adds the information for 2016 to what was presented for 2017 and 2018 in Figure 10.8.)

Leon's Furniture Limited Consolidated Statements of Income (partial) As at December 31, 2018, 2017 and 2016			
($ in thousands)	**2018**	**2017**	**2016**
Revenue	$2,241,437	$2,215,379	$2,143,736
Cost of sales	1,264,561	1,261,112	1,228,499
Gross profit	$976,876	$954,267	$915,237
Operating expenses			
Selling, general and administrative expenses	825,276	809,025	786,568
Operating profit	151,600	145,242	128,669
Finance costs	(9,396)	(11,952)	(14,481)
Finance income	2,468	1,450	-
Change in fair value of derivative instruments	5,918	(3,311)	-
Net income before income tax	150,590	131,429	114,188
Income tax expense	39,560	34,836	30,597
Net income for the year	$111,030	$96,593	$83,591

For demonstration purposes, information from Leon's Furniture Limited's Consolidated Statements of Income for 2018 and 2017 has been put together in this figure. Values for 2018 and 2017 are taken from the 2018 report; those for 2016 are taken from the 2017 report.

FIGURE 10.45

The comparative income statement allows the company to quickly see whether revenue and expenses have increased or decreased and whether net income is rising or falling. Leon's Furniture has seen a large increase in revenue, perhaps attributable to an increased advertising budget. The company's net income has increased by almost a third since 2016, which is a good sign of profitability. However, other trends should be examined.

Figure 10.46 lists the key figures from the income statement for the previous three years as dollars, percentage of the base year of 2016 and percentage changed from the base year of 2016.

Leon's Furniture Limited Key Figures ($ in thousands) For the Year Ended December 31, 2016–2018			
	2018	**2017**	**2016**
Total Revenue	$2,241,437	$2,215,379	$2,143,736
Cost of Sales	1,264,561	1,261,112	1,228,499
Gross Profit	976,876	954,267	915,237
Total Operating Expenses	825,276	809,025	786,568
Net Income	111,030	96,593	83,591

Leon's Furniture Limited Percentage of 2016 Base Year For the Year Ended December 31, 2016–2018			
	2018	2017	2016
Total Revenue	105%	103%	100%
Cost of Sales	103%	103%	100%
Gross Profit	107%	104%	100%
Total Operating Expenses	105%	103%	100%
Net Income	133%	116%	100%

Leon's Furniture Limited Percentage Changed with 2016 Base Year For the Year Ended December 31, 2016–2018			
	2018	2017	2016
Total Revenue	5%	3%	0%
Cost of Sales	3%	3%	0%
Gross Profit	7%	4%	0%
Total Operating Expenses	5%	3%	0%
Net Income	33%	16%	0%

FIGURE 10.46

The above analysis reveals that Leon's sales, cost of sales and operating expenses increased proportionately over the base year (2016); however, the net income increased substantially, at 33% in 2018 and 16% in 2017. How could this be possible? For the answer, we need to analyze the items on the income statement reported below the line showing operating profit. Here we see that Leon's reported less interest expense plus some non-operating revenues that were the result of book entries to adjust some balance sheet items to fair values. Notwithstanding the above, Leon's does appear to be a profitable company.

Vertical Analysis—Income Statement

Finally, we will perform a vertical analysis on Leon's income statement by converting everything to a percentage of total revenue for each year, as shown in Figure 10.47.

Leon's Furniture Limited Percentage of Base Figure Total Revenue For the Year Ended December 31, 2016–2018			
	2018	2017	2016
Total Revenue	100%	100%	100%
Cost of Sales	56%	57%	57%
Gross Profit	44%	43%	43%
Total Operating Expenses	37%	37%	37%
Net Income	5%	4%	4%

FIGURE 10.47

This analysis reveals that gross profit and operating expenses have remained quite steady in relation to total revenue. This indicates that sales have risen without causing much of an increase to operating expenses, allowing for more net income per dollar of sales.

Considering all of the indicators examined, it is apparent that Leon's Furniture has been growing steadily over the past three years and is in a healthy enough financial position to expand operations if it chooses to.

We have used horizontal and vertical analysis tools to examine the financial statements of Leon's Furniture. While these tools provide some insight regarding a company's financial position, there are limitations to what they can actually show. The tools do not consider errors in the figures. Also, the trends may not continue because businesses change and evolve constantly. Fortunately, there are many other analysis tools available to users, including the ratio analysis covered in the previous sections of this chapter.

Pause & Reflect

Exercise 10-5

The following summarizes key financial information for Industrial Furnishing's previous four years.

	2020	2019	2018	2017
Total Revenue	$610,000	$600,000	$525,000	$500,000
Cost of Goods Sold	155,000	150,000	110,000	100,000
Gross Profit	455,000	450,000	415,000	400,000
Total Operating Expenses	385,000	375,000	325,000	315,000
Net Income	70,000	75,000	90,000	85,000

a) Calculate the trend precentage for each account, using 2017 as the base year.

Industrial Furnishings
Percentage of 2017 Base Year
For the Year Ended December 31, 2017-2020

	2020	2019	2018	2017
Total Revenue				
Cost of Goods Sold				
Gross Profit				
Total Operating Expenses				
Net Income				

b) Based on the trend percentage calculated in part a), analyze why net income has been decreasing in the past two years.

See Appendix I for solutions.

Computerized Financial Analysis

Financial analysis can help a company assess its performance and make decisions about its operations. However, completing this process manually is time-consuming and can lead to error. Access to timely and accurate reports is necessary for a company to make informed decisions. Accountants often use spreadsheets to calculate ratios and create comparative financial statements, and spreadsheet templates can make formatting reports easy.

To increase efficiency even further, a company can use a computerized accounting system to create instant real-time reports. Products like Intuit's QuickBooks or Sage 50 provide financial statements that allow for quick year-to-year comparisons. The reports can also be exported into spreadsheet software for further analysis and customization.

Horizontal, vertical and ratio analysis can also be completed through financial analysis software. For example, Sage provides an Intelligence Reporting solution that pulls data from Sage accounting software. The software consolidates and calculates the data, which can be exported to Microsoft Excel for further manipulation. Options for reports also include dashboards that show key figures at a glance. Some reporting tools have predictive functions that help with budgeting and forecasting. Using software can increase efficiency and ensure decision-makers have access to current and accurate information.

Limitations of Financial Analysis

LO 8

Although financial analysis of a company's statements can be beneficial, there are specific situations where the comparison will not be entirely accurate or the information provided may not be useful.

For example, when results are compared between companies, different accounting policies can alter the values and make a direct comparison more difficult. Such accounting policies could include how inventory is valued (specific identification, FIFO or weighted average), and how property, plant and equipment is depreciated (straight-line, declining-balance, double-declining-balance or units-of-production). Also, Canadian corporations following ASPE may find it difficult to compare with international competitors that follow IFRS.

To work around this challenge, accountants may adjust the stated values in the financial statements *for comparison purposes only*. The statements are not reissued; this is simply an internal process for ratio comparison. By changing the account values based on similar accounting policies, a more accurate comparison can be made.

A second limitation arises from how IFRS presents certain information. Comprehensive income is not usually included in profitability or other ratios. In most cases, using net income instead of comprehensive income will not cause any significant change in the ratios presented. For example, a change in the profitability ratio from 6.3% to 6.6% due to including comprehensive income will not affect decision-makers. However, if comprehensive income makes up a large portion of the income reported by a company, the company may wish to include comprehensive income in the ratio calculations so the relevant information is available to users.

Lastly, the economy and other external factors can affect how ratios are interpreted. For example, if a company is affected by a recession and reports a net loss for the year, comparing the current year to previous years really does not provide much useful information. A net loss can also cause other ratios to lose their meanings. For example, a company may have a negative price–earnings ratio and a negative dividend yield, but that information alone does not mean much.

When a company experiences a loss, in which case some ratios and analyses are not productive, it may be more beneficial to examine what caused the loss. If the loss is due to an economic downturn, is the company able to survive the loss and is it positioned to bounce back once the economy recovers? If the loss is due to selling off a portion of the company and restructuring, does the company have a sound plan in place to maximize remaining resources to begin generating a profit again? Financial statement analysis can begin to provide a better understanding of a company's financial position and performance. Still, it is just a starting point in the decision-making process and does not eliminate or replace the need for sound expert judgment.

In Summary

LO 1 Explain the importance of analyzing financial statements

- There are different ways to analyze a company's financial statements, such as financial ratio analysis, horizontal analysis and vertical analysis.
- Internal users, such as managers and executives, analyze financial information to correct negative results and take advantage of positive results.
- External users, such as investors and suppliers, analyze financial information to determine whether to invest money or extend credit terms.

LO 2 Calculate and apply liquidity ratios

- A company's liquidity can be assessed using working capital, current ratio and quick ratio.
- Working capital measures a company's ability to cover current liabilities using current assets.
- The current ratio assesses a company's liquidity by determining the extent to which current assets can cover current debts.
- The quick ratio assesses the ability of the company to meet its short-term debt obligations using only highly liquid assets.

LO 3 Calculate and apply profitability ratios

- A company's profitability can be assessed using gross profit margin, net profit margin, return on equity, return on common shareholders' equity, return on assets and asset turnover.
- Gross profit margin measures the percentage of sales revenue left after deducting cost of goods sold.
- Net profit margin assesses a company's profitability after deducting all expenses.
- Return on equity is a measure of what the shareholders are getting out of their investment in the company.
- Return on common shareholders' equity is a measure of the profitability of shareholders' investments.
- Return on assets measures every dollar of net income earned against each dollar's worth of assets.
- Asset turnover is a measure of a company's ability to generate sales revenue from asset investments.

LO 4 Calculate and apply operations management ratios

- A company's operations management can be assessed using inventory turnover, days' sales in inventory, days' sales oustanding and accounts receivable turnover.
- Inventory turnover measures the efficiency of inventory management.
- Days' sales in inventory measures the average number of days it takes a company to turn over inventory during the year.

- Days' sales outstanding measures the average number of days a company takes to collect accounts receivable.
- Accounts receivable turnover measures the efficiency of accounts receivable collections.

LO 5 Calculate and apply solvency ratios

- A company's solvency can be assessed using the debt-to-equity ratio, times interest earned ratio and debt-to-total-assets ratio.
- Debt-to-equity measures the relative amount of debt versus shareholders' equity being used to finance a company's assets.
- Times interest earned measures a company's ability to cover interest on its debt.
- Debt-to-total-assets measures the amount of debt being financed by creditors.

LO 6 Calculate and apply capital market ratios

- Public corporations can be analyzed to determine if they are desirable as investments.
- Book value per common share measures the theoretical value of a share based on shareholders' claims to a company's assets.
- Dividend yield measures the rate of return to common shareholders.
- Earnings per share measures profit earned by investors per common share.
- Price-earnings ratio measures the market value of a common share related to its earnings.

LO 7 Conduct a horizontal and vertical analysis of financial statements

- The comparative balance sheet is used to perform a horizontal analysis because it compares information from one accounting period to another.
- One way of conducting a horizontal analysis is by calculating the succeeding years' balance sheet items as a percentage of the base year's number. Another way is by calculating the percentage change from a base year to show the percentage increase or decrease of each balance sheet item over time.
- A vertical analysis is conducted by converting each separate line item in a financial statement into a percentage of the base figure within the specific year.

LO 8 Identify the limitations of financial statement analysis

- Ratio analysis may not present an accurate picture if the companies being compared use different accounting policies, or if one follows ASPE while another follows IFRS.
- Under IFRS, comprehensive income is usually not included in ratio analysis. Comprehensive income may need to be included if the amount is significant.
- Economic situations or company losses can cause some ratios to lose their meaning. A closer look at the cause of a loss, in addition to ratio analysis, may be beneficial.

Review Exercise 10-1

Basil's Bakery has provided you with the following financial statements.

Basil's Bakery
Balance Sheet
As at December 31

($ in thousands)	**2020**	**2019**
Assets		
Current Assets		
Cash	$1,605	$987
Accounts Receivable	1,175	573
Merchandise Inventory	396	256
Other Current Assets	301	103
Total Current Assets	3,477	1,919
Property, Plant & Equipment	2,034	1,170
Total Assets	$5,511	$3,089
Liabilities		
Current Liabilities	$1,474	$547
Long-Term Liabilities	104	58
Total Liabilities	1,578	605
Shareholders' Equity	3,933	2,484
Total Liabilities and Equity	$5,511	$3,089

Basil's Bakery
Income Statement
For the Year Ended December 31, 2020

	($ in thousands)
Sales Revenue	$6,009
Cost of Goods Sold	2,928
Gross Profit	3,081
Operating Expenses	
Depreciation Expense	108
Interest Expense	518
Other Operating Expenses	723
Total Operating Expenses	1,349
Income from Operations	1,732
Investment Income	79
Operating Income before Tax	1,811
Income Tax	516
Net Income	$1,295

Assume all sales are credit sales.

In addition to the financial statements, the following data is known. Basil's Bakery does not have preferred shares. The bakery industry average for gross profit margin is 49% for 2020, and the industry average for net profit margin is 20% for the same time period.

In 2019, Basil's Bakery had a gross profit margin of 52% and a net profit margin of 22%.

Required

a) Perform a horizontal and vertical analysis of Basil's Bakery.

Basil's Bakery Percentage Change and Vertical Analysis As at December 31				
($ in thousands)	**2020**	**2019**	**% Change**	**% of Base Figure 2020**
Cash	$1,605	$987		
Accounts Receivable	1,175	573		
Merchandise Inventory	396	256		
Other Current Assets	301	103		
Total Current Assets	3,477	1,919		
Property, Plant & Equipment	2,034	1,170		
Total Assets	$5,511	$3,089		
Current Liabilities	$1,474	$547		
Long-Term Liabilities	104	58		
Total Liabilities	1,578	605		
Shareholders' Equity	3,933	2,484		
Total Liabilities and Equity	$5,511	$3,089		

b) Calculate the financial ratios and figures for 2020.

Financial Ratio or Figure	**Calculation**	**Result**
Working Capital		
Current Ratio		
Quick Ratio		
Gross Profit Margin		
Net Profit Margin		
Return on Equity		
Return on Common Shareholders' Equity		
Return on Assets		

Financial Ratio or Figure	Calculation	Result
Asset Turnover		
Inventory Turnover Ratio		
Days' Sales in Inventory		
Days' Sales Outstanding		
Accounts Receivable Turnover		
Debt-to-Equity Ratio		
Times Interest Earned		
Debt-to-Total-Assets		

c) For each ratio, comment on the result. In your explanation, state whether or not the result is favourable for the company and include your reasons.

See Appendix I for solutions.

Appendix I

SOLUTIONS FOR PAUSE & REFLECT AND REVIEW EXERCISES

CHAPTER 1 SOLUTIONS

Pause & Reflect Exercise 1-1

JOURNAL			
Date	**Account Title and Explanation**	**Debit**	**Credit**
2020			
Dec 31	Bad Debt Expense	6,500	
	Allowance for Doubtful Accounts		6,500
	To record estimated bad debt		
2021			
Mar 5	Allowance for Doubtful Accounts	2,100	
	Accounts Receivable—Basil's Hotel		2,100
	To write off bad debt		

Pause & Reflect Exercise 1-2

a)

Aging Category	Bad Debt %	Balance of Accounts Receivable	Estimated Bad Debt
30 days	1%	$200,000	$2,000
31-60 days	5%	120,000	6,000
More than 60 days	10%	80,000	8,000
Total		$400,000	$16,000

b)

JOURNAL			
Date	**Account Title and Explanation**	**Debit**	**Credit**
Dec 31	Bad Debt Expense	12,600	
	Allowance for Doubtful Accounts		12,600
	To record bad debt expense		

Pause & Reflect Exercise 1-3

JOURNAL			
Date	**Account Title and Explanation**	**Debit**	**Credit**
2020			
Nov 1	Notes Receivable	6,000	
	Accounts Receivable		6,000
	To convert account receivable into note receivable		
Dec 31	Interest Receivable	50	
	Interest Revenue		50
	To accrue interest on the note receivable		
2021			
Apr 30	Cash	6,150	
	Interest Receivable		50
	Interest Revenue		100
	Notes Receivable		6,000
	To record receipt of payment of note plus interest		

Pause & Reflect Exercise 1-4

a)

$$\text{Accounts Receivable Turnover Ratio} = \frac{\text{Net Credit Sales}}{\text{Average Net Accounts Receivable}}$$

$$= \frac{\$278{,}000}{\$23{,}000}$$

$$= 12 \text{ times}$$

The accounts receivable turnover is 12 times. This means that the company collects the entire amount of accounts receivable about 12 times a year, or approximately once a month.

b) $$\text{Days' Sales Outstanding} = \frac{\text{Average Net Accounts Receivable}}{\text{Net Credit Sales}} \times 365$$

$$= \frac{\$23{,}000}{\$278{,}000} \times 365$$

$$= 30 \text{ days}$$

The days' sales outstanding is 30 days. This means that the company collects the entire amount of accounts receivable in an average of 30 days, or approximately one month.

Review Exercise 1-1

a)

JOURNAL			
Date	**Account Title and Explanation**	**Debit**	**Credit**
Dec 31	Cash	70,000	
	Accounts Receivable	280,000	
	Sales Revenue		350,000
Dec 31	Cash	250,000	
	Accounts Receivable		250,000
Dec 31	Allowance for Doubtful Accounts	1,500	
	Accounts Receivable		1,500
Dec 31	Accounts Receivable	1,500	
	Allowance for Doubtful Accounts		1,500
Dec 31	Bad Debt Expense	2,500	
	Allowance for Doubtful Accounts		2,500

b)

Cash

Debit	Credit
$70,000	
250,000	
$320,000	

Accounts Receivable

Debit	Credit
Beg. Bal. $35,000	$250,000
280,000	1,500
1,500	
$65,000	

Sales Revenue

Debit	Credit
	$350,000

AFDA

Debit	Credit
$1,500	$2,500 Beg. Bal.
	1,500
	2,500
	$5,000

Bad Debt Expense

Debit	Credit
$2,500	

c)

ABC Company
Balance Sheet (partial)
As at December 31, 2020

Accounts Receivable	$65,000
Less: Allowance for Doubtful Accounts	5,000
Net Accounts Receivable	$60,000

d)

JOURNAL			
Date	**Account Title**	**Debit**	**Credit**
Dec 31	Bad Debt Expense	2,800	
	Allowance for Doubtful Accounts		2,800
	To estimate bad debt for the year		

If the company uses the income statement approach, it does not take the AFDA beginning balance into account when it records the journal entry to estimate bad debt. Simply calculate 1% of credit sales (350,000 × 0.8 = 280,000), which is equal to $2,800, and use this number in the journal entry.

Review Exercise 1-2

JOURNAL			
Date	**Account Title and Explanation**	**Debit**	**Credit**
Jun 30	Accounts Receivable	5,000	
	Sales Revenue		5,000
	To record sale on credit		
Jul 31	Notes Receivable	5,000	
	Accounts Receivable		5,000
	To convert account receivable to a note receivable		
Aug 31	Interest Receivable	25	
	Interest Revenue		25
	To record accrued interest revenue		
	($5,000 × 6% × 1/12)		
Dec 31	Cash	5,125	
	Interest Receivable		25
	Interest Revenue		100
	Notes Receivable		5,000
	To record receipt of note principal and interest		
Dec 31	Accounts Receivable	5,125	
	Interest Receivable		25
	Interest Revenue		100
	Notes Receivable		5,000
	To record a dishonoured note		

CHAPTER 2 SOLUTIONS

Pause & Reflect Exercise 2-1

a)

Asset	Appraised Value	Percentage	Book Value
Building	$1,000,000	50%	$900,000
Land	600,000	30%	540,000
Parking Lot	400,000	20%	360,000
Total	$2,000,000	100%	$1,800,000

b)

JOURNAL			Page 2
Date	Account Title and Explanation	Debit	Credit
May 1	Building	900,000	
	Land	540,000	
	Parking Lot	360,000	
	Cash		1,800,000
	To purchase assets with cash		

Pause & Reflect Exercise 2-2

Year	Beginning of Year Book Value	Depreciation	Remaining Book Value
2020	$5,000,000	$2,000,000	$3,000,000
2021	$3,000,000	$1,200,000	$1,800,000
2022	$1,800,000	$720,000	$1,080,000
2023	$1,080,000	$432,000	$648,000
2024	$648,000	$248,000	$400,000

Pause & Reflect Exercise 2-3

JOURNAL			
Date	Account Title and Explanation	Debit	Credit
Dec 31	Depreciation Expense	260,000	
	Accumulated Depreciation—Equipment		260,000
	To record annual depreciation		
Dec 31	Cash	360,000	
	Accumulated Depreciation—Equipment	2,340,000	
	Loss on Disposal of Asset	300,000	
	Equipment		3,000,000
	To record sale of asset for cash		

Pause & Reflect Exercise 2-4

a) Depletion Rate $= \dfrac{(\$21{,}000{,}000 - \$1{,}000{,}000)}{500{,}000 \text{ ounces}}$
$= \$40/\text{ounce}$

b)

JOURNAL			
Date	**Account Title and Explanation**	**Debit**	**Credit**
Dec 31	Depletion Expense—Mineral Deposit	560,000	
	Accumulated Depletion—Mineral Deposit		560,000
	To record depletion of gold mine		

Review Exercise 2-1

a)

JOURNAL			
Date	**Account Title and Explanation**	**Debit**	**Credit**
Dec 31	Computer	3,000	
	Office Equipment	10,000	
	Cash		13,000
	To record purchase of computer and office equipment for cash		

b) A reasonable life for a computer would be three years, and for equipment would be 5–10 years. Students will arrive at various numbers based on their research.

c) Because computers are upgraded quickly, a declining-balance method would be appropriate with large amounts of depreciation early on. For office equipment, straight-line depreciation would be reasonable.

d) Computer

Year	Cost	Depreciation	Accumulated Depreciation	Net Book Value
2021	3,000.00	1,000.00	1,000.00	2,000.00
2022	2,000.00	666.67	1,666.67	1,333.33
2023	1,333.33	444.44	2,111.11	888.89

Office Equipment

Year	Cost	Depreciation	Accumulated Depreciation	Net Book Value
2021	10,000	2,000	2,000	8,000
2022	10,000	2,000	4,000	6,000
2023	10,000	2,000	6,000	4,000
2024	10,000	2,000	8,000	2,000
2025	10,000	2,000	10,000	0

e) The profit or loss on disposal of a long-term asset is the difference between the amount received and the net book value of the asset at the time of disposal.

Review Exercise 2-2

JOURNAL			
Date	Account Title and Explanation	Debit	Credit
Jan 1	Assets	500,000	
	Goodwill	50,000	
	Liabilities		300,000
	Cash		250,000
	To record purchase of assets and liabilities of Regnier Ltd.		
Jan 1	Patents	50,000	
	Cash		50,000
	To record purchase of patents for cash		
Jan 1	Trademarks	20,000	
	Cash		20,000
	To record purchase of trademarks for cash		
Jan 30	Mineral Deposit	100,000	
	Cash		100,000
	To record purchase of mineral deposit for cash		
Jun 30	Impairment Loss	25,000	
	Goodwill		25,000
	To record impairment of goodwill		
Dec 31	Amortization Expense—Patents	6,250	
	Accumulated Amortization—Patents		6,250
	To record amortization for the period		
	[(50,000 ÷ 4) × ½ year]		
Dec 31	Amortization Expense—Trademarks	1,244	
	Accumulated Amortization—Trademarks		1,244
	To record amortization for the period		
	[((20,000 − 100) ÷ 8) × ½ year]		
Dec 31	Depletion Expense—Mineral Deposit	2,000	
	Accumulated Depletion—Mineral Rights		2,000
	To record depletion for the period		
	[10,000 × (100,000 ÷ 500,000)]		

Review Exercise 2A-1

a) The following shows both calculation methods, either of which is correct. Fair market value is shortened to FMV in the table below.

Exchange of Asset with Commercial Substance—Worksheet		
Method: Difference between FMV (new asset) and book value (old asset) plus cash paid on exchange		
Price (FMV) of New Machinery		$150,000
Less: Value of Assets Given Up in Exchange		
Book Value of Old Machinery *($125,000 – $103,750)*	$21,250	
Cash Paid on Exchange	120,000	141,250
Gain on Exchange of Assets		$ 8,750
Method: Difference between FMV (trade-in allowance) of old asset *and* book value of old asset		
FMV (Trade-In Allowance) of Old Machinery		$30,000
Less: Book Value of Old Machinery *($125,000 – $103,750)*		21,250
Gain on Exchange of Assets		$8,750

b)

JOURNAL			
Date	**Account Title and Explanation**	**Debit**	**Credit**
Nov 30	Machinery (new)	150,000	
	Accumulated Depreciation—Machinery (old)	103,750	
	Machinery (old)		125,000
	Cash		120,000
	Gain on Exchange of Assets		8,750
	To record exchange of old machinery and cash for		
	new machinery		

c)

JOURNAL			
Date	**Account Title and Explanation**	**Debit**	**Credit**
Nov 30	Machinery (new)	141,250	
	Accumulated Depreciation—Machinery (old)	103,750	
	Machinery (old)		125,000
	Cash		120,000
	To record exchange of old machinery and cash for		
	new machinery		

Review Exercise 2A-2

a) The following shows both calculation methods, either of which is correct. Fair market value is shortened to FMV in the table below.

Exchange of Asset with Commercial Substance—Worksheet		
Method: Difference between FMV (new asset) *and* book value (old asset) plus cash paid on exchange		
Price (FMV) of New Delivery Vehicle		$60,000
Less: Value of Assets Given Up in Exchange		
Book Value of Old Delivery Vehicle *($45,000 – $39,000)*	$6,000	
Cash Paid on Exchange	55,000	61,000
Loss on Exchange of Assets		($1,000)
Method: Difference between FMV (trade-in allowance) of old asset *and* book value of old asset		
FMV (Trade-In Allowance) of Old Delivery Vehicle		$5,000
Less: Book Value of Old Delivery Vehicle *($45,000 – $39,000)*		6,000
Loss on Exchange of Assets		($1,000)

b)

JOURNAL

Date	Account Title and Explanation	Debit	Credit
Apr 30	Delivery Vehicle (new)	60,000	
	Accumulated Depreciation—Delivery Vehicle (old)	39,000	
	Loss on Exchange of Assets	1,000	
	Delivery Vehicle (old)		45,000
	Cash		55,000
	To record exchange of old delivery vehicle and		
	cash for new delivery vehicle		

c)

JOURNAL

Date	Account Title and Explanation	Debit	Credit
Apr 30	Delivery Vehicle (new)	61,000	
	Accumulated Depreciation— Delivery Vehicle (old)	39,000	
	Delivery Vehicle (old)		45,000
	Cash		55,000
	To record exchange of old delivery vehicle and		
	cash for new delivery vehicle		

CHAPTER 3 SOLUTIONS

Pause & Reflect Exercise 3-1

JOURNAL

Date	Account Title and Explanation	Debit	Credit
Apr 30	Salaries Expense	10,000	
	Employee Income Tax Payable		2,500
	CPP Payable		490
	EI Payable		190
	Health Insurance Payable		200
	Salaries Payable		6,620
	To record payroll for pay period		
Apr 30	Employee Benefits Expense	956	
	CPP Payable		490
	EI Payable		266
	Health Insurance Payable		200
	To record employer share of employee benefits		

Pause & Reflect Exercise 3-2

JOURNAL

Date	Account Title and Explanation	Debit	Credit
Mar 13	Cash	56,500	
	Sales Revenue		50,000
	HST Payable		6,500
	To record cash sale of goods		
Mar 13	Cost of Goods Sold	22,000	
	Merchandise Inventory		22,000
	To record cost of goods sold and reduce inventory for items sold		

Pause & Reflect Exercise 3-3

JOURNAL

Date	Account Title and Explanation	Debit	Credit
2020			
Sep 1	Cash	20,000	
	Notes Payable		20,000
	To borrow cash from the bank, due in six months		

JOURNAL			
Date	**Account Title and Explanation**	**Debit**	**Credit**
Dec 31	Interest Expense	400	
	Interest Payable		400
	To accrue interest on note payable		
2021			
Feb 28	Notes Payable	20,000	
	Interest Payable	400	
	Interest Expense	200	
	Cash		20,600
	To record payment of note and interest on due date		

Pause & Reflect Exercise 3-4

JOURNAL			
Date	**Account Title and Explanation**	**Debit**	**Credit**
Dec 31	Warranty Expense	400,000	
	Estimated Warranty Liability		400,000
	To record estimated warranty liability		

Review Exercise 3-1

JOURNAL			
Date	**Account Title and Explanation**	**Debit**	**Credit**
Jan 15	Merchandise Inventory	105,000	
	HST Recoverable	13,650	
	Accounts Payable		118,650
	To buy machine for resale		
Jan 30	Cash	241,820	
	HST Payable		27,820
	Sales Revenue		214,000
	To record sale of machine for cash		
Jan 30	Cost of Goods Sold	105,000	
	Merchandise Inventory		105,000
	To record COGS for above sale		
Jan 30	Warranty Expense	20,000	
	Estimated Warranty Liability		20,000
	To accrue estimated warranty costs		

JOURNAL			
Date	Account Title and Explanation	Debit	Credit
Jan 30	HST Payable	27,820	
	HST Recoverable		13,650
	Cash		14,170
	To pay HST to the government		
Feb 15	Accounts Payable	118,650	
	Cash		118,650
	To pay for machine bought on account on Jan 15		
Mar 27	Estimated Warranty Liability	200	
	Parts Inventory		200
	To record inventory for warranty work		

CHAPTER 4 SOLUTIONS

Pause & Reflect Exercise 4-1

JOURNAL			
Date	Account Title and Explanation	Debit	Credit
Sep 1	Cash	5,000	
	Building	275,000	
	Notes Payable		80,000
	Akazi, Capital		200,000
	To record investment by Miko Akazi into partnership		
Sep 1	Cash	15,000	
	Equipment	20,000	
	Accounts Payable		10,000
	Warren, Capital		25,000
	To record investment by Gayle Warren into partnership		

Pause & Reflect Exercise 4-2

a)

	Total	Eric Banner	David Martin
Net Income	$90,000		
Salary to Eric	−45,000	$45,000	
Salary to David	−35,000		$35,000
Remainder	10,000		
Share of profit to Eric	−5,000	5,000	
Share of profit to David	−5,000		5,000
Transferred to capital accounts	−$90,000	$50,000	$40,000

b)

JOURNAL			
Date	**Account Title and Explanation**	**Debit**	**Credit**
Dec 31	Income Summary	90,000	
	Banner, Capital		50,000
	Martin, Capital		40,000
	To allocate net income to capital accounts		

Pause & Reflect Exercise 4-3

	Kelsey	Zac	Yelena	Total
Capital balance before admission	$110,000	$150,000		$260,000
Admission of new partner	−10,000	−10,000	$120,000	100,000
Capital balance after admission	$100,000	$140,000	$120,000	$360,000

Pause & Reflect Exercise 4-4

JOURNAL			
Date	**Account Title and Explanation**	**Debit**	**Credit**
Nov 30	Cash	200,000	
	Loss on Sale of Assets	40,000	
	Assets		240,000
	To record sale of assets for a loss		
Nov 30	Diana, Capital	20,000	
	Kate, Capital	20,000	
	Loss on Sale of Assets		40,000
	To allocate loss to partners		
Nov 30	Liabilities	110,000	
	Cash		110,000
	To pay partnership liabilities		
Nov 30	Diana, Capital	50,000	
	Kate, Capital	70,000	
	Cash		120,000
	To distribute cash to partners		

Review Exercise 4-1

a)

	Total	Zelma	Serena	Sharon
Cash Contribution	$30,000	$10,000	$10,000	$10,000
Contribution of Equipment	25,000	25,000		
Partner Contributions	$55,000	$35,000	$10,000	$10,000
Net Income	$25,000			
Salaries	−15,000	5,000	5,000	5,000
Equipment Rental	−3,000	3,000		
Interest	−1,500	500	500	500
Division of Income	5,500	1,834	1,833	1,833
Addition to Partners' Capital		$10,334	$7,333	$7,333
Capital Balance, December 31, 2020	$80,000	$45,334	$17,333	$17,333

b)

JOURNAL

Date	Account Title and Explanation	Debit	Credit
2020			
Jan 1	Cash	30,000	
	Rapoza, Capital		10,000
	Dennen, Capital		10,000
	Thorne, Capital		10,000
	To record set up of partnership		
Jan 1	Equipment	25,000	
	Rapoza, Capital		25,000
	To record contribution of equipment		
Dec 31	Income Summary	25,000	
	Rapoza, Capital		10,334
	Dennen, Capital		7,333
	Thorne, Capital		7,333
	To adjust partners' capital accounts for their share of net income		
2021			
Jan 2	Thorne, Capital	17,333	
	Rapoza, Capital		10,000
	Dennen, Capital		7,333
	To record Thorne's withdrawal from partnership		

CHAPTER 5 SOLUTIONS

Pause & Reflect Exercise 5-1

JOURNAL			
Date	**Account Title and Explanation**	**Debit**	**Credit**
Jan 7	Cash	57,000	
	Preferred Shares		25,000
	Common Shares		32,000
	To issue preferred and common shares for cash		
Jan 8	Land	400,000	
	Common Shares		400,000
	To issue common shares in exchange for land		

Pause & Reflect Exercise 5-2

JOURNAL			
Date	**Account Title and Explanation**	**Debit**	**Credit**
May 25	Cash Dividends—Preferred, cumulative	40,000	
	Cash Dividends—Preferred, noncumulative	50,000	
	Cash Dividends—Common	30,000	
	Dividends Payable		120,000
	To record declaration of cash dividends		
Jul 15	Dividends Payable	120,000	
	Cash		120,000
	To record cash payment of dividend		

Note: Preferred, cumulative dividends per year are 10% × $40 × 5,000 shares = $20,000. Total cumulative preferred dividends for 2019 and 2020 are $20,000 × 2 years = $40,000. Preferred, noncumulative dividends are 20% × $25 × 10,000 shares = $50,000.

Pause & Reflect Exercise 5-3

a) The 2-for-1 stock split will double the quantity of common shares from 400,000 to 800,000. The total book value of common shares will remain unchanged.

b) The value of retained earnings will remain unchanged.

c) The market price will likely be halved, to $40 per share.

Review Exercise 5-1

a)

JOURNAL			
Date	Account Title and Explanation	Debit	Credit
Mar 3	Assets	2,000,000	
	Liabilities		1,250,000
	Common Shares		750,000
	To issue common shares for net assets of partnership		
Apr 15	Cash	1,000,000	
	Common Shares		1,000,000
	To issue common shares for cash		
Apr 30	Accounting Fees Expense	100,000	
	Preferred Shares		100,000
	To issue preferred shares for accounting services		
May 10	Equipment	250,000	
	Common Shares		250,000
	To issue common shares for equipment		
Sep 15	Retained Earnings	135,000	
	Common Stock Dividends Distributable		135,000
	To record declaration of 5% common stock dividends		
	(2,250 × $60 = $135,000)		
Oct 2	Common Stock Dividends Distributable	135,000	
	Common Shares		135,000
	To record distribution of stock dividends		
Oct 15	Cash Dividends—Preferred	30,000	
	Cash Dividends—Common	150,000	
	Dividends Payable		180,000
	To record declaration of cash dividends on common and		
	preferred shares		
Dec 15	Dividends Payable	180,000	
	Cash		180,000
	To record payment of cash dividends declared		

b)

Camphamel Inc.	
Balance Sheet (partial)	
As at December 31, 2020	
Shareholders' Equity	
Contributed Capital	
Preferred Shares, 30%, 200,000 shares authorized,	
10,000 shares issued	$100,000
Common Shares, unlimited shares authorized,	
47,250 shares issued and outstanding	2,135,000
Total Contributed Capital	2,235,000
Retained Earnings	585,000
Total Shareholders' Equity	$2,820,000

Notes:

Common Shares = $750,000 + $1,000,000 + $250,000 + $135,000 = $2,135,000

Retained Earnings = Net Income − Stock Dividends − Cash Dividends
= $900,000 −$135,000 −$180,000
= $585,000

Review Exercise 5A-1

a)

JOURNAL			
Date	**Account Title and Explanation**	**Debit**	**Credit**
Mar 10	Common Shares	75,000	
	Contributed Surplus		5,000
	Cash		70,000
	To record reacquiring and retiring of shares		
	[($1,000,000 ÷ 200,000) × 15,000]		

b) Average cost of shares remains unchanged at $5. [($1,000,000 – $75,000) ÷ 185,000 shares]

c)

JOURNAL			
Date	**Account Title and Explanation**	**Debit**	**Credit**
Jun 15	Common Shares	75,000	
	Contributed Surplus	5,000	
	Retained Earnings	10,000	
	Cash		90,000
	To record reacquiring and retiring of shares		
	(15,000 shares × $5 per share)		

CHAPTER 6 SOLUTIONS

Pause & Reflect Exercise 6-1

Earnings per share from continuing operations	Earnings per Share = $\frac{(\$850,000 - \$0)}{100,000}$ = \$8.50
Basic earnings per share	Earnings per Share = $\frac{(\$925,000 - \$0)}{100,000}$ = \$9.25

Pause & Reflect Exercise 6-2

a) Dividend per common share = \$300,000 ÷ 100,000 = \$3

Dividend Yield = \$3 ÷ \$50 = 6%

Dividend Payout Ratio = \$300,000 ÷ \$1,462,000 = 20.5%

b) Price-Earnings (P/E) Ratio = \$17.42 ÷ \$3.15 = 5.53

Review Exercise 6-1

a)

Shah Company Income Statement For the Year Ended December 31, 2020		
Sales Revenue		$710,000
Less: Sales Discounts		15,000
Net Sales		695,000
Cost of Goods Sold		380,000
Gross Profit		315,000
Operating Expenses		
Selling Expenses	$42,000	
Administrative Expenses	20,000	
Total Operating Expenses		62,000
Income from Operations		253,000
Other Income and Expenses		
Interest Expenses	(30,000)	
Loss Due to Lawsuit	(11,000)	(41,000)
Income (Loss) from Continuing Operations before Income Tax Expense		212,000
Income Tax Expense		74,200
Income (Loss) from Continuing Operations		137,800
Discontinued Operations		
Income from Operating Discontinued Operations (net of $12,250 tax)	22,750	
Loss on Sale of Discontinued Operations (net of $14,000 tax)	(26,000)	(3,250)
Net Income (Loss)		$134,550

Note: Basic earnings per share is $8.36. Since this company follows ASPE, EPS can be reported in the income statement or in the notes.

b)

Shah Company Statement of Retained Earnings For the Year Ended December 31, 2020	
Retained Earnings, January 1, 2020, as Originally Reported	$110,000
Prior Period Adjustment	
Retained Earnings Overstated	(7,500)
Retained Earnings, January 1, 2020, as Adjusted	102,500
Net Income	134,550
Less: Cash Dividends—Common	20,000
Cash Dividends—Preferred	5,000
Retained Earnings, December 31, 2020	$212,050

c)

Shah Company		
Balance Sheet (partial)		
As at December 31, 2020		
Shareholders' Equity		
Contributed Capital		
Preferred Shares, 10% noncumulative		
10,000 shares authorized, 1,000 shares issued and outstanding	$50,000	
Common Shares, unlimited shares authorized,		
15,500 shares issued and outstanding	155,000	
Total Contributed Capital	205,000	
Retained Earnings	212,050	
Total Shareholders' Equity		$417,050

d) Since preferred dividends equal $5,000 ($5.00 × 1,000), and assuming the same number of shares has been outstanding throughout the year, earnings per share is calculated as follows.

$$EPS = \frac{\text{Net Income} - \text{Preferred Dividends}}{\text{Weighted Average Number of Common Shares Outstanding}}$$

$$= \frac{\$134{,}550 - \$5{,}000}{15{,}500}$$

$$= \$8.36$$

CHAPTER 7 SOLUTIONS

Pause & Reflect Exercise 7-1

JOURNAL			
Date	**Account Title and Explanation**	**Debit**	**Credit**
Jan 1	Cash	300,000	
	Bonds Payable		300,000
	To issue 1,500 five-year bonds at par		

Pause & Reflect Exercise 7-2

a)

Straight-Line Amortization Table of Bond Discount					
Semi-Annual Interest Period	Interest Payment	Discount Amortization	Interest Expense	Discount Balance	Bond Book Value
0				3,546	96,454[1]
1	4,000	887	4,887	2,659	97,341
2	4,000	887	4,887	1,772	98,228
3	4,000	887	4,887	885	99,115
4	4,000	885[2]	4,885	0	100,000
Total	16,000	3,546	19,546	0	-

[1] Using the tables, the value is $96,454. [($100,000 × 0.8227) + ($4,000 × 3.5460)]
Using a financial calculator, the value is also $96,454. (FV = $100,000; n = 4; I/Y = 5; PMT = $4,000)
[2] $885 is due to rounding.

b)

JOURNAL			
Date	Account Title and Explanation	Debit	Credit
Jan 1	Cash	96,454	
	Discount on Bonds Payable	3,546	
	Bonds Payable		100,000
	To issue $100,000 worth of bonds at a discount		

Pause & Reflect Exercise 7-3

a)

Straight-Line Amortization Table of Bond Premium					
Semi-Annual Interest Period	Interest Payment	Premium Amortization	Interest Expense	Premium Balance	Bond Book Value
0				7,092	207,092[1]
1	12,000	1,773	10,227	5,319	205,319
2	12,000	1,773	10,227	3,546	203,546
3	12,000	1,773	10,227	1,773	201,773
4	12,000	1,773	10,227	0	200,000
Total	48,000	7,092	40,908	0	-

[1] Using the tables, the value is $207,092. [($200,000 × 0.8227) + ($12,000 × 3.5460)]
Using a financial calculator, the value is the same. (FV = $200,000, n = 4; I/Y = 5; PMT = $12,000)

b)

JOURNAL			
Date	Account Title and Explanation	Debit	Credit
Jan 1	Cash	207,092	
	Premium on Bonds Payable		7,092
	Bonds Payable		200,000
	To issue $200,000 worth of bonds at a premium		

Pause & Reflect Exercise 7-4

JOURNAL			
Date	**Account Title and Explanation**	**Debit**	**Credit**
Jun 30	Bonds Payable	1,000,000	
	Premium on Bonds Payable	40,000	
	Cash		950,000
	Gain on Bond Redemption		90,000
	To redeem $1,000,000 worth of bonds		

Pause & Reflect Exercise 7-5

JOURNAL			
Date	**Account Title and Explanation**	**Debit**	**Credit**
Jul 1	Interest Expense	927	
	Notes Payable	4,734	
	Cash		5,661
	To record monthly payment of principal and interest on note payable		

Review Exercise 7-1

Premium bond price = $2,000,000 + $142,968 = $2,142,968

a)

	A	B	C	D	E
Semi-Annual Interest Period (Date)	**Interest Payment ($2,000,000 × 2%)**	**Premium Amortization (Total Premium ÷ 40 periods)**	**Interest Expense (A – B)**	**Premium Balance (D [Previous Period] – B)**	**Bond Book Value ($2,000,000 + D)**
0				$142,968	$2,142,968[1]
1 (Sep 30, 2020)	$40,000	$3,574	$36,426	139,394	2,139,394
2 (Mar 31, 2021)	40,000	3,574	36,426	135,820	2,135,820
3 (Sep 30, 2021)	40,000	3,574	36,426	132,246	2,132,246
4 (Mar 31, 2022)	40,000	3,574	36,426	128,672	2,128,672
5 (Sep 30, 2022)	40,000	3,574	36,426	125,098	2,125,098
6 (Mar 31, 2023)	40,000	3,574	36,426	121,524	2,121,524
7 (Sep 30, 2023)	40,000	3,574	36,426	117,950	2,117,950
8 (Mar 31, 2024)	40,000	3,574	36,426	114,376	2,114,376
9 (Sep 30, 2024)	40,000	3,574	36,426	110,802	2,110,802
10 (Mar 31, 2025)	40,000	3,574	36,426	107,228	2,107,228

(1) Using a financial calculator, the value is $2,142,971. (FV = $2,000,000; n = 40; I/Y = 1.75; PMT = $40,000)

b)

JOURNAL			
Date	**Account Title and Explanation**	**Debit**	**Credit**
2020			
Apr 1	Cash	2,142,968	
	Premium on Bonds		142,968
	Bonds Payable		2,000,000
	To issue $2 million worth of bonds at a premium, due in		
	20 years		
Sep 30	Interest Expense	36,426	
	Premium on Bonds	3,574	
	Cash		40,000
	To record payment of interest and amortization of premium		
2021			
Feb 28	Interest Expense	30,355	
	Premium on Bonds	2,978	
	Interest Payable		33,333
	To accrue interest at year end		
	(Interest Expense: $36,426 × $^5/_6$ = $30,355)		
	(Interest Payable: $40,000 × $^5/_6$ = $33,333)		
2025			
Mar 31	Cash	2,200,000	
	Bonds Payable		2,200,000
	To issue new bonds		
Mar 31	Bonds Payable	2,000,000	
	Premium on Bonds	107,228	
	Loss on Bond Redemption	2,772	
	Cash		2,110,000
	To redeem bonds		
Sep 30	Interest Expense	22,000	
	Cash		22,000
	To record interest		
	($2,200,000 × 2% × $^6/_{12}$)		

Review Exercise 7-2

a)

Date	A Cash Payment	B Interest Expense (D × 4% × 6/12)	C Reduction of Principal (A – B)	D Principal Balance (C – D)
May 1, 2020				$200,000
Nov 1, 2020	$52,525	$4,000	$48,525	151,475
May 1, 2021	52,525	3,030	49,495	101,980
Nov 1, 2021	52,525	2,040	50,485	51,495
May 1, 2022	52,525	1,030	51,495	0

b)

JOURNAL

Date	Account Title and Explanation	Debit	Credit
May 1, 2020	Equipment	200,000	
	Notes Payable		200,000
	To issue note payable of $200,000, at 4%		
	annual interest rate, payable semi-annually		
Nov 1, 2020	Interest Expense	4,000	
	Notes Payable	48,525	
	Cash		52,525
	To record installment payment of principal and interest		
Mar 31, 2021	Interest Expense	2,525	
	Interest Payable		2,525
	To recognize accrued interest at year end		
	(Interest Expense: $3,030 × 5/6 = $2,525)		
May 1, 2021	Interest Expense	505	
	Interest Payable	2,525	
	Notes Payable	49,495	
	Cash		52,525
	To record payments of interest and principal		
	(Interest Expense: $3,030 × 1/6 = $505)		

Review Exercise 7A-1

a) Discount bond price = $200,000 – $15,443 = $184,557

Semi-Annual Interest Period (Date)	A Interest Payment ($200,000 × 4%)	B Interest Expense (D × 5%)	C Discount Amortization (B – A)	D Bond Amortized Cost (D + C)
0 (Jan 1, 2020)				$184,557
1 (Jun 30, 2020)	$8,000	$9,228	$1,228	185,785
2 (Dec 31, 2020)	8,000	9,289	1,289	187,074
3 (Jun 30, 2021)	8,000	9,354	1,354	188,428
4 (Dec 31, 2021)	8,000	9,421	1,421	189,849
5 (Jun 20, 2022)	8,000	9,492	1,492	191,341
6 (Dec 31, 2022)	8,000	9,567	1,567	192,908
7 (Jun 30, 2023)	8,000	9,645	1,645	194,553
8 (Dec 31, 2023)	8,000	9,728	1,728	196,281
9 (Jun 30, 2024)	8,000	9,814	1,814	198,095
10 (Dec 31, 2024)	8,000	9,905	1,905	$200,000
Total	$80,000	$95,443	$15,443	

b)

JOURNAL

Date	Account Title and Explanation	Debit	Credit
2020			
Jan 1	Cash	184,557	
	Discount on Bonds Payable	15,443	
	Bonds Payable		200,000
	To issue $200,000 worth of bonds at a discount		

c)

JOURNAL

Date	Account Title and Explanation	Debit	Credit
2020			
Jun 30	Interest Expense	9,228	
	Discount on Bonds Payable		1,228
	Cash		8,000
	To record semi-annual interest and amortization		
	of the bond discount		

d)

JOURNAL

Date	Account Title and Explanation	Debit	Credit
2024			
Dec 31	Bonds Payable	200,000	
	Cash		200,000
	To record repayment of $200,000 to bondholders		

Review Exercise 7B-1

Market Interest Rate	Bond Price
2%	$3,664,971
3%	$3,500,000
4%	$3,344,186

CHAPTER 8 SOLUTIONS

Pause & Reflect Exercise 8-1

JOURNAL			
Date	Account Title and Explanation	Debit	Credit
Jan 21	Cash	5,550	
	Short-Term Investment—Bonds		5,000
	Gain on Sale of Investment		550
	To record sale of bonds		

Pause & Reflect Exercise 8-2

Initial investment: $250,000

Andover's share of Blackstar's profit: $200,000 × 30% = $60,000

Andover's share of cash dividend received: $10,000 × 30% = $3,000

Net Investment in Blackstar Limited = Initial Investment + Revenue from Investment – Cash Dividend Received

= $250,000 + $60,000 – $3,000

= $307,000

Review Exercise 8-1

JOURNAL			
Date	Account Title and Explanation	Debit	Credit
Jan 1	Investment in Tamalie Inc. Shares	450,000	
	Cash		450,000
	To record purchase of 6,000 common shares of Tamalie Inc.		
Apr 1	Long-Term Investment—Bonds	101,500	
	Cash		101,500
	To record investment in bonds with intent to hold to maturity		
May 10	Short-Term Investment—Pergola Inc. Shares	50,000	
	Cash		50,000
	To record purchase of common shares		

JOURNAL			
Date	**Account Title and Explanation**	**Debit**	**Credit**
Jul 1	Cash	3,000	
	Interest Revenue		3,000
	To record interest received from bonds purchased Apr 1		
Jul 10	Cash	100	
	Dividend Revenue		100
	To record dividend from trading equity securities		
Jul 31	Investment in Tamalie Inc. Shares	24,000	
	Revenue from Investment in Tamalie Inc.		24,000
	To record 30% profit on equity investment in Tamalie Inc.		
Aug 20	Cash	3,000	
	Investment in Tamalie Inc. Shares		3,000
	To record dividends received from Tamalie Inc.		
Oct 1	Cash	10,000	
	Loss on Sale of Investment	150	
	Long-Term Investment—Bonds		10,150
	To record sale of 10% of bonds purchased Apr 1		
Dec 15	Cash	26,800	
	Short-Term Investment—Pergola Inc. Shares		25,000
	Gain on Sale of Investment		1,800
	To record sale of half of Pergola shares		
Dec 31	Valuation Allowance for Fair Value Adjustment	650	
	Unrealized Gain on Fair Value Adjustment		650
	To record fair value adjustment for bonds		
	[$92,000 – ($101,500 – $10,150)]		
Dec 31	Unrealized Loss on Fair Value Adjustment	1,000	
	Valuation Allowance for Fair Value Adjustment		1,000
	To record fair value adjustment for Pergola shares		
	[($50,000 – $25,000) – $24,000]		

CHAPTER 9 SOLUTIONS

Pause & Reflect Exercise 9-1

Reconciliation of Net Income to Net Cash Provided (Used) by Operating Activities	
	Add or Subtract?
Net Income	
Adjustments to Reconcile Net Income to Net Cash Provided (Used) by Operating Activities	
Depreciation	Add
Amortization	Add
Loss on Sale of Land	Add
Gain on Retirement of Debt	Subtract
Changes in Current Assets and Current Liabilities	
Increase in Accounts Receivable	Subtract
Increase in Prepaid Expenses	Subtract
Decrease in Merchandise Inventory	Add
Decrease in Accounts Payable	Subtract
Increase in Salaries Payable	Add
Decrease in Interest Payable	Subtract
Increase in Income Taxes Payable	Add
Net Cash Provided (Used) by Operating Activities	

Pause & Reflect Exercise 9-2

Altitude Sportswear Inc. Statement of Cash Flows (partial) For the Year Ended December 31, 2020	
Cash Flow from Investing Activities	
Cash paid for new office equipment	($250,000)
Cash received from sale of long-term investments	80,000[1]
Cash received from sale of land	900,000 [2]
Cash received from sale of old production equipment	15,000[3]
Net Cash Provided (Used) by Investing Activities	$745,000

[1] Cash received from sale of long-term investments = ($155,000 − $70,000) − $5,000 = $80,000

[2] Cash received from sale of land = $850,000 + $50,000 = $900,000

[3] Cash received from sale of old production equipment = $200,000 − ($130,000 + $30,000 − $0) − $25,000 = $15,000

Pause & Reflect Exercise 9-3

a) Pacific's free cash flow is $157,000, calculated as follows:

Free Cash Flow = Net Cash Provided by Operating Activities − Net Cash Used byInvesting Activities
= $235,000 − $78,000
= $157,000

b) This is a favourable indicator of the company's financial health. It indicates the company has $157,000 remaining after it has covered its operating activities and capital expenditures. It may choose to use the cash to reduce debt, buy back shares or pay dividends.

Review Exercise 9-1

a)

Dellray Inc.		
Statement of Cash Flows		
For the Year Ended December 31, 2020		
Cash Flow from Operating Activities		
Net Income	$986,700	
Adjustments to Reconcile Net Income to Net Cash		
Provided (Used) by Operating Activities		
Depreciation	80,000	
Loss on Sale of Equipment	10,000	
Gain on Sale of Investments	(8,000)	
Changes in Operating Assets and Liabilities		
Decrease in Accounts Receivable	30,000	
Increase in Merchandise Inventory	(40,000)	
Increase in Prepaid Expenses	(8,000)	
Increase in Accounts Payable	119,000	
Net Cash Provided (Used) by Operating Activities		$1,169,700
Cash Flow from Investing Activities		
Sale of Equipment	160,000	
Sale of Investments	48,000	
Purchase of Equipment	(400,000)	
Net Cash Provided (Used) by Investing Activities		(192,000)
Cash Flow from Financing Activities		
Proceeds from Notes Payable	70,000	
Proceeds from Bonds Payable	6,000	
Payment of Cash Dividends	(75,000)	
Proceeds from Issuance of Common Shares	80,000	
Net Cash Provided (Used) by Financing Activities		81,000
Net Increase (Decrease) in Cash		1,058,700
Cash at the Beginning of the Year		27,000
Cash at the End of the Year		$1,085,700

Cost of equipment sold	= $1,100,000 + $400,000 – $1,300,000
	= $200,000
Depreciation of equipment sold	= $156,000 + $80,000 – $206,000
	= $30,000
Book value	= $200,000 – $30,000
	= $170,000 – $10,000 loss
	= $160,000 cash received on sale of equipment
Cost of investment	= $600,000 – $560,000
	= $40,000 + $8,000
	= $48,000 cash received on sale of investments
Proceeds from notes payable	= ($75,000 + $275,000) - ($65,000 + $215,000)
	= $70,000
Dividends paid	= $1,210,000 + $986,700 – $2,121,700
	= $75,000

b) Free Cash Flow = Net Cash Provided by Operating Activities – Net Cash Used by Investing Activities

= $1,169,700 – $192,000

= $977,700

Dellray has a positive free cash flow, which means that the company generated more than enough cash from operations to cover its capital expenditures in 2020. It has $977,700 remaining cash that it could have used to reduce debt, buy back shares or pay dividends. In addition, Dellray's free cash flow is more than enough to cover its total current liabilities, which is equal to $536,000 at the end of 2020. Analysis of Dellray's free cash flow together with the income statement and balance sheet reveals favourable conditions for Dellray because the company is profitable and would not have a liquidity crisis even if it has to repay all of its current liabilities right away.

Review Exercise 9A-1

Harmony Inc.		
Statement of Cash Flows		
For the Year Ended December 31, 2020		
Cash Flow from Operating Activities		
Cash Receipts		
Cash Received from Customers		$5,630,000
Cash Payments		
Payments for Inventory	$2,889,000	
Payments for Insurance	16,000	
Payments to Employees	766,000	
Payments for Other Operating Expenses	367,300	
Payments for Income Taxes	422,000	
Total Cash Payments		4,460,300
Net Cash Provided (Used) by Operating Activities		1,169,700
Cash Flow from Investing Activities		
Sale of Equipment	160,000	
Sale of Investments	48,000	
Purchase of Equipment	(400,000)	
Net Cash Provided (Used) by Investing Activities		(192,000)
Cash Flow from Financing Activities		
Proceeds from Notes Payable	70,000	
Proceeds from Bonds Payable	6,000	
Payment of Cash Dividends	(75,000)	
Issuance of Common Shares	80,000	
Net Cash Provided (Used) by Financing Activities		81,000
Net Increase (Decrease) in Cash		1,058,700
Cash at the Beginning of the Year		27,000
Cash at the End of the Year		$1,085,700
Reconciliation of Net Income with Net Cash Provided (Used) by Operating Activities		
Cash Flow from Operating Activities		
Net Income		$986,700
Adjustments to Reconcile Net Income to Net Cash		
Provided (Used) by Operating Activities		
Depreciation		80,000
Gain on Sale of Investments		(8,000)
Loss on Sale of Factory Equipment		10,000

Changes in Operating Assets and Liabilities		
Decrease in Accounts Receivable		30,000
Increase in Merchandise Inventory		(40,000)
Increase in Prepaid Expenses		(8,000)
Increase in Accounts Payable		119,000
Net Cash Provided (Used) by Operating Activities		$1,169,700

*Note that the investing and financing sections are calculated the same way under both direct and indirect methods.

Calculations for the Operating Activities—Direct Method

Cash Received from Customers	
Sales of 2020	$5,600,000
Add: Increase of Account Payable Changes ($400,000 – $370,000)	30,000
Cash Received from Customers	$5,630,000
Payments for Inventory	
Cost of Goods Sold for 2020 (from income statement)	$2,968,000
Add: Increase in Merchandise Inventory for 2020	40,000
Inventory purchased on credit during 2020	$3,008,000
Balance of Accounts Payable, Jan 1, 2020 (from balance sheet)	$342,000
Add: Merchandise purchased on credit during 2020	3,008,000
Less: Balance of Accounts Payable, Dec 31, 2020 (from balance sheet)	461,000
Cash payments for merchandise	$2,889,000
Payments for Insurance	
Insurance Expense for 2020 (from income statement)	$8,000
Add: Change in Prepaid Insurance for 2020	8,000
Cash payments for insurance during 2020	$16,000
Payments to Employees	
Salaries Expense for 2020 (from income statement)	$766,000
Add: Change in Salaries Payable for 2020	0
Cash payments to employees for salaries during 2020	$766,000
Payments for Other Operating Expenses = Other Operating Expenses	$367,300
Payments made for Income Taxes	
Income Tax Expense for 2020 (from income statement)	$422,000
Less: Change in Income Tax Payable for 2020	0
Cash payments for income tax during 2020	$422,000

Cost of equipment sold	= $1,100,000 + $400,000 – $1,300,000
	= $200,000
Depreciation of equipment sold	= $156,000 + $80,000 – $206,000
	= $30,000
Book value on sale of equipment	= $200,000 – $30,000 = $170,000
Proceeds from sale of equipment	= $170,000 – $10,000 loss
	= $160,000
Cost of investment sold	= $600,000 – $560,000 = $40,000
Proceeds from sale of investment	= $40,000 + $8,000
	= $48,000
Dividends paid	= $1,210,000 + $986,700 – $2,121,700
	= $75,000
Proceeds from bank loan	= ($75,000 + $275,000) – ($65,000 + $215,000)
	= $70,000

Review Exercise 9B-1

Mountain Slope Merchandise Inc. Spreadsheet for Statement of Cash Flows For the Year Ended December 31, 2021						
	Balance		Changes			Balance
	Dec 31, 2020		Debit		Credit	Dec 31, 2021
Balance Sheet Accounts						
Cash	69,000			(i)	62,700	6,300
Accounts Receivable	36,000	(c)	27,000			63,000
Inventory	75,000			(d)	12,000	63,000
Land	300,000					300,000
Equipment	450,000	(f)	60,000			510,000
Accumulated Depreciation	(75,000)			(b)	10,800	(85,800)
Accounts Payable	(99,000)	(e)	30,000			(69,000)
Current Portion of Note Payable	(36,000)					(36,000)
Non-Current Portion of Note Payable	(180,000)	(g)	36,000			(144,000)
Preferred Shares	0			(h)	15,000	(15,000)
Common Shares	(45,000)					(45,000)
Retained Earnings	(495,000)			(a)	52,500	(547,500)
Totals			153,000		153,000	
Statement of Cash Flows						
Operating Activities						
Net Income		(a)	52,500			
Depreciation		(b)	10,800			
Increase in Accounts Receivable				(c)	27,000	
Decrease in Inventory		(d)	12,000			

Decrease in Accounts Payable				(e)	30,000
Investing Activities					
Purchase of Equipment				(f)	60,000
Financing Activities					
Decrease in Note Payable				(g)	36,000
Increase in Preferred Shares		(h)	15,000		
Net Decrease in Cash		(i)	62,700		
Totals			153,000		153,000

CHAPTER 10 SOLUTIONS

Pause & Reflect Exercise 10-1

a) Working Capital (2019) = Current Assets – Current Liabilities
= ($6,501 + $220 + $4,368 + $123 + $190 + $0) – $11,061
= $11,402 – $11,061
= $341

Working Capital (2020) = Current Assets – Current Liabilities
= ($10,918 + $81 + $4,026 + $221 + $485 + $699) – $23,684
= $16,430 – $23,684
= ($7,254)

b) Current Ratio (2019) $= \frac{\text{Current Assets}}{\text{Current Liabilities}}$

$= \frac{\$11,402}{\$11,061}$

= 1.03

Current Ratio (2020) $= \frac{\text{Current Assets}}{\text{Current Liabilities}}$

$= \frac{\$16,430}{\$23,684}$

= 0.69

Pause & Reflect Exercise 10-2

a) Gross Profit Margin (2019) $= \frac{\text{Gross Profit}}{\text{Sales Revenue}}$

$= \frac{\$23,134}{\$27,188}$

= 0.85 or 85%

$$\text{Gross Profit Margin (2020)} = \frac{\text{Gross Profit}}{\text{Sales Revenue}}$$

$$= \frac{\$20{,}493}{\$28{,}172}$$

$$= 0.73 \text{ or } 73\%$$

b) $$\text{Net Profit Margin (2019)} = \frac{\text{Net Income}}{\text{Sales Revenue}}$$

$$= \frac{(\$7{,}369)}{\$27{,}188}$$

$$= -0.27 \text{ or } -27\%$$

$$\text{Net Profit Margin (2020)} = \frac{\text{Net Income}}{\text{Sales Revenue}}$$

$$= \frac{(\$27{,}032)}{\$28{,}172}$$

$$= -0.96 \text{ or } -96\%$$

Pause & Reflect Exercise 10-3

$$\text{Days' Sales in Inventory (2019)} = \frac{\text{Average Inventory}}{\text{Cost of Goods Sold}} \times 365$$

$$= \frac{\$130}{\$4{,}054} \times 365$$

$$= 11.7 \text{ days}$$

$$\text{Days' Sales in Inventory (2020)} = \frac{\text{Average Inventory}}{\text{Cost of Goods Sold}} \times 365$$

$$= \frac{\$172}{\$7{,}679} \times 365$$

$$= 8.2 \text{ days}$$

Pause & Reflect Exercise 10-4

$$\text{Book Value per Common Share} = \frac{\text{Shareholders' Equity} - \text{Preferred Equity}}{\text{Number of Common Shares Outstanding}}$$

$$= \frac{\$24{,}994{,}000}{\$12{,}830{,}945}$$

$$= \$1.95$$

Pause & Reflect Exercise 10-5

a)

Industrial Furnishings Percentage of 2017 Base Year For the Year Ended December 31				
	2020	**2019**	**2018**	**2017**
Total Revenue	22%	20%	5%	0%
Cost of Goods Sold	55%	50%	10%	0%
Gross Profit	14%	13%	4%	0%
Total Expenses	22%	19%	3%	0%
Net Income	−18%	−12%	6%	0%

b) Net income has been decreasing in 2019 and 2020 despite a steady increase in revenue because the expenses have been increasing more than the increase in revenue. While the cost of goods sold increased quite significantly from 10% in 2018 to 50% and 55% in 2019 and 2020, respectively, there was still a modest increase in gross profit year after year. The most important factor causing a decrease in net income is the increase in total expenses, which jumped from 3% in 2018 to 19% and 22% in 2019 and 2020, respectively.

Review Exercise 10-1

a)

Basil's Bakery Percentage Change and Vertical Analysis As at December 31, 2020				
	2020	**2019**	**% Change**	**% of Base Figure 2020**
Cash	$1,605	$987	63%	29%
Accounts Receivable	1,175	573	105%	21%
Merchandise Inventory	396	256	55%	7%
Other Current Assets	301	103	192%	5%
Total Current Assets	3,477	1,919	81%	63%
Property, Plant & Equipment	2,034	1,170	74%	37%
Total Assets	$5,511	$3,089	78%	100%
Current Liabilities	$1,474	$547	169%	27%
Long-Term Liabilities	104	58	79%	2%
Total Liabilities	1,578	605	161%	29%
Shareholders' Equity	3,933	2,484	58%	71%
Total Liabilities + Equity	$5,511	$3,089	78%	100%

b)

Financial Ratio or Figure	Calculation	Result
Working Capital	$3,477 – $1,474	$2,003
Current Ratio	$\frac{\$3,477}{\$1,474}$	2.36
Quick Ratio	$\frac{\$1,605 + \$1,175}{\$1,474}$	1.89
Gross Profit Margin	$\frac{\$3,081}{\$6,009}$	0.51 or 51%
Net Profit Margin	$\frac{\$1,295}{\$6,009}$	0.22 or 22%
Return on Equity	$\$1,295 \div \frac{(\$3,933 + \$2,484)}{2}$	0.40 or 40%
Return on Common Shareholders' Equity	$\frac{(\$1,295 - 0)}{(\$3,933 + \$2,484) \div 2}$	0.40 or 40%
Return on Assets	$\$1,295 \div \left(\frac{(\$5,511 + \$3,089)}{2}\right)$	0.30 or 30%
Asset Turnover	$\frac{\$6,009}{(\$5,511 + \$3,089) \div 2}$	1.40 times
Inventory Turnover Ratio	$\$2,928 \div \left(\frac{(\$396 + \$256)}{2}\right)$	8.98
Days' Sales in Inventory	$\frac{(\$396 + \$256) \div 2}{\$2,928} \times 365$	40.6 days
Days' Sales Outstanding	$\frac{(\$1,175 + \$573) \div 2}{\$6,009} \times 365$	53 days
Accounts Receivable Turnover	$\$6,009 \div \left(\frac{(\$1,175 + \$573)}{2}\right)$	6.9
Debt-to-Equity Ratio	$\frac{\$1,578}{\$3,933}$	0.40 or 40%
Times Interest Earned	$\frac{\$2,329}{\$518}$	4.50 times
Debt-to-Total-Assets Ratio	$\frac{\$1,578}{\$5,511}$	0.29 or 29%

c) A positive **working capital** of $2,003 indicates that the company has enough liquid assets to pay off its upcoming short-term debts.

A **current ratio** of 2.36 indicates that the business has a little more than twice the amount of current assets to pay for its current liabilities. It could be argued that the bakery has enough of a cushion that it could afford to have more cash tied up in current assets, such as inventory and accounts receivable. It could also invest a small portion to earn more investment income.

A **quick ratio** of 1.89 indicates that the business can meet its most immediate debt obligations without relying on the liquidation of inventory. In terms of liquidity as a whole, Basil's Bakery is highly liquid based on the above three financial ratios and figures, indicating a strong financial position in meeting short-term debt obligations.

A **gross profit margin** of 51% means that, after deducting cost of goods sold from sales revenue, the company still has a little more than half of sales revenue left to cover other expenses. Compared to 2019, the gross profit margin declined, indicating that the company is either generating less revenue, has experienced an increase in inventory costs or both. This should be a point of concern, indicating a downward trend. Comparing 2020's gross profit margin to the industry average of 49% shows that the bakery is doing better than the average company in the same industry. It must work to ensure that it remains above this amount by setting appropriate prices and properly managing inventory costs.

A **net profit margin** of 22% means that the company is earning $0.22 of net income for every dollar of revenue earned. Compared to 2019, the net profit margin declined, indicating that the company's costs have increased. This should be a point of concern, indicating a downward trend. Comparing 2020's net profit margin to the industry average of 20% shows that the bakery is doing better than the average company in the same industry. It must work to ensure that it remains above this amount by managing costs and expenses.

Basil's Bakery has a positive 40% **return on equity (ROE)**, which is favourable for investors. As always, shareholders can compare the company's ROE with other companies' ROE to see whether the return from investing in Basil's Bakery provides at least as high a return as they could have received if they had invested elsewhere. In terms of profitability, the company is doing well.

Because Basil's Bakery does not have preferred shares, its **return on common shareholders' equity** is equal to its ROE of 40%. Similar to the ROE, the return on common shareholders' equity indicates that approximately $0.40 of net income was earned for every dollar invested by the common shareholders. By comparing this rate of return to that of other companies in the industry, investors can determine if this is a good rate of return, and whether they made a good choice to invest in the company. Good returns can also attract potential investors to purchase shares and benefit the company's value.

Basil's Bakery had a **return on assets** of about 30%. This means the company made a profit of $0.30 for every dollar invested in assets in the business. This appears to be a good return, but can be compared to other bakeries for a more thorough assessment.

The **asset turnover** is 1.4 times. This means the bakery generates $1.40 of revenue for every dollar of assets. This is a good indicator that the company is using its assets efficiently.

Basil's Bakery has an **inventory turnover ratio** of 8.98, which represents the number of times that the company sold its entire inventory within the year. Bakeries should have a higher turnover ratio because some of the input products they use can expire, such as milk and eggs. Once items are baked, they have a short shelf life.

A **days' sales in inventory** of 40.6 days indicates that the inventory is sold rather slowly. This, paired with the inventory turnover ratio, shows that the bakery could be selling inventory faster. This is a point of concern. In terms of operations management, inventory must be addressed immediately. Inventory should be turning over more quickly to ensure that the bakery is not throwing out expired products. A turnaround in operations management could mean more success in profitability and liquidity.

The **days' sales outstanding** and **accounts receivable turnover** ratios indicate the company collects its accounts receivable every 53 days, or turns over its accounts receivable almost seven times a year. This is not a very healthy ratio. Long collection periods can mean that the company's credit policy is too lenient, or that there are billing disputes, resulting in a delay in receivables collection from customers. It can lead to cash flow problems if cash is not being received in a timely manner.

A **debt-to-equity ratio** of 40% indicates that the total debt is significantly lower than equity. Having relatively low debt compared to equity is considered low risk because the company has a low cost of debt in the form of interest. Therefore, the company's leverage appears to be at an acceptable level.

The **times interest earned** appears healthy. Basil's Bakery has enough cash to cover its interest obligations 4.5 times. The bakery currently has a debt-to-equity ratio of 40%, but if the amount of debt were to increase, the bakery should still be able to cover the interest on the debt. This should be monitored to ensure the times interest earned does not get too low.

The **debt-to-total-assets ratio** is sitting at about 29%. This may be a relatively low value for debt-to-total-assets, which would indicate the company is not relying too heavily on debt to finance its assets. A comparison with other bakeries would place this in perspective.

Appendix II
PRESENT VALUE FACTORS

Present Value Factors for a Single Value

Period	Interest Rate																			
	1%	2%	3%	4%	5%	6%	7%	8%	9%	10%	11%	12%	13%	14%	15%	16%	17%	18%	19%	20%
1	0.9901	0.9804	0.9709	0.9615	0.9524	0.9434	0.9346	0.9259	0.9174	0.9091	0.9009	0.8929	0.8850	0.8772	0.8696	0.8621	0.8547	0.8475	0.8403	0.8333
2	0.9803	0.9612	0.9426	0.9246	0.9070	0.8900	0.8734	0.8573	0.8417	0.8264	0.8116	0.7972	0.7831	0.7695	0.7561	0.7432	0.7305	0.7182	0.7062	0.6944
3	0.9706	0.9423	0.9151	0.8890	0.8638	0.8396	0.8163	0.7938	0.7722	0.7513	0.7312	0.7118	0.6931	0.6750	0.6575	0.6407	0.6244	0.6086	0.5934	0.5787
4	0.9610	0.9238	0.8885	0.8548	0.8227	0.7921	0.7629	0.7350	0.7084	0.6830	0.6587	0.6355	0.6133	0.5921	0.5718	0.5523	0.5337	0.5158	0.4987	0.4823
5	0.9515	0.9057	0.8626	0.8219	0.7835	0.7473	0.7130	0.6806	0.6499	0.6209	0.5935	0.5674	0.5428	0.5194	0.4972	0.4761	0.4561	0.4371	0.4190	0.4019
6	0.9420	0.8880	0.8375	0.7903	0.7462	0.7050	0.6663	0.6302	0.5963	0.5645	0.5346	0.5066	0.4803	0.4556	0.4323	0.4104	0.3898	0.3704	0.3521	0.3349
7	0.9327	0.8706	0.8131	0.7599	0.7107	0.6651	0.6227	0.5835	0.5470	0.5132	0.4817	0.4523	0.4251	0.3996	0.3759	0.3538	0.3332	0.3139	0.2959	0.2791
8	0.9235	0.8535	0.7894	0.7307	0.6768	0.6274	0.5820	0.5403	0.5019	0.4665	0.4339	0.4039	0.3762	0.3506	0.3269	0.3050	0.2848	0.2660	0.2487	0.2326
9	0.9143	0.8368	0.7664	0.7026	0.6446	0.5919	0.5439	0.5002	0.4604	0.4241	0.3909	0.3606	0.3329	0.3075	0.2843	0.2630	0.2434	0.2255	0.2090	0.1938
10	0.9053	0.8203	0.7441	0.6756	0.6139	0.5584	0.5083	0.4632	0.4224	0.3855	0.3522	0.3220	0.2946	0.2697	0.2472	0.2267	0.2080	0.1911	0.1756	0.1615
11	0.8963	0.8043	0.7224	0.6496	0.5847	0.5268	0.4751	0.4289	0.3875	0.3505	0.3173	0.2875	0.2607	0.2366	0.2149	0.1954	0.1778	0.1619	0.1476	0.1346
12	0.8874	0.7885	0.7014	0.6246	0.5568	0.4970	0.4440	0.3971	0.3555	0.3186	0.2858	0.2567	0.2307	0.2076	0.1869	0.1685	0.1520	0.1372	0.1240	0.1122
13	0.8787	0.7730	0.6810	0.6006	0.5303	0.4688	0.4150	0.3677	0.3262	0.2897	0.2575	0.2292	0.2042	0.1821	0.1625	0.1452	0.1299	0.1163	0.1042	0.0935
14	0.8700	0.7579	0.6611	0.5775	0.5051	0.4423	0.3878	0.3405	0.2992	0.2633	0.2320	0.2046	0.1807	0.1597	0.1413	0.1252	0.1110	0.0985	0.0876	0.0779
15	0.8613	0.7430	0.6419	0.5553	0.4810	0.4173	0.3624	0.3152	0.2745	0.2394	0.2090	0.1827	0.1599	0.1401	0.1229	0.1079	0.0949	0.0835	0.0736	0.0649
16	0.8528	0.7284	0.6232	0.5339	0.4581	0.3936	0.3387	0.2919	0.2519	0.2176	0.1883	0.1631	0.1415	0.1229	0.1069	0.0930	0.0811	0.0708	0.0618	0.0541
17	0.8444	0.7142	0.6050	0.5134	0.4363	0.3714	0.3166	0.2703	0.2311	0.1978	0.1696	0.1456	0.1252	0.1078	0.0929	0.0802	0.0693	0.0600	0.0520	0.0451
18	0.8360	0.7002	0.5874	0.4936	0.4155	0.3503	0.2959	0.2502	0.2120	0.1799	0.1528	0.1300	0.1108	0.0946	0.0808	0.0691	0.0592	0.0508	0.0437	0.0376
19	0.8277	0.6864	0.5703	0.4746	0.3957	0.3305	0.2765	0.2317	0.1945	0.1635	0.1377	0.1161	0.0981	0.0829	0.0703	0.0596	0.0506	0.0431	0.0367	0.0313
20	0.8195	0.6730	0.5537	0.4564	0.3769	0.3118	0.2584	0.2145	0.1784	0.1486	0.1240	0.1037	0.0868	0.0728	0.0611	0.0514	0.0433	0.0365	0.0308	0.0261
21	0.8114	0.6598	0.5375	0.4388	0.3589	0.2942	0.2415	0.1987	0.1637	0.1351	0.1117	0.0926	0.0768	0.0638	0.0531	0.0443	0.0370	0.0309	0.0259	0.0217
22	0.8034	0.6468	0.5219	0.4220	0.3418	0.2775	0.2257	0.1839	0.1502	0.1228	0.1007	0.0826	0.0680	0.0560	0.0462	0.0382	0.0316	0.0262	0.0218	0.0181
23	0.7954	0.6342	0.5067	0.4057	0.3256	0.2618	0.2109	0.1703	0.1378	0.1117	0.0907	0.0738	0.0601	0.0491	0.0402	0.0329	0.0270	0.0222	0.0183	0.0151
24	0.7876	0.6217	0.4919	0.3901	0.3101	0.2470	0.1971	0.1577	0.1264	0.1015	0.0817	0.0659	0.0532	0.0431	0.0349	0.0284	0.0231	0.0188	0.0154	0.0126
25	0.7798	0.6095	0.4776	0.3751	0.2953	0.2330	0.1842	0.1460	0.1160	0.0923	0.0736	0.0588	0.0471	0.0378	0.0304	0.0245	0.0197	0.0160	0.0129	0.0105
30	0.7419	0.5521	0.4120	0.3083	0.2314	0.1741	0.1314	0.0994	0.0754	0.0573	0.0437	0.0334	0.0256	0.0196	0.0151	0.0116	0.0090	0.0070	0.0054	0.0042
40	0.6717	0.4529	0.3066	0.2083	0.1420	0.0972	0.0668	0.0460	0.0318	0.0221	0.0154	0.0107	0.0075	0.0053	0.0037	0.0026	0.0019	0.0013	0.0010	0.0007
50	0.6080	0.3715	0.2281	0.1407	0.0872	0.0543	0.0339	0.0213	0.0134	0.0085	0.0054	0.0035	0.0022	0.0014	0.0009	0.0006	0.0004	0.0003	0.0002	0.0001

Present Value Factors for an Annuity

Period	Interest Rate																			
	1%	2%	3%	4%	5%	6%	7%	8%	9%	10%	11%	12%	13%	14%	15%	16%	17%	18%	19%	20%
1	0.9901	0.9804	0.9709	0.9615	0.9524	0.9434	0.9346	0.9259	0.9174	0.9091	0.9009	0.8929	0.8850	0.8772	0.8696	0.8621	0.8547	0.8475	0.8403	0.8333
2	1.9704	1.9416	1.9135	1.8861	1.8594	1.8334	1.8080	1.7833	1.7591	1.7355	1.7125	1.6901	1.6681	1.6467	1.6257	1.6052	1.5852	1.5656	1.5465	1.5278
3	2.9410	2.8839	2.8286	2.7751	2.7232	2.6730	2.6243	2.5771	2.5313	2.4869	2.4437	2.4018	2.3612	2.3216	2.2832	2.2459	2.2096	2.1743	2.1399	2.1065
4	3.9020	3.8077	3.7171	3.6299	3.5460	3.4651	3.3872	3.3121	3.2397	3.1699	3.1024	3.0373	2.9745	2.9137	2.8550	2.7982	2.7432	2.6901	2.6386	2.5887
5	4.8534	4.7135	4.5797	4.4518	4.3295	4.2124	4.1002	3.9927	3.8897	3.7908	3.6959	3.6048	3.5172	3.4331	3.3522	3.2743	3.1993	3.1272	3.0576	2.9906
6	5.7955	5.6014	5.4172	5.2421	5.0757	4.9173	4.7665	4.6229	4.4859	4.3553	4.2305	4.1114	3.9975	3.8887	3.7845	3.6847	3.5892	3.4976	3.4098	3.3255
7	6.7282	6.4720	6.2303	6.0021	5.7864	5.5824	5.3893	5.2064	5.0330	4.8684	4.7122	4.5638	4.4226	4.2883	4.1604	4.0386	3.9224	3.8115	3.7057	3.6046
8	7.6517	7.3255	7.0197	6.7327	6.4632	6.2098	5.9713	5.7466	5.5348	5.3349	5.1461	4.9676	4.7988	4.6389	4.4873	4.3436	4.2072	4.0776	3.9544	3.8372
9	8.5660	8.1622	7.7861	7.4353	7.1078	6.8017	6.5152	6.2469	5.9952	5.7590	5.5370	5.3282	5.1317	4.9464	4.7716	4.6065	4.4506	4.3030	4.1633	4.0310
10	9.4713	8.9826	8.5302	8.1109	7.7217	7.3601	7.0236	6.7101	6.4177	6.1446	5.8892	5.6502	5.4262	5.2161	5.0188	4.8332	4.6586	4.4941	4.3389	4.1925
11	10.3676	9.7868	9.2526	8.7605	8.3064	7.8869	7.4987	7.1390	6.8052	6.4951	6.2065	5.9377	5.6869	5.4527	5.2337	5.0286	4.8364	4.6560	4.4865	4.3271
12	11.2551	10.5753	9.9540	9.3851	8.8633	8.3838	7.9427	7.5361	7.1607	6.8137	6.4924	6.1944	5.9176	5.6603	5.4206	5.1971	4.9884	4.7932	4.6105	4.4392
13	12.1337	11.3484	10.6350	9.9856	9.3936	8.8527	8.3577	7.9038	7.4869	7.1034	6.7499	6.4235	6.1218	5.8424	5.5831	5.3423	5.1183	4.9095	4.7147	4.5327
14	13.0037	12.1062	11.2961	10.5631	9.8986	9.2950	8.7455	8.2442	7.7862	7.3667	6.9819	6.6282	6.3025	6.0021	5.7245	5.4675	5.2293	5.0081	4.8023	4.6106
15	13.8651	12.8493	11.9379	11.1184	10.3797	9.7122	9.1079	8.5595	8.0607	7.6061	7.1909	6.8109	6.4624	6.1422	5.8474	5.5755	5.3242	5.0916	4.8759	4.6755
16	14.7179	13.5777	12.5611	11.6523	10.8378	10.1059	9.4466	8.8514	8.3126	7.8237	7.3792	6.9740	6.6039	6.2651	5.9542	5.6685	5.4053	5.1624	4.9377	4.7296
17	15.5623	14.2919	13.1661	12.1657	11.2741	10.4773	9.7632	9.1216	8.5436	8.0216	7.5488	7.1196	6.7291	6.3729	6.0472	5.7487	5.4746	5.2223	4.9897	4.7746
18	16.3983	14.9920	13.7535	12.6593	11.6896	10.8276	10.0591	9.3719	8.7556	8.2014	7.7016	7.2497	6.8399	6.4674	6.1280	5.8178	5.5339	5.2732	5.0333	4.8122
19	17.2260	15.6785	14.3238	13.1339	12.0853	11.1581	10.3356	9.6036	8.9501	8.3649	7.8393	7.3658	6.9380	6.5504	6.1982	5.8775	5.5845	5.3162	5.0700	4.8435
20	18.0456	16.3514	14.8775	13.5903	12.4622	11.4699	10.5940	9.8181	9.1285	8.5136	7.9633	7.4694	7.0248	6.6231	6.2593	5.9288	5.6278	5.3527	5.1009	4.8696
21	18.8570	17.0112	15.4150	14.0292	12.8212	11.7641	10.8355	10.0168	9.2922	8.6487	8.0751	7.5620	7.1016	6.6870	6.3125	5.9731	5.6648	5.3837	5.1268	4.8913
22	19.6604	17.6580	15.9369	14.4511	13.1630	12.0416	11.0612	10.2007	9.4424	8.7715	8.1757	7.6446	7.1695	6.7429	6.3587	6.0113	5.6964	5.4099	5.1486	4.9094
23	20.4558	18.2922	16.4436	14.8568	13.4886	12.3034	11.2722	10.3711	9.5802	8.8832	8.2664	7.7184	7.2297	6.7921	6.3988	6.0442	5.7234	5.4321	5.1668	4.9245
24	21.2434	18.9139	16.9355	15.2470	13.7986	12.5504	11.4693	10.5288	9.7066	8.9847	8.3481	7.7843	7.2829	6.8351	6.4338	6.0726	5.7465	5.4509	5.1822	4.9371
25	22.0232	19.5235	17.4131	15.6221	14.0939	12.7834	11.6536	10.6748	9.8226	9.0770	8.4217	7.8431	7.3300	6.8729	6.4641	6.0971	5.7662	5.4669	5.1951	4.9476
30	25.8077	22.3965	19.6004	17.2920	15.3725	13.7648	12.4090	11.2578	10.2737	9.4269	8.6938	8.0552	7.4957	7.0027	6.5660	6.1772	5.8294	5.5168	5.2347	4.9789
40	32.8347	27.3555	23.1148	19.7928	17.1591	15.0463	13.3317	11.9246	10.7574	9.7791	8.9511	8.2438	7.6344	7.1050	6.6418	6.2335	5.8713	5.5482	5.2582	4.9966
50	39.1961	31.4236	25.7298	21.4822	18.2559	15.7619	13.8007	12.2335	10.9617	9.9148	9.0417	8.3045	7.6752	7.1327	6.6605	6.2463	5.8801	5.5541	5.2623	4.9995

Appendix III
SUMMARY OF FINANCIAL RATIOS

The following is a guide to some common ratios used to measure the financial performance of a company. Different industries have different benchmarks for each ratio. It is important to understand the trends in a company's performance from period to period and the relative performance of a company within its industry for each ratio.

Note that the purpose of ratio analysis is to help the user of financial statements ask the appropriate questions and understand which issues need to be addressed. No single ratio will provide the complete story; all the pieces are needed for informed decision-making.

Ratio	Formula	Is a measure of
Liquidity		
Working Capital	Current Assets − Current Liabilities	Ability to cover current liabilities using current assets
Current Ratio	$\frac{\text{Current Assets}}{\text{Current Liabilities}}$	Ability to cover current liabilities using current assets
Quick Ratio	$\frac{\text{Cash + Short-Term Investments + Accounts Receivable}}{\text{Current Liabilities}}$	Ability of highly liquid assets to cover current liabilities
Profitability		
Gross Profit Margin	$\frac{\text{Gross Profit}}{\text{Net Sales}}$	Percentage of profit remaining after deducting cost of goods sold
Net Profit Margin	$\frac{\text{Net Income}}{\text{Total Revenue}}$	Percentage of profit remaining after deducting all expenses
Return on Equity	$\frac{\text{Net Income}}{\text{Average Shareholders' Equity}}$	Profitability of shareholders' investments
Return on Common Shareholders' Equity	$\frac{\text{(Net Income − Preferred Dividends)}}{\text{Average Common Shareholders' Equity}}$	Profits earned on investment of common shareholders
Return on Assets	$\frac{\text{Net Income}}{\text{Average Total Assets}}$	Effectiveness of the company's investment in assets
Asset Turnover	$\frac{\text{Total Revenue}}{\text{Average Total Assets}}$	Ability to generate sales revenue from asset investments
Operations Management		
Inventory Turnover Ratio	$\frac{\text{Cost of Goods Sold}}{\text{Average Inventory}}$	Efficiency of inventory management
Days' Sales in Inventory	$\frac{\text{Average Inventory}}{\text{Cost of Goods Sold}} \times 365$ or $\frac{365}{\text{Inventory Turnover Ratio}}$	Average number of days to turn over inventory during the year

Ratio	Formula	Is a measure of
Days' Sales Outstanding	$\frac{\text{Average Net Accounts Receivable}}{\text{Net Credit Sales}} \times 365$	Average number of days to collect accounts receivable
Accounts Receivable Turnover Ratio	$\frac{\text{Net Credit Sales}}{\text{Average Net Accounts Receivable}}$	Efficiency of accounts receivable collections
Solvency		
Debt-to-Equity Ratio	$\frac{\text{Total Liabilities}}{\text{Total Shareholder's Equity}}$	Relative amount of debt vs. shareholders' equity that is being used to finance a company's assets
Times Interest Earned	$\frac{\text{Earnings before Interest Expense and Income Tax}}{\text{Interest Expense}}$	Ability to cover interest on debt
Debt-to-Total-Assets Ratio	$\frac{\text{Total Liabilities}}{\text{Total Assets}}$	Amount of debt being financed by creditors
Capital Market Performance		
Book Value per Common Share	$\frac{\text{Shareholders' Equity} - \text{Preferred Equity}}{\text{Number of Common Shares Outstanding}}$	Theoretical value of a share based on shareholders' claims to a company's assets
Dividend Yield	$\frac{\text{Cash Dividends per Common Share}}{\text{Market Price per Common Share}}$	Rate of return to common shareholders
Earnings per Share	$\frac{\text{Net Income} - \text{Preferred Dividends}}{\text{Weighted Average Number of Common Shares Outstanding}}$	Profit earned by investors per common share
Price–Earnings Ratio	$\frac{\text{Market Price per Share}}{\text{Earnings per Share}}$	Market value of a common share related to its earnings

Appendix IV

ASPE vs. IFRS

Topic of Interest	ASPE	IFRS
Chapter 1		
Revenue recognition	Companies are allowed to use the percentage-of-completion method as well as the completed-contract method.	The completed contract method is not allowed.
Chapter 2		
Capital expenditures	Assets do not have to be broken down into significant parts to be capitalized and depreciated.	Each significant part of an asset needs to be separately capitalized and depreciated.
Depreciation vs. amortization for property, plant and equipment	The periodic allocation of property, plant and equipment cost is called amortization, although the term depreciation is also allowed. The amount of depreciation charged to income is the greater of • Cost less salvage value over the life of the asset • Cost less residual value over the useful life of the asset	Only the term depreciation is used. Depreciation is the allocation of the cost less residual value over the asset's useful life.
Re-measuring the value of long-term assets	Only the cost model is allowed, so long-term assets must always be recorded at cost (less accumulated depreciation and impairment). An annual review of useful life and residual value estimates is not required.	Companies may choose to account for long-term assets using either the cost model or the revaluation model. Under the revaluation model, assets are revalued periodically to reflect their fair market value. An annual review of useful life and residual value estimates is required.
Impairment	The book value of an impaired plant asset is written down to its fair value. An impairment loss that has been previously recorded can never be reversed.	The book value of an impaired plant asset is written down to its recoverable amount. Previously recorded impairments may be reversed for all tangible and intangible assets, except goodwill.
Reconciliation of property, plant and equipment balances	Reconciliation of beginning and ending balances for each class of property, plant and equipment is not required.	Every company must show the reconciliation of the beginning and the ending balances for each class of property, plant and equipment.
Amortizing intangible assets	Intangible assets are reported and amortized only when they are purchased.	Any internally generated intangible asset can be capitalized and amortized as long as it provides future benefits to the company.
Impairment	A company must conduct impairment tests whenever it becomes aware of an impairment indication.	A company must conduct impairment tests on goodwill and intangible assets with indefinite lives every year, even if there is no indication of impairment. For intangible assets with finite lives and for property, plant and equipment, a company must actively look for impairment indicators every year, and conduct impairment tests only if indicators exist.

Topic of Interest	ASPE	IFRS
Chapter 3		
Contingent liabilities	A contingent liability must be recognized as an actual liability when the company determines that the payment is probable, defined as "likely to occur."	A contingent liability must be recognized as an actual liability when the company determines that the payment is probable, defined as "more likely than not."
Chapter 5		
Organization costs	Organization costs may be capitalized as an intangible asset or treated as an expense, as long as the same accounting policy is applied to all such costs.	Organization costs are treated as an expense, except in special circumstances.
Disclosure of share classes	Only the classes of shares that have been issued are required to be disclosed.	All classes of shares authorized must be disclosed, even if they are not issued.
Issuing shares in exchange for non-cash assets or services	The fair market value of either the asset given up or the shares issued may be used, whichever is more reliable.	The fair market value of the asset must be used first. If that is not determined, then the fair value of shares can be used instead.
Chapter 6		
Income statement or statement of comprehensive income	The name used is income statement, or statement of income. There is no specific rule on how to present the expenses as long as all items that are required are included. All profit and loss items are included in net income without being separated into other comprehensive income. Earnings per share is not mentioned.	The name used is statement of comprehensive income, or statement of income and comprehensive income. Expenses should be classified by either their nature or their function. Items must be classified as either comprehensive income or net income. Other comprehensive income must be presented either in a stand-alone statement or as a separate section within the statement of comprehensive income. Basic and diluted earnings per share must be presented in the statement.
Statement of retained earnings or statement of changes in equity	The name used is statement of retained earnings. Only changes in retained earnings are presented on the face of the statement. Changes in other shareholders' equity accounts are presented in the notes to the financial statements.	The name used is statement of changes in equity. Changes in all equity accounts are presented on the face of the statement.
Balance sheet or statement of financial position	Both balance sheet and statement of financial position are acceptable, although balance sheet is more often used. Listing order is not specified, but companies adopting ASPE tend to list items from most liquid to least liquid. Liabilities are usually presented before shareholders' equity. Because companies that use ASPE do not report other comprehensive income, the accumulated other comprehensive income (reserves) account does not exist on the balance sheet.	Both balance sheet and statement of financial position are acceptable, although statement of financial position is more often used. Listing order is not specified, but companies adopting IFRS tend to list items from least liquid to most liquid. Shareholders' equity is usually presented before liabilities. Retained earnings and accumulated other comprehensive income (reserves) are reported separately.

Topic of Interest	ASPE	IFRS
Change in accounting policy	A company does not need to meet the reliability/relevance test to change an accounting policy.	A company can change an accounting policy only if the change is required by IFRS or if the change will result in more reliable and relevant information for users of its financial statements.
Chapter 7		
Straight-line vs. effective-interest amortization of bonds	The effective-interest method is supported, but the straight-line method is also allowed, if the results are not significantly different from the effective-interest method.	Companies are strictly required to use the effective-interest amortization method.
Leases	An operating lease is permitted.	Almost all leases must be recognized as finance leases, meaning that they would be recorded on the balance sheet.
Chapter 8		
Accounting for short-term debt (bonds)	The fair value through net income (FVTNI) method is used. The historical cost method can be used if no market value is available.	The fair value through net income (FVTNI) method is used. The historical cost method can be used if no market value is available.
Accounting for long-term debt (bonds)	The amortized cost (AC) method is used. Any premium or discount can be amortized using either the straight-line method or the effective-interest rate method.	The amortized cost (AC) method is used. Any premium or discount must be amortized using the effective-interest rate method.
Accounting for equity with insignificant influence (less than 20% ownership, non-strategic)	The fair value through net income (FVTNI) method is used. The historical cost method can be used if no market value is available. Gains and losses are reported in net income.	The fair value through net income (FVTNI) method or the fair value through other comprehensive income (FVTOCI) method is used, depending on the circumstances. Gains and losses are reported in either net income or other comprehensive income (OCI).
Accounting for equity with significant influence (20% to 50% ownership, strategic)	The equity or historical cost method can be used.	The equity method is used.
Equity with controlling influence (greater than 50% ownership, strategic)	The consolidation method can be used, if the parent company chooses to.	The consolidation method is required.
Chapter 9		
Reporting interest and dividends on cash flow statements	Interest or dividends received from a short-term or long-term investment are reported as operating activities. Interest paid on loans is an operating activity, and dividends paid to shareholders are a financing activity.	Interest or dividends received from a short-term or long-term investment are allowed to be reported as either operating or investing activities. Interest paid on loans and dividends paid to shareholders are allowed to be reported as either operating or financing activities. Once a decision is made about where to report interest and dividends, they must always be reported in that manner.

Topic of Interest	ASPE	IFRS
Reporting cash flows to pay tax	Cash outflows for income tax must always be classified as operating activities, but separate line disclosure is not required.	Cash flows to pay taxes are reported as a separate line in the operating activities, unless they are specifically identified with financing or investing activities.
Reconciling net income to net cash used (provided) by operating activities	Net income must be reconciled to net cash provided (used) by operating activities under both direct and indirect methods.	Net income must be reconciled to net cash provided (used) by operating activities only under the indirect method.
Chapter 10		
Comprehensive income	All profit and loss items are included in net income and therefore included in ratios.	Comprehensive income is not usually included in ratios. However, if it makes up a large portion of the income reported, a company may wish to include it in the ratio calculations so the relevant information is available to users.

GLOSSARY

A

accounts receivable subledger a subledger that contains individual customer accounts and is used to record the details of transactions affecting each account

accounts receivable turnover ratio (ART) a measure of how often during the year a company collects its entire accounts receivable amount

accrual-based accounting a type of accounting where revenue and expenses are recorded in the period in which they occur, regardless of when cash is received or paid

accumulated depreciation the contra asset account for property, plant and equipment (PPE); reflects the decrease in the net book value of PPE without changing the original cost of the asset

adjunct account an account linked to another account to record increases in the value of that account; the opposite of a *contra account*

aging method a method to estimate bad debt by which percentages are applied to groupings based on the age of outstanding accounts receivable amounts

allowance for doubtful accounts (AFDA) a contra asset account that records bad debt in a way that satisfies the expense recognition principle

allowance method a method to estimate bad debt and record it in the books

amortization the process of allocating the cost of intangible assets over their useful life

amortized cost (AC) method an accounting method used to report long-term debt investments

amortizing the discount the process of allocating the total cost of borrowing (interest and discount) to the interest expense account over the life of a bond

amortizing the premium the process of allocating the total cost of borrowing (interest payment less premium) to the interest expense account over the life of a bond

annuity a stream of periodic and recurring fixed payments, such as interest payments, over a period of time

articles of incorporation government documents filed when a corporation is formed, containing the operational details of the corporation; also called a *corporate charter*

Accounting Standards for Private Enterprises (ASPE) standards developed by the Accounting Standards Board in Canada; private companies may choose to follow these standards instead of IFRS

asset turnover ratio a measure of how quickly a company converts total assets, including long-term assets, into revenue

authorized shares the maximum number of shares that can be legally issued by a company

average cost per share a value calculated by dividing the book value of the common shares account by the number of common shares issued and outstanding at the transaction date

B

bad debt an uncollectible account resulting from customers who will never pay their bills

balance sheet approach a method by which a company calculates allowance for bad debt using either the percentage of total accounts receivable method or the aging method

bank overdraft a financial institution's extension of credit to cover the portion of cash withdrawal that is more than the account's balance

base figure a total dollar amount used in a vertical analysis to determine the relationship between line items on a financial statement

base year the earliest year shown on a comparative balance sheet; used as a basis for comparison in a horizontal analysis

basic earnings per share earnings per share (EPS) that is based on actual shares that have been issued to shareholders

betterment an improvement that increases an asset's efficiency or effectiveness without necessarily increasing the asset's useful life

bond a type of long-term debt in the form of an interest-bearing note

bond certificate a document that is issued as an official record to investors when they purchase bonds

bond indenture a contract between a bond issuer and a bondholder

bond issuer a company that issues a bond

bondholder an investor who purchases a bond

book value per common share a value that indicates what a common share would be worth to common shareholders if the company were to be liquidated

book value per share a value that indicates what a share would be worth to shareholders if the company were to be liquidated

business combination a transaction that occurs when one company purchases more than 50% of the outstanding share of another company

business segments different lines of business within a company that serve different types of customers or provide different goods and services

C

capital deficiency a debit balance in a partner's capital account

capital expenditure expenses paid for a change to an asset resulting in benefits extending beyond the current period

cash flow from financing activities the movement of cash within a business received from investors and lenders to help run, or finance, a business; also cash paid back to investors and lenders

cash flow from investing activities the movement of cash in a business on the basis of purchases and sales of long-term assets

cash flow from operating activities the movement of cash within a business as a result of day-to-day activities

change in accounting estimate the change in an estimate, such as useful life of an asset, to reflect new information

change in accounting policy the decision to change an approach to documenting information, such as a change in depreciation method

classified balance sheet a document that provides details of a company's assets, liabilities and shareholders' equity, under ASPE; also called a *statement of financial position*

common shares a type of equity that gives shareholders ownership in a corporation, voting rights to elect a board of directors and potential to receive dividends

comparative balance sheet a balance sheet that shows the balances for multiple years for easy comparison

compound interest the growth effect of applying the same interest rate on an account over a period of time

comprehensive income the total of net income plus other comprehensive income (or loss)

consolidated financial statements a set of financial statements that combine the details for both the parent and subsidiary companies

contingent liabilities financial obligations that occur only if a certain event takes place in the future

continuing operations a company's normal day-to-day activities that are expected to continue in the near future

contra account an account linked to another account to record decreases in the value of that account; the opposite of an *adjunct account*

contractual interest rate the annual percentage rate of interest an investor receives on the face value of a bond; also called the bond's *coupon rate*

contributed capital the total amount of assets that shareholders contribute to the corporation to receive the corporation's shares in return; generally comprised of two subcategories called *share capital* and *contributed surplus*

contributed surplus additions to shareholders' contributions other than capital raised from the sale of shares

controlling influence a situation where one shareholder or investor owns more than 50% of the outstanding common shares and therefore has control over how the company operates

convertible bonds bonds that give bondholders the option of converting or exchanging them for a specific number of the company's shares

copyright the exclusive right of ownership given to a person or group that has created an artistic work

corporation a type of business that is a legal entity separate from its owners

coupon bonds bonds that contain detachable coupons stating the amount and due date of the interest payment

cumulative shares a type of preferred shares that give shareholders the right to be paid the current year's dividends and to accumulate any unpaid dividends from previous years

current ratio a measure of a company's ability to pay off short-term debt

customer loyalty programs rewards given to customers that can be redeemed in future for a product or service

D

date of declaration the date on which a board of directors announces dividends will be paid to shareholders

date of payment the date on which a company makes dividend payments to eligible shareholders

date of record the date on which a corporation lists all those who currently hold shares and are eligible to receive dividend payments

days' sales in inventory a measure of how many days inventory will last given the current rate of sales; also called *inventory days on hand*

days' sales outstanding (DSO) a measure of how long customers take to pay their bills

debenture bonds unsecured bonds that are backed only by a bondholder's faith in a company's reputation; also referred to as *debentures*

debt investments investment through lending money to a company in return for interest income; also called *debt instruments* or *debt securities*

debt-to-equity (D/E) ratio a measure of how much of a company is being financed by lenders and how much is being financed by shareholders

debt-to-total-assets ratio a measure of how much of a company's assets are financed through total liabilities

declining-balance method a depreciation method that applies an annual percentage to calculate depreciation against the net book value of an asset

depletion the process of allocating or expensing resources as they are harvested or mined and sold

depreciation the allocation of the cost of a long-term asset over its useful life

determinable liabilities liabilities with a precise value

direct method a method of preparing cash flow statements that calculates cash flow from operating activities by directly analyzing cash received from sales and collections and directly analyzing cash spent on expenses

direct write-off method a method to account for bad debts in which an account receivable is not written off until it has been determined to be uncollectible, and then is then written off directly to bad debt expense

discontinued operation a business segment that is no longer part of a company's regular operating activities

discount the difference between the price paid and the par value of a bond, when the price paid is lower

dishonoured note a note receivable that is not paid at maturity

dividend a distribution of a company's earnings to shareholders

dividend payout ratio the percentage of company earnings that is paid out to shareholders in dividends

dividend yield the percentage of company earnings paid out to shareholders in cash dividends

dividends in arrears unpaid dividends on cumulative preferred shares from prior periods

double taxation a situation in which a corporation pays income tax on its earnings and shareholders pay personal income tax on their dividends

double-declining-balance method a depreciation method that doubles the declining-balance rate of depreciation

E

earnings per share (EPS) a ratio that indicates the profit earned by each common share

effective-interest amortization method a method that uses the market interest rate at the date the bonds are issued as the basis to calculate the interest expense

equity investments investment through buying a stake in the ownership of another organization; also called *equity instruments* or *equity securities*

equity method a method used to record and report strategic equity investments when the investor owns 20% to 50% of the investee's outstanding common shares

estimated liabilities financial obligations a company cannot exactly measure

expense recognition an accounting foundation that states that an expense must be recorded in the same accounting period in which it is used to generate revenue

expenses by function a method of classifying related expenses together, such as selling expenses or administrative expenses, and presenting them as such on the statement of comprehensive income under IFRS

expenses by nature a method of classifying expenses in which they are presented based on their natural classification, such as salary expense or advertising expense, and presenting them as such on the statement of comprehensive income under IFRS

F

face value the amount on a bond to be paid to an investor upon maturity; also called the bond's *par value*

factoring the practice whereby a company sells all or a portion of its accounts receivable to a factor, such as a bank or financial institution, in exchange for cash

fair value the amount an asset could be sold for in the open market

fair value adjustment recording changes in the carrying value of an investment due to changes in fair value

fair value through net income (FVTNI) method an accounting method used to report short-term investments in bonds; also known as *fair value through profit or loss*

fixed interest rate an interest rate that remains constant for the entire term of a note

franchise a contract that allows the franchisee to operate a branch using the franchisor's brand name and business model

free cash flow the amount of cash remaining after a company has covered its operating activities and capital expenditures required to maintain its existing production capacity

fully diluted earnings per share earnings per share (EPS) that is based on actual and potential shares that have or could be issued

future value the value of money that will be in an account after a number of years

G

general partner a partner with unlimited liability who is legally authorized to manage the day-to-day operations and make decisions on behalf of the partnership

general partnership a form of partnership in which all partners share responsibilities of the business and have unlimited liability

good and services tax (GST) a sales tax imposed by the federal government on most transactions between businesses and between businesses and consumers

goodwill an intangible asset that can be attributed to factors such as a recognizable brand name, experienced management, a skilled workforce or a unique product

gross profit margin the difference between sales revenue and cost of goods sold expressed as a percentage of sales; also called *gross margin*

GST recoverable a contra liability account that records the amount of GST that a business spends; that amount can be deducted from the GST collected to reduce the total amount payable to the government

H

harmonized sales tax (HST) a sales tax that combines the provincial and federal taxes into one sales tax amount

horizontal analysis a method to compare information from one accounting period to another, usually from year to year

I

impairment the permanent drop of an asset's fair value to a point that is below its net book value

income (loss) from continuing operations the results of the company's operations that are ongoing

income statement a record used to show a company's revenue and expenses to provide the net income figure for a period

income statement approach a method that uses credit sales from the income statement as a basis to predict future bad debt; also known as the *percentage of sales method*

income tax the amount of taxes on its net income that a corporation is obligated to pay to the government

indirect method a method of preparing cash flow statements that indirectly analyzes cash flow from operating activities by adjusting accrual-based net income based on information from the income statement and balance sheet

insider trading the use of a company's private information to trade in the stock market for personal gain before the information is released publicly

installments periodic payments made on a note payable

intangible assets conceptual assets that have no physical form and largely consist of intellectual property, such as patents and trademarks

International Financial Reporting Standards (IFRS) standards created by the International Accounting Standards Board (IASB), which provide guidance on how financial information should be reported

inventory turnover ratio an estimate of how many times a year a company is selling its entire inventory

investee a company that issues (sells) debt or equity to another company

investor a company that purchases and owns the debt or equity issued by another company

issued shares authorized shares that are sold to shareholders

L

lease a contract between the owner of an asset and another party who uses the asset for a given period of time

licence a contract that permits the licensee to use the licensor's product or brand name under specified terms and conditions

limited liability a type of liability that extends only to the amount a person has invested in a partnership or a corporation

limited liability partnership (LLP) a business legal entity used to protect one partner from another partner's negligence

limited partner a partner with limited liability who is responsible only for providing the capital to finance a business

liquidity the ease with which an asset can be converted to cash

long-term assets assets that are used to operate a business and are not expected to turn into cash or be used up within the next 12 months; also called *noncurrent assets, long-lived assets, fixed assets* or *capital assets*

long-term debt investment a debt investment that will take more than 12 months to mature

long-term investment an investment intended to be held for longer than a year that is reported under the long-term assets section of a balance sheet

long-term liabilities amounts due to be paid after 12 months; also referred to as *noncurrent liabilities*

long-term notes payable a long-term liability due beyond 12 months of the date of issue

lump sum purchase a purchase of property, plant and equipment from the same vendor in one transaction, as opposed to buying the assets separately from different vendors; also called a *basket purchase*

M

maker a customer (borrower) of a note receivable who makes a promise to pay

Management's Discussion and Analysis (MD&A) a special section included in a company's annual report filed with security regulators that provides shareholders with an analysis of the company's past and current performance, and a discussion of its future plans and projected performance

market interest rate the interest rate that investors can demand in return for lending their money

market value the price shares are sold for, determined by the amount investors are willing to pay for them

materiality a measure of the significance of information to the users; a piece of information is material if it could influence or change a user's decision

maturity date the date on which the final payment of a bond is due to the investor

measurement the process of determining the amount at which an item is recorded in the financial statements

money market instrument a short-term debt investment that is highly liquid and low-risk, such as a treasury bill, term deposit or money market fund

mortgage bonds bonds for which a company puts up specific assets as collateral in the event it defaults on interest or principal repayments; also called *secured bonds*

mortgage note a note secured by an asset

mutual agency in a partnership, the ability of each partner to speak for the other partners and bind them to business contracts

N

natural resources assets with a physical nature that are different from property, plant and equipment, such as metal ores, minerals, timber or petroleum

net profit margin a measure of a company's profitability after all expenses have been deducted

net realizable value (NRV) the price that a company can realistically expect to sell an item for, less any costs incurred to make the item ready for sale

noncumulative shares preferred shares that do not have the right to receive any accumulated unpaid dividends

noncurrent an alternative term for *long-term*, commonly used under IFRS

non-determinable liabilities unknown liabilities including estimated and contingent liabilities

nonparticipating preferred shares shares with a limit to the dividends that can be issued each year

non-strategic investment an investment where the purpose is to generate investment income without intending to establish a long-term business relationship with, or to influence or control, the investee

no-par value shares shares issued with no assigned value

note payable a legally binding document that obligates the borrower to follow certain terms, much like a loan

note receivable an agreement that makes an account receivable resemble a formal loan by adding precise terms of repayment and the customer's signature; also called a *promissory note*

O

operating lease a form of a lease where ownership is not transferred to another party over the term of the agreement, such as for a car rental

operating line of credit the maximum loan balance a business may draw upon at any time without having to visit or request approval from the bank

operations management the ability of a company to manage its assets, such as inventory and accounts receivable

organization costs initial costs incurred to organize or form a corporation

other comprehensive income (OCI) a category of income under IFRS resulting from transactions that are beyond company owners' or management's control

other income (expenses) items that are not part of a company's regular day-to-day operations

outstanding shares shares that are still held by shareholders; may be equal to the number of issued shares

P

par value shares shares that are issued with an assigned value

parent company the investor in a business combination

participating preferred shares shares that entitle preferred shareholders to share with common shareholders any dividends paid in excess of the percentage stated on the preferred share certificate

partnership an association of two or more people who jointly own a business, its assets and liabilities, and who share in its gains or losses

partnership liquidation a process to dissolve a partnership; involves selling assets, paying off liabilities and distributing any proceeds to the partners according to individual profit and loss ratios

patent the exclusive right to an invention for a set period of time, including all rights to make, use, sell or distribute the patented invention

payee the company (lender) to whom a note receivable is payable

payment terms conditions by which a vendor expects to be paid by a customer

percentage of completion a method of revenue recognition in which a company can recognize a percentage of revenue for a service that is partially completed

percentage of total accounts receivable method a method by which a company uses a percentage of receivables to estimate bad debt

pledging the practice whereby a company offers its receivables as collateral for a loan, but retains ownership of the receivables

preferred shares a type of equity for which dividends must first be paid before those on common shares

premium the difference between the price paid and the par value of a bond, when the price paid is higher

present value the amount that needs to be invested today to produce a specific amount in the future; also referred to as *discounting*

price–earnings (P/E) ratio a measurement of share price compared to actual earnings of a corporation

prior period adjustment a correcting entry that is made to a previous period

private corporation an incorporated company that does not offer its shares to the public

profitability the ability of a company to generate profits

promissory note an agreement that makes an account receivable resemble a formal loan by adding precise terms of repayment and the customer's signature; also called a *note receivable*

prospective approach the use of a new estimate to adjust records for the current and future periods, such as for the useful life of an asset

provincial sales tax (PST) a tax imposed by the province and paid by the final consumer of a product

public corporation an incorporated company that trades its shares on a stock exchange

Q

quick ratio a measure of a company's ability to pay off short-term debt, based on liquid assets; also known as the *acid test*

R

redeemable bonds bonds that the issuer has the right to buy back before maturity; also called *callable bonds*

registered bonds bonds that list bondholders as registered owners who receive regular interest payments on interest payment dates

residual value estimated value of an asset at the end of its useful life; also referred to as *salvage value* or *scrap value*

retained earnings earnings that are kept and accumulated by a company after dividends have been paid to shareholders

retroactive approach the approach of changing accounting information on the financial statements of a prior period when there is a change in accounting policy

return on assets (ROA) a measure of the relationship between net income and assets

return on common shareholders' equity a measure of the profits earned on an investment of common shareholders

return on equity (ROE) a measure of what the owners are getting out of their investment in the company

revenue expenditure expenses paid for a change to an asset that benefits the current period

revenue recognition the concept that revenue can only be recorded (recognized) when goods are sold or services are performed

S

sales tax a tax applied by the government to goods or services that are sold

serial bonds a set of bonds that mature at different intervals

share a unit of equity in a corporation

share capital capital raised from the sale of shares

share issue costs costs associated with the share issue, such as registration fees, legal and accounting fees, regulatory fees and printing of share certificates and other required documentation

shareholders owners of a corporation who own equity in a corporation in the form of shares

shareholders' equity the partial ownership of a shareholder in a company

short-term debt investment a debt investment that will mature within 12 months; a short-term investment in bonds

short-term investment an investment intended to be held for less than a year that is reported under the current assets section of a balance sheet; also called a *temporary investment*

short-term notes payable a short-term liability paid in full at its maturity date, usually within 12 months of the date of issue

significant influence a situation where a company owns between 20% and 50% of another company's common shares outstanding

solvency a company's ability to cover its long-term debt obligations; relates to the amount of debt and risk a company has

statement of cash flows a statement that tracks the sources and uses of cash in a company; also called the *cash flow statement*

statement of changes in equity a statement required under IFRS reporting changes to all equity accounts

statement of comprehensive income a statement in which comprehensive income is reported as well as earnings per share; under IFRS, the statement can be presented by function or by nature

statement of financial position under IFRS, the equivalent of a balance sheet, showing a company's assets, liabilities and shareholders' equity

statement of partners' equity a partnership's statement explaining changes to the balance of each partner's capital account from the beginning to the end of a year

statement of retained earnings a statement required under ASPE reporting changes in the retained earning account

stock dividend shares issued in lieu of a cash dividend

stock split an action that increases the number of a corporation's outstanding shares, decreasing the individual price of each share traded on the stock market

straight-line amortization method a method in which the same amount of bond discount is recorded each period

straight-line method of depreciation a method that produces an average depreciation expense, which is applied each year until the asset is sold or reaches the end of its useful life

strategic investment an investment where the investor intends to establish a long-term business relationship with, or to influence or control, the investee

subsidiary company the investee in a business combination

T

tangible assets assets that have a physical existence, such as a machine or a building

term bonds bonds that mature on a specific date

time value of money a basic principle of economics and finance that shows how the value of money changes over time

times interest earned ratio a measure of whether a company is able to cover the interest charged on its debt

trade name a company or product name to which a company has exclusive rights for commercial purposes, even though its legal or technical name might differ

trademark a recognizable symbol or logo to which a company has ownership rights

treasury shares shares that are bought back from shareholders by the corporation

trend analysis a comparison of similar line items in a comparative balance sheet to see how an item has changed from year to year; a *horizontal analysis*

U

units-of-production method a depreciation method that estimates the number of units used for the entire life of the asset and bases each period's depreciation amount on the actual units used for that period

unlimited liability a type of liability under which owners or partners can be held personally liable for all financial obligations if the company is unable to pay its debts

V

variable interest rate an interest rate that fluctuates according to market interest rates; also called a *floating rate*

vertical analysis a method to compare a line item on a financial statement to a base figure within the same year

W

weighted average number of common shares outstanding the number of shares outstanding multiplied by the fraction of the year during which those shares were outstanding

working capital the difference between current assets and current liabilities

PHOTO AND INFORMATION CREDITS

Chapter 1

Chapter opener: © surasaki / Shutterstock.com. *Making It Real to You:* © Igor Kardasov | Dreamstime.com

In the Real World: With information from Berman, D. (2018, May 17). Canada's biggest banks moving to analytics for credit assessments. *The Globe and Mail.* Retrieved from https://www.theglobeandmail.com/report-on-business/canadas-biggest-banks-moving-to-analytics-for-credit-assessments/article32486204

A Closer Look: Screenshot courtesy of Sage Intelligence, https://www.sageintelligence.com/blog/2018/07/collect-your-cash-with-the-analysis-of-accounts-receivable-report

Chapter 2

Chapter opener: © Alexey Sk | Dreamstime.com. *Making It Real to You:* © Geckophotos | Dreamstime.com. *Figure 2.2:* Excerpt from *Canadian Tire Corporation 2018 Report to Shareholders.* Retrieved from https://s22.q4cdn.com/405442328/files/doc_financials/en/2018/q4/CTC-2018-Annual-Report_Online_EN.PDF. Used with permission. *Figure 2.26:* © Srki66 | Dreamstime.com. *Figure 2.27:* © Guryanov Andrey / Shutterstock. *Figure 2.31:* Schedule 8, Capital Cost Allowance, Canada Revenue Agency, https://www.canada.ca/en/revenue-agency/services/forms-publications/forms/t2sch8.html. *Figures 2.45 and 2.51:* Excerpts from *Suncor Annual Report 2018.* Retrieved from https://www.suncor.com/en-CA/investor-centre/financial-reports/annual-disclosure. Use with permission.

In the Real World: With information from Beatty, A. & Weber, J. (2006). Accounting discretion in fair value estimates: An examination of SFAS 142 goodwill impairments. *Journal of Accounting Research, 44*(2), 257; and Finch, N. (2012). Detecting abonormal goodwill impairment practices. *The Journal of Applied Research in Accounting and Finance, 6*(2). Retrieved from https://papers.ssrn.com/sol3/papers.cfm?abstract_id=2470899

Chapter 3

Chapter opener: © Anthony Berenyi / Shutterstock. *Making It Real to You:* © Kaspars Grinvalds | Dreamstime.com. *Figure 3.6:* © Dusan Petkovic / Shutterstock, © Vlue | Dreamstime.com, © Martine Oger | Dreamstime.com

In the Real World: With information from *Warranty Week.* (2017, March 23). Fourteenth Annual Product Warranty Report. Retrieved from https://www.warrantyweek.com/archive/ww20170323.html; and IBM. (2015, May 12). Redbooks: Transforming warranty processes with the IBM warranty analytics solution. Retrieved from https://www.redbooks.ibm.com/technotes/tips1254.pdf

Chapter 4

Chapter opener: © Ammentorp | Dreamstime.com. *Making It Real to You:* © Benzoix | Dreamstime.com

Chapter 5

Chapter opener: © Rawpixel.com | Dreamstime.com. *Making It Real to You:* © Astra490 | Dreamstime.com

Chapter 6

Chapter opener: © Vinnstock | Dreamstime.com; © Leonid Sorokin | Shutterstock; © Casper1774 Studio | Shutterstock. *Making It Real to You:* © Fsstock | Dreamstime.com

In the Real World: With information from Deloitte. eXtensible Business Reporting Language. https://www2.deloitte.com/us/en/pages/audit/solutions/extensible-business-reporting-language-xbrl.html; and Ontario Securities Commission. (2019). XBRL. Retrieved from https://www.osc.gov.on.ca/en/xbrl_index.htm

Chapter 7

Chapter opener: © Alexskopje | Dreamstime.com. *Making It Real to You:* © Rmarmion | Dreamstime.com

In the Real World: With information from Kricheff, R. (2014). Data analytics for corporate debt markets: Using data for investing, trading, capital markets, and portfolio management. Upper Saddle River, NJ: Pearson Education; and Ro, S. (2015, Feb 12). Here's what the $294 trillion market of global financial assets looks like. *Business Insider Australia*. Retrieved from https://www.businessinsider.com.au/global-financial-assets-2015-2

Chapter 8

Chapter opener: © Chaiyapak Mankannan | Dreamstime.com. *Making It Real to You:* © Monkey Business Images Ltd. | Dreamstime.com

Chapter 9

Chapter opener: © Wisitporn Cheyasak | Dreamstime.com. *Making It Real to You:* Tirachard Kumtanom | Dreamstime.com

Chapter 10

Chapter opener: © Yurolaitsalbert | Dreamstime.com. *Making It Real to You:* © Dragonimages | Dreamstime.com. *Figures 10.1, 10.8, 10.39, 10.45 and data used throughout chapter:* Excerpts from *Leon's Furniture Limited 2017 Annual Report* and *Leon's Furniture Limited 2018 Annual Report.* Retrieved from https://www.leons.ca/pages/annual-reports

INDEX

A

D

E

F

M

N

O